All My Best,
David Kroese

THE *Centennial*

A Journey through America's National Park System

DAVID KROESE

The Centennial: A Journey Through America's National Park System

Published by Wheatmark®
2030 East Speedway Boulevard, Suite 106
Tucson, Arizona 85719 USA
www.wheatmark.com

ISBN: 978-1-62787-657-5 (paperback)
ISBN: 978-1-62787-658-2 (ebook)
LCCN: 2018913736

Bulk ordering discounts are available through Wheatmark, Inc. For more information, email orders@wheatmark.com or call 1-888-934-0888.

The journey continues at www. Centennialjourney.com

For my mother, Juanita.
This book is a reflection of a lifetime of love.

Contents

Acknowledgments

THE 2016 NATIONAL Park Service centennial celebration inspired multiple personal projects. In the first, I acquired commemorative lapel pins for an exhibit now touring the parks. I also collected the NPS (National Park Service) passport program's centennial cancellations, dated ink impressions made by stampers available throughout the park system. Merged with the original goal to see all the parks, these projects pushed me to visit as many parks as possible in 2016. The centennial projects challenged me through a grand adventure. The third and final centennial project became this book. I never considered putting the year to paper until halfway through it. Following these adventures via social media, my mother asked, "Will you please write your story?"

Without giving it much thought, I said, "I'll write something for you." Months later, I understood. This story would be her trip to these places, most of which she will never see in person.

The 2016 park journey would not have been possible without support from my wife, Kareen. We did have our challenges. As the effort grew, it tested her understanding and patience. We spent weeks apart. Some months included only a few days together. Kareen later said, "At first I thought you were crazy. Then I thought you were seriously crazy. I finally realized you were obsessed." But Kareen always understood the journey's fundamental drivers and eventually supported it. She saw the year as I did, an achievement unto itself. This crazy whirlwind park tour morphed into a unique, once-in-a-lifetime experience requiring complete commitment. Kareen came full circle, encouraging me to continue when exhaustion took hold. I'm blessed to have her companionship and support and, when lucky, her participation. She has been my pillar of rock, my "El Capitan," through the journey.

She also advised me to include the final twenty-three parks visited in 2017 to complete the story of both the parks and projects. The narrative continues with three additional chapters through all 418 NPS units. I'm thrilled to tell their story. I committed to add the remaining parks during my second trip to Alaska after rangers at Glacier Bay and Kotzebue, both 2017 park destinations, insisted that I must include their parks. One even quipped, "We know where you live, and we have lots of bears."

The centennial projects grew under the care of many. I'm indebted to my friends who read early drafts of the manuscript, offering priceless input that improved the writing. The final product speaks to their contributions and guidance. Thanks to my fellow park travelers Deborah Archer, Leland Warzala, and Chris and Bill Balcerski for their input. Thanks to Kimberly Watley, who graciously shared some of her professional expertise and encouragement. Thanks to my high school English teacher Carolyn Gallo for her high standards all those years ago and her review of this project. Thanks to rangers Eric Leonard and Bob Boensch at Minuteman Missile for reviewing their park's information for accuracy. Thanks to all the rangers who contributed their vast knowledge to help me get it right, including Dave at Big Bend, Mike at Redwood, and John at Fossil Butte, among many. Thanks also to Dorothy at the Bell County Historical Society and Tom Shadick for sharing his extensive knowledge of the Cumberland Gap area. Thanks to David Bates and my lifelong friend, Greg Kelly, for their comments. At Wheatmark, I would like to thank my project manager, Lori Conser, for her considerable time and effort, Grael Norton for his encouragement from our initial conversation, Mindy Burnett for her work on the book's website, and Atilla Vekony for his suggestions. A special thanks goes to Steve OKrepky for his work on the book's Facebook page. Last, but not least, thanks to my mother for starting me on the adventure of writing this book, reading the early chapters, and offering her opinion.

I'm fortunate, thankful, healthier, and happier for these park experiences. Many people reminded me, "You're a lucky guy," to paraphrase a line I heard dozens of times. "Yes, I am," I agreed. I hope my experience inspires others to follow their passions without regret.

The simple kindness and enthusiasm that filled my year is truly heartwarming. The journey included many who provided a spiritual boost. They're the glue that held it all together. So many park personnel and staff helped and encouraged me as I traveled to one site after another. I hope that I reflect the enthusiasm and compassion shared from Alaska to the Caribbean, Maine to American Samoa, and all parts in between. To everyone who engaged me along the way, please accept my sincerest and heartfelt thanks. All of you made my journey an experience of human goodwill and kindness befitting the momentous history and stunning natural beauty. In the end, the simple grace of these people transcended even these majestic places.

Introduction

THE FIRST TRIP that I can remember to a national park happened in July of 1977. As a curious six-and-a-half-year-old, I couldn't wait to see what lay ahead. We were headed to Colorado's Rocky Mountain National Park. I was about to see real mountains for the first time! As we scrambled into the car, I grabbed our road atlas and a couple of worn, folded state maps, examining the areas we would cross from our starting point in southern Illinois, across the Mississippi and Missouri Rivers, up and down the rolling hills of Kansas, and finally over the arid plains of eastern Colorado, where the foothills of the Rocky Mountains trace a faint outline on the horizon. That trip is memorable for many reasons. I can still remember studying the distant but growing profile and my father saying, "Those are only the foothills. You can't even see the bigger mountains yet."

I replied, "Those aren't the big mountains?"

We left the sweltering ninety- to one-hundred-degree temperatures and high humidity of the Mississippi River Valley to encounter snow at the park's higher elevations. We spent one frigid night shivering in our pop-top camper before retreating to Estes Park the next morning to raid an army surplus store. We bought anything and everything to keep warm, from woolen blankets to socks and sweaters. The haul included a pair of thick leather hiking boots. We put on our game faces and reentered the fray, better equipped for the cold than the 101st Airborne had been around Bastogne.

As an extra, adventurous thrill, our green Buick kept cutting out as we climbed to twelve thousand feet on Trail Ridge Road. Our car would shut off, taking out the power steering as we rounded tight corners with no guardrails and straight drop-offs of hundreds of feet. Thankfully, my father managed to keep us on the road despite terrifying moments around 180-degree switchbacks. He later discovered the distributor shaft had a bad bearing, stalling the car. Watching him manhandle the steering wheel and restart the engine as we passed within feet of the great void became the stuff of vacation legend.

I still remember seeing the expanses of high alpine country for the first time, with numerous signs asking visitors to stay off the fragile tundra and people stomping right past the signs as if illiterate. The widespread disregard for clear and logical park rules left an impression as a footnote of sorts to the park's rugged beauty. The mountains proved every bit as captivating as I had imagined. The jagged peaks and treeless high country with its crystal-clear lakes and streams formed a fierce natural beauty beyond any imagining, despite the car troubles, snow in July, and morons walking across the tundra.

In August 2012, Kareen and I took our first US vacation together to Washington, DC, and eastern Virginia's Civil War battlegrounds. To be more accurate, I chose the destination, and Kareen agreed to come along. I learned quickly that they didn't cover Grant's 1864 Overland campaign in her Jamaican history class. Over time, we adjusted our park experience to provide the introduction to American history that Kareen needed, both as a visual learner and a naturalized citizen. For her part, her mind works like a highly advanced Pentium chip *if* you have her attention. My attempts at explaining the history in advance, as driving conversation, stalled much like that old Buick in the mountains. She needed a more comprehensive, audio-visual presentation. Ironically, Kareen triggered my epiphany to see the parks. During our first park visit in eastern Virginia, Kareen picked up a little blue book with *Passport to Your National Parks* in gold lettering across the top. Passport program enthusiasts use the books to collect dated ink impressions (also called cancellations) available across the park system. Each stamp identifies the park and location where it is kept. Some parks have dozens of unique stamps. She was responding to my excitement over the places on our itinerary. She handed me the little book and said, "You seem to really like all this history. This looks like something you would enjoy." I had never heard of the passport program before that moment.

From a modest beginning would come great enterprise. We purchased the book and took out a folded National Park System map included in a clear, plastic sleeve inside the front cover. As I unfolded the map, my eyes darted from one region to another, studying these sites scattered about the country. The intriguing blend of familiar and unfamiliar park names sparked an aspiration. Could I see them all? I couldn't remember seeing a National Park System map, much less studying it. In that moment, my deepest personal passions linked to a quantifiable goal. I'd visited about fifty parks at the time, personal interests having led me to them as the opportunity arose. I had discovered a personal quest to fill the void of challenge, growth, opportunity, and achievement my career had ceased to offer. I didn't realize all these things in the moment. Only after years of traveling to the parks, nearing completion of the goal, did I comprehend all the forces that had driven me into America's National Park System.

Having a vacation list of over four hundred destinations, spread across every state and five American territories, is a weighty thing. In 2013, we adjusted vacation plans to include twenty-seven new parks. In March 2014, I got knowledgeable and serious. I joined the National Park Travelers Club (NPTC), an invaluable resource for the park visitor and passport stamp collector. The NPTC is a non-profit group of over two thousand avid park enthusiasts who share travel tips and information about the US National Park System. One NPTC member resource is a database of passport-stamping locations nationwide, with a current list of the stamps available at each location. Collecting stamps attracted me for the dated visit log it creates and the targeted motivation to visit locations that might otherwise be missed. Finding all the passport locations in a large park or along a trail becomes a fascinating and educational scavenger hunt. Some parks, trails, and national heritage areas have dozens of unique cancellations. Passport enthusiasts had additional motivation during the centennial, trying to collect over 450 special fixed-date centennial cancellations around the country. Nearly all the four hundred–plus NPS units and some of the national trails and heritage areas had commemorative centennial cancellations. Most passport enthusiasts endeavored to visit as many units as possible throughout the year. For many, this included revisiting familiar parks. I had visited 318 NPS units by the start of 2016.

Though I've always loved history, I didn't seek a career in it. Rather, I chose engineering after observing my father, an electrical engineer, at his work while I was a young boy. I liked the concept of using math and science to solve real-world problems and never doubted or regretted my decision. Academic demands restricted history to a few electives. I graduated from the University of Illinois at Urbana-Champaign with a BS in chemical engineering in May 1993.

After working the first six years of my career in engineering roles for a corn wet milling company in Tennessee and a bio-technology company in Iowa, I accepted an offer to move to a business group within the latter. Over the next eighteen years, I held regional and global roles in sales, marketing, and account and group management. Much of that time, I filled two or more full-time roles simultaneously. By the end of my sixteenth year, I had filled assignments for ten full-time-equivalent years in addition to my primary job. The extra assignments never included additional pay, just the work. Before Kareen handed me that little blue book, my career progression had stalled indefinitely, leaving me seeking growth and challenge elsewhere.

As 2015 closed, I considered how to visit as many parks as possible in 2016. Could I see parks and fulfill my essential job responsibilities? Kareen convinced me I should try. I had been making full use of off-hours, working before 8:00 a.m. or after

5:00 p.m. since the multiple assignments started years ago. Heavy workloads resulted in late nights. After midnight, my yellow lab would wedge his wriggling body between the desk and chair and put his big paw on top of the keyboard. As the scene repeated itself, I started negotiating, saying, "Just fifteen more minutes," or "I'm almost done with this email." The first few years, he yielded and lay back down. If I abused his good graces, I would feel his nose again, and the ominous paw would return with more force. I saved some drafts during those years with an ending of "Shfshffhhhhh…." That's Labrador retriever for "You're an idiot!" After a few years of that bedtime routine, he reacted to entreaties to continue working by cocking his head and wagging his tail furiously without yielding an inch, as if to say, "You're insulting my intelligence!" Fortunately, he had enough sense for both of us.

Over most of my career, I worked odd hours in addition to a normal working day. The fundamental difference in 2016 is that I worked off hours to *free up* time in the day. In this professional purgatory, I had limited responsibilities and no direct reports. The home office and a hotel room served the same function. I scheduled park visits around work commitments. If trips took me completely out of touch or I could not work in the early morning or late evening, I used vacation, weekends, and holidays. I eliminated anything from my personal and professional schedule that did not further the park goals or add critical value at work.

I launched an adventure more in concept than plan. The priority shifted from professional to personal. I started the centennial journey without understanding my deepest motivations for doing so. What lay at the end? Would a year in the parks take my life in a new direction? I hadn't a clue.

1 *Charleston*

A LIGHT RAIN patters against the hotel room window, muffling a smattering of fireworks and occasional dull thunder rumbling in the distance. The weather front moving through Charleston, South Carolina, is dampening the local holiday celebrations. I'm staring at my watch as it turns midnight. My beautiful bride, Kareen, is fast asleep. She's an extreme morning person. I've never seen someone with more natural energy at 4:00 a.m. It's sacrilegious to night owls like me. After dinner, the countdown begins on her nightly transformation into a pumpkin. Her hibernation is usually underway by 8:00 p.m. Kareen's dead to the world on this New Year's Eve. I've never seen her awake at midnight on New Year's Eve. I nudge her at 12:01 a.m. She mumbles, "Is it twenty-whatever?" and rolls over.

"Yes, it's twenty-whatever." Before my reply is finished, her slow and steady breathing announces a return to unconsciousness.

She will start a movie on her computer and watch less than five minutes before fading away. Whatever she's started will keep playing until I come to bed and close her laptop, only to have her awaken and mumble, "I was watching it."

My standard reply: "Yeah, I can see that." She's notorious for watching the same ten minutes of a show over and over. It's like watching Sisyphus roll the stone up the mountain. Her computer's silent on December 31, 2015. And I'm up alone, lost in thought. The subtle background noises fail to break a deafening silence.

I'm restless. My excited mind moves from one destination to the next, reviewing the new year's calendar month to month. I've been thinking about the new year with greater frequency for six months. This new year is special. It's the start of the National Park Service's centennial anniversary. I hope to visit as many parks as possible in 2016, beyond progress on the goal to see all the NPS units. The challenge enhances the normal excitement I've felt planning visits to new sites over the past few years. This year, the parks dominate. In that spirit, a few months ago I told Kareen, "I'm leaving my job after my twentieth service anniversary in early February 2016 and spending the year in the parks. Whatever and whenever my next job might be, it can wait until 2017."

Kareen and I are both professionals with a modest standard of living. When we met in July 2010, at ages forty-one and thirty-nine, the decision point to have children had come and gone. That's okay with us. Neither of us feels the burning drive that moves others to procreate. As a result, we have more options than most couples our age. I can entertain plans to hit the road. The personal factors aren't prohibitive. The enormity of the task is the issue. I've already been to over three hundred of the more than four hundred parks in the National Park System. What I'm contemplating tonight is visiting as many in one year as I've visited lifetime to date. Just thinking about it is tiring. It's also exciting. I'm ready to see what I can do. Untold thrills and new adventures await.

Kareen talked me out of leaving my job in 2016, pointing out that, with the nature of my work and my low internal visibility, I can fulfill work obligations and visit parks simultaneously. Her initial concern had been that I might drift without the job. She came to realize that I have too much energy and passion to languish in despair. We'll be okay. I concurred, delaying any career change, and shifted to planning the year with the continuing restriction of a full-time job. I'm reconciling the situation and what it portends when we arrive in Charleston. I'm blissfully ignorant that I'm about to embark on a quest that will challenge the limits of my physical and mental endurance in a twelve-month test of passion against stamina.

Our 2016 New Year's Day in Charleston is our second consecutive New Year's Day in South Carolina. The winter trips south are mutually agreeable. I'm trying to familiarize Kareen with southern cities, hoping we'll move farther south. In recent years, each winter feels colder and more uncomfortable than the last. We both appreciate a break in the monotony of Chicago's long winters. I thrive on outdoor recreation and the chance to explore. Long winters thwart these basic needs. Moreover, a change extracts us from a corrupt, failed state government, and Kareen's medical practice, in much the same condition. Most importantly, a joint move will finally consolidate our homes and lives.

Our circumstances led to separate homes ninety miles apart. Her condominium in Chicago's Lakeview neighborhood is too small for both of us to occupy full-time as an exclusive residence and doesn't allow pets to even visit, precluding the two Labrador retrievers I had when we met. My house in Rockford is much too far away for her to commute. She regularly works twelve consecutive days since she works twenty-four weekends each year. When we met, Kareen's US travel experience wanted. After her residency in Washington, DC, and first three years as a practicing nephrologist in the underserved community of Decatur, Illinois, a requirement for her H-1 visa and permanent US residency, she moved to Chicago on her first day of eligibility. She felt isolated and starved for cultural stimulation in Decatur. Since we got engaged, I tried suggesting other places in the country for a home together. Kareen rejected each location without any real knowledge of it. I sympathized, grasping the difficulty and loneliness for her starting life anew in a small midwestern town. I felt similarly misplaced when my company moved me to Elkhart, Indiana, for three years in 1999. The area never felt like home. I gained ground with Kareen on our first trip to Charleston. She loved the city. I promised her that the beautiful historic homes, great cuisine, and mild climate fuse into a unique experience. But she's naturally resistant to change in a life built around routine.

Her career began draining her vitality away before we met. She works sixty-hour weeks and almost half her weekends and holidays. An uneven work distribution pervades within the practice, sometimes to extremes. The clinic staff, knowing some pages go unanswered, often call Kareen for other doctors' patients. Contractual obligations are selectively enforced or ignored. The entity moves on inertia, absent of management or strategy. The constant strain debilitates Kareen and affects our marriage. I watch her grow weaker under the workload and stress. We don't need this burden and cannot survive under it indefinitely. Mostly, I'm concerned about her health. Yet, she resists change. I couldn't understand why for the longest time.

Kareen's major life ambition included US citizenship and a dynamic medical practice in a diverse urban setting. She's achieved her goal and wants to maintain it. But at what cost? Something in her mind views leaving the practice as a personal failure. The stress and negativity is a price she's been willing to pay, literally the frog in boiling water. Every time she experiences some unethical or nasty thing at work, she vents her rage at me, not to me, avoiding professional confrontation. It's left a cumulative set of scars. As I'm sitting in the silence of the new year, watching raindrops hit the glass, I can only speculate on the extent to which Kareen's toxic work environment will affect us in 2016.

New Year's Day, we walk two miles east from our hotel to Liberty Square, the visitor center and departure point for Fort Sumter. Kareen and I visited **Fort Sumter National Monument** a year ago, though the park's closed today. The isolated brick guardian of Charleston's harbor gained permanent fame on April 6, 1861, as the recipient of the Civil War's opening salvo. On our boat ride, we left a beautiful, sunny, sixty-degree day in Charleston only to find an isolated dark cloud hanging over the outer harbor and island fort. We could see rain falling on the structure as we approached the dock. It rained for the first forty-five minutes of the hour-long tour. This day marked my third visit to the island. The rain confined us to sheltered areas like the fort's museum. We studied the Palmetto flag raised by victorious southern troops after

Union forces commanded by Major Robert Anderson surrendered the fort on April 14, 1861. The action created the Civil War's first two military heroes: Major Anderson in the North for his gallant defense of the besieged fort without reinforcement or resupply, and Brigadier General Pierre G. T. Beauregard in the South for his command of the forces that evicted the hated Yankees from Charleston Harbor. Beauregard would become the first Confederate promoted to the rank of full general. The fort's capitulation gained control of the important southern port for the Confederate States of America.

New Year's Day 2016 consists of touring Charleston Aquarium at Liberty Square, followed by a midafternoon meal at a seafood house in old Charleston. The next morning, we return prepared to revisit Fort Sumter. At the Liberty Square Visitor Center, we examine part of the thirty-four-star American flag flown above the fort during the bombardment. Only a small section is displayed at any one time to minimize fabric degradation.

Hoping to collect the fort's centennial cancellation, we change plans when we learn they don't yet have one. We decide to spend our time at **Fort Moultrie National Monument** on Sullivan's Island. Enjoying sunny skies and a cool breeze, we stroll through the grounds and amuse ourselves with a picture of Kareen looking down the barrel of one of the cannons lined up on exhibit beside the fort.

As an active military post for 171 years from the American Revolution through World War II, Fort Moultrie is an excellent example of US coastal defense evolution. The original structure consisted of two palmetto-log walls bracketing earthen fill. The soft, spongy palmetto wood absorbed the shot from the British navy's smoothbore cannon during the bombardment on June 28, 1776, allowing the fort's thirty guns to drive off the two-hundred-gun British fleet. The British didn't make the same mistake twice, avoiding the fort when they captured Charleston as part of Cornwallis's southern campaign in 1781.

Our next stop is Charleston's other NPS unit, **Charles Pinckney National Historic Site**. The unit preserves the surviving 28 acres of Snee Farm, originally part of 715 acres Charles inherited from his father in 1782. The Pinckney's owned the plantation for over sixty years, selling it in 1817. None of the structures built during the family's era remain. The surviving home sits on the foundation of the original Pinckney plantation house and dates to the late 1820s, after Pinckney's 1824 death. Pinckney served as a delegate and signer at the 1787 Constitutional Convention. His ideas for reforming weaknesses in the Articles of Confederation influenced the US Constitution.

We warm ourselves in the sun as we follow the trail around the tidewater cottage, reading about plantation life in the late 1700s and early 1800s. Pinckney regarded Snee Farm as a favorite among his seven plantations, though he made his primary residence in a Charleston townhouse. Many of his papers burned in the Charleston fire of 1861. Most of what is known about the farm during Pinckney's lifetime is based on archeological evidence.

Charles Pinckney National Historic Site and the other coastal park units, extending from Wilmington to Jacksonville, are part of the **Gullah Geechee Cultural Heritage Corridor**, which celebrates the culture and language of the formerly enslaved who gathered in nineteenth-century barrier island communities. Both names have, in turn, been used to describe the African descendants living in these communities and their English-based creole language. Gullah represents a blend of British, American, and West African culture, food, religion, and traditions, including the creole language spoken in these communities. Geechee generally describes African Americans living on the Atlantic Coast of South Carolina, Georgia, and northern Florida. The island community culture has direct connections to the West African Coast. Many of the sea islands were only accessible by boat in the nineteenth century. The relative isolation helped preserve African linguistic and cultural heritage among the Geechee to a greater extent than for any other African American community in the United States.

At least forty major African coastal slave castles served the slave trade in the eighteenth and nineteenth centuries, though the Geechee are most closely connected to Bunce Island. Englishmen owned the Bunce Island slave castle, and the majority of the enslaved leaving the island ended up in the West Indies and North America. Overall, during the African slave trade, only 4 percent of enslaved Africans were brought to North America, compared to the 96 percent destined for Brazil and the Caribbean.

Traders operating out of Liverpool, Bristol, London, and Newport, Rhode Island, carried their human cargo from Bunce Island during its period of English control, from 1670 until Great Britain banned the trade in 1807. Located twenty-five miles up the Sierra Leone River, feeding the largest natural harbor on the West African Coast, the island survived four French attacks from 1695 to 1794—two by pirates led by Bartholomew Roberts (more famously known as Black Bart) in 1719 and 1720.

Bunce Island lies at the furthest point of navigation for ocean-going sailing vessels on the Sierra Leone River. Traders operating the fortress extracted captives from outposts stretching over six hundred miles, from Senegal and Gambia in the north to Sierra Leone and Liberia in the south.

Enslaved workers brought to the South Carolina coast important knowledge of rice cultivation previously unknown to English planters, such as the tidal flow method to power rice irrigation. Henry Laurens, who succeeded John Hancock as president of the Continental Congress, served as one of the United States' three representatives for the 1783 Treaty of Paris, ending the Revolutionary War. Laurens, one of the wealthiest plantation owners in South Carolina, functioned as the largest agent for Bunce Island trade in the southern American colonies. The principle owner of Bunce Island, Richard Oswald, represented England as one of his counterparts.

With a few hours left in our day, we take advantage of Kareen's first opportunity to see Savannah, Georgia, 120 miles south. Kareen doesn't want to spend four hours on the road, preferring a relaxed agenda. She relents at the promise of a delicious meal in Savannah. My idea seems a catastrophic error as mile after mile of bumper-to-bumper traffic crawls north on I-95. The solid mass continues with few interruptions most of the way to the Savannah exit. Choked with East Coasters returning home after spending the holiday week in Florida, I shudder to think of the hundreds of miles remaining for these travelers. Looks like we'll be taking another route back to Charleston. Fortunately, the lighter southbound traffic doesn't impede us, leaving time to tour **Fort Pulaski National Monument**.

James Madison authorized Fort Pulaski. Built from 1829 to 1847, it still awaited full armament and a garrison when tensions rose between the states in late 1860. Then Georgia governor Joseph Brown seized the fort without a fight on January 3, 1861. An imposing structure, the pentagonal fort has seven-and-a-half-foot thick brick walls surrounded by a forty-foot wide moat. A triangular demilune built outside the gorge, or back wall, after the Civil War connects the fort and surrounding land via a drawbridge and appears as several earthen mounds protecting magazines and passageways between gun emplacements. Both military leaders of the time and Savannah-area residents considered the fort impregnable. The fortification commanded Cockspur Island's swampy landscape, controlling the Savannah River channel between the key southern port and coastal shipping lanes.

After launching a southern Atlantic coast campaign in late 1861, the Union retook the fort. The decisive thirty-hour bombardment on April 10, 1862, inflicted heavy damage from the use of a new military innovation, the rifled cannon. As we walk around the southeast corner of the fort, I show Kareen the massive hole blown through this corner by artillery positioned a mile away on Tybee Island. The damage shows in color variation between original and replacement bricks. Passing the moat's eastern side reveals round and cylindrical projectiles imbedded in the brick. The success at Fort Pulaski marks a major turning point in military strategy and defense. Typical smoothbore cannons of the period had an effective range under a half mile and were virtually useless in attack of strong defensive positions farther out. Rifling a gun barrel dramatically increases the effective range and punching power for artillery and small arms alike. Rifled artillery not only reduced Fort Pulaski but made brick and mortar forts obsolete. The same innovation in small arms made an equally profound impact on Civil War infantry combat.

Though the Union's capture of Fort Pulaski limited commercial traffic to Savannah, blockade runners could still reach the port while friendly forces controlled the inland waterways. The Union did not attain total control over Savannah until Sherman's March to the Sea ended here in December 1864. Sherman closed the march by penning his famous telegram to President Lincoln, offering the town as a Christmas present.

Across the parking lot from the fort, a trail leads to the site of the fort's former supply dock. A spur trail reveals another interesting piece of history within the park, commemorated on a brick column called the Wesley Monument. John and Charles Wesley made landfall on Cockspur Island, first setting foot on North American soil in February 1736. John remained in Savannah, while Charles continued farther south on the Georgia coast to the town of Frederica. The missionary expedition ended unceremoniously for both Wesley brothers. Charles returned home from Frederica in May 1736, and John followed in December 1737 after what amounts to a case of jilted love. John Wesley recovered from his misadventures to establish the modern Methodist Church. Charles nicely summarized his feelings about Georgia with the statement, "I was overjoyed at my deliverance out of this furnace..." He is remembered today as the writer of over six thousand Christian hymns, some of which remain popular. I love the Wesley story for how it humanizes the brothers as men with ordinary weaknesses long before their historical status as religious icons.

Ready for dinner, we stop at the Pirates' House Restaurant in Savannah. The building dates to 1753 and has quite a history. A dark passage, now behind protective bars, appears to our left as we're led to our table in a newer dining area. According to legend, unsuspecting tavern-goers would be encouraged to drink to intoxication and, when incapacitated, would be carried through this waterfront tunnel to a waiting ship on which they would wake up the next morning well out to sea. Given the colonial history of press gangs, it's possible such stories have basis in fact. "Efficient concept," Kareen notes. We survive an excellent seafood feast without being pressed into service. The return to Charleston by the alternate coastal route gets us back to our hotel room in time for a blissful rest.

After returning to Chicago, I have a week to catch up on life before the next park visit, this one close to home. The following Sunday, January 10, in bone-numbing cold at two degrees, I roll up and down the hills of southwestern Wisconsin's "Driftless Zone," named as such because the glaciers that flattened much of the upper Midwest during the last ice age ten thousand years ago did not cover this area. The glaciers bypassed southwestern Wisconsin but continued farther south, leveling much of Illinois into the prairie that gave the state its nickname.

Today marks the first of more than 350 parks I'll visit solo throughout the year. I miss Kareen's company. The excitement of park exploration combats loneliness, but today's frigid temperatures curtail any impulse to hike. An upside of solo travel will be the countless books on tape I'll enjoy while logging over eighteen hundred hours of windshield time this year.

Today's destination lies on the Mississippi River bluffs north of Harper's Ferry, Iowa, and across from Prairie du Chien, Wisconsin. **Effigy Mounds National Monument** splits into a north and south unit. The more frequently visited north unit's main trail starts behind the visitor center. I walked the north unit trail during my first three visits, enjoying the 850-to-1,400-year-old mounds and views from the high river bluff of eagles bouncing in the air currents only feet away. During my last visit, I explored the south unit's Marching Bear Mound Group. Many visitors skip the four-mile roundtrip hike from a small parking area along State Highway 76 to the park's southern boundary and miss this spectacular sequence of well-preserved mounds shaped into ten bears and three birds in flight.

With the bitter cold outside, I enter the theater to watch some park service videos as part of a special film review taking place this weekend. The first film is a documentary on world population growth and its impact on fish populations. Much of the footage features Jamaica. The island's coastal waters have been overfished in the past half century. Most larger fish have vanished, leaving only immature specimens. I think about our upcoming trip to Jamaica and eating some of those fish. Meanwhile, I'm anxious to schedule more park travel. The cold keeps me off the trails at Effigy Mounds, but it won't at my next destination in the southern Arizona desert.

2 The Mighty Cacti

EARLY THURSDAY MORNING, January 14, I board a United flight bound for Arizona's second largest city, Tucson. Scattered across the Sonoran Desert, six unexplored southern Arizona parks await. Thursday's objective is the east unit of **Saguaro National Park**, my first new park in 2016. Saguaro's two units bookend Tucson east-west. Both areas protect the ecosystem of the mighty saguaro cactus rising from the dusty hillsides. The giant saguaro's image adorns Arizona's license plates and symbolizes the desert southwest. The cactus can live 175–200 years, grow to over fifty feet in height, and weigh more than sixteen thousand pounds at full maturity.

From the airport, I'm off in a white Nissan Sentra rental to Western National Association's headquarters store in the northern suburbs. The nonprofit Western National Association (WNA) runs stores at over seventy NPS units, all west of the Mississippi. I'm here to ask about centennial promotional items like lapel pins and T-shirts. When I explain the visit's purpose to the lady staffing the counter, her eyes widen, and she bursts, "You're the guy who ordered all those pins last year! We were just talking about you yesterday!" She doesn't share a context.

I smile nervously, afraid to ask. I might be the lapel pin maniac from Illinois, featured on some unsolved crime show. "I've started a new project with the centennial and Find Your Park lapel pins, and I'm wondering if I can buy them directly from Western," I inform her.

"We're working on putting them on our website today," she shares. "You can probably place an order in about a week."

"That's great news. I'm not sure I'll make it to all the Western parks this year. I visited over half of them last year. Even if I make it back, it will be late in the year."

With the information and two new centennial T-shirts, because the twenty or so I've purchased in the past five months aren't enough, I return south to the Rincon Mountain Visitor Center at Saguaro East to solicit hiking advice. It's a good idea to get recommendations. I frequently adjust plans based on staff suggestions and real-time information. A thin, gray-haired gentleman volunteering in the park smiles as he outlines my visit today. "Start on Cactus Forest Drive, an eight-mile loop passing multiple trails. Stop at the Desert Ecology Trail, an easy, quarter-mile paved information path next to Javelina Wash. The road passes hillsides covered with saguaro. I would also check out the one-mile Freeman Homestead Trail. You can see the visible foundations of the 1929 Freeman family homestead." Homesteading plays a crucial role in Tucson area development as in many western states. Immersed among the cacti, I'm struck by how the saguaro dominate the landscape. The giant cacti tower over the undulating ground. These "sentinels of the desert" command the view in every direction.

Saguaro National Park's two units, the eastern Rincon Mountain District and the western Tucson Mountain District, carry the name of their respective mountains. From the higher points in the park, I follow the Rincon and Tucson Ranges running latitudinally away from the city tucked into the alluvial plain between them. The saguaro-studded slopes distract me until dusk. The receding sun splits the cactus fields into shadowed and brightly lit areas. The contrast is striking as night beckons across the desert. It's time to find my hotel east on I-10. Tomorrow requires an early start to reach three more parks.

Friday morning, I'm awake by four o'clock for work tasks

before a two-hour commute. **Fort Bowie National Historic Site**, one of the ten least-visited parks in the Lower 48, hosts just over eight thousand centennial visitors. Physically healthy visitors hike one and a half miles one way to reach the visitor center adjacent to the fort's newest rendition. Although an annoyance to the sedentary, this unique and clever feature embodies the park's history, passing the ruins of the original Fort Bowie, explored via a short side trail, the remnants of an old station for the short-lived Butterfield Overland Mail stagecoach route, the fort's cemetery, and the site of the Battle of Apache Pass. The trail ends at the last and largest fort site.

From 1862 to 1889, when the Chiricahua Apache leader Geronimo surrendered with his last band of holdouts, Fort Bowie dominated US Army operations against the Apache resisting westward expansion. In the Battle of Apache Pass, July 15–16, 1862, native warriors ambushed an army in route to confront Confederates in New Mexico. Fort construction began the following month. The post protected Apache Pass and Apache Spring with its precious water amid the dry, inhospitable climate. The original fort, a hasty, three-week construction effort, proved insufficient. Needing more protective and durable structures, the army built the second, larger Fort Bowie in 1868 on a plateau in the pass about three hundred yards to the southeast of the first fort.

On the walk to the fort, I meet a ranger who explains how to spot rattlesnakes. If you listen for the sound of rustling leaves aside the trail, you can sometimes spot rattlers fleeing the perceived threat of a larger animal. Last year in West Texas, I learned about snakes' keen sense of vibration. I try to use the trait to my advantage by stepping purposefully in rattlesnake country. The most important rule is to avoid putting your hands anywhere you can't see. Give the snake some space and route of escape, and it will generally flee.

At the visitor center, a kind and enthusiastic ranger shares the site's history. His welcoming exuberance seems incongruent to this lonely place. After exploring the first and second fort, I return to the trail head for the short half-hour drive to the next park, one of the most memorable new parks I'll see all year, **Chiricahua National Monument.**

The Chiricahua Apache called it the land of "standing up rocks." I've described the park as a set of canyons carved by a thousand stone masons who vanished, leaving nothing other than their creation. The park covers a mountainous area amid the desert called a sky island. The sky island rises to elevations over ninety-seven hundred feet at the confluence of four ecosystems. Two mountain chains, the Sierra Madre and Rocky Mountains, and two deserts, the Sonoran and Chihuahuan Desert, converge here. Massive volcanic eruptions a short distance to the south created this sky island around twenty-seven million years ago. The surviving eroded rock rises in carved spires left behind after ash and softer rock washed away. I consider Chiricahua to be one of the park system's hidden gems.

The visitor center lies a few miles from the west entrance on the eight-mile Bonita Canyon Drive. The park's single road climbs from an elevation of 5,124 feet at the entrance to Massai Point at 6,870 feet, offering access to many hiking trails that skirt canyon rims or drop to the canyon floor.

I start in Echo Canyon with one of the spectacular canyon rim trails, this one leading to the Echo Canyon Grotto, a place where twisted and irregular-shaped openings in the rock are large enough for the trail to pass through. Given we're less than fifty miles from the Mexican border, it's mildly surprising to see snow and thick ice covering shaded sections of trail. The altitude brings winter weather and temperatures to the higher elevations despite the sixty to seventy degree temperatures and sunshine on the surrounding desert floor. Ice-covered trail sections partially exposed to sunlight require extreme caution. The morning melt leaves a thin layer of water over the ice, rendering it void of traction. The same freeze-thaw cycle has carved the stone along the canyon walls for millennia. Today's temperature at altitude stays in the low forties and sunny, pleasant hiking weather in my jacket and gloves.

The canyon trails reveal a never-ending series of stone columns both attached to the canyon wall and free standing. As the trail winds its way around the shifting canyon rim, each blind turn exposes a new panorama of pinnacles and pillars across the canyon, similar yet unique. The views could be an endless series of Ansel Adams photographs. On the wet ice, I bob my head up and down, shuffling forward while taking pictures. It's hard to stop taking pictures as each section of canyon and its rock spire cathedral burst into frame.

Chiricahua rock columns

I cover several miles between Echo Canyon and additional trails before the cold air drains my camera's dying battery. It seems wrong to be here without a functional camera, even though I've already taken lots of pictures. Such is the challenge of Chiricahua. On my exit, I stop again at the visitor center, mostly to offer high praise. The rangers ask, "How are the trail conditions?"

I reply, "The sections with wet ice are treacherous. And I have a complaint."

"Oh?" a younger female ranger asks with a raised eyebrow.

"This park is so captivating, you can't put your camera down long enough to enjoy it! Work on it before my next visit," I say over my shoulder as I open the door to leave. I can hear the rangers laughing as the door closes behind me.

With the early start, I have enough time to reach the day's third new park. **Coronado National Memorial** lies on the Mexican border about seventy miles west of the New Mexico state line. Upon arrival, I've got a couple of hours to orient myself. Current conditions on the dirt and gravel road to Montezuma Pass require a four-wheel drive. The Sentra won't cut it. I hoped to see Montezuma Pass Overlook and walk the southern terminus of the **Arizona National Scenic Trail**, which runs eight hundred miles north to Utah. I'll cross the trail again near its northern terminus later this year.

Instead, I hike the one-mile trail to Coronado Cave, penetrating the north side of Montezuma Canyon, with Montezuma Peak's 7,676 feet looming above. I pause to catch my breath, wipe the sweat from my brow, and gaze east over the San Pedro River Valley. Francisco Vasquez de Coronado's 1540–1542 expeditionary route followed the river north seeking the Seven Cities of Cibola, the mythical land of gold and jewels falsely reported by others that had motivated his quest.

From the trail's switchbacks, I see the border wall glistening in the afternoon sun. The wall stops near the western park boundary, replaced by a fence to permit wildlife migration. I'm winded by the four-hundred-foot elevation gain. I'm thinking, "It's an easy trail with nice scenery. Why the struggle?" It's a theme that will repeat itself this year. It occurs to me that the collective effects of yesterday's early flight, today's early start, seven miles of hiking, and five hours of driving are testing the limit of my endurance. I force myself to keep moving. Some new experience ahead always vindicates the effort. Today's finish is anticlimactic. The cave mouth appears as an uninviting black hole contracted by piles of fallen rocks. I'm losing momentum. Retreating from the cave, I descend as darkness falls over the valley.

As for Coronado, he never found his seven cities of gold, and returned to Mexico City in shame, spending the next four years trying to clear his name and dying in obscurity ten years after his return. He died unaware he had earned something rarer than gold, historical immortality.

Saturday begins with the first three locations, from south to north, on the **Juan Bautista de Anza National Historic Trail**. The trail follows the 1776 journey of Juan Bautista de Anza from Mexico to establish a settlement at San Francisco. The third trail stop, **Tumacacori National Historical Park** protects the native (Pima) settlement site where, in January 1691, Jesuit Eusebio Francisco Kino established the mission San Cayetano de Tumacacori on the east bank of the Santa Cruz River. The mission remained active for 157 years, the first in a series extending north into central Arizona. After touring the grounds and river trail, I continue following the Juan Bautista National Historic Trail to the town of Tubac. In 1751, Spanish soldiers established a presidio, or fort, at Tubac after the Pima attacked Tumacacori.

Continuing the historic trail as far as the Presidio of Tucson, I divert across the Sonoran Desert to **Organ Pipe National Monument**, which covers the southernmost twenty-two miles of State Highway 85 to southwestern Arizona's international border. Organ Pipe's Kris Eggle Visitor Center honors a young park ranger killed by drug smugglers using the park as a travel corridor. Frequent signs warn visitors about dangerous criminals. The warnings don't detract from the grandeur of the park's namesake, the large organ pipe cacti growing on the southern sunbaked desert hillsides.

The twenty-one-mile Ajo Mountain Drive leads me to several trailheads highlighted by a trek into Arch Canyon. The box canyon features an arch high on the heavily eroded bluff skirted by the trail entering the canyon, where another arch appears high on the canyon's far wall. The Ajo Mountain Drive makes a loop in the park area east of Highway 85, while the North Puerto Blanco Drive runs from the visitor center ten miles west. The sun drops to the horizon as I exit the park, exhausted but exhilarated.

Sunday morning, I arrive at the Tucson Mountain District of Saguaro National Park, driving the Scenic Bajada Loop Drive through the subunit's saguaro-covered hills and walking some short trails before an NPTC meet-up event at the Red Hills Visitor Center. The meet-ups started last year to encourage group activities. This is my second meet-up, having attended one at Pullman National Monument in Chicago last October. The club distributes special passport stamps for the meet-ups, with a different stamp in a different color for each of the nine regions designated by Eastern National Association (EN), the nonprofit that operates most park bookstores in the eastern half of the US. EN launched the Passport to Your National Parks program in 1986.

The like-minded park enthusiasts attending these gatherings are a fascinating, diverse mix with a wealth of knowledge about the parks and related activities. Before the meet-ups, most prearranged member connection had been limited to the club's internet forum, annual conventions, and trips among friends. Each member chooses a user name. My NPTC user name is Cardinal Dave, for my favorite baseball team. I've worn a Cardinals hat in every NPS unit I've visited. Because I am a heavy park traveler and forum contributor, it seems like more people know me than I remember, though I often struggle with names and faces I've only heard or seen once. The many enthusiastic and kind members I've met through club activities are a joy and motivational boost.

Members occasionally share significant park experiences in the forum. One example is a centennial thread that another member, Lee, and I started in December 2015, challenging each other to collect the most cancellations and visit the most parks in 2016. The running exchange became the year's most widely read club thread.

In December, I met Lee by coincidence at George Washington Carver National Monument in southwest Missouri. A bespectacled, medium-build, gray-haired retiree from Springfield, Illinois, Lee plans every detail of his trips, each day mapped out on a spreadsheet. He developed these meticulous travel planning habits during his career as a pharmaceutical sales rep. Curious, I asked him about his experience collecting all the special commemorative cancellations for the passport program's twenty-fifth anniversary in 2011. He interpreted my question as a competitive challenge, and I agreed to play along by posting a provocative account of our discussion concluded later that same morning at Wilson's Creek National Battlefield. Kareen later described the resulting mano-a-mano challenge as, "I'm crazier than you are and I'm going to prove it!" Her observation has merit. The thread title "Centennial Madness" proved prophetic.

Seventeen members, mostly from the southwest, attend the Saguaro event, my trip's finale. Soaking in the last bit of heat, I bid farewell to catch my return flight back to the dead of winter. I'll be home less than twenty-four hours for laundry, mail, and preparation. Tomorrow, I begin a return to warmth in the Sunshine State.

3 *The Gulf Coast*

TWELVE HOURS AFTER returning home from Tucson, the wheels roll again to my seventh St. Louis Cardinals Fantasy camp in Jupiter, Florida. These camps have brought some remarkable people into my life. I think of my friends in three separate spheres, or families: a park family, a baseball family, and a track and field family. I've been a certified track and field official since 1994, working mostly collegiate meets. Although I've cut back on the number of track meets in the past few years, I appreciate the good people I've met in the track and field community over thirty years of officiating and competing. Spring brings all three groups to the forefront on a revolving basis.

The ambitious eighteen-day itinerary begins Monday, January 18. I'm meeting two friends in Mississippi to visit park and heritage area sites. Next, I'll swing through Louisiana, following the Gulf Coast east and south to Everglades City. After traversing southern Florida's wetlands, I'll continue to Key West. Returning through Miami and the camp in Jupiter, I'll travel north along the Atlantic Coast.

Today's outbound route passes the Illinois capital of Springfield and the first park. **Lincoln Home National Historic Site** preserves the only house the sixteenth president of the United States ever owned. In addition to Abraham and Mary Todd Lincoln's home, the park includes the surrounding Jackson and Eighth Street neighborhood and its Lincoln-era structures. I've learned something new on each of my four home tours in Lincoln's world. Entering this house elicits a momentousness, as if American history has enveloped me in the weight of a nation's fate that so aged Lincoln during his presidency, accentuating the sunken cheeks and deeply carved facial lines familiar to us on the five-dollar bill.

Springfield forms the center of the **Abraham Lincoln National Heritage Area**. The heritage area highlights important places in Lincoln's life, mostly as a lawyer traveling the state judicial circuit. For sixteen years of his legal career, Lincoln spent twenty weeks a year in the county seats across central Illinois. During my youth we visited many antebellum Illinois homes, observing that each site's caretakers now claim a Lincoln overnight stay. In truth, Lincoln did sleep in many places while traveling with the state circuit court and his fellow jurists. From Springfield, I conclude the day south of Memphis. I'm meeting two other NPTC members tomorrow morning to tour locations in the **Mississippi Delta National Heritage Area** and **Mississippi Hills National Heritage Area**.

Deborah, Lee, and I will travel among participating sites in both heritage areas for the next two and a half days. Deborah is a trim professional retiree with short-cropped gray hair and a friendly smile reflecting her kind and thoughtful disposition. She's keeping the peace between Lee and me during this brief armistice from our centennial challenge. After visiting multiple Mississippi Delta locations Tuesday morning, we make an afternoon stop at Tupelo and the headquarters of the **Natchez Trace National Scenic Trail** and the 444-mile long **Natchez Trace Parkway**. The trail parallels the parkway over sixty miles in five different areas from the parkway's southern terminus at the Mississippi River town of Natchez to its northern terminus entering Nashville. I've been on both the trail and parkway countless times during childhood visits to my mother's family in Mississippi and Louisiana. The trace's pines, swamps, and live oaks adorned with Spanish moss bring fond memories of family excursions, the scented, humid air, and delicious home-cooked meals. Natchez Trace National Scenic Trail includes sections of the original footpath used before steamboats made travel up the Mississippi River feasible. Prior to the mid-1820s, traders shipping goods to lower Mississippi markets floated downriver on flatboats, returning north via the trace. Long before settlers used the trace, Native Americans traveled and traded over the route.

The Parkway headquarters also administers **Brices Cross Roads National Battlefield Site and Tupelo National Battlefield**. At Brices Cross Roads, southern forces led by one of the Civil War's most successful generals, Major General Nathan Bedford Forrest, fought a northern army led by Brigadier General Samuel Sturgis on June 10, 1864. The Union withdrew from a defensive position at the cross roads under heavy pressure, fracturing into a chaotic retreat northwest over an overflowing Tishomingo Creek. Forrest utilized his characteristic tactics during the engagement, compensating for his outnumbered force with cunning, guile, deception, and bravery.

We stop at the Brices Cross Roads Visitor and Interpretative Center off Highway 45 near Baldwyn, Mississippi and talk with the staff about our battlefield tours. Most visitors start with the center's documentary film narrated by the famous Civil War historian and writer Shelby Foote. An enthusiastic docent educates us on the origin of several unique artifacts, offering fascinating and sometimes sad anecdotes beyond the interpretive descriptions. "A man donated this gun his family recovered after the battle," he explains, pointing to a muzzle-loading hunting rifle. "It belonged to a local Confederate boy who died fighting on his own farm."

Tupelo National Battlefield Site is a one-acre town parcel. Interpretive panels there and at a few rural locations tell the story of the July 14–15, 1864 battle. Confederate forces including Forrest's men under overall command of Major General Stephen D. Lee fought a bloody and indecisive engagement with Union forces under Major General Andrew J. Smith, charged with the difficult task of keeping Forrest occupied in the west, away from Sherman's Nashville–Chattanooga supply line.

Deborah split from us this afternoon, having visited Tupelo a month ago. Both Lee and I have visited these park units separately several times. We stop at the Parkway Visitor Center north of Tupelo to chat with the staff. The rangers enjoy hearing of our extensive park travels and passport stamp collections. They take a picture for the park's social media page of us posing with our passport books.

Deborah rejoins us for dinner in Clarksdale, Mississippi Tuesday night. Wednesday morning, the three of us visit the Mississippi Delta National Heritage Area headquarters on the campus of Delta State University in Cleveland, Mississippi, and across the street from the Grammy Music Awards Museum. We're greeted with great cheer and hospitality by the heritage area's friendly staff. The Mississippi Delta National Heritage Area and their partner sites celebrate the delta's rich history and musical legacy. Later today, they feature a picture of us in social media. We also appear in the heritage area's next newsletter. The energy, enthusiasm, and kindness at the heritage area office lifts our spirits, and we depart amid smiles aplenty. In keeping with their cultural education mission, the staff provided a firsthand experience in southern hospitality.

After Deborah's departure Wednesday evening, Lee and I complete the heritage area itinerary Thursday morning before splitting up. By noon, I'm passing through **Vicksburg National Military Park** on a restricted agenda compared to prior tours, beginning with a photo stop at the Illinois Memorial and the section of scarred battleground it overlooks. These areas reveal the remnants of deep trenches and earthworks dug by both sides during the forty-seven day siege, ending in Confederate capitulation on July 4, 1863. The intimacy of Vicksburg's siege and combat has always struck me. Combatants could and did speak to each other across lines that sometimes approached within fifty feet. The humanity within the tragedy of Americans killing one another leaves a lingering sadness every time I visit.

One of the park's newer features is the USS *Cairo*, a Union gunboat sunk by a mine in the Yazoo River. I walk around the exhibit's covered platform supporting recovered pieces of the gunboat reconstructed around a wooden frame. Naval gunboats played a crucial role in the Union's campaign to reduce Vicksburg and gain control of the Mississippi.

The detached park locations of South Fort, Navy Circle, and Louisiana Circle represent Confederate gun batteries blocking northern traffic on the Mississippi River bend below Vicksburg's bluffs. Rear Admiral David Dixon Porter ran his gunboats past these batteries in April 1863 as Grant's Union army bypassed the town on the Louisiana side. Circumventing Vicksburg's commanding river defenses proved the campaign's decisive stroke. Grant's force crossed the river well south of Vicksburg at Bruinsburg, Mississippi, and defeated Confederate forces in multiple battles before enveloping General John C. Pemberton and his thirty thousand troops. The river reopened to commerce following Vicksburg's surrender and Port Hudson's reduction five days later, inspiring Abraham Lincoln's famous line, "The Father of Waters again goes unvexed to the sea."

One of the two most recently designated US World Heritage Sites, northeastern Louisiana's **Poverty Point National Monument** features mounds and earthworks constructed between 1750 BC and 700 BC. After walking through the mounds last year, heavy rain this afternoon forces me to settle for collecting cancellations and reviewing the indoor exhibits. I stop for the night in Natchitoches, Louisiana, awaiting the first new park of the trip tomorrow morning.

Cane River Creole National Historical Park preserves the Oakland and Magnolia Plantations near the Cane River southeast and downstream of Natchitoches. I seem to be the Oakland Plantation's only visitor on this January weekday. A maintenance project forestalls home tours, but I walk among both plantations' surviving structures reading descriptions of the free and enslaved inhabitants. My solitary stroll ends when I meet a lonely ranger in the back building serving as a small visitor contact station. The park lies within the **Cane River National Heritage Area** and its story of the original Native American, Spanish, French, and African people.

Natchez National Historical Park features two primary locations, the Melrose mansion and estate and the William Johnson House. Both tell unique and interesting stories about the structures and people who lived in the antebellum river town. Many consider

Melrose to be one of the Natchez area's finest historical homes. A combination of enslaved and free laborers constructed the mansion in the 1840s on 132 acres of land owned by John McMurran, a successful Natchez lawyer. Visitors can walk the grounds and join a ranger-guided tour to see how McMurran reflected his wealth in the home's amenities.

William Johnson, born in 1809 and believed to be the son of his owner and a mulatto slave, gained his emancipation from his probable father at eleven. He apprenticed as a barber with his uncle and eventually owned three barbershops and a bath house. By the 1840s, Johnson's commercial success extended into the agrarian countryside to include farming with enslaved labor. Johnson's story survives through a daily diary covering sixteen years, from 1835 until his 1851 death. While providing an entertaining account of local events and personalities, the diary reveals little about his personal feelings on much of anything. He moved into the building now preserved by the park service in March 1841 and used the main floor space for a barbershop while he and his family lived in the rooms above. I toured both the Melrose and Johnson homes in the past two years. Today's stops are shorter, as I have another three-hour drive south in the twilight, bound for New Orleans.

Friday night's arrival at my airport hotel brings a welcome pause for a good meal and a cold beer at the sports bar next door. My road routine systemizes such meals. I eat sparingly and stay active by day, steadily losing weight as the year progresses. I only eat to avoid the discomfort of hunger. Park activities preempt meals in daylight hours. Kareen, who exercises intensely each morning, sarcastically dubs my dinner convention the "steak and beer diet." She declares it unjust that I roam through parks all day, losing weight exploring history and beauty, then eat whatever I like at night. In her mind, I'm always eating some delicious and exotic local food contrasting with her Spartan lifestyle. My food consumption is much more Epicurean in her imagination than reality. Seizing the opportunity, I keep her informed when I do eat something delicious. I describe the dish in detail to convince her I'm rapturous in my culinary infidelity. Tonight, I convince her that my mediocre Cajun chicken sandwich is a delicacy fit for kings. At least the beer is always cold.

Saturday, I stop at the French Quarter visitor centers on Decatur Street for the first two parks, **Jean Lafitte National Historical Park and Preserve** and **New Orleans Jazz National Historical Park**. Kareen and I visited both parks last March during a long weekend in the Crescent City. New Orleans Jazz National Historical Park is the only park unit in the country dedicated to a form of music and one of two dedicated to the performance arts. We toured all six visitor centers in Jean Lafitte National Historical Park, named after a New Orleans smuggler and privateer turned patriot in the War of 1812. Lafitte and his brother fought courageously under Andrew Jackson in the war's final major conflict at Chalmette Battlefield. The park service preserves the center of the battleground, which occupies a section of the Mississippi River's north bank a few miles east of the French Quarter.

Jackson and his troops defeated the British army on January 8, 1815. The battle took place after the countries agreed to peace at Ghent, Belgium, in December 1814, but the pace of Atlantic travel delayed this news to the participants. Andrew Jackson gained national fame through the victory. The strength of that popularity earned him two terms in the White House from 1829 through 1837.

The furthest of the six visitor centers from New Orleans, the Jean Lafitte NHP Prairie Acadian Cultural Center is located nearly three hours west in Eunice, Louisiana. The Eunice facility and the Acadian Cultural Center in Lafayette focus on southern Louisiana's Creole and Cajun culture. They tell the story of the local amalgamation of French, Spanish, Native American, Caribbean, African, and British peoples. The park film dramatizes the story of the French-speaking Acadians, or Cajuns, who were evicted by the British from their Nova Scotia homeland in the late 1700s after France ceded its claims over Canada. We stopped near Lafayette for a lunch of boiled and seasoned crayfish, a childhood favorite from those Louisiana trips. In the afternoon, we visited the two ecologically themed visitor centers, the Wetlands Acadian Cultural Center in Thibodaux and the Barataria Preserve in the wetlands south of New Orleans. The Barataria Preserve includes some of the same swampland and bayou waterways used by Jean Lafitte and his Baratarian smugglers in the early 1800s.

From the French Quarter, I go east through the **Mississippi Gulf Coast National Heritage Area**, stopping at a few heritage area locations on the way to the next new park in Ocean Springs, Mississippi. **Gulf Islands National Seashore** has two subunits, one in Mississippi and an eastern subunit near Pensacola, Florida. We'll revisit the wonderful folks in the Mississippi Gulf Coast National Heritage Area in chapter 40.

It's midafternoon when I arrive at the William M. Colmer Visitor Center in Ocean Springs. After watching the park film and sharing my story, a ranger gives me one of the rectangular centennial lapel pins for employees and volunteers, which I immediately fasten on my red Cardinals hat. The ranger's kind gift is appreciated and a bit of karma.

Last summer, I sought to accomplish something during the centennial beyond seeing parks and collecting passport stamps. I wanted to create something to acknowledge these places and express my gratitude to the rangers and park staff that have helped me so much along the way. The project concept derived from a framed display of all thirty national trails signs at the Ice Age National Scenic Trail headquarters in Madison, Wisconsin. The symmetrical display caught my attention and reminded me of my trail experiences. Might I do something similar for the parks?

In early August 2015, two new promotional lapel pin sets appeared in park stores. A bright-gold-colored pin featured the centennial logo on the top half and the park's name below, and a white pin had the multicolor Find Your Park logo above the gold-lettered park name. In total, the pins represented 248 National Park Service locations across forty-six states and territories. I began collecting the sets, 483 pins in all, to have them mounted and framed as a traveling park exhibit and eventual donation to the park service. Though the concept seemed simple enough, the project became a twenty-month effort to complete the displays and a multiyear obligation to see the traveling exhibit become reality.

Cumberland Gap, Centennial and Find Your Park lapel pin exhibit

At Mississippi's Gulf Islands, I pick up the unit's pins and drive the park road through Davis Bayou inside the mainland park boundary. Gulf Islands National Seashore includes five barrier islands off the Mississippi Gulf Coast, and Santa Rosa Island and Presidio Key off the Florida Gulf Coast. During the summer months, boats run to the Mississippi barrier islands, including the Civil War–era Fort Massachusetts on West Ship Island. For this midwinter visit, I walk the Nature's Way Loop Trail before watching an alligator and some turtles perched on a log warming themselves as the afternoon sun drops low over the bayou.

The park's Florida attractions are accessible by car from the mainland. From a Gulf Breeze hotel, I start Sunday with a short trip across Santa Rosa Sound to the western end of Santa Rosa Island and Fort Pickens. The oldest part of Fort Pickens was constructed in 1829 as part of the Third System of US Coastal Defenses. Third system fortifications built between 1817 and 1867 include twenty-nine major installations protecting the country's coasts and borders. Twelve surviving structures are protected in nine separate NPS units. Posts within park units include Ft. Wadsworth, Ft. Monroe, Ft. Moultrie, Ft. Sumter, Ft. Pulaski, Ft. Jefferson, Ft. Pickens, Ft. Barrancas, Ft. Massachusetts, Ft. Union, Ft. Point, and Alcatraz Island. These forts are all based around the brick construction preferred before the era of rifled artillery.

Fort Pickens served as the primary defense for Pensacola Bay from the Civil War through World War II. I tour the older areas of the fort, defended in January of 1861 after the Union commander, Lieutenant Adam Slemmer, consolidated the three harbor entry defense garrisons into Fort Pickens, the most defensible of the locations. Fort McRee, Fort Barrancas, and Fort Pickens formed a triangular line of crossfire covering the port's inlet. Fort McRee's ruins now lie underwater as the Gulf of Mexico's winds and waves steadily push Presidio Key and the other islands west. Fort Barrancas survives as a separate area of the park on the north side of the bay's inlet.

My tour of Fort Pickens includes tunnels leading to three powder charges under the fort's northwest corner. The charges would destroy the fort in case of an irreversible breech. From the walls of the parapet, I look to the west, south, and east over the more recent batteries dating from the Spanish-American War to World War II. Fort Pickens also anchors the northern terminus of the thirteen-hundred-mile **Florida National Scenic Trail**, which ends in southern Florida at Big Cypress National Preserve.

After the morning at Fort Pickens, I return to the mainland through Pensacola to reach the solid, intact brick structure of Fort Barrancas. The initial Spanish fortification dates to 1698. After a brief French possession, followed by British control in the 1700s, the Spanish returned during the American Revolution. The current water battery below the fort's southern rampart dates to the postrevolutionary Spanish era. The US Army built Fort Barrancas between 1839 and 1844. The visitor center houses an excellent model of the structures. A third fortification, the Advanced Redoubt of Fort Barrancas, built between 1845 and 1870, protects the northern side of the peninsula and the nearby naval yards. After touring the three structures, I exit the park to enter the National Naval Aviation Museum.

The navy's aviation museum earns its exceptional reputation. The planes, aircraft carrier models, and stories of combat and heroism are well presented and can fascinate a student of twentieth-century military history for a day or longer. After a full day exploring Gulf Islands National Seashore and the introductory tour of the Naval Aviation Museum, I ease onto eastbound I-10 for a seven-and-a-half-hour drive to Bradenton, Florida. I'm starting to lose focus by the time I reach the Hampton Inn parking lot at 1:30 a.m. Sleep comes easy on this night.

De Soto National Memorial represents Hernando De Soto's May 1539 landfall. The expedition's landing began a four-year odyssey wandering through modern America's southeastern states. De Soto did not survive, dying three years into the journey in May 1542. The survivors spent the expedition's last winter in the Mississippi River Valley before making their way downstream and back to Mexico City with only a story to show for the effort. The Memorial Trail loops through the park past the Holy Eucharist Monument and the Memorial Cross. Placards placed in the ground at regular intervals give information about area natives and their interaction with the expedition. I find one particularly memorable for its macabre account of Spaniards punishing disfavored native guides by throwing them to vicious dogs that literally tore them apart. It reminds us that the interaction between Europeans and natives could go horribly wrong.

My route south along the Gulf Coast terminates at Everglades City, Florida, the literal end of the road. The Gulf Coast Visitor Center of **Everglades National Park** represents the conclusion of my 850-mile drive from New Orleans through parts of five Gulf Coast parks. The visitor center is my preswamp pit stop.

The Big Cypress Swamp Visitor Center heralds entrance into **Big Cypress National Preserve**. We'll explore farther into Everglades National Park, but for now I continue east on US Highway 41 through Big Cypress National Preserve to the Oasis Visitor Center.

Mature alligators sun themselves next to a canal beneath the fronting boardwalk. Some South Florida alligators have exceeded fifteen feet in length. Behind me in the short grass, markers announce the Florida National Scenic Trail's southern terminus. Two loop roads off US 41 take visitors deeper into the preserve.

My preserve visit is augmented with a stop at the Kirby Storter Boardwalk Trail, a one-mile roundtrip above swampy terrain to a gator hole. Alligators dredge these shallow water holes with their snouts and tails, maintaining them generationally as warm-weather cooling stations. I find the hole temporarily converted to a real-world snake pit with countless serpents warming themselves on exposed sections of partially submerged tree limbs. More snakes are visible below the surface of the dark and murky water. A young, two-foot alligator is the species' lone visible representative.

The day concludes traveling Everglades National Park's main park road, all thirty-eight miles from the Ernest E. Coe Visitor Center at the park entrance to the southern end at Flamingo. An NPS law enforcement SUV speeding south passes me, emergency lights flashing. I arrive in Flamingo to the whirring blades of a medivac helicopter landing and watch a ranger bodily carry someone from the SUV to the helicopter.

After the helicopter rises and disappears to the north, I follow on the road through the mangroves dominating the southern end of the park, pausing about five miles out of Flamingo to wander down Snake Bright Trail. Lacking strong repellent, I venture far enough to appreciate the trail's shaded mangrove setting through standing water on both sides before the mosquitoes launch an all-out assault. The swamp trail should be named Snake and Mosquito Bite Trail. I continue north for an evening drive across the Florida Keys. Tonight, I'm staying in Marathon, about fifty miles short of Key West. I've got an early start to catch a ferry boat departing Key West at 8:00 a.m.

Dry Tortugas National Park consists of seven small keys seventy miles distant at the western end of the 330-mile Florida Archipelago. The trip is two and a half hours each way by boat, leaving day trippers four hours to explore the picturesque spot. The bright-blue Caribbean water contrasts with the tiny, isolated coral island shoreline. There is sufficient history and bird species for amateur historians and birders alike. Our time at the park allows a relaxed pace to absorb the place's inherent beauty.

The park's centerpiece is Fort Jefferson, the product of an uncompleted 1846 construction project spanning thirty years on Garden Key. The largest nineteenth-century masonry fort on United States soil served to protect Mississippi River–Gulf of Mexico shipping lanes but never saw active combat and became a post–Civil War prison. I visit the second-level casemate cell above the sally port that housed the fort's most famous inmate, Dr. Samuel Mudd, convicted of conspiracy in Abraham Lincoln's assassination based on his treatment of John Wilkes Booth's broken leg. The assassin suffered the injury jumping from the presidential box in Ford's Theatre. Booth stopped at Mudd's Maryland country home in flight from Washington. After the post doctor and commandant died from illness, Mudd treated dangerously sick soldiers and inmates suffering through a malaria outbreak. He earned numerous letters of accommodation from the prison staff supporting a less-vengeful view of his role after Lincoln's death and a presidential pardon from Andrew Johnson after four years.

Another interesting and more recent piece of Fort Jefferson history is the chug boat display in the southwest corner's ground level. These keys comprise the closest US land to Cuba, just over eighty miles across the Florida Strait. Groups of desperate Cuban refugees targeted the islands as their destination. The boats came to be called "chugs" for the sound carried across the water from the variety of makeshift inboard and outboard motors powering the vessels. The official US policy on Cuban refugees through most of the period without formal diplomatic relations rendered no assistance or returned to Cuba those found at sea but granted asylum to those landing on US soil. A casemate exhibit features two ramshackle boats used for this purpose. Their condition and size are such that few would dare take them on a small lake, much less the open ocean. They are fifteen feet or less in length with a capacity under ten. They overflowed with thirty or more people when they made landfall at Garden Key. Their dilapidated condition, with patched hulls and retasked motors put together with homemade replacement parts, speak to the refugees' desperation and courage. Some chugs rode so low in the water that refugees reported fatalities from shark attack. Many highly educated professionals, including doctors, lawyers, and engineers, are counted among those landing within the park. The history of Cuban migration to south Florida is a complex story, from the 1980 Mariel boatlift, which saw as many as 125,000 Cubans flee to US shores in six months, to the division created between Cubans and others in the Hispanic community due to the special immigration status derived from the US "dry land" policy.

Dry Tortugas, Fort Jefferson on Garden Key

I meet some interesting fellow visitors on the boat, including an art professor taking a sabbatical to visit all fifty-nine national parks and creating one or more paintings based on each park. We share stories of our experiences, making the trip seem shorter and the world smaller. Dry Tortugas is his fifty-seventh national park. We dock in Key West as darkness falls. Having concluded my purpose in the eclectic town, I begin retreating up the island chain for a night's rest near Homestead, Florida.

Wednesday's schedule requires another early start. The day begins at the Dante Fascell Visitor Center in **Biscayne National Park**. The park's surface area is 95 percent water, from Biscayne Bay into the Atlantic Ocean. Biscayne National Park hosts four distinct ecosystems, including the longest continuous mangrove shoreline on Florida's east coast, the bay, the islands composed of coral deposits that comprise the northern end of the Florida Archipelago and Keys, and the living coral reef. It's my second visit at the visitor center, but I'm still waiting to get on the bay. I have a great conversation with Ranger Gary, sharing comments about Dry Tortugas. He suggests that since I'm alone, they could ask for permission to join a school group taking a boat out to one of the keys. It's very tempting, but I need to keep moving. I will have to wait until January 2018 to get on the water here with a trip across the bay to Boca Chita Key, formerly owned by millionaire industrialist Frank Honeywell.

I've got a hard stop on park activities today. I'm picking up one of my fellow fantasy campers at the Miami airport at 1:00 p.m. The interim leaves time to see the Everglades National Park's Nike missile exhibit. The Nike Hercules Missile system is an antibomber aircraft defense system and one of several major deployments triggered by the Cuban Missile Crisis. After being initiated during the October 1962 crisis, HM-69, the base in the park, remained active until abandoned in 1979. The site is one of the best preserved in the country. Only in South Florida and Alaska are Nike missile sites above ground due to the impracticality of in-ground silos in either area. Earthen berms constructed around the launch pads protect adjacent areas and structures from blast damage.

A right turn off the road to the Royal Palm area leads to the missile site not far from the park entrance. The area is staffed for a few hours a couple of days a week. The exhibit's been open less than a year. When I pull up to the main exhibit building, I'm greeted by two veteran volunteers. Both served with different parts of the Nike operation. They walk me through the exhibit, including a complete de-armed, forty-one-foot Nike Hercules missile and its various components. The Hercules missile is one of the fastest missiles ever designed, and it needed to be for its intended purpose. The missile reached the speed of sound (760 feet/second) at launch, and a top speed three and a half times faster. The two ex-military men are delightful in conversation, and the exhibit is fascinating. Having the good fortune of being their only customer, I find myself here for well over an hour mentally downloading information.

The intention of the Hercules missile is to explode above a squadron of bombers rather than targeting individual aircraft. The Soviets had brought the IL-28, a lightweight nuclear-capable bomber, to Cuba with the land-based missiles, making the Nike system essential to defense operations. The Hercules can carry up to a forty-kiloton nuclear warhead. The size and proximity of the shock wave can knock a formation of planes out of the sky. I'm parked on the former launching pad, now identifiable only by marks on the pavement. The area around the pad contains twenty-two buildings and structures associated with the missile squadron. HM-69 housed three launch pads with three missiles each. Each launch pad had one nuclear-armed missile marked with a dark-green tip. The Everglades site is one of four south Florida Nike missile sites. Due to its distance from Cuba, only 160 miles by air, the south Florida Nike missile sites played a critical role.

President Kennedy recognized the important role the air defenders in South Florida played during the Cuban Missile Crisis by traveling to Homestead a month later and personally awarding the US Army's 2nd Missile Battalion, 52nd Air Defense Artillery the army's Meritorious Unit Commendation. The honor is usually only given during wartime, but such is Kennedy's estimation of the air defense group's importance in deterring escalation to conflict.

I'm running behind schedule. I could spend hours with the veterans, listening to their stories and experiences or wandering about Everglades National Park, but I have obligations and promises to keep. It's time to leave the parks for a few days and indulge another lifelong passion for America's greatest pastime.

4 The Atlantic Side

AFTER COLLECTING MY friend Mark, a middle aged, balding lawyer with a permanent smile and boundless enthusiasm, at the Miami Airport, we head north toward Jupiter to check in for the St. Louis Cardinals Fantasy Camp at our Palm Beach Gardens hotel. Smiling broadly, Mark asks, "Are you excited about camp?"

"I'm tired," I reply, sharing the essence of my year to date.

"Won't they fire you when they find out you're spending all this time in national parks?" Mark asks.

"I stopped growing at work four years ago," I reflect. "I guess it will be interesting to see whether they fire me or I quit first."

Camp structure and format vary among the MLB teams that offer them. They've grown in popularity over the years as most teams now sponsor one. They're typically held at the site where the MLB team conducts spring training, offering a few days' break in the winter. The most unexpected aspect of the camps has been meeting fellow campers, well-accomplished individuals from a broad geographical and vocational range. Many returning campers are friends who I occasionally see at ballparks across the country. Years before the park goal, I started taking advantage of heavy business travel to watch games in stadiums around the country. By the start of 2016, I'd seen games in twenty-eight of the thirty active MLB stadiums and six retired venues.

From the file of fellow campers I admire, Freddy has been my teammate at multiple camps. Slight of build with neatly cropped graying hair, the West Memphis police detective runs like a gazelle with the grace and poise of a natural athlete and has a positive attitude that is both gracious and infectious. The fact he's able to play in any game is a miracle. In 2002 as a patrol officer, he was shot in the face by an armed felon that had fled a traffic stop. The assailant opened fire at Freddy from close range through his open driver's side window while Freddy was still in his police cruiser. Despite being hit in the head, Freddy managed to stumble out of his patrol car and find cover, returning fire as best he could. One of his shots silenced the gunman permanently, but Freddy had to be transported by Medivac to a Memphis hospital where doctors discovered the bullet had deflected off his cheekbone and lodged in his neck, only a quarter inch away from a major artery and his spinal cord. Today Freddy is a positive force for good in his community and a genuine hero by any definition.

While fellow campers offer social humility, playing baseball provides plenty of the physical variety. My 2016 camp starts with Game 1 on Thursday afternoon. I go 2–2 with four RBI in a 4–4 tie, including the game-tying two-run double down the right field line with our team down to one strike during my final at bat. But it should have been a 5–4 victory. Shortly after reaching second base with my double, the next batter hit a clean single into right field. In my haste to run around third base, I stumble and face-plant into the grass about ten feet past the bag. I still have time to get up and come home with the winning run, but the other campers and our ex-pro coach at third base are so shocked by my human lawn dart impersonation and too concerned about my immediate physical condition to tell me to get up and keep running, and I'm too disoriented to confidently run home. I crawl back to third base to gather my wits. I swear I used to be a better athlete. I think it's better to give us another chance than walk into an out at home, but the next batter promptly grounds out. I could have walked home from second on that hit. I went from team hero to team jackass in one misstep. The camp humbles the average Joe and gives the typical fan an appreciation of just how hard it is to play the sport at its highest level. Looking back at my camp experiences, connection with so many phenomenal people is the greatest takeaway. It's an honor to meet the pros and fellow campers like Freddy that remind you how precious and precarious life can be and what can be accomplished with a second chance.

Fantasy camp concludes Sunday. After enjoying a relaxing final night in Palm Beach Gardens, it's up the coast to visit Florida's Atlantic Coast parks. From Jupiter, the first destination is north on I-95 to **Canaveral National Seashore**. The park came about after the government collected land for the nearby NASA facility, protecting the undeveloped coastline not needed for the space center as a national seashore. I enjoy a few ocean views and walk the short boardwalk trail through the vegetation at Turtle Mound adjacent to Mosquito Lagoon, separating the thin barrier land and mainland. A detached park area, Seminole Rest protects a collection of oyster shell mounds as high as eighteen feet that date from 2000 BC to AD 1565. The Snyder family incidentally preserved the mounds by building a home on them in the early 1900s, living here from 1911 to 1988.

From Canaveral, it's seventy miles north to **Fort Matanzas National Monument**. The Spanish constructed the fort from 1740 to 1742 to guard the southern passage to St. Augustine. Matanzas Inlet, a backdoor to St. Augustine, created a natural military weakness and threat to Spain's stronghold fourteen miles north. In 1565, a few months after establishing St. Augustine, Spanish soldiers killed nearly 250 French soldiers and settlers at this inlet. The French had established Fort Caroline farther north on Florida's coast near present-day Jacksonville over Spanish protests. Spain wanted them gone. After a forced surrender, the Spanish executed French Huguenots refusing to reject Protestantism and proclaim themselves Catholic. The Spanish named the inlet Matanzas, which translates to "slaughters." The fort's ownership follows Florida's colonial history. The events of 1565 preceded almost two hundred years of Spanish rule before the British gained Florida in the 1763 Treaty of Paris that ended the Seven Years War, known in America as the French and Indian War. The British ceded Florida back to Spain in the 1783 Treaty of Paris, ushering in another thirty-eight years of Spanish rule. The United States finally took possession of Florida in the Adams-Onis Treaty of 1821.

Visitors take a short boat ride across the channel to see the small coquina fort. The readily available raw materials of sand, broken shells, and calcium carbonate comprise the concrete-like substance of coquina, an invaluable construction material in the remote, wild country.

A short drive north to St. Augustine brings me to the first major Spanish fortification in Florida, **Castillo de San Marcos National Monument**. The Spanish built the imposing coquina fortress from 1672 to 1695 to protect the oldest town in the United States.

The Spanish laid claim to Florida based on Ponce de Leon's 1513 exploration of the Florida coast. In that expedition, the Spanish discovered the Gulf Stream, powerful sea currents wrapping around Florida from the Gulf of Mexico. The current carried ships from Spain's New World possessions north along the Florida coast before sailing to Europe on the North Atlantic Drift. The Florida Coast had to be fortified to protect against potential pirates who might otherwise use its numerous bays and inlets as lairs to launch raids on Spanish cargo ships.

Castillo de San Marcos' impressive structure, the oldest masonry fort in the continental United States, commands visitor attention as it once did the harbor. Europe endured frequent instability in the 1500s. The major colonial powers, including England, France, and Spain, maneuvered for position to expand and enrich their empires. Indeed, the fort received its first test shortly after construction. The British attacked and laid siege to Castillo de San Marcos for fifty days in 1702 and again for twenty-seven days in 1740, the latter battle led by troops from the British post of Fort Frederica up the coast. Surrounded by a moat (now dry) and earthworks, the Spanish fortress forms a square with diamond-shaped bastions at each corner, permitting fire in all directions and along each exterior wall.

The fort's material of construction sustains its strength. Coquina makes the walls hard and stable yet compressible, absorbing hard projectiles like cannonballs rather than shattering. The resilient material survived the bombardment by enemy warships that accompanied each siege. I enjoy a brisk walk around the fort, outside and in, but I'm not loitering. After the refreshing stroll, I continue north to see more colonial history.

Fort Caroline National Monument, on the south side of the St. Johns River inlet at Jacksonville, offers the opposing view to Spanish disputes. As I walk the short trail from the Timucuan Preserve Visitor Center to enter the wooden reconstructed version of the 1564 French palisade along the riverbank, a spray of mist carried by the overwater breeze splashes the right side of my face. As I wipe the water from my cheek, I contemplate the tragedy that befell the settlers here.

French Huguenot settlers established the fort and settlement two years after starving and desperate settlers aborted an earlier attempt and set sail for France. The second group of settlers had reached much the same condition in 1565 when a relief expedition arrived in May. Unfortunately, the relief is transitory. The Spanish, aware of the French settlement, sent an expedition nearly simultaneously to the French voyage. The Spanish expedition created their own permanent settlement on the Florida coast at St. Augustine, with orders to drive off the French by whatever means necessary. The Spanish eradicated the French fort and colony. Although a French contingent did the same to a Spanish garrison down the coast three years later, France never again seriously challenged Spain's North American claims by direct military action. The next major North American land exchange between France and Spain is diplomatic, in a sequence of events culminating in the Louisiana Purchase.

The memorial is jointly managed and operated with another park unit, **Timucuan Ecological and Historic Preserve.** The preserve carries the name of the native Timucua people, who occupied

Florida's coast for thousands of years. Opposite the entrance to Fort Caroline, I walk trails through coastal wetlands populated with pines and live oaks dressed in Spanish moss.

North of the St. Johns River inlet, the Kingsley Plantation Visitor Center on St. George Island shares the story of Zephaniah Kingsley, who settled on this sea island cotton plantation in 1814. At the peak of his holdings, Kingsley possessed over thirty-two thousand acres split among four major plantation complexes and served by more than two hundred enslaved workers. Built in 1798, the St. George Island plantation house and grounds predate Kingsley.

Kingsley's wife, Anna, was born in Senegal and purchased by Kingsley in Havana, Cuba. After Kingsley manumitted Anna and her three children in 1811, she acquired land and slaves. The interracial couple coexisted under liberal Spanish policies, but their lifestyle and beliefs conflicted with the oppressive laws that followed 1821 when Florida transferred to the United States. In 1837, Anna and her two sons fled to a free colony in Haiti established by Zephaniah. He sold the St. George Island plantation in 1839 and died in New York City a few years later. Anna died in 1870 after returning to Jacksonville. The Kingsley relationship is an interesting historical anecdote to the contemporary visitor, an anomaly of its time that includes an interracial marriage with a black, female slave owner and successful plantation manager.

The ranger and I share stories about our favorite parks before I continue north for an overnight stay across the Georgia state line. My fourteen-hundred-mile trip paralleling the Florida Coast required twenty-two hours of driving to visit the state's eleven national park units.

The next morning, I start at the **Cumberland Island National Seashore** visitor center in St. Marys, Georgia. I took the ferry to the island during my first visit in 2014. Today, my schedule limits me to acquiring lapel pins and stamps. The island offers fifty miles of trails over 36,400 acres and plenty to explore, including eighteen miles of undeveloped beaches. The largest of Georgia's coastal barrier islands, Cumberland Island became the winter home of the heir to the Carnegie fortune who enticed her children to join her by building them impressive homes such as Orchard Plum. The island's isolation and limited ownership preserved much of the habitat. It became a park in 1972 due in large part to the efforts of the heiress's grandchildren.

Located an hour north, **Fort Frederica National Monument** tells yet another side of the colonial power struggle. Through the early 1700s, modern-day Georgia remained disputed territory between England and Spain. The English hoped to formalize land claims and establish a buffer between the Carolinas and Spanish Florida. England sent James Edward Oglethorpe to Georgia with a group of "worthy poor" to create a settlement south of the Carolinas. Oglethorpe and his entourage landed on Georgia's coast in January 1733, founding the city of Savannah. Oglethorpe knew he must establish defensive coastal positions farther south. Fort Frederica is the most important of these positions.

The monument includes the remnants, mostly foundation outlines, of the town and fort built on the west side of St. Simons Island along the inland waterway. A military road ran south from the fort to a position at the island's southern tip, garrisoned and fortified as Fort St. Simons. Frederica thrived as a small town and military post from 1736 through 1749 when the military attachment disbanded. In July 1742, the English garrison defeated an invading force from Spanish Florida in the post's only military engagement. I walk across the grass to remnants of the shoreline fort on what had been the town's Broad Street. Despite the surrounding modern suburbia, the site feels isolated behind the park's wooded boundary. After the post's military necessity faded, the town soon followed. Settlers abandoned the site a few years after the soldiers departed. Fort Frederica concludes ten days on the coast. The road home turns west through the middle of Georgia.

5 *In the Heart of Dixie*

Ocmulgee National Monument in Macon, Georgia, protects AD 900–1100 Indian mounds remaining from a once-thriving village. Exhibits tell the site's story over ten thousand years of human activity. On the paved walking path through the park, I first encounter a reconstructed earthen lodge. The interior, with seating areas built around an open circular area, surprises me with its spaciousness. Farther down the trail, I climb the fifty-foot Great Temple Mound to enjoy the view. Several mounds have been destroyed or partially destroyed by the Norfolk Southern Railroad's 1870 track construction and much later when Interstate 16 passed through the southwestern boundary. Two Civil War engagements, extensions of Sherman's 1864 campaign, crossed park boundaries. Confederates thwarted both of Sherman's probes south from Atlanta. Macon, the temporary state capitol after Atlanta fell, did not surrender to Union forces until ten days after Lee's surrender at Appomattox.

About ninety miles northwest of Macon, **Martin Luther King Jr. National Historical Park** in Atlanta remembers the civil rights leader's legacy and honors nonviolent civil disobedience as advocated by MLK and the Southern Christian Leadership Conference he led from its 1957 inception. Panels in the visitor center walkway highlight global civil rights advocates, ending at a statue of Ghandi.

Exhibits address the civil rights movement of the 1950s and '6os. Visitors can tour Martin Luther King, Jr.'s birth home on Auburn Avenue, his gravesite, and the Ebenezer Baptist Church as it stood when MLK led the congregation. King Jr. became copastor with his father after returning to Atlanta from Montgomery, Alabama, where he served as the public leader of the Montgomery bus boycott of 1955–1956. On my most recent visit, I toured the Ebenezer Baptist Church, walking past the pulpit and chrome microphone where Martin Luther King Sr. and Jr. preached to their congregation.

Kennesaw Mountain National Battlefield protects key locations in the Civil War engagement. The battle began on June 27, 1864, with continued action along these lines until July 2. Sherman's Georgia campaign from Chattanooga south to Atlanta deployed a series of flanking maneuvers around the Confederate left. The Union's flanking marches continually forced southern forces back to prepared defensive lines blocking the route to Atlanta. During the Chattanooga to Atlanta campaign, Union forces dug over three hundred miles of rifle pits, discharged nearly 150,000 artillery rounds, and fired over 22 million rounds from small arms. At Kennesaw Mountain just over twenty miles from downtown Atlanta, Sherman's army confirmed they had been correct to avoid a general engagement with the Confederates in their entrenched positions.

In intense fighting, the Union army attacked in force near the center of the line and stalled downhill within thirty feet of the earthworks. Union troops found themselves pinned down below the defenders' trench. Nowhere on the battleground is this more apparent than at Cheatham Hill. I walk the trail around the trench to the Illinois Monument where attacking soldiers, unable to advance or retreat without incurring direct fire, attempted to tunnel through the top of the hillside under the Confederate works. The battle's participants called this hotly contested spot the Bloody Angle. The Union soldiers pinned beneath the earthworks remained trapped in this position, save a brief ceasefire to attend to the wounded and bury the dead, for the four days the armies stood deadlocked on the mountain.

While talking to volunteers at the visitor center, I share my first memories of Kennesaw Mountain from 1995. At Civil War sites, I never have enough time. There's always something to see and learn at these parks. As the day concludes, I take the short drive to the top of Kennesaw Mountain, directly behind the visitor center, to walk the summit trail and watch the sun drop low over North Central Georgia.

I leave Kennesaw at dusk, stunned by the area's residential growth over the past two decades. Suburban sprawl encroaches on all sides, threatening to swallow up the battlefield. Rush hour traffic chokes the once-rural two-lane roads connecting park areas. The fragility of these sacred places never fails to give pause. The land and sites protected by the National Park Service and other conservation-minded entities would be forever lost to the crush of population growth otherwise.

Chattahoochee Ford Island river trail

The morning of February 2, I arrive at my first new park on the return home. **Chattahoochee River National Recreation Area** consists of divided areas totaling forty-eight river miles north of Atlanta. Atlanta's northern suburbs wrap around the river, disguising the park's atmosphere and creating a rather remarkable contrast. My early-morning, three-mile hike of the Island Ford area river bank proves one of the year's most serene park experiences. Autumnal foliage blankets the trail and surrounding ground, coloring the wooded landscape. The only audible sounds are the rushing current, the crunch of leaves, and singing birds. The peace and contentment along the Chattahoochee remain with me long after the visit. I close my eyes and can still hear the rushing water and rustling leaves underfoot. This delightful first exposure validates the 1978 creation of this suburban park.

Pacified by the wooded river bank, I'm in good spirits driving north on I-75 to **Chickamauga and Chattanooga National Military Park**. I first visited these pivotal Civil War battle sites in 1994, during a work tenure in Knoxville, Tennessee. I walk into the Chickamauga Battlefield Visitor Center this afternoon for my fifth visit. The unit includes three principle battle locations: the Lookout Mountain area and Point Park; Chickamauga Battlefield, named for the creek that runs through it; and Missionary Ridge, a ridgeline that runs across the state line angling to the northeast and forms a natural eastern boundary for Chattanooga and the Tennessee River corridor.

The Chickamauga Battlefield lies in Georgia, bordering the town of Fort Oglethorpe a few miles from Tennessee. In these woods the seventy-thousand-man Union army under Major General William Rosecrans engaged a sixty-six-thousand-man Confederate army under General Braxton Bragg in September 1863. The core of these two armies had battled each other for months between Nashville and Chattanooga, with the stronger Union army driving Southern forces into tactical retreats after several engagements. After Bragg's early-September reinforcement with additional troops under Major General James Longstreet, he

maneuvered his army between the Union forces and their Chattanooga–Nashville supply line.

On September 19, 1863, both armies clashed on a four-mile
front from north to south with Confederate troops gaining ground
but failing to accomplish the objective. The battle resumed the
next morning, turning into a decisive Confederate victory when
shifting Union troops created a gap in the line as a Confederate
attack launched into the void. The attack cut the Union army in
two, leading to a desperate Union retreat west and north into Chattanooga. Union troops under Major General George H. Thomas
made a stand on a new line astride Snodgrass Hill, holding their
position against repeated assaults to give the balance of the federals
time to retreat. The determined resistance under dire circumstances
earned Thomas the nickname he carries ever after, The Rock of
Chickamauga.

After the South laid siege to the Union army in Chattanooga
through October and most of November, a reinforced Union
army, now led by Major General Ulysses S. Grant, broke out of
the predicament with victories over the Confederates at Lookout
Mountain on November 24 in the Battle Above the Clouds and
a decisive engagement at Missionary Ridge on November 25 in
what would be one of the war's most famous successful attacks
against a strongly entrenched position. Bragg's army disintegrated
into a disorganized retreat south into Georgia, thus beginning the
campaign that moved to Kennesaw Mountain and Atlanta. After
stopping at the Chickamauga Battlefield and visitor center, I visit
the Lookout Mountain Battlefield Visitor Center. At the top of
Lookout Mountain, Point Park offers a view over Chattanooga and
the Tennessee River for dozens of miles in each direction. Chickamauga and Chattanooga National Military Park is one of the first
four military parks authorized by Congress in 1890 and became
the model for future preservation efforts at other battle sites. The
other military parks authorized in the 1890s are Shiloh, Gettysburg, and Vicksburg.

Moccasin Bend, another detached park area, includes a portion of the 1805 Federal Road that bisected the area, as well as an original section of the 1838 Trail of Tears. **Trail of Tears National Historic Trail** commemorates the routes used for the forced removal of over sixteen thousand Cherokee from their ancestral lands in the southeast to reservations in modern-day Oklahoma over the winter of 1838–1839.

The Federal Road became critical to the relief of the besieged Union army in Chattanooga as part of the "cracker line" created in October 1864 to supply the starving garrison. Remnants of Brown's Ferry, the last river crossing utilized in the supply line, are visible today from the end of the trail across Moccasin Bend.

The next park on the road home is **Stones River National Battlefield** in Murfreesboro, Tennessee. Stones River, along with other state battle sites including Shiloh, form the **Tennessee Civil War National Heritage Area**. Tennessee saw the second-most Civil War battles of any state fought on its soil, after Virginia. The Battle of Stones River engaged the core of the two armies that fought later at Chickamauga. My travel from Atlanta to Nashville retraces the two armies' movement from 1863 to 1864 in reverse. The conflict at Stones River started on December 31, 1862 and continued through January 2, 1863. Two days of combat bracketed a quiet day on January 1 when both sides remained in position.

The engagement's vicious and bloody combat gives Civil War and American history some of its most notorious battlefield locations, including the Slaughter Pen and Hell's Half Acre. Walking the trails through the Slaughter Pen remains an eerie experience today. The path leads through a wooded area of cedars sprinkled with rounded limestone rocks protruding from the ground. The rocks provided minimal cover for a defensive position but made orderly movement through the area difficult and advancing field artillery over this part of the battleground impossible, a factor in the first day's battle as many Confederate units charged Union lines without artillery support. The rounded rocky ground appears today like a field of natural tombstones overtaken by the woods. The allusion of a natural graveyard matches the battle's events. Union troops mounted a determined defense here despite grievous losses on December 31, giving the rest of the Union forces enough time to reform along a fall back defensive line on the Nashville Pike. Many of the units fighting in these woods lost more than a third of their number.

Farther back and to the north of the Slaughter Pen is the Hazen Brigade Monument marking Hell's Half Acre. This spot on the battlefield marks the Union line's anchor on the Nashville Pike and the only Union position held throughout the first day's action. A brigade led by Colonel William B. Hazen held the line here, supported by cannon firing canister across their front to deadly effect. Wave after wave of Confederate attacks were brutally broken up assaulting this point. One Alabama regiment sustained nearly 80 percent casualties. Both sides knew if the Union line broke here, a Confederate rout would ensue. Hazen's brigade paid in blood for their courageous resilience with over four hundred casualties. Brigade survivors erected the monument in 1863, making it the oldest Civil War battlefield monument.

Detached park areas include McFadden's Farm, where the Union left flank beat back a Confederate attack on the last day, and Fortress Rosecrans, the surviving earthworks from a two-hundred-acre fort constructed in 1863 for up to fifteen thousand troops. At McFadden's Farm, it's hard to fully imagine the difficulty of the Rebel approach across the West Fork of Stones River. Wading across the freezing water, attacking soldiers suffered a hail of grape and canister from Union artillery in addition to infantry small arms' fire. Surveying the ground, it's not surprising that the rebel charge faltered, the river running red with their blood. Federal infantry discharged over 2 million rounds of ammunition during the Battle of Stones River. Union artillery fired another 20,300 rounds, over 375,000 pounds of projectiles, at Confederate positions. The total carnage from the three days of Stones River, 24,645 casualties out of about 80,000 participants, exceeded 30 percent of the two armies' combined strength, the highest total casualty rate in any major Civil War battle.

After dinner in Murfreesboro, I pass through Nashville to stop at

Clarksville for the night. I pull into a Budget hotel off Interstate 29, waking up several times to a raging thunderstorm. We'll return to the Deep South in September to visit the remaining Southeastern parks.

6 Hills of Kentucky

FEBRUARY 3 DAWNS crisp after the storm. By 8:00 a.m., I'm westbound on US 79 for the forty-five-minute drive to **Fort Donelson National Battlefield**. A temporary visitor center in the county tourism board's building replaces the one under renovation. It's a quiet morning, more so in this location away from the park.

Fort Donelson represents a pivotal Civil War event after the north suffered a morale-deflating series of early setbacks. General Ulysses Grant's momentous victories at Fort Henry and Fort Donelson, resulting in the capture of Fort Donelson's twelve-thousand-man garrison, gave federal arms a much-needed boost. This first substantial Union victory triggered celebratory reaction throughout the north. Most importantly, the victory launched Grant's career into a meteoric ascendency as a national hero that culminates in the White House.

Fort Henry on the Tennessee River and Fort Donelson on the Cumberland River guarded the approaches to Nashville and the Deep South. Taking them, or holding them, loomed paramount for both sides. The Confederacy sought boundary security while the forts blocked the Union plan to subdue the rebels in the heart of the Confederacy.

The army-navy joint operation at Forts Henry and Donelson

offered a model for future cooperation. Grant coordinated strategy with Flag Officer Andrew H. Foote and his fleet of steam powered, ironclad Union gunboats. The oft-flooded Fort Henry, now permanently under Kentucky Lake, capitulated first on February 6, 1862. Most of the troops at Fort Henry and Fort Heiman, a supporting work only partially completed across the Tennessee River from Fort Henry, escaped via a twelve-mile logging road to Fort Donelson, strengthening that garrison by almost twenty-five hundred men. Fort Henry capitulated under bombardment from the navy's gunboat fleet before Grant's army arrived.

Fort Donelson lies due east of Fort Henry, about a mile from the town of Dover. By February 13, Grant's fifteen-thousand-man army encircled Fort Donelson's outer defenses. The naval flotilla arrived late after steaming downstream to the Ohio River and returning on the Cumberland River to engage Fort Donelson on the morning of February 14. The fort's river batteries pounded the gunboats, forcing their retreat. I visit these batteries for the irresistible pictures of the Cumberland down the gun barrels. After its initial success, a breakout attempt by the fort's defenders on February 15 fell apart due to poor coordination. The fort's surrender imminent, Lieutenant Colonel Nathan Bedford Forrest led his cavalry across swollen Lick Creek in the predawn hours of February 16, skirting the river at the Union's extreme right. Meanwhile, two Confederate co-commanders, General John B. Floyd and Brigadier General Gideon J. Pillow, escaped upriver to Nashville with about two thousand troops, leaving in command Grant's prewar army friend Brigadier General Simon B. Buckner. Grant's note informing Buckner that "no terms except an unconditional and immediate surrender can be accepted" received condemnation from Buckner as "ungenerous and unchivalrous." The two commanders finalized the surrender at the Dover Hotel, this visit's primary destination. I found the hotel closed two years earlier, but it's now open during regular park hours. Interpretive boards on the main floor share the surrender's details while the upper floor contains NPS offices. Public acclaim and newspaper coverage of the Union triumph gave the victorious general a popular moniker playing on his initials: "Unconditional Surrender" Grant.

From Fort Donelson, I travel into Kentucky's **Mammoth Cave National Park**. My first look underground came in 2014 on the two-hour Historic Cave Tour. Today's schedule precludes an underground excursion. And my lapel pin project hits a snag. Mammoth Cave is the first park I find sold out of the centennial pin and won't be the last.

Mammoth Cave contains more than four hundred miles of surveyed passageways. Geologists believe as many as six hundred miles of unexplored cave might await discovery. New passages are found regularly. Mammoth Cave derives from a continual process over millions of years. Groundwater seeps through cracks in the sandstone cap rock, absorbing enough carbon dioxide to become weakly acidic carbonic acid. The acidic water dissolves limestone layers under the sandstone, forming caves big and small and the world's largest cave system. Mammoth Cave has more than twice the known length of the next largest cave, Mexico's Sac Actun, the world's largest underwater cave. The Mammoth Cave area is typical of karst topography (eroded limestone landscapes). The park contains diverse ecosystems above and below ground.

Though I've enjoyed visiting the National Park System's caves, I'm mildly claustrophobic. The wild cave tours where visitors often crawl and in places even wriggle through a passageway hold no temptation. I can enjoy the caves on the popular tours that keep visitors upright. It's perhaps for this reason that the Floyd Collins story leaves me cringing. In 1925, Collins, from a local family making money by selling admission to a privately owned cave, was investigating relatively unexplored Sand Cave in search of new business opportunities when a twenty-seven-pound rock dislodged as he squeezed through a tight passage, pinning his ankle behind him. Searchers discovered him and initiated rescue attempts, eventually trying to tunnel to him. All efforts proved futile, and Collins died from exposure after seventeen days trapped underground in the tiny passageway. As the crisis continued, it developed into a national news story. One reporter even took tremendous risk to crawl down to Collins and interview him several times. I can't imagine the suffering that Collins endured as he died this slow, agonizing death.

From Mammoth Cave, I travel an hour northeast to Hodgenville, Kentucky, the birthplace of our sixteenth president and site of the **Abraham Lincoln Birthplace National Historical Park**. Thomas and Nancy Lincoln welcomed their newborn Abraham on February 12, 1809, in their small cabin at Sinking Spring Farm, a three-hundred-acre tract Thomas purchased for $200 in December 1808. The spring flows today near the spot where an oak sapling started life about the same time as Abraham, growing into a mighty tree called The Boundary Oak. The National Park Service removed the tree after its death in 1976.

Built on site from 1909 to 1911, a marble and granite memorial holds a Lincoln birth cabin. The memorial and farm site became a park in 1916. Years later, scholars and historians confirmed the memorial's cabin is not actually Lincoln's birth cabin but typical of period construction. The NPS considers it a symbolic cabin. The park contains a separate area of land ten miles north of the visitor center and birthplace where the Lincolns owned a farm at Knob Creek from 1811 to 1816, when Thomas moved his family, including seven-year-old Abe, across the Ohio River from slave to free state.

The **Lincoln Boyhood Home National Memorial** in Lincoln City, Indiana, commemorates the family's next home. The future president lived here until 1830 when the family moved again to Illinois. The site's memorial doubles as the visitor center. The memorial features two ornately trimmed, wooden interior chapels flanking a concave corridor. A walking trail across the parking lot passes the Pioneer Cemetery and through a wooded area past the cabin site to a living history farm. After the obligatory stamping and pin purchase, I pause to admire the memorial's handsome design.

My resting place this evening is my parents' home in Lawrenceville, Illinois, across the Wabash River from Vincennes, Indiana. I share some adventures through the first forty-four parks of the year and sink into an upholstered chair near the family room window.

This isn't my childhood home or hometown, but it's nice to see my parents on the last night of this eighteen-day trip.

The next morning, I cross the river into Vincennes for the trip's final stop. **George Rogers Clark National Historical Park** celebrates the Revolutionary War contributions of the twenty-six-year-old Clark and his men who secured the Old Northwest Territory north of the Ohio River. George is the older brother of William Clark, coleader with Merriweather Lewis of the 1803 Corps of Discovery. The elder Clark excelled as a leader and parlayed these skills and a small compliment of men to conquer British outposts in Kaskaskia, Cahokia, and Vincennes for the patriot cause. The park's centerpiece, sitting near the Fort Sackville site on the Wabash, is a granite-faced, Greek-style memorial rotunda completed in 1931 to celebrate Clark's accomplishments for the revolution's 150th anniversary. The limestone and marble interior, depicting scenes from the campaign, compliments Clark's statue at its center.

George Rogers Clark and his men endured a remarkable nineteen day journey to attack Fort Sackville. In February 1779, Clark and his men crossed flooded wetlands and rivers in freezing temperatures over the last ten days. Clark's victories secured American claims over the present states of Ohio, Indiana, Illinois, Michigan, Wisconsin, and part of Minnesota.

I share with the rangers that George Rogers Clark National Historical Park is the thirty-fifth and final park visited on this thirty-five-hundred-mile roundtrip from Chicago to Key West. I wish the rangers a great centennial year, stop in Lawrenceville to bid my parents farewell, and begin the last leg home. It's been a long road.

Author's note: In October 2018, **Camp Nelson National Monument** became the 418th unit in the National Park System. About twenty miles south of Lexington in central Kentucky, Major General Ambrose Burnside created Camp Nelson as a supply depot for military operations into East Tennessee. The camp's location is shielded from attack on the south and west sides by the 500-foot limestone bluffs along the Kentucky River and on the southeastern side by Hickman Creek and its heavily wooded, 300-foot ravine.

The Lexington-Danville Pike, the region's only north-south, Civil War-era road bridging the river, bisected the camp. Modern US Highway 27 occupies the historic pike's right-of-way. Eight earthen fortifications connected by trenchworks anchored the 1.5-mile northern boundary. Trails follow the boundary and tour the surviving earthworks. The post served as an entry, processing and training depot for over 10,000 US Colored Troops (USCT) during the Civil War, making it the third largest USCT recruiting facility in the country.

7 O-hi-o

A TRUNK FULL of laundry and a long to-do list shortens the three-day weekend. Monday, February 8 brings a Minneapolis work trip, concluding Tuesday afternoon with a detour to Coldwater Spring and Fort Snelling in the **Mississippi National River and Recreation Area**. The park runs seventy-two river miles through the Twin Cities, though the NPS owns only thirty-five of the fifty-four thousand acres within the corridor. I've leveraged past work trips to see the park's multiple locations though today's midwinter visit to Coldwater Spring is my first. It's also the first of three centennial visits to Mississippi National River and Recreation Area.

Coldwater Spring lies north of Fort Snelling and the confluence of the Minnesota and Mississippi Rivers. During Minnesota's frontier days, travelers often camped here next to the fort's water supply. Completed in 1825, Fort Snelling marks the northern-most post in a defensive line of frontier forts across the eastern Plains. Farther south, two NPS units at Fort Scott and Fort Smith form part of this fortified boundary. As the forts are completed, the pull of land and trade pushed settlers past them into the Great Plains, rendering the forts obsolete. As the process repeated with another set of forts farther west, the encroachment on the Plains tribes meant the end of a centuries-old way of life.

After a late-week work trip takes me to Ohio for an overnight stay, Friday begins at **Dayton Aviation Heritage National Historical Park**, the center of the **National Aviation Heritage Area**. The Wright Dunbar Interpretative Center and Aviation Trail Visitor Center pays tribute to three of Dayton's most cherished native sons, Orville and Wilbur Wright and the poet Paul Lawrence Dunbar. Over the last few years, I've been able to tour each of the six separate park areas. This morning I return to the Paul Lawrence Dunbar home, finding a sign on the door, announcing the ranger will return after a tour. Dunbar purchased this house in 1904 for himself and his mother. After a prolific literary career in which he produced four novels, twelve books of poetry, four books of short stories, and some popular song lyrics, he died from tuberculosis at the age of thirty-three. I toured the Dunbar home early last year, and later in 2015, the magnificent Wright home at Hawthorn Hill.

After about fifteen minutes, some movement inside catches my eye. Looking through the glass door, my park friend Lee follows the ranger into the room. Neither notice me waiting in the vestibule. After the ranger unlocks the door, I quietly slip past him and approach the front desk. As Lee raises a stamper to ink it, I reach around his shoulder and grab the handle. He resists, confused by the sudden interruption, before losing his grip. He turns around, revealing a bewildered expression. As he recognizes the culprit, he exclaims, "I thought, 'What kind of jackass would take the stamper right out of my hand?' Now I know!" We haven't spoken in recent days, but it turns out we have identical itineraries planned today. Centennial madness strikes. We agree to tour today's parks jointly, driving separately, as our plans diverge this evening. It's nice to have the company.

Our next stop is the Huffman Prairie Interpretive Center perched on a hill overlooking the field where Orville and Wilbur perfected their flying machine. Five miles east of Dayton, Huffman Prairie Flying Field is chosen to avoid prying eyes. The location lies past the end of Dayton's streetcar system, which the brothers used for their daily commute. The Wright Memorial next to the Interpretive Center also overlooks Wright-Patterson Air Force Base's main runway. Watching modern air force jets take off adjacent to the Wright's experimental field, with its circle of white poles marking the test flight path, presents a striking contrast. The Wright Brothers conducted 155 test flights over this field from 1904 to 1905. We leave Huffman to make a scheduled appointment. Lee prearranged a morning tour at our next stop, **Charles Young Buffalo Soldiers National Monument**, less than thirty minutes southeast, near Wilberforce, Ohio.

Born to enslaved parents in 1864 Kentucky, Colonel Young overcame prejudicial obstacles in and outside the military establishment to serve with distinction as a US Army officer. Young graduated from West Point in 1889, the third African American to do so, and served in western "buffalo soldier" units. A source of pride in the black community, his achievements stood out in the period of 1880–1920, often characterized as "the nadir of race relations in America." His southern Ohio house became a park in March 2013. Young made his home here while teaching military science at Wilberforce University. Although the unit doesn't have regular visitor hours, tours of the home are available on special request and pending staff availability. An NPS student intern meets us with a smile as we enter. Dating to 1839, the two-story home may have been part of the underground railroad. Young purchased the property in 1907, calling it Youngsholm. Colonel Young died while serving overseas in 1922 and is buried in Arlington National Cemetery.

Continuing across southern Ohio, our next unit is **Hopewell Culture National Historical Park** in Chillicothe. The Hopewell built mound groups throughout southern Ohio between 200 BC and AD 500. The Hopewell mounds are not living quarters but burial and ceremonial complexes. Construction of Camp Sherman, a World War I army training facility, partially destroyed the dense collection of twenty-three mounds known as the Mound City Group next to the present-day park visitor center. The mounds gained protection as a national monument in 1923. The park includes five separate mound groups. I've toured the four open to the public: Mound City Group, Hopewell Mound Group, the Seip Earthworks, and Hopeton Mound Group. A careful eye and written guide are supplemented by interpretive mowing to help delineate the earthworks today. Worn down by decades of plowing in the rich agricultural Scioto River Valley, some of these mounds once towered over the surrounding terrain with walls over ten feet high and fifty feet wide.

Moving south to Cincinnati, we end the day at **William Howard Taft National Historic Site**, the 1857 birth home of the twenty-seventh president of the United States, from 1909 to 1913. Taft trained as a lawyer, serving on the bench and as US solicitor general. He also served as governor of the Philippines after the Spanish-American War. As President Roosevelt's secretary of war from 1904 to 1908, Taft held special status with Theodore as one of his closest and most trusted advisors. He followed Roosevelt as his handpicked successor. Though Taft only served one term as president, he earned the legacy of a responsible and impactful leader. He remains lauded by many presidential scholars for his ethics and distinguished public service. Taft finished his career as chief justice of the US Supreme Court from 1921 until his death in 1930. A respected jurist, he turned down two earlier nominations to the court. Taft lived in the home until leaving for Yale in 1874. Exhibits tell the story of Taft's family life and impressive public career. Lee and I go our separate ways from the site, fleeing the downtown area ahead of Cincinnati's rush hour.

After another night in Dayton, northbound I-75 brings me to the Toledo area and first Saturday stop at **Fallen Timbers Battlefield and Fort Miamis National Historic Site**. Next to a new visitor center at the Fallen Timbers site, a statue of General Anthony Wayne commemorates the August 1794 victory here over a confederation of Ohio and Great Lakes warriors. Presaging the battle, the British constructed Fort Miamis nearby in defiance of obligations in the 1783 Treaty of Paris to relinquish the Northwest Territory. Wayne's victory has been called the final battle of the American Revolution.

River Raisin National Battlefield Park in Monroe, Michigan, came into the park system in 2010. The park protects the grounds for two War of 1812 battles fought on January 18 and 22 between the fledging United States and the British and their Indian allies. The battles in the village of Frenchtown beside River Raisin ended in a clear British victory. After thirty to sixty Americans wounded and scattered about the battlefield were slaughtered on January 23, American forces evoke their memory throughout the war with the battle cry, "Remember the Raisin!"

From River Raisin, I spend the weekend visiting greater Detroit area locations in the **MotorCities National Heritage Area**. Motor-Cities highlights the area's automobile history. I'm not a car buff but enjoy the Detroit History Museum exhibits and the Ford Piquette Avenue Plant, the oldest purpose-built automotive factory in the world open to the public. The plant dates to 1904 and housed much of Ford's Model T production capacity until Studebaker purchased the factory in 1911. I stop at the Henry Ford Museum to collect the heritage area cancellation but elect to save my first tour as an adult for a future visit. Our family visited the museum and its famous Greenfield Village in the late '70s, a memorable vacation, as I almost drowned in our Detroit-area hotel's swimming pool at the age of seven. After being sent out to tell my brother to leave the pool and get dressed for dinner, an unruly young boy snuck up behind me unseen and pushed me in fully clothed. After I went under, two adults swam to my aid and pulled me out as my lungs took in water. Excepting my brother, all present were strangers.

We will return to Ohio several times this year for work and stops at four northern Ohio NPS units. Back in Chicago, Kareen and I discuss plans for our next trip to the bright-blue waters of the Caribbean.

8 The Caribbean

ON THURSDAY, FEBRUARY 18, Kareen and I fly to San Juan, Puerto Rico, to begin a trip through the US Caribbean territories in route to Jamaica, where we'll attend a wedding reception for one of Kareen's medical school classmates. After landing, we catch a taxi to the decidedly modest Old San Juan hotel Kareen booked months ago. Exhausted from working up to the time of our departure, Kareen declines my offer to tour the park and changes into her threadbare sleeping clothes as I leave for Castillo San Cristobal in **San Juan National Historic Site**.

Construction of Castillo San Felipe del Morro, commonly called El Morro, began in 1539 and continued for 250 years, while work on Castillo San Cristobal started in 1634. The citadels fortify Old San Juan's oceanside and harbor entry. El Morro guards the narrow harbor mouth while Castillo San Cristobal provides protection landward on the islet, adding firepower against approaching ships. The arrangement uses the military concept of "defense in depth." Two lines of defensive works against land attack extend east of Castillo San Cristobal. The citadel itself forms the third line of defense. Another less visited park structure, Fortin San Juan de la Cruz (commonly known as El Canuelo), sits on the small island across the port inlet from El Morro. The park also includes about three-quarters of the protective wall and bastions built around the old city. I walk a mile from our hotel to Castillo San Cristobal at double time. I'm excited to see the old fort and begin exploring its rich history.

Entering the citadel, I tell two rangers how excited I am to see San Juan National Historic Site, the 52nd NPS unit I've visited this year and 329th lifetime. We share enthusiastic conversation and take a picture for the park's social media page. My two-hour self-guided walking tour includes the ravelin and stratified outer defenses allaying an eastern land attack. Castillo San Cristobal's high stone seawall and complimentary landward defensive works create an imposing image exactly as its Spanish builders intended. Sequenced construction across 150 years tells in structural layers. The historic entrance and visitor passage leads into the main plaza, where I start my tour. The plaza's far corner draws me into a damp, cool tunnel winding down to subterranean levels and the visitor center. It feels like descending into the depths of a natural cave. The lower level houses a gift shop, administrative offices, and a musty-smelling theater playing the park film alternately in Spanish and English.

After exploring the eastern fortress, I walk the mile to El Morro before closing, hoping to get my bearings and collect the passport cancellations, allowing me to leave my park backpack at the hotel tomorrow. The thirty-five-pound backpack containing my national park passports, reference materials, and other park-related items weighs more this year since I'm carrying a collector's edition passport book as a centennial year log. Stamping the special passport book with every dated cancellation I come across in 2016 records my stops throughout the National Park System, totaling over twenty-two hundred cancellations by year's end.

A fast walk west to El Morro follows the top of the fortified town wall past a sea-level ghetto and cemetery. I hurry across a grass field to a freestanding bookstore east of the fort to pick up the park's centennial pin and guzzle a bottle of water. I'm a sweaty, overheated mess. Continuing through the fort's main entrance, I complete the mission minutes before closing.

Back at the hotel, I enter the darkened room to find Kareen

sleeping. I wash my face in cool water and lay down. Her soft, steady breathing is the only sign of life. Over a dinner of fresh fish, we discuss our plans for El Morro tomorrow and five more new parks over the next six days. It's going to be a wonderful week.

As morning breaks, I prod Kareen, whose chronic fatigue has bested her circadian rhythm. We start our stroll, for Kareen a slow trudge, to San Cristabol about 9:00 a.m., retracing yesterday's steps through the fortress.

At El Morro, we enter the main plaza, the fifth of six levels, wandering about the courtyard and connecting areas to kill the fifteen minutes before the park film plays in English. Kareen appreciates an audio-visual introduction to each site's history. I conceded to the park films after my early attempts at reviewing park history suffered from my overexuberance and the marital adaptation that attenuates the spousal voice.

San Juan, El Morro

After the film's narrative of the islet's defenses and their importance to three hundred years of Spanish rule and New World wealth extraction, we walk down the ramp, once used for cannon, to the fourth level. A triangular open area overlooks the harbor entrance and El Canuelo opposite the channel. Any vessel running this gauntlet would be pounded in a murderous crossfire. A sloping tunnel along the ocean wall descends to an exposed part of the original fort construction dating to 1540. From this lowest, original level, we peer upon brick and mortar laid almost five centuries ago before climbing back to the fifth level to take the obligatory visitor picture in the iconic sentry boxes with the rounded top capped by a stone ball on three short cylinders. Level six atop the fortress offers a panorama of the islet in every direction, overlooking the fort's land defenses and the crowded, crooked streets of Old San Juan.

With the balance of our morning, we read El Morro's rich history of Spanish colonial rule, spanning five major attacks by the English, Dutch, and finally the Americans, who took possession of Puerto Rico after the Spanish-American War of 1898. It speaks to the solid construction of these fortresses that they were not fully transitioned from the army to the National Park Service until 1961.

From El Morro, we walk through the old city center, pausing for lunch at Barrachina, one of two Old San Juan locations claiming to be the origin of Puerto Rico's native cocktail, the piña colada. The Barrachina piña colada is refreshing after our extended walk under a bright sun, but one's plenty. I almost fall asleep at the table. We retire to our hotel for a nap before resuming our senior citizen dinner schedule.

Saturday morning, an island hopper takes us from San Juan International Airport to the island of St. Croix. After procuring the rental car, we're off to the island's most populous town, Christiansted. **Christiansted National Historic Site** contains structures extant to the island's Danish rule. After its 1733 purchase from France, Denmark ruled the island until its 1917 sale to the United States. The island's greatest prosperity, from 1760 to 1820, coincided with government-managed trade based off the island's sugar plantations. The age of sugar and slavery represented the peak of prosperity for Caribbean landowners, many of them absent European aristocrats. The next similarly dominant island industry would be tourism.

We turn right from King Street among the park's bright yellow buildings. The vivid color helped incoming travelers identify key government buildings from the harbor. We walk the grounds surrounding Fort Christiansvaern, completed in 1749, the customs house dating to 1841, the scale house from 1856, the government house completed in 1830, the Danish West India & Guinea Company Warehouse from 1749, and the exception to the yellow color scheme, the Lutheran Church built in 1744 as the Dutch Reformed Church.

In a light rain, more a mist, we enter the fort at 9:00 a.m. The fort's parapet supports a battery of cannon facing the water and affords us a perch above the harbor. The fort served multiple functions, including a jail. The west side rooms confined male and female prisoners separately. A more modern-looking cell, partitioned with floor to ceiling bars, occupies the southwest corner ground level. Near its entrance and built into the foundation of the southwest bastion, stairs penetrate the fort's dungeon. The foreboding space divides into two rooms with a low ceiling, requiring a crouch. The first room, lighted through a small window originally only nine inches square, includes an iron staple anchored to the floor for leg or ankle irons. The outer room's shadowy light falls away to the cramped back room's darkness. Presumably used for solitary confinement, the still lower ceiling in this aphotic recess embodies solitary's modern slang name, "the hole." Very little air circulates through either space. It must be a living hell confined in this space, a literal proxy of being buried alive. The dungeon reminds us of the harsh treatment meted out to lawbreakers in the colonial world, especially the enslaved.

Throughout the Caribbean Islands, chattel slavery manifests horrors and abuse incomprehensible today. Any offense, a perceived slight or disobedience, could be punished by extreme violence such as severing a hand or finger. Enslaved workers greatly outnumbered the white ruling class on St. Croix and other Caribbean islands, often by ratios of eight to one or greater. The imbalance supported persistent fear of revolt. Though rare, a few occurrences of Caribbean unrest bolstered these fears.

Slave labor remained readily available and relatively cheap in eighteenth-century Caribbean commerce. Slave traders, following the trade winds and ocean currents across the Atlantic from West Africa, typically stopped in the islands before continuing to mainland destinations. Christiansted served as a primary port of call for trans-Atlantic slavery's cruel Middle Passage. Harsh treatment, malnutrition, and tropical illness perpetuated a 60 percent death rate for new African arrivals in their first five years in the West Indies. The shocking mortality rate accentuates Caribbean slavery's brutality. Exposure to such inhumanity strongly influenced St. Croix's most famous and accomplished resident and one of American history's most remarkable self-made men to take a lifelong public stance against slavery. Alexander Hamilton, born on the island of Nevis in 1757, grew up in Christiansted.

Hamilton's checkered family history ties to the fort. After leaving a brief, unhappy marriage, his mother, Rachel, remained confined for several months of 1750 in one of the small ground-floor cells within Fort Christiansvaern's west curtain at the behest of her estranged husband. After release, she left for St. Kitts, where she entered an unofficial common-law marriage with James Hamilton. The couple had two sons, James Jr. and, after the family relocated to Nevis, Alexander. She could not legally remarry under Danish law, leaving Alexander and his brother illegitimate.

After relocating again to St. Croix around 1760, James Sr. abandoned the family. Rachel earned a living running a small general store in a building owned by two New York merchants operating a trading firm. After she died from fever in 1768, Alexander gained attention for his intelligence and maturity as a young teenager, eventually managing the merchants' trading business in Christiansted. By the age of fourteen, Alexander functioned as the acting operating manager of the international trading business on King Street.

The town's residents recognized Hamilton's exceptional gifts.

His life's work later confirmed a prodigious work ethic and a rare natural genius. By 1772, supportive townspeople had raised funds to send Alexander to the British North American colonies for a proper education. He entered New York City's King's College (now Columbia University) in late 1773 as rebellion fomented.

After touring the fort and remaining park buildings, Kareen and I walk King Street, a one-way street that dead-ends at the park. The young Hamilton's lodging and business stood a couple of blocks down King Street. Standing out among the founding fathers, he formed an accurate vision of the United States' destiny as a nation outgrowing subsistence agriculture and developing into a global industrial and economic power. His fundamental design of the US Department of Treasury survives today. He is the only founding father to never own slaves, though John Adams only did briefly before manumitting an inherited bondsman. Though his pride and vanity led him to some serious missteps, namely a lurid public affair and the duel with Aaron Burr that ended his life in 1803, Hamilton triumphs as an early manifestation of the American Dream, rising from his station as the "bastard brat of a Scotch peddler," per John Adams, to make lasting contributions as a political leader and visionary in his adopted country. For the full story, Ron Chernow's *Hamilton* is one of the best biographies I've ever read.

We have lunch at a waterfront bar down the boardwalk from the park, conversing with the owner, an East Coast transplant, about his move to the island. Throughout our time in the islands, we hear stories from transplanted Lower 48 residents living out their lives in America's tropical paradise. Though Kareen has no desire to return to the islands, I turn to her and suggest, "Doesn't sound half bad, especially compared to Chicago in the winter."

"You would get bored," she offers. "What would you do all day?"

A cool breeze passes through the open-air bar as I glance up at a bright blue sky and reply, "I could figure it out."

After lunch, we drive five miles west along the north coast to **Salt River Bay National Historical Park and Ecological Preserve.** The bay signifies Christopher Columbus's only landfall on US territory during his four voyages to the New World. Columbus anchored his fleet here in 1493, sending a party ashore to get fresh water. A Carib village on the bay's west side served as the source of contact between Columbus's men and the native islanders. The sailors returned with some newly liberated Taino slaves, fighting a group of Caribs in a canoe in action that killed a Spanish sailor and Carib warrior. The incident represents the first documented case of native resistance to European exploration or settlement in the Americas.

On this Saturday afternoon, we skip the closed hilltop visitor contact station and stop beside the road near a parking lot by the coast to avoid driving through a mud slough with standing water. A trail through the trees to the ocean turns east to follow the rocky shoreline and continues around the northwest corner of the inlet for a view of the entire bay. I take some pictures of Kareen standing in front of the gray and blue water we presume to be Columbus's anchorage, though its exact location is speculative. As part of our trip preparation, I'd questioned a coworker raised on the island. Regarding Salt River Bay, he'd cautioned, "There's not much there." We failed to disprove his assertion. Some visitors explore the park by kayak. Despite Kareen's island upbringing, neither she nor I seek water activities unless a boat tour's our only option as is the case tomorrow. We climb across the rocks, returning to our car to find our Airbnb lodging.

After turning off the two-lane highway that is the main coastal artery, we navigate a series of rutted gravel roads to the residence. Our host, Gail, and her husband, John, greet us with a warm smile as she shows us to our well-situated, comfortable room. We're on a hillside overlooking the north coast about ten miles east of Christiansted, with a clear view of tomorrow's destination and our next park.

In the morning, we return to Christiansted for our boat to **Buck Island Reef National Monument**. Though we don't have plans to snorkel, a popular activity for those exploring the reef, we bring gym clothes, suspecting we might get wet. About a mile long and under a half mile wide, Buck Island lies a mile and a half from

Christiansted. Approaching the small island's west end, we spot a long concrete pier to the right of a large anchorage area holding fifteen to twenty boats of various size and type scattered offshore. As the engines throttle back, a boat hand shares the news we're swimming the final one hundred yards to the beach. The operator left out this small detail in the tour information. Since Kareen and I are not adept swimmers, we watch preparations for reaching shore nervously and wonder at the pier's apparent lack of purpose. We let them unload most of the boat before they first haul Kareen and then me to shore by having us hold on to a life ring tied to a rope with our arms extended while a fit, twenty-something guide tows each of us to shore like stranded whales. A five-gallon bucket on the life ring carries any personal effects. It's painless but would have been good to know in advance.

On the island, we follow the trail from West Beach to Die-drichs Point, crossing over the island's east-west ridge. The trail's upper sections offer vistas of the bright-blue water atop the island reef. We scan the reef from the observation point near the peak of the trail, enchanted by the scenery. Buck Island Trail's panorama counts as one of my favorite centennial scenes. The water's bright-blue color seems aglow under the midday sun. We rejoin the trail from the observation deck, crossing the ridge supporting the island's peak 328 feet above sea level.

Several bottlenose dolphins join us partway for the afternoon return to the harbor, racing beside the boat to oohs and aahs as they leap from the water. The group lines the port side watching the show. I find myself receiving the glare of a yuppie princess who apparently perceives I've violated her personal space along the crowded rail at an arm's length away. I look at her with one eye crossed, mouth slightly agape, and a protruding lower lip. Motioning toward the dolphins breeching the surface, I say in a low, guttural voice, "Them's sum tasty water varmints." The princess stares at me in shock and horror, backing away slowly. Now I have plenty of space along the rail.

When I tell Kareen the story at dinner, she shakes her head and says, "You're terrible. At least you didn't tell her she had nice teeth."

Buck Island Reef, view of coral from overlook

Buck Island Reef, dolphin escort

"She left before I had the chance," I admit.

We enjoy a relaxing dinner on the coast, sitting down for a meal of tasty water varmints. We're in one of these places that likes to claim famous guests. Vice President Joe Biden dined here a few weeks earlier. Sadly, we're not added to their celebrity list. Our St. Croix park exploration concluded, we're ready for our morning plane to the Cyril E. King Airport in Charlotte Amalie, St. Thomas, to catch a ferry to St. John.

We land in St. Thomas at 7:45 a.m., but it's after 9:00 a.m. before we get our Budget rental, a beat-up minivan. Nothing thrills like waiting ninety minutes at a tiny airport for a trashed rental. We head east through town to the St. John ferry at Red Hook on the island's east end. We're about halfway to Red Hook when the low tire pressure warning flashes. I pull over at a gas station to find the tires at eighteen, forty, forty-one, and forty-two psi. "Well, that's reassuring," I tell Kareen. After I equalize the pressures and enter the ferry que, Kareen and I have a short discussion guessing when the tire will go flat. "Don't worry," I reassure her. "I'll watch for traffic while you change the tire."

We land in Cruz Bay, heading directly to the visitor center for **Virgin Islands National Park**. From there, we hike the Lind Point Trail, winding our way around switchbacks through dense tropical foliage in a big loop.

Most of our exploring's tomorrow, so we stop in Cruz Bay to eat a late lunch before continuing east on 10, the island's main east-west route. I'm already a little nervous about our accommodations after calling our Airbnb host from Cruz Bay. After asking for my name repeatedly, he replies that the room is not reserved this weekend. I reassure him that we have the correct dates. Realizing his weekends are mixed up, he tells us the room will be ready after he moves a friend out of it. I gather the gist from sentence fragments. We manage to locate the correct driveway for the house on a hilltop off Route 10 after passing it once and turning around. Our host greets us and lets us unload our bags before we park off the shoulder of the main road. The multilevel, hillside house is quite different than the one on St. Croix, though our hosts are friendly and welcoming. Our lower-level room will serve our basic needs, though I nervously watch Kareen take in the whole scene of our temporary cliff dwelling. The good doctor doesn't stay in places like this. She fixes me with a stare, and I look at her like a puppy dog that just peed on the carpet. She takes pity on her large canine, gamely keeping her disapproval nonverbal. To the positive, the view over the hillside of Coral Harbor and Coral Bay, a steep slope of dark-green jungle flowing to the bright-blue water and countless anchored sailing vessels, is captivating.

Virgin Islands, Coral Bay

Since we still have daylight, we leave to explore the East End down Route 10 all the way to its end beyond the park boundary.

For our last Caribbean park, **Virgin Islands Coral Reef National Monument**, we enter the NPS unit by standing in Princess Bay. Earlier at the visitor center, a ranger confirmed the boundary. "It's the waterline." We take pictures of each other in ankle deep water, our last park boundary penetrated, albeit unexplored.

St. John comes highly praised. Several friends raved about the island. It's easy to see why. The beautiful weather and scenery offer an ideal atmosphere for quiet, secluded getaways. Covering 60 percent of the island, the national park derives from Laurance Rockefeller's purchase of five thousand acres on St. John in 1956. The Rockefellers' philanthropy directly contributed to twelve of the sixty national parks in existence today, including Acadia, the Great Smoky Mountains, Grand Teton, Yosemite, Yellowstone, Shenandoah, and Virgin Islands. They also contributed to over a half dozen other park units, including the John D. Rockefeller Jr. Memorial Parkway in Wyoming, named after Laurance's father, and the Marsh-Billings-Rockefeller National Historical Park in Vermont. We'll visit all these parks in 2016, my way of thanking the Rockefellers for their contributions to our park system.

Tuesday begins on Reef Bay Trail. The trail runs south 2.2 miles one way from the Route 10 trailhead downhill to Reef Bay, passing the decaying ruins of four sugar plantations and mills. In sugar's heyday, planters cleared 90 percent of the island's native vegetation. Fortunately, the native tropical forest made a comeback. The trail leads steadily down the ridge through a canopy of tropical trees and plants. We meander downhill, stopping to explore sugar mill ruins and native etchings down the 0.3-mile Petroglyph Trail spur. Reaching the water and ruins of Reef Bay Sugar Mill, we're amused by countless small crabs scurrying everywhere. As the trail nears sea level, it's hard to avoid them. We walk a half mile along the hillside overlooking Genti Bay before retracing our steps on the ascent. We go uphill in forty-five minutes after the 75-minute downhill trek. I probably look a bit crazed, sweat falling from my face, as a ranger-led group passing us suddenly grows quiet, stepping aside. Mostly, they are practicing good trail etiquette, yielding to climbing hikers.

After lunch in Coral Bay and copious fluids, we complete our day exploring the Annaberg Sugar Mill ruins over Leinster Bay and walking the Francis Bay Trail on the north side of the island. The Annaberg Sugar Mill ruins are among the island's most extensive. The plantation and mill date from 1797 to 1805. Among the surviving structures, the windmill crushed the cane, beginning the separation process courtesy of the trade winds. The ruins overlook the bay, the Narrows, and Sir Francis Drake Channel, separating St. John and the British Virgin Islands, which rise under a blanket of dark-green against the blue water. I study the last few interpretive panels while Kareen lays on a bench. We've covered thirteen miles today, and she's done. The scenery merits the effort, in my opinion. It's time to return to our cliff dwelling for a shower and a relaxing Coral Bay dinner.

Virgin Islands, Rams Head

Our last day on the island dawns with a burst of sunlight glistening across Coral Bay. Achy joints aside, we target Rams Head Trail. From its junction with the Salt Pond Bay Trail, the trail runs one mile each way on the thin peninsula jutting out from the island's southeast end. The rocky prominence resembles a ram's head across the bay. The peninsula sits between Drunk Bay on the east and Saltpond Bay. Standing on the sea cliff, or ram's head, we gaze across the southern coast and its multiple bays and inlets as we're buffeted by easterly trade winds. Near the end of the trail, the path drops into a break in the peninsula that serves as a natural wind tunnel. Air compressed against the peninsula pours through the gap at high velocity. It's like putting your face near the open window of a moving car. As the warm wind blasts us, breakers crash against the jumbled rocks below. Kareen and I reach the area simultaneously with a female couple. We take pictures against the beautiful coastal backdrop before returning on the trail. Our host had suggested we hike here in the moonlight. We shudder imagining navigating these rocky ocean cliffs in the dark. We're happy to tackle the cliffs in daylight. The Rams Head Trail is our favorite among the beautiful scenery we've enjoyed the past several days. It's the perfect ending to our first trip in the US Virgin Islands.

Midday Thursday, we're greeted by Kareen's parents, George and Constance, outside the Montego Bay Airport. We're staying with them near St. Ann's Bay, an hour east on Jamaica's northern coast. Knowing of my recent travels and passion for history, George and Constance planned stops Friday morning at two interesting coastal historical sites. Our first stop is only a few miles from their home. Nueva Sevilla National Historic Site lies between St. Ann's and Discovery Bay, where Columbus landed in 1494 to claim the island for Spain. Columbus's crew marooned him at St. Ann's Bay for a year (1503–1504) during his fourth voyage to the New World. Spain's first island settlement, Sevilla served as the colonial capital from 1509 to 1524 when it was abandoned in favor of a south coast location called Spanish Town. The museum and grounds show artifacts spanning the island's human history, including the native

Arawak and Taino tribal stories. Disease, warfare, and enslavement wiped out the native Caribbean islanders. Needing a labor force, the Spanish imported African slaves. Displays in the plantation great house cover Jamaican history through English rule, from 1655 to 1962.

From Sevilla, George drives us west to Rose Hall Plantation near Montego Bay and our resort hotel, the Hilton at Rose Hall. The Rose Hall Plantation tour emphasizes alleged paranormal events surrounding the sugar plantation's legendary mistress. As we tour the Georgian-style great house built in the 1770s, our guide does an excellent job recounting the estate's exciting and scandalous past. The infamous lady of the house is the "White Witch Annie Palmer." Anne married John Palmer, the estate owner, before murdering him, two subsequent husbands, and an unknown number of slave lovers. She met a similar fate at the hands of her last intended lover-victim. Annie's restless spirit allegedly haunts the estate, with numerous stories of unexplained and bizarre events.

As we walk from Annie Palmer's gravesite, I ask Kareen, "You wouldn't off me for another guy, would you?"

Smiling, she replies, "That depends on the other guy."

"Well, that's sweet," I mumble.

9   *Philadelphia Flower Power*

AFTER A TWIN Cities business trip March 2, I revisit Mississippi National River and Recreation Area locations the next day, including the Mill City Museum and St. Anthony Falls. Another work trip to Dayton, Ohio follows a fourteen-hour turnaround at home. By late Friday afternoon, I'm crossing central Ohio. The weekend destination is the Philadelphia Flower Show. The 2016 show's theme is the National Park Service centennial celebration with an NPTC member meet-up Sunday morning. A younger me couldn't imagine driving nine hundred miles to attend a flower show. The trip also presents an opportunity to stop at sixteen parks in Pennsylvania, Maryland, and West Virginia. I need the pins from all these sites to complete my project. Having visited these parks in the past two years allows a faster pace.

Saturday begins entering Pennsylvania through Wheeling, West Virginia. The history of the town and surrounding area is documented in the **Wheeling National Heritage Area,** which commemorates the 1849 completion of the suspension bridge extending the National Road into Ohio and the prairie beyond. The heritage area also celebrates Wheeling as the Civil War birthplace of West Virginia statehood.

Friendship Hill National Historic Site sits on a river bluff above the Monongahela River in southwestern Pennsylvania. Albert

Gallatin, the secretary of the treasury for thirteen years under Presidents Jefferson and Madison, built the home beginning in 1789 and used it as a primary residence until 1825. Exhibits throughout the home review the Swiss-born Gallatin's life, including the tragedy of his first marriage, ended by his wife's death a few months after they wed.

A thirty-minute drive east, **Fort Necessity National Battlefield** marks the place where twenty-one-year-old Lieutenant Colonel George Washington, with his militia and Indian allies, surprised French soldiers camping in a nearby glen and ambushed them on the morning of May 28, 1754. The clash opens hostilities in the French and Indian War. Washington and his command constructed a fort nearby at the Great Meadows. By early July, a French and Indian force doubling the size of the British garrison enveloped the fort. The French commander, the brother of the deceased French leader at the glen, allowed Washington to surrender under generous terms.

Washington returned the next summer as an aide-de-camp for Major General Edward Braddock. Braddock's twenty-four-hundred-man army planned to attack the French in Fort Duquesne at modern-day Pittsburgh. The French ambushed Braddock and his advanced detachment of thirteen hundred men about eight miles south of Fort Duquesne, cutting the British troops to pieces and mortally wounding the general. Braddock died a few days later as the British retreated near the Great Meadows. His men buried him in the middle of the wilderness road, presumably to prevent desecration of the body.

Continuing over the hills and curves for fifty-four miles farther east and north, I stop at the **Flight 93 National Memorial** near Shanksville, Pennsylvania. During my first visit in 2014, the visitor center location consisted of leveled ground on a hill overlooking the crash site. Since visiting the memorial near the crash site, I've been anticipating seeing the new visitor center. Stories across the park system of heroism and tragedy are moving, but none feel as raw as at Flight 93. Like most Americans, I remember 9/11 vividly, including the story of the people who boarded United 93 in Newark, New Jersey, and gave their lives to thwart a fourth terrorist attack that day. The exhibits contain items recovered from the crash, along with passenger names and pictures. One exhibit features three voicemail recordings from among the thirty-seven phone calls made from Flight 93 between 9:28 a.m. and 10:03 a.m. These heartbreaking messages, each about a minute long, play through a handset. Listening to one on the first pass through the displays is heart wrenching. Tissue boxes located on the window sills suggest I'm not alone. When I'm ready to exit, I return to the audio exhibit and listen to the last two messages. I'm afraid I'll start crying as they replay in my head.

Inscriptions of the September 11, 2001, timeline augment the walkway and wall connecting the parking lot and visitor center. Both the wall and sidewalk align with the flight path of Flight 93, as does the memorial near the point of impact. I pull out of the parking lot with echoes of those passengers' voices in my head. What would you say to those you love if you knew it's the last time they'll ever hear your voice? What words might come, amid the swirling chaos and terror, given a minute to say good-bye? I imagine most would say something similar to what these three passengers said. I barely make it out of the parking lot before the tears start rolling down my cheeks. Thirty-three passengers and seven crew members, all here today, gone tomorrow. Only once can I remember feeling so affected amid history. Standing on the cliff above Omaha beach in Normandy, thinking of all the brave men cut down in the prime of their lives defending my right to stand on this sacred soil, many of them still behind me under a field of white headstones, I bowed my head, and cried.

The last park today covers another tragedy of a different nature. I first read of the events memorialized at the **Johnstown Flood National Memorial** in a *Reader's Digest* article I came across as a child. Years later, I listened on CD to David McCullough's riveting account of the catastrophe in *The Johnstown Flood*. The South Fork Dam failed on the morning of May 31, 1889, releasing the contents of Lake Conemaugh, 20 million tons, in a massive wall of water and debris moving down the steep Little Conemaugh River Valley, wiping out small towns over fourteen miles before hitting Johnstown at forty miles per hour. A forty-five-acre debris pile developed at a stone railroad bridge over the Conemaugh River and caught fire with people still trapped in the wreckage. After the flood waters receded, the apocalyptic nightmare of flood and fire left 2,209 dead while Johnstown lay in ruin.

The story embodies an ironic and symbolic twist. The reservoir, 450 feet higher in elevation than Johnstown, served as a playground for the South Fork Fishing and Hunting Club, mostly rich industrialists from Pittsburgh. The park today includes the surviving section of the earthen dam and the former clubhouse in the small town of Saint Michael. The park film portraying these horrible events is one of the most referenced and memorable films among park enthusiasts. Miles to go, I leave Saint Michael as the sun loses its grip on day. Nightfall compliments my somber mood, an afternoon immersed in tragedy. I pass Harrisburg before exhaustion compels me to stop south of Reading.

At dawn, my adrenaline overcomes lingering fatigue. I can't wait to reach Philadelphia. I launch this day in the parks at the visitor center for **Independence National Historical Park**. After chatting with a ranger, I walk over to Old City Hall on the corner of Fifth and Chestnut, buy the park unit's lapel pins for the project in the bookstore, and take a few minutes to admire the old Supreme Court Chamber on the building's main floor. During four prior visits, I've explored the park's major attractions, such as Independence Hall. Several years ago, I drew a wry smile from a ranger in the Liberty Bell Center when I pointed to the cracked bell hanging in the circular exhibit hall and said, "I know a couple of metal workers back home that could probably fix that for you." Independence National Historical Park takes me on a journey through layers of rich, important history. Every visit reveals something new. We will return for the NPTC convention in August, counting Independence National Historical Park as one of 190 NPS units I visit at least twice in 2015–2016. This morning, I'm anxious to reach the convention center.

The Philadelphia Flower Show is a perfect example of a special place or event I've experienced only because of my park goals or NPTC membership. Though I'm challenging my sanity driving over two thousand miles in the last four days, the effort proves well rewarded with the flower show's mixture of color and creativity. At least one third, if not half, the exhibit space features national park–themed creations. A large timbered A-frame forms the entrance to the park display with the NPS arrowhead on stone-tiled columns. To the left of the entrance are some strange but very colorful mushrooms covered with every conceivable color of flower. The Yellowstone section includes a model of the Grand Prismatic Spring and its intoxicating bands of blue, yellow, reds, and greens all depicted florally, and a standing grizzly made of brown wood chips. A wooden-framed bison grazes on wildflowers near a colorful giant panel with EXPLORE AMERICA emblazoned in brown block letters against an ivy background. A red, white, and blue Liberty Bell, the same size as the original and complete with a flowery crack, hangs above us. Our member meet-up goes quickly. The exhibits are beautiful, but as the crowd builds at midday, I depart to visit more parks in eastern Pennsylvania.

About a mile away is **Edgar Allan Poe National Historic Site**. The famous author rented this house from 1843 to 1844 during the six years he lived in Philadelphia. The ranger at the desk is familiar. She'd been working at the house the last time I visited in November 2014 when I joined Kareen in Philadelphia for a conference. While Kareen sat through over eight hours a day of lectures on every aspect of nephrology, I visited every NPS site I could reach in three days before she came along for the fourth day. During that visit we waited outside for the fire department to give the all clear, our tour aborted by a suspected gas leak. Kareen posed for a picture beside a post outside sporting a large black raven. The photograph appeared eerily symmetrical. I posted the picture on social media with the question, "Can you find the raven?"

At **Valley Forge National Historical Park**, Washington's bedraggled Continental army ushered Valley Forge into American history as their winter campsite in 1777–1778. The British army occupied Philadelphia when the campaigning season ceased. The army camp's compromised conditions and privation became the stuff of legend. The park's position in American lore symbolizes struggle and sacrifice to sustain the new country and its founding principles of self governance and personal liberty.

Edgar Alan Poe raven

My first visit here took on a clandestine form during a business trip in October 2013. The date fell during a government shutdown, leaving the park buildings and visitor center closed. I managed to see several park areas accessible via public roads. I returned last year for a complete visit, exploring places like Washington's headquarters without the *Mission Impossible* aspect.

Two hours to the southwest of Valley Forge lies another small Pennsylvania town immortalized for sacrifice under great peril. **Gettysburg National Military Park** protects the battleground known as the "high water mark of the Confederacy," acknowledging the northern-most advance of Lee's Army of Virginia. Gettysburg weighed heavily toward the war's outcome. The engagement opened as Lee's fabled force reached its strategic and psychological peak. Ironically, Lee's belief in his army's infallibility proved the Confederates' undoing.

Critical decisions loomed large at the onset. Had the Confederates pushed their advantage on the first day, they could have taken the heights of Cemetery Ridge before scattered Union forces gathered to full strength. Historians have long speculated that the strategic blunder in failing to press the advantage on the first day might be a critical aftershock of losing Stonewall Jackson's brilliant aggression to friendly fire at Chancellorsville three months earlier.

I first saw the park when I drove my parents to Washington, DC, in August 2007. We spent one and a half days touring legendary sites on the Civil War's most famous battleground. We walked up Little Round Top, where the 20th Maine under Colonel Joshua Lawrence Chamberlain defended the Union left flank against a relentless assault by John Bell Hood's Alabamans. Chamberlain, awarded the Medal of Honor for his leadership, is immortalized in the film *Gettysburg*. We visited the battle's notorious sites of fierce combat, such as Devil's Den, the Wheatfield, and Culps Hill, where the federals anchored their right flank. We traveled the length of the Union and Confederate positions a mile apart on Cemetery and Seminary ridges, respectively.

Visiting the battlefield gives an appreciation for how narrowly the contest swung in the Union's favor. The decimation of southern troops in "Pickett's Charge" on the third day, when five thousand Confederates fell in an hour, belies how close the South came to breaking the Union line on the second day, thwarted across a contracting two-mile line in the shape of an upside-down fishhook. Wave after wave of Confederate attackers forced heroic Union efforts to maintain a tenuous hold on the high ground, exemplified by the 1st Minnesota near the center and the Maine and New York regiments on the left. I stop on Cemetery Ridge at the monument erected to the memory of the 1st Minnesota Volunteer Infantry Regiment, ordered into a gap in the line where attacking troops outnumbered them five to one. The regiment, largely of Scandinavian decent, rushed into the gap amid dense, acrid smoke and a torrent of fire. Despite near annihilation at an 82 percent casualty rate, these young sons of Norwegian and Swedish frontier farmers refused to yield, buying precious minutes for reinforcements to fortify the position to their rear. Visualizing cries of agony as they are torn to pieces by .58-caliber lead pouring through their flesh, I lean forward, hand against stone, and for the second time in two days am overcome with grief.

At the visitor center, I catch the last shuttle of the day to the **Eisenhower National Historic Site**, the thirty-fourth president's Gettysburg farm. Ike grew attached to the town during a World War I army tank corps training assignment at Gettysburg College. The farm, purchased in 1950, is the only place that the Eisenhowers truly called home. Eisenhower gained global renown as the Supreme Allied Commander in Europe for the 1944 invasion of France. Ike served two terms as president from 1953 to 1961. Dwight D. Eisenhower and his wife, Mamie, deeded the farm over to the US government in 1968. Dwight died the following year, and Mamie lived on the property until she passed in 1979, after which it transitioned to the care of the NPS as a national historic site. The farm opens a telling window into the Eisenhower's world.

Unknown to me during my first Gettysburg visit, I toured the house and farm last year on my second trip to the town. Today, I'm the only visitor on the last bus. After collecting the pins and cancellations in the gift shop, I meet the ranger on duty. She's a history student doing her doctoral dissertation on Eisenhower, so I pepper her with questions about Eisenhower's life and career. It's always a special treat to get a solo NPS site tour, and I overstay the twenty minutes I promised to the bus driver asking about the young ranger's research. We discuss one of my favorite items in the home. Mamie's guest book contains the signatures of world and American political leaders who visited the farm, leaving a roll call of post–World War II world history.

Staying overnight in Gettysburg, I enjoy a memorable dinner at the Blue & Gray Bar & Grill on the square. The grill's craft burgers are named for Union and Confederate generals who fought in the battle, with the applicable battle flag flying atop the burger. I like the fried egg–burger combo, despite Kareen's dire warnings that it's a heart attack on a plate. I'm a lost cause tonight, ordering the General Jubal Anderson Early burger. I contemplate the symbolism of the small Confederate flag, wondering whether a cheeseburger can be racist. I conclude the only way to deal with this politically incorrect burger is to eat it. Sometimes you've got to get tough. Tonight, Old Jube's Confederate flag symbolizes a delicious dinner and cold beer, a sanctioned meal on the steak and beer diet.

Monday morning I'm up early, on a mission to collect pins and cancellations at seven recently visited park units before turning for home. The first park, thirty minutes southwest of Gettysburg and over the border in Maryland, is **Catoctin Mountain Park**. The park is popular for its hiking and camping opportunities. It's best known as the location of Camp David. The presidential retreat is not marked on any public maps to reduce the temptation to visitors and random psychotics that might wander into the restricted area.

From Catoctin, I continue south to Frederick, Maryland, and **Monocacy National Battlefield**. The engagement at Monocacy was a delaying action fought on July 9, 1864, between a Confederate army led by Lieutenant General Jubal Early (my burger's namesake), and a Union force commanded by Major General Lew Wallace. Early's force emerged from the Shenandoah Valley on their way to attack Washington, DC from the north. Wallace, outnumbered more than two to one by Early's force of fifteen thousand, wasn't trying to stop Early but slow him long enough for Union reinforcements to reach Washington from the main Union army encircling Petersburg, Virginia. Lee hoped the attack might relieve pressure on his troops, who'd been fighting the much larger Union army in costly major engagements the past two months. Grant's strategy to vanquish Lee's Army of Virginia resulted in a bloody battle of attrition across eastern Virginia. Wallace successfully stalled Early's march, buying several precious days before Early could bring his troops in sight of Washington's defenses.

The reinforcements arrived just in time. Early engaged newly reinforced federal troops at Fort Stevens, including two divisions Grant sent north from Petersburg. The Union force was too large for Early to dislodge. The battle at Fort Stevens is best known as the location where a curious President Lincoln, who came out to witness the battle, peaked above the parapet as rebel bullets whizzed past. According to army lore, a young Captain Oliver Wendell Holmes, not realizing the identity of the tall, gangly man in the top hat, shouted at Lincoln, "Get your damn head down before it gets shot off!" At least, Holmes is reputed to have said this, but no evidence survives confirming the story. What is known is Lincoln was fired upon while viewing the action, becoming the only US president to ever come under fire in combat. We'll visit Fort Stevens in chapter 22.

From Frederick, I continue to **Harpers Ferry National His-torical Park**. Harpers Ferry is loaded with history and serves as a primary resource center for the National Park Service. The town sits at a major travel junction, situated in a steep valley at the con-fluence of the Potomac and Shenandoah Rivers. It's best known for the federal arsenal attacked by John Brown and his militant aboli-tionists in October 1859. Brown and his followers hoped to foment a rebellion by arming the local enslaved population in Maryland and Virginia. Instead, his small group is captured by a company of US Marines led by US Army Colonel Robert E. Lee and Lieutenant J. E. B. Stuart. Brown's execution by hanging on December 2, 1859, in nearby Charles Town created a martyr and rallying cry for the growing abolitionist movement. For the South, the raid reinforced their worst fears and inflammatory predictions about the true intent among the hated abolitionists. For the park service, the town hosts the NPS Media Design Center, where many of the exhibits and displays shown in parks around the country area are created. Next to the Media Center is the Mather Training Center, one of two major training centers for the NPS, the other being the Albright Training Center at Grand Canyon National Park in Arizona.

Harpers Ferry also hosts the Appalachian Trail Conservancy office. The trail runs directly through the town. After stopping at the Mather Training Center and Media Design Center to collect their passport stamps, I walk to the lower town via a section of the **Appalachian National Scenic Trail** along the high cliff above the Shenandoah before it meets the Potomac. The one-mile walk offers a view of the steep valley and the river confluence. The Appalachian National Scenic Trail runs a total length of 2,170 miles from Mt. Katahdin in Maine to Springer Mountain in Georgia.

Three NPS units converge here. The Appalachian National Scenic Trail and the **Potomac Heritage National Scenic Trail** both pass through Harpers Ferry National Historical Park. The Potomac Heritage National Scenic Trail includes 710 miles of trail from the Allegheny Plateau south of Pittsburgh to the Potomac River at Chesapeake Bay. The trail commemorates the tremendous history along the Potomac River corridor in Pennsylvania, Maryland, West Virginia, Virginia, and the District of Columbia. The Appalachian, Potomac Heritage, and Natchez Trace National Scenic Trails are the only three among the thirty trails in the National Trails System designated as NPS units.

At the Lower Town Visitor Center, the ranger on duty is listening to a spring training game radio broadcast. I can tell immediately it's a Cardinals game by the players mentioned and familiar voices. As I greet him, I realize the older ranger is blind. "Are you a Cardinals fan?" I ask.

In a light, wavering voice, he replies, "I've been a Cardinals fan my whole life."

I remember the ranger from a previous visit and ask, "How long have you worked for the park service?"

He replies, "I've been a park ranger for thirty-six years. Do you like baseball, too?"

"Yes, I'm a big baseball fan," I reply.

"What's your favorite team?" he asks, unable to see my sweat-stained Cardinals hat adorned with national park pins.

"I was born in St. Louis, so you can probably guess. I've supported the Cardinals since I can remember," I answer. He smiles at the surprise of a visitor who shares his passion for the Cardinals. "I'm visiting as many national park units as possible to celebrate the centennial," I tell him. "Harpers Ferry is number seventy-one." As I finish stamping and turn to go, I say, "Have a wonderful centennial year."

He smiles and replies, "And you as well. Safe travels and go Cardinals."

I remember as I exit that I spoke with him about the park's history at some length during my last visit. I recall admiring his enthusiasm for the park he represents and his dedication of service. I did not know during that visit what I just discovered in today's exchange, that we share two personal passions. Our connection vibrates an emotional string within me. Perhaps it's the irony of the question and how small the world can seem. I'm touched by the exchange as my feet hit the bricks of the Lower Town street for the uphill hike back to the car.

From Harpers Ferry, I continue on rural, two-lane roads over hills and curves to **Antietam National Battlefield** in Sharpsburg, Maryland, following the same path that Stonewall Jackson used to march his troops sixteen miles at double time from Harpers Ferry to reinforce Lee's embattled army at Sharpsburg. The Battle of Antietam developed after a copy of Lee's orders dividing his command into three separate forces is discovered by two Union soldiers wrapped around some cigars at a recently vacated Confederate campsite on a farm located within Monocacy National Battlefield near Frederick. The normally overcautious Union General George McClellan chanced into a perfect opportunity to strike at Lee's divided army with its back to the Potomac River, making a quick retreat impractical. These events triggered the bloodiest day in the Civil War on September 17, 1862. Of over one hundred thousand troops engaged at Antietam, twenty-three thousand are casualties of the one-day battle.

Last year, I returned to the park for my second visit to explore some places I'd missed, such as the Pry and Newcomer Houses. The Pry House served as McClellan's battle headquarters and as one of many field hospitals in the following days. The organization of battlefield triage advanced greatly based on observations at Antietam and that history is explained in the Pry House exhibits.

Gettysburg, Monocacy, Harpers Ferry, and Antietam are part of the **Journey Through Hallowed Ground National Heritage Area,** which includes historical sites in Maryland, Pennsylvania, Virginia, and West Virginia. The aptly named heritage area covers 175 miles along the corridor of US Highway 15, including the greatest concentration of Civil War battle sites within any national heritage area.

I'm hoping to visit the day's last park in two parts. From Antietam, I have another half hour to reach the **Chesapeake and Ohio Canal National Historical Park** headquarters. The twelve-foot-wide canal connects the Potomac at sea level near Washington, DC, to the Ohio River beyond the Allegheny Divide, spanning a 605-foot change in elevation. Construction occurred from 1828 to 1850, by which time railroads began bridging the commercial transportation gap from east to west. The canal remained in service until 1924, after which it sat abandoned for thirty years. By the late 1960s, concerned citizens realized the historical and recreational value of the extant canal right of way and its towpath. Chesapeake and Ohio Canal National Historical Park preserves this legacy to America's transportation history.

After the headquarters stop for passport cancellations, I continue west to the Canal Visitor Center in Cumberland, Maryland. I arrive at 4:02 p.m. and find the doors locked, a surprise since I'd checked the hours on both the park site and NPTC database, which gave a 4:30 p.m. winter closing time. On the door though is a white sheet of paper stating the visitor center closes at 4:00 p.m. on Monday and Tuesday during the winter. They might as well have added a "Hey, Dave" over an extended middle finger. It fits a pattern. Over the past three years, I've visited all the park's six visitor centers along its 185 miles and found the visitor center closed each time. At least the park headquarters had been open. At some point, I hope to take a couple of days and drive the canal's length. I'll call first beforehand. Only then will I learn that the park has an annual strategy session on how to keep me out of its visitor centers. In truth, budget cuts and reduced staffing have cut hours across all the park's visitor locations. A similar story is playing out at parks across the country.

Now, I have only 645 miles to drive to complete my 3,000-mile travel week. "No problem," I tell Kareen over the phone. "It's as easy as eating a racist cheeseburger."

10 The Great Plains

It's Tuesday, March 8, and I'm off to North Dakota for work after a few hours at home. By Wednesday, I've continued to Bismarck, North Dakota. It's an ideal starting place into the heart of the **Northern Plains National Heritage Area**, with historical sites along the **Lewis and Clark National Historic Trail**. At Fort Mandan State Historical Site, I walk into the reconstructed timber and earthen fort built by the Corps of Discovery during the expedition's first winter of 1804–1805. After departing St. Louis in May 1804 and traveling sixteen hundred miles up the Missouri, the party secured shelter here from the harsh Northern Plains winter.

Mandan and Hidatsa Sioux in nearby settlements assisted the corps. Remnants of their villages are now protected as **Knife River Indian Villages National Historic Site**. The tribes occupied earthen lodges near the confluence of the Knife and Missouri Rivers. I study a reconstructed earthlodge next to the visitor center before walking the 1.3-mile Village Trail through two of the park's three village sites. Depressions in the ground mark the former location of lodges and other earthen structures. Archeological study here reveals over five hundred years of habitation. The Sioux abandoned the villages in 1845 after smallpox epidemics devastated their population. Before breaking camp, Lewis and Clark hired French fur trapper Toussaint

Charbonneau, who was living among the Hidatsa, as a guide. His teenage wife, Sacagawea, joined the expedition as an interpreter and earned immortal fame for her invaluable contributions.

From the villages, I have a three-hour trip to **Fort Union Trading Post National Historic Site**. Near the Canadian border and Yellowstone and Missouri River confluence, the 1828 fort's strategic location for commerce on the upper Missouri made it a vital trading post for thirty-nine years. The park straddles the North Dakota–Montana state line. I park in the Montana lot and cross into North Dakota to enter the reconstructed trading post. The full-scale replica enclosure and main building doubles as the visitor center. It's quiet. The ranger seems distracted by whatever task he paused in order to greet me. I'm more interested in walking around the stockade anyway as I did last year, so I use the site's stampers and exit.

From Stanton, it's a two-hour drive south on North Dakota Highway 16 skirting the Montana state line to Medora and the headquarters and south unit of **Theodore Roosevelt National Park**. I visited the north unit last year, driving the tour road through North Dakota's badlands, an irregular and strangely attractive landscape with its buttes, multi-colored hills, and eroded rock. At the south unit, I stopped at Painted Canyon Visitor Center along I-94, surveying the panorama of colorful topography at the overlook. I arrived to find a lone bison bull sitting in front of the building. The same bull stood in the parking lot near my passenger door when I returned. It looked like he was waiting for me to unlock the car. As I opened the driver's side door, I announced to the one-ton bull, "Sorry pal. I don't pick up hitchhikers."

The Painted Canyon Visitor Center is closed today. In Medora, I get the park's stamps and pins before walking 150 feet or so to peer into Theodore Roosevelt's relocated Maltese Cross cabin, his first North Dakota residence, dating to September 1883. He later moved to the Elkhorn Ranch, now an isolated park property between the north and south units.

On the south unit's thirty-six-mile scenic drive, I climb into the hills to wind through the rugged reds, browns, greens, and yellows of the badlands. The park's resident bison amuse me with their use of the road. On the north side of the drive, I approach a bison standing perpendicular to the road on the right shoulder and waiting to make eye contact. He strolls across the road after I stop. If the bison could speak, I imagine him saying into my open window, "I'm the boss and you'll like it. You'll like it a lot! Plus, I'm the National Park Service's mascot, and you are…? I didn't think so." A few miles down the road, a series of bison meet me walking in a straight line, one after the other in the opposite lane like a series of cars. I guess if you weigh two thousand pounds, you're close enough to a moving vehicle. Along the west section of the road, the Little Missouri River Valley overlook reveals a large bison herd grazing below in the river's flat, fertile floodplain. I now understand how Theodore Roosevelt found the solace to recover from tragedy in this place. He departed Manhattan destined for the North Dakota's badlands after losing his mother and wife on the same day, February 14, 1884, prompting Roosevelt to make a single entry into his diary that night, a large 'X' followed by, "The light has gone out of my life."

Today's visit in Medora leaves me a 340-mile drive through southwestern North Dakota into western South Dakota and Deadwood. I detour into northeastern Wyoming to drive by **Devils Tower National Monument**, passing the closed park under a clear western nighttime sky decorated by the Milky Way spanning its length. Devils Tower is one of many parks that takes advantage of its remote setting and minimal light pollution to host stargazing programs. I visited the unique geological feature last year but don't count it among the parks visited this year. The igneous intrusion, standing 867-feet above the rocks piled at its base, holds the distinction of America's first national monument, courtesy of Roosevelt in 1906. Wyoming also boasts the first national park, Yellowstone in 1872, and the first national forest, Shoshone in 1891. After entering Deadwood exhausted and hauling my bags to the room, I trudge across Main Street to a saloon for a burger and beer. Sleep comes easy tonight.

Friday starts at **Jewel Cave National Monument**. I stopped here in February 2015 but couldn't tour the cave beyond the large underground entry chamber since I was the only park visitor. The park requires two or more visitors for a tour. I have better luck today. There are five more visitors waiting for the day's first cave tour. I join them for the eighty-minute underground walk. The impressive natural features created by calcite crystal formations lend the cave its name. Varying mineral content creates different colors in the sparkling crystals. Some formations are large, like the five-foot striped drapery known as "The Bacon" because it looks like a giant strip of bacon hanging from the cave wall. It doesn't appear as tasty as I imagined a human-size strip of bacon might look.

Next in the Black Hills is **Mount Rushmore National Memorial**. Work began in 1927 on Gutzon Borglum's shrine to America, with the fourth presidential head dedicated in 1939, only to be completed in 1991 by Lincoln Borglum fifty years after his father's death. During this visit, my third, I walk the Presidential Trail along the Avenue of Flags to stand on the Grand View Terrace, gazing at the sculpture of Washington, Jefferson, Roosevelt, and Lincoln. I find the giant granite sculpture irresistible. Despite having been here thirteen months ago, I linger to stare at the art. When I returned here in February 2015, sixteen and a half years after my first visit, the facilities and added NPS presentation impressed me. The Avenue of Flags and Lincoln Borglum Visitor Center had been added. The constant thread, the sculpture, remains unchanged from afar, an iconic American image.

South of Rushmore and Jewel Cave is **Wind Cave National Park**. I first toured the cave in February 2015, detouring a work trip to take advantage of a fluke weather system that brought sixty- to seventy-degree temperatures to the Black Hills. I walked to dinner in nearby Hot Springs, South Dakota, in a short-sleeve T-shirt. Wind Cave is most famous for its box-work formations, with more than any other cave. A popular example is the "post office." Countless box formations on the walls and above give the impression of a vast, 360-degree mailroom. Today's visit is shorter. I share a short summary of my park travels with a couple of the rangers, collecting the project pins and stamps. Leaving the visitor center, I take a few bison pictures en route to the next stop and one of my favorite NPS hidden gems.

Minuteman Missile National Historic Site requires a two-hour drive north through Rapid City and east along I-90. Minuteman Missile is a preserved missile silo (with an unarmed training missile) and launch control facility from the Minuteman II defense system. The Minuteman I and II systems served as America's primary nuclear defense for thirty years from October 1962 until deactivated in favor of its smaller, more advanced replacement, the Minuteman III, from December 1991 until Ellsworth Air Force Base 44th Missile Wing's formal deactivation in 1994. The intercontinental ballistic missile, or ICBM, can carry a nuclear warhead to any global target within thirty minutes. Over one thousand Minuteman missiles dotted the upper Plains. The park's missile silo and launch control facility went active in 1966. Both are the only remaining examples of the early designs in these facilities.

The park's history held limited interest before I visited. It's perhaps the best example of an amazing unit and related history that I might have missed without the park goal. In February 2015, the unit's month-old visitor center felt bare without exhibits. I received an unofficial personal tour of the launch control facility as the park's sole visitor that day. I felt like I stumbled into this fascinating place. The ranger and I strolled the grounds in a relaxed manner, having more conversation than presentation.

The site's security procedures speak to solemnity, starting with the ominous, heavily armored Hummer in front named the Peacekeeper. I can visualize teenagers having a keg party on some country road interrupted when this thing rolls up complete with occupants carrying fully automatic weapons.

The surface facility is a bland, one-story sheet-metal construction, uninteresting inside and out except for the not-so-subtle park service humor evident in a game of Battleship set up on a mess table. Access underground requires passing through the site's security room with steel-plated doors and gun ports. Only the two missileers on duty and the cook went underground. The cook needed to bring meals during shifts varying from twenty-four to forty hours.

The launch control center (LCC) is a self-contained, oblong metal capsule supported by four massive shock absorbers preventing direct ground contact. The metal capsule sits within a reinforced concrete bunker with an escape tunnel. Small models of the Minuteman and its predecessors, such as the Atlas, are in the outer room, an entry area between the elevator and bunker. Other show-and-tell exhibits include pieces of normal rebar and the heavy rebar used here. When constructed, these bunkers must have been among the most heavily reinforced structures ever built.

The first thing one notices is the mural painted on the eight-ton steel bunker door. The mural spoofs the original Domino's Pizza delivery promise of thirty minutes or less or your next one's free. Inside the metal capsule, necessities of prolonged shifts are met with a toilet and bunk. The missile commander and deputy's stations and panels display the system's contemporary technology. The launch procedure includes a two-person key turn, requiring verification at another LCC. The fail-safe meant no single LCC could launch a missile without confirmation.

Missileers received occasional false alerts and performed the launch procedure up to authorization. The early-launch-detection satellite used during most of the system's service life incorrectly identified solar flares and volcanic eruptions as nuclear missile launches. Primary control over America's nuclear defense system resides at North American Aerospace Defense Command (NORAD) headquarters in Colorado. As a back-up, SAC (strategic air command) has kept a Boeing jet, originally known as Looking Glass, flying random patterns over the United States twenty-four hours a day since the program began. Former members of the missile groups have contributed much to the park's interpretation and some even conduct tours as seasonal rangers or volunteers.

Today, I meet the park superintendent, Eric, and share my enthusiasm for the unit. He mentions that the visitor center is closing for April to install the permanent exhibits. They are near completion at the Harpers Ferry Design Center I visited earlier this week. I tell Eric, "I can't wait to visit the site after the exhibits are installed, hopefully with my wife so she can tour the launch control facility too."

Minuteman Missile Launch Control

He walks me through mock-ups hanging on the walls. Among the information, I read the account of Russian Lieutenant Colonel Stanislav Petrov, who chose to ignore an alarm indicating an American nuclear attack on September 26, 1983. The Russian system warned the Soviet command center that the United States had just launched five ICBMs at the Soviet Union. The colonel reasoned that the US would never begin a nuclear attack by launching just five missiles. Petrov took a dire, calculated risk by exercising his discretion and delaying reporting the situation, but his judgment stood vindicated when system checks revealed that sunlight reflected off high-altitude clouds triggered the warning. The story isn't shared with the West until after the Cold War. As the incident happened at an especially tense time in international relations, a retaliatory strike order loomed as a real possibility had Petrov immediately reported the "attack." In 2006, the United Nations honored the colonel, dubbing him "the man who saved the world." Below the story is a photograph of the retired Russian colonel with one of the park's rangers during a 2007 visit. It's a modern heroic tale woven into park history. Colonel Petrov's courageous decision and visit to Minuteman Missile National Historic Site constitute one of my favorite National Park System stories.

This day in the parks concludes with my fifth visit to **Badlands National Park**. Though the familiar rugged and bizarre landscape impresses at first glance, I find the eroded rock formations always offer something new. The park's complex beauty reveals itself over time and repeated exposure, in synchronicity to its creation. After a long day driving, I'm ready to take a walk and stop at the Door, Window, and Notch Trails near the park's eastern entrance.

The Doors Trail leads across hopelessly complex rocky ground, misshapen from heavy erosion with an irregular furrowing leaving gullies without any discernible pattern. Taller rock features rise to the south and in the distance. The Notch Trail leads one up to and along a cliff at the rim of a small canyon to the trail's ultimate destination, a notch in the rock, offering an overlook of the White River Valley. It's a thoroughly enjoyable trail, with the climactic view exposing the transition from the dry plain to the badland's broken landscape across the valley below. After hiking several miles, I start the drive south into Nebraska. I'll stay in Chadron overnight, tired but content with a day well spent. We'll visit Badlands National Park and the other Black Hills area parks again in chapter 39.

The Saturday morning drive passes through Crawford, Nebraska, and Fort Robinson State Historic Site. The famous Sioux war leader Crazy Horse died on September 5, 1877, while confined at Fort Robinson. My first visit to **Agate Fossil Beds National Monument** took me through this isolated part of northwestern Nebraska. Fort Robinson and the fossil beds are near the Wyoming state line at the western end of the sparsely populated Nebraska sand hills.

I arrive at the visitor center as it opens at 9:00 a.m. I covered the Daemonelix and Fossil Hills Trails a year earlier. It's taken time to develop a strong interest in the NPS fossil beds. But they've grown on me, and now I consider myself a fan. In that progression, Agate didn't resonate during my first visit. Literally in the middle of nowhere, the park has some interesting fossils and an exhibit built around the Native American artifacts collected by local rancher James H. Cook, who befriended the famous, never-defeated-in-combat Sioux chief Red Cloud. Cook once owned much of the park's land, thus the site connection.

The ranger greets me as I share Agate Fossil Beds National Monument is the eighty-second NPS unit I've visited on my centennial park-a-thon. When I suggest that Agate didn't capture my full interest, Ranger Stephan jumps into action with the park's story. I think, "He must be lonely and bored," but as the tale unfolds in his telling, it comes alive from his enthusiasm. I feel his genuine appreciation for the location and its unique attributes as he continues the spontaneous revelation.

Discovered in 1904, the animals represented in the primary fossil bed at this spot on the Niobrara River are not dinosaurs but died after the age of dinosaurs, nineteen to twenty million years ago in the Cenozoic Era of paleontology, which continues today. A vast floodplain covered far western Nebraska, subject to alternating droughts and floods. An extended drought left animals dying of dehydration in shallow water holes, covered over time by sand, silt, and ash that preserved the fossil record. Ranger Stephan explains suspected characteristics of the more common animals found here. I ask how he manages the solitude of this remote place. He shares that he's enjoyed his four years at Agate but is seeking a transfer. He hasn't decided his favorite among three or four openings he's considering, but I record his email address to share additional references on Red Cloud and other subjects I can't recollect in the moment without internet access. After returning home, I send him those reading recommendations, including the excellent, best-selling biography by Bob Drury and Tom Clavin, *The Heart of Everything That Is: The Untold Story of Red Cloud.* I leave wondering where Stephan will land. I'll find out later this year when I visit his new park.

Eastern Wyoming's **Fort Laramie National Historic Site** is the next stop. Robert Crawford and William Sublette built the original fort at the confluence of the Laramie and Platte Rivers in 1834. After being rebuilt and converted from log to adobe construction in the 1840s, the US Army purchased the post in 1849 to protect the nearby emigrant trails. The fort evolved from a trading post to the most important military post in the Northern Plains, hosting more treaty negotiations than any other army location. The Treaty of 1868, Fort Laramie's most important treaty, promised western South Dakota and the sacred Black Hills to Native Americans. Prospectors and other opportunists broke the treaty in 1874 after reports of gold. The ensuing war led to the Battle of Little Bighorn. The army abandoned the post in 1890 after the conclusion of the Indian Wars.

Modern-day Fort Laramie consists of surviving structures, ruins, and building outlines. The oldest documented building in Wyoming survives in the fort. The 1849 bachelor officer quarters is known by its nickname, "Old Bedlam." I can only imagine the name was well earned.

After touring the fort and grounds, I stop to walk four hundred feet on the Old Army bow bridge over the North Platte River. The King Iron Bridge Company completed the wooden-planked, triple-span bridge, pedestrian-only nowadays, in 1876 as the Great Sioux War erupted. The historic bridge became part of the park after a new, adjacent concrete bridge replaced it in 1957.

An hour east of Fort Laramie, **Scotts Bluff National Monument** earned a place in American history as one of the most well-known markers along the **California National Historic Trail**, **Oregon National Historic Trail**, **Mormon Pioneer National Historic Trail**, and **Pony Express National Historic Trail**, all of which passed the sandstone and siltstone monolith along the North Platte River. During the first decade of trail migration, traffic had to bypass the landmark as deep ravines in its western flank made the route impassable until a single-wide wagon path was cut around the base in 1851.

The top of the rock overlooks the path west taken by three hundred fifty thousand pioneers between 1841 and 1869. Scotts Bluff signaled a transition from the Great Plains to eastern Wyoming's arid open country and the mountains beyond. I summited the five-hundred-foot promontory a year ago. The road's closed today from storm damage in the form of fallen rocks.

Of numerous trail stories, one that symbolizes courage, determination, faith, and heroism is that of one thousand Mormon emigrants hauling handcarts and stranded in central Wyoming when an October 1856 blizzard locked them in place with little to no food or shelter. A group of well-equipped rescuers, ordered to retrieve the stranded itinerant travelers by Brigham Young, located them in treacherous conditions and successfully brought them to the safety of Salt Lake, but not before exposure and starvation killed 25 percent of their number. Considering the normal migrant fatality rate for wagon passage stood at about 10 percent, the survival of so many counted as miraculous. The Mormon Church still maintains many important historical sites along the Mormon Pioneer National Historic Trail, including a fascinating museum at the Winter Quarters in Omaha (then Florence, Nebraska) where the first of over seventy thousand emigrants sought shelter from 1846 to 1847. My stops at the church-managed historic trail locations have been marked by the kindness of my hosts. I applaud the church's historic preservation efforts.

From Scotts Bluff, a short half-hour drive east leads to **Chimney Rock National Historic Site**. The Nebraska State Historical Society operates the park, an NPS-affiliated location. I focus on the large historic western trails wall map that's caught my attention on each of my three visits. It's my favorite among dozens of similar maps I've seen in the parks. The rock outside is currently 325 feet tall with a 125-foot spire. The sandstone continues to erode from the taller column travelers noted in their accounts of westward migration.

After Chimney Rock, I gas up, buy a Slim Jim and a Mountain Dew from a minimart in Bridgeport, Nebraska, and take a short detour for a picture of Courthouse and Jail Rocks, another popular trail landmark about thirteen miles east of Chimney Rock. Highway 88 runs east of the four-hundred-foot rocks, far enough to spoil my picture against the setting sun. I lack the energy to drive around seeking better lighting. I'm ready to move on after opening the Slim Jim and taking a bite to discover it's over five years old. Expelling the hardened beef with the mouthfeel of a pretzel stick out the open window, I'm thwarted in this sad attempt to expand beyond liquid calories. I tell myself I'll stop in an hour, but I drive for three more before stopping in Gothenburg, Nebraska. Another steak and beer dinner at a saloon-style trucker bar across from my motel satiates my hunger before some much-needed rest.

Sunday begins on a disappointing note at **Nicodemus National Historic Site** in north central Kansas. I find the visitor center closed, a fact noted on the door but not on the website. Later, I use the Contact Us feature at the bottom of the park's webpage to alert them about the omission so some other fool doesn't drive out of their way on a Sunday. Driving out of the way is the *only way* to get to the tiny town of Nicodemus, with a population under fifty.

Formerly enslaved people moving north and west in the decades after the Civil War founded Nicodemus and similar towns to escape discrimination and limited economic opportunity in the Jim Crow south. The unit features two local churches and a hotel property with the former town hall converted into a visitor center, the only one of the buildings regularly open. After striking out at the visitor center, I stop at the old AME church to peer in on the dusty, dilapidated entryway before passing the Old First Baptist Church on the way out of town.

A two-hour drive south through the rolling hills of central Kansas brings me to **Fort Larned National Historic Site**. Today's my second visit in the past eighteen months. As with Fort Laramie, Fort Larned is a frontier fort along an important trail. The **Santa Fe National Historic Trail** connects Independence, Missouri, to Santa Fe, New Mexico. The original fort consisted of simple adobe structures built in 1860. More durable stone and wood construction replaced the original buildings during an 1868 expansion. Most of the structures I see today lining the fort's rectangular parade ground date to the makeover. Fort Larned's history tells of southwest trade and expansion, along with Indian control and removal to reservations in Oklahoma. We're fortunate the fort survived eighty years of private ownership after the federal government sold the property and buildings at auction in 1884. It returned to the public trust as a unit of the National Park Service in 1964.

Channeling my inner bison, the stampede across the plains continues for three and a half hours into Oklahoma and **Washita Battlefield National Historic Site**. Arriving about 2:45 p.m., I greet the ranger on duty and mention the unit is my 335th visited lifetime. She's unimpressed, so I avoid mentioning the current odyssey and request advice on the park. After studying the exhibits, I move about a mile west to the battleground trailhead. Some six thousand Cheyenne, Arapaho, and Kiowa men, women, and children sheltered in Washita River Valley villages at the time of the winter attack. A short, one-mile trail leads down a sloping hillside to the riverbank where Cheyenne Chief Black Kettle's band lodged in the early morning hours of November 27, 1868. The trail leads through grassland to the water, following the tree-lined bank a short distance before turning away to the right and up a slope through a rail cut back to the parking area. Ribbons tied to tree branches at the river represent spiritual and religious offerings from the villagers' descendants.

Lieutenant Colonel George Armstrong Custer led 7th Calvary troopers against the sleeping village. The action is cruelly ironic. Black Kettle advocated for peace among native leaders and had survived what would be known as the Sand Creek Massacre four years earlier. He did not survive Custer's attack, an initiative from his departmental commander Major General Phillip Sheridan's policy of either killing the native populations or driving them on to reservations notorious for squalid living conditions. Many groups resisted this forced cultural assimilation under great hardship.

The park's brochure includes a summary of Native American treaties. From 1778 to 1871, the US government negotiated approximately eight hundred treaties with Native groups, though Congress ratified fewer than four hundred. The United States and its encroaching citizens rarely observed treaty provisions for long. The government honored boundary conditions only when convenient.

Underfunded mandates doomed most treaty promises to failure for lack of support and unethical behavior among agents designated to carry them out. The resulting mistrust and bad faith led to repeated uprisings and tragedy for one Native American population after another until the army subdued and resettled the last of them in 1890. The extermination and forced relocation of Native Americans constitutes a sad and shameful chapter in American history.

My day ends two hours east in Oklahoma City. After getting a room south of town, I arrive downtown at the **Oklahoma City National Memorial** at dusk. The memorial offers a stunning nighttime visual. The museum and memorial are an NPS-affiliated site managed by the Oklahoma City National Memorial Foundation. The memorial features two large black stand-alone frames bracketing east-west ends of a reflecting pool on part of NW Fifth Street. The Alfred P. Murrah Federal Building's foundation follows the pool's south side. The building's footprint, the memorial centerpiece, is a grass field with 168 metal chairs. Each chair sits on a semitranslucent square plastic base illuminated at night, creating a field of 168 lights against the darkness. Each chair and light represent one of the people lost on April 19, 1995, when a Ryder rental truck packed with explosives detonated in front of the Murrah Building at 9:02 a.m. The blast destroyed the building and set off a chain of events chronicled in the adjacent museum. The bomber, Timothy McVeigh, was convicted and later executed in 2001 at the federal prison in Terre Haute, Indiana.

I remember the day. I heard about the incident at my first full-time job in a plant along the Tennessee River. The initial reports shocked us in our naivete of the age of terror. What kind of person willfully causes the death of hundreds of innocent people? It's a question I ponder again as I walk beside the reflecting pool from the east, or 9:01 gate, to the west, or 9:03 gate. Near the east gate, a small section of the Murrah Building's foundation remains in the memorial. Opposite the chairs, the north side of the memorial features the Survivor Tree, a lone over-ninety-year-old American elm that survived the explosion and aftermath. The tree symbolizes resilience. I spend more time at the memorial than I'd intended. I take one last picture of the illuminated field of chairs before slipping away into the night.

Oklahoma City Memorial at night

The next morning's visit is for a set of daytime pictures and museum tour. The national memorial and museum are one of the year's most impressive new experiences. The museum follows the events of April 19 and their aftermath. Shortly after the incident, Oklahoma State Trooper Charles Hanger pulled over Timothy McVeigh, northbound on I-35. Hanger noticed McVeigh's car lacked plates. It's fascinating that someone with the will and presence of mind to plan and execute a bombing of this magnitude would drive a getaway car without license plates. Hanger arrested McVeigh after finding him illegally in possession of a handgun. McVeigh remained in custody three days later when FBI agents connected him to the bombing. The museum displays the shirt McVeigh wore during his arrest, presumably the same shirt he wore as he drove the Ryder truck to the Murrah Building, and his possessions at the time of his arrest, including the handgun tucked into his waistband. McVeigh's 1977 yellow Mercury Marquis, the car he was driving when stopped, is on display along with other items that connect the bombing and its perpetrator.

After Oklahoma City, I continue the drive south to **Chickasaw National Recreation Area** in Sulphur, Oklahoma. This first visit starts at the visitor center in Sulphur before continuing to the Travertine Nature Center. I walk the trails behind the nature center leading past Antelope Springs and Buffalo Springs. It's a beautiful day in south-central Oklahoma, and I seem to have a lot of company from local families with children, perhaps on spring break. From the trails behind the nature center, I drive to the Bison Pasture parking area and walk the trail around the pasture, up and over Bromide Hill. It's a modest but pleasant walk, among nine miles covered today in the park. The good weather and sunshine lift my spirits. It's after 5:00 p.m. before I'm back on the road, continuing south on US 271 and crossing the Red River into Texas before turning east, and past 9:00 p.m. when I check into a motel room in Texarkana, Arkansas.

Tuesday, March 15, the trip's last park day, starts with my third and final new NPS unit of the trip, **President William Jefferson Clinton Birthplace Home National Historic Site** in Hope, Arkansas. Today the home remains closed to tours due to a fire intentionally set near the back of the residence some weeks earlier. Fortunately, the fire caused only minor damage. Changes at the site sparked by the incident include a new security fence around the side and back of the house and yard. Without the house tour, there isn't much I can do at the unit, so it's a quick visit.

Hot Springs National Park is only ninety miles northeast on I-30. I visited the park and bathhouses on Central Avenue in downtown Hot Springs last year. On this visit, I stop at the

Fordyce Bathhouse visitor center and walk the self-guided tour, reflecting the glory years of Hot Springs in the late nineteenth and early twentieth centuries when the thermal waters were a popular treatment to improve health and combat illness. The forty-seven springs that surface at the base of Hot Springs Mountain have an average 143-degree temperature. Congress protected the springs in 1832 as Hot Springs Reservation. Hot Springs became a part of the NPS as Hot Springs National Park in 1921. The initial congressional protection gives Hot Springs National Park the distinction of being the oldest federally protected location for its natural features. Since Hot Springs Reservation functioned much like a park since its 1832 creation, many park reference books claim it as the oldest unit in the park system. Congress passed legislation tasking the reservation as a park in 1880. The oldest unit by date of federal protection is the National Mall, dating to 1790. After collecting the pin set and stamps at Hot Springs, I head north on I-30 to the state capital.

Little Rock Central High School National Historic Site protects the 1927 high school and the two-block area of land behind it as the scene of Little Rock High School's integration by nine African American students in September 1957. Little Rock Central High is still an active high school, so tours of the school are ranger led. The incident marks the first prominent test of the 1954 *Brown v. Board of Education* ruling by the US Supreme Court that effectively outlaws educational segregation as unconstitutional. The ruling reversed the Supreme Court's 1896 *Plessy v. Ferguson* ruling, which established the legal rationale of "separate but equal." The effort to test the Brown ruling set off a series of events with Little Rock Central High School and the "Little Rock Nine" in the middle. Arkansas Governor Orval Faubus actively attempted to block the students from attending classes, mostly for perceived political gain, thwarted when President Eisenhower federalized the Arkansas National Guard and used them, supported by twelve hundred soldiers from the US Army's fabled 101st Airborne Division, to protect the nine students, who attended class until the emotion and community resistance lost momentum. The abuse suffered by the Little Rock

Nine shocks any sensible human and reminds us of the sacrifices and bravery that led the way in the civil rights movement.

From Little Rock, I travel west on I-40, leaving the interstate at several points to stop by state parks affiliated with the Trail of Tears National Historic Trail. My final park today is another trail location, **Fort Smith National Historic Site** in Fort Smith, Arkansas. Fort Smith is built on the banks of the Arkansas River at the eastern boundary of Indian, or Oklahoma Territory. Only the foundation outline remains from the initial fort built here in 1817 and abandoned in 1824. The second Fort Smith operated from 1838 to 1871. Thereafter, the grounds housed the federal court for the Western District of Arkansas, the center for law and order over a vast and often lawless area that included most of modern-day Oklahoma. The federal judge seated at Fort Smith, Isaac C. Parker, became the inspiration for Hollywood's version of the stereotypical "hanging judge" portrayed in the Clint Eastwood movie *Hang 'Em High*. My first visit to Fort Smith National Historic Site had been difficult due to intermittent heavy rains, so I use this opportunity in good weather to walk the grounds, taking pictures in the last hours of daylight. The large gallows, built to hang as many as six condemned inmates simultaneously, is one of the more popular attractions. After walking the fort grounds and enjoying an early evening barbecue dinner at a downtown restaurant, I begin the 720-mile drive home.

11 Viva Las Vegas

A HECTIC MARCH continues west. Month to date, I've covered over fifty-five hundred miles through parts of nineteen states, visiting thirty-five NPS units in route. The big finish is another three thousand miles bouncing through twenty parks in southern Utah, Nevada, and southeastern California, hiking days and traveling evenings.

Las Vegas is a recent target destination for reasons having nothing to do with the city itself. The city has a plethora of parks within striking distance in either direction. Unexplored are three southern Utah national parks in the Colorado River Plateau: Zion, Bryce, and Capitol Reef. And there are three more parks in southern Utah or northern Arizona I haven't seen—Pipe Spring, Cedar Breaks, and Natural Bridges. West of Las Vegas, I'm eager for my first look at Death Valley, Manzanar, Mojave, and Joshua Tree. Its proximity to these parks represents the extent of my interest in Sin City.

Since I told Kareen about the Vegas trip, she keeps asking for the dates. She's struggling to keep track of my whereabouts. "You're in so many places, I can't keep them straight," she complains. I'm able to convince her to join me for the second leg of the trip when we'll see eight new southeastern California parks.

I'll pass through Vegas three times, staying in town three nights.

An early-morning flight from Chicago to Las Vegas on Tuesday, March 22, returning late on April 4, leaves fourteen days of exploration. The recent heavy travel doesn't diminish my enthusiasm. The general plan of attack is to devote a full day to each new park, starting early each morning and hiking different trails chosen to see the park's major features. In the evening, I'll drive to a new park location and repeat. During the first week in the Colorado Plateau, I will average nine miles a day on the trails in Zion, Bryce, Capitol Reef, Natural Bridges, and Great Basin before picking Kareen up on Sunday night, March 27, in Las Vegas. That will prove to be a day I'll never forget.

Arriving at McCarren International Airport about 9:30 a.m. on United 1858, I immediately get lost searching for baggage claim. I travel with two backpacks, my regular backpack with two laptops plus work-related items, and my park backpack. The two carry-ons force me to check a bag. Our flight arrives in the desert fifteen minutes early, but exiting the jetway, the airport I enter looks nothing like the one I vaguely remember two decades ago. The only familiar aspect at McCarren are the slot machines clustered near the gates. McCarren seems at least twice the size. The directional signs point to a lower level for baggage claim and the train connecting the two major terminals. I look around, even backtracking to look for other signs. Finding none, I ask an airport employee and get a vague point to the lower level. "It's down there," he says. I get on the train, assuming baggage claim must be consolidated at the other terminal's ground level. It's not. You can't ride the train back after descending to terminal 2 baggage claim without clearing security. Twenty minutes later, after catching the shuttle bus back to terminal 1, I walk through the ground floor hunting the correct conveyor. Exiting the National rental lot, I've managed travel by plane, train, bus, automobile, and walking in under an hour. I've only skipped travel by boat, horse, mule, camel, and dogsled, but the day's still young.

Happy to be clear of the airport, I head to Hoover Dam and **Lake Mead National Recreation Area**. After stopping by the Boulder City headquarters for some cancellations, I arrive at the

Alan Bible Visitor Center to review park destinations with the rangers. I intend to collect Lake Mead's available passport cancellations, requiring a driving tour to seven different locations including the Katherine Landing Ranger Station at the park's southern tip.

We'll return for the driving tour of Lake Mead at the end of the trip. Today, I backtrack through Henderson and the outskirts of Las Vegas to I-15, going north into Arizona on the three-hour commute to **Pipe Spring National Monument**. I explore the principle feature of the park, Winsor Castle at Pipe Spring Ranch. Pipe Spring lies in the Arizona Strip's high desert north of the Grand Canyon. The arid appearance of this harsh living environment indicates scarce water and alternating temperature extremes. Survival here demands a reliable water source, thus Pipe Spring's historical importance.

Puebloan peoples, who gave way to Paiutes, originally settled Pipe Spring and the Arizona Strip. In 1863, Mormon rancher James Whitmore became the first permanent white settler with his 160-acre homestead. Navajo raiders killed Whitmore three years later. Brigham Young purchased the property from Whitmore's widow on behalf of the Mormon Church to keep church-owned cattle tithed by Mormon farmers and ranchers. The remote location also sheltered polygamous wives, avoiding trouble from federal marshals. Young appointed Anson Perry Winsor as the first ranch manager of the Southern Utah Tithing Office. The church built Winsor Castle in 1870 and 1871, but sold Pipe Spring Ranch in 1895 to avoid having the property and cattle confiscated as government sanction for violating antipolygamy laws passed by Congress in the 1880s. In 1907, the Kaibab Paiutes regained a portion of their traditional lands in a reservation surrounding Winsor Castle and the historic ranch, declared a national monument in 1923 by President Warren G. Harding. I tour the castle and fort, taking pictures of the two-story structure restored to its late-nineteenth-century appearance. Pipe Spring completes the Arizona NPS units and is the first of fifteen new park units I'll see during the trip. The day ends in Hurricane, Utah, with a barely edible barbeque dinner. We're not in Kansas City, Toto.

Like thousands of nineteenth-century settlers, I enter Utah seeking a new adventure. The story of westward migration and early settlement is the focus of the **Mormon Pioneer National Heritage Area**. The heritage area extends across six Utah counties centered around US Highway 89, running north-south through the middle of the state.

Wednesday begins at the south entrance of **Zion National Park**. I enter Zion Canyon Visitor Center a few minutes after 8:00 a.m. I skip suggestions from the staff, overwhelmed with unprepared, clueless visitors intent on reviewing every minute of their day with a ranger, sometimes asking the same question several times. "So where on the park road can I see the canyon?" and "Are there any hiking trails in the park?" are two questions I overhear in the space of thirty seconds. I look at the poor ranger and imagine what he must be thinking. It would take the patience of Job. Instead, I review the park layout, making a mental note not to spend the whole day on one trail. I'll save some of the longer trails and their views for a future visit.

I catch the park bus all the way to the end of the road and walk as far I can get without waders or a wetsuit into the park's most well-known feature, The Narrows, stopping at the Zion Human History Museum on the way. The Narrows is the descriptive name of the Zion Canyon section where the canyon closes over the river channel running wall to wall. Local park outfitters do a booming business by renting waders to visitors to walk through the normally shallow water. I'm thankful I started early, as the buses are already full. I stand most of the way to the Temple of Sinawava, the last stop and trail head for The Narrows. The steep canyon grows narrower, casting the river into shadow. Many hikes to various canyon rim overlooks are popular, such as the trek to Angel's Landing. Zion National Park is one of the most popular hiking destinations among the national parks, but since I don't have time to walk multiple trails in both the southern and northern sections, I opt for peace and solitude away from the crowd in the less frequently visited northern Kolob Canyons area. When I return to the visitor center, the park bus que extends past the building and into the parking lot.

It's an hour or longer wait to catch a park shuttle bus. The line of cars at the south entrance station stretches a quarter mile. It pays to arrive early at Zion.

An hour later, I'm pulling into the Kolob Canyons area. After picking up a one-page trail summary at the Kolob Canyons Visitor Center, I travel east on the five-mile Kolob Canyons Road to Kolob Canyons Viewpoint. At road's end, the one-mile roundtrip Timber Creek Trail leads to an overlook from an angled rock slab. I scramble over tilted rocks up to the edge, the trail's highest point. The angled rock falls away into the void with a sheer drop. I sit straddling the summit and gaze out in wonder at the view of the park's tree-covered mountainous interior to the east and south and the Hurricane Cliffs to my left. I take a photograph with my iPhone pointed into the abyss below the summit. I post it to social media with the message "Found phone on rock. Last picture attached."

From the overlook, I return west for the five-mile roundtrip Taylor Creek Trail to the Double Arch Alcove. The trek to the double arch leads deeper into the canyon. As the walls slowly close in above, lighting and shadow alter depth perception. The rock's color seems more vivid. It's a smaller and drier example of the gradual change in Zion Canyon. The afternoon hike exposes large areas of shadow and sunlight on the valley floor and canyon walls, making photography tricky, extra so for me since I never bothered to read my Canon digital camera's instructions. On the way to the arches, I pass a family wearing traditional conservative dress, the type of clothing worn by Christian fundamentalists. I wonder if it's a family or group from one of the area's estranged polygamous communities. As the passing party stares at me, I notice four or five women of child-bearing age and only one middle-aged man, with the party split into three or four groups of two to four people each. Other than two other pairs of hikers, they are the only park visitors I see this afternoon. The double arch is carved into the southwestern corner of the canyon like a giant relief sculpture, and the trail is challenging and quiet. Fortunately, I'm too early in the season to encounter any of the rattlesnakes that frequent the trail. I've hiked twelve miles by the time I exit the park after 5:00 p.m. It's a short drive to the hotel in Cedar City. A hot meal with a cold beer or two awaits. Nothing refuels the body after a long day of hiking like the steak and beer diet.

Thursday begins collecting passport cancellations at **Cedar Breaks National Monument** headquarters. My route goes right by the road to Cedar Breaks from the south, Utah Highway 148. The state highway and park are over ten thousand feet in elevation and typically snow-covered until late May or even June. The state DOT only clears Highway 14 from Cedar City over the edge of the Markagunt Plateau to US Highway 89, but not Highway 148, which connects Highway 14 and the park. Highway 14 summits at the junction. The DOT plows about two thousand feet of Highway 148 to maintain access to their summit maintenance post. The park boundary for Cedar Breaks lies four miles farther north on Highway 148, under four to five feet of snow beyond a barricade. I hoped to break the boundary for this unvisited park unit somehow. I'm so close, but there's no way without a snowmobile or dogsled. I will have another shot at Cedar Breaks later this year. I continue the drive to **Bryce Canyon National Park**.

Bryce Canyon's nucleus is an eighteen-mile drive on the Paunsaugunt Plateau rim's eroding slopes revealing a fantastic array of hoodoos and fins dropping to the Paria Valley 2,000 feet below. The concave plateau escarpment faces east with bright red limestone chiseled into an astonishing density of irregular shapes, spires, and rock cathedrals. Some rock formations cluster together resembling an ancient stone city's abandoned ruins. The park road gains elevation moving north to south, rising from 7,894 feet at the visitor center to 9,115 feet at Rainbow Point overlooking the canyon. A Rainbow Point interpretive panel reveals a key meteorological fact explaining Bryce's eroded rock formations. The park's temperature crosses water's freezing point more than 240 days a year on average. The freeze-thaw effect separates and carves rock from the plateau. Bryce Canyon's stunning natural beauty began forming over sixty million years ago and continues today.

Bryce Canyon, Rainbow Point

I venture south past the overlooks, stopping at each one before choosing today's hikes. The park offers a range of experiences. Visitors can travel the road, enjoying brilliant views, or pick one of dozens of trails through and among the rock features. I choose a popular hike to the valley below Sunset Point. The trail passes Thor's Hammer and descends among the fins to the Navajo Loop Trail on its way to "Wall Street." The return through the "city" is closed today due to dangerous conditions. The roundtrip hike's ascent gets the blood pumping as the grand finale of my seven miles in the park. Among numerous stunning visuals, Rainbow Point's overview is my favorite. The park's high point is also mine on this wonderful day in Bryce Canyon National Park.

My day ends at Richfield, Utah, where I start the next day collecting a passport cancellation for the **Old Spanish National Historic Trail**, one of nearly eighty trail cancellations spread across six southwestern and mountain states to commemorate early overland routes across the region's challenging topography. The broken and obstacle-filled southwest separating Santa Fe and Los Angeles gave rise to variations in a route so rugged it remained impassable to wagons for long distances. The difficulty delayed commerce for over fifty years after Father Escalante's nascent 1776 journey. The NPS trail counts twenty-seven hundred miles among these lines to cover the twelve hundred miles along the early route. Leroy Hafen described the trail as "the longest, crookedest, most arduous pack mule route in the history of America." I'll travel sections of multiple Old Spanish Trail routes throughout the year. The BLM Field Office stamp location opens at 7:30 a.m., a good thing for Friday's aggressive itinerary.

From Richfield, **Capitol Reef National Park** awaits seventy-three miles southeast. Capitol Reef intrigues me. Despite reading the park's brochure, a mental image remains elusive. Although fourth in visitation among southern Utah's five national parks, the "reef" leaves an immediate impression. Capitol Reef's central and most visible feature, the north-south ridge called the Waterpocket Fold, towers one thousand feet above the surrounding terrain. Approaching the park on Utah Highway 24, the fold dominates the eastern horizon. Early explorers called this enormous bluff a reef, as it limits east–west passage along its one hundred miles, much like ocean reefs impede ships. The fold developed fifty to seventy million years ago when a fault buckled the earth's crust. The massive uplift created an enormous bend or fold of rock. Erosion over tens of millions of years wore layers from the original fold, leaving the impressive remnant visible today. In geological terms, the fold is a monocline, a warped horizontal rock layer. I'm splitting my time in Capitol Reef since tomorrow's route west to Nevada returns directly through the park.

Most of Capitol Reef National Park's quarter-million acres is backcountry accessible only via unpaved roads or hiking trails.

Today, I focus on the scenic drive and sights along Highway 24, which cuts through the middle of the park. The park's scenic drive runs eight miles one way south from the visitor center and leads to an unpaved road entering Capitol Gorge, a steep-walled, narrow canyon explorable on foot from the parking area at the end of the dirt and gravel road. The dusty road at the end of the scenic drive heads east for a couple of miles before reaching the trailhead. Driving the dirt road to the Gorge trail head leaves a massive dust cloud hanging in the air, blotting out hikers who park their vehicles at the alternative parking area near the paved road. Lacking time to hike an extra four or five miles, I spread a cloud of dust over two miles to the gorge at the twenty-mile-per-hour speed limit.

Capitol Reef, the reef

The trail into the narrow, flat gorge passes petroglyphs and etchings carved into the canyon wall, marking its human history. The gorge served as the primary travel corridor through the fold during early western settlement. Inscriptions from this period are known collectively as the Pioneer Register.

The Capitol Gorge Trail is listed as a mile each way through the gorge and up the rocks, ending at rock depressions holding water called "the Tanks." The ascent begins on a clearly defined trail but less so farther up. After scaling the smooth, eroded rock, or "slick rock," above the gorge floor, rock cairns (small stacks of stones) mark the trail. After ten minutes scrambling atop the rocks, I struggle finding the next cairn. At the Tanks, the higher purview offers a view of the eroded rock cliffs surrounding the gorge.

On the return I spend a few minutes wandering, searching for a reference point. Possible routes over the rock seem endless. I feel like part man, part mountain goat. After making a couple of correct guesses on direction, I recover the more obvious section of the trail about halfway down the rock.

It's always advisable to stay on the trail for personal safety and environmental stewardship. Some parks permit hiking off trail and others do not. I strongly recommend confirming the status of an area before exploring it. A few questions in advance and a trail map can even save your life.

Back on the scenic road, I stop several times to photograph the vivid rock colors. The bright pinks and purples visible in the fold towering above me immediately to the right and continuing north to the horizon produce a stunning landscape. I resist the temptation to stop for more hiking. The additional trails can wait for tomorrow.

The John Wesley Powell River History Museum in Green River, Utah, is on the way to the next park destination in Moab, Utah, 140 miles away. The museum is one of two named after Powell that I visit this year and honors his southwest exploration, including his 1866 Colorado River expedition through the Grand Canyon. Powell cuts quite an image as a one-armed Civil War veteran leading his men through Colorado's previously unrecorded rapids and perils as it descends through Utah and Arizona.

The brief museum tour leaves time for quick stops at two more parks. The first one, on Moab's north side, is **Arches National Park** visitor center. The plateau's rock features of Park Avenue, the Courthouse, the Organ, and Three Gossips are briefly exposed from US Highway 191 before it starts downhill from the north. I stopped to stare at the enchanting Three Gossips during my visit here last June. The three massive rock towers with sharply cornered rocks precariously balanced atop them look like ridiculously large sculptures of maidens in decorative Renaissance-style hats. As with most of Arches' rock features, the towers strain plausibility that natural forces left *this* behind.

Arches, Three Gossips

Represented on Utah's license plates in the image of Delicate Arch, Arches symbolizes the eroded beauty of Utah's Colorado Plateau for many regional residents, making it a coveted holiday and weekend getaway. Last year, rangers shared Memorial Day weekend horror stories. The entry line extended from the gates over a mile on to the highway, stopping traffic. The Utah State Patrol forced the park service to close the entrance for a few hours to avoid gridlock.

An ancient seabed here created a sandstone layer thousands of feet thick in places. Shifting faults cracked the surface rock layers, allowing water to erode the Entrada and Navajo Sandstone into an endless variety of spectacular rock formations. The park's playground of awesome rock features stimulates the imagination. Last year, I amused myself by sending Kareen a picture of a massive, phallic rock spire with the question, "Guess this rock feature's name." She replied only with the recrimination, "You have a dirty mind." One of my favorite park features is the trail past the Parade of Elephants to the Double Arch. A short distance away, another trail leads to the North and South Window and Turret Arches. I hope to take Kareen on a future visit to this must-see park.

Arches, Double Arch

From Arches, I cross Moab to **Canyonlands National Park** headquarters south of town. The administrative ranger happened to be in the office on a Saturday last June and kindly let me in to collect the passport cancellations kept there. Originally from Des Moines, Iowa, it seemed like a small world when I shared that I've officiated at the Drake Relays for twenty years. She remembers last year's discussion and my park goal and asks about my progress. I report Capitol Reef is the 341st NPS unit visited lifetime and Canyonlands is the 98th unit I've visited thus far in 2016.

Last June's trip included a full day in Canyonlands National Park's Island in the Sky District after the day at Arches. Canyonlands National Park has three major districts with names describing their unique landscape. The Maze and The Needles districts lie below and south of Island in the Sky. Canyonlands' endless combinations of canyons, basins, and mesas surround the confluence of the Colorado and Green Rivers between The Maze and The Needles. The least visited of Utah's five national parks with less than a fifth of Zion's visitation, Canyonlands contains personal unfinished park business, as I've yet to hike in The Maze or The Needles.

During my first visit, I explored Island in the Sky, a large mesa separating the Green and Colorado rivers before they come together farther south in the park. I walked the one-mile Grand View Point Overlook Trail at the mesa's southern tip. The trail overlooks the other two park districts within a hundred-mile horizon. The island stands twelve hundred feet above a nearly continuous sandstone layer called the White Rim, with the rivers another one thousand feet lower. I found myself drawn farther down the trail by the complex scenery. The deep river canyons are barely visible to the east and west amid countless bluffs and rock columns near and far. Each turn of the head yields an endlessly dynamic landscape. No matter how hard I focused, I couldn't absorb it all. The never ending columns and spires of The Maze and The Needles to the south appear like an undulating sea of rocky prominence and shadowy void stretching away seemingly forever. At trail's end, I met a Salt Lake City physician on a regular weekend visit to unwind from long hours of rounding. The intoxicating view under a blazing sun melts stress away. My supply of water exhausted, the kind doctor gave me a bottle of water out of his pack. We sat on the edge of the bluff and absorbed the vista's majestic tranquility. As we walked the mile back to the parking lot together, he gave me a brief synopsis of southern Utah's parks. We wished each other well before going our separate ways. The island trail concluded a great day, and this year, Canyonlands once again bookends my day in the Colorado River Plateau. I head south to a hotel room in Monticello, Utah, for some much-needed rest.

Canyonlands, Island in the Sky

Each day of this trip feels more tiring than the last. Tomorrow will raise the stakes again. Indeed, it figures to be one of the most exhausting days of the year. I have some inclination that I might be challenging my physical limits on this grandiose tour but have no idea in this last week of March that I'll push myself to the boundary and beyond before it's over.

Saturday starts with a seventy-five-minute drive through southeastern Utah's open spaces to **Hovenweep National Monument**. Hovenweep protects six groups of structures built by thirteenth century Puebloans. These larger villages are built nearer to water sources than the scattered mesa top settlements preceding them, suggesting proximity to water influenced early settlement patterns across the area as the climate grew arid.

Last year's visit to Hovenweep focused on walking the two-mile paved loop trail around the Square Tower Group next to the visitor center. The visitor center and two closest villages are in Utah while the other four ruins are in Colorado. The bistate unit covers a twenty-mile span of mostly empty, remote space. The natives who built these structures abandoned them in the same century after the area grew less hospitable. I hope to return one day in a high clearance vehicle to visit Hovenweep's outlying ruins. The rental cars I've taken on my visits to date are ill-suited to the road conditions. Hovenweep marks the trip's eastern extent. I arrive as the visitor center opens at 9:00 a.m., anticipating the five hundred miles and eight and a half hours of driving to three more parks on my way west to Ely, Nevada. It's going to be a long day.

A one-and-a-half-hour drive west from Hovenweep, **Natural Bridges National Monument** protects three striking natural bridges in southeastern Utah. On the nine-mile loop drive, I encounter the bridges in order from the highest span above the canyon floor to the shallowest. It's a fortunate park feature since I'm exploring each bridge by descending to the river bed below.

From the White Canyon rim overlook, I descend to the canyon floor beneath Sipapu Bridge, a 500-foot elevation change over 0.6 miles each way. I repeat the pattern at each bridge. Sipapu is 220 feet high and spans 268 feet.

After Sipapu Bridge, I proceed on the loop road to the Horse Collar Ruin Overlook. These ancient Indian dwellings built high into the walls of White Canyon leave one wondering how agile the occupants must have been to live in such a challenging place. The second span is Kachina Bridge at the junction of White and Armstrong Canyons. The hike down to the modest stream of water flowing underneath drops 400 feet over 0.75 miles each way. The bridge is 210 feet high and spans 204 feet. Kachina is easily the largest bridge in terms of rock volume, at 93 feet thick and 44 feet in width.

Natural Bridges, Sipapu Bridge

Owachomo Bridge is the third and smallest at a height of 106 feet and span of 180 feet. It's also the thinnest, only nine feet thick, and looks fragile compared to the other two. The short, 0.2-mile trail to the base drops only 180 feet, good news, as I've expended some energy climbing down underneath the first two bridges at the pace demanded by my schedule. More aggressive visitors can hike the 8.6 miles from Sipapu through White Canyon and under Kachina into Armstrong Canyon and Owachomo Bridge on an unmaintained trail, meaning you can't always see the rattlesnakes. I'm happy with the 3.5 miles and 1,000 feet in elevation change I've navigated in just over an hour and a half today, but I have many miles to go and more trails to hike.

The drive northwest passes through the northern end of **Glen Canyon National Recreation Area**. As it bursts into view from the east, a trick accomplished by turns in the highway around rocky bluffs in the foreground, Glen Canyon National Recreation Area presents a stunning landscape of towering discontinuous sandstone mesas with profiles sharpened by erosion. The red rocks rising from the horizon on my approach are lit in full contrast under the midday sun and clear-blue skies. I fight the urge to stop and take a picture. I have so many miles left to drive.

The Hite Ranger Station at Lake Powell's north end is a mile off the highway. I observe evidence of the long-term drought in America's southwest several times throughout the year, though few locations highlight the drought like Hite. The large boat ramp next to the ranger station slopes into clumps of tall weeds popping up intermittently across the dusty ground. Water hasn't extended to the ramp in quite some time. From the ranger station, the Colorado River flows unseen below the far west cliff face. The lakebed's north end is now a river with a one-sided flood plain.

Leaving the ranger station, I climb to higher elevations west of the river off Utah Highway 95, stopping at an overlook of Dirty Devil Canyon dumping its raging contents into the Colorado as it exits a long sequence of steep, narrow canyons that include the famous Cataract Canyon. On the map, the Colorado enters Lake Powell beneath me, but it actually remains a formidable river just out of sight below the cliff edge until Lake Powell deepens farther south.

Highway 95 connects to Highway 24 and the return trip through Capitol Reef National Park. Over the twenty miles before the park boundary, brightly colored rock strata, mostly greens and yellows with some reds appearing as mesas and formations both near and far, accentuate the scenic drive. Back in Capitol Reef National Park, I stop at the two-mile Hickman Bridge Trail, which climbs the reef and passes underneath a 133-foot natural bridge. The trail offers views of the reef's dome shapes and peaks on both sides of the road. I get good pictures of Capitol Dome at a pullout east of the bridge. This second visit to the park concludes at the petroglyphs along Utah 24 just east of the visitor center. With four miles in Capitol Reef, today's hiking reaches nine miles. Exiting the park at dusk, I'm tired and hungry with almost three hundred miles and over four and a half hours of driving remaining. I open the window, turn up the stereo, and start down the two-lane highway through the vastness of southern and west-central Utah.

I pull into the hotel in Ely at 9:00 p.m. Ely is more than sixty miles past the next park, traveling from the east. It appeared to be the closest decent lodging option in the middle of the Great Basin Desert. I'm exhausted. As a final blow to my energy and spirits, I wait over twenty minutes to check in at the front desk while the clerk tries to find a pillow for another guest. "My wife left it here a week ago. It's her favorite pillow," he explains after he arrives at the front desk seconds before me. The confused clerk asks for a detailed description. I'm wondering, "How many guest pillows can you have in lost and found?" Lost and found storage is in a small room about the size of a broom closet to the right of the desk. He could've brought out all the pillows the room could hold in a few minutes, but instead he disappears into the closet on his knightly quest. The pillow guy starts to squirm as we pass fifteen minutes, and I'm glaring at him, envisioning a late-night murder sequence. In my mind, I grab the lost pillow and smother them both with it. The guest probably had no idea it would take the guy over twenty minutes to find a pillow in a broom closet. When the desk man finally emerges with a pillow, the right one thankfully (perhaps the only one in the closet), there are three guests waiting behind me, all in various stages of anger from annoyed to livid. I can feel the veins protruding from my forehead, and I'm wondering, "Is this real, or is there a hidden camera somewhere?"

After seven hours of sleep, an Egg McMuffin, a Coke, and coffee,

I'm running mostly on adrenaline as I turn east on US Highways 6 and 50, which combine for 150 miles across the Great Basin Desert from Delta, Utah, to Ely, Nevada. I'm excited to see my next new unit, **Great Basin National Park**, which lies just inside the Nevada state line. The park consists of 13,000-foot Mt. Wheeler and its shoulder peaks, a mountainous oasis surrounded by the Great Basin Desert's flat, desolate expanse. The **Great Basin National Heritage Route** crosses the Nevada-Utah state line and includes the park and surrounding area's cultural history.

As with many first-time visitors, I start with a morning tour of Lehman Caves, hollowed into the core of the Snake Range to which Mt. Wheeler belongs. Having plenty of time to explore the visitor center and gather the usual collection of tokens, pins, and stickers that I've been collecting across the park system for some unknown purpose, I use the time to plan an afternoon hike. Since spring hasn't arrived at higher elevations, park roads above 8,000 feet remain snow-packed and closed. Wheeler Peak Scenic Drive is open only as far as Upper Lehman Creek Campground at 7,752 feet. A ranger suggests I explore the higher elevations via the Lehman Creek Trail from the trailhead at Upper Lehman Campground to at least the Mather Overlook, about three miles up the 6.8-mile trail that ends at the drive's summit, 9,886-foot Wheeler Peak. The overlook sits beside a meadow and offers a beautiful view of the mountain and desert below.

The tour of Lehman Caves, named for local rancher and miner Absalom Lehman, who first explored it in 1885, is an hour-long walk through cave formations that have grown familiar in the park caves: stalactites, stalagmites, columns, draperies, and soda straws all made from limestone dissolved by mildly acidic water and redeposited into wondrous shapes. Among the more famous here are the massive shields, adorned with stalactites and other natural ornaments appearing like sculpted decoration. I'm nearing the end of my first tour through the park system caves and feel a little spoiled since seeing Carlsbad last July. Nonetheless, each cave has unique attributes. It's probably uncommon for someone to tour all of them in a three-year time frame. As we complete the cave tour, I fall into a conversation with two vacationing seasonal rangers from Utah's Timpanogos Cave, one of my last two unexplored NPS cave units. "I've been looking forward to seeing Timpanogos Cave," I share, "and hope to do so this year." I'll make it to Timpanogos in early August, though I don't know this at the time of the conversation.

Our discussion turns to other destinations, including Alaska. I tell them I'm scheduling my first trip to the last frontier in June without help, so I'm a little nervous. One of them refers to an air charter outfit that served them well in a great park trip a few years ago. They take my email address, promising to send me the name of the charter service.

Before my hike, I have another interesting conversation in the visitor center with Ranger Matthew, who started as a ranger in the eastern Civil War battlefields, completing graduate work that tied his family history to the Civil War. His ancestors fought with the south. We discuss some of our favorite Civil War books. Later, I would barely remember these conversations given the course of events to follow. But I will see Ranger Matthew again today and during my second trip to Alaska in 2017.

By late morning, I'm parked and ready to hike. After signing the trail log shortly after noon, I start up the Lehman Creek Trail from the trailhead at the north end of Upper Lehman Campground's parking lot. Although the elevation gain is steady and the ground open and stable, permitting good traction, I struggle mightily to establish my usual pace. I feel like I'm hauling a heavy pack, but I'm unburdened, carrying only a camera and small knapsack for water. My labored breathing reminds me of the hike to Coronado Cave on a bigger scale. I charged over similar challenges all week hiking in elevation as high as today's eight thousand feet plus. In hindsight, I realized that I averaged about nine miles of hiking a day for five straight days, with over six hundred miles in the car yesterday. I'm gassed and hoping for a second wind. Struggling over the first two miles, I stop several times to enjoy the magnificent view of the pancake flat Great Basin stretching away to the north, west, and south. The Lehman Creek Trail is not a switchback trail but climbs south up the west side of Mt. Wheeler over the first few miles. The view north overlooks the desert plains with the evergreens and mountain side on the periphery. It's one of the year's most impressive panoramas.

I also discover the open nature of the trail yields a cell phone signal almost two miles up after Kareen calls to update me on her progress in packing and heading to the airport for her flight to Las Vegas, where I am scheduled to pick her up tonight. I enter the snowpack after the short phone call and finally gain my stride. Dressed in layers, I'm wearing a long-sleeve T-shirt and a National Park Service centennial hoodie covered by a rain-resistant wind jacket from the Big Ten Track and Field Championships. The jacket has a convenient zipper pocket over the right chest where I tuck the Canon camera with the strap around my neck to prevent it from swinging out and bouncing off my chest with each uphill lunge. I'm past two and a half miles on the trail and approaching my destination at the meadow overlook. I take the camera out and snap pictures of the mountain and desert below. With the iPhone I take a picture of the trail ahead. The evergreen-lined, snow-covered trail turns about twenty degrees to the left as it climbs out of view. The scene conjures thoughts of Robert Frost.

Great Basin, Lehman Creek Trail

I reestablish my pace on the snow and ice, trying to step on the harder snow for better traction. I'm back into the rhythm of the climb as I round the bend to the left before stopping dead in my tracks. Ahead of me, about fifty feet uphill, a mountain lion stands perpendicular to the trail. My eyes focus first on the only thing moving, its tail. Two to three feet long and moving through the air, the tail curls into a U-shape as my eyes focus amid my utter astonishment. I've read a fair amount of reference material on wild animals, in part because of frequent solo hiking. I know the tail is the best way to identify North America's predatory cats. A long tail confirms that it's a mountain lion and not a lynx or bobcat. The animal a stone's throw away from me up the trail is also much too large to be either a bobcat or lynx. The back paws are resting on the west or right side of the trail, and the front paws are on the east, or mountain side of the trail, completely spanning the opening between the trees. The cat is larger than either of the two male Labrador retrievers I've raised in the past fifteen years. This animal is easily over one hundred pounds in size. I stand frozen in silence, stunned to see a mountain lion standing still in the open, completely exposed. It's rare to see a mountain lion in the wild, but rarer still to see one purposefully exposed in the open. I encountered a mountain lion once before, hiking in my early twenties. That cat had the conventional beige or tan color with short fur and in hindsight acted as eager to avoid me as I of it after dashing in front of me across another mountain trail. But this cat is standing still in the open, blocking the trail I'm climbing. My eyes track from back to front as the cat turns its head to look straight at me. This cat is mostly gray with some black patches of fur on its belly. The fur is long all over its body. In late March at the change of seasons, it's sporting a full winter coat. As it turns and we're staring eye-to-eye, I notice the long fur on its neck forms a miniature mane around the distinct outline of a cat face. Its retinas glisten back at me in a reddish sparkle.

I'm frozen in my stance. I know not to make sudden movements that could signal panic or flight. My mind moves from the instinctual process of identifying the animal to the realization that this cat heard me coming up the trail and intentionally placed itself uphill in my path. It has perfect positioning to flee to cover in case of a threat by leaping into the trees—or attack downhill in case of a hunting opportunity. At such a close distance, a couple of bounds over a second or two and the cat would be on top of me. I wait for the animal to decide. I have nothing with which to defend myself but my hands. After several seconds staring at each other, the cat hops into cover in the trees to its front. My climb is over. I know big cat behavior suggests this cougar will track me for some distance from the cover of the trees. It will know my whereabouts, but I will be blind to its location. Its reaction on the trail, by hopping into the trees instead of sprinting away, doesn't betray fear but a deliberate calculation of risk. The prey cutoff for mountain lions is usually around 200 pounds, and I'm tipping the scales at 206.

I turn and, being careful not to run, start retreating down the trail as fast as I can without losing balance on the snow and ice. I'm sliding and skipping on my own tracks, eyes darting side to side for any signs of movement. Having retreated about three to four hundred yards, I freeze a second time. From some indiscernible location not far distant among the evergreens comes a loud screech. I've never heard this sound before in person or in any TV show. It isn't a roar or a cry but something in between not mistakable for any other animal sound I've ever heard. It fills the air through the trees and reverberates across the snow-covered mountainside around me. The loud guttural peal sends chills down my spine, followed by a wave of terror. I've read about the panther's scream many times in both early pioneer historical accounts and in wilderness adventure stories. It always seemed fantastical, beyond comprehension. The panther's loud scream is as blood-curdling as those historical accounts by early American explorers indicated. I have no illusions of its source, though the intent remains a mystery. That I'm in mortal danger seems obvious enough. Am I going to die on this mountain?

My pulse rate soars, and sweat rolls down my face as I survey the ground around me for anything I can use in self-defense. After picking up and discarding a couple of rotten tree limbs, I dig out a round rock protruding from the snow. It's just large enough for the palm of my right hand. I figure it weighs about five pounds. I grip the rock tightly, figuring in the event of an attack at least I can try to whack the cat in the head and stun it or scare it away. It seems a vast improvement from nothing. In this state, my down-climb continues, not in a run but as fast a pace as I can maintain without tumbling downhill or slipping and falling. Looking side to side in raw terror, I start audibly repeating, "Please let me live. Please let me live." I don't know whether the plea is intended for the cat or a higher power. But it helps me stay focused on the retreat. I improve my time a bit when I clear the snowline. Shortly thereafter, I start checking my phone for a signal. Nothing yet. I want someone to know my location and what's happened, in case the worst is yet to come. I hear a sound to the side, in the trees, but see nothing. I'm trying hard to stay calm and deliberate. I'm sweating from more than the physical exertion as I think of all the things I haven't done. I don't want to die on this mountain, but that decision is no longer mine. How would Kareen know? I picture her waiting in Las Vegas and me torn up and bleeding, lying some-where off this trail. I want to say good-bye to someone, anyone.

After a few more minutes, but what seems much longer, a signal reappears on my phone and I dial 9-1-1. I reach the county sheriff's dispatcher and tell her of my situation and the events of the past fifteen minutes. After answering a standard series of ques-tions, the dispatcher keeps asking for my location. I realize she's keeping me on the phone until I reach safety. When I clear the trail head and start across the camping spots to the area at the northern end of the campground where I'm parked, I tell her I'm safe and will make it from here, thanking her several times for staying on the phone and talking to me for the last ten minutes. She did all she could to help me in the moment. Talking with someone calmed me during the descent. I'm forever thankful to this dispatcher, who did her job and did it well. As I open my car door, I drop the rock I've been carrying since the cat screamed. I'm so grateful to be alive and unharmed.

I enter the visitor center a disheveled, sweaty mess with eyes dilated. As I step to the desk, Ranger Matt looks at me and asks, "What happened to you?" I describe the experience in detail to the rangers. After the first few minutes of the story, Matt turns to the other ranger and, pointing a finger, proclaims, "That's why I don't hike that trail!" I think, "Thanks for telling me, guys!" But I know my experience is a very rare occurrence. Mountain lions are seldom seen by park visitors, and even rarer do they expose themselves intentionally with plenty of cover readily available. I realized all this in the moments the cat and I stood staring at each other, in a blend of dire concern and amazement. I didn't have time to fully process the terror of the moment until I heard the cat scream. Then I just did what I thought gave me the best chance to survive.

After driving over three hundred miles south from Great Basin National Park to McCarren International Airport, I pick up Kareen a few minutes after 8:00 p.m. She's agitated, per normal at the beginning of a trip, and complaining about the delays and American Airlines' customer service. She barely hears me say, "I'm so happy to see you." It isn't until after we've checked into our hotel on the Vegas Strip and are eating dinner at a nearby P. F. Chang's when she unwinds enough to really hear my story. She can see the earnest feeling of gratitude and relief in my eyes as I say in a quivering voice, "I'm so thankful to be sitting here enjoying a meal together. I thought I might never see you again."

She finally processes that I stood face-to-face with the fourth largest big cat on earth, only a few pounds on average smaller than the muscular and deadly jaguar, totally unprotected and at its mercy. "You were really afraid for your life," she says.

"Yes," I tell her, "you have a mountain lion to thank for your dinner companion tonight." Staring off into space, I add, as an afterthought, "It was a beautiful animal." We sit quietly, both acknowledging the moment.

We navigate the fine line between getting a good night's rest and getting up and out Monday morning. The last bit of encouragement to start moving comes when I pay five dollars at the hotel lobby Starbucks for a small cup of coffee . We throw our bags in the car and drive away from the hotel, happy to trade the Vegas Strip for the open desert.

12 *The California Desert*

LEAVING LAS VEGAS and its suburban sprawl, we skirt past Red Rock Canyon National Conservation Area to Pahrump in route to **Death Valley National Park**. Pahrump remained a small Nevada desert town for decades until it exploded to over thirty-five thousand residents with the addition of gaming, multiple RV parks, and an assortment of other vices. We stop at a Walgreens so Kareen can buy some hair oil. The TSA disposed of her bottle since the container exceeded three ounces. No telling what some madman might do with hair oil on a plane.

Our first stop this morning, hair oil secured, is Ash Meadows National Wildlife Refuge. I want to collect an Old Spanish Trail stamp at the visitor center. The drive is quiet. I'm smiling and relaxed. Not even twenty-four hours prior, the sum of my wishes had been to be alive today. It might seem excessive, but the lion encounter shook me up. Perhaps it's because I read stories about park and wilderness fatalities and understand incidents can happen to normal people. They're not confined to the stupid, though bad behavior and ill-conceived actions are probably the leading cause. In 2016 at Yellowstone National Park alone, there are at least a half dozen reported incidents of visitors suffering injury from bison. Common sense should dictate not approaching a two-thousand-pound wild animal for a selfie. A recent story about wildlife selfies in social media included over a dozen pictures with *bears* in the wild! The recklessness it takes to stand, back turned, feet away from a bear for a picture, then share your mental limitations with the world, confounds the imagination! In another 2016 Yellowstone incident, a visitor placed a bison calf in their car and drove it to a ranger because it "looked hungry and lonely." The park staff had to euthanize the calf after the herd refused to take it back. Stupidity seems to know no boundaries.

At Ash Meadows, I share yesterday's encounter with a wildlife biologist familiar with mountain lions. The refuge and town of Pahrump lie in a travel corridor for the roaming cats. Unwelcome cats create occasional problems. The Department of Natural Resources staff assists in such cases. She believes that I likely encountered a lioness with a nearby den. I had considered the scream might be intended for cubs as I descended the mountain. She states, "Face-to-face encounters are rare. A mountain lion only stands fully exposed near humans with intent." There seems little doubt the cat heard me coming. She continued. "You're a lucky fellow having lived to tell the tale. Had the animal been starving, you would have likely been attacked." I summarize my feelings to Kareen and the biologist with, "I'm so thankful to be here."

We bounce our way through the wildlife refuge on grated gravel roads, happy to exit south on paved Nevada Highway 127. Crossing into California, we turn west on US 190 at Death Valley Junction. Death Valley lies between southeastern California's Amargosa and Panamint Ranges running north-south in the east and west, respectively. Death Valley is the first of six Mojave Desert NPS units we'll visit during this trip. It's easy for the unfamiliar to dismiss Death Valley as a novelty attraction due to its extremely arid and oppressively hot environment. Death Valley's famous as the "hottest, driest, lowest." Among national parks in the contiguous United States, it's also the largest. It's 3.37 million acres are tops outside of Alaska, as are its 3.1 million acres of wilderness. Furnace Creek boasts the hottest temperature ever recorded in the United States at 134 degrees. The average daily highs for July and August are 116 and 115, respectively, and highs in the 120s are common. Badwater

Basin's salty crust drops to an elevation of 282 feet below sea level, the lowest elevation in North America. The park's average annual rainfall is less than two inches. Rather than barren and devoid of life, the valley's home to over one thousand native plant species and a variety of animals specially adapted to its harsh conditions. The park's amazing natural wonders surprise many first-time visitors. I'm expecting a spectacular experience based on glowing accounts from fellow park travelers.

After entering the park, we stop at Furnace Creek Visitor Center. At 10:30 a.m., the temperature's in the upper eighties according to the digital temperature display beside the entrance. I'm enjoying the heat after chilly weather last week. Today's breaking story is a windstorm sweeping across the valley floor, producing sustained south and southwesterly winds of 30 to 50 mph with gusts over 60 mph. Departing Furnace Creek, we follow Highway 190 northwest and southwest to Stovepipe Wells Village. I'm relieved to buy the park's centennial lapel pin after finding them sold out at Furnace Creek. Death Valley is one of thirteen park units outside of Eastern or Western National that ordered one or both exhibit pins.

The Mesquite Flat Sand Dunes lie a mile east of Stovepipe Wells Village. We fight the windstorm as we enter the dunes. A massive wall of sand and dirt looms to the south, seemingly moving up the valley. We walk a half mile, turning our heads downwind to avoid getting sand in our eyes. In the distance, another large cloud of sand towers over the dunes at the base of Tucki Mountain to the southwest. The looming wall of sand appears to threaten our present location, but it's mostly an optical illusion. Tired of being sandblasted, we reverse into the wind toward the car, leaning forward to keep our balance. Kareen has a black scarf wrapped around her head, looping over her hair bun. Her eyes peak through a narrow slit. She looks like a Bedouin.

Safely back at our camel, we make our way to the Salt Creek Interpretive Trail, a half-mile looped boardwalk running east to west beside the creek. Countless pupfish dash wildly here, there, and everywhere in the salty stream. The tiny fish species are exclusive to Salt Creek.

We pass Furnace Creek heading south, continuing seventeen miles to Badwater Basin. The parking area sits beneath a cliff on the valley's east side. A painted wooden sign affixed nearly three hundred feet up the irregular rock wall reads SEALEVEL. Another sign next to the boardwalk reads, "BADWATER BASIN, 282 FEET, 85.5 METERS BELOW SEA LEVEL." Kareen dons the scarf around her head again and we trudge west down the boardwalk to the salt flat. The sustained southerly wind blows so hard, we face north and balance ourselves reclining backward. The actual lowest point is over a mile out. Fighting the gale and our schedule, we turn around at a half mile, far enough that other visitors appear as specks on the distant sand. We step deliberately through today's second sandblasting. I shout to Kareen, "It's great for wrinkles! It takes ten years off your face!"

Death Valley, Devil's Golf Course

From Badwater Basin, we go north to the Devil's Golf Course. At first glance, the area resembles recently ploughed earth without pattern or arable soil. Closer inspection reveals undulating, irregular chunks across the valley floor. I venture about one hundred feet onto the buckled earth comprised of rock, salt, and sand, imagining pioneers traversing the area. Navigating the ground reminds me of hiking across a lava field. The broken and twisted tract must have been impassable for early settlers. It's harsh, intimidating terrain.

After our round with the devil, we proceed to the nine-mile Artist's Drive loop. The road twists and turns through the Artist's Palette. The Palette boasts the largest variety of vivid, natural rock colors I've ever seen. The hills appear in a spectrum of pastels. The astonishing array of natural colors are derived from the rock's varying and unusually high rare mineral content. Death Valley's color surprises me. Kareen and I compromise our way through the hills. I keep stopping to take pictures as different color sequences come in view around every turn. Red and pink mounds sit aside green, purple, blue, and yellow. It seems like every pastel tone pops up somewhere around the corner. Kareen appreciates the color and beauty, but she's tired and hungry and not in the mood to stop every quarter mile for landscape shots. She sees how enthralled I am by the unique scenery and patiently waits out my exuberance.

Intense colors also dominate the landscape at today's final park stop. Zabriskie Point, located along US 190 near the eastern entrance, offers distant views of the Artists Palette and the flats beneath the surrounding mountains. In the colorful mudstone badlands immediately surrounding the Point, distinct features unfold in every direction. Ridges of tan and beige sandstone with intermittent hues of pink, red, and yellow look like eroded mini mountain ranges in series. As we turn ninety degrees, the tan ridges of the mudstone badlands running in every direction give way to higher, darker brown and harder rocky peaks in the distance. Zabriskie Point's landscape holds iconic status as the most photographed in the park.

Death Valley, Zabriske Point

It's late afternoon and Kareen's struggling. "I'm not feeling well. I probably just need to eat," she shares. Her body language betrays an unusual discomfort. We drive north on 190 to Daylight Pass Road and the small town of Beatty, Nevada, where we'll stay tonight.

Tuesday morning begins at Dante's View. Dante's View offers Death Valley in spectacular panorama. The overlook, at 5,475 feet atop the Amargosa Range, reveals the entire park below as an open desert nestled between two north-south mountain ranges. Badwater Basin is directly below, a massive white blotch that looks like spilled milk. Dante's Ridge Trail extends over eight miles of ridgeline. We walk south along the trail to another popular overlook with a less-obscured view of the valley. Though the wind mercifully abated overnight, the ridge's elevation and breeze make chilly conditions. The scenery and pictures from Dante's View count among my favorites in the park system. The valley runs to as far as the eye can see to the north and south. Death Valley National Park manages to exceed every expectation. As we prepare to exit the valley, I'm forever a fan.

Death Valley, Dante's View

We leave the valley with unfinished park business. Scotty's Castle is closed due to flood damage sustained last October. Another area of Death Valley we'd hoped to see is the Racetrack: a flat, dry lakebed in a remote north central section of the park known for the large stones that mysteriously migrate across the desert floor. Visiting the Racetrack requires a full-day commitment in a high-clearance, four-wheel-drive vehicle for the eight-hour roundtrip from Furnace Creek.

After crossing the park on Highway 190, we exit past Panamint Springs near the main western entrance before turning north on US 395 at Lone Pine, California. We continue twenty miles north up the Owens Valley east of the Sierra Nevada Mountains to **Manzanar National Historic Site.**

Manzanar is one of ten internment camps the US government established in remote areas of the west, forcibly detaining over one hundred ten thousand Japanese Americans during World War II. President Franklin D. Roosevelt's Executive Order 9066 on February 19, 1942, proves to be the most regretted and misguided government domestic policy decision made during World War II. It arises from the fear of a Japanese fifth column. Having been shocked out of neutrality by the Japanese navy's surprise attack on Pearl Harbor, the American people, and more critically, the military and civilian defense leadership, lobby Roosevelt to thwart the imagined threat. Military leaders express great concern over potential espionage and sabotage by Japanese Americans loyal to the emperor. The solution to the perceived threat confines Japanese American residents in remote camps without due process and in violation of their constitutional rights. The injustice arising out of fear and prejudice is important to remember, lest we repeat the mistake.

Authorized as a park site in 1992, Manzanar offers the most interpretation among the four 1942 internment sites preserved in the park system. The camp opened with poor living conditions. Almost nonexistent facilities provided little protection from the harsh valley weather. High winds carrying sand scoured the camp, tearing through hastily thrown up makeshift structures. Left to build and do what they must, the internees survived.

After speaking with rangers in the visitor center, we pause next to the exhibits to hear a Q and A between park visitors and Arthur Ogami, a former camp resident speaking from a wheelchair. Arthur lives in southern California, and his son brings him to the park a few times each year to share his story. Today, the park service opens a new exhibit on life in Manzanar that includes interviews with Arthur and his wife. Touring the park grounds, we end up at the new exhibit by chance at the same time as the Ogami family. I have a moment to thank his son for bringing him to the park and letting us hear his story.

Visiting Manzanar Tuesday afternoon brings us a full day ahead of schedule. Over our evening meal in Lone Pine, Kareen and I discuss options. We're headed to Barstow for two nights. I offer to drive straight to Barstow so Kareen can get some rest, but she wants to join me for another option. We decide to drive around a break in the Sierra Nevadas to the south through Bakersfield and visit **Sequoia National Park** and **Kings Canyon National Park** before backtracking to Barstow. The ambitious diversion sets up a long Wednesday. I never imagined we might stop in Sequoia or Kings Canyon when I planned this trip. If I had, we would have stayed near those parks Wednesday night and made our way to Barstow on Thursday. The roundtrip requires ten and a half hours of driving, excluding time in the park. Kareen's not feeling well, having caught a cold either just before or during her flight, so I'm reluctant to attempt such a long day with her in tow. I do want to show her the beautiful sequoias. The closest she's come to truly large trees is a two-hour visit to Muir Woods. I know she'll enjoy seeing the sequoias and redwoods in their namesake national parks. We've planned to see the redwoods in August, but the sequoias elude my planning until this opportunity. The long day has personal appeal as my first opportunity to get inside both parks. Until recently, I thought I visited Sequoia National Park in 2002 but had mistaken it with the Mariposa Grove at Yosemite. We opt for the long day.

Wednesday, we're off by 7:00 a.m. The first three hundred miles are blasé. Entering Sequoia National Park about midday, we stop at the Foothills Visitor Center before climbing into the heart of the park on Generals Highway. Sequoias grow between 3,500 and 7,700 feet in elevation, but optimally between 5,500 and 6,500 feet, consistent with the greatest precipitation on the Sierra Nevada's western slope. After stopping at the Giant Forest

Museum, we continue to the largest living tree on earth, General Sherman. Growing in Sequoia's Giant Forest, General Sherman is 275 feet tall, weighs 1,385 tons, and its ground circumference is 102.6 feet with a base diameter of 36.5 feet. The trunk volume exceeds 52,500 cubic feet at an estimated age between 2,300 and 2,700 years. Larger trees are referenced in California history. Two coastal redwoods, the Crannell Creek Giant and the Lindsey Creek Tree, are recorded as substantially larger. The latter had been reported with a trunk volume of 90,000 cubic feet. Of the thirty largest living giant sequoias (ranked by trunk volume), fourteen grow within Sequoia National Park. The Giant Forest is home to three of the top four and ten of the top thirty. Four more in the top thirty grow within Kings Canyon National Park. The second largest tree, General Grant, is found in Kings Canyon's Grant Grove, as is the eleventh largest, Robert E. Lee. No record exists suggesting the latter two trees have led other trees into combat against each other.

As we approach the Giant Forest, heavy snow falls, leaving a fresh layer on the ground for our short walk. I take some pictures of Kareen in front of General Sherman. We marvel at the outline of the tree's base on the concrete at the overlook. With the snowfall, the high-altitude road connecting the two parks is temporarily closed, forcing us to exit on Generals Highway and enter Kings Canyon by a circuitous route. We navigate an astonishing number of switchbacks on Highway 245. The one-and-a-half-hour drive features constant 180 degree turns, many one right after the other. I can feel a tinge of motion sickness, unusual for me in a car. Kareen's gamely braving the storm, but she doesn't look well. I'm worried she's coming down with something worse than a cold. We make it to Kings Canyon with enough time to stop at the Kings Canyon Visitor Center in Grant Grove Village. With five hours of driving yet ahead us, we grab a few snacks at the small general store and start back to Barstow, leaving considerable unfinished park business at Sequoia and Kings Canyon.

Our seminal experience at Kings Canyon must wait. During the preparation of this book in 2018, we stay several days in the park lodge near the visitor center. Our first look into the park's namesake comes on the Kings Canyon Scenic Byway at Junction View. From the higher elevation, we gaze down upon two canyons converging to form a *V* and carrying the Kings River and South Fork of the Kings River. The park road dives down into Kings Canyon and follows the South Fork to Roads End. The two rugged, tree-covered canyons fall away, leading to distant peaks.

Kings Canyon

We take the park road to Roads End, but the highlight of our time in the canyon is the walk through Zumwalt Meadow. The wetland and wavy green meadow, bracketed by tall evergreens, fronts the high mountain backdrop of the canyon wall. We walk the trail around the meadow, taking pictures of one real-life Bob Ross painting after another. Looking at the scene live, I can picture him painting the exact same scene, brush in hand, and saying, "And now a tall tree goes behind the meadow, and shorter trees go here at the base of the mountain."

We end our time in 2018 surveying the largest collection of old growth trees in the park, the Redwood Mountain Grove in

Redwood Canyon, from the two-mile Buena Vista Peak Trail off the main park road. Though the trail only gains about 450 feet in elevation over a mile to 7,600 feet, it feels like a steeper climb. The overlook of the massive trees beneath the ridge to the northwest rewards our sweat and panting. They look impressive reaching toward the sky even from 2,000 feet higher and two miles away.

Kings Canyon, Zumwalt Meadow

Back in our story, it's 10:00 p.m. when we pull into Barstow. After a Spartan dinner, we're ready to rest. Thursday morning, I let Kareen sleep and go solo on a short road trip over one hundred miles west to **Cesar Chavez National Monument**, an NPS unit since 2012. We drove past it twice the day before on our way to see the big trees. Before leaving the hotel, I explain the unit to Kareen to the best of my ability. Feeling weary, she chooses rest.

Cesar Chavez National Monument protects Chavez's home and office location through the end of his life. I appreciate the history despite the lack of NPS presence. Cesar Chavez led and organized immigrant farm workers in California, growing to sym-

bolize migrant farm laborer rights in the 1960s. The most interesting exhibit in the site's museum is his office desk. I love pieces of
history like original office spaces. They offer a connection to the
historical figures that used them. In total, the site comes across as
a family shrine rather than a historical location. I had hoped for
something more in the interpretation of Chavez and the migrant
workers he represented.

Back in Barstow, I stop at the **Mojave National Preserve** headquarters to collect their passport stamps and advice. Ranger Dora
suggests activities in the preserve and offers driving directions to
one of the newest NPS units in the country, designated on February
12, 2016, **Castle Mountains National Monument**. Mojave National
Preserve dates to 1994 and surrounds the new monument formerly
set aside from the preserve for mining interests.

I collect Kareen at noon. Castle Mountains National Monument
is today's objective, leaving the balance of Mojave National Preserve
for tomorrow. It's a two-and-a-half-hour trip to the new unit. The
drive across the desert, mostly on Interstate 15 and state highways,
ends with a turn on to Walking Box Ranch Road, a brutal gravel
mining road. We bounce along the minimally maintained road for
ten miles before arriving at the new sign for Castle Mountains
National Monument. Ranger Dora advised me that several recent
park visitors have overturned a vehicle proceeding deeper into the
new park. We take pictures next to the sign against a background
of the Castle Mountains alight in the afternoon sun and retreat for
a second jolting ride. Kareen informs me, "You're seeing the remote
Alaskan parks on your own."

Low on gas, we drive a bit farther east across the state line into
Searchlight, Nevada to fill up before venturing into the preserve in
twilight. After twenty-eight miles west on Nipton Road to Ivanpah
Road, we turn south into the preserve. We take pictures of the
Castle and New York Mountains in silhouette as darkness settles
over the desert.

Friday morning April 1, we're off for a full day in Mojave
National Preserve, the namesake of the rain shadow Mojave Desert
system between the Great Basin Desert to the north and Sonoran

Desert to the south. The Mojave Desert's rain shadow derives from coastal mountain chains to the west that extract moisture out of storm systems coming off the Pacific, casting a rain "shadow" over the desert to the east. The desert ecosystem features an extreme temperature range. High and low temperatures can differ by fifty degrees. Minimal cloud cover and sparse vegetation allows 90 percent sunlight penetration to the earth's surface. More thickly vegetated areas might receive only 40 percent penetration to ground level. The same clear sky reverses the process at night, radiating 90 percent of absorbed heat back into the atmosphere while wetter areas only lose about 50 percent. Radiative heat loss can be a factor for humans and other animal life in nondesert environments as well, particularly in dry northern winters. Most of the Mojave Desert lies between three thousand and six thousand feet in elevation, though it includes the lowest spot in North America at Badwater Basin and peaks above eleven thousand feet.

We enter Mojave from the south via I-40 and Kelbaker Road, passing the Granite Mountains Natural Reserve on our way to the Kelso Depot Visitor Center. Kelso Depot is a partially restored train depot at the park's center. On Kelso Cima Road we continue to Cedar Canyon Road. The hillsides at the junction explode with the color of wildflowers. Yellows and purples cover the dry ground. Wildflowers bloom throughout the park, adding a surprising layer of beauty over an unforgiving environment. After six miles on Cedar Canyon Road, we turn south on Black Canyon Road to Wild Horse Canyon Road, arriving at the Hole-in-the-Wall Information Center.

Kareen and I set out on the Hole-in-the-Wall Nature Trail and the Rings Loop Trail. The loop trail passes through a rock formation and the literal "holes in the wall." We clamber up and onto the rock using iron rings permanently screwed into the rock. It's a fun trail to navigate, with rewarding views. The bright yellow and purple wildflowers' vivid color contrasts with the tan desert rock at points on both trails.

After Mojave, we cross three hours of desert in the late afternoon to reach our Palm Springs, California, hotel. We pass through the towns of Twentynine Palms and Joshua Tree, both entrance points for **Joshua Tree National Park**. Kareen's struggling and needs to lay down. Exploring must wait. After checking in, hunger trumps rest, so we walk down the boulevard to eat in an Italian steakhouse owned by transplanted New Yorkers. It's almost 9:00 p.m. when we return to the room. Kareen's in a downward spiral. "Can I help?" I ask.

"Let's wait until morning to see how I feel," she replies. She's fighting a virus, and the virus is winning. It's probably a matter of time before I'm sick, too. I feel helpless as we lay down to restlessness for me and a dizzying descent to the lowest level of hell for Kareen.

Early Saturday morning, Kareen's immobile, unable to rise. I feel so sorry for her. She thinks she caught a bug on the plane from a guy coughing with reckless abandon on everyone. It's also possible she acquired it at work. She's around dangerously sick patients every day. "Want me to take you to a hospital or urgent care?" I ask.

"No, they won't do anything for me," she laments. Instead, I hit a local grocery store with a list of supplies: cold medicine, orange juice, fruit, and water. We agree that staying in the room and watching her sleep will only guarantee both of us are sick, potentially stranding us if I become immobile, too.

I let her rest, admonishing, "Call me if you need anything," and head out for an abbreviated tour of Joshua Tree. I'll hope four more hours of sleep improves her condition. I've never seen her this sick.

Joshua Tree National Park begins with stops at Black Rock Education Center just beyond Yucca Valley, Joshua Tree Visitor Center in the town of Joshua Tree, and finally the Oasis Visitor Center at Twentynine Palms, where I enter the park. Joshua Tree intensifies my newfound appreciation for flowers. Floral beauty highlights my year in the parks. A little early in Death Valley, we hit peak bloom farther south. The Mojave wildflowers serve as an appetizer for the main course at Joshua Tree. Two desert ecosystems, the Mojave to the north and the Colorado to the south, are alive in color. The boundary between these distinct desert ecosystems runs directly through Joshua Tree.

The exploration begins at the Jumbo Rocks area off Park Boulevard on the 1.7-mile Skull Rock Trail. The relatively flat trail makes a big circle intersecting Skull Rock. I walk right past the feature several times before recognizing it. It's a disfigured skull at best. Perhaps the challenge of climbing over the rocks and the plethora of wildflowers and cacti distract me. The two most common wildflower colors on the trail are the same as for Mojave National Preserve, bright yellow and purple, though in Joshua Tree, there's plenty of interposing red, pink, and white.

Pinto Basin Road drops from over four thousand feet in elevation to nearly three thousand feet at the transition between ecosystems. The park road's scenery highlights the contrast. At the higher elevation, the park's namesake, Joshua tree, dominates the landscape, though it isn't really a tree but a large species of the yucca plant that can grow forty feet or more in height. The "trees" grow in groups and clusters, or isolated. Pinto Basin Road passes impressive specimens before dropping through Wilson Canyon to the south.

In the Cholla Cactus Garden, I walk the short, quarter-mile boardwalk looping through a vast field of cacti. The garden features seemingly endless cholla cacti in full flower. A few miles south, the Ocotillo Patch blooms. These ocotillo shrubs look like small trees sporting bright red flowers, magnificent bursts of color at the flowery tips of each branch. I walk among them taking pictures, unsure which one's most brilliant. The drive continues to Cottonwood Visitor Center. Just escaping the crush of visitors milling about the visitor center, I end with the Bajada Nature Trail near the south entrance. The trail's a desert botany lesson in a symphony of color. The whites, reds, pinks, yellows, purple, and blues of alternate blooming trees and plants play to the senses' visual notes in an intoxicating sequence. I'm most surprised by the sage, covered in brilliant yellow flowers. It's a beautiful plant. I wish Kareen could have enjoyed the stunning desert color of Joshua Tree National Park.

Back in Palm Springs, Kareen's stabilized but not better. We waste no time starting our four-hour drive to Las Vegas. She needs bedrest. In Vegas, Kareen goes immobile again. "I'm going to a strip bar," I tell her as I venture into Fremont Street's lights and noise seeking Kareen's dinner. The food options vary between cheap and bad. I finally settle on Chinese takeout since she loves rice and comfort food seems the best option. We still have the liquids, more important for her than food. After bringing Kareen her meal, I return to "The Fremont Street Experience" for my own meal. Still unimpressed, I enter the Heart Attack Grill at the end of the street, having seen it on some show. It's a little closer to the strip bar than intended. I'm not looking for swats from a busty dominatrix. I just want a cheeseburger. Nothing like combining pleasure food and S and M. I don't eat enough anymore to consider ordering the sillier "Bypass" burgers they dub as "Triple," "Quadruple," etc. by how many meat patties and layers of bacon are jammed into the burger. I order the "Single Bypass" cheeseburger, plenty of food without fries or any sides. I watch a couple of guys who can't finish their ridiculous cheeseburgers get spanked while holding onto what looks like a set of dipping bars from a gym. It seems absurd. I'm an old geezer now, I conclude, as I finish and return to the room to check on Kareen.

Sunday morning, Kareen marshals the strength to clean up and ride to the airport. She's feeling slightly better, strong enough to make her flight, but weak. She won't fully recover for several weeks. We flew out separately and are returning that way. I'll fly to Chicago tomorrow afternoon. I drop her off at the terminal and head into the north suburbs of Las Vegas via US Highway 95 to the location of a new NPS unit, **Tule Springs Fossil Beds National Monument**. Located less than twenty miles north of the Strip, Tule Springs is a large fossil bed protected by Congress in December 2014 after it was uncovered by contractors expanding a subdivision. The park preserves a collection of Columbian Mammoths, sloths, American lions, and camel fossils. These fossils date to the Pleistocene Epoch, when the Las Vegas area had been a wetland. Since it's such a new unit, the only thing located at the site is a sign identifying the open desert beyond the subdivision as a national monument and some adjacent parking spaces. Finding Tule Springs proves challenging until I put clues together with the substandard directions on the park's webpage. From the fossil bed, I head south through Henderson, returning to Lake Mead National Recreation Area to visit the remaining passport locations. The furthest is Katherine's Landing at the far southern end of Lake Mohave, the second of two reservoirs in the recreation area, and over one hundred miles south of central Las Vegas. Lake Mead National Recreation Area is large, at 1.5 million acres, 87 percent of which is Mojave Desert. The desert acreage gets overshadowed by the two large lakes. I make five stops in Lake Mead today before returning to Las Vegas on US 95.

Monday morning starts relaxed. After stopping at the Las Vegas BLM Field Office for an Old Spanish Trail stamp, I tour Red Rock Canyon National Conservation Area. The park's beautiful, though the most interesting part of the day is watching one of the park volunteers play with a rescued desert tortoise living outside the visitor center. The large turtle serves as the park's unofficial mascot. The perfectly camouflaged desert tortoise suffers from its biggest predator, vehicle traffic. I take a few pictures of the desert shellbacks and Red Rock's scenery before returning to McCarren for my flight back to the chilly upper Midwest.

13 Meet Me in St. Louis, or Ohio

SPRING IS HERE. Four opportunistic road trips highlight the next seven weeks. A weekend near home offers the chance to revisit sites in the nation's first national heritage area, **Illinois and Michigan Canal National Heritage Corridor**. After opening in 1848, the Illinois and Michigan Canal and the Illinois River link Chicago and the Great Lakes to the Mississippi River. The national heritage corridor commemorates canal history in the communities along its one hundred miles, from the eastern boundary at Lake Michigan to the western boundary at the contiguous municipalities of LaSalle-Peru. Located within the corridor, the **Chicago Portage National Historic Site** has been called the "birthplace of Chicago." The portage crosses a narrow strip of marshy land, called Mud Lake, that forms a natural barrier between the Mississippi River drainage via the Des Plaines River flowing westward to the Illinois River and the Great Lakes drainage via the south branch of the Chicago River. Early French explorers Father Marquette and Louis Joliet recognized the significance of this continental divide between the Atlantic and Gulf of Mexico drainages.

Monday, April 11, brings the home opener for the St. Louis Cardinals against the Milwaukee Brewers at Busch Stadium III. Born at Barnes Hospital in December 1970 and raised near St. Louis, my baseball allegiance came naturally. Opening Day is an annual rite in St. Louis. My father and I watch the game together, enjoying a pregame celebration of the Cardinals' rich baseball history. From Busch, I drive to Ohio for a work trip extended to three Ohio NPS units.

First Ladies National Historic Site is the combination of the Education and Research Center, the former 1895 City Bank Building on Market Avenue in downtown Canton, Ohio, and the former home of William and Ida McKinley one block south. William McKinley, the twenty-fifth president of the United States, served from 1897 to 1901. His September 1901 assassination by a deranged gunman at the Pan-American Exposition in Buffalo, New York, put forty-two-year-old Theodore Roosevelt in the White House as the youngest president. McKinley's widow, Ida, returned to their Canton home for her last six years. The McKinley home exhibits honor our first ladies' service to the nation. Having toured the home in 2014, today I share a few stories from the year's travels and collect the unit's lapel pins for my project in the second-floor bookstore.

North central Ohio's **Cuyahoga National Park** covers land surrounding 22 miles of the Cuyahoga River and Ohio & Erie Canal. The canal served as a major industrial shipping lane in the 1830s, the heyday of America's canal systems. The **Ohio & Erie National Heritage Canalway** includes sections of canal with towpath and stops over 100 miles of the 308-mile canal built for commercial traffic from Lake Erie near Cleveland to the Ohio River east of Cincinnati. I stop first at the Peninsula Depot, a station for the Cuyahoga Valley Scenic Railroad running through the park between Cleveland and Akron. From Peninsula, I enjoy the roar of rushing water over Brandywine Falls, followed by the Boston Store Visitor Center. Not far away is an area called The Ledges, with a two-mile wooded loop around sandstone outcroppings on a plateau I hiked during my first visit. From the Boston Store, I stop at the Canal Exploration Center, picking up the location's passport stamp and sharing a few more park stories to close my fourth visit to Cuyahoga National Park.

Next is an O&E Canalway stop in Cuyahoga Heights, the Leonard Kreiger Canalway Center, managed by Cleveland Metroparks. A short walk from the Center over to the canal and towpath converted to walking trail stretches my legs in the warm afternoon sun. Interpretive panels clustered in a small area near the canal explain part of its history and that of the railroad bridge passing high overhead.

An affiliated NPS site at the Mandel Jewish Community Center in the eastern Cleveland suburb of Beachwood, Ohio, **David Berger National Memorial** venerates the only American citizen among eleven Israeli athletes killed by Palestinian terrorists during the 1972 Munich Olympic Games. Raised near Cleveland, Berger had joint US-Israeli citizenship and represented Israel in weightlifting. I pause to take a picture of the metal sculpture depicting the Olympic rings split in halves, symbolizing the tragic events that temporarily halted the 1972 Summer Olympics.

A short Thursday morning drive northeast along Lake Erie's shoreline ends in Mentor, Ohio, the location of **James A. Garfield National Historic Site**. Garfield became the twentieth president of the United States after his inauguration in March 1881. He died less than six months into his term, on September 19, after being shot on July 2 by Charles Guiteau in a Washington, DC, train station. Well-regarded by his contemporaries, all indications suggest Garfield would have been an effective president, but history denied him the chance. Guiteau, a disaffected and psychologically disturbed office seeker, felt rejected after his requests for patronage went unanswered in the early days of the Garfield administration. Guiteau deluded himself, believing his support critical to Garfield's election.

The park isn't open for the season yet during this third visit to the Garfield home, all restricted to the exhibits and grounds. I call, asking if someone can let me into the visitor center briefly for stamps and lapel pins. A kind ranger accommodates the request but informs me the staff is unavailable for a house tour, though I hadn't asked. I'm happy with the pins and cancellations. It's time to go home.

The week finds me back in St. Louis, attending games included in my regular season weekend ticket plan. I've had the twenty-seven game season ticket package since 2004. The baseball schedule presents the opportunity to revisit two local NPS units. Sunday, I enjoy nice weather with a leisurely morning drive to southwest St. Louis and the **Ulysses S. Grant National Historic Site**. The site's original home dates to 1818. Grant's father-in-law, Frederick Dent, called his family home White Haven. Ulysses and Julia lived on the property for several years while Grant unsuccessfully tried scratching a living from the land. Though Grant purchased the property from the Dent family in the 1860s, he and Julia never returned to live here. I've toured the home several times while hosting out of town guests for baseball weekends. This morning I watch the park film, an exceptional production focusing on Grant's overlooked civil rights legacy. He stands alone as the only president over the century spanning the Civil War's conclusion and the 1960s civil rights movement that actively supported meaningful national civil rights reform during his tenure in office. In the interim, progress made by more reform-minded presidents, such as Theodore Roosevelt, retrograded under later administrations such as Woodrow Wilson's. Unfortunately, rampant prejudice and his administration's shortcomings fail to match Grant's admirable aspirations.

Today's visit marks the first of three centennial visits to Ulysses Grant National Historic Site. I'll return twice during baseball weekends, enjoying an NPTC member meet-up on May 1, and another visit during a living history event reenacting the 1872 presidential election, the first in US history to include a female presidential candidate. I chat with the living historians portraying candidates supplemented with twenty-first-century park rangers in period attire. Visitors are offered information on reconstruction issues and policy in this election pivoting on reestablishing southern states in the union and the protection of freedmen's rights in the Deep South.

The second pregame stop is the Old Courthouse and visitor center under the Gateway Arch, both part of the **Jefferson National Expansion Memorial**, JNEM for short. (Author's note: In February 2018, a congressional act changed the park's name to **Gateway Arch**

National Park.) Architect Eero Saarinen designed the memorial's centerpiece, the Gateway Arch, reaching 630 feet high above the raised bank of the Mississippi River. Construction crews inserted the arch's final keystone section in October 1965. The triangular stainless-steel outer skin, structural as well as cosmetic, covers a carbon steel inner skin and framework reinforced by concrete poured between the inner and outer skin up to 300 feet. The underground Museum of Westward Expansion and most visitor facilities under the arch will be closed soon as part of a major renovation project that has already closed most of the surrounding grounds.

The Old Courthouse, completed in 1845, is one of the oldest structures in downtown St. Louis. The most famous and important historical event in the courthouse are the initial court actions from 1846 to 1850 in the Dred Scott case, a suit filed by a slave (Dred Scott) for his freedom after he had been moved from slave to free state by his enslaver. In 1857, the United States Supreme Court, led by proslavery zealot Chief Justice Roger B. Taney, issued an uncompromising reversal of lower court rulings favoring Scott. The decision, *Dred Scott v. Sandford*, provided a spark to the Civil War. I visit both the Old Courthouse and visitor center under the arch before enjoying a game at Busch Stadium under sunny skies. It's a welcome relaxing afternoon. The next ten days will be another test of stamina.

14 *New England*

THE SUNDAY AFTERNOON game ends at 4:00 p.m. Less than ten minutes later, I'm across the new Stan Musial Bridge, heading east on I-70. Friends and family who go to games with me watch in amused amazement at my practiced skill of exiting downtown St. Louis after watching the final pitch of a baseball game. I'm sure it gives the appearance of a man possessed. But when the drive home is 300 miles, you learn to be efficient over thirteen years. Tonight, I'll drive over 550 miles to make the east side of Cleveland, part of the same road I covered earlier in the week. Coupled with losing an hour going from Central to Eastern time, I net less than four hours of sleep. Over the next six days, I intend to repeat the park stops made during two trips through upstate New York and New England in 2014. For the whole ten-day trip, I'm hoping to revisit twenty-six NPS units and visit three additional units for the first time. The 3,000-mile trip will require about forty-eight hours of driving.

Monday morning, I'm dragging but still manage to get up and out by 7:00 a.m., trying to complete the three-hour drive to my first destination by 10:00 a.m. **Theodore Roosevelt Inaugural National Historic Site** occupies the Ashley Wilcox residence on Delaware Avenue in Buffalo, New York. Theodore Roosevelt took the oath of office in the home's library on September 14, 1901, becoming the twenty-sixth president of the United States after William McKinley succumbed to bullet wounds suffered at the hands of anarchist Leon Czolgosz. It's the second time in just over twenty years, and the third time in just over thirty-six years, that a madman assassinates the president at close range with a handgun. Despite this onerous record, the Secret Service will not protect the president in a way resembling modern security for more than forty years, after a failed assassination attempt on President Harry S Truman's life in 1944, again with a handgun.

The next stop along the New York State Thruway (I-90) is the **Women's Rights National Historical Park** in Seneca Falls, New York. Visitors can see the Wesleyan Chapel, site of the first convention devoted specifically to women's rights on July 19–20, 1848, with some three hundred in attendance. On this Tuesday, the drive from Buffalo to Seneca Falls puts me at the visitor center during the lunch hour. There's only one problem. The park's not open on Tuesdays in April. I tried calling the park yesterday, and try again several times in route, to ask if someone can at least let me in briefly to get the passport stamps and buy the lapel pins. I don't reach anybody, so I decide to wing it and take my chances. If I stand at the door and look sad enough, hopefully some kindhearted ranger will let me in for a few minutes to complete my tasks. The plan almost proceeds to perfection, except the kindhearted ranger who lets me in to collect the stamps is in the maintenance department and cannot turn the register on to sell me the lapel pins. I will have to go through the time-consuming process of ordering them by phone. It will be after hours when I pass the park again on my way home.

Today's driving route runs along the **Erie Canalway National Heritage Corridor**, roughly paralleled by the thruway. After its completion in 1825, the 363-mile long Erie Canal is the first commercially viable transportation link between the Great Lakes and Atlantic Ocean entirely under US control. The success of the canal and the growth and prosperity in the towns adjacent to it spawned a major canal building effort throughout the developed United States between 1820 and 1840. Major canals, attempting to duplicate the success, are constructed in Ohio, Illinois, Pennsylvania, Maryland, Virginia, and other states. The canal system, along with the major river systems in the country, remained the backbone of domestic commercial transportation until the railroads began displacing water transport in the 1850s.

The third stop off the thruway is Rome, New York, between Syracuse and Utica. **Fort Stanwix National Monument** features the reconstructed fort garrisoned by Revolutionary War continental soldiers during the British siege in August 1777. The engagement, as well as the related Battle of Oriskany, comprises one part of the three-pronged assault by the British through upstate New York to cutoff the New England states from the other colonies. The English planned to surround and isolate the northern Continental army and supporting militia forces under the overall command of Major General Horatio Gates. American forces resisted the siege, and patriot reinforcements forced the British to withdrawal before the end of the month. The American victory at Fort Stanwix, combined with British Major General John Burgoyne's defeat and surrender at Saratoga two months later, and Sir William Howe's decision to abandon the enterprise with his sizable British force in New York City, represented the first major American strategic military success in the Revolution and became the turning point of the war when the victory convinced France to formally support the American cause with money and military forces. I enjoy my second visit to Fort Stanwix, mostly because of the staff's encouragement and enthusiasm. Fort Stanwix is the 120th NPS unit visited this year. I enjoy walking into the fort and taking some pictures of the detailed model on display in the West Barracks. I buy a rain jacket with the centennial logo on it from the gift shop while I share the year's adventures to date with the rangers on duty. The ranger who's handling my purchase remembers me from two years earlier. She wishes me good luck and tells me she's looking forward to seeing the exhibit I hope to create with the lapel pins, which now includes Fort Stanwix.

My final stop of the day is **Saratoga National Historical Park.** This afternoon, it's a race to make the two-hour drive before the visitor center closes at 4:30 p.m. During my initial visit, a careful tour of the battlefield helped me finally understand exactly how the American forces had defeated Burgoyne's more experienced British army. The essential role in the victory of Polish Colonel Thaddeus Kosciuszko stands out, particularly his decision to fortify the ground at Bemis Heights. The American defensive position forces Burgoyne, who's already committed to the march on Albany by breaking his supply train to Canada, to attack and dislodge the Americans in their strengthened, fortified positions or risk destruction in detail passing downstream alongside the river commanded by the same fortified heights overlooking the valley. The selection of the battleground boxed Burgoyne into a no-win scenario if the Americans defended their positions on the battlefield, which they did under the brave and inspired combat leadership of men like Benedict Arnold and Daniel Morgan. The park tour brings the events and outcome into specific relief for the amateur historian in a way that reading accounts of the battle cannot. I arrive at the visitor center fifteen minutes before closing, just enough time to get my stamps and lapel pins to end a long day. Visiting the four NPS units along the New York State Thruway is a great start to National Parks Week in 2016.

Though I entered it yesterday in route to Saratoga, Tuesday is the Hudson River Valley day in my centennial journey. Today, I'll revisit the group of four park units between Albany and Poughkeepsie. The first of these parks is **Martin Van Buren National Historic Site** near Kinderhook, New York. Kareen and I visited the home during our New England vacation at the end of the summer of 2014. During our tour of the home, I asked the ranger if he thought President Van Buren got a fair representation by Hollywood in the movie *Amistad*. He replied, "No, I don't think he was nearly as stupid as he's portrayed." I think he's probably right. It's also likely that Van Buren wasn't as pliable as he's portrayed in the movie either, though it's just as likely that Vice President Calhoun's threats about southern insurrection were more articulate and less obvious than Hollywood's interpretation for the sake of the modern viewer. Regardless of the nuances, the facts remain that Van Buren supported what he believed to be his party's interests in appealing the *Amistad* decision and found himself on the wrong side of history as a result. As incorrect as Van Buren's stance seems to us now, John Quincy Adams's participation stands the test of time as noble and honorific. It's an unfortunate representation for Van Buren, as it sells his legacy short.

Martin Van Buren called his yellow country home, completed in 1797, Lindenwald. Van Buren purchased the home in 1839. He put a great deal of time and effort into home improvements. Lindenwald served as the site for numerous political meetings during his presidential campaigns of 1844 and 1848. The artifact that intrigued me most during our first visit is the cane on Van Buren's bed inscribed and given by Andrew Jackson to his protégé. What a special piece of history. This morning, I have no ambition to challenge the rangers with complex questions about modern interpretations of President Jackson's hand-picked successor. Van Buren carried the moniker the Little Magician for his adeptness in building and handling the machinery of party politics. He's considered by many historians to be the father of modern party politics in the United States.

Martin Van Buren National Historic Site is still closed for the season during my visit, but I knock on the door of the NPS office and get Ranger Dawn, who guides me back to the passport stamps while I excitedly explain my grand centennial journey in progress. I entertain Dawn and the park superintendent with the story about my mountain lion encounter at Great Basin, and they congratulate me on making it to 122 NPS units thus far this year without being eaten. Dawn decides that I can be the park's honorary visitor for National Parks Week. She gets a life-sized cutout of Martin Van Buren from the storage room, and we pose for a picture next to the Little Magician himself. She then places the cutout in her vehicle because who leaves home, or work, without a life-sized cutout of Martin Van Buren? I just feel lost without mine. Dawn and the superintendent at Martin Van Buren are great company. Thanks to their exceedingly good will and humor, I enjoy the return considerably more than I'd anticipated.

The next three parks in my daily target package are all clustered together in Hyde Park, New York. They are **Vanderbilt Mansion National Historic Site, Home of Franklin D. Roosevelt National Historic Site**, and **Eleanor Roosevelt National Historic Site**. Although I manage another tour through the Roosevelt Presidential Library, a perfect companion to the Roosevelt family home tour, a place the family calls Springwood, my visits to these three units today are mostly motivated by collecting the centennial stamps and lapel pins. I stop at Vanderbilt first, where I buy the Find Your Park pins for all three sites, the only one made for these three units. They chose the Find Your Park pin since the unit name shows up much better in the design. The three Hyde Park units will join Hawaii Volcanoes as the only four units in the country to elect to get only the Find Your Park pin from the two sets I'm collecting for the exhibit. During my last centennial park trip of the year in December, I'll learn that Hawaii Volcanoes had a very different reason for only ordering the Find Your Park pin.

Another challenge on the day is that Val-Kill, Eleanor Roosevelt's personal cottage on the Roosevelt property, is still closed on Tuesdays in April. The best I can do is pull into the driveway and take a picture. From Eleanor's driveway, I'm off to a few stops in the **Hudson River Valley National Heritage Area**. The heritage area covers historical properties, museums, and other interesting spots in the history-rich and beautiful valley. The valley's dense historical layers are indicated by over one hundred participating locations within the national heritage area. The most notable one I visit on this Tuesday afternoon is the Walkway Over the Hudson in Poughkeepsie, where I enjoy the views up and down the river valley from the railroad-turned-pedestrian bridge.

After making a few additional heritage area stops for the sake of curiosity and passport stamps, I'm off to my last park of the day and the only one currently in the state of Connecticut, **Weir Farm National Historic Site**. Weir Farm is the only park dedicated to American painting. The site protects the summer home of painter J. Alden Weir, who used the home from his purchase of the property in 1882 until his death in 1919. The park promotes the visual arts by sponsoring and hosting artists. Weir Farm is also closed on Tuesdays, but fortunately they leave their passport stamps in a box outside the visitor center door for off-day traffic. The property is bucolic, and I can't resist the temptation to walk around a little while, even though I'm tired from a long day and still have a two-hour drive through Hartford to Springfield, Massachusetts. The views of the Weir Home against the trees and around Weir Pond are living landscape portraits.

While passing through Hartford, I can see the dome built by Samuel Colt, soon to be included with his 1859 gun factory in **Coltsville National Historical Park**, a pending unit already authorized by Congress. "God didn't make all men equal, Samuel Colt did." Or so goes the phrase attributed to William Cody. As I'm driving by Mr. Colt's future park, I realize I forgot to get the lapel pins at Martin Van Buren and will also have to get them by phone from Weir Farm. Ranger Dawn isn't done with me yet.

Wednesday morning begins at the **Springfield Armory National Historic Site**. The park has one of the world's most comprehensive collections of small arms. After the obligatory stamps and pins, I start roaming through the irresistible collection again. Most of the exhibit space is dedicated to the gun collection, though another part covers the mechanical evolution of small arms and their manufacture. It's absorbing to both the gun aficionado and history buff. The Springfield Armory has supplied small arms to the US Army for 174 years.

After mentioning passing through Hartford and the future Coltsville National Historical Park, the ranger on duty gets out a map showing the boundary and various buildings and features in development. Coltsville will be a fascinating new park, and I eagerly anticipate its inception. My stay in Springfield is also an intersection with the New England National Scenic Trail, a hiking trail that runs directly through Springfield on its 215 miles from Long Island Sound in Connecticut to the Massachusetts–New Hampshire border.

From Springfield, I head east on the Massachusetts Turnpike, stopping at the Old Sturbridge Village near Sturbridge, Massachusetts. The drive cuts through the northern part of the **Quine-baug & Shetucket River Valley National Historical Corridor**, also known as **The Last Green Valley**. The national historical corridor covers the extreme eastern section of Connecticut, extending into south-central Massachusetts, and a narrow area of western Rhode Island. The corridor, centered upon the Thames River watershed and its tributaries, the Quinebaug and Shetucket, claims to be the last stretch of dark nighttime sky between Washington and Boston. The real charm of the corridor comes in the peaceful blend of pastoral farmland and native forest. The living history at Old Sturbridge offers a glimpse of New England colonial life.

From Old Sturbridge, I come to **Blackstone River Valley National Historical Park**, created in December 2014. The park features water-powered remnants of the industrial revolution highlighted in the **John H. Chafee Blackstone River Valley National Historical Corridor**, the forerunner of the historical park. Today, I begin my visit to the park, spread out among multiple locations and in partnership with state and local entities, with a stop at the headquarters in Whitinsville, Massachusetts. The ranger on duty helps me plan this first visit. Mills constructed along the Blackstone River as early as the late 1700s and operational through the 1800s form the essence of the park.

The Kelly House in Lincoln, Rhode Island, is a great place to learn about the development of the Blackstone River Valley. Captain Wilbur Kelly built the house in the early 1800s and played a pivotal role in area development, including the forty-eight-mile Blackstone Canal completed in 1828, connecting Worcester to the port of Providence. An adjacent remnant of the canal survives. Across the Blackstone River sits the new Kelly Mill, a post–Civil War construction replacing the original mill, whose footprint remains visible next to the house and opposite its replacement. The Kelly House exhibits introduce the area's industrial history, embodied in the rise and decline of the mills.

Next up is the Pawtucket Visitor Center. Across the street, the Slater Mill (1793) and the Wilkinson Mill (1810) sit perched on the Blackstone riverbank. Samuel Slater built the first successful water-powered cotton spinning mill in the United States in 1790. The enclosed overwater area housing Slater Mill's water wheel appears to be open, so I enter and read the interpretive board on the railing before noticing restoration underway. I escape out the open exit before a worker looking in my direction can ask me to leave. The mills built along the Blackstone River in southern Massachusetts and Rhode Island represent the vanguard of America's Industrial Revolution.

Roger Williams National Memorial is a small park in the middle of downtown Providence. Roger Williams established Providence in 1636. An outspoken rebel from the Puritan church in Massachusetts where he objected to the church's pervasive civil authority and control over matters of conscience, he fled to Narragansett Bay after spending some time as a refugee among the Wampanoag tribe. Williams' 1663 colonial charter establishing Rhode Island inspired later statesmen such as Thomas Jefferson for its positions on liberty and freedom of religion.

After Providence, I head east on I-195 back into Massachusetts to the town of New Bedford for today's last objective, **New Bedford Whaling National Historical Park**. The park highlights New Bedford's history as the whaling capital of the world. In the 1850s, more whaling ships departed New Bedford than all the other ports in the world combined. New Bedford is the scene for a young Herman Melville, who will retell of his adventures on a whaling ship in his epic novel *Moby-Dick*.

Kareen and I visited the park, including the New Bedford Whaling Museum, in 2014. I took one of my favorite pictures of Kareen standing next to the sculpture of a whale's fluke before the museum entrance. History-rich New Bedford is also a major stop on the underground railroad. Many former slaves found work in the whaling fleet then at its peak. After the visitor center, I eat next to the docks, sharing details about the fresh seafood dinner with an envious and hungry Kareen on the phone. She begins to hunt for her next meal about midafternoon, so the timing's perfect.

New Bedford Whaling Museum, Kareen and whale fluke

Thursday morning, I'm up early and headed farther east on I-195 and US Highway 6 to **Cape Cod National Seashore**. Kareen and I enjoyed Cape Cod in 2014, traveling to Provincetown, the literal end of the road. After visiting the Coast Guard's Old Harbor Life-Saving Station Museum, we ventured into Provincetown for lunch. I fell in love with fried, whole-belly clams, then in season. I ate a plateful of whole-belly clams for dinner every night of our stay on the Massachusetts coast. Kareen thought I might turn into one, conjuring an image of her waking up next to a large, off-white clamshell. I never tired of them.

From the Salt Pond Visitor Center near the entrance, I proceed to the park headquarters and the Marconi Station Site, where Guglielmo Marconi transmitted the first transatlantic, two-way wireless message on December 17, 1902. I bypass the ongoing ranger talk. I usually join ranger talks only for special topics, tours, and ranger-guided activities. It elicits memories of approaching a group during my first visit at Manassas only to hear the ranger explaining that slavery was a primary cause of the Civil War. I slipped away as quietly as I'd come, like a ghost from Stonewall Jackson's army. After taking a few pictures of the Atlantic, I do the same today.

The second and final park for the day is **Adams National Historical Park**. I'm among the legions of history lovers who gained a new appreciation for John Adams and his contributions as a founding father through David McCullough's Pulitzer Prize–winning book, *John Adams*. I also enjoyed the HBO series adaptation, starring Paul Giamatti and Laura Linney as John and Abigail Adams. It's nice to see individuals who gave so much of their lives to our country honored in modern America, even by Hollywood. I first stop at the Adams Visitor Center, in a downtown Quincy, Massachusetts, office building, to secure the park's stamps and pins, before moving along to the home the Adams family called the Old House at Peace field. John and Abigail Adams called Peace field home after his return from duty as a diplomat and foreign minister in 1788. Four generations of Adams lived a world of history and public service at the Old House, from John and Abigail to their son, John Quincy Adams, the sixth president of the United States, to his son, Charles Francis Adams, who served as the US minister to Great Britain during the Lincoln and Andrew Johnson administrations, to his son, the famous historian Henry Adams. A kind ranger lets me obtain a passport stamp in the carriage house on the Peace field property. He smiles as I mention his uncanny resemblance to a hanging portrait of postpresidential John Quincy Adams.

Kareen and I had seen the birthplaces of both John Adams and John Quincy Adams two years ago. These two homes are the nation's oldest surviving presidential birthplaces and remain on their original foundations, though the surroundings were substantially more rural in the 1700s. From Quincy, I reach the Boston suburb where I've booked a hotel room for two nights. Friday, I'll revisit the other seven Boston metro-area parks. It will be another exhilarating but exhausting day.

Friday begins at 8:30 a.m. at the Minute Man Visitor Center near Lexington, Massachusetts, part of **Minute Man National Historical Park**. Minute Man protects important locations and landmarks to the story of April 19, 1775, when Paul Revere rode (one if by land, two if by sea) across the countryside to warn patriots that British forces had left Boston to march on Concord and capture rebel leaders and arms. From Lexington, I drive to Concord, Massachusetts, and arrive at the North Bridge Visitor Center as it opens at 9:00 a.m. Patriots and British regulars exchanged musket fire across the North Bridge during the Battle of Concord. Minute Man is the most famous park within **Freedom's Way National Heritage Area**, dedicated to the Revolutionary-era history of forty-five communities across Massachusetts and New Hampshire.

Two years earlier, Kareen and I walked down to the North Bridge, finding two living history volunteers. Before us stood a British regular and colonial minuteman, deep in conversation. I walked up to the pair and asked, "Shouldn't you guys be shooting at each other?"

Checking my smart remark, the minuteman replied, "We just might load up and start shooting at you." I love the people of New England! Fortunately, no patriots or British regulars have shot at me as of this writing.

Next, I'm off to the **Frederick Law Olmsted National Historic Site**. Olmsted earned fame as a landscape designer and planner of many treasured urban green spaces, including New York City's Central Park and Boston's city park system. Olmsted is considered the nation's first professional landscape architect. Olmsted moved his home and office from New York to the Boston suburb of Brookline in 1883. Built between 1889 and 1925, he named the home, office, and property Fairsted. After getting the pins and stamps at the Olmsted house, I ask about **John Fitzgerald Kennedy National Historic Site**, the Brookline birth home of our thirty-fifth president. The Kennedy site is closed on weekdays in April, but I'm hoping to catch a ranger on-site for stamps and pins. I'm told the site's rangers are at off-site training today. I try anyway, confirming them absent. Add another phone order to the list.

The next stop is **Longfellow House—Washington's Headquarters National Historic Site**. The beautiful historic home in the shadow of Harvard University in Cambridge has the unique historical distinction of being both the house George Washington used as his residence and headquarters during the siege of Boston in 1775–1776, and the home of the famous poet Henry Wadsworth Longfellow from 1843 to 1882. Kareen and I toured the home in 2014. The house is also not yet open for the season, but I find a ranger and ask if I might be able to get the stamps and pins for my project. I thank the kind ranger for her assistance and continue to the next stop north of Boston, in Saugus, Massachusetts.

The **Saugus Iron Works National Historic Site** features the first successful cast and wrought iron production facility in North America. Iron production on-site dates to 1646. Most of the historical buildings are reconstructions, although the iron works house dates to the 1600s. Like the last two parks, Saugus is still closed to the public but several rangers are present. One senior ranger, impatient because he's supposed to begin a training exercise, lets me into the visitor center to get my passport stamps. I feel too guilty about keeping him from his scheduled task to ask about the lapel pins. That becomes a costly mistake later when I'm charged triple the normal shipping cost. Buying pins by phone is always time-consuming, and the punitive shipping charge would be trivial if not for the project requiring about 500 pins spread across 250 locations. Thankfully, it's the only time I'm overcharged. The cost of the pins alone approaches $3,000. Creating the exhibit will cost over $5,000.

From Saugus, I loop back to the outskirts of Boston, parking in a commuter parking garage for the Tee, Boston's subway system, to take mass transit into the heart of the city, exiting at Boston Common. My first destination downtown is the Robert Gould Shaw and 54th Massachusetts Regiment Memorial, a relief sculpture by Augustus Saint Gaudens on Beacon Street across from the state capitol. Many art historians consider the work to be among the finest relief sculptures ever done. From Saint Gaudens' tribute to Shaw and the all-black enlisted men of the 54th Massachusetts, I walk past the capitol to the Abiel Smith School, the visitor center for **Boston African American National Historic Site**. From the Abiel Smith School, the 1.6-mile Black Heritage Trail leads past historic homes, businesses, and meeting places in Boston's black community during the 1700s and 1800s. My path leads back to Boston Common and the Freedom Trail, a 2.5-mile walking path from the common to significant Revolutionary War–era locations. I've walked the Freedom Trail at least once the last two times I've been in Boston, 2009 and 2014, and will do so again today, and then some. After walking off the path to explore one thing or another, and some backtracking, I return across the whole route with tired legs. Encouraged by today's beautiful weather (it's sunny and in the seventies) I tote my thirty-five-pound backpack over fourteen miles on and off the Freedom Trail.

The spiritual and historical center of the Freedom Trail is Faneuil Hall, the "the Cradle of Liberty" since many important meetings held here presaged conflict with England. Faneuil Hall serves as the primary visitor center for **Boston National Historical Park**. The trail passes the outdoor information area and pier to **Boston Harbor Islands National Recreation Area**, though the boats aren't yet running. During our 2014 trip, Kareen and I visited Fort Warren on Georges Island, one of the more popular destinations among the thirty-four sites in the recreation area. Four peninsulas in the national recreation area are accessible by car, while thirty sites are only accessible by water.

In Boston's North End, the Freedom Trail passes Paul Revere's House and the Old North Church, then crosses the Charlestown Bridge to the Charlestown Navy Yard and Bunker Hill. The navy yard houses another visitor center next to the USS *Constitution*, the oldest active ship in the US Navy. Docked alongside Old Ironsides, the USS *Cassin Young*, a World War II destroyer, is also on permanent exhibit. From the yard, I walk to the Battle of Bunker Hill Museum next to Bunker Hill Monument. It's challenging to imagine exactly how the surrounding area appeared when the battle took place in June 1775, but detailed models and descriptions in the museum offer excellent interpretation to educate the visitor.

I talk to the rangers on duty at the museum and tell them Boston National Historical Park is the 139th NPS unit I've visited this year. "Have a great centennial year," we exchange as I turn to start the hike to Boston Common.

Passing the common into Chinatown, then to Downtown Crossing, I give up on plans to eat a nice meal and find a Subway for sustenance. A group of young guys in the Subway wear lanyards sporting conference badges that say "PAX." I ask, "What brings you to town?"

"Gaming conference," one replies, which makes sense considering the guys wearing the lanyards. I wish them well at their conference, refilling my soft drink for the third time. It's hard to rise from the curved, yellow bench. I trudge back to the Tee station to ride to the end of the line, where I retrieve my car and drive to the hotel and a much-needed night of sleep for my bone-weary body. One of the five most exhausting days in my year is now a speck of Freedom Trail history.

Saturday morning, I'm up early, on schedule to arrive in Salem, Massachusetts, by 9:00 a.m., when the visitor center opens for **Salem Maritime National Historic Site**. Salem reigned as a maritime trading nexus during the age of sail, and the park commemorates that history. After the usual routine at the visitor center, I drive a few blocks to Derby Wharf. Dating to 1762, it's the oldest and largest of the major wharves for sailing vessels. I slip into the Public Stores building behind the 1819 Custom House to use another set of passport stampers kept there. From the historical buildings near Salem's waterfront, I drive a short distance north to the John Cabot House in Beverly. The home of the wealthy local businessman and ship owner dates to 1781 and is the first brick mansion built in town. It's one of the sites in the **Essex National Heritage Area**, which highlights locations in the five-hundred-square mile area of eastern Massachusetts north of Boston for their contributions to native, colonial, maritime, and industrial New England history.

My next and last park stop for the day is **Lowell National Historical Park** in Lowell, Massachusetts. The park focuses on the story of Lowell's large textile mills and their role in America's industrial revolution. The mills in Lowell utilize the hydraulic power from the Pawtucket Falls on the Merrimack River, which drops thirty-two feet at this location in less than a mile. The city of Lowell originated as an industrial enterprise. Boston merchants, perceiving the natural advantage afforded by the falls, founded Lowell in 1821–1822. Francis Cabot Lowell copied the design and techniques of British textile production and collaborated with a mechanic, Paul Moody, to build the first working loom operated with water power in America. The profit potential of larger operations spurred the creation of a much bigger capital enterprise. The town of Lowell and its textile mills were born. By 1850, the town had grown to a population of 33,000, the second largest in Massachusetts. Over ten thousand residents worked in the mills, most of them women and girls deemed particularly suited for the work required in the large factories. The mills of Lowell attracted immigrant and country girls to the city for the better part of the nineteenth century.

Lowell's history intertwines into the fabric of American history, as the town's production capacity helped clothe the Union army in the Civil War and provided a backdrop for the burgeoning issues of labor welfare and reform. Kareen and I spent a whole day walking through the exhibits and historical structures two years ago. Today, I start at the visitor center, sharing a summary of the year with two rangers. Taking advantage of the beautiful spring day, I walk to Boott Mills, where the exhibits include a floor of working looms in the same construction and approximate condition as would be typical in the 1860s. One aspect that strikes me as I watch the looms churning away is the incredible noise level, abated from the nineteenth century. The place where these women and girls as young as ten worked twelve-hour days, six days a week, for little more than subsistence wages, and the sacrifices involved, shock the modern sensibility. The work came with lodging and three meals a day, a greater assurance of life and stability than many poor immigrant or rural children might otherwise have had. The Mill Girls and Immigrants Exhibit tells the story of Lowell's workers at a personal level. The exhibit resides in a reconstructed corporation boardinghouse.

Today's visit is anything but grim. I soak in sunshine on a leisurely stroll through town, taking in its history for a second time. By midafternoon, I'm satisfied with the effort and experience. I've walked almost six miles today, farther than I anticipated after the 14-mile forced march over five hours yesterday. It's time to get in the car for a 170-mile drive north, to be in position to strike out early tomorrow morning for the next park.

Saturday night, I pull into a Best Western along I-95 near Waterville, Maine, and after checking in and dining on lobster rolls at a local restaurant, decide to have a beer in the hotel's basement lounge. The place is dark and nearly empty, except for a couple of guys sitting on stools at the bar. I pull up a stool next to them and proceed to learn they are over-the-road truckers from southern Louisiana who are hauling oil drilling equipment up to Canada for ocean transport to an oil rig. The two gentlemen instruct me on the proper procedures for a crab and crawfish boil, which sounds delicious. They are intrigued by my cross-country adventure, and we enjoy a long conversation. The friendly banter provides much-needed humanity to the dungeon-like atmosphere of our surroundings. The whole time we're talking, I keep studying a life-size cutout of John F. Kennedy standing in the corner of the bar. I ask the bartender, "What's JFK doing here?"

"No idea," she replies.

Maine, me and JFK

It's so dark, the cutout blends into the room, looking eerily lifelike. JFK appears to be standing over in the corner having a beer, enjoying a conversation as if whispering to a cutout of a model, actress, or secretary, "You mustn't say anything about tonight." After several beers, I decide JFK needs more company, so I walk over to introduce myself. Tomorrow begins with a laugh when I open social media to see a picture of me smiling, my arm around JFK. It's the second presidential photo-op of the trip. I think one of the truckers took the picture but can't recall. It may have been the female cutout.

As day breaks, I'm contemplating the mechanics of the crawfish boil on the drive east over two-lane Maine highways for my first visit to **Acadia National Park**. Acadia is the 355th NPS unit visited lifetime and the thirty-sixth new park I've visited year to date. Mount Desert Island forms the center and largest area within Acadia National Park. The island's name derives from French explorer Samuel Champlain's trip to the area in 1604. Champlain used the word *desert* referring to the barren rocky mountaintops on the island. Acadia is the first national park declared east of the Mississippi River, under its original name of Lafayette National Park. Acadia only exists today due to the benefice of John D. Rockefeller Jr. and other private landowners on the island who donated property to the federal government. Rockefeller's gift of eleven thousand acres is the largest single donation and comprises over 20 percent of the park's land today.

Making this trip in late April in the park's off-season has two major trade-offs. By coming early, I miss the big summer crowds and get to enjoy the scenery's peace and solitude. On the other hand, most of the visitor facilities remain closed. I start with a stop at Hulls Cove Visitor Center, open year-round and located off Maine Highway 3 before it enters the town of Bar Harbor, pronounced "Baa Habba" by locals. The letter *r*, when it appears as the last letter in a word, is a rejected suggestion in New England dialect. After getting feedback on today's plan of attack, I begin the park's 27-mile loop road at Sand Beach. From the sea cliffs, the tiny rock island known as Old Soaker guards the little cove. South of Sand Beach, the Ocean Path offers an overlook of the rock-strewn coast and excellent picture location. I trade picture-taking duties with a couple basking on the rocks, taking in the view and the late April sun. It's in the low sixties today, but the sun and wind make it feel much hotter or colder, depending on the location. I leave my car at Sand Beach to walk the Ocean Path down the coastline, pausing at Thunder Hole. Trapped air in a cavity underneath the rock makes a roaring or gurgling sound when released by the combined action of waves and tide. The turnaround destination for my walk is Otter Point, with a high and low overlook area at the edge of Otter Cliff. The walk between Thunder Hole and Otter Point has a sojourn into the pines growing on the rocky coast, where ground stability and soil support the trees. The coastal hike is a perfect introduction to Acadia's beautiful rugged coast. Attractions along the way include a cobblestone beach and plenty of sea cliff views above the ocean crashing ashore.

Acadia, cobblestone beach on Ocean Path

After returning to the car, I follow the park road to the Jordan Pond House, not yet open for the season. I notice volunteers stocking merchandise in the gift shop and one of them is kind enough to let me in briefly to stamp my passport. The next stop's another hiking opportunity at one of the park's most famous locations, Cadillac Mountain. I hike the North Ridge Trail, listed as 4.4 miles roundtrip. The trail climbs the 1,530-foot summit, the tallest mountain on the US Eastern Seaboard, for views of the surrounding water and land. On the mountain, I find numerous erratics, glacially deposited rocks appearing strangely out of place. These rocks are left by the massive sheets of ice that once covered the area, dropping their cargo during melt and recession. Many of these rocks sit on sloped surfaces, deceptively appearing on the verge of tumbling down the mountain. Appropriately sized erratics make for great benches to catch one's breath and take in the view. I finish my day with an early seafood dinner in a Bar Harbor pub. A bowl of chowder and a cold pint are the perfect nutritional replenishment after nine miles of hiking. I fall into a deep sleep Sunday night, dreaming of Acadia's coastal views and fully appreciating why someone might come here year after year. Indeed, I'll return as well in chapter 39 with the good doctor in tow.

Monday at 8:00 a.m., I start at park headquarters to add a few of their passport cancellations to my collection. I share a summary of the year's journey with the ranger on duty at the information center. Mentioning that I need to hit the road for the 2.5-hour drive northeast to **Saint Croix Island International Historic Site**, the Acadia ranger calls the permanent ranger stationed there and asks if I can get the passport cancellations during my visit. Saint Croix Island hasn't opened for the season. Luckily, she'll be around today. Saint Croix Island International Historic Site lies in the St. Croix River between New Brunswick, Canada, and Maine. St. Croix Island is the site of one of the first European settlements in North America. The French, on the same voyage when Champlain named Mount Desert to the south, explored the various inlets and rivers along the coast before deciding to establish a settlement on an island in the middle of the St. Croix River, a tributary to Passamaquoddy Bay. The expedition, led by Pierre Dugua, Sieur de Mons, hoped to profit from the fur trade. With no prior knowledge of the severity of North American winters, they were cut off from the mainland after the river became impassable, freezing into massive chunks of ice. Many settlers suffered from scurvy and died of malnutrition. When resupply ships found the settlement in June of the following year, Dugua used the opportunity to move to a safer location, founding Port Royal, Nova Scotia. Due to the fragility of the small island's historic remnants, visitors are encouraged to view it from the riverbanks. Canada has interpretive panels on their side of the river as well. A short walking path through the trees on the American side leads to a circular shelter exhibiting the ill-fated settlement's story. Complimentary sculptures of important figures adorn the walking path.

From Saint Croix Island International Historic Site, I drive an hour south to **Roosevelt Campobello International Park** on Campobello Island in New Brunswick. The park is not an NPS unit but an affiliated site on Canadian soil. Campobello Island is the summer vacation home for the Roosevelts of Hyde Park. Franklin Roosevelt had been enjoying another summer retreat at the family's 10,000-square-foot, thirty-four-room cottage in 1921 when struck with polio, causing a life-altering disability. He briefly returned to the island only three more times in his life.

Like the other parks, none of the buildings in the park have opened for the season, but the grounds are accessible, and I make use of the walking trails to take pictures of the Roosevelt's beautiful home. Leaving the Roosevelt cottage, I head northeast to the island's tip at Head Harbor Light. The walking path to the light had been recommended without mention of the thirty-five-foot tides around the island that bury the bottom half of the metal staircases and beach path out to the lighthouse in eight to ten feet of salt water. I'm amused by the warning sign erected at the start of the disappearing walking trail. It reads: "EXTREME HAZARD: Beach exposed only at low tide. Incoming tide rises at five feet per hour, and may leave you stranded for eight hours. Wading or swimming are extremely dangerous due to swift currents and cold water." I shake my head, looking past the sign at the stairway into the ocean. These tides demand serious attention. The Bay of Fundy boasts the highest measured tides in the world, over fifty-three feet at Burntcoat Head, Nova Scotia.

The only problem with the trip to Maine's coast is the drive back. I make it to the town of Falmouth before calling it a night. Falmouth resembles a ski resort town with designer stores and high-end shopping, though little is open after nine o'clock on an April Monday night. I wake up the next morning to a steady snowfall. I waste no time getting in the car to go south.

After a slow drive through Portland on snowy I-95, I turn west toward my next destination at Concord, New Hampshire. The snow has turned to a wintry mix when I reach **Saint-Gaudens National Historic Site**. After our visit to the home of Augustus Saint-Gaudens in 2014, Kareen and I enjoyed walking through Chicago's parks admiring some of his most famous sculptures. My favorite among Chicago's Saint-Gaudens sculptures is the statue of General John A. Logan on horseback in Grant Park. The sculptor's best-known Chicago works are his Sitting Lincoln in Lincoln Park, the former site of the city cemetery, and the Standing Lincoln in Grant Park.

The house and grounds of the New Hampshire park served as Saint-Gaudens' summer home from 1885 to 1897, and his permanent home from 1900 until his death in 1907. This is another park representing history and art that I would have missed without the park goal. Having toured Saint-Gaudens' home and studio, and admired some of his work, I've gained a deep appreciation for the artist. Saint-Gaudens National Historic Site has yet to open for the season during my April 28 visit, but they're busy preparing to open in May despite the inclement weather. I meet a ranger at the visitor center who greets me and lets me do the stamping and purchase the lapel pins. From Saint-Gaudens, it's a short thirty-five-minute drive to the trip's last park, **Marsh-Billings-Rockefeller National Historical Park** in Woodstock, Vermont.

Marsh-Billings-Rockefeller National Historical Park is a historical home that serves as the residence of three major conservationists, starting with George Perkins Marsh, then railroad tycoon Frederick Billings for whom Billings, Montana, is named, and last for Laurance S. Rockefeller, who continued his family's tradition of conservation and environmental stewardship with his gift of the land and farm for this park. Kareen and I enjoyed the house tour during our 2014 visit. The National Park Carriage Barn Visitor Center is still closed for the season, but a kind volunteer lets me repeat the tasks of stamping and buying lapel pins. Before leaving, I ask her to take my picture beneath the park's name in raised metal letters on the brown-paneled wall behind the ranger desk.

Marsh-Billings-Rockefeller, author

I'm headed west again toward the Adirondacks, a route that takes me south of Fort Ticonderoga and through the **Champlain Valley National Heritage Partnership**. I've always wanted to visit the fort, but I'm too late to do so now and will be well on my way across New York State by tomorrow morning. My first real exploration of the Champlain Valley, holding Lake Champlain and nestled between Vermont's Green Mountains and New York's

Adirondacks, will take place in 2018 during the preparation of this book. The highlight is a chance to walk the ruins of the French and British forts constructed at Crown Point next to a narrow section of Lake Champlain, and Fort Ticonderoga. These sites played paramount roles in the French and Indian War that secured the American colonies under British rule.

My last stop on the trip home is a brief one at Niagara Falls, represented in the park system by the **Niagara Falls National Heritage Area**, featuring several War of 1812 sites. From the falls, it's time for a return across northern Ohio and Indiana on the trip home.

15 The UP

I'M HOME LESS than twenty-four hours, with enough time to unload clothes from the New England trip and replace them with my track and field gear. I never forget to include a rain suit. I'm going to need it. I'm off to Des Moines, Iowa, and the Drake Relays. It's always nice to see the great people in Des Moines, and we all enjoy good weather on Thursday and Friday. Only one day to go, but Saturday is a different animal. And this animal is vicious. A front brings steady rain and plunges the temperature by thirty degrees overnight. Strong winds drive intermittent heavy rain. It's impossible to stay dry or warm. My Saturday event is the hammer throw, memorable as it's the coldest I've ever been at a meet. With many cold and wet meets to my credit over two decades in the upper Midwest, I've worked in some bad conditions. None are colder or more miserable than Saturday at the 2016 Drake Relays. I find myself shaking uncontrollably, barely able to move my hands as we enter the men's hammer final, our last event of the day. I'm the head event official for the hammer and am blessed and thankful to have a remarkable crew working the event who seem to hold up better than I do today. Somehow my clothing gets wet under my rain suit, as do my fingers despite gloves. Once I'm wet to the skin, my body cannot retain heat, and the day turns truly ugly. I can't stop shaking, sliding into hypothermia.

From Des Moines, I drive, still wet, to St. Louis to dry out Saturday night before beginning May watching the Washington Nationals play the St. Louis Cardinals at Busch Stadium. After the Sunday game, I have two days at home to work and prepare for a three-day trip through Wisconsin and Michigan's Upper Peninsula.

Wednesday morning, May 4, I start early on a five-hour drive to St. Croix River Visitor Center in St. Croix Falls, Wisconsin, part of **St. Croix National Scenic Riverway.** The park covers 252 miles of the St Croix and Namekagon rivers, including the St. Croix's 155-mile southern section of Minnesota and Wisconsin's shared border and the entire length of the Namekagon, its principle tributary. The park extends south to the St Croix-Mississippi confluence at Prescott, Wisconsin. The past two years I've taken advantage of work trips through the area to explore the St. Croix River in 2014 and the Namekagon in 2015.

St. Croix Falls is also the western terminus of the **Ice Age National Scenic Trail,** stretching twelve hundred miles across Wisconsin's terminal moraine, or the last glacier's furthest advance across the state about ten thousand years ago. Nine areas of special interest in the glacially formed landscape are included in the **Ice Age National Scientific Reserve** and administered by the Wisconsin Department of Natural Resources. Though I've visited all nine locations, I found the most illustrative at Chippewa Moraine State Park, about seventy miles east of St. Croix Falls. The park's visitor center provides a comprehensive and easily understood explanation of glaciated land forms. The interpretive exhibits compliment the view from the visitor center's hilltop location. One can look out the exhibit area's panel windows or stand at the outdoor overlook and survey excellent examples of almost all the major landscape features described in the exhibit. I learned more about glacial impact on terrain at Chippewa Moraine State Park than I had previously understood from all sources combined. Both the trail and reserve lie entirely within the state of Wisconsin.

Another three hours brings me to Wisconsin's Lake Superior shoreline and the Northern Great Lakes Visitor Center, an interagency visitor center near Ashland, Wisconsin. After a short stamping stop, I proceed to the **Apostle Islands National Lakeshore** headquarters and visitor center in Bayfield, Wisconsin. Apostle Islands National Lakeshore includes twenty-one islands and over twelve miles of Lake Superior's Wisconsin shoreline. In summer months, tourists take boat and camping excursions to the islands. The boats haven't begun yet for the season, so I satisfy myself admiring the largest of the Great Lakes from the shore after my usual routine in the visitor center. I've squeezed almost eight hours of driving into today and will push another hour farther to Ironwood, Michigan, just across the border into Michigan's Upper Peninsula, or the "UP" to midwesterners.

Thursday is the UP day of the centennial tour. I first visited the UP units during a beautiful September weekend in 2014. I hit upper Michigan at peak color, driving through intense yellow, red, and orange hardwood countryside for two days. Today's visit begins in the center of the Keweenaw Peninsula at Calumet, Michigan. **Keweenaw National Historical Park** protects many historical sites and locations from the peninsula's copper mining era. Keweenaw Peninsula natives used surface deposits of the area's high-purity copper ore for tools and jewelry. After Keweenaw's confirmed ownership as part of the United States in 1842, commercial mining ventures extracted the high-value deposits. This morning, I stop at the visitor center and admire a few of the historical pictures, my favorite being one of a locomotive pictured with cumulative snowfall equal in height to the body of the engine. Railroad workers pose in the photograph standing aside one another on the engine and surrounding snow. During my first visit to Keweenaw National Historical Park on that September weekend, I spent a full day exploring the park's sites. On this May centennial day, I leave Calumet for the forty-five-minute drive to Copper Harbor and Fort Wilkins, built here in 1844 to maintain peace in the burgeoning mining community. After walking the grounds, I retreat south to Houghton, Michigan, the location of the headquarters for **Isle Royale National Park.**

Kareen and I experienced an unforgettable first encounter with Isle Royale. Late July 2015, we visited both the Windigo Visitor

Center at the west end of the forty-five-mile long island and Rock Harbor Visitor Center at the southeastern end on the same day. We planned visits to both locations around an overnight stay, going from Grand Portage, Minnesota, to Rock Harbor on Wednesday and returning Thursday. It takes seven to eight hours to reach Rock Harbor from Grand Portage with the smaller boats used by the concessionaire, so the boats stay at Rock Harbor overnight and return the next day. The day we booked happened to be the fourth day in ten years that the company canceled the trip due to high winds and swells on Lake Superior. They don't take the boats on the lake in swells six feet or higher. We discovered why the next day.

The wind storm continued throughout Wednesday. Our tickets transferred to Thursday, but we couldn't spend the night on the island since they had to bring the boat back on its normal schedule. That meant circumnavigating the island and returning to Grand Portage the same day, a fourteen-hour ride. They normally do it only once a year to open the summer season. Our trip marked the first fourteen-hour ride in memory through six-foot swells. I left the decision to go or pass up to Kareen. She thought I would regret not making it to the island park having come so far and concluded we should take the boat.

The thoughtful captain offered us two options. We could debark at Windigo and hike for the day. He would pick us up on the return. Or we could ride the boat around the island, getting out for a few minutes at both visitor centers. Again, I left the decision with Kareen. She decided to ride around the island. I leaned toward staying in Windigo given the punishment underway. The waves tossed the boat like a bob. Several younger passengers fed fish off the back rail. Thankfully, we'd both taken meclizine, which kept us from joining the chum challenge. Some of the teenagers must have eaten big breakfasts that subsequently floated on Lake Superior. The motion sickness pill did not prevent the physical pounding from all sides. The high swells rocked us side to side eastward, then up and down as we churned west. We learned firsthand that wave impact is enhanced on the Great Lakes near land, something mariners call the washtub effect. Intermittent rain and waves breaking over the rails soaked anyone daring to breathe fresh air. We felt like we spent fourteen hours on a teeter-totter bobbing up and down while someone to the side rhythmically smacked us with a broom. The only thing missing was Gordon Lightfoot's *Edmund Fitzgerald* playing on repeat over the boat's speakers. Like the ill-fated iron ore freighter, we waited to break up and take water. Let there be no doubt, the gales of July are remembered. At least the plunge to the deepest Great Lake's bottom would end the misery. Kareen declared, "If you visit Isle Royale again, you'll be going alone." No need. I've conceded Lake Superior to the fish that inhabit it.

On this centennial visit, I'm limited to the park headquarters in Houghton. The rangers and I discuss some of the parks I've toured this year and our Magellan-esque Isle Royale experience. The regular boats aren't running yet, thus I avoid temptation to give the evil lake another chance to finish me off. I remind the rangers to order centennial stampers for both island visitor centers, something they hadn't done yet. I'd hate for someone to narrowly escape Lake Superior's clutches and not even get the centennial stamp for their masochism.

From Houghton, I'm off to **Pictured Rocks National Lakeshore**. I spent a day at the lakeshore during the 2014 trip, thrilled by the park's beauty dressed in spectacular color. My centennial visit starts with a stop at the interagency visitor center in Munising, Michigan, near the park's western boundary. From town, I drive a few miles east to Sand Point. The headquarters occupies a house completed in 1933 as part of the Munising United States Coast Guard Life Saving Station. I entertain several park rangers with tales from the year's travels. Pictured Rocks National Lakeshore is my 150th NPS unit visited this year. They're not yet open for the season, with new merchandise and materials still in boxes awaiting distribution among the visitor facilities. The park's lapel pins remain in unpacked boxes, but one of the rangers finds a set of samples for the two pins to give to me for the exhibit. It's an example of the kindness and enthusiasm that originally inspired the project. Before leaving, the rangers take a picture of me next to a large seven-foot vertical Find Your Park banner featuring Pictured Rocks. The whole experience is the perfect complement to my first visit exploring the lakeshore's trails and views. After walking about Sand Point taking pictures of the lifesaving station remnants, I head back to Munising to travel northeast across the landward side of the park to the Grand Sable Visitor Center at the park's eastern end near Grand Marais, Michigan. The route through Pictured Rocks National Lakeshore runs along the **North Country National Scenic Trail**, a forty-six-hundred-mile trail through seven states from Crown Point, New York, to North Dakota's Lake Sakakawea. I'll loosely follow UP trail sections running to lower Michigan.

From Grand Marais, I drive south and east along the lake to the **Father Marquette National Memorial** commemorating the accomplishments of the French priest and explorer, Jacques Marquette. An NPS-affiliated site, the memorial sits next to Mackinac Bridge's north end at Straits State Park in the town of St. Ignace, Michigan. Father Marquette established the first two European settlements in what is now the state of Michigan at Sault Ste. Marie and St. Ignace in 1668 and 1671, respectively. Interpretive panels within the memorial's open shelter review Marquette's expeditions with Louis Joliet exploring inland waterways in hope of finding the mythical all-water route through North America to the Pacific. From 1666 until his death in 1675, Marquette and Joliet become the first Europeans to travel the Chicago and Illinois Rivers to the Mississippi, which they navigated to present-day Arkansas.

After walking the short memorial trail, I continue south into lower Michigan for the trip's final park. It's nearly three hours more of driving, so I close the distance this evening, stopping in Petoskey. The lakefront resort town has plenty of hotel rooms available this early in the year. I stop at an inviting restaurant on the way into town, sit at the bar, and ask, "What's good here?" In a strong New York accent, the bartender advises, "Try the special, spaghetti with meatballs." I figure a guy straight out of *The Godfather* ought to know good Italian food, so I order the special. The spaghetti is wondrously delicious. While I'm enjoying the meal, Kareen calls, so I can tell her all about it. It's a perfect ending to a long day spanning the southern shore of Lake Superior and the eastern shore of Lake Michigan.

Early Friday morning I depart en route to the Philip A. Hart Visitor Center for **Sleeping Bear Dunes National Lakeshore** in Empire, Michigan. It's my second trip to Sleeping Bear Dunes. Two years ago, I did the park's obligatory Dune Climb and toured the length of the lakeshore. Walking on loose sand is not among my favorite activities. It's punishing to feel yourself sinking with each step. From the visitor center, I repeat the activity I enjoyed the most during the first visit, the 1.5-mile roundtrip hike out to the edge of the dune cliff at Empire Bluffs. The steep sand cliff lakeshore extends north towering four hundred feet over the water. South Manitou Island, also a part of the park, is clearly visible across the water, as is North Manitou Island in the distance. Standing on the edge of the sand cliff high above Lake Michigan, I marvel at how the delicate balance of vegetation, compaction, wind, and wave maintains the massive wall of sand dominating my sightline. It's blissful.

From Empire, I follow the North Country Trail southeast of Grand Rapids to the town of Lowell, Michigan. Lowell is home to the North Country Trail Association office and the trail's superintendent, though the trail's administrative functions are handled by the staff at the Ice Age National Scenic Trail office in Madison, Wisconsin. I leave Lowell with a stamp and shirt from the association office and a warm meal in my stomach, ready for the four-hour drive to Chicago. Every trip to the UP and Michigan's beautiful Great Lakes shorelines dazzles and soothes the soul.

16 *Colorado*

THE NEXT ADVENTURE begins with an officiating assignment. The University of Nebraska-Lincoln, my father's alma mater, hosts the Big Ten Outdoor Track and Field Championships May 13–15, 2016. I've looked forward to helping at a track meet in Lincoln since the school entered the Big Ten conference. It's an honor and privilege to help at the 2016 Big Ten Championships. The hosts and fellow officials are as wonderful as I knew they would be. I've found the Big Ten host schools to be magnificent everywhere I've worked a conference championship. In addition to Nebraska, the list includes Illinois, Indiana, Iowa, Purdue, Ohio State, and Wisconsin. The exceptional staffs speak to the high quality of what I consider to be the country's most impactful pubic university conference. Ten of the fourteen Big Ten schools were designated by the 1862 Morrill Land Grant College Act signed by President Abraham Lincoln. The roll call of conference land grant universities includes Illinois, Maryland, Michigan State, Minnesota, Nebraska, Ohio State, Penn State, Purdue, Rutgers, and Wisconsin. Founded in 1855, both Michigan State and Penn State predate the act and have been commemorated as the first of the land grant colleges.

After a business meeting early in the week, I have an extra day before the meet to revisit a couple of Nebraska parks. Thursday morning, I stop in Yankton, South Dakota, at the **Missouri National Recreational River** headquarters. Ranger Dugan and I discuss my park travels and lapel pin project. "That's quite a year you're having," he offers. "Good luck with the project."

Missouri National Recreational River has two free-flowing regions, the 59-Mile District in the east and the 39-Mile District in the west. The eastern area begins about twenty-five miles west of Sioux City, Iowa, continuing to Gavins Point Dam in South Dakota. The dam created Lewis and Clark Lake, which separates the districts. The eastern section maintains the river's original dynamic characteristics while the western section features captivating plains landscapes.

After Yankton, the next stop's Niobrara State Park, encompassing the Niobrara and Missouri River confluence at the eastern end of the 39-Mile District. I find the confluence of rivers fascinating, perhaps because they are the major intersections of historical travel. After getting the passport stamp at the visitor center, I make my way to a wooden-decked pedestrian bridge spanning the fast-moving Niobrara as it enters the Missouri. The former railroad bridge offers a nice view of the river junction. Crossing into a wetland, the trails are empty and quiet except for the Niobrara's rushing water.

From Niobrara State Park, I continue two and a half hours west to Valentine, Nebraska, the "Gateway to the Sandhills." Northwestern Nebraska's vast, desolate sandhills are an ancient seabed. The sandhills spread west and south of Valentine, the host of **Niobrara National Scenic River**'s visitor center and headquarters. The park starts south of Valentine at the Borman Bridge, another converted crossing, and runs seventy-five miles east.

At Fort Niobrara National Wildlife Refuge, the park road crosses the river and climbs a slight hill where I acquire a bison escort from the resident herd. They're lounging across the road, mindful of the car but moving at their own pace. For two hundred feet, I crawl along among bison on all sides. The beasts finally part to let me slip past. A bison to the left looks through my open window as if to ask, "Where are you going?" Good question. "You don't want any of this," I reply, slowing back to the bison's pace. Channeling

Eddie Murphy's Billy Ray Valentine, I say, "I'm a karate man! Karate man bruise on the inside!" The bison snorts.

After returning through town, I walk across the Borman Bridge spanning the Niobrara under a clear-blue, sunny sky. The 1916 bridge carried auto traffic in and out of town. Today, it's a pedestrian and bike path across the river with elevated views of the Niobrara turning through a wooded landscape up- and downstream.

After five hours across the farmland of eastern Nebraska, I reach my downtown Lincoln hotel at dusk. The three-day meet goes quickly. I spend some spare time Friday morning catching up on work and contemplating the next park excursion. My inclination is to drive west after the meet ends Sunday afternoon and do a sweep of Colorado's national park units, but it's a tall order and a lot of driving. After working the men's shot put Sunday, I'm finished with my assignments by 3:00 p.m. and ready to head west.

With the reasonable start time, I hope to get close enough to **Rocky Mountain National Park** to reach it early Monday morning. After a nice weekend and a good night's sleep, my energy level is good. I set the GPS destination for Estes Park, Colorado, eight hours and over five hundred miles away. The first seven hours go smoothly. The last sixty minutes between Loveland and Estes Park unravel to terror. It's alternating rain, snow, and freezing rain as a dense fog settles into the foothills. I've traveled this highway but don't know it well. Gripping the steering wheel with both hands, I concentrate my full attention on the barely visible lane markings, crawling at times around one blind curve after another. Oncoming cars induce a moment of panic. Each one blinds me a few seconds when its headlights refract off the water hanging in the air. Darkness and fog has one benefit, obscuring the sheer roadside drops. The high rock wall rising on my right and the sharp curves indicate increasingly larger precipices. If I'd known of the conditions, I would have stopped in Loveland. I regret it throughout the drive. I'm a nervous wreck, and it's all I can do not to become a physical one. Relief washes over me when I pull into Estes Park, the eastern gateway to Rocky Mountain National Park.

Off early again Monday, I arrive at Beaver Meadows Visitor

Center as it opens. After acquiring the standard stamps and pins and a long-sleeve centennial T-shirt with the park's name emblazoned on the sleeve, I head through the entrance station to the Moraine Park Discovery Center.

I drove a group of colleagues through Rocky Mountain National Park last June as a team-building exercise. We traveled Trail Ridge Road (also US 34), the highest major highway in North America, reaching an altitude of 12,183 feet near Alpine Visitor Center. A short trail leads from the parking lot to 12,000 feet. The uphill walk demonstrates the lower oxygen levels at altitude. As part of our team-building exercise, I purchased little blue passport books for everyone in our group. If they weren't interested, I suggested they give the book to a relative. We ate our picnic lunch and tried some hiking near Timber Creek but retreated under attack by relentless mosquitoes. I forgot to bring repellent, an inexcusable omission considering my park experience. At the western end of Trail Ridge Road, we stopped at Kawuneeche Visitor Center before enjoying a short walk to Adams Falls near Grand Lake.

My centennial visit is abbreviated. I follow US 34 east past Sheep Lakes, stopping to talk to a ranger getting ready for a talk on bighorn sheep before continuing to Fall River Visitor Center, the only visitor center we didn't visit last June. I'd love to spend all day in the park, but I've got twelve Colorado NPS units to cover, excluding the ruins of Hovenweep, visited in March. I've visited eleven of them in the past two years, leaving one new park this week. I exit Rocky Mountain National Park and begin the three-and-a-half-hour drive to **Florissant Fossil Beds National Monument**.

Located thirty-five miles west of Colorado Springs, the monument protects one of the most extensive fossil records on earth, yielding samples from over seven hundred species, most of which date to the Eocene epoch 34 MYA (million years ago). South-central Colorado's high plains had a warm, temperate climate in the Eocene epoch, from 55 MYA to 33.8 MYA. Over several million years, a period of substantial global cooling ended the Eocene epoch. Volcanic activity covered the area in ash, preserving a rich collection of plants and insects in shale.

I stretch my legs on the Petrified Forest Loop, a one-mile hiking trail passing fossilized tree trunks and other fossil excavations. My last park stop is the Hornbek Homestead. The home and surrounding buildings, the homestead of Adeline Hornbek, date to 1878. After losing her second husband, Hornbek and her teenage children started life anew in Florissant Valley. I overlooked the homestead during my first visit here. From Florissant, I have another three-hour drive to today's last park stop, **Great Sand Dunes National Park & Preserve**. In route, I pass through part of the **South Park National Heritage Area** focused on central Colorado's mining and ranching history. The heritage area includes nineteen working area ranches and multiple mines.

North America's tallest sand dunes reach 750 feet above the San Luis Valley floor and cover over thirty square miles. The dune field lies at the foot of the Sangre de Cristo Mountains to the east. A westerly wind pattern across the valley swept up loose sand for millions of years. Unable to pass, sand collected at the foot of the mountains. The valley stretches from the San Juan Mountains, a volcanic mountain chain about sixty-five miles west, to the tectonic Sangre de Cristo Mountain Range towering over the park and dunes piled under its shadow.

Visitors who access the dune field walk across Medano Creek's shallow water. Several creeks carry melt water from the mountains and reposition sand to the south and west of the dune field. Most of it is blown back into the dunes. The sand dunes' configuration and appearance are remarkably stable. Century-old photographs show the dune field much the same as today. The complex system of wind and water forces maintain the dune system's size and major features. I hiked across the creek and into the dune field during my first visit, but today's is shortened by my tight schedule.

The park and preserve are part of the **Sangre de Cristo National Heritage Area**. The heritage area covers the adjoining part of the San Luis Valley, the first area settled in Colorado.

After crossing the valley and Monarch Pass at 11,312 feet on US 50, Monday ends at Gunnison, Colorado. The route and towns have a strong air of familiarity, as I followed the same path last year on my initial visits to these parks.

Tuesday starts with a thirty-minute drive to Elk Creek Visitor Center in **Curecanti National Recreation Area**, consisting of reservoirs created by three Gunnison River dams. US Highway 50 follows the northern bank of the Blue Mesa Reservoir, over twenty miles long and the largest body of water in the state, before cutting across to the south bank on the appropriately named Middle Bridge. The other two reservoirs, Morrow Point and Crystal, are narrower bodies of water, as the river tightens entering the steep canyons downstream. Boat tours of Blue Mesa are a popular park activity.

I continue west on US 50 to the next park, **Black Canyon of the Gunnison National Park**, one of the most beautiful and awe-inspiring places on the continent. The park includes fourteen of the forty-eight-mile long Black Canyon, where the Gunnison River loses more elevation than the Mississippi River does in fifteen hundred miles from Minnesota to New Orleans. The river drops an average of 96 feet per mile in the park and 480 feet in a two-mile stretch. The fast-moving water creates the power necessary to cut through hard rock layers and create the park's steep-walled canyons. Most visitors see the park from the seven-mile South Rim Road. The road ends at High Point, the deepest part of the canyon, with the river over 2,700 feet below the rim. The overlooks include a glimpse of the river twisting far below and vertical rock faces like the 2,250-foot Painted Wall, Colorado's tallest cliff. At its narrowest, Black Canyon, so named because sunlight only reaches the river at midday, spans 1,100 feet compared to the river's 40-foot wide channel below.

Today, I stop for pictures of southern Colorado's expanse from State Highway 347, connecting US 50 to the park. At the South Rim Visitor Center, I walk to the overlook at Gunnison Point. To the north, the river turns west under the canyon's towering walls. I continue to the overlooks at the Painted Wall and High Point, snapping pictures and soaking in more of the canyon before the press of time forces my departure.

Black Canyon of the Gunnison, Painted Wall

I must drive four hours to reach the last two parks of the day. From Black Canyon, I stop at the BLM Field Office in Montrose, Colorado, for an Old Spanish Trail passport stamp, then proceed to Dolores, Colorado, and the Anasazi Heritage Center for the same. A topographical map of the Canyons of the Ancients National Monument, a BLM-managed area to the west along the Utah border, gives me another location for a Word document I will create for Kareen containing thirty-five numbered bullets and titled Unfinished Park Business.

From Dolores, I pass through Cortez, Colorado, to the next park, **Yucca House National Monument**. Yucca House lacks visitor facilities. Visiting the location requires parking in front of a rancher's house and taking a walking trail. Other than a sign at the trailhead cautioning visitors to watch for rattlesnakes hiding among the scattered brush, there are no interpretive panels or visual aids. Although protected in 1919 and officially managed by the NPS, the ruins remain unexcavated for their own preservation. About the only people that bother to visit this unit are park enthusiasts trying to visit all the units or serious students of Native American history.

From Yucca House, I return through Cortez and ten miles east on US 160 to **Mesa Verde National Park** Visitor and Research Center. I visited the impressive Native American cliff dwellings on Chapin Mesa and Wetherill Mesa within Mesa Verde National Park last July. Today's stop is short. I don't have time for the twenty-one-mile, one-hour trip to the park's closest ruins.

Today's last stop is the BLM Field Office in Durango. An extremely kind USFS employee loads me up with Smokey the Bear rulers, erasers, stickers, and other items left over from past promotions. I'm tired, but the day's not over. I have a two-and-a-half-hour drive north through three separate mountain passes to Montrose. That gets me close enough to reach my first park at 9:00 a.m. tomorrow. I navigate the 10,640-foot Coal Bank Hill Pass without issue. In the second pass, 10,910-foot Molas Pass, it snows heavily as I round sharp blind corners with shear drop offs to the right. I descend to Silverton, taking US 550 to 11,075-foot Red Mountain Pass. It's sunny here. Each mountain creates its own weather pattern. The ski resort town of Telluride sits on the other side of this mountain. I manage to stay awake through a fifteen-minute construction delay for single-lane traffic. Back in Montrose, another steak and beer dinner completes a long day. Tomorrow will be even longer, much longer.

Wednesday, I start north at 7:30 a.m., hoping the coffee lifts my tired eyes. Back on US 50, I'm driving to one of my favorite parks and the last of the three hidden gems mentioned earlier, at **Colorado National Monument** in Grand Junction, Colorado. The park blew me away during my visit last June. When I mentioned my surprise, a ranger told me they meet awed visitors on a regular basis who are lifelong area residents and only see the park when visiting friends ask about it.

On the way to the visitor center located four miles into the twenty-three-mile park road, I stop at the Redlands Fault overlook. The monument occupies the ridge south of Grand Junction, named for the confluence of the Gunnison and Colorado (Grand) Rivers. Massive erosion from the two rivers and uplift at the Redlands Fault raised the park's ridge two thousand feet above the Grand Valley. At the overlook, I scan east and south across the face of the plateau, following the fault line indicated by large sections of rising rock broken off and slanting at dramatic angles to the valley below. It's one of the most striking fault lines I've seen in the parks and underscores tectonic uplift.

Visitors tour the park via Rim Rock Drive south and east across the heavily eroded face. As the plateau rose and water drained from it into the valley, erosion cut a series of box canyons that continue to grow into the higher terrain. Many rock features are remnants of fins, the disappearing walls of ancient box canyons. The park so impressed me last year, I didn't miss a single stop noted in the park brochure. Knowing nothing about the park previously, I left it thrilled by its powerful geological origin. After a short visit this morning, my next destination and the week's only new park, **Dinosaur National Monument**, is two and a half hours due north.

The route cuts through the highlands across Grand Valley next to the Bookcliffs. As I ascend to 8,268-foot Douglas Pass, I navigate around several dual-axle pick-up trucks carrying drilling equipment and other supplies up the steep grades. The scenic road covers interesting topography. I guess I expected a barren wasteland north of Grand Valley.

The first stop in the new park is Canyon Visitor Center near the small town of Dinosaur, Colorado. Here, Harpers Corner Road leads into the middle of the monument, where visitors can explore canyons carved by the Green and Yampa rivers. The park is centered about their confluence. I'll have to explore the park's interior and canyons during a future visit, more unfinished park business. Today, I'm touring the famous Quarry Exhibit Hall, accessed through the tiny town of Jensen, Utah. Over the twenty-five miles between Dinosaur and Jensen, I feel a gnawing hunger, reminding me I skipped breakfast. In Jensen, the only food option seems to be a gas station with a takeaway order menu. "Whaddya want?" the woman in the station asks. Her twenty-something body and deeply carved facial features don't match. Ordering something here feels like a bad idea. But an intense hunger supersedes my better judgement. I mumble, "I'll have a double cheeseburger," hoping somebody will walk in and stop me.

I eat half the burger to abate my hunger before the river of grease in the aluminum foil and the burger's empty taste convince me to stop. I've consumed enough calories to survive. From Jensen, it's a seven-mile drive to the Quarry Visitor Center, filled with small plastic dinosaurs and other items for enthusiastic children. Quite a few parents probably leave the park with a new ten-dollar plastic dinosaur.

Built in the 1950s as an art-deco masterpiece with its angled, multilevel construction and overhanging checkmark-shaped roof, the exhibit hall protects the fossil bed and is a national historic landmark. Inside, an unexcavated section of the original quarry tilts at a sixty-degree angle, leaving the quarry face directly in front of visitors on either of the hall's two levels. Paleontologist Earl Douglass discovered the large dinosaur fossil bed and began excavation for the Carnegie Museum in 1909. The Douglass Quarry, also called the Carnegie Quarry, represents one of the most impressive discoveries of late-Jurassic period bones in the world. Twenty-three different geologic formations lie exposed in the park, each representing an extinct ecosystem.

I find the fossil bed and how it came to be in this position fascinating. The uplift that created the Uinta Mountain Range across southern Wyoming to the north also lifted the fossil bed at the Carnegie Quarry, tilting it. A ranger educates me on the decision to leave the quarry face unexcavated for future visitors, and I ask him to take my picture next to the four-foot long femur standing on end in the hall, presumably with this purpose in mind. "Okay, I'll bite," I say as I hand him my camera. It's hard not to feel a little like a kid again in such a place. Maybe I'll buy my own plastic dinosaur.

Dinosaur femur and me

From the quarry, I make my way down Cub Creek Road along the tributary to the Green River, stopping to walk the Sounds of Silence Trail featuring native petroglyphs. Next, I descend to the Split Mountain parking area next to the river to walk the Desert Voices Trail. The trailhead offers a view of the entrance to Split Mountain Canyon, where the river appears to split the 1,000-foot-high rock. The geological feature develops from the uplift occurring at nearly the same rate as the water channel's erosion. Dinosaur National Monument offers more than one of the world's best Jurassic fossil records. It's a geological wonderland through 150 million years of uplift and erosion.

After hiking at Split Mountain, I return to the visitor center overcome with drowsiness. I've never experienced such a sudden wave of fatigue. It's only 3:00 p.m., so I lie down across a couple of chairs in the park's empty theater and close my eyes for thirty minutes, hoping the feeling passes. The burger's hitting my body like a wrecking ball. Miraculously, it works. I feel better, ready for the five-hour drive over the Rocky Mountains to Denver. The drive's long and tiring with a dash of excitement added. Shortly after turning east on State Highway 64, about twenty miles from Dinosaur, I pass a series of racing cars going west. They look like Porches but could be Ferraris or something else. They're going fast enough the other way around successive curves as to be a blur. It's clear these are very pricey foreign performance cars. Each car's covered in sponsor decals and advertisements, with a large number on the door. I'm shocked to see competitive race cars apparently running on an open public highway. I'm still puzzling over it ten minutes later when I pass another race car off the roadway to the right, facing in the opposite direction of the other racers. A van is parked on the elevated roadside about fifteen feet higher than the thickly weeded marsh where the car sits. I find the scene comical. A guy in a racing suit, presumably the driver, and a couple of other guys, apparently from the van, stand around this very expensive racing car in the mud. It's going to take them a while to get a wrecker out here to the middle of nowhere to extract that car out of the muck.

The rest of my two-hour drive on the two-lane roads to the town of Rifle, where I pick up Interstate 70 East, is my own race trying to pass slow-moving, rock-hauling trucks. I'm spent when I reach Rifle but still have three hours through the mountains and into Denver. Tonight's drive through rain and poor visibility stresses me further when the temperature drops below freezing in the mountains. As the rain turns to snow, I'm doubtful I've got the endurance to handle a treacherous road surface. I manage to clear Denver, completely shot mentally and physically.

Thursday begins traveling south on I-29 through Colorado Springs. Construction and traffic slow the pace. At Pueblo, I go east on US 50 to La Junta. My first stop in town is the Comanche National Grassland Visitor Center for a Santa Fe Trail stamp. Next, I stop at the Amtrak station, hunting a passport stamp for the

Trails and Rails partnership, an NPS-affiliated program based on major historical train routes. The La Junta Amtrak station stamp is a Santa Fe Trail passport stamp for Amtrak's Southwest Chief, running daily service between Chicago and Los Angeles. After calling a contact for the local rail ranger club, the keepers of the stamp, the Amtrak agent and I find the stamp in a storage room next to the ticket counter. From La Junta, today's first park stop is eight miles to the east.

Bent's Old Fort National Historic Site features the reconstructed frontier fort built by William and Charles Bent in 1833. Located on the Arkansas River and the original Mountain Route of the Santa Fe Trail, the fort's the only significant settlement on the route between Missouri and New Mexico. The fort lay abandoned in 1849 as the railroad took over commercial transportation.

I continue to another Santa Fe Trail location, Boggsville State Historic Site. One of the first nonmilitary settlements in southeastern Colorado started here in the 1860s. The site retains the ambiance of a remote location, largely because it still is. The place is deserted today.

Sand Creek Massacre National Historic Site is seventy-five miles northwest of La Junta. The park acknowledges a disgraceful and sad event in American history. US Army soldiers, led by Colonel John Chivington, slaughtered men, women, and children inhabiting a peaceful village of plains tribespeople camped along the Big Sandy Creek in southeastern Colorado on November 29, 1864. About two hundred of the seven hundred Cheyenne and Arapaho in the village are killed, and many defenseless women, children, and elderly are killed and mutilated with some soldiers taking body parts as trophies. The army's actions at Sand Creek ended hope of an early peace between settlers and Native Americans, preceding decades of hostility.

Today's my second visit to Sand Creek Massacre. The rangers are holding a pair of the park's lapel pins for the exhibits, ensuring the unit is represented. I cross the vast expanse of eastern Colorado and western Kansas for another four and a half hours to Salina before stopping for the night.

Friday morning starts in Lawrence, Kansas, at the **Freedom's Frontier National Heritage Area** headquarters. The heritage area recently acquired their first passport stamp. Hardly a soul can be found in the building when I arrive at 9:30 a.m., but I eventually find someone in the empty offices who guesses correctly at the stamp's storage place. Freedom's Frontier National Heritage Area tells the story of Bleeding Kansas, or Bloody Kansas, the 1850s frontier battle over Kansas's status as a free or slave state based on popular sovereignty, and the Civil War engagements across eastern Kansas and western Missouri. From Lawrence, I have a few trail related stops in the greater Kansas City area to make today before visiting the last park of the week.

Harry S Truman National Historic Site includes Harry and Bess Truman's home in Independence, Missouri, and the Truman farm south of town where the thirty-third president of the United States worked as a young boy. The Truman home remains as it appeared in 1972 at Harry's death. Bess lived in the house until 1979 but meticulously kept her husband's things as they'd been during his life and at his passing. Visitors today see his hat on the rack as he hung it upon returning home from his library office. In a pre-arranged scenario like that of the Eisenhower's Gettysburg home, the Truman house transferred to the National Park Service after her death in 1982. The Truman's down-to-earth midwestern nature shines through in viewing the simple place they called home. The Harry S Truman Presidential Library, a mile away, compliments the historic site.

From Independence, a two-and-a-half-hour drive across north central Missouri brings me to the trip's final stop. The town of La Plata, Missouri, serves as home for a group of railroad enthusiasts who call themselves the APRHF Rail Rangers. A major commercial rail link between Chicago and the southwestern United States passes through the rural town. It's also a stop for the Amtrak's L.A.– Chicago Southwest Chief. Both passenger and freight trains pass through La Plata, the freighters blowing through town near top speed several times each hour. It's a great place to watch trains up close. The rail rangers even have a viewing platform built next to the tracks outside of town. I'm after a couple of trails and rails stamps at the station and hope to catch the station manager as he opens an hour before the daily LA-bound Southwest Chief arrives at 8:00 p.m.

I'm nearing town almost two hours early when I discover the route into town from the west is closed for bridge repair. Since the all-highway detour forms a thirty-mile loop, I shorten the distance on local mud and gravel roads. On today's tour through the Missouri wilderness, I learn that, like most other midwestern states, Missouri has an Amish country. I pass countless horse and buggy setups. Friday evenings appear to be socially active in the Amish community. After about fifteen miles of mud and gravel, my gray Chevy Malibu looks two-toned like a paneled station wagon with the bottom half spattered in solid brown. I snap a photo of the car and post it to social media with the following explanation:

> *Just rolled over 4,000 miles on my current trip through Nebraska, crisscrossing Colorado into Utah and back through Kansas via Pueblo. Now I couldn't get to St. Louis by driving I-70 but had to go through the north part of the state into Amish country (who knew Missouri has an Amish country?) where it would appear they aren't fond of strangers and some of the holes in the road are big enough for the car. Why did I torture myself thus? A) because I'm an idiot B) to get more Passport stamps C) both A and B are correct.*

The station manager doesn't show up until 7:30 p.m. and is consumed checking in boarding passengers and completing his daily southbound paperwork. During my wait, I stand on the station's platform as a speeding freight train passes. The train shakes the platform as it subtly rocks side to side and bounces over connecting joints in the track, pushing a sustained blast of wind over and around me. The sense of power from a train moving at 60 mph only ten feet away is overwhelming. When the Amtrak arrives at 8:00 p.m. sharp, I watch the conductor step off and check for incoming passengers before giving the okay for a hoard of smokers to come outside and smoke furiously at one end of the platform before herding everyone back onboard, all in under ten minutes. It's quite impressive, both the whirl of the conductor and the power smoking event. One guy inhales a cigarette in about four massive puffs. As the conductor sweeps the last of the smokers on board and bids adieu to the station manager, he leans out the door as the train pulls away, nods at me, and says, "I'm a White Sox fan, not a Cubs fan, but I still don't like your hat." Smiling and tipping my pin-laden Cardinals hat, I shout back, "Have a safe trip!" in a scene a century removed. He smiles and waves, pulling himself inside as the train shrinks into the distance.

17 *New York City*

THE TIMING FOR my centennial trip to New York City must meet two requirements. First, it must be a weekend from Memorial Day through Labor Day, since the only NPS unit I've yet to see in the NYC metro area is only open on these weekends. Second, it needs to coincide with a Yankees home game, as the new Yankee Stadium is one of only two active MLB stadiums where I've not seen a game. Memorial Day weekend meets both criteria. The Yankees host the Toronto Blue Jays on Thursday afternoon and Governors Island opens for the season on Saturday.

Thursday, I depart on a 7:00 a.m. flight from Chicago O'Hare to LaGuardia, landing at 10:00 a.m. NYC's weekend forecast predicts sun and unseasonable heat, with highs in the nineties through Sunday. After a cab ride to my Allen Street hotel, the extended weekend begins with a fifteen-minute walk to **African Burial Grounds National Monument** in lower Manhattan. Proclaimed in February 2006, the monument developed after workers excavating ground for the new federal office building in the 200 block of Broadway discovered human remains. The location, on the outskirts of town during its century of use (1690s to 1790s), functioned as an African American cemetery. Following the initial 1991 discovery, workers excavated 419 sets of remains over two years.

The monument encompasses the reinternment location adjacent to the Ted Weiss Federal Building and serves to honor and memorialize the deceased buried here.

The first-floor visitor center in the federal building requires full security screening. Retrieving my backpack, I greet the ranger at the desk inside the gift shop. "I'm excited to be here. I'll get to see my last NPS unit in the metro area this weekend!" He informs me, "We're not supposed to tell the public, but there's gonna be a new Manhattan unit declared next month." I had read a story leaked to the press that **Stonewall National Monument** will be created sometime in June, coinciding with the Stonewall protest anniversary. We'll stop at the new park location after today's game.

After grabbing a quick lunch and checking in, I ride the subway north to Yankee Stadium for the 4:05 game. I buy a ticket in the stadium's second deck, entering after the gates open to explore. Yankee Stadium's museum chronicles franchise history, the most celebrated in baseball, with twenty-seven World Series titles and nearly fifty appearances in the Fall Classic. It's loaded with memorabilia, including several of the Highlanders' Commissioner's Trophies.

I've had many delightful experiences conversing with fans around the country. This afternoon, I sit among several older Yankee fans who share their experiences and passion for the game. We all relate to the perpetual blend of frustration and joy in baseball. The game concludes, a 3-1 Blue Jays' victory, and I join the crowded southbound subway, headed to the center of Greenwich Village.

Stonewall National Monument features the facade of the Stonewall Inn and the small triangular park across the street known as Christopher Park. The Stonewall Inn and surrounding area has been called the birthplace of the gay rights movement. Repeated raids by the NYPD on gay establishments culminated in an attempted raid of the Stonewall Inn on June 28, 1969. The resultant clashes with police and six days of protests generated nationwide attention, launching the LGBT rights movement. Though the park won't be officially proclaimed for a month, I want to learn as much of the history as possible. After reading plaques in Christopher Park detailing the events of 1969, I enter the Stonewall Inn and order a beer. The bar's wooden interior, high top tables and cheap cushioned stools appear exactly as I would expect of any neighborhood bar except for the history preserved in newspaper articles and large photographic prints on the walls.

After finishing my beer, I walk to the subway to return to my SoHo hotel, shortened from South of Houston Street. I find a small neighborhood bar down the street that serves cold beer and hot food. The bar facade is open air, blending the patron's noise with the sounds of the street. I settle in at a small table for a relaxing meal and reflect that tonight's the last time my legs, ankles, and feet will feel normal during the trip. I walked myself to exhaustion during my first NYC park trip, and I'm about to repeat the experience at a faster pace going solo. Poor Kareen felt battered by the end of our week in the city two years ago. She smartly and happily conceded this trip to me alone.

To collect the exhibit pins, I booked a return to the **Statue of Liberty National Monument** and the Ellis Island Immigration Museum on the first boat Friday. From NPTC member reports, I know both the Statue of Liberty and Ellis Island have a centennial stamper and suspect each has the lapel pin set as well. The only way I'm collecting both is in person. Not that it's a hardship. Kareen and I enjoyed our first visit here in April 2014.

Manhattan boats to the statue depart from another NPS unit, **Castle Clinton National Monument**. The "castle" is a round, sandstone battery erected from 1808 to 1811 as one of five key War of 1812 defensive positions in New York Harbor. Though the castle never fired a shot in anger, the southern tip of Manhattan is still known as "the battery." After military use ceased in 1822, the structure functioned as a public venue and aquarium and preceded Ellis Island as the city's immigration station from 1855 to 1892.

This morning, I take pictures of the statue from the ferry in route to Liberty Island. The copper-skinned sculpture by Auguste Bartholdi, dedicated in 1886, is 151 feet tall from pedestal to torch but towers 305 feet above ground level. After securing the pins, I set out on a walk around the statue as the day warms. The morning sunlight illuminates Manhattan's iconic skyline. High-rises glisten as their glass reflects the light. I rejoin the ferry for the short trip to Ellis Island, where I repeat the same activities. There are two sets of lapel pins as suspected, one set with "Statue of Liberty" and another with "Ellis Island" on the bottom. I walk around the island's Immigration Museum on the same ground that 12 million immigrants trod from 1892 until 1954.

After a ten-minute walk from the battery, I enter **Federal Hall National Memorial**. Federal Hall sits on Wall Street next to the New York Stock Exchange and, the centerpiece of the fronting pedestrian mall, its famous bull sculpture. A few minutes of observation leads to the conclusion most tourists at the junction of Wall and Broad streets fall into two classes: those who grab the anatomically correct bull's testicles, and those who are tempted to do so. Who doesn't want to brag that they had the bull by the balls? The author would never do such a thing despite any photographic evidence to the contrary.

Federal Hall served as the first capitol of the United States. George Washington took the oath of office as the first president of the United States on its balcony. Walking through the building today, it's hard to fathom how Congress, even a much smaller one, could have conducted its business inside the building before the temporary capitol moved to Philadelphia in 1791. Federal Hall witnessed the establishment of precedents for newly created offices and governing bodies under the Constitution, and the addition of the first ten amendments, the Bill of Rights. The building is the design of architect Pierre L'Enfant, who would have an even more ambitious project awaiting him in the coming decade designing the country's new capital city on the banks of the Potomac River. Federal Hall offers a sense of the profound. Looking up at the second-floor balcony, I imagine straining to hear a reserved and nervous George Washington utter his barely audible words on April 30, 1789. A large statue of Washington stands in front of the building below that same balcony.

From Federal Hall, I take the subway on a forty-five-minute trip north, past Olmsted's Central Park, to the banks of the Hudson River at West 122nd Street and the **General Grant National Memorial**, better known as Grant's Tomb. The eighteenth president of the United States and Union army leader lies entombed here with his beloved wife, Julia. Following the Civil War, the nation needed a leader who could stand above the animosity of divisive sectional politics that continued to plague the country. Grant unfortunately lacked the political skill and sense of his wartime chief, Abraham Lincoln, and fell victim to men less honest than himself. But history is kinder to Ulysses Grant on reflection, despite his shortcomings. He proves the most enlightened president of the postwar nineteenth century. His aspirations for civil rights in America shine with the nobility fitting his exceptional character. He stands on his record as a good, honest man truly ahead of his time. After adding the General Grant National Memorial pins to the collection, I walk around the memorial's interior, taking pictures of the famous mausoleum from the stone-tiled patio in front of the structure before continuing my day with a one-and-a-half-mile walk to the next destination honoring my personal favorite among the founding fathers.

Hamilton Grange National Memorial is the home of the first secretary of the treasury for the United States, Alexander Hamilton. It is the only home he ever owned. I knew little about Hamilton until I read Ron Chernow's book, mentioned in chapter 8. At Hamilton Grange, I join another tour of the historic home. The preservation of Hamilton's beloved Grange is an interesting story. The current house location is its third. When Hamilton built the house from 1800 to 1802, he took great pains in the design of his country estate, then six miles north of the city. As New York and the surrounding Harlem neighborhood grew around the home, it had to be relocated twice to save the structure. The first move, in 1889, sandwiched the home between an apartment house and a church. It had to be moved in 2008 a second time to its current location by the park service. A film reviewing the project is shown to visitors in a rear first floor room. I enjoy my second tour through the Grange, though I'm disappointed to find the gift shop built into the ground floor is out of the unit's centennial lapel pins. After walking a modest three and a half miles on Thursday, today I trek eight miles toting my hefty pack in the unseasonable heat. I look like someone sprayed me with a hose. After walking back to the subway, I return on a southbound train to the lower east side of Manhattan. I've got one stop left today.

The **Lower East Side Tenement National Historic Site** is an NPS-affiliated site. Kareen and I joined one of the several tours that take visitors through reconstructed tenements in Manhattan's lower east side. Tours follow the story of one of the families struggling amid the crushing poverty and deplorable conditions in New York City's infamous tenements. Many of these first-generation immigrant families faced daily challenges to their survival.

I consider taking the subway to another park unit I've left off the itinerary. The **Theodore Roosevelt Birthplace National Historic Site** on East Twentieth Street in lower Manhattan remains closed for renovations. The timing of its reopening seems to be a mystery among Manhattan rangers. Kareen and I toured the home two years ago. Exhibits include the shirt Teddy wore during an attempted assassination in Milwaukee after he returned to politics for the 1912 presidential campaign. The bullet might have been fatal if not slowed by his eyeglass case and the thick manuscript of his speech. Both items are on exhibit. Roosevelt added another remarkable aspect to that event by refusing medical care and insisting to continue with his speech. He stood delivering his address for about two hours after being shot. Roosevelt's level of determination and disregard for his own convenience and comfort had already achieved legendary status. Since the site's closed to the public, I skip it. Later in the year, I will regret not returning, even if just for a picture from the street. If Teddy could give a two-hour speech after being shot, I certainly could have mustered the energy to walk to his birthplace. On Memorial Day weekend, I have no idea I'll visit nearly four hundred parks by year's end.

As Saturday dawns, I'm anxious with excitement. The first stop today, **Governors Island National Monument**, is my 357th NPS unit visited. In 2014, I tried unsuccessfully to find a way to the island on my own. I ceased trying before checking into options like water taxis. I preferred to see it when the park's visitor services are open anyway. The monument opens for the season today, and I'm on the first ferry. Two of New York Harbor's earliest defensive fortifications, Fort Jay and Castle Williams, are located here. Castle Williams, constructed simultaneously with Castle Clinton, also has a circular design though much larger. I join a ranger-led tour of Castle Williams' interior. The fort, converted to a prison before the Civil War, held Confederate POWs. As with Castle Clinton, no foreign power ever tested Castle Williams or Fort Jay. Both structures are part of the country's initial system of coastal defenses conceived and initiated in the 1790s. Castle Williams is named after Colonel Jonathon Williams, who designed and constructed New York Harbor's defenses in the first decade of the nineteenth century. The harbor defenses did serve a military end. The strength of these installations is one of the reasons the British chose not to attack New York City during the War of 1812. The island's facilities also became a staging ground for soldiers preparing for combat overseas as recently as the 1944 Allied invasion of Normandy. The island served as an army headquarters post for over two hundred years. The post closed in 1996, and the island became an NPS unit in 2001. As I stand beside Castle Williams, army helicopters circle the island. They appear to have left from the island's airstrip and circle overhead for about ten minutes as I stroll to the island's oldest defensive structure. I walk into Fort Jay, built in 1794, through its sandstone entrance gate over a dry moat. A collection of brick buildings sit within the perimeter.

Returning to Manhattan, the next destination is the Brooklyn Bridge. I visited the famous bridge two years ago, but that was prior to reading David McCullough's book, *The Great Bridge*. I cross the bridge again, studying details in its appearance and design and imagining the workers in the caissons sunk and filled with compressed air to build the two anchor towers. Those who got sick with the bends, not yet understood in the 1870s, included the chief engineer, Washington Roebling, son of the bridge's designer, John Augustus Roebling. Roebling's landmark use of wire rope originally replaced hemp ropes used for the Allegheny Portage Railroad, an NPS unit we'll visit later this year. The strength of wire rope wrapped in bundles revolutionized design possibilities, strength, and capacity for suspension bridges.

From the bridge, I travel north on the subway to Yankee Stadium. There, I take a cab to the northernmost Manhattan NPS unit, **Saint Paul's Church National Historic Site.** Today's visit is a blunder. I had enough time to visit the church yesterday, but tired from walking in the heat, I opted to wait until today, forgetting the site's only open on weekdays. I realize my mistake as the cab pulls away.

The church dates to 1763 and served as a hospital after the island's 1776 Revolutionary War battles. Kareen and I took the #5 subway line to its northern terminus, then walked a mile to tour the church in 2014. I retrace those steps back to the subway to find the #5 line out of service this weekend. Taking the alternative forty-five-minute bus ride to reconnect with the subway, I discover the second seven-day transit pass I've purchased since arriving has stopped working. The first seven-day pass worked for about twenty-four hours. I had to purchase a second one to keep moving. I've been careful throughout to keep the pass isolated in a dedicated pocket, away from anything magnetic. Fortunately, this commute is the trip's last on mass transit. I'm able to slip through a gate to make the final subway ride south.

Returning to SoHo, I shower, eat a sandwich, and sit down to catch my breath. I decide to walk the mile and a half to the last Manhattan destination, the 9/11 Memorial. The underground museum opened in May 2014. We walked the surface Memorial two years ago, pausing in somber reflection at the fountains built on the footprints of the World Trade Center's North and South Towers. This evening, I watch one of several films offered in the theater, followed by the museum exhibits, an impressive and moving experience. I recall watching the buildings collapse on 9/11 in shock and horror. The bent and split I-beams included in the exhibits testify to the enormous force generated after the buildings' infrastructure failed. From the memorial, I meander back to the hotel, totaling fourteen walking miles in the concrete jungle. I'm exhausted. After tomorrow, the weekend's walking will top thirty miles.

Sunday morning, I check out of the hotel early and catch a cab to the National rental car location across from LaGuardia. I'm renting a car because it's the most convenient way to see the three Long Island parks before my 7:00 p.m. flight back to Chicago. The first of those parks is **Sagamore Hill National Historic Site.** Sagamore Hill is Theodore Roosevelt's 1884 country home on the northern shore of central Long Island near the town of Oyster Bay. Doubling as his presidential summer retreat, he lived at the estate until his death in 1919. The home had been closed for renovation during our last visit. Today, I arrive at the visitor center about 8:45 a.m., and the line to sign up for a house tour already stretches into the parking lot. I bypass the line to enter, ignoring dirty looks from people who don't comprehend or care that I'm entering to get lapel pins and passport cancellations. After these tasks, I walk around the grounds for some pictures, visiting the Museum at the Old Orchard, a short walk away.

My next destination is a home tour at the William Floyd Estate, part of **Fire Island National Seashore.** Fire Island includes most of the thirty-two-mile barrier island off Long Island's southern coast. The diverse park has multiple locations, ranging from historical sites to sandy beach areas. William Floyd signed the Declaration of Independence and supported the patriot cause in a place and time when both distinctions brought peril. The Mastic Beach, New York, estate is near the seashore's east end. The family home, the Old Mastic House, dates its earliest construction to 1724, when William's father Nicoll first constructed a two-story, six-room wood frame house on the site. William inherited the home in 1755 at the age of twenty and significantly expanded the house after he returned following the Revolutionary War. He entertained distinguished houseguests, including Thomas Jefferson and James Madison. The estate remained in the Floyd Family over 250 years, ending when the family gave the house, its contents, and 613 acres of land to the National Park Service in 1976.

The Floyd home tour and the Fire Island Wilderness Visitor Center on the beach a short distance away comprise today's seashore stop. On our first visit to the park, Kareen and I enjoyed exploring the famous Fire Island Lighthouse. I hope to see more of the park on a future trip.

The trip's final park destination is **Gateway National Recreation Area**, consisting of three major areas, each with multiple destinations covering a diverse range of locations and topics. The major areas of the recreation area are Jamaica Bay, Staten Island, and Sandy Hook, New Jersey. We'll visit the Staten Island and Sandy Hook areas in Gateway National Recreation Area later this year. Today I'm stopping in the Jamaica Bay unit, specifically at Floyd Bennett Field, which served as NYC's first municipal airport beginning in 1931. After visiting the terminal at the airfield, now the park visitor center, I make a side trip to a small gift shop in a temporary structure a few miles away to buy Gateway's centennial and Find Your Park lapel pins.

Although a short distance, the heavy traffic through Brooklyn and Queens results in a forty-five-minute drive to LaGuardia. Returning the rental refueled, I don't bother to look at the receipt, failing to notice the charge for a half tank of gas. National refunds the refueling charge when I call to complain, but the oversight offers a clue that I'm not personally running on full. I'm tired and need a rest. I'm not going to get it.

18 *The Breaking Point*

As the year of park immersion therapy progresses, my perception and views evolve. Seeing expansive land development throughout the country speaks to a population explosion. Open cornfields and undeveloped pasture land two decades ago now hold subdivisions. Man's footprint is growing at a prodigious pace. I've always accepted the concept of limited resources, but like most, never gave it much thought. Most people practice denial on topics like overpopulation and environmental damage. I know. I used to be one of them. I've heard religious people wave their hands and say, "God will take care of it. I have faith." Maybe so, but I would like to believe we have brains for a reason. Environmental stewardship has moved from an abstract concept to a pressing concern. In some places, the parks represent the last green space. How many animal species will we wipe from the face of the earth before we start to ask, "How many people can this planet hold?"

Some people argue that science and progress, in the form of crop yields and other advances, make our planet boundless. Yet, the scientist within me cannot help but see this orbiting rock we call home as a finite mass. And all the resources our planet provides are finite as well. The unlimited meadows and woodlands that Lewis and Clark explored and the Native Americans deemed sacred have vanished under plow and bulldozer. Is man destined to be the instrument of his own destruction?

Since my encounter with North America's big cat at Great Basin, I fear I may be among the last generations to see this beautiful animal in the wild. I feel a sense of debt. I owe the cougar and all the wild creatures that share our home this opportunity to plead their case. They are running out of space and time. Can we confine them all within park boundaries like animals in a zoo? I don't think so, not without losing many of them and destroying our ecosystem. If the cat spared me, am I not obligated to return the favor to the utmost of my ability? We owe the life that shares our precious planet more than a nonchalant wave of the hand.

The last vestige for many of these wild animals, our federal park lands, are also at risk. The National Park Service will welcome 331 million visitors in 2016 and again in 2017, a 20 percent increase from ten years ago after little change between 1996 and 2006. Meanwhile, we haven't funded a major park infrastructure project since the Mission 66 program over fifty years ago. A considerable amount of park infrastructure dates to the CCC and the 1930s. Annual visitation system-wide has roughly tripled since the conclusion of Mission 66. Many units let established ranger positions go unfilled to finance critical repairs essential to keep the parks open. We trample and take from these priceless places that offer us so much. Perhaps it's time we gave something back.

The parks aren't the only thing threatened as the year nears its midpoint. My return home to Chicago begins a weeklong nightmare. I've departed for all my flights commuting to O'Hare from our Chicago condominium. I return on Memorial Day weekend knowing that Kareen's upset again by some nasty work episode. Kareen is both committed to the status quo and angry about its problems, leaving her in perpetual conflict. Since we've been married, she's vented to me about all manner of observed bad behavior. Unrelenting long hours compound her stress. I can see her unraveling after more than a dozen years working with fewer days off than someone who works full time with no vacation.

We've settled into a damaging pattern. She vents at me rather than to me about nasty work situations. The result is some quasi-lecture in sharp, harsh tones that grows more aggressive as the one-sided conversation continues. It begins as a story. After a few minutes, the account moves from third person to second person, as in "you." I hear a barrage of "you did this" or "you did that" as we seamlessly shift from a story to role play with me cast as the villain. These episodes usually play out over several days, several times each day, until the rage subsides. It's like a psychological volcanic eruption. I've tried every possible reaction. I have tried being quiet, supportive, and agreeable, to which Kareen claims I don't care. When she insists that I provide some suggestion or active input, she rejects my comments, often repeating the same observation later in the conversation. When I've explained the pain of being berated for something I didn't do, she claims I'm oversensitive. She sees protestations as silly because she feels a lot better after yelling at me. Presumably, I should feel better, too. To this, I explain that it isn't sustainable if one person is verbally bludgeoned for the temporary mental health of another. After going through this cycle countless times in the past two years, I've reached the end of my mental capacity to absorb anger for actions and events in which I played no part. I've hidden in the parks from my own negative work situation, but my phone delivers vitriol several times a day. I'm under siege. The angry phone calls have a cumulative effect, like mental poison. It's impossible to maintain a good relationship when our primary communication revolves around work hostility. Kareen's a good person, but she struggles to see other perspectives. This coping mechanism is unsustainable.

When this year's heavy travel became reality, it increased our time apart, but not as it would for a couple who lives together. Since it's out of my control and my pleas for change stand rejected, I'm resigned to let Kareen come to an understanding of her toxic work environment on her own terms. The life plan of literally working to death is one I reject. I marvel at the efficiency of the thing. You collapse in the hospital, they pick you up, place you on a gurney, and wheel you down to the morgue. Then your practice "partners" fight among themselves for your patients, thrilled with the windfall.

This is our state of being when I arrive home from NYC on Sunday night. I arrive at the condo, greeted by another terrible work story. She's already yelled at me about this issue several times over the phone. I can't absorb the anger any longer, so I've started hanging up when the tirade tears into me. Refusing to be yelled at makes the situation worse and shifts her anger squarely at me. With Kareen yelling over my shoulder, I pick up my bag, turn around and leave the condo, driving to my Winnebago County home. The phone stays off until the next morning. When I turn it back on, a series of texts spanning melancholy to anger flashes on the screen. I turn the phone back off. I'm attending a three-game series at Miller Park between the Cardinals and Brewers, hoping the games will be a temporary distraction from a world unrecognizable, unacceptable, and incomprehensible.

The one safe place through it all is the parks. In the parks, animosity falls away. People are essentially good and happy to help others. Motivation comes from things other than money, and nearly all of them are more important. I am now the frightened animal fleeing to safety in the wild. I have no refuge in the human world.

The games in Milwaukee pass in a haze. Kareen exhausts herself attacking me by Wednesday and realizes it's not having the therapeutic benefit she expected. I just want peace without being berated. By Wednesday night, I agree to speak with her if she promises not to yell at me. We agree to a fragile armistice. Kareen resolves not to talk to me about work, since, according to her, I perceive her comments incorrectly. For me, I don't have the energy to sustain my protestations of innocence. It's a waste of time. I'm asking only for the time to complete the park projects I've started and not live under a fundamentally unfair construct. The societal model seems to be: Work throughout your functional life until you can work no longer and when your health is gone, your body broken, you retire and wait to die. This model lacks appeal for obvious reasons. The fortunate among us blend vocation and passion, altering the supposition. I had a long run among the fortunate. When any sense of accomplishment, respect, and growth vanished at my workplace, I climbed out of the pit and left the venomous snakes behind. Kareen's paralyzed by change and keeps getting bitten, biting me in turn. At some point, one either evolves or dies from the bites. That's the choice.

After a melancholy Thursday, a respite comes from a trip to South Central Missouri to meet up with Lee. Tomorrow, we'll drive into Missouri's Ozarks to **Ozark National Scenic Riverways**. We booked rooms in the same motel off I-44 in Cuba, Missouri. I arrive Thursday evening to find Lee hanging out in his room with the door wide open, his car parked in front. We share stories of our centennial travels. Between us, that includes over four hundred NPS units year to date.

Early Friday, we're driving south to the 134 miles of southeastern Missouri's Current and Jacks Fork rivers within the park. The rivers form a giant, crooked Y, with the open end facing west. The Current River forms the main diagonal, running 105 miles from northwest to southeast. The Jacks Fork River park boundary runs for almost thirty miles of its length before its confluence with the Current River at mile marker 55.

We start our adventure following one another south on Missouri Highway 19 through a twisting, hilly blend of wooded forest and cleared farmland. We reach our first destination at Pulltite, a Current River park stop with a cabin, camping area, and visitor contact station. We find a ranger in the station and get the site stamp. After our conversation, we both regain our vehicles and drive eight miles to Round Spring where I purchase the unit's lapel pins for the exhibit.

From Round Spring, we continue south to the town of Eminence, turning right to drive four miles to the remnants of the late-nineteenth-century community Alley Spring. The main attraction is Alley Mill, built in 1894 using hydraulic power from the river currents and still containing much of its original equipment. On this early June morning, cool temperatures following rain and high humidity leave a fog over the water's surface around the mill built over a race off the Jacks Fork River. Cloaked in haze rising several feet above the surface, the mill and surrounding water present a surreal setting in the mist. I take multiple pictures, hoping to capture the scene's magic in at least one or two of these shots. From Alley Mill, Lee and I split up. We have two park areas with stamps to cover today. I want to continue downstream and visit the headquarters in Van Buren and from there stop at Big Spring. Lee visited both locations earlier this year and wants to return upstream to Akers Landing, the site of another Current River visitor contact station.

Ozark, Alley Mill

I cannot remember any of these specific locations from multiple childhood visits. It feels like my first time in the park. I walk the short trail from the parking area over to Big Spring, flowing at a high rate today due to the recent rains. I also stop at the CCC Historic District, an old hotel and cabins built in the 1930s. None of the areas reveal signs of life. The park road spans a scenic river section via an old bridge. I walk the road and river trail to take pictures of the sleepy river and overhanging foliage under the blanket of fog in this serene, soul-soothing atmosphere. It's a memorable and gratifying visit to Ozark National Scenic Riverways.

The weekend brings two more baseball games in St. Louis against the San Francisco Giants. It's a chance to relax and recalibrate before the complete novelty of the next trip to Alaska. Kareen and I slowly begin functioning together again. We need an understanding more than a healing. The resolution we reach in the early days of June extracts vocational hostility from our marriage. Our breaking point becomes a turning point.

19 *Alaska*

ONE OF THE most anticipated trips of the year kicks off June 6 with a United flight from O'Hare to Anchorage. The next eleven days will be spread among eight Alaskan parks and America's last vast wilderness. Travel to over three hundred parks in the past two years leaves me confident tackling itineraries to almost anywhere in America. Alaska is the exception. The remoteness of Alaskan parklands among the state's twenty-four NPS units makes for special challenges. Only four are accessible from the Alaskan road system. The others require flying from Anchorage, Fairbanks, or Juneau and/or catching subsequent charter flights. Alaskan charter air providers and backcountry guides vary widely in service and reliability. I've heard horror stories. One traveler shared that his group arrived for their charter trip six months after the booking and discovered the pilot too hungover to fly. Given air service variability, I'm hesitant to make charter reservations without referrals. Months earlier, I hoped for guidance from more experienced Alaskan travelers. Instead, I'm on my own. I build the itinerary around Alaska's road system.

After landing Monday at 7:30 p.m., I check into my downtown hotel and enjoy a delicious fresh salmon meal down the street. I have no problem resting or sleeping in daylight. Conversely, the infamous midnight sun proves a great travel convenience in the days to come.

Tuesday morning, I enter the National Park Service building lobby in Anchorage, where the first person I see asks, "Are you here for the bear conference?"

I smile. "Good morning. No. And you?"

"No," he says, cocking his head at me, as it's obvious I don't work here.

I see a whiteboard on an easel with instructions for bear experts attending the international conference. I wait until he disappears in the elevator to make my escape. I'm not even sure what I'm doing here. Since my daily attire includes the pin-adorned hat and a centennial T-shirt from my growing collection, other visitors and even rangers often ask if I work for the National Park Service. Kareen has quipped, "You could be their spokesman." The visitor services helpful to my true role as an Alaskan newbie are a few blocks away at the Alaska Public Lands Information Center in the Old Federal Building. I ask the staff questions on specific parks and collect a few missing park brochures.

Next up is the BLM Anchorage Field Office. They have a stamp for the **Iditarod National Historic Trail**. The BLM administers the trail's 2,350 miles from Seward to Nome along multiple routes. The Anchorage to Nome segment is famous for the February dogsled race contested annually since 1973. The race among over fifty teams alternates between a northern and southern route of 975 and 998 miles, respectively. Last year, the race started in Fairbanks due to insufficient snow farther south. I enjoyed reading about the Iditarod in Gary Paulsen's *Winterdance: The Fine Madness of Running the Iditarod*. Participant experiences make captivating reading. Winners finish in under ten days. It's cool to see part of the trail.

From the BLM, Alaska Highway 3 takes me north toward Fairbanks. The Alaskan highway system has several primary numbered highways, most of them connecting Anchorage to other towns. Nearly all the highways and significant roads are better known by their given names. Highway 3 is the George Parks Highway. Those renting cars from major national chains must pay attention as their rental contracts ban over a dozen named roads across the state.

The 230-mile drive north on the George Parks Highway from Anchorage to **Denali National Park & Preserve** takes four hours. My first park-related stop is a side trip to Talkeetna Ranger Station. The small town is a popular tour group stop, and several buses are parked near the village center as I navigate among the throngs of tourists spilling onto the streets. At the ranger station, two rangers offer several planning suggestions and congratulate me on making it to 181 NPS units thus far this year. I leave with a wave and say, "Thanks! Happy centennial year!"

Returning to the George Parks Highway via the fourteen-mile Talkeetna spur road, I continue north, arriving at the park about 3:30 p.m., enough time to get my bearings and secure a reservation on a park shuttle bus tomorrow. Personal vehicle traffic is limited to the first fifteen miles of Denali's ninety-two-mile park road. The narrow gravel road can't handle unregulated traffic into the interior.

Visitors not staying overnight often do the roundtrip to Eielson Visitor Center at mile marker sixty-six. Everyone who visits the park hopes to see a clear view of Denali. Early Alaskan adventurers christened the park's namesake peak Mt. McKinley, though William McKinley never came near here.

Denali is the tallest North American peak and the second-highest peak in the western hemisphere to Argentina's Aconcagua in the Andes Mountain chain that forms South America's spine along the Argentina-Chile border. I had the good fortune to see Aconcagua from the southern side of the mountain via the main highway connecting the two countries when my good friend and longtime business colleague Nestor drove me to the Andes in March 2010. After walking a mile or two up the valley trail toward the southern base camp, we returned to his car and climbed the old road to the original mountain pass. A long series of switchbacks on a dirt and gravel road lead up to a border crossing at four thousand meters. A ferocious wind poured through the pass, so violent it made it difficult to stand upright or open a car door. The two countries' flags flapped atop adjacent poles with a loud *crack, crack, crack,* leaving them shredded. After a very stressful period at work, Nestor asked me to visit him in Buenos Aires out of concern for my health. He had me stay at his home office for a week of peace and quiet. He ascertained I needed a break. We combined a customer visit with our drive into the Andes to see the magnificent mountain and historical pass.

A clear view of Denali is more challenging than Aconcagua because clouds obscure the summit on 70 to 80 percent of the days during the summer tourist season. Various references available in the park quote slightly different odds the visitor will see Denali's 20,230-foot peak. I get a reservation for the 7:00 a.m. bus out to Eielson so I can enjoy the views during the ride and return to the main visitor facilities before they close. It takes a full day to travel out to Eielson and back. On this first day I make it to Denali Visitor Center and the Wilderness Access Center (WAC), where the park's shuttle buses originate. From the WAC, I drive fifteen miles to Savage River to hike the full length of the Savage River Loop Trail, an easy, flat trail along the river that runs north nearly a mile into the valley. Glaciers gouged out this river valley, leaving large erratics dotting the valley slopes. On this first hike in the park, I take in the sparsely vegetated, rock-strewn hillside against Denali's snow-capped mountainous backdrop. A good night's rest in a rented cabin at McKinley Creekside Cabins follows another salmon dinner in their small but cozy restaurant.

Wednesday morning, the WAC is abuzz with tourists cautiously snapping pictures of a moose eating foliage between the pines near the front of the building where the buses load. The bus has two main stops after crossing the Savage River before reaching Eielson. The first is Teklanika River, with bathroom facilities and views of the river valley. Between the first and second stop at Toklat River Ranger Station, we pass a mother grizzly and her two cubs lounging in some bushes and small pines south of the road. Since the road hugs the valley's north side, most wildlife appears on the south side as the bus heads west through the park. I've gotten a good window seat for the caribou, elk, and grizzlies. At Toklat, I move quickly into the ranger station to get the passport stamp and use the bathroom before returning to a row of buses that seem indistinguishable. I board the wrong bus, realize my error, and sheepishly wave as I exit to find the correct bus. I think I mumbled thank you as I waved, as if this had been a scheduled appearance for the other tourists. I later learn that a couple I know in the NPTC is on the bus that I inadvertently boarded, but I'm too embarrassed to pause and recognize anyone.

When we reach Eielson, we're in luck with the weather. It's a mostly clear day, and we have a good view of Denali to the southeast. The peak of the south summit, taller than the north summit by 850 feet, is barely obscured by clouds that move over and around the mountain, but the view is generally excellent. I'm able to get some good pictures of the park's namesake geological resident. We have about thirty minutes before our bus begins the return trip. Since this is my last day in the park, I must choose between walking one of the trails across the tundra and returning on a later bus or returning on our bus to catch the two visitor locations I missed yesterday. I elect to return with my bus. I figure I'll eventually return to the park for several days with Kareen. Better to hike with someone else to give the bears an option.

On our return, we again spot grizzlies. One bear amuses us. The grizzly is out in the open tundra, meandering about with an eye on a group of caribou about two hundred yards west. The herd largely ignores the bear though aware of his presence. He decides to check their awareness by charging about twenty yards toward the herd. They sprint a few steps in multiple directions before stopping and resuming their meal. They don't seem to take the grizzly seriously, knowing they can easily outrun the bear should he get too curious. We leave the bear and caribou in the same relative situation as we found them and move along. We observe a couple of additional bears, some sheep on a distant rocky hill, and numerous elk. The decision to return early proves beneficial, as we arrive at 3:30 p.m. and I have time to stop at the Murie Science and Learning Center before my last park destination, the Sled Dog Kennels. I'm just in time to attend the 4:00 p.m. sled dog demonstration. I arrive to find the walking trail blocked, but the rangers wave me through and I'm able to join the crowd. It's a great finish to the day in Denali.

Wednesday ends in Fairbanks. After checking in at the Best Western, I enjoy more fresh salmon at a small strip mall pub recommended by the hotel clerk. It's delicious. I tell Kareen about all the fresh fish I'm eating when she calls, and she accuses me of living high on the hog. Since I'm in parks by day and eating fresh salmon each night, it's hard to argue the point. I'm eating so much salmon, I'm starting to ponder sleeping through the winter.

After a restful hibernation, I start Thursday with a stop at the Interagency Morris Thompson Cultural and Visitor Center in Fairbanks for passport cancellations and guidance for today's destination, **Gates of the Arctic National Park and Preserve**. I have little idea of what I'll find farther north. I'm both a little intimidated and excited about the day's adventure. I've heard plenty about the infamous Dalton Highway. My plan is to drive 270 miles north on the Steese and Dalton Highways to Coldfoot and Wiseman for a hike into the park at its closest point to the road system, about a mile away. Coldfoot is at mile marker 175 on the Dalton, and Wiseman is at mile marker 189. Google Maps tells me the trip is seven hours each way. Wiseman is almost halfway to the Arctic Ocean. Prudhoe Bay is 500 miles from Fairbanks, a fourteen-hour drive through the Brooks Mountain Range and across the North Slope. It's nearly 9:00 a.m. when I leave Fairbanks.

The Dalton Highway has gained a great deal of notoriety due to reality TV shows such as *Ice Road Trucker* and *Alaska State Police*. I thought the Dalton ran from Fairbanks to the Arctic Ocean and North Slope oil fields. However, the road that heads north out of Fairbanks is Steese Highway, which continues to the town of Circle. Steese connects to Elliot Highway, which leads to the southern terminus of the Dalton Highway nearly one hundred miles north of Fairbanks. All three roads are on the rental car banned list, so knowledgeable tourists use special rental outfits in Fairbanks to rent "Dalton-ready" vehicles, cars more aptly described as tanks on wheels with a full-size spare, sometimes two. Vast distances and the lack of almost any civilization encourages safety measures.

The most dangerous aspect of the Dalton is the changing nature and unpredictability of driving conditions. The two-lane highway is paved for long stretches, followed by an approximate thirty-mile stretch of gravel going through twisting, mountainous terrain with curves requiring 30 mph or less. The speed limit on the entire Dalton Highway is 50 mph. Even the seemingly good sections hold unexpected surprises, such as deep potholes created by the heavy trucks that frequent the road. Hitting some of these potholes at 50 mph will blow a tire and crack a rim. It can easily be hundreds of miles to a tire repair shop or wrecker. The gravel stretches often require much slower speeds to avoid fishtailing or sailing off the road. Mountainous, gravel segments with sharp curves demand controlled speeds and punish the noncompliant.

Rapid deceleration on gravel can have disastrous consequences, indicated by multiple wrecked autos off the roadway. Some road sections are elevated by fifteen to thirty feet above the surrounding terrain. I pass two vehicles that slid off the road and landed twenty to thirty feet below on a tree, totaling each vehicle. I stop to take a picture of a silver pickup truck resting on its wheels in the trees below the road bed, still facing south in its presumed direction of travel. During the slide, the driver took out the yellow-and-black caution sign for the upcoming curve to the left, with 35 mph noted underneath it. The truck remains as a warning for the curve in lieu of the flattened sign. I also pass a car that had smashed into the back of a truck or heavy vehicle at a turnout, compressing the car like an accordion. The crushed passenger compartment speaks to the high price of mistakes on the Dalton. Inattentiveness is life-threatening.

I don't encounter many potholes in the paved sections, but a few are deep enough to cause problems. Alaska's 663,000 square miles are equal to more than 21 percent of the contiguous United States. Part of the challenge driving the Dalton is staying focused during hours of monotony across the vast open space. It's easy to lose concentration.

Mercifully, I have good weather for my three-hundred-mile trip north. I have clear conditions throughout, minimizing drive time. It takes about five hours to reach my first destination in Coldfoot, one of the few places along the Dalton where travelers can get gas and a hot meal. The drive to Coldfoot passes over the Yukon River at Dalton mile marker fifty-five. I'm struck by the river's size. I incorrectly imagined the river as a rocky mountainous stream. But the Yukon is a large river where it crosses the highway, reminding me of the upper Mississippi River between Illinois and Missouri.

Between the Yukon River and Coldfoot, I pass the Arctic Circle at sixty-six degrees of latitude and mile marker 115. A roadside state park called Arctic Circle Park offers tourists a photo op. Few roads cross the geographical boundary. The Arctic Circle's actual location isn't fixed. It moves about two degrees in latitude every forty thousand years from fluctuation in the earth's axial tilt. Tidal forces, influenced by the moon, cause our planet to wobble as it spins. The same phenomenon changes the North Star over time from its current location in the Little Dipper. The actual Arctic Circle shifts north almost fifty feet (fifteen meters) every year. That's a significant change. Over forty thousand years, it's a shift of over one hundred miles. I'm not quite certain where the real Arctic Circle is during my visit, but it's still cool to take a picture next to the park's sign that reads "Arctic Circle." Travelers past this point do cross the boundary, though it might be a few hundred feet down the road.

Just south of the Arctic Circle stop is Finger Rock on Finger Mountain at Dalton mile marker 97.5. Finger Rock is old granite rock in the shape of a giant finger protruding out of the mountain and pointed south to Fairbanks. The rock has long served as a landmark for pilots navigating the Arctic between Prudhoe Bay and Fairbanks.

The Dalton Highway is formidable enough that several of the curves and hills have popular names. North of the Arctic Circle, I crest an uphill grade to find a steep one-mile descent on gravel ending in a ninety-degree left turn at the base of a mountain. I later learn the sharp curve, at mile marker 126, is called "Oh Shit Corner," the first two words being exactly what I uttered when I crested the hill. I imagine more than one trucker's experience contributed to the curve's name.

I arrive in Coldfoot and the Arctic Interagency Visitor Center about 2:00 p.m. Gates of the Arctic remains undeveloped within its boundaries. Intentionally preserved in its wilderness state, it easily ranks as the least visited national park among the sixty, with just over ten thousand centennial visitors. The only evidence of civilization within the park's boundaries is Anaktuvuk Pass, a small Inuit village located on an easement in the park about seventy-five air miles northwest of Coldfoot. The park covers nearly two hundred miles of the central Brooks Range, which stretches for seven hundred miles from Canada's Yukon to northwestern Alaska. The park is remote, wild, and cold. Average daily high temperatures in the winter range from negative twenty-two to negative eight at Anaktuvuk Pass, while the summer highs usually range between thirty-seven and sixty-one.

I share a bit of my story with the ranger at the visitor center and get specific directions for my hike. The closest point between a public road and the park boundary is off a spur from the Wiseman Road. The Wiseman Road splits shortly after it begins at the Dalton. The right fork of the road leads to a mining operation next to the park identified by the town name Nolan. I will drive the twenty-one miles to that point in a couple of hours, but first I soak in the exhibits, including a large globe in the middle of the visitor center. It's impossible not to notice upon entering. A ranger takes my picture in front of the globe. I can't resist buying a long-sleeve T-shirt for the park, because how often am I going to be in the middle of the Brooks Range and headed into Gates of the Arctic National Park?

Before hiking, I drive across the highway to a truck stop. The facility is not exactly like the familiar Lower 48 truck stops. I load a plate at the buffet and eat at a small table across from the cash register. After filling up the rental SUV I'm driving, a Toyota RAV4, I turn back onto the Dalton, thinking about the hike ahead of me and operating subconsciously. I pay no attention to speed as I accelerate north until I see an Alaska state trooper in a pickup truck coming toward me. Looking down at my dash, I'm doing 70 mph! I hit the brakes, but it's way too late. The RAV4 accelerates a lot faster than the four-cylinder Chevy Malibu I drive back home. I slow down to pull over as the trooper turns around with his lights on in my rearview mirror. As he pulls up behind me, I roll down the window and shut the engine off, pulling out my license with that awful feeling you get when you know you've done something stupid. He asks, "Do you have any guns or other weapons in the vehicle?"

"No," I reply.

"Why are you going so fast?" he asks.

"Because I wasn't paying attention. I'm thinking about hiking into the park near Nolan and wasn't watching my speed."

He reacts as if I didn't even try to answer his question with, "Why are you speeding? Speed is the number-one cause of serious accidents on the Dalton."

"I understand," I start to say.

To which he replies, "Just be quiet and answer my question!"

I say nothing, unsure how to respond to that request. He proceeds to lecture me about how dangerous speeding is. I don't think he understands or cares that I'd been on the road less than a mile when he clocked me. I realize this trooper assumes I'm some deadbeat who is hopelessly stupid. At least, that's the message that comes across. I wait for him to finish and pause for a response before I say, "I'm sorry, officer. I have no excuse. I wasn't paying attention to my speed." He takes my license and rental agreement back to the truck.

After about ten minutes, he returns and points out on the rental agreement as he hands it back to me that I'm not allowed to take the car I'm driving on the Dalton Highway. He's also kind enough to point out that we're having this conversation about 176 miles up the Dalton Highway, as if I didn't know. "It's not against the law. But if you get in an accident, you are financially liable," he explains.

"I don't plan on getting into an accident," I think, but just listen, using my stupid look of amazement for effect. I have the gift, if you can call it that, of being able to mislead people as to my intelligence. Unfortunately, this has happened several times to my disadvantage. It bothered me for years.

As I'm waiting in my SUV and considering what hard time is like in an Alaskan prison, I've resolved to just run with my presumed low IQ. He tells me to follow him to the station, making a point to say he doesn't plan to arrest or detain me, just give me a ticket. Since he's starting to soften a little, I mention, "I have the feeling I've seen you somewhere. Were you on *Alaska State Troopers?*"

"Yeah, they used me for most of the footage on snowmobiles or in Arctic scenery."

"Is there anything from the episodes you appeared in that I might remember?"

"I was the trooper that found the guy shaving his cat," he admits. "Follow me to the station."

I contemplate his last words, "the guy shaving his cat," as we drive about a mile to the state trooper office next to the town's airstrip. He says, "I'll be right back," and disappears into the station with my driver's license. I'm waiting and imagine him exiting the station holding a cat, or pulling out his handcuffs, having changed his mind about the jail bit, but when he reappears after another ten minutes, he's holding a ticket and my driver's license. I sign it and bid him farewell. Before I leave, I ask him what it was like to film the TV series. He shares, "Most of the troopers didn't like it because we have so little room in our vehicles. We had to haul three people with us in that," he says, pointing to his pickup truck. "That's why they canceled it after the sixth season."

"Interesting. I didn't know that," I reply, as I shut the door and pull away to continue to Nolan. Good thing I'm not in a hurry. It takes forty-five minutes to get a speeding ticket in Alaska.

The spur road to Nolan off the Wiseman Road goes uphill and has some deep ruts that hold water. It's navigable with regular passenger cars, but I'm thankful I've got a 4-wheel-drive SUV for good measure. About four miles down the road, it curves around an incline on the right and the mine comes into view about a half mile ahead on the side of a large hill. The park boundary is directly west of the road, a one-mile cross-country hike through groups of pines, Alder thickets, and numerous tussocks. After the curve, the gravel road runs north to the mine entrance. The ranger in Coldfoot explained to me that the park boundary lies on a north-south line between two peaks that bracket a valley running west away from the road. A small pond even with the boundary lies in the valley between the slopes. The hike looks simple from the road, but I've never hiked on permafrost or in terrain quite like the Arctic valley in front of me.

I turn around and park behind a hatchback car that four guys are systematically emptying as they spread their gear on the ground, packing and arranging it for a wilderness trek. I greet them as I leave the vehicle and ask if they're familiar with the ground below us or if they've hiked in the area. One answers, "We've never been here before. We're going backcountry for five days."

I reply, "I want to break the park boundary, so I'm headed down the valley to the pond."

"Good luck," they offer in unison.

The ground is good down the hill, but after I cross a stream running across the field, I enter a permafrost swamp. The ground everywhere has standing water since the frozen soil and rock beneath it blocks surface drainage. The only way to keep your feet dry is to step on the middle of the tussocks, large clumps of grass that rise above the water level. They are stiff and large enough for a foothold at the beginning of my short hike. There's no trail or path of any kind, and no indication where there's solid ground and where there's so much water that even the tussocks can't keep your feet dry. When I get halfway across the field, my socks and shoes are soaking wet, but I've almost gained the hillside on the right where at least I can stay on solid ground. The downside to hiking on the hillside is the pines and thickets obscure the view. I can't see where I'm going, and soon I've lost any view of the guys on the road. It makes me a little nervous because the water-laden ground silences noise from my movement. I could break through a thicket and be standing right in front of a bear in a swamp. I put the thought out of my mind and continue moving forward to the line bisecting the pond. I'm still navigating the hillside into the valley when I see through a clearing in the trees that I've passed the pond on my left. It's time to turn around. That's far enough for the day. It's impressive to me how quickly you can lose all trace of civilization and your bearings. When I make it across the swamp, I'm relieved to climb the steep bank back up to the road. The guys ask, "How was the ground over the first mile?" I tell them, "I hope you're wearing waterproof footgear for the swamp. Good luck!"

The drive back to Fairbanks is tedious and long. On the return, the road's familiarity lends some comfort. It's almost 1:00 a.m. when I reach my hotel in Fairbanks. No fresh salmon tonight. I'm awake again at 6:00 a.m. to be at the airport for a 6:45 a.m. check-in for my flight to Anaktuvuk Pass.

After calling the Gates of the Arctic Anaktuvuk Pass ranger station last month, the ranger informed me that two companies offer regular commercial service to outlying northern Alaskan communities. I might be able to fly some place in the morning and return that afternoon. The kind ranger's helpful tip expands my trip, leading to today's reservations with Wright Air Service.

At the airport, I realize that the check-in time for these flights isn't meant to be taken literally. The office isn't even open yet, and my flight doesn't board until 9:00 a.m. It leaves about 9:15 a.m. I spend an idle hour at the Wright Air terminal. On most summer days, the service to a few villages includes morning and afternoon flights. I want to see more of the Gates of the Arctic National Park and booked a round trip today between Fairbanks and the Inuit village.

The process of flying with Wright to these remote places is low-key, though all the employees are professional and helpful. They also seem organized, which surprises me given the relaxed atmosphere. I notice that there's a small office to the side of the main counter for charter services. I ask the lady in the office if, by any chance, they might have a plane available tomorrow. I know the odds are slim, but it can't hurt to ask. She tells me she'll have to check with the guy who runs their charter services when he comes in a little later. I promise, "I'll check back when I return to Fairbanks this afternoon." As we board the plane, the pilot informs us we are making an unscheduled stop at another village for a cargo delivery and to drop off a passenger. I don't even catch the name of the isolated airfield where we land but watch as the people greeting the plane gleefully unload cases of soft drinks and snacks. It's the first time I've ever seen anyone visibly excited to grab a whole case of vanilla wafers. It's a reminder that these flights and the deliveries that come on them are a lifeline for the people that live out here in the Alaskan wilderness.

The aerial view of the Brooks Range exposes these rugged, wild mountains stretching as far as the eye can see east and west. With wondrous scenery out each side of the plane, our time in the air seems short. After the long wait this morning and the detour, I'm happy to be on the ground at Anaktuvuk Pass. The police and several other people gather as the plane unloads. Here, you can screen the traffic in and out of town by watching who and what deplanes. My happiness is only dampened somewhat as I exit the airstrip and feel the cold wind. I'm wearing a hoodie, jacket, jeans, and gloves, but it's about thirty-five degrees in a biting gale. The town is appropriately named, situated in a mountain pass opening to the North Slope. Ernie Creek and John River run through bordering valley passes to the east and southwest. The south end of the village abuts the headwaters of the **John Wild River**, one of six national wild rivers within Gates of the Arctic National Park. When I spoke with the ranger a month ago, he told me he would be out of town during my visit. He informed me that a graduate student at the station as a research guest might let me in to get the three passport stamps kept here.

I walk to the ranger station, closed and locked as expected. I knock on the front door of the adjoining residence, and a young guy answers in his shorts with his toothbrush in his mouth. I introduce myself and ask if he wouldn't mind letting me use the passport stampers the ranger left out. He nods and muffles, "No problem." I find the stampers all out and ready for me on the counter. It is thoughtful that the ranger remembered our conversation and left them out for my arrival. I write him a short thank-you on a scrap sheet next to the stamps. I thank the student researcher and leave.

Gates of the Arctic, Brooks Mountains

The rest of my village day is less productive. There's a museum for the handful of tourists who come here, but the only curator is out of town for several days tending a sick relative. I had hoped to hike a few miles down one of the rivers, but the bone-numbing cold is too much. The day turns into a cultural experience.

Since I have five hours to kill and no place to go, I wander around the village, about two blocks long in any direction. Entering the small village supermarket, I look around and smile politely, but I'm not really interested in buying anything, just trying to get out of the cold wind for a few minutes. After twenty minutes, I start walking around outside again, which is noisy from the numerous angry, barking dogs chained outside almost every raised home. I decide to get a better view of the terrain south of town, so I climb a snow-covered hill behind the school at the south end of the village. I make it on top of the hill to scan the landscape and the John River headwaters. Descending the hill, I sink to my knees in a snow drift.

Back at the grocery store, I ask about the village restaurant. They explain it's on the south side of the village. I return through the gauntlet of snarling dogs, looking over the buildings next to the school and finding no evidence of any restaurant. Through a dirty window, there appears to be a small hardware store. The only identified building is the high school. They don't get many visitors. Villagers know each house and building. Returning to the airstrip, I discover the mayor's office in the adjacent building, so I go in and plant myself on the couch to wait. That works for an hour until they close for lunch. Returning to the grocery store, the guy working there asks what I'm doing here. It's a good question. I'm tempted to say, "I decided to live here as a transient." Instead, I explain that I had planned to visit the museum and take a short hike but didn't expect the museum to be closed and a wind chill in the single digits. I ask him if he and the other villagers ever get cold in winter. He tells me, "No, we do indoor activities and look out after each other." Residents connect with a sense of community and shared fellowship characteristic of native communities. I ask another lady who walks into the store if she ever gets cold, and she gives me the same answer. The Inuit villagers I meet on this day are kind. I admire their spirit and togetherness. The interaction with the villagers becomes today's park experience. Several more villagers approach me wondering why the big white guy with the backpack is wandering aimlessly through their village. Perhaps that will become my Inuit name if I'm stranded here: Big White Guy Wandering with Backpack.

The flight to Fairbanks has another detour. We touch down eighty-five miles south in Bettles to pick up a passenger and drop off packages. I can see the NPS ranger station two hundred feet away and wish I had a few minutes to get their cancellations, but our unscheduled stop serves to unload one passenger and the consumables and we're back in the air without delay. The mosquitoes are so thick at Bettles, they create a haze. The folks at Wright Air do a tremendous and flexible service for these small communities. I can see they make regular stops to accommodate situations outside their normal schedule.

We land in Fairbanks at 4:30 p.m. I'm hungry and tired. I check with the Wright Air charter office before leaving, and they tell me the guy in charge got my message. I'm told he has my number and will give me a call in the next hour. On the way to the hotel, he calls to share they have an open plane and a pilot available to take me to **Yukon-Charley Rivers National Preserve**. It's going to be my most expensive park unit of the year, since I will absorb the $1,450 cost of the charter myself, but it's worth it to see another park in what might have been a slow day.

Rejuvenated by another fresh salmon and beer dinner and eight-hour hibernation, I'm back at the Wright Air terminal Saturday for my 9:00 a.m. flight to the preserve. Yukon–Charley is one of twenty Alaskan NPS units inaccessible by road from Anchorage. Visitors to the preserve reach it in one of three ways. They float down the Yukon or Charley River, they fly to one of the park's air strips, or they trek through backcountry. The preserve centers about the confluence of its two namesake rivers, protecting 128 miles of the 1,900-mile Yukon River and all eighty-eight miles of the **Charley Wild River**. The Charley River's remote and rugged nature renders it accessible only to experienced wilderness explorers. Larger than the state of New Jersey, the preserve lies between the towns of Circle and Eagle and has only twenty year-round residents, fewer than one hundred years ago when gold mining dominated the area.

My pilot, Mike, recently retired from the Army after two tours in Afghanistan flying Black Hawk medivacs, proves a polite, reliable, and conscientious companion. It's an honor to fly with him today. We climb into our Cessna for the flight east to our destination, the gravel landing strip at Coal Creek twelve miles downstream on the Yukon from its junction with the Charley. Our flight takes about an hour. Mike scours the mountain sides for a large herd of caribou he spotted three days ago. We see a few small groups, but not the massive herd Mike observed. We circle to land on the airstrip from the north, or river side. After landing, Mike inquires as to my plan. "I'm hiking the three and a half miles to Slaven's Roadhouse on the southern bank of the Yukon, following the old gold dredging operation next to Coal Creek." The roadhouse is a restored 1932 two-story cabin built by prospector and long-time resident Frank Slaven. The cabin, restored by the National Park Service in the 1990s to its 1930s appearance, serves as a stopping point and shelter for river floaters and boaters, backcountry hikers, and dogsled mushers during the winter. Recently, I hear it's become a seasonal ranger residence.

Mike replies, "I don't feel safe letting you hike alone and unarmed. I'll join you, if that's okay."

"Outstanding," I reply. "Would love your company!"

He tucks a loaded .45 into his pants as an emergency bear deterrent, and we're off.

We walk the half-mile gravel strip and continue down a muddy lane of sorts—calling it a road would be a stretch—along the channel dug by the abandoned gold dredge next to the trail. Gold Placers, Inc. mined several claims purchased from Slaven and other prospectors between 1935 and 1957. After the claims were deemed as played out, abandoning the equipment cost less than any salvage from such a remote location. It remains today as a sort of full-scale exhibit of the area's mining history. The dredging operation simplified is industrial-sized panning for gold.

As Mike and I pass the dredge, we enter a mosquito fog. Since the creek returned to its natural, parallel course, the old mining channel's stagnant water offers a perfect breeding ground for Alaska's giant mosquitoes. They are huge, numerous, and relentless. Good thing I brought 50 percent DEET repellent. It's the first time I've needed it on the trip. We spray each other thoroughly, including our clothes as these mosquitoes attempt to bite through any material, including shoes. There are mosquitoes trying to bite Mike through the back of his blue jeans as I spray them. I watch them fall dead while others circle the mist for an unprotected spot of fabric or skin. I've never seen insects this aggressive. They swarm like small birds in a Hitchcock movie.

After we escape the wrath of the flying blood donor crew, we make it to the roadhouse elevated on the Yukon riverbank. I take plenty of pictures. Mike snaps a few of me. I thought a passport stamper existed with "Slaven's Roadhouse" as its location. Another NPTC member reported the cabin as a stamp location. Mike and I spend about fifteen minutes scouring the cabin, looking through drawers and even the desk in the second-floor bedroom to no avail. I've found hidden stampers in bizarre places at other parks, but not here. We meet a maintenance ranger working on the primitive road between the river and airstrip, and he assures us there had been a stamper at the cabin no more than a week ago. We reenter the cabin and watch as he performs an abbreviated version of the same search. Again, no luck. We start back for the plane empty-handed but having enjoyed seeing the river and roadhouse. About halfway back, the maintenance ranger catches up to us on his ATV to tell us they have the stamper at the NPS/BLM employee cabin west of the landing strip. Another ranger is bringing it down to our plane. When we meet her, I share that Yukon–Charley is my 362nd NPS unit visited lifetime and the 44th new park out of 184 total this year. When I test the stamp, I see the location on the bottom reads "Coal Creek." I confused the Slaven's Roadhouse stamper location with the park location on the stamp. But the idea of a stamp for the roadhouse sticks with me. On Monday, I call Ranger Kris who works out of Fairbanks. She's responsible for Yukon–Charley's stampers. I share a brief version of our adventure and suggest they add a Slaven's Roadhouse stamp for such a unique location. A month or two later, I'm thrilled to see the list of new stamps from Eastern National includes Yukon–Charley NP—Slaven's Roadhouse! A couple of weeks after that, I get an envelope from Fairbanks with copies of the new Slaven's Roadhouse stamp and the date of my visit. Throughout the year, thoughtful kindnesses such as this endear park service personnel to me. On our return flight, Mike indulges me by flying directly over the confluence of the Yukon and Charley rivers. The Charley looks like a coiled snake striking the larger Yukon from the side. The aerial image of the river junction is probably the most recognizable preserve image and worth seeing in person.

Yukon-Charley confluence

Sunday morning, I start on the four-and-a-half-hour drive from Fairbanks to Slana, the northern entrance road into **Wrangell–St. Elias National Park and Preserve**. The national park's 8.3 million acres and the preserve's 4.85 million acres combine into the largest park in the system at over 13.1 million acres, 8.7 of which is designated wilderness. Wrangell-St. Elias is almost four times the size of the largest national park in the Lower 48, Death Valley National Park, and six times the size of Yellowstone National Park. The park features the second-highest peak in North America, Mt. St. Elias, at 18,008 feet and fifteen of the twenty highest peaks in Alaska.

There are two roads that enter Wrangell–St. Elias. Both named roads make the rental car banned list. Nabesna Road starts at the northern entrance and Slana ranger station. The southern entrance road, McCarthy Road, runs sixty-one miles between Chitina and McCarthy, a two-hour drive. A short distance from McCarthy is the Kennecott Visitor Center, a popular destination for park visitors.

For my Sunday park experience, I stop at the Slana ranger station and enjoy a wonderful conversation with the incredibly kind Ranger Dora. She explains points on Nabesna Road and suggests I might first enjoy a nearby hike to Copper River to see a working fish wheel spinning in the river's current. It feels good to get out of the car and hike a couple of miles.

I share a summary of my year with Dora, explaining how excited I am to finally see Alaska and Wrangell–St. Elias. She gives me a massive Wrangell–St. Elias wall map. I ask her if the map is full scale to the park's 20,500 square miles. Even rolled tightly, it won't fit in my large suitcase. I'll have to fold it to get it home. With the appreciated gift in tow, I start down Nabesna Road. There are multiple interesting places, scenic trails, and stops over the forty-five miles to the old mining community of Nabesna. The mountains to the south of the road are volcanic, and some give strong clues in their shape. As the road passes deeper into the park, the valley narrows, and the mountains loom higher. I don't have time to do my preferred extent of hiking but settle for several short walks in places of note along Nabesna Road.

My bed tonight is at a location found with the help of Ranger Dora. I overshot my original reservation, sixty-four miles north in Tok. She called the number at the new place, about forty miles south, on my behalf and handed the phone to me. They had an open cabin, and I agreed to rent it for the night. The couple who owns the cabins and RV park are kind and enthusiastic about my park journey and first Alaska trip. After I inquire as to any place I can buy something to eat, they tell me the only options are at least twenty miles away. Realizing I haven't eaten all day, they offer to share their evening meal with me, a gracious gesture I thankfully accept.

They ask if I've seen the PBS film about Richard Proenneke, a mechanic and carpenter from Iowa who moved to Twin Lakes, a remote area in what is now Lake Clark National Park, in May 1968 at the age of fifty-two to build a cabin and live out his life in the wilderness. What made Proenneke's story lasting for future generations is the written and visual chronicle he left. He kept both a detailed journal and 8-mm video of his efforts to build the cabin on Upper Twin Lake. He films himself constructing his cabin with local supplies and handmade tools. He also records his subsistence lifestyle, including hunting, fishing, and other ways he coexists in nature. The journal is narrated over clips of Proenneke's film to make the documentary, *Alone in the Wilderness*, a PBS staple. At the age of eighty-two and no longer able to take care of himself, he departed the Twin Lakes cabin. He left the property in the care of the National Park Service upon his death in 2003. The cabin is one of Lake Clark's most popular visitor attractions. I've never heard of Proenneke's story or seen the film. The proprietors offer to show it to me. We watch it together after dinner from an old videotape buried in their TV cabinet. I agree with their assessment. It's a remarkable story. The handmade cabin is an amazing example of craftsmanship considering the primitive circumstances. I make a mental note to visit the Proenneke cabin when I return to Alaska to see Lake Clark and the remaining Alaskan parks. It's an educational ending to another full day.

Monday begins at the Main Park Visitor Center in Copper Center, Alaska. Multiple exhibits review the geology, ecology, environment, and native peoples. There are also a lot of aggressive mosquitoes lurking about nearby trails. After the nature hike, I'm returning to the car and hear someone call out, "Dave!" Looking around clueless, assuming it can't be me, I start walking again and hear another "Dave!" this time by a chorus of voices. I look over to some picnic tables and see Donna and Paul, two NPTC members and St. Louis-area residents and friends. I know there are some NPTC members traveling in Alaska concurrently with my trip and even tried to arrange something with Paul beforehand to link up with his family and see one of the parks together. We never could make our schedules sync.

I walk over to greet my friends and ask them how their trip is going. They tell me, "We saw you in Denali! You got on our bus and exited when you realized you were on the wrong bus."

"So much for the old saying, 'No one here knows us or will ever see us again!'" I reply. At least they didn't see me wave or hear me say thank you.

They tell me another group of NPTC members are traveling through Chitina today. That's my next and last stop in the park. I realized yesterday that I would have to turn around at Chitina to complete the drive back to Anchorage, since my hotel tonight is in Seward, a six-hour drive from Chitina. I don't have the time and stamina to drive into the park on the southern entrance road and make Seward tonight. I wish them well and start for Chitina.

At the ranger station, I run into the NPTC group. They introduce themselves, but I'm so hazy and tired from all the driving, I don't fully register who I'm greeting. There are too many names for my muddled mind. After getting the passport cancellation, I stop at Gilpatrick's Hotel and enjoy a meal before the long drive.

The commute between Wrangell–St. Elias and Anchorage travels the Glenn Highway, part of the Alcan Highway, with views of the Chugach Mountains to the south and the Talkeetna Mountains to the north. Someone could easily spend the whole day driving the road and taking pictures of the Alaskan ranges and the occasional moose, elk, or bear. I limit myself to only a few photo stops and make those short. The highway has alternating passing lanes in each direction, a common feature for the more heavily traveled roads so that faster cars can pass slower-moving heavy trucks and RV's. It's a challenge to travel at a reasonable pace with the slow-moving traffic and distracting scenery. I'm more concerned about fatigue. I don't have a specific time to be in Seward other than for some sleep before tomorrow's eight-and-a-half-hour boat tour. The Glenn Highway has a thirty- to forty-five-minute stretch of almost all two-lane road, with no passing lanes around steep grades and hairpin turns. It can be frustrating following an RV or truck for fifteen to twenty minutes or even longer, going 15 to 30 mph. There's a law in Alaska that slower-moving vehicles that have five or more vehicles stacked up behind them are supposed to use the turnouts provided to let the traffic pass, but most people driving RVs either don't know about the law, feign ignorance, or don't care. The best way to give yourself relief from the drive time is to schedule extra time for each commute. In my case, I don't want to lose a full day to travel.

Passing Anchorage, I continue another two hours into the Kenai Peninsula and another scenic drive on the Seward Highway. It's about 9:00 p.m. when I pull into my hotel parking lot, completely exhausted but happy to be here.

Tuesday, I join a full-day boat tour of **Kenai Fjords National Park**. We pull away from the Seward docks at 8:00 a.m. The boats travel south out of Resurrection Bay to one of the park's fjords. Named park glaciers originating out of the Harding Icefield calve into the ocean at the end of narrow, glacially carved inlets. The first views through Resurrection Bay are the peaks on either side. A series of peaks surround Sargent Glacier on the Resurrection Peninsula to the east. Our boat passes through the Harding Gateway between the Chiswell Islands in the Alaska Maritime National Wildlife Refuge and into Harris Bay.

Over one hundred years ago, the Northwestern Glacier met the ocean at the edge of Harris Bay. In the interim, the glacier retreated inland, creating Northwestern Lagoon and Striation Island, which splits two channels into the lagoon. The boat pauses for multiple humpback whale sightings from Resurrection Bay to the lagoon, where we spot two pairs of humpbacks, one of which breeches the water with a characteristic flip. Farther toward the Harris Peninsula shoreline, another humpback appears to be doing some sort of whale calisthenics, rolling from side to side, first sticking one fin vertically out of the water and then another. It's entirely unclear to all on board exactly what the exercising whale is doing or why. The guide gives me a derisive look when I suggest the whale's *Sweatin' to the Oldies* or working through a *Buns of Steel* routine. We see about two dozen humpbacks today, though only the one pair breeches for us. Mostly, it's a lot of humpbacks feeding solo or in pairs. We spot the whales surfacing in the water before diving to feed with a flip of their fluke. We spend about forty-five minutes at the end of the lagoon, so everyone has plenty of opportunity to photograph the Northwestern Glacier and the others above us.

Kenai Fjords, Northwestern Glacier

The glacier's terminus appears in a brilliant baby blue. Glacial ice appears blue after enormous pressure exerted on the ice squeezes air out, making it denser. The dense ice, like the ocean, absorbs colors at the red end of the visible spectrum more efficiently than longer blue wavelengths that are reflected to create the blue color we see.

We observe an impressive array of wildlife. The boat stops once so we can photograph a seal bobbing in the water eating an octopus. The beautiful terrain combined with the wildlife make the boat tour of Kenai Fjords a trip highlight.

Upon our return to the docks, I've got sufficient time today to stop at the Kenji Fjords National Park Visitor Center in the Seward harbor and drive to the Exit Glacier Nature Center north of town. I want to hike the Harding Ice Field Trail, considered a strenuous 8.2-mile trek. The rangers at the visitor center tell me that a female black bear with two cubs has been reported every day for the past week near the trail, closed today as a result.

I take the easier and flatter trail out to the Exit Glacier. As I walk toward the glacier receding into the narrow valley, signs show the year the Exit Glacier's terminus rested there. The increasing pace of glacial retreat is shocking, hundreds of feet in the past decade. It speaks directly to rising global temperatures over the past two hundred years. Since my hiking is limited, I return to the docks for another salmon and beer dinner. After all the salmon I've eaten on this trip, I now have the urge to swim upstream and spawn. I resist, as I would certainly be eaten by a bear. There's still the possibility of that as it is.

Wednesday, my next-to-last day in Alaska, starts without specific plans, though I still hope to hike to the ice field. There's a ranger-led hike about halfway to the ice field each day at 9:00 a.m. It seems the better solution this morning, so I join the group. The trail is open, but the bear remains. We start the hike with a report that some rangers have gone up to the place where the bear has taken temporary residence next to the trail, and she's engaging them with aggressive behavior, snapping and snarling according to the accounts we can hear over the volunteer's radio. We only hike about a half mile when someone in charge informs her our hike is canceled and the park's bear response team is headed up. Most Alaskan parks have a formal bear response team, available for events like this one when bear activity conflicts with human activity, creating danger to both species. We reverse and begin descending. We're about ten minutes into our return when we cross paths with the team headed to the incident. As they stall trying to pass our group, I ask them what they use on the bear. They have shotguns that shoot beanbags, noisemakers, and other items designed to annoy the bear into leaving by choice. We leave the bear team to their uphill climb and task and continue downhill. Since I now have unexpected time on my hands, I read the nature center exhibits again. I notice a wildlife information panel. For bears, it has three columns: If You See a Bear, If a Bear Charges, and If a Bear Attacks. The display educates visitors on the difference between black bears and grizzly (brown) bears in terms of their behavior. Brown bears are curious and have been known to charge or approach people out of curiosity without attacking. Black bears are not naturally curious, and if they charge, they mean to do harm. The last line under If a Bear Attacks reads, "If it starts to eat you, fight back." Sage advice, indeed.

After the bear excitement on the Harding Ice Field Trail, I check back late in the day to find they've reopened the trail. Apparently, the bear response team successfully annoyed the bear and her two cubs away. It's too late to hike it now, so I leave the goal uncompleted.

Thursday is an easy day. My flight home to Chicago isn't until 8:45 p.m. I have all day to make my way north from Seward. I explore locations in the **Kenai Mountains–Turnagain Arm National Heritage Area**. The heritage area commemorates settlement history in the rugged mountain corridor of Kenai Peninsula's northern neck. The first stop in Hope, population two hundred, is a small museum covering town history and the mining that spawned the settlement. From Hope, I have a short drive into the narrowest part of the peninsula to the Chugach National Forest Visitor Center. The last stop is the Alyeska Ski Resort in Girdwood. I ride the ski lift to the top of the mountain to visit the Roundhouse Museum and enjoy the view of the town, valley, and the Cook Inlet. Over lunch in the cafeteria on the mountaintop, I process all the things I've seen the past ten days. It's been an incredible trip. I look forward to returning to see the remaining Alaskan NPS units.

20 *In Search of Sasquatch*

As much as I've enjoyed Alaska, it feels good to be home. After catching up on work and other items throughout the day Friday, the weekend brings the first of six consecutive Cardinals games I'll attend. I drive to St. Louis for a weekend series between the Cardinals and Texas Rangers. The Cardinals manage to lose eighth-inning leads in both the Saturday night and Sunday afternoon games. They bounce back to surprise everyone by sweeping three from the first-place Cubs at Wrigley, their first series at the "friendly confines" this season.

The park journey turns to the Pacific Northwest. I fly to Seattle from O'Hare early Friday morning, looking forward to seeing more of Washington, including three new parks near the Washington-Oregon border. The first stops in downtown Seattle are the **Wing Luke Museum of the Asian Pacific American Experience**, an accurately self-described location, and the **Klondike Gold Rush National Historical Park**. At Wing Luke, I enjoy the exhibits, learning more about Asian immigration and the challenges of discrimination during the settlement and development of the Pacific Northwest. I like the gallery featuring the story of Seattle's hometown hero, karate artist and movie star Bruce Lee.

Klondike Gold Rush National Historical Park has two units, one in Seattle and the other in Skagway, Alaska. Most 1896 and

1897 gold rush prospectors started their expedition in Seattle. Crowded boats departed daily, teeming with men determined to strike it rich in the Canadian Yukon and Alaskan goldfields. The gold rush became more of a windfall to the merchants of Seattle and entrepreneurs willing to brave the harsh frontier than for most prospectors. Only a few prospectors struck it rich, but the boom helped pull the US economy out of a depression that had languished since earlier in the decade. The Seattle unit's visitor center is in the former Cadillac Hotel, opened in 1890. The Cadillac Hotel is one of many historic gold rush–era buildings within the Pioneer Square National Historic District in the heart of Seattle. Exhibits review the gold rush and its noteworthy characters.

The historic district is a few blocks north of the football and baseball stadiums for the Seahawks and Mariners. I stop to peek into the football stadium, CenturyLink Field, said to be the NFL's loudest stadium, on my way to Safeco Field to buy a ticket for tonight's game against the Cardinals. President Obama is visiting Seattle today, and the authorities have announced they are shutting down I-5 between the city and airport. I have no interest in getting snarled in traffic. I'm staying south of downtown near the airport. The nearby mass transit station is about a mile from my hotel. I return, clean up, and head for the station.

At the ballpark, I enjoy a front-row seat down the right field line where I have an excellent view of the two-run home run hit by the Mariners off the Cardinal's closer to turn a 3–2 Cardinals lead into a 4–3 Mariners walk-off victory. I leave the stadium with the same feeling as last weekend's games, though replayed in a different stadium against a different team. I enjoyed the game and my second visit to Safeco nonetheless.

Saturday morning begins with a two-hour drive to Sedro-Woolley, Washington, and the Interagency USFS and NPS Information Center. I'm hosting an NPTC member meet-up in **North Cascades National Park**. The members gather between 8:00 a.m., when the building opens, and 8:30 a.m. This is my first member meet-up as the organizer and host.

Sedro-Woolley is also home for the Pacific Northwest National Scenic Trail Association office. The **Pacific Northwest National Scenic Trail** covers twelve hundred miles from the Continental Divide at Glacier National Park in Montana across the northern end of Idaho and Washington to the Pacific Ocean adjacent to Olympic National Park in the Olympic Peninsula. The trail connects the Continental Divide National Scenic Trail and the Pacific Crest National Scenic Trail and claims to be one of the world's most scenic trails. Our group will hike a short section today.

Seven other members show up in quick succession for our hike into North Cascades National Park. North Cascades is the closest mountain experience in the contiguous states to the wild, jagged peaks of Alaska. The park covers the northern most fifty miles of the Cascade Range south of the Canadian border. The Cascades run from southern British Columbia to northern California. The volcanic mountain chain derives from tectonic activity, the sub-duction of the Pacific plate (Juan del Fuca plate) underneath the North American plate, destabilizing the mantle and creating uplift where the Cascade Range exists today. The Cascade Range has produced all the contiguous United States volcanic eruptions for the last two hundred years. The most recent High Cascades eruptions occurred at Mount St. Helens in 1980 and Lassen Peak from 1914 to 1921. Lassen anchors the range's southern end. The Cascades form part of the Pacific "ring of fire," which includes Alaska's Aleutian Islands, the Japanese Islands, and Indonesia. The North Cascades' rugged beauty is no longer volcanically active but contains the largest number of glaciers in the Lower 48, though these glaciers are retreating quickly with rising global tempera-tures.

When Congress established the park in 1968, some local groups expressed concern that national park status would eliminate estab-lished recreational activities in the park. The legislation addressed these concerns by creating the North Cascades National Park Service Complex, which includes a North Unit and South Unit of North Cascades NP divided by the **Ross Lake National Rec-**

reation Area. The park complex extends south to include Lake Chelan National Recreation Area. Primary public access is via US 20, which crosses the park boundaries east to west entirely within Ross Lake National Recreation Area. The goal for our group today is to enter North Cascades National Park proper via one of the two most commonly used routes.

After everybody has gotten the special meet-up stamp and posed for a group picture, we drive separately to the Baker River Trail. The trailhead is east of Baker Lake and north of US 20. The Baker River Trail is 2.6 miles one way, extending into North Cascades National Park for one mile. At just over a half mile, the trail forks with the Baker River Trail to the national park on the left and a pedestrian suspension bridge on the right spanning the Baker River. The trail takes us through old-growth forest along the river. Our party hits a snag after the suspension bridge. The trail crosses a gully wash requiring passage over wet, smooth rocks covered by running water. We have seven adults, including two couples and two solo males. One of the couples is a delightful retired couple from the East Coast. Bob and Betty are taking their RV north into Canada for a grand tour of the Pacific Northwest. The other couple includes Alex, a Seattle pediatrician, and his wife, mother-in-law, and young daughter. The other member of our hiking party is an experienced and amiable park traveler named Dan who's wearing a brown T-shirt and tan cargo shorts. I like these people. They are precise examples of why I think of my NPTC friends and others I've met in these places as a park family. Alex and his wife are carrying their daughter in a child carrier. After careful consideration, they decide it's unsafe to cross the wash with the child carrier, so the two ladies turn back to the trailhead with the young girl in tow, leaving the four men in the party to cross the stream and continue.

As we enter the national park, we take a few pictures at the boundary marker. The trail ends at a spot on the park map called Sulphide Camp. On our return trip, I pause the group briefly to have Alex take a couple of pictures of me up ahead, obscured by ferns and other foliage. I'm planning to post these pictures as evidence of sasquatch, but it's so difficult to see that I'm in the pictures, my plans for riches and fame are dashed.

North Cascades, Alex, Dan, and Bob

I enjoy hiking in these cool forest environments. I hike at a quick pace, often passing people. Nearly all my hiking this year has been solo. Our surroundings and the pleasant company renders me oblivious to the pace. The distractions of the scenery and my fellow park cohorts also seem to inhibit fatigue. Just being in the parks gives me energy, and the comradery is a further boost. Dan tugs on my sleeve and asks, "Can we slow down?" I turn around and see my three companions with heads down, sweating profusely and breathing like racehorses. Now I feel like an ass. I like to get a good sweat going but forget others may prefer a more relaxed gait. Moreover, I've had a lot of activity-specific training this year, including time at high altitude. "I'm so sorry," I say. "Dan, why don't you take the lead? I don't trust myself." We make our way back across the wash, which gives us a short pause. For the rest of our 5.2-mile excursion, I stop to take pictures at several spots, and Dan keeps us at a nice pace. Despite the unplanned aerobic workout, I'm getting to know these gentlemen better and enjoy their company.

After the Baker River Trail, the participants go separate ways, though I do join Bob and Betty for a quick lunch in the small town of Rockport. From the lunch, I stop at the North Cascades National Park Wilderness Information Center near Marblemount for passport stamps. I continue into Ross Lake National Recreation Area on US 20 to the North Cascades National Park Visitor Center and the North Cascades Environmental Learning Center near Diablo Lake. These are mostly cancellation stops, as my primary destination for the rest of the day is Cascade Pass Trail.

To reach the trail, I backtrack to Marblemount on US 20 and take the twenty-three-mile Cascade River Road heading southeast into the park to the road's end at the trailhead. I've heard that Cascade Pass is the most beautiful and easily accessed representative park area. Only within a few miles of the trailhead do I begin to see the jagged, glaciered peaks of the park's interior. The mountains surround the trailhead parking area on three sides, giving way to more open terrain in the north and west, the Cascade River Road's direction of entry.

The 3.7-mile, one-way hike to Cascade Pass has seventeen hundred feet of elevation gain beginning at the parking lot. The trail climbs straight up the side of the mountain in a series of switchbacks through a dense fir forest. There are several points with openings in the trees, offering a series of higher mountain views across the valley to the south. Rain and melting snow muddy the path. Large trees lie across the trail in three different places. One fallen tree requires an impressive limbo while another creates an impromptu obstacle course. The sunlight starts to dim as I near the top of the climb. As much as I want to continue across the icefield, I know the fading light means I have a limited amount of time to downclimb the switchbacks and exit Cascade River Road to the highway at Marblemount. I'm not equipped to be on the trail in darkness and prefer not to drive the park road at night either. I decide to yield to my fatigue and these safety concerns and retreat. The Cascade Pass Trail is one that should be prioritized and done earlier in the day. I didn't leave myself enough time to do both these park entrance trails. Seeing the Cascade Pass area for the first time is still rewarding. It's a stunning scenic location with a glimpse of the mountainous park interior's hidden wonders. When I return to my hotel room tonight, I've covered fifteen miles of hiking today. And I feel it. Tomorrow's plan is equally ambitious.

North Cascades, Cascade Pass Trailhead

During this journey, I'm attempting multiple arduous travel itineraries that I will never repeat. Sunday's tour qualifies in that category. I start at 6:00 a.m. for the two-and-a-half-hour drive to Lake Quinalt at the south end of **Olympic National Park**. Kareen and I visited Olympic during our 2013 Washington trip. We entered the park in the north at Port Angeles. From there, we visited Hurricane Ridge to hike several shorter trails and finished the day with a long hike along the Elwha River. Today, I'm prioritizing the other side, among the massive old-growth trees of the Quinalt and Hoh Rain Forests. Amid the hiking, I will circumnavigate the park clockwise.

The world champion Sitka spruce tree grows outside the park at Quinalt's outskirts. The massive spruce spreads out from its enormous trunk, casting the surrounding meadow in shadow. It's difficult to photograph the whole tree in one shot from within the meadow. Persistent mosquitoes dissuade me from lingering. I move on to the Quinalt Rain Forest ranger station on the other side of Lake Quinalt. A hike to the Quinalt Big Cedar Tree, a very muddy trail passing some impressive old-growth specimens, ends anticlimactically. The big cedar is dead, and the trail end around its rotting base is a mud pit.

The massive trees that call the park home grow under an annual rainfall of 140–167 inches. The park's namesake 7,980-foot Mt. Olympus receives as much as 220 inches of precipitation, half in snow. The description "rain forest" applies literally to the coastal old-growth stands.

From Lake Quinalt, I start around the park on US 101, stopping at the Kalaloch ranger station and again for a short hike through a big cedar grove to the north. Next, it's onward to the day's most anticipated attraction, the Hoh Rain Forest. I've been excited about returning to see the Hoh since our visit to Hurricane Ridge three years ago. Old growth stands are perhaps my favorite park feature.

These cool, damp woods seem to draw me into an unseen embrace with a flowing, three-dimensional space teeming with life. I lose myself here. Nursery logs litter the forest floor. These decomposing fallen trees provide nutrients for the younger trees emerging from them. A ranger I encounter in the forest stops to share, "These Sitka spruces have interconnected root systems, enabling them to share water and nutrients." The whole place is a giant, living thing. Larger trees can top three hundred feet and twenty feet in diameter. Western hemlocks, Douglas firs, and western red cedars join the spruces across the forest floor while ferns, mosses, and lichens compete for real estate under the towering green canopy.

As I stroll through the forest, I reflect on the life I'm now living compared to my vocational years. Happy with my career when it mattered, I've stopped pretending. This year's grand journey is an acknowledgment that my time at work is in its epilogue. Standing beneath a towering western hemlock, I'm humbled but connected, one small living thing in the larger one's shade. I belong here, and I'm beginning to understand why. Professionally, I've been ignoring the disintegration of my prospects. This thousand-year-old tree has a quality unapproachable and incomprehensible to the charlatans that ceased to assign me personal value. I refuse to stay in a workplace defined entirely by self-interest. The delight that abates the fatigue of arduous adventure fills my heart. Though my house be two thousand miles distant, I'm home.

From the forest, I need almost three and a half hours to reach tonight's destination. I'm staying with a couple of good friends and fellow track and field officials in Bremerton, Washington. Lane, a retired educator, and Deanna, a retired advertising professional, are the type of people you feel privileged to know and call friends. They have a beautiful home in the navy port town. Kareen and I stayed with them during our last trip to Washington, and I'm thrilled to see them again as part of this grand tour of America. Two magnificent days full of natural beauty and wonder followed by their warm blanket of friendship blunts the bone-weariness I feel after seventy trail miles over the past week.

Despite another ambitious plan Monday, I loiter with Lane and Deanna, sharing news of the life change underway. They think I'm making a bold decision to chart my own course and fulfill these important goals while I'm still able. By year's end, I'll spend nearly two hundred days of the year in parks seeking the rainbow's end. I appreciate their support. It's cathartic to discuss the situation with people who believe in and care about me.

Olympic, nursury log

Olympic, Hoh Rain Forest

The mental boost precedes a late start to **Mount Rainier National Park**. After a brief stamping stop at the park headquarters near Ashford, I enter at the southwest Nisqually Entrance and stop at the Longmire Museum and Wilderness Information Center. The day at Rainier includes another hike up the paved trail behind the Henry M. Jackson Visitor Center at the Paradise Inn. Stepping carefully to avoid snow and ice, I climb high enough to gaze up at Columbia Crest, the 14,410-foot summit. I've got a good sweat going despite the cool air. The descent includes some freestyle sliding across wet ice, but I stay on my feet and avoid the ascending visitors glancing about for cover like they would before a skidding bison.

After stops at the Ohanapecosh Visitor Center at the southeastern park entrance and the White River Entrance to the yet-to-open Sunrise Visitor Center, I make my way west to I-5 and then south to Kelso, Washington, where I stop for the night to refuel on another steak and beer dinner.

Tuesday begins early at Fort Clatsop in the **Lewis and Clark National Historical Park**. After traveling large sections of the Lewis & Clark National Historic Trail and reading Stephen Ambrose's Pulitzer Prize-winning *Undaunted Courage*, I've awaited my first visit to Lewis and Clark National Historical Park. After arriving at the Pacific Ocean, the Corps of Discovery spent the expedition's second winter at a small wooden fort on the banks of the Netul River, a modest Columbia River tributary. The visitor center stands next to the reconstructed 1805 fort. The group sheltered here from December until they began their return in March 1806.

At Fort Stevens State Park south of the Columbia River mouth, I climb a berm to look upon the treacherous passage. Licensed pilots, familiar with the navigable channels through numerous shoals, currents, and changing conditions, guide ships through the river inlet. Fort Stevens witnessed the only World War II attack on a US mainland military post, launched by a Japanese submarine in June 1942. The seventeen 14-cm shells fired from the submarine's deck gun succeeded only in the destruction of the post baseball field's backstop.

Crossing the river on the Astoria Bridge to explore the Washington sites, I stop at Dismal Nitch, the north riverbank location where a severe November storm pinned the group down for six days. Opposite Fort Stevens, Cape Disappointment State Park owes its name to Clark, a self-explanatory assessment. I visit the Lewis and Clark Interpretive Center and walk the trail to Cape Disappointment Lighthouse, an active coast guard light station, enjoying the cool breeze off the Pacific.

State Highway 4 passes through a large wetland in the southern part of Pacific and Wahkiakum counties. For dozens of miles, the road crosses vast fields of mud. The two-hour drive ends at **Fort Vancouver National Historic Site**. I use the remaining time this afternoon to plan tomorrow's exploration with the rangers.

The Hudson Bay Company built Fort Vancouver in 1825 to control their Pacific Northwest fur-trading empire. Many Oregon Trail pioneers stopped here before settling to the south in Williamette Valley's fertile farmlands. Most new arrivals from the trail are Americans, strengthening the 1847 agreement dividing Canada and the United States at their modern-day boundary on the 49th parallel.

After the Hudson Bay Company abandoned the site, the US Army built Vancouver Barracks on a rise twenty feet above the fort, making it the first US Army post in the Pacific Northwest. The army maintained a presence here through World War II. Latter-day post activity centered about military and civilian air traffic based at Pearson Field. Fort Vancouver's aviation history is on exhibit today in the Pearson Air Museum. With tomorrow's agenda complete, I pause for an evening of much-needed rest.

Fort Vancouver is the 50th new NPS unit among the 194 parks I've visited this year. It's the halfway point of my centennial journey, though I have no idea of this at the time. My time at Fort Vancouver includes a walk through the reconstructed 1840 frontier outpost. At Pearson Field, I examine the wood-framed early aircraft models after a discussion about the site's history with Robert, the museum manager. Among the famous military assignees to the post, Ulysses Grant was assigned to duty here in the early 1850s, as his career and commercial prospects languished. I sympathize, Sam.

John McLoughlin, the Hudson Bay Company's chief factor at Fort Vancouver, played a key role in the area's settlement. Called the "Father of Oregon," he provided land and other resources to early valley settlers. A half hour south of Fort Vancouver, the McLoughlin House in Oregon City stands as detached park property. John McLoughlin lived in the home from 1846 until his death in 1857. Unfortunately, the home is not open for tours on Wednesday, so I walk around the property on the Williamette River, reading the historical markers.

On the drive east to this trip's last two parks, I make a couple of stops on the Lewis and Clark Trail. The first is forty miles east of Portland. Bonneville Dam at the Cascade Locks on the Columbia River, a 1930s public works project, provides hydroelectric power and replaced the 1896 Cascade Locks and Canal for river navigation. The Bonneville Dam and the Grand Coulee Dam in west central Washington's Lake Roosevelt National Recreation Area are efforts to harness the enormous power of the Columbia River's elevation change.

The dam includes a fish ladder, a passage allowing fish through the dam to spawn. The bottom floor of the Army Corps of Engineers visitor center has a fish ladder viewing area. I watch different species work their way upstream in the plexiglass cutout. It's surprisingly mesmerizing, like a constantly changing fish tank.

On the Columbia's northern bank about five miles west of the dam, Beacon Rock is an 848-foot tall monolith that sits on the Washington side of the river within the Columbia River Gorge National Scenic Area. Lewis and Clark made note of the landmark when they stopped here to measure the river level. Their measurements indicated a tidal variation and the ocean's proximity, the easternmost point on the river where tidal influence is observed. A man named Henry Biddle purchased the rock in 1905 for one dollar and spent an enormous amount of time and effort building a stairway and paved trail to the top. It took another Herculean effort by Biddle's family to get the state of Washington to accept the rock as part of a state park and save it from planned destruction by the corps of engineers, who had designs to use the rock to help build the large jetty at the mouth of the river. I'm struck by Biddle's extraordinary passion for the landmark. The view at the top of Beacon Rock is worth the climb. I trade picture-taking duties with a couple at the summit after we collectively catch our breath. From here, I continue more than 150 miles east and about 30 miles north to overnight in Richland, Washington.

As the temperature rises Thursday morning, I begin a final day of exploration with the B Reactor tour at the US Department of Energy's Hanford site, part of the newly created **Manhattan Project National Historical Park**. The park is a unique NPS unit, with subunits in three different states and regions. The other two subunits are in Oak Ridge, Tennessee and Los Alamos, New Mexico. We'll visit both later this year. The tour turns out to be a fascinating trip through time.

B Reactor is the world's first full-scale nuclear reactor. The reactor converts uranium 235 to plutonium 239. The Hiroshima bomb's plutonium came from B Reactor. Although most of the surrounding support equipment, such as the cooling water facility, is gone, the main reactor building remains intact and restored to its basic World War II appearance. Its design and operation are centered about the reactor's 2004 aluminum charging tubes. Uranium fuel plugs spend one hundred days on average in the reactor before moving to recovery for ninety days. The original yield from two thousand pounds of enriched uranium 235 is half a pound of plutonium. Each aluminum tube holds thirty-two fuel elements, called slugs, for a total reactor fuel weight of five hundred thousand pounds, or 250 tons. Standing before the reactor, the complexity in this first-of-its-kind facility, and the inherent risks are compelling and obvious. The plant's successful operation without a major catastrophe was an extraordinary accomplishment given the full-scale deployment of this radical new technology in the 1940s. Even the layman visitor can appreciate the tremendous scientific and engineering achievement Reactor B represents. A mechanism on top of the reactor handled twenty-nine boron-spiked, stainless-steel rods that served as an emergency shutdown system. The facility used seventy-five thousand gallons per minute of Columbia River water to cool the reactor, though the reactor's water volume is only four hundred gallons. The average one-second contact time for reactor water increased its temperature from ambient, around 55 degrees, to 195 degrees.

Manhattan Project, Reactor B

Only project participants with the highest security clearance got as close as we are today. The control room and process control equipment are equally impressive considering the limitations compared to modern control systems. At peak capacity, the Hanford site included nine reactors and five chemical separation plants for fuel processing.

After two more brief stops on the Lewis and Clark Trail, I arrive at the final NPS unit for the trip and June, **Whitman Mission National Historic Site**. Early pioneers and missionaries, Marcus and Narcissa Whitman are forever linked with the settlement of the Pacific Northwest. As devout Methodists, the Whitmans accepted the call of the Second Great Awakening in the 1830s to share their faith with the Oregon Territory's native population. They traveled to Oregon country in 1836 and established a settlement and mission among the Cayuse tribe. The Whitmans became the first nonnative couple to cross the continent overland, traveling on what would be known as the Oregon Trail. The mission served as an important way station for the thousands of pioneers to follow. Sadly, Marcus and Narcissa lost their lives during a Cayuse raid on the mission in November 1847. The attack was triggered by native fear after local tribes suffered grievous losses in pandemics caused by exposure to the settlers.

Whitman Mission is near the Walla Walla River in present-day southeastern Washington. I walk the site behind the visitor center. Outlines on the ground are all that remain of the buildings that once stood here. I climb the hill to the Whitman Memorial, an obelisk on top of a stone base overlooking the site and river beyond. At the foot of the hill lies the mission grave site. The Whitman story is a fascinating one about accomplishment in the face of tremendous obstacles and selfless sacrifice to a greater cause, ultimately ending in tragedy. Sadly, the theme of the Whitman's story replayed many times during nineteenth-century America's westward expansion.

As the late-afternoon sun moves across the sky to the northwest, I start across the state to Seattle for tomorrow morning's flight home. I've left only two parks unvisited in Washington state, Lake Chelan National Recreation Area and Lake Roosevelt National Recreation Area. I also failed to return to two of the parks Kareen and I visited in 2013, **Ebey's Landing National Historical Reserve** on Whidbey Island, and **San Juan Island National Historical Park** in the Salish Sea island chain of the same name northwest of Seattle. The historical park preserves two military posts occupied for a year while the US-Canadian boundary remained under arbitration, originating in a dispute over a farmer's pig. The English and American camps showed little heart for war, even inviting their opposites to attend picnics. History is murky on the fate of the pig, but I like to think it served as the guest of honor at one of the camp picnics.

Our visit to Friday Harbor on San Juan Island over Labor Day weekend is particularly memorable. Kareen gamely played along with our challenging park itinerary, insisting only that we take a whale-watching boat tour out of Friday Harbor. We scheduled the tour on a small boat restricted to groups of four or five at a time. Most people join tours on much larger boats with open-air top decks and metal benches. I had no enthusiasm to join a large, crowded boat.

When we left the dock, the captain admitted to his now-committed audience, "We haven't seen an orca around the island in weeks and haven't spotted a whole pod in over two months." The orca pods had been out to sea hunting. Knowing there's a lot of chance involved in wildlife viewing, we didn't have much time to let the disappointment settle before we rounded a narrow peninsula off the island's southeastern corner to find a whole pod of orcas in the channel between San Juan and Lopez Islands. The thirty or forty killer whales, spread over two to three square miles in the strait, breached the surface on all sides of our boat for over an hour. We twisted our heads from side to side as if watching a tennis match. The beautiful ocean mammals seemed delighted to be home, almost as delighted as a smiling Kareen seemed watching them. I've rarely seen her so thrilled. She'd been insistent about the whale watching, an activity I mustered little enthusiasm for in advance. During our unexpected run-in with the prodigal pod, watching Kareen became as enjoyable as watching the whales.

As we continue to visit parks together, wildlife repeatedly appears out of nowhere for Kareen's viewing pleasure. Bison, bears, elk, bighorn sheep, orcas, humpbacks, dolphins, and birds all answer her siren call. She is a wildlife magnet. I told Kareen, "You fell off a pirate ship as an infant and an orca pod raised you." The flying orcas had come to see an old friend.

21 *Beltway or Bust*

EARLY TUESDAY MORNING, July 12, my flight lands at Reagan National, ushering the National Capital Region into my centennial story. I'm excited to be in this target-rich environment. The itinerary includes fifty-two NPS units over the next eleven days. The only new park among them is a DC unit created in April. After stops in the District of Columbia and the surrounding areas of Maryland and Virginia, we go south into Virginia's Tidewater region and west across the Piedmont. Next, we'll travel through western North Carolina and South Carolina to complete centennial visits in the Palmetto State. I'm angling for new experiences at familiar parks in this history-rich region. It's time to get busy.

Waiting on the rental car shuttle outside the terminal, the sun bakes my skin in this outdoor sauna of thick, humid air. The forecast warns of temperatures in the high nineties for the next week. From Reagan National, I blast the A/C and head north on the **George Washington Memorial Parkway**. The parkway runs alongside the Potomac for 25 miles, preserving the natural beauty of the river's Virginia shoreline. George Washington's Mount Vernon home and I-495 bookend the parkway. As an NPS unit, the parkway includes multiple subunits and a 6.8-mile section across the Potomac in Maryland renamed the Clara Barton Parkway. The Clara Barton Parkway runs past Clara Barton's home and her former base of operations as the founder and leader of the American Red Cross. Another parkway subunit is the Mount Vernon Trail, a walking and biking trail running parallel to the parkway from Mount Vernon to Theodore Roosevelt Island.

I navigate the ebbing rush hour to stop at the **Lyndon Baines Johnson Memorial Grove on the Potomac**. The seventeen-acre memorial to our thirty-sixth president lies between the parkway's north and southbound lanes. I walk among the five hundred white pine trees interspersed with Johnson quotes inscribed in Texas granite, passing the forty-three-ton, nineteen-foot central monolith. Venturing past the Navy-Marine Memorial, honoring Americans lost at sea, I conclude my time in Lady Bird Johnson Park, formerly known as Columbia Island, to park the car a mile north at Arlington National Cemetery.

Our most famous national cemetery since its Civil War establishment, Arlington National Cemetery honors our military dead on its 624 acres. Today marks my fourth visit. The solemnity of these hallowed grounds feels palpable. A wave of heat and humidity washes over me as I start for **Arlington House, The Robert E. Lee Memorial**. The cemetery occupies the former estate of the US Army officer, US-Mexican War veteran, and Civil War field commander of all Confederate Armies. The first president's adopted grandson, George Washington Parke Custis, constructed the Greek Revival home from 1802 to 1818. Lee moved into the house after his 1831 marriage to Custis's daughter, Mary. Declining President Lincoln's offer of a federal army command at the Civil War's onset, Lee penned his resignation letter from the US Army here on April 20, 1861. Virginia had seceded from the Union a day earlier, and Lee cited loyalty to Virginia in his decision. He departed Arlington House on April 22, never to return. The cemetery's establishment on Lee's family estate in 1864 served the practical need for a national cemetery to bury the mounting war dead and as retribution by US Army leaders for Lee's decision.

The blistering hot day is in full swing for the climb to Arlington House. The home sits atop a hill overlooking the cemetery and, more distant, the National Mall extending to the US Capitol.

Hauling my backpack, I zigzag up the circuitous route to the mansion. When the home's portico with its Greek-style columns emerges, perspiration streams down my face. My centennial T-shirt is soaked. Pausing to catch my breath, I drop the pack next to the roped barrier opposite the portico. Pierre Charles L'Enfant's grave lies a few feet away. Reinterred here in 1909, L'Enfant's final resting place commands the center of Washington, DC, the city he designed in 1791.

Arlington Cemetery, L'Enfant's Grave

I take pictures of the city across L'Enfant's memorial and return my attention to Arlington House. After my third time through the self-guided tour, I visit the bookstore behind the house, located inside former slave quarters. Guzzling a bottle of water between gasps for air, I wish the bookstore manager a happy centennial as I don my backpack to return into the midsummer heat.

A mile north off the GW Parkway, **Theodore Roosevelt Island** remembers our twenty-sixth president's meaningful reforms and conservation efforts. Although Yellowstone National Park dates to 1872 and the Grant administration, the concept of protecting lands for public benefit owes much to Theodore Roosevelt's leadership. We owe a great debt to Roosevelt for championing what has been called, "America's Best Idea." I cross the pedestrian bridge over the

Potomac channel that creates the island to study Teddy's statue centerpiece flanked by stone tablets inscribed with his quotes. After walking a section of the two and a half miles of mostly shaded walking trails serving the midday exercisers moving about, it's time to continue north.

At Turkey Run Park, the parkway headquarters maintains over forty passport stampers representing many locations within or near the parkway. This year, the headquarters also keeps four of the over 450 special, fixed-date centennial stampers scattered around the country. Before year's end, I will collect 432 of these in person. The four units I've visited so far today bring the year's total to 200.

From Turkey Run, I take the Beltway (I-495) one exit north to the Clara Barton Parkway for the short drive east to Glen Echo Park and **Clara Barton National Historic Site**. Built in 1891 as a storage location for disaster relief supplies, the home served as Clara Barton's residence and the American Red Cross headquarters from 1897 until her death in 1912. Clara Barton National Historic Site holds the distinction of being the first unit created to honor a woman's accomplishments. Barton began her charitable work in earnest in 1862 during the Civil War. She served as a battlefield nurse and played a major postwar role identifying deceased prisoners of war in Confederate prisons such as Andersonville. She championed the 1864 Treaty of Geneva, launching the International Red Cross. After the US ratified the treaty in 1882, she led the American Red Cross as president for twenty-three years. The American Red Cross first gained public acclaim during disaster relief efforts following the Johnstown Flood.

I toured the home, presently closed for renovations, two years ago. Today, I settle for a picture of the home behind a chain-linked fence securing the building materials stacked on site. From the construction zone, I cross the parking lot to Glen Echo Park, a partially restored amusement park that dates to the 1890s.

Returning to Virginia, Great Falls Park is seven miles northwest of the Beltway at the Great Falls of the Potomac. Great Falls Park includes some of the world's most dangerous and popular rapids for kayakers. The Potomac River drops seventy-six feet in less than a mile through multiple twenty-foot waterfalls as it narrows from one thousand feet to less than a hundred. Considered extremely hazardous to any but the most experienced and prepared, Great Falls are the only Class V rapids in the world navigable by kayak and located near a major metropolitan area, fifteen miles distant from the capital. Per the NPS website, "the Great Falls of the Potomac display the steepest and most spectacular fall line rapids of any eastern river." I first visited the Maryland side two years ago. Today is my first chance to see the rapids up close in Virginia, though the falls and Potomac River are in Maryland since the state line follows the south bank of the river.

I recently watched an episode of Showtime's *60 Minutes Sports* that featured a story about twenty-three-year-old Shannon Christy, who died before the annual Great Falls kayak race in July 2013. During an early-morning practice run, Christy became trapped and drowned under the torrent of a deadly chute known as the "subway." Christy became the third kayaker to drown in the rapids since 1998. I scan the rapids, the subway flowing ominously at its center, and cringe at the tragedy of such a young person, full of life and good spirits, helplessly pinned under the raging water.

From Great Falls, I'm off to **Manassas National Battlefield Park** in Manassas, Virginia. Manassas saw two major Civil War battles, including the first major battle in the war's Eastern Theater. The First Battle of Manassas (Bull Run), took place in July 1861. General Thomas Jackson led southern troops in a fierce rally that forever after gave him the nickname Stonewall. Jackson and his troops made their famous stand on Henry Hill, behind the park's visitor center. Two years ago, I toured the battlefield following the course of battle. Today's stops include the Stone House, in sight of Henry Hill at the junction of Highways 234 and US 29, and Brawner Farm on the western end of the battlefield. The Second Battle of Manassas took place in August 1862. Close fighting and desperate combat ended in another Confederate victory. In the aftermath of the second battle, Union commander General John Pope was relieved and assigned to command troops combating a Sioux uprising in Minnesota.

Moving along in eastern Virginia, **Wolf Trap National Park for the Performing Arts** features an outdoor amphitheater among multiple performance venues and is the only NPS unit dedicated to presenting the performing arts. No performances are scheduled today. I snap a picture of the Feline Center and collect the passport stamps. It's my second visit to Wolf Trap, but I've yet to attend an event here. I continue twenty miles west in anticipation of a relaxing dinner and a good night's rest.

Wednesday begins with a couple of stops at affiliated locations in the **Shenandoah Valley Battlefields National Historic District**. During the Civil War, the valley saw almost continuous conflict up and down its length. Nestled between the Blue Ridge and Appalachian Mountains, the valley runs from the Potomac to the James River. This productive agricultural area held the moniker "Breadbasket of the Confederacy." It's also a natural travel corridor from southwestern Virginia to Maryland and Pennsylvania. The valley played a major role in both of Lee's northern campaigns. I'm passing through the north end this morning, stopping in Front Royal and Strasburg, Virginia, before visiting **Cedar Creek and Belle Grove National Historical Park**.

The Battle of Cedar Creek, October 19, 1864, proved a decisive event in the four-year struggle for the Shenandoah Valley. Union General Philip Sheridan secured his place in American history and folklore for his dramatic midmorning return to the battlefield, rallying Union troops after a predawn Confederate assault across Cedar Creek threw the federals into retreat northward. Sheridan's Union forces waged an afternoon counterattack that scattered southern troops down the valley in defeat. Over 8,600 casualties made it one of the valley's bloodiest engagements. I spent a day exploring the grounds last year. Today, I stop at the visitor contact station in Middletown, Virginia, and amuse myself rereading the information panels and watching the electronic battlefield exhibit, out of order during my previous visit.

From Cedar Creek, I cross the valley to the headquarters of one of my favorite parks. **Shenandoah National Park** strikes me as four parks in one. The 105-mile Skyline Drive follows the crest of the Blue Ridge Mountains north and south on a two-lane road that weaves among and over the peaks separating the Shenandoah Valley and the endless hills of Virginia's Piedmont. Over two days last year, I traveled Skyline Drive north and south, noting the directional difference in scenery. Hikes varying in length and exertion level beckon the visitor to scenes over the valley backdropped by the Appalachians and the rounded hills of the Piedmont stretching east to the horizon. The panorama changes further from morning to afternoon as the sun and shadows move, leaving the piedmont's hills in profile as they transition from green to black. Shenandoah strikes me as addictive. The more you see of it, the more you want. Today's visit is much shorter. Only a commitment to the schedule overcomes the urge to head in either direction for a few hours on one of the park's trails. I have a specific location within the next park, sixty miles east, that has eluded me during earlier visits but is open today.

The ranger staffing the headquarters front desk listens with great enthusiasm about my year through over half the National Park System. She educates me on earthcaching, which is like geocaching except participants hunt natural features and landscapes rather than a physical cache. Shenandoah's elevated command over western Virginia offers an ideal location to hunt extraordinary landscapes.

Shenandoah, Piedmont at dusk

The Ellwood House, also called the Lacy House, dates to the 1790s and served as staff headquarters for Union Generals Gouverneur Warren and Ambrose Burnside during the Battle of the Wilderness on May 5–6, 1864. In prior visits to the battlefields protected within **Fredericksburg and Spotsylvania County Battlefields Memorial National Military Park**, the Ellwood House had been closed but is open today. The park protects much of the remaining undeveloped ground from the Battle of Fredericksburg, December 11–13, 1862, the Battle of Chancellorsville, April 27–May 6, 1863, the Battle of the Wilderness, and the Battle of Spotsylvania Court House, May 8–21, 1864. I discuss war history with the Ellwood docents, listening to the story of the plantation house, its occupants, its role during the Battle of the Wilderness, and its famous gravesite for Stonewall Jackson's amputated arm.

After Ellwood, the next stop is the Chancellorsville Battlefield Visitor Center. I walk the short trail to the spot where Jackson was shot by friendly fire. Jackson had returned to Confederate lines after reconnoitering the Union rear guard. North Carolina troops mistook him for a Union patrol and opened fire, hitting him twice in the right hand and left arm. Earlier in the day, the Confederates routed the Union right flank due in large part to Jackson's strategic genius and determination. The defeat at the Battle of Chancellorsville led to the demotion of Union General Joseph Hooker, just as the defeat at Second Manassas had exiled Pope to the western frontier. The Battles of the Wilderness and Spotsylvania Court House represent Grant's push south across Virginia during the final year of the war, when he famously cabled President Lincoln, "I've determined to fight it out on this line if it takes all summer."

I skip the Spotsylvania Court House Battlefield on this trip due to time constraints. Kareen and I walked the battlefield in August 2012, stopping for reflection at the Bloody Angle in the Confederate defensive salient. It's hard to stand in this quiet place and imagine bodies buried so deep they filled the ten-foot trench. The battle's horrors defy comprehension. During the peak of the battle, heavy small-arms fire passing over the salient trench felled at least one mature tree. The Smithsonian Museum of American History in Washington, DC, displays a tree trunk taken from the battlefield near the Bloody Angle, cut in half by shot and shell.

Major General John Sedgwick fell mortally wounded early at Spotsylvania from the bullet of a rebel sharpshooter fired from approximately one thousand yards away. The .58-caliber slug hit Sedgwick below the left eye. Minutes earlier, he scolded those around him seeking cover as bullets landed in their midst, reportedly saying, "They couldn't hit an elephant at this distance." Sedgwick became the highest-ranking member of the Union army to die in the Civil War. Previously, Major General John Reynolds, also shot by a sniper, died on the first day of Gettysburg. Contemporaries held both generals in high esteem. Though Reynolds led an army and Sedgwick led a corps, Sedgwick held senior rank at the time of his death by date of promotion. A statue of Sedgwick at West Point Military Academy sits across from Trophy Point next to the parade grounds. At the academy, legend suggests cadets who spin Sedgwick's spurs at midnight while in full dress uniform have good luck with subsequent exams.

From Chancellorsville, it's a short drive to the Fredericksburg Battlefield Visitor Center, followed by the park headquarters at Chatham. Dating to before the American Revolution, the house at Chatham served as the Union headquarters before the Battle of Fredericksburg. General Ambrose Burnside ordered thousands of northern troops to their deaths, charging the protected Confederate position behind a stone wall along a sunken road on Marye's Heights. More Union soldiers died in one hour during the ill-conceived advance than in any other hour during a Civil War engagement. Troops making the assault suffered over five thousand casualties in two hours. It's a one-sided slaughter that led directly to Burnside's demotion back to corps command from his disastrous tenure in command of the Army of the Potomac. Having explored battlefield sites around the town in earlier visits, this is my first visit at Chatham. The mansion sits atop a hill overlooking Fredericksburg across the Rappahannock River. Walking the estate grounds reading interpretive panels, I resist the urge to get lost in the history of the place. I could spend hours here. The list of famous people who stopped at Chatham includes George Washington, Thomas Jefferson, Abraham Lincoln, Clara Barton, and Walt Whitman. At least eleven NPS units are namesakes of this famous entourage.

Today's last stop requires a half-hour drive toward DC to **Prince William Forest Park**. The park covers over seventeen thousand acres of Piedmont forest. A preserved woodland and water shed to the DC metro area, the park offers a refuge for camping, hiking, orienteering, and a peaceful woodland respite. Neighboring the Marine Corps base at Quantico, Virginia, the Marines still conduct exercises within park boundaries.

Arriving late in the day, I ask a ranger to take my picture standing within the Dutch door frame next to the visitor center for a social media post celebrating my two hundredth NPS unit visited this year. I discover later that I omitted seven units in my park planning journal, throwing the count off. When the year started, I had no idea how travel would literally fill the year and never imagined that something as simple as tracking parks visited could get complicated by the sheer size and spontaneity of the endeavor.

During my first visit to Prince William Forest Park, I learned of the National Museum of the Marine Corps a mile away. The museum's lure proved overwhelming, so I followed the scenic drive through the forest and spent the balance of the day at the marine museum, a fascinating presentation of Marine Corps and US military history.

Today's visit at Prince William Forest Park must include a walk in the woods. I need to break a sweat after a day of driving across Virginia. After receiving hiking suggestions, I leave the car on the scenic drive and start on a five-and-a-half-mile hike on the South Valley and Turkey Run Ridge Trails. It's hot and humid, especially on the South Valley Trail that hugs the bank of the South Fork of Quantico Creek. The Turkey Run Ridge Trail, passing through both dense and open stands of forest, isn't much cooler. Fortunately, some trail sections provide shade. I return to the rental at 6:00 p.m. with every item of clothing saturated. I've even managed to sweat through my cargo shorts. I look like someone thought I caught fire and tried to put me out. Nonetheless, I'm thrilled with the scenery and exercise during this selective exploration of Prince William Forest Park. It's a perfect finish to another great day.

Thursday begins with a trip across the Potomac into Maryland. It's my third visit to **Fort Washington Park,** protecting the massive brick masonry fort built to guard the capital's river approach. The grounds exhibit the evolution of US coastal defense systems, with the original fort constructed here in 1809 and subsequently destroyed by the British during the War of 1812. The army began building the brick structure visible today in 1814. Pierre Charles L'Enfant supervised the fort's initial construction until L'Enfant parted ways with his sponsor, acting Secretary of War James Monroe. Lieutenant Colonel Walker K. Armistead continued the project in 1815 as a peacetime initiative. Armistead's brother George led the valiant defense of Fort McHenry in Baltimore. His son, Lewis, is remembered for his brave leadership and death at Gettysburg during Pickett's charge. Declared finished but unarmed in October 1824, the structure was remodeled extensively in the 1840s with eighty-eight permanent gun platforms.

At a critical location commanding Potomac navigation south of the capital, the post anchored Washington's Civil War defenses as the only established fort protecting the capital at the start of hostilities. Over the following decades, the army modernized the armament to include new, more powerful weaponry. Fort Washington continued as an active military installation until its transfer to the Department of Interior in 1939. I enjoy a quiet early-morning walk in the park until the visitor center opens.

Today's second park is a short fifteen-minute drive downriver to **Piscataway Park,** protecting the Potomac's Maryland shoreline opposite George Washington's Mount Vernon estate. The park features the National Colonial Farm, a reconstructed 1770s farm and living history exhibit. Piscataway is operated under a partnership between the NPS and the Accokeek Foundation.

While at Piscataway, a rare situation develops, putting the parks and work in apparent conflict. Dialing the number for a scheduled conference call, I enter the call on time but for some reason my line is muted. It's maddening to listen to the others speculate as to why

I haven't joined the call, unable to correct them. Disconnecting and redialing the numbers fails to give me a voice. I'm forced to call one of the participant's cell phones and have him place his mobile phone on speaker mode next to the office phone dialed into the call. I so seldom work with internal colleagues these days, no one knows or cares if I'm connected.

A half hour south on two-lane, rural Maryland highways brings me to **Thomas Stone National Historic Site**. Stone served in the Continental Congress and signed the Declaration of Independence. Built in the 1770s, Stone called the home Haberdeventure and lived at the 1,077-acre plantation until he moved his family to Annapolis in 1783. Though he died in 1787, the home remained in the Stone family until 1936. Privately owned in the interim, a fire destroyed the center of the house in 1977. The National Park Service purchased the structure and property in 1981. One of the few surviving homes of a Declaration signer that dates to the same era, the park service opened the home to the public in 1997 after restoration to its earliest known layout. Amid Maryland's history-rich western neck, Thomas Stone National Historic Site connects both the **Star-Spangled Banner National Historic Trail** and the **Captain John Smith Chesapeake National Historic Trail**.

Per the trail's brochure, the 290-mile Star-Spangled Banner National Historic Trail connects the places, people, and events that led to our national anthem. Francis Scott Key penned the anthem after observing the twenty-five-hour bombardment of Fort McHenry from a British naval vessel in Baltimore Harbor. The Captain John Smith Chesapeake National Historic Trail commemorates British explorer and settler John Smith's exploration of the Chesapeake Bay area and its tributaries from 1607 to 1609. The trail's multiple segments represent Smith's voyages and extend beyond his early travels to the far reaches of the Chesapeake Bay Watershed. The trail travels nearly three thousand miles in aggregate and extends as far north as Cooperstown, New York.

From Thomas Stone, I make several stops at state parks and affiliated locations on the Captain John Smith Chesapeake National Historic Trail and Potomac Heritage National Scenic Trail, including Stratford Hall along the southern shore of the Potomac River in Tidewater Virginia. Henry "Lighthorse Harry" Lee, winner of the Congressional Medal of Honor for his service in the Revolutionary War, named his plantation home Stratford Hall. Henry Lee's son, Robert Edward, born in this house on January 19, 1807, would surpass his father in fame.

Eight miles upriver from the Stratford Plantation, **George Washington Birthplace National Monument** preserves the location of a small farm home on the bank of Popes Creek near the Potomac where George Washington was born to Augustine and Mary Ball Washington on February 22, 1732. The original house disappeared long ago. The park features a 1931 memorial house next to the outline of the suspected original farm home. The unit shares Washington family history and information about the early settlers in colonial Tidewater Virginia.

Washington's birthplace lies directly between the water and land routes, to the east and west respectively, commemorated by the **Washington-Rochambeau Revolutionary Route National Historic Trail**. The trail covers over one thousand miles of land and water routes used by Washington and French General Jean Baptiste Donatien de Vimeur, comte de Rochambeau, to move the Continental and French Armies from upstate New York and Rhode Island to Yorktown, Virginia, during the summer of 1781. Relocating both armies proves a brilliant military stroke. The combined force besieged the British army commanded by Lord Charles Cornwallis. We'll visit all the NPS units along the trail this year, including Yorktown. From the banks of the Potomac, I start the hour-and-a-half drive north to my hotel room across the street from Nationals Park in Washington, DC.

Friday morning breaks at six o'clock as I bounce out of bed to begin this much-anticipated day. Since my objectives have shifted to visit as many NPS units as possible this year, today is literally the tree of low-hanging fruit. Fourteen units are found on the National Mall or within a few blocks. Expanding the area another mile adds four more units. Except for one new unit, I've visited all these sites multiple times. Today's visits target any missing lapel pins for the exhibit and collecting the centennial passport stamps. I visited DC last September and collected most of the lapel pins representing units on the Mall. Today I'm checking for any I missed. I'm also armed with a list of twenty-seven of twenty-eight centennial stamps located in the District of Columbia. Though using the stampers is always free, today's haul comes with a physical price.

I begin by driving to locations too distant from the Mall to efficiently walk, then return the car to the hotel and take public transit to the Mall for a walking tour of the city center. Others suggested I use the people mover or hire a cab to curb the walking distance, but I opt for the physical challenge of walking between the units despite the oppressive heat.

I leave at 7:45 a.m. for the **National Capital Parks-East** headquarters in Anacostia Park. The NPS unit National Capital Parks–East provides oversight for fourteen NPS locations in and around Washington, DC. The park contains over eight thousand acres of varied natural, historic, and recreational areas. The administrative structure can be confusing. Seven of the fourteen sites within National Capital Parks–East are counted as separate units.

The first park ground I enter today, Anacostia Park, includes over twelve hundred acres and eleven miles of Anacostia River shoreline before it meets the Potomac. I'm seeking the park's centennial stamp at the park headquarters. Inside, I ask a nice gentleman at the front desk for the stamp, but he's unsure where it is. As we talk, Ranger Vince stops and motions for me to join him down the hall at his office. He compliments me on my centennial T-shirt and the NPS pins on my hat. I summarize my tour de force centennial celebration. He offers me a bottle of water, which I graciously accept, and tells me I must get an NPS centennial hat when I stop at Frederick Douglass National Historic Site later today. The hat has Anacostia Park on the side, and Anacostia Park is the first NPS location that had their name added to the side of the centennial hats on sale this year. Interesting, I think, for someone who finds the centennial merchandise irresistible and has over thirty-five centennial T-shirts at home to prove the point. I've been collecting centennial merchandise across the system. His enthusiasm is a spark for the day, in case I'm in want of motivation for the forced march I've planned around the city. His smile and good cheer intensify my own, shaking off the last threads of morning cobwebs. I'm a bit shocked that this busy park ranger is taking time out of his day to talk to me about my projects and park promotional items. I thank him for his time, say good-bye, and head for the parking lot.

Frederick Douglass National Historic Site is about a mile away. I've toured the 1850s home of the ex-slave-turned-champion of human rights, Frederick Douglass, on two prior visits in 2007 and 2012. I stopped here at least three other times after passport stamps or other specific items. The gift shop manager hands me one of the NPS centennial hats with Anacostia Park on the side and informs me it's a gift from the National Park Service for visiting over two hundred parks already this year. Ranger Vince had phoned these folks ahead of my arrival. I'm touched by the gesture.

From Frederick Douglass National Historic Site, I return to the Hampton Inn to ditch the car. I'm traveling on the DC Metro and then by foot for the next parks. I still have fourteen more units to visit today and other stamping stops for a total of over twenty locations. I walk for the exercise and the additional time among the monuments and memorials. With temperatures soaring to the high nineties, I expect to be less energetic by tomorrow night.

After exiting the Metro at the L'Enfant Plaza station, I start west on D Street, headed for the **National Mall and Memorial Parks** headquarters. Collecting the location's two passport cancellations, I angle across Fourteenth Street toward the Tidal Basin and the **Thomas Jefferson Memorial**. After its 1934 authorization, the park service dedicated the colonnaded memorial honoring our third president in April 1943. From the memorial, I walk across the Tidal Basin inlet and through the Japanese Yoshino Cherry Trees planted here to the **Franklin Delano Roosevelt Memorial**.

The FDR Memorial honors our thirty-second and longest-serving president with four outdoor rooms covering the history of FDR's administration. Inside the gift shop, I purchase two bottles of water, guzzling one at the counter. My backpack in tow, I'm already a sweaty mess. This plan begins to feel more like a military exercise than a delightful stroll in the park.

I continue the walk between the Tidal Basin and West Potomac Park to the **Martin Luther King, Jr. Memorial.** The memorial honors the Georgia minister and civil rights leader, remembering his aspiration for equal treatment of all Americans under the law. It's the newest completed memorial near the Mall, dedicated in August 2011. The memorial's gift shop on West Basin Drive yields stamps, another bottle of water and a soda. I'm losing fluids quickly. After discarding the first empty bottle, I keep the next two to refill them. I drain both bottles at least half a dozen times by day's end.

Crossing Independence Avenue, I turn right at the DC War Memorial and walk to the ranger station and information kiosk past the John Paul Jones Memorial. The Mall's multiple ranger stations and information kiosks are staffed on a rotating basis depending on manpower. Six different centennial stampers are scattered among these stations.

Directly north looms the **Washington Monument.** The monument's construction dates to July 1848 and continued for ten years until funding ran out. The 555-foot, 5-inch white obelisk stood uncompleted for eighteen years until President Ulysses Grant approved an act to finish the project in 1876. The capstone was set in 1884 before its dedication in February 1885.

From the ranger station, I follow the paved walking path on the right and turn left, passing the **World War II Memorial,** honoring the men and women from all fifty states and the US territories who served in our military during the Second World War. Some personalities and historians have called World War II–era Americans the greatest generation for their sacrifice and patriotism. The moniker is fitting, in my own humble opinion.

Walking west along the Reflection Pool, I come to the **Korean War Memorial** on the left. The memorial honors those who served during the hostilities on the Korean Peninsula from 1950 to 1953, when a cease fire ended the bloodshed but not the acrimony between ideologies that triggered the conflict. I had the opportunity to visit the Korean DMZ (demilitarized zone) in 2006 during a work trip. Seeing the heavily fortified border is a heavy dose of reality. Buffered by a no-man's land between high, chain-link fencing topped by razor wire, both sides maintain opposing armed guards at frequent intervals. DMZ visitors are not allowed to approach the actual fence line but must remain about ten feet behind a painted yellow line. Taking a picture of the DMZ is considered a hostile act as a form of intelligence gathering. To avoid the provocation, photography and visitation is strictly controlled. The harrowing centerpiece of the Korean War Memorial features nineteen statues of soldiers with combat accoutrements. It's a unique and impactful design. I take a few pictures to add to my existing collection and move on to the ranger information station northwest of the memorial to collect the unit's centennial stamp.

I step a couple hundred feet north before turning west, to my left, to snap a picture of the **Lincoln Memorial** at the west end of the Mall. Up the steps sits the iconic statue of our beloved sixteenth president, Abraham Lincoln, sitting as if pondering some momentous issue. It is certainly true that Lincoln had many moments of somber reflection during his presidency. Lincoln led the nation through four years of unparalleled bloodshed during our civil war. His wisdom and political genius guided the nation to the abolition of slavery and the brink of reunification before his assassination. Though I've visited the memorial many times and read the inscriptions and interpretive displays in their entirety, I always pause at the top of the steps, under the shelter of the recess where the sculpture sits. As if it's an instinctual reaction, I read the passages from the Gettysburg Address and his Second Inaugural Address carved on the north and south walls. I think of achievement from humble beginnings, of enormous sacrifice and perseverance, and I reflect in sadness on how this man and our nation were robbed of his second term in office. It's a powerful experience, 151 years after his death.

In front of the memorial and to the left is the glossy, angled black wall that is the **Vietnam Veterans Memorial**. The wall serves as a tablet for 58,267 names (as of this writing), in chronological order of the date of casualty. The memorial includes two statues, The Three Servicemen and the Vietnam Women's Memorial. Congress authorized the memorial in July 1980 and the dedication took place on Veterans Day in 1984 when President Ronald Reagan accepted the completed memorial on behalf of the nation.

Continuing across the grounds, I turn north, passing **Constitution Gardens** on my right. Constructed for the American Bicentennial celebration in 1976, the forty-acre park contains the fifty-six Signers of the Declaration of Independence Memorial on a small island in the pond at the park's center. From Constitution Gardens, I cross Constitution Avenue to Twentieth Street, turning right at C Street to arrive at the Department of the Interior.

The DOI houses a small museum dedicated to America's public lands. Outside the museum on a pedestal are passport stamps for the DOI and National Park Service headquarters in the same building. Centennial stampers for both are added this year. I use the stamps before going to the second floor to check out the collection of park brochures outside the NPS offices. I'm looking for a few that I've missed. I use them to prepare for park trips, supplementing the information as the complexity of the park dictates. Most of the current brochures for the more than four hundred units in the park system are kept in stock in a set of magazine racks in the hall. I find a couple of unfamiliar brochures, putting one of each in my backpack. The set at home is nearly complete. (Author's note: The hallway brochure stands have since been removed.)

From the DOI, I'm back into the heat and headed east across the Ellipse, forming the southern section of **The White House** unit. The unit includes Lafayette Park across a pedestrian mall from the north side of the White House. My walks today through the Ellipse and Lafayette Park and my next stop at The White House Visitor Center are the extent of today's visit. I collect The White House centennial stamp, then walk across Pennsylvania Avenue South to Pershing Park, renamed the **World War I Memorial** by an act of Congress signed on December 19, 2014. Plans are underway to transform the small park east of the White House. As the work remains uncompleted, the official unit exists but awaits dedication.

Turning east from Pershing Park, I enter Freedom Plaza, part of **Pennsylvania Avenue National Historic Site**. The unit, designated in 1965 and adjusted and expanded in 1996, includes the statues and small parks adjacent to Pennsylvania Avenue, often dubbed "America's Main Street." The avenue connects the White House with the US Capitol. It's a short distance between Freedom Plaza and the next unit, **Ford's Theatre National Historic Site**.

Ford's Theatre, the site of President Abraham Lincoln's assassination on April 14, 1865, remains a functioning venue. Some of the lower-level museum artifacts are fascinating yet ghastly. The single-shot derringer pistol John Wilkes Booth used to assassinate Lincoln is displayed with other items found on Booth when he died trapped in a rural Maryland barn eleven days after the assassination. Lincoln's famous top hat is on exhibit, as is the blood-stained pillow placed under Lincoln's head. Carried across the street to the Petersen House and placed in a back bedroom, Abraham Lincoln died at 7:22 a.m. on April 15, 1865, punctuated by Secretary of War Edwin Stanton's comment, "Now he belongs to the ages."

From Ford's Theatre, I walk to the Smithsonian Museum of American History for a Star-Spangled Banner National Historic Trail stamp at the information desk. One of the most famous items in the museum's amazing collection is the original forty-two-foot by thirty-foot American flag that flew above Fort McHenry the morning after the 1814 British bombardment. To preserve the priceless relic, the flag remains in controlled conditions behind the museum's lobby. I feel as beaten and tattered as the 202-year-old flag. Covering over fifteen miles walking distance with my thirty-five-pound pack and consuming well over a gallon of water plus an unknown quantity of other fluids, my feet and ankles ache with each step. I've made it to sixteen NPS units today. It's my highest single-day total this year. Returning to the Metro station from whence the tour of the National Mall began, L'Enfant Plaza, I exit the Metro and shuffle back to the Hampton Inn opposite Nationals Park.

Back at the hotel, I request my car from the valet and go up to my room for a quick break. I've got just enough time to make it the two miles over to East Potomac Park and the National Capital Region headquarters for a final passport stamp. It's about 4:00 p.m., and I figure I might as well check out tomorrow's first stop, Oxon Hill Farm in Oxon Cove Park at the Maryland border with DC. The farm and park are managed as one of the fourteen locations within National Capital Parks–East. I pull into the parking lot at 4:30 p.m., after my GPS takes me into the adjacent neighborhood for an entrance that no longer exists. I've never been to this site, so I'm looking forward to seeing it. I ask a ranger leaving the parking lot about the farm's hours. It opens at 8:00 a.m. tomorrow.

As I'm making a note on the itinerary, I'm surprised by my ringing phone. It's a work colleague who rarely calls. I answer and am a bit shocked when he explains the subject. I've heard through the grapevine that our technical services group leader is leaving. The long hours and regular onboarding have worn him thin. I haven't thought much about the situation until my colleague, who is the position's hiring manager, explains why he believes I would be a good fit and should apply. He compliments my managerial performance when we worked together and believes my skill set matches the role. Am I interested? I would have to navigate the formal application process. The conversation surprises me, in part because it's the first time in over four years that anyone at a higher level has said anything complimentary about my managerial performance. I'm flattered by the kind words. He suggests I consider it over the weekend and call him early next week. While we're talking, I inform him about a customer who's an experienced manager and is looking for a new opportunity. This custermer had asked me if I might discreetly inform our leadership. If I pursue the opening, it's self-defeating to introduce an alternative candidate. This opportunity is my final lifeline in the company. If I say no, I will be gone in a matter of months. Of that, I'm certain.

After returning to the hotel, I walk a short distance east to a newly gentrified area of shops, restaurants, and bars to eat an early dinner at a sports bar. After dinner, I return to the room for a shower and change of clothes before heading across the street for a baseball game between the Washington Nationals and Pittsburgh Pirates, a

5-1 Washington victory. It's more relaxing watching an MLB game as a carefree, neutral observer than as a diehard fan. Oddly, during the game, the customer who I'd earlier recommended calls me to offer his personal email and phone number. I tell him, "You might be contacted about a role in our company." As we conclude the call, I'm undecided. I've got lots of drive time in the next few days to consider it. Since I haven't abused my body enough, I return to the sports bar to have a beer and some sliders for a postgame snack. Returning to my hotel room, I leave a path of clothes from the door to the bed. Somebody, in a fit of passion, tore my clothes off before throwing me on the bed for a night of lustful savagery. At least, that's how it looks the next morning. I'm asleep when my head hits the pillow.

Saturday starts at Oxon Cove Park. I walk the dirt lane from the parking area to Oxon Hill Farm, a working farm and agricultural living history exhibit managed by the NPS and opened to the public in 1967. Agricultural activities here go back to the 1600s. The interpretive displays along the lane explain the area's agricultural history. Bonded workers labored these fields until the Civil War. Visitors are encouraged to volunteer for activities, with different ones scheduled depending on the time of year. I'm not interested in feeding the chickens today. Instead, I'm after the site's lapel pins for the exhibit. It's unclear to me which subunits have the pins. I didn't have the time to visit all the NPS locations around the DC area last September. After collecting the passport stamps and buying the pins, I return to my car for the twenty-minute drive to another subunit for National Capital Parks–East, Kenilworth Aquatic Gardens.

When I scheduled this trip, I had no idea that today is the annual Lotus and Water Lily Festival held at Kenilworth Gardens, located within the northern part of Anacostia Park. The mid-July event highlights the water-borne flowering plants at full bloom. I'm excited to see the beautiful flowers on this first visit. Arriving before 9:00 a.m. keeps me ahead of the crowd. After the site's stamps and pins are secured, it's time to tour the gardens. As I'm returning from putting my backpack away in the car, I run into my park friend Deborah. I heard she would stop by the festival today. She's completing her garden tour as I'm beginning.

The lotus bloom in brilliant pinks, purples, and white. The water lilies appear in white, yellow, and shades of pink and purple. The festival features some of the most beautiful flowers I've seen. I take dozens of pictures with the Canon and enough with the iPhone for a social media photo album. I pass a guy sitting on the ground using a massive telephoto lens to take a picture of a lotus about two inches from the end of the lens. A butterfly flutters past my head as stare at a flower. It's beauty over beauty, a highlight of this DC trip.

Kenilworth lotus

The next stop is the nature center at **Rock Creek Park,** one of the country's largest natural urban parks and one of the oldest federal parks, created in 1890 and transferred to the NPS in 1933. Rock Creek Park extends over ten miles north from the creek's Potomac discharge.

From the nature center, I drive a mile and a half to Fort Stevens, managed by Rock Creek Park and part of the twenty miles of trenches and earthworks in the Civil War defenses of Washington. Confederate General Jubal Early appeared before Fort Stevens with fourteen thousand soldiers on July 11–12, 1864. Having led his forces through the Shenandoah Valley to attack Washington from the north, Early hoped to find the city's defenses weakened by the draw of soldiers away from the capital to replace massive combat losses suffered earlier in the year by the main Union army, now camped around Petersburg. Southern strategy gambled that Early's forces could defeat the Union garrison in the city and give the south leverage to sue for peace. Confederate leaders know Early's chances of breaking through and holding the capital for any length of time are slim, but they hope the move forces Grant to transfer enough soldiers north to permit a break out action through the Petersburg siege.

Two major things happened that doomed Early's campaign. First, his approach to Washington stalled during a delaying action fought by outnumbered federals at Monocacy. The rebels gained the field and resumed their advance but lost critical time. Secondly, the city's remaining garrison did not panic. They commandeered available manpower, including office clerks and the wounded who could operate a weapon, and manned the defenses with a stubborn resistance. These factors bought the time necessary for reinforcements to take positions in the defensive line and secure the capital. I enjoy my walk on the preserved Fort Stevens grounds, reading the interpretive panels covering the battle.

From Fort Stevens, I drive south to **Mary McLeod Bethune Council House National Historic Site**, a Victorian townhouse purchased by Mary McLeod Bethune in 1943. Her enduring legacy advocates education and its importance to personal empowerment and community development. The home served as her residence for six years and the National Council of Negro Women headquarters from 1943 to 1966. The council maintains the National Archives for Black Women's History. The archive includes personal papers, organization records, and photographs. I toured the home two years ago. Today, I'm buying the unit lapel pins for my exhibit and collecting the passport stamps for this unit and the **Carter**

G. Woodson Home National Historic Site. The Carter Woodson Home unit, created in 2006, preserves the residence and working space for Carter Woodson, who became the first major historiographer of African American history. Woodson lived in the home from 1922 until his death in 1950. I pass by the Woodson Home after leaving the Council House. Undergoing extensive renovation, the building opens for public tours in 2018.

My last driving stop today is the US Botanic Gardens near the Capitol. The US Botanic Gardens are not a part of the NPS but administered by the Architect of the US Capitol. I booked a room tonight at the Hyatt downtown and head there now, ready to park the car and move my bags into the room before one last DC park excursion. From the Hyatt, it's a walk to the Metro to ride to the Judiciary Square station. From there, I walk a mile past Union Station Plaza and the Senate office buildings to one of the newest NPS units.

Formerly known as the Sewall-Belmont House National Historic Site until its designation as a national monument in April 2016, **Belmont-Paul Women's Equality National Monument** protects an historic brick home dating to around 1800. The National Women's Party has operated out of the house since 1929. The site served as the home of the party's founder and famous suffragette leader, Alice Paul. The suffrage movement succeeded in championing the Nineteenth Amendment to the US Constitution, ratified in 1920. Campaign banners and flags adorn the walls. Some of the displayed items are pictured in parades and demonstrations next to the banners. Demonstrations outside the White House put tremendous pressure on President Woodrow Wilson, who finally capitulated, reluctantly supporting the women's vote. I've long admired Alice Paul for her courage, determination, and intelligence. She's a true hero of American history. It's an honor to tour her former home. Belmont-Paul Women's Equality National Monument is the 370th NPS unit I've visited lifetime.

From Belmont-Paul, I have one final National Mall walking tour. This afternoon's trek starts with the full two miles from the capitol to the Lincoln Memorial. Thousands crowd the Mall, gathered for an event called "Together 2016." It's a Christian rally to bring the message of Jesus into contemporary America. I navigate among the temporary barriers and fencing that the contractors and the park service use to segment areas of the Mall for large events. I slip past the rally's main stage north of the Washington Monument, my first destination. I skipped the monument bookstore yesterday, deferring it for today. Passport enthusiasts allow time at the bookstore to use the over thirty passport stampers the bookstore maintains. Soaked again, I'm struggling to stay cool and hydrated. As I'm finishing with the stampers, word circulates that the ninety-eight-degree temperature and onset of heat-related illness has led authorities to truncate the Together event. High humidity adds punching power to the temperature.

I exit the bookstore and continue past the Reflection Pool, temporarily leaving the festival crowd behind. The Vietnam Veterans Memorial information kiosk is open today. I use two additional centennial stampers kept at the kiosk and begin my final walk of the day on the Mall. Penetrating the dispersing throngs to return to the Hyatt via the Federal Triangle Metro station, it's frustrating navigating the crowd. I'm hot, tired, and dehydrated despite copious water consumption. I walk faster than the shuffling crowd, but rally attendees part, moving aside to yield the right of way to my determined gait. It's the nicest, most courteous crowd of this size I've encountered. The kindness touches me. I force a nod and smile at everyone as I move through each group. I'm passing eleven walking miles today on hot concrete.

Relieved to reach the hotel lobby, I remove my pack and sling it over my right shoulder. My left shoulder hurts too much from bearing a disproportionate burden. Back in the room, every piece of clothing comes off, hung up somewhere around the room to dry. I yank back the bedspread and lay in the center of the king-sized bed, spread eagle like Leonardo Da Vinci's Vitruvian Man. It's all I can manage to take a shower and limp across the street for a modest meal at a downtown pub. I'm shot. It's not long before I'm back on the bed, resting and cooling from stops at twenty parks and nearly thirty miles walked over the past two days in blistering heat. Maybe the people mover hadn't been such a bad idea after all.

22 *Equine Beach Bums*

DAWN BREAKS OVER the National Capital as I awake from a deep sleep, rolling out of bed and gimping across the room in pain. Hoping another hour of sleep will mitigate the agony, I return to bed and manage a few minutes of light sleep before rising for good. Swaying in the shower as warm water rolls down my body, I shift to spread the pain of bearing my weight. Speed walking on concrete over fifteen miles in ninety-five-degree weather on successive days has reduced me to a quivering wreck.

Despite an effort to move efficiently, it's 7:40 a.m. by the time I drive east out of DC. Shortly after crossing into Maryland on the Baltimore-Washington Parkway, I enter **Greenbelt Park**, an outdoor recreational area for the metro area not unlike Prince William Forest Park in Virginia. While Prince William lies adjacent to the Marine base at Quantico, Greenbelt's boundaries border the US Secret Service Academy in Maryland. NPS land buffers multiple government facilities. In Virginia, the Claude Moore Colonial Farm, a part of the George Washington Parkway, borders the FBI's Langley headquarters.

A federal project spawned Greenbelt in the 1930s as the first planned US community. Greenbelt Park became a unit in the National Park Service in 1950. A part of the unit, the Baltimore-Washington Parkway accessing the town and park opened in

1954. I enter the park today and pull into the headquarters parking lot. The small visitor contact station in the lobby has moved to a ranger station farther into the park. I continue past camping and hiking locations and find the ranger station using the park map. I collect the cancellations, but no pins are for sale. I will learn later in the year that the park administration ordered the unit's centennial pin, but only as a gift for park personnel. It will take plenty of communication and help to acquire a Greenbelt pin for the exhibit.

Continuing to Baltimore, the most famous among today's stops is **Fort McHenry National Monument and Historic Shrine**. Fort McHenry gains immortal status in American history from the garrison's successful defense of the British naval attack on September 13–14, 1814. Major George Armistead, commanding about one thousand men, celebrated the triumph on the morning of September 14 by raising the large American flag currently at the Smithsonian. The massive flag flown over the fort does not see action during the battle. A smaller flag flies amid the barrage of iron shell and shot. The victory secures Fort McHenry and, most importantly, the city of Baltimore. The fort never again sees hostile action. The victory saved the city from certain destruction at the hands of the British army who had sacked and burned Washington three weeks earlier. The British fleet and forces regrouped in Jamaica before reappearing at New Orleans, where the British suffered the decisive defeat at Chalmette by a mixed force of militia, regular army, local civilians, and assorted scalawags under General Andrew Jackson.

Fort McHenry elicits a patriotic sense, the country's only park with a dual official designation of national monument and historic shrine. I feel a sense of pride each time I come into view of the flag flying above the fort. The structure's firepower has range on the Patapsco River and its Northwest Branch as it merges with Baltimore Harbor. The battles fought over Fort McHenry and the city of Baltimore represent one of the three most important strategic victories in the War of 1812, the other two being Perry's Lake Erie naval victory and Jackson's victory in New Orleans. Baltimore is a major British target as the city's port served American privateers bent on disrupting British Atlantic commerce. Many of the most successful converted raiders originated in Baltimore shipyards. British Vice Admiral Alexander Cochrane, the English naval commander, referred to the city as a "nest of pirates." The city's rich history is shared in part through sites in the **Baltimore National Heritage Area.**

As I finish my tasks in the visitor center, the staff announces, "They're going to fire the cannon!" several times, referencing a living history program. I join other visitors inside the fort watching an artillery gun crew march out to the piece. The crew loads the barrel with harmless wood chips and a partial powder charge. The cannon's report shakes the ground as fire flashes and smoke emerges from the end of the barrel. I think about the roar of an actual battle with artillery firing at will. Accounts liken it to a constant rolling thunder at a distance. And the smoke from multiple cannon would shroud the area in a thick cloud in all but the windiest conditions.

Nine miles north of Baltimore's city center, the eighteenth century estate established by Colonel Charles Ridgely in 1745 survives as **Hampton National Historic Site.** His son, Charles Ridgely Jr., built a Georgian mansion on the property starting in 1783. At its 1790 completion, the mansion stood as the country's largest private residence. The estate expanded to more than twenty-five thousand acres with wealth generated from multiple business interests. Enslaved labor operated the plantation until the Civil War.

I toured the home two years ago. Heirlooms and furnishings speak to the occupants' family history over 150 years and six proprietors. The Ridgely family owned the property until 1948, when it became a national historic site. The site covers sixty-two acres, including slave quarters and some of the original farm buildings. Gardens and a greenhouse flank the home. My visit today is brief. I collect the site's cancellations and lapel pins before leaving for today's final park.

Assateague Island National Seashore protects the 37-mile barrier island on the coast of Maryland extending south into Virginia. It's impossible to drive the island's length, as no continuous public road exists. Visitors enter the island either from the Maryland or Virginia entrance. Visitors on the Virginia side enter Chincoteague National Wildlife Refuge while the northern entrance passes through Assateague State Park. The island shelters Chincoteague Bay from the Atlantic Ocean. The seashore's famous wild horses, a nonnative species originating from animals brought here by colonists in the 1600s, roam the island. The horses have adapted well to the island's harsh environment. I had the opportunity to visit both the Maryland and Virginia sides of the park during my first visit. The southern side features a wildlife loop circling Snow Goose Pool, the Woodland Trail, and Assateague Lighthouse warning seafarers away from the island's southern tip. This afternoon, I enter in Maryland, stopping first at Assateague Island Visitor Center. After getting hiking suggestions, I cross the Verrazano Bridge to the island.

Bayberry Drive enters the north side. Turning right on Bayside Drive, the salt marsh boardwalk trail stretches my legs. The island's ecosystem is a complex interplay between the open ocean and tidal marshes. Heavier foliage grows on the leeward, protected side of the island. Sand moved by wind and wave sculpts the oceanside's stark landscape. The tide flushes marshes and sheltered bays, transferring animals into the open ocean and back. Barrier islands like Assateague are constantly evolving under the forces that create them.

From the marsh, I continue farther on Bayside to a beach area facing the bay to the south. Past the knoll that bounds the beach, a large group of horses lounge in a circle on the sand. Some are lying down on one side as if enjoying a good nap as they work on their tan. "Wilbur, put a little more lotion on my baaaaaack!" Human beachgoers give the horse beach party a broad cushion on both sides. Nobody crowds the equine beach bash fun zone. Long hair flowing from the manes of the standing partiers floats in the southerly breeze off the water. From her visit here earlier this year, Deborah posted a picture on social media of a beach restroom with ponies standing in line at the entrance. I wouldn't want to be in line behind the horses! I would like to hear a talk by the ranger who taught them how to form a powder room que. I walk several miles of beach here and on the small peninsula's bayside to conclude my time in the park.

Assateague, equine beach bash

Tonight's stopping point, Salisbury, Maryland, halves the distance to Monday's first destination, **Harriet Tubman Underground Railroad National Historical Park**, declared a national monument in 2013 and redesignated the following year. Born in 1822 on a Dorchester County plantation, Harriet Tubman won her freedom in 1849 at the age of twenty-seven. She risked her life guiding others out of Maryland's Eastern Shore wetlands to freedom, completing thirteen trips to help over seventy to free northern or Canadian soil. Her navigational skill benefited the Union cause during the Civil War. She served the federal army as a nurse and spy and guided an armed assault. She became the only woman to lead assaulting troops during the Civil War. Her heroism in the face of great danger, and her sacrifices for others, inspire the sobriquet the "Moses of her people."

The new, developing park experience starts at the Blackwater Wildlife Refuge Visitor Center. The new park borders the refuge. With the park in its infancy last year, I spent the morning of my first visit watching a pair of nesting bald eagles sharing a large ever-green branch in the wetland refuge.

This morning, I stop at the NPS offices next to the new, still unopened visitor center. A Maryland state park ranger greets me in the office. The National Park Service and Maryland State Parks will jointly manage the unit. I'm looking for a unique passport stamper unavailable at the refuge. After striking out with the state ranger, I run into Superintendent Robert in the parking lot. He has the stamper I'm seeking and invites me into his office, sharing information about progress at the new park throughout our delightful conversation. Robert adds, "Go through the visitor center and have a look at the mock-ups of the permanent exhibits."

"I would love to see them," I reply to the kind offer.

As I'm walking about the exhibits, another park employee approaches me and starts, "You can't be in—" but stops after spotting my centennial T-shirt and pin-adorned hat. "Oh, it's okay," he finishes, apparently assuming I work for the park service.

Since I'm inside on Robert's invitation and have no ulterior motives, I respond with a silent smile. The mock-ups sharing Tubman's inspirational story survive my walkthrough unmolested.

From the park, I head north through several state parks and museums affiliated with the Captain John Smith Chesapeake National Historic Trail. At the Annapolis NPS office and the trail headquarters, I find the cubicles deserted as I locate six passport stampers left on a cabinet for public use. The staff is crowded into the conference room. After stamping, I pause to study the large wall map near the entrance showing the trail, its many branches and affiliated locations. Some unfamiliar sites catch my attention. Meanwhile, the meeting breaks up and a ranger in uniform asks, "Can I help you?"

"I just stopped by to get your passport stamps," I explain. "I've made it to over half the NPS units this year as a kind of personal centennial celebration." He listens as I explain the lapel pin endeavor.

"That's quite a project," he replies. "Have you been on our trail in Pennsylvania? We're opening up a new visitor location this year." He explains that new trail sections are filling in some gaps. "You've got quite a year going. I'll bet people tell you they're jealous all the time."

"They do. I'm very fortunate to have an opportunity to spend this year in the parks," I reply. "What is your role here?"

"I'm the trail superintendent," he tells me. "Wait a minute. I want to give you something." Returning, he's holding a couple of lapel pins and a coin. The pins, the NPS arrowhead and a small version of the triangular trail marker, I affix to my hat. The commemorative coin honors the tenth anniversary of the Captain John Smith Chesapeake National Historic Trail, established in 2006. "That's so kind of you," I say to the superintendent.

"Thanks for supporting your national parks," he replies, "and good luck with the rest of your year and getting to all the units."

I exit the office and walk to the car, feeling so good I ignore the pain from each step.

Returning to Virginia, today's final stop is the Battle of Bladensburg site on the Star-Spangled Banner National Historic Trail. The decisive British victory at the Battle of Bladensburg, August 24, 1814, exposed the capital to capture and burning. The Maryland State Historical Site visitor center is closed today, but I stop to explore and read the interpretive panels. The battle represents an American military debacle. Strategic weaknesses and a general lack of preparation and leadership all contributed to the defeat.

I continue driving past the District of Columbia to I-95 southbound and Richmond, shifting from the War of 1812 this afternoon to the Civil War tomorrow.

23 *Parks in the Piedmont*

DUSK DESCENDS AS I enter my Richmond hotel. It's the same hotel my father and I used during our trip last December. We spent two days exploring Richmond-area battlefields and parks. Before dinner, I buy an Apple Watch. Since Kareen and I had purchased Microsoft Bands on Christmas Eve, I had a total of four fail in under three months. Two stopped taking a charge and died, and the other two stopped working altogether. I didn't physically damage any of them. After discussion with my local Best Buy manager, I exchanged the fourth failed Band for a Polar fitness watch. I liked the product's functions. Unfortunately, the watch would not synchronize with the corresponding smart phone application after three weeks. I even tried direct connecting the watch to my laptop. Neither phone nor laptop could link with the watch. I purchased Kareen a Fitbit after her second Microsoft Band failed at the same time my fourth Band stopped working. When she misplaced the watch a few weeks later, I bought her a Garmin fitness watch, which seems to work. Many of these companies hurried their fitness watches to market and failed miserably at product reliability.

Tuesday morning, July 19, begins at Richmond's Tredegar Iron Works, now a **Richmond National Battlefield Park** visitor center. The park contains thirteen subunits with five visitor centers. On this, my fifth visit, I'll complete the tours of all thirteen locations. Regardless of how much time I spend at these places, it seems like I'm always finding new information and unknown aspects of the story. Today's agenda is compressed.

From Tredegar, I visit Richmond's other unit, **Maggie Walker National Historic Site**. My father and I enjoyed the ranger-led tour at Maggie Walker's former Richmond home last December. In 1903, Maggie Walker chartered a bank and became the country's first African American female bank president.

Drewry's Bluff lies nine miles due south and commands the approach to Richmond high above the northern bank of the James River. Union gunboats tested Confederate defenses here during the 1862 peninsula campaign, only to be pounded and driven back. As I stand in the earthworks, the position seems impregnable to river-based Civil War–era armament. About a mile east, I continue my morning walk around the ruins of Fort Harrison, one of the major defensive earthworks in the line circumnavigating the city.

Kareen and I visited the Cold Harbor battlefield during our trip to eastern Virginia in 2012. Even today, the Confederate position's strength leaves an impression, protected by trenches and log breastworks behind which the defenders' field of fire would have been murderous to attacking federal forces. From the battle's onset, troops attacking the fortified line fall in detail. After the war, Grant referred to the attack at Cold Harbor as his only regret in combat strategy. It gained nothing and resulted in carnage. The strategic error at Cold Harbor stems from a miscommunication among the Union army's leadership. In his memoirs, Grant states that he incorrectly assumed that the corps commanders had reconnoitered the ground before the attack. The corps and divisional commanders assumed that Grant personally had seen to battlefield reconnaissance. In fact, neither evaluated the ground and Confederate position. Cold Harbor stands with Fredericksburg and Pickett's Charge as ghastly slaughters deriving from frontal assaults on heavily fortified positions.

Last December, our history tour included Cold Harbor, a

walking tour of the Malvern Hill battlefield and Totopotomoy Creek Battlefield, and the Chimborazo Medical Museum. Chimborazo served as Richmond's largest hospital during the war. Today, the museum's exhibits focus on Civil War medical practices.

About seventy-five miles west of Richmond, **Appomattox Court House National Historical Park** marks the Civil War's effective end. Robert E. Lee, commanding the south's largest fighting force, succumbed to attrition and harsh reality. Lee surrendered his army to US Army Lieutenant General Ulysses S. Grant in Wilmer McLean's parlor. In one of history's great ironies, Wilmer McLean had moved his family to this rural Virginia location from the site of the first major battle, Manassas, during the fall of 1862.

My first visit to Appomattox fell during the 150th Civil War anniversary. The Appomattox Court House Sesquicentennial celebration ran for several days across key events surrounding Lee's surrender to Grant on April 9, 1865. I arrived at the park on Saturday, April 10, 2015, to witness the memorable spectacle. The Appomattox festivities followed among the last in the 2011–2015 sesquicentennial celebrations at the National Park Service's Civil War sites. I missed most of these events since I didn't learn about the program until late 2014. The sesquicentennial celebration presented challenges to see the park. With thousands of visitors, the park service arranged parking miles away with shuttle service. Pullouts remained closed to vehicle traffic. The celebration attraction revolved about the park's center. The place came alive with living historians, reenactors in period dress and uniform, cavalrymen displaying their skill on horseback, and a general buzz that thousands of guests give a park. I took note of the reenactors playing Grant and Lee. They looked the part. I walked past Grant and asked him if he "could give Lee a break, for old time's sake." He ignored me with a slightly bewildered expression. Apparently, General Grant hasn't seen *The Godfather.*

Today, I explore the park with its normal access and quiet, spending more time reviewing the impressive courthouse exhibits.

Walking through the reconstructed McLean House highlights this park for many Civil War buffs. Very little remains of the original home furnishings after the surrender as Union officers and soldiers, understanding the momentous occasion, purchased or confiscated everything not permanently affixed in the house. Only a few items eventually found their way back. The rest are scattered in other museum collections or have been lost to time.

During a pit stop to buy a sandwich, I call my work colleague who'd asked about the technical service group leader position. I inform him that I've thought about the opportunity and will apply for the position. I've struggled with the question all weekend. If I apply and am chosen, I must give up this park journey wherever it stands. If I decline, I'm accepting the imminent end of my time with the company after twenty years. After consulting further with Kareen over the next two weeks, we decide our marriage will suffer if both of us are working sixty-plus hours each week in high stress jobs. I reverse myself and withdraw from consideration. I've already started a new life and am committed to go down this path wherever it may lead.

Another fifty-five miles southwest in rural western Virginia, **Booker T. Washington National Monument** is a small, restored Civil War–era farm. Born enslaved here in 1856, Booker T. Washington went on to create the Tuskegee Institute. He left the farm at the age of nine as the Civil War closed and slavery ended. Washington understood the importance of education to societal progress. He championed literacy and higher education throughout his life. I toured the farm last year, the day after visiting Appomattox. Later in 2015, I made it to Washington's Tuskegee Institute, another NPS unit, and his home there, "The Oaks." We'll visit Tuskegee again later this year.

Continuing west across rural two-lane highways over and around the hills toward Roanoke, I arrive at Virginia's Explore Park Visitor Center on the **Blue Ridge Parkway**. The parkway runs 469 miles, from the southern end of Shenandoah's Skyline Drive to Great Smoky Mountains National Park near Cherokee, North

Carolina. I've been on the parkway in one place or another many times, but I've never driven the whole distance in one trip. All the sections I've traveled feature attractive Appalachian topography. Today I drive sixty miles south on the parkway before leaving the road's tranquil scenery to continue farther west for an evening meal and a night's rest in Wytheville, Virginia.

24 Over the Holler and into the Swamp

THE TRIP'S FINAL leg extends into the Carolinas. Wednesday begins early with a wake-up call to address work tasks, followed by a drive deeper into the Appalachians and Abingdon, Virginia. Late in the summer of 1780, backcountry patriots gathered to answer the call for the defense of southern Appalachia and eviction of British forces menacing rural Carolina. The mountain settlers and frontiersmen who started their journey from Abingdon on September 24 marched over two hundred miles to surround Loyalists at Kings Mountain, South Carolina. Militia and men from North Carolina's piedmont start in Elkin on September 27. The groups rendezvous at Morgantown on September 30. Other groups joined en route. The combined force totaled over two thousand men. The military victory on October 7, 1780, encouraged British commander Lord Cornwallis to withdraw northward to Virginia.

The **Overmountain Victory National Historic Trail** covers 330 miles, originating from Abingdon and Elkin, connecting in Morgantown, and continuing to Kings Mountain about 30 miles southwest of Charlotte. We will visit the trail's destination and battle site at Kings Mountain tomorrow. Today at the trail headquarters,

I study the exhibits covering the events of September and October 1780. The docent gives me a trail lapel pin like the one received in Annapolis. I wish her a great centennial and exit to continue my travel into Tennessee.

The **Andrew Johnson National Historic Site** in Greeneville, Tennessee preserves two personal residences, Johnson's tailor shop and a national cemetery named in his honor. A small brick structure next to the tailor shop, purchased in 1831, served as the original Johnson home until 1851. The family moved two blocks to a larger home they called "The Homestead." The Johnsons lived in The Homestead for twenty-four years, surrounding four years at the White House from 1865 to 1868.

Johnson presents a complicated figure. He inherited one of the greatest challenges any president has faced, reconstruction after decades of growing division, four years of war, and 620,000 Civil War military deaths. The House of Representatives impeached Johnson. The Senate absolved Johnson by one vote. Johnson's historical complexity lay central to his acrimony with Congress. A staunch Tennessee unionist during the war who served as the state's military governor under heavy criticism from southern sympathizers, Johnson and his presidential policies contrasted with the Republican-dominated Congress. He opposed the Thirteenth Amendment as vice president and fought the Fourteenth and Fifteenth Amendments as president. After defying the southern aristocracy in his home state, he did everything possible to restore them to power as postwar president. One could conclude the major driving force throughout his career was a bitterness at being excluded from the ruling elite. Once he had real power, he appeared to do everything possible to ingratiate himself to the same class he earlier opposed. Johnson's presidential record does not engender sympathy through modern eyes.

I'm headed east to Asheville, North Carolina, and the Blue Ridge Parkway's headquarters and visitor center. The **Blue Ridge National Heritage Area**, also based in the Asheville visitor center, celebrates the history and culture of North Carolina's mountain country and includes the state's twenty-five westernmost counties.

After a brief stop at the parkway's Folk Art Center, I travel south on I-26 to the next park, **Carl Sandburg Home National Historic Site**. The famous author and poet spent his last twenty-two years at Connemara Farm in Flat Rock, North Carolina. Sandburg moved to the small Appalachian foothills town at the age of sixty-seven after earning fame for his work.

I love the view of the house from the parking area, across a pond known as Front Lake. Walking the quarter-mile lane to the house, a one-hundred-foot rise, I enter the gift shop on the home's ground floor. During my home tour two years ago, I admired Sandburg's storage and filing system. According to rangers, Sandburg knew where items were and could retrieve them when needed. Papers, magazines, and an impressive book collection filled the middle of the upstairs living area. His study revealed some personal organization system combining shelves, stacks, and piles. He appeared to be a man constantly into something. The farm includes Sandburg's prized goats, kept in the goat barn among other farm buildings near the house.

Oconaluftee Visitor Center sits outside **Great Smoky Mountains National Park**'s east entrance, the southern terminus of the Blue Ridge Parkway. After a dozen or so visits to Great Smoky Mountains National Park, I'm approaching America's most heavily visited national park from the North Carolina side for the first time. Great Smoky Mountains National Park exceeds 11.3 million visitors in 2016. The next highest total among the sixty national parks is Grand Canyon National Park at nearly 6 million, followed by Yosemite National Park with over 5 million. Among all NPS units, Great Smoky Mountains trails both Golden Gate National Recreation Area and the Blue Ridge Parkway, which count over 15 million centennial visitors.

I reenter the parkway south of Maggie Valley at Soco Gap, fifteen miles from the southern terminus at mile marker 469. I'm taken by the scenery. The rounded, hardwood-covered Smoky Mountains are picturesque. I struggle to keep focus on the road. Adding to the view, ominous storm clouds loom over the mountains to the open, south side of the road. The rainstorm appears to be moving closer. I'm driving under the 45-mph speed limit much of the time. Sometimes the road requires a slower speed despite light traffic. Other times, I'm glancing across the landscape. I'm nearly to Big Witch Gap, about nine miles from the end, when I ease into a pullout for a better view. As I gaze over the mountains, I don't notice my foot relaxing on the brake pedal or think to put the car in park. The car inches up to the side of the relatively high stone curbing at the edge of the pullout. The curb is too high and sharp-edged to harmlessly roll up on like municipal curbing. I hit the curb creeping forward, driving the tire against the five-inch barrier. The jolt wakes me out of my haze as I brake and back away. I get out to see the right front tire torn open and flat, a hole in the sidewall. I mutter, "Dumbass!" to myself and start unloading bags to reach the emergency spare beneath the trunk's baseboard. The overlook offers plenty of space, but the ominous storm clouds looming above the mountains suggest urgency. I put the damaged tire in the cavity under the trunk and replace it with the spare. The donut-style spares typically have a maximum speed rating of 50 mph and are intended for short distances. That's not my problem today. My problem, other than blowing my time in the park because I'm an idiot, is finding a tire shop in Cherokee, the small town outside the park, before the end of the business day and hoping they have a suitable tire. I have long distances to cover before returning the car at Reagan National on Friday.

While the new, self-inflicted problem is swirling in my mind and the storm clouds approach overhead, a couple of motorcyclists pull into the overlook to admire the view. They ask if I need help. Just a new brain, I think. "I hit a rock in the road," I say, too embarrassed to admit the truth. I thank both for offering. I'm about finished. "Do you think the rain will hit us?" I ask.

"Looks like it's moving off to the east," says one of the cyclists.

"Well, thanks again, and have a safe ride. Try not to get wet," I reply, lifting my roller bag back into the trunk. They wish me a safe drive as well, and I wave good-bye as I close the car door. My cell phone has no signal. I plan to stop at the visitor center, my plan anyway, and ask the rangers about a tire place in Cherokee.

I keep my eyes on the road through the parkway's end. Exiting on to US 441, I turn right behind cars pulled to the side and an NPS law enforcement vehicle with flashing emergency lights. Scanning the landscape, a herd of elk, including a couple of bucks with massive racks, are grazing to the right. Traffic is stopped along the road as people snap pictures.

At the visitor center, I ask about the tire shop. A ranger reaches under the front desk, extracts a phone book, and looks up the number for a garage in town. He dials the number and hands me the phone. "I need to replace a tire," I explain. The repair shop guy advises me to hurry, since they are getting ready to close. It's 4:20 p.m. I thank the ranger and exit, heading across Cherokee amid the late afternoon pedestrian and auto tourist traffic.

At the shop, they go to work. In a stroke of luck, the small shop has one new tire of the size and brand on the car. They've got the new tire on in less than fifteen minutes and I'm on my way. All's well that ends well. My punishment is losing the two-hour hike I had planned in the park.

I point the car toward Greenville, South Carolina and begin working through the foothills. Instead of going the fastest route via the interstates, I take the longer route south via US 74 and 23, eventually connecting to I-85 about thirty-seven miles southwest of Greenville. The thirty miles between Cherokee and Franklin, North Carolina have classic Smoky Mountain scenery. I'm told that one of the more scenic points on that road is widely used for photographic representations of the mountains. I recognize the view of dark green, smoothly curved mountains offset right and left as far as the eye can see. It's about 7:45 p.m. when I pull into my hotel between Greenville and Spartanburg.

A motorcycle club is having a charity fundraiser, selling chances on a draw for a new Harley-Davidson at the hotel where I'm staying. I'm eating, enjoying another steak and beer refueling at the hotel's bar when a socializing member of the club sits next to me and applies her charm to sell a chance at the motorcycle. I explain my predicament. "If I won the bike, I don't have the slightest idea how I'd get it back home." Furthermore, when I considered getting another motorcycle a few years ago, Kareen vetoed the idea with an offer I couldn't refuse. She suggested that if I didn't die in some horrific motorcycle crash, she would kill me for making her worry about me dying in a horrific motorcycle crash. In the end, I decided riding in the Chicago area too dangerous. I buy a five-dollar raffle ticket anyway, mostly so she'll go away feeling a sense of accomplishment.

Thursday begins at **Cowpens National Battlefield**. Continental troops defeat a force under hated adversary Colonel Banastre Tarleton at Cowpens on January 17, 1781. Loosely represented with substantial creative license, Tarleton inspires the Hollywood character of Colonel William Tavington in *The Patriot*. Much of Tarleton's nasty reputation derived from the slaughter of surrendered Continental soldiers at the Battle of Waxhaws. At Cowpens, Brigadier General Daniel Morgan led the Americans to a decisive victory over Tarleton's cavalry and light infantry. Morgan deployed the military principle of defense in depth by placing successive defensive lines at intervals. Each defensive line weakened the attacking British before retreating to the main defensive line and counterattacking in force with the benefit of enfilade fire on the British flanks. Despite some hiccups in execution, the plan worked to great success, gaining a conclusive victory and avenging American ire against Tarleton.

I toured the battlefield in December 2014 but walk the 1.25-mile battlefield trail again to test my recollections from the first visit. In the visitor center, I discover this park has also sold out of the unit's centennial pins. They used the pins as promotional giveaways to every fiftieth visitor earlier this year. That's two missing pins in the last two parks that had them. I hope for better success at the last three South Carolina NPS units.

Kings Mountain National Military Park protects the wooded ridge topped by a treeless plateau where backcountry and piedmont patriots, marshalled from across the western Carolinas and Virginia, encircled a force of about one thousand Loyalists led by British Major Patrick Ferguson. Killed during the action, Ferguson's hillside marker identifies his final resting place. As at Cowpens, I visited

Kings Mountain late in December 2014, but elect to walk the mile-and-a-half Battlefield Trail again this morning across the wooded hillside. Kings Mountain better fits the description of a tree-covered Carolina backcountry hill than its name suggests.

Kings Mountain is a much-needed victory for the Americans after defeats at Charleston, Camden, and Waxhaws. Morgan's victory at Cowpens followed a few months after Kings Mountain, which was in turn followed by a bloody engagement at Guilford Courthouse near Greensboro, North Carolina, and the successful Loyalist defense of their fort at the small hamlet and crossroads of Ninety-Six, South Carolina. Though the British commanded the field at both Guilford and Ninety-Six, they suffered significant losses hampering their ability to maintain an effective offensive force after Guilford and abandoned Ninety-Six the month following that engagement to consolidate their regional forces.

The turning point of American fortunes in the Carolinas coincided with the consolidation of the Continental southern theater command under General Nathanael Greene's steady leadership. The Fabian strategy of the southern Continental force paralleled that deployed by Washington with the main army farther north. Lacking the resources to defeat the British in head-to-head conventional engagements, patriot leaders chose engagements that made it too costly and impractical for Cornwallis to hold territory or chase the mobile patriot forces across the countryside.

I'm greeted with a surprise at Kings Mountain. Walking out the back of the visitor center, I run into Ranger Stephen, the ranger who made my time at Agate Fossil Beds National Monument back in March so memorable. I recalled Stephen explaining his pending move to another NPS unit, though he didn't know where. I greet him with a smile and congratulations on his new assignment. A little stunned, he shakes my hand. It's not shocking I would run into a familiar ranger considering Kings Mountain National Military Park is the 248th NPS unit I've visited year to date.

After the battlefield walk, I return to the car for the two-hour trip south across the state to yet another Revolutionary War battlefield, **Ninety-Six National Historic Site**. In keeping with the strategy to harass British outposts, patriot forces target a star-shaped earthen fortification near the frontier town of Ninety-Six in southwestern South Carolina. Greene and his troops laid siege to the fort, too strong a defensive position for a direct, frontal assault. The Americans arrived on May 21, 1781, and worked to improve their advantage before attempting to reduce the fort. They attacked on June 18, taking a wooden stockade but failing to take the fort. The Americans quietly retreated on the morning of June 20. The pro-British forces withdrew the following month to the protection of the coast.

On this second visit to the site, I repeat the mile-and-a-half battlefield walking tour, enjoying the company of another middle-aged gentleman with a shared passion for history. We discuss my journey and some of his memorable park visits. We both enjoy the company for our battlefield review before splitting up at the wooden stockade near the tour's end. The only Revolutionary War battle site I've missed today among NPS-affiliated locations is the **Historic Camden Revolutionary War Site**. I visited Camden, site of a devastating American defeat and humiliation for General Horatio Gates, in January 2015 with Kareen.

On the way to the east side of the state capital of Columbia, I cut through the middle of the **South Carolina Heritage Corridor**, covering centuries of native, colonial, and modern history from South Carolina's Low Country to the High Country of the Appalachians. The destination is the largest remaining eastern, old-growth bottomland forest in the United States. Before its settlement, the coastal wetlands of the southeast held vast old-growth wetland forests. As settlers moved inland, easily reachable stretches of forest fell to create arable land for farms and massive plantations. Large forest expanses remained in some wetlands until late in the nineteenth century. **Congaree National Park** protects one of the last remaining vestiges of wetland habitat and old-growth forest in a remarkable ecosystem nearly wiped off the North American continent.

Kareen and I first visited this park on January 1–2, 2015. The winter proved a great time to walk Congaree's trails. The insects are gone, and the swamp's resident snakes are deep in their winter slumber. Our 2015 New Year's Day activity featured ten miles across Congaree's boardwalks and trails, passing massive bald cypress and loblolly pine trees. Congaree boasts world champions of five different tree species, including a loblolly pine over 170 feet in height and 15 feet in circumference. We thrilled at the massive trees. Beneath the champion loblolly, which lies a short distance off the trail, I told Kareen, "I think loblolly pines might be carnivorous. That's why I'm having you pose for the pictures." This throwaway comment sparked an idea in my incongruent mind: "What if we learned the hard way that my favorite species of tree is carnivorous?"

I use this late July visit to retrace our steps on the boardwalk, though my walking is truncated from that first visit. I'm disappointed to find Congaree is the third park in two days sold out of their unit's centennial pins. I didn't expect to have this problem so early in the year. After this trip, I will spend a few hours calling the remaining parks with pins that I've yet to visit, asking each to save a pair for my visit later in the year. When I explain the purpose, every park store agrees to save a set for my arrival.

This evening grows long, covering most of the five hundred miles back to Washington, DC, where my flight from Reagan National to O'Hare leaves late Friday afternoon. Slipping into DC after the morning rush, I still have time for a few final stops in the national capital. I return to Frederick Douglass and National Capital Parks–East to collect cancellations requested by other NPTC members. The balance of my time is spent at the Washington Navy Yard museum. It's my first visit to the Navy Museum, and it's the perfect way to conclude the trip. I've visited fifty-two NPS units in eleven days, completing at least one visit to every park in Maryland, the District of Columbia, and South Carolina in 2016, and setting the stage to complete visits in the remaining eastern states this year. The sheer density of park locations on the eastern seaboard yield the high numbers. Despite the shortened visits, I've walked over sixty miles among and within parks in the past eleven days.

25 Northern Rockies

AFTER STRUGGLING TO find a window for the northern Rocky Mountain parks we visited last year, the process of elimination leaves a long weekend trip bridging July and August. The Saturday and Sunday after flying home from Washington, DC, brings another baseball weekend in St. Louis. The Cardinals host the Los Angeles Dodgers, and I take advantage of the weekend for a return visit to the arch, part of the Jefferson National Expansion Memorial and amid a multiyear renovation project. The following week gives me a few days at home to catch up on work and personal items lagging after the long East Coast trip.

As 2016 progresses, I find it hardest to schedule returns to some of the more than 150 parks visited in 2015. Such is the case for the northern Rockies and much of the Southwest. Can I push myself to cover the vast distances necessary to hit these parks in quick succession? After the northern Rocky Mountains, I've sketched out three major trips to get back to all these units, with new destinations blended into each itinerary. I fly to Phoenix to visit the remaining units in Arizona and southern California. A trip to Albuquerque will serve to reach the parks in New Mexico and West Texas. And I will need to fly to San Antonio to see the parks of East and Central Texas.

The adventure begins with an early-morning flight to Salt Lake

City on Thursday, July 28. It's bright and warm as I leave the airport. The trip's core includes stops at fifteen parks Kareen and I visited last August and September but starts today with two new locations. The first destination is the NPS Intermountain Region National Trails Office in Salt Lake City, serving the four western trails that cross northern Utah. The office helps coordinate trail activities and manages the Mormon Pioneer National Historic Trail. A friendly office staffer retrieves a trail poster from storage and hands it to me. "I hope to see the exhibit and read your story. Good luck with the rest of your centennial."

South and east from Salt Lake City, I enter the Wasatch Range and the Uinta National Forest location of **Timpanogos Cave National Monument**. Located on a steep mountainside, the Trail to the Caves climbs 1,092 feet over one and a half miles. In today's heat, I'm getting the full experience. It's a tiring start in the parks. The physical effort of climbing and hiking compliment the natural wonder. At least I'm whole from the DC trip. And the caves will cool me off with a constant interior temperature of forty-five degrees. The roundtrip three-mile hike, plus another half mile inside the caves, takes about three hours.

Timpanogos Cave National Monument encompasses three caves. Ranger-guided tours pass through Hansen Cave, Middle Cave, and Timpanogos Cave, in that order. As he harvested timber high up the southern slope of the American Fork Canyon, Martin Hansen discovered the first cave here in 1887. Legend has it that he tracked a mountain lion to the cave named after him. Hansen Cave's popularity led to permanent damage. Souvenir hunters and miners stripped many features and natural formations, selling rock fragments to museums and companies making objects from the materials. Fortunately, the second cave remained undiscovered until 1915, when two teenagers exploring the slope face found an opening near Hansen Cave. They had discovered the natural entrance to Timpanogos Cave. The third cave, Middle Cave, between Hansen and Timpanogos Caves, was discovered in 1921. Local citizens united that year seeking protection for the two newly discovered caves lest they also be vandalized and stripped of their natural features.

President Warren G. Harding recognized these efforts the following year by creating Timpanogos Cave National Monument.

Timpanogos Cave, helictites

My cave tour starts slow in Hansen Cave, an exhibit on the fate of unprotected natural wonders. The long-lost original beauty of the cave requires the imagination, though a few natural features too large to easily remove survive. As the tour moves into the Middle Cave, formations increase in number and variety. The Middle Cave's Big Room reveals a comprehensive speleothem exhibit. Groundwater containing carbonic acid dissolves calcium carbonate in the bedrock before redepositing it. Calcareous formations form as water trickles into the cave. Calcium carbonate deposits crystalize as calcite or aragonite, chemically identical but structurally unique. Depending on the chemical composition of the rocks and water, deposits of calcium sulfate (gypsum) develop. Trace minerals create color variation. Nickel gives some formations a green hue. Yellow-colored formations are calcite, and greenish formations are mostly aragonite. The Middle Cave's formations include stalactites, stalagmites, draperies, flowstone, and helictites. Helictites are small stalactites that have a nonvertical element and seem to defy gravity. The Timpanogos Cave system is famous for its large number of fragile helictites, rarely seen in reach of accessible areas in publicly toured caves. Timpanogos Cave's Chimes Chamber sparkles with brilliant white helictites several feet in length.

Timpanogos Cave's most famous feature is known as the "Great Heart of Timpanogos." Draperies connect multiple stalactites to form this massive, heart-shaped feature. Descending from the cave, I pause on the trail to snap pictures of American Fork Canyon and Utah Valley to the west. The trail to the National Park Service's cave system entrance at 6,730 feet, and exit at 6,717 feet, affords a view of the steep canyon walls surrounding it and the broad, flat Utah Valley with its thriving metropolitan population and Great Salt Lake.

From the caves, I travel north past Salt Lake City to Ogden. Noting a low tire pressure warning light flashing on my rental car's dash, I stop at a tire shop for a quick repair job. I've learned to travel with a tire gauge after getting several rentals with tire issues. They patch a nail puncture and get me back on the road. It's a relief to have the problem fixed. The mountain roads on this itinerary are not good places to have a flat. After finding a steakhouse for an early dinner, I check into my hotel north of Ogden to do a few hours of work and rest for tomorrow's road trip.

Friday begins at 4:00 a.m. with more work before my 8:00 a.m. departure for the one-hour drive to **Golden Spike National Historic Site**. The transcontinental railroad's completion here provided the first rail link from coast to coast on May 10, 1869. Prior to the Civil War, disagreement between congressmen arguing for northern or southern routes stalled the legislation. With the southern faction absent, Congress authorized the project in 1862 along a northern route generally following the Mormon and California Trails. Central Pacific received the contract for the section from Sacramento, California to the east. Union Pacific received the lucrative bid for Omaha going west.

I arrive at the park as the visitor center opens. Kareen and I also started an August day at Golden Spike. We screened the park's film and watched the two restored engines, the Central Pacific's Jupiter, and the Union Pacific's No. 119, pull up to each other behind the visitor center at 10:00 a.m. We found ourselves absorbed in the story and completed our time in the park following the West and East Grade auto tours.

This massive and momentous project's unification of the North American continent progressed slowly until the Civil War's conclusion. With men and material no longer diverted by the war effort, the pace quickened, exceeding everyone's expectations. On flat ground, rail crews laid between two and five miles of track a day. Graders pushed ahead, pressured by both companies seeking the valuable land subsidies awarded with the contract. At Promontory, visitors see the parallel grades created by both teams. Before the companies settled on a meeting point, the grading teams passed each other and carved parallel grades for over 200 miles. The Central Pacific got the harder assignment, blasting their way through the Sierra Nevadas across Donner Pass. As a result, Central Pacific completed 690 track miles compared with the 1,086 miles laid by Union Pacific. With the Western labor pool diminished by a gold rush followed by a silver rush, Chinese immigrants formed the core of the Central Pacific's work force. The Union Pacific used between eight thousand and ten thousand workers, drawn mostly from unemployed European immigrants. One can only imagine the chaos in the work camps as the line moved across the open frontier. The traveling carnival of businesses and opportunists, gambling and prostitution aplenty, gave entry to the phrase "hell on wheels" in the American lexicon.

A year ago, Kareen and I spent the second half of our day hiking and scrambling among the strange and curious collection of rocks in the middle of nowhere at **City of Rocks National Reserve**. We took pictures of each other standing in the park's famous Window and drove among the named rocks and features. The California Trail's primary route traverses the reserve, named City of Rocks by an early immigrant in 1849. I don't have time today to repeat or expand upon last year's hiking. After the brief visit, I'm off to two more southern Idaho parks.

Hagerman Fossil Beds National Monument in Hagerman, Idaho, requires a two-hour drive north on Highway 77 and west on I-84. Crossing the Snake River, I stop at the Oregon Trail Overlook and pick out trail ruts still visible running uphill in the brown grass. You can see the deformity in the slope's contour from the traffic of 170 years ago. At the Snake River Overlook, the monument's high cliff along the river's western bank reveals six hundred feet of sandstone layers containing an amazing variety of fossils spanning 550,000 years. The layers at the river level are 3.7 million years old, while the top layer is 3.15 million years old, representing the Pliocene epoch of the Cenozoic period.

From Hagerman, I take the interstate and then two-lane highways east to drive through **Minidoka National Historic Site**, a Japanese internment camp operating from August 1942 to October 1945 on 33,000 acres and housing almost 9,400 Japanese-American internees at its peak. In total, over thirteen thousand internees stayed at Minidoka. The relocation center included six hundred buildings, most condensed on to 946 acres. Only a few structures survive. The camp's living areas consisted of thirty-six residential blocks. Each block contained twelve housing units, designed as barracks, with each unit split into six one-room apartments with communal dining halls and bathrooms. The site's most obvious landmark is the guard tower next to the camp's former entrance.

There are no staffed, on-site visitor services. Last year, Kareen and I walked the grounds, reading the interpretive panels and pondering the hardships faced by those interned here. Today, I stop to take another picture at the surviving guard tower and read a few interpretive panels. Seems like there are more panels now than last year, but that could be an illusion due to greater familiarity with the site.

The next park requires driving ninety-five miles though it's less than fifty air miles to the northeast. **Craters of the Moon National Monument and Preserve** originates from the same hot spot responsible for Yellowstone National Park's thermal wonders and super volcano. As the North American plate shifts in a southwesterly direction, the center of the hot spot moves on the surface about two inches per year. Though the hot spot lay underneath Craters of the Moon long before Yellowstone, these massive lava fields derive from eruptions through a series of deep fissures collectively known as the Great Rift. These cracks developed as continental drift stretched the Earth's crust, creating the fifty-two-mile Great Rift on a northwest to southeast line roughly perpendicular to the continental drift. Eight major periods of eruption created three lava fields between fifteen thousand and two thousand years ago. The largest, the Craters of the Moon lava field, contains about sixty lava flows and twenty-five volcanic cones covering 618 square miles. Geologists believe future activity is likely. Past eruptions occurred on average at two-thousand-year intervals.

Kareen and I spent a day exploring lava tubes and wandering trails around cinder cones and across lava fields stretching to the horizon. We walked past blocks of lava the size of small buildings and varying flows and features such as squeeze-ups, where enormous pressures force molten lava through a crack in the solidified surface. I took a picture of Kareen emerging from a lava tube, visible from the waist up. She looks like a prairie dog popping out of its hole. I captioned the photo, "What comes out of a lava tube."

Craters of the Moon, "What comes out of a lava tube"

Today's visit focuses on something we missed last year. Kareen and I marveled at the change in terrain entering the lava fields and park. We wanted to get out of the car and walk the ominous volcanic landscape. I regretted not stopping off US Highways 93 and 20 to absorb the views. Today, I use highway pullouts near the park boundary to study the transition from flat, arid scrubland to endless expanse of lava. The park derives its name from early visitors who imagined this bizarre landscape of massive black rock might resemble the moon's surface.

From the lava fields, I have a 3.5-hour drive, mostly on US Highway 20, to Boise, Idaho. As I get closer to the interstate at Mountain Home, Idaho, I see an extraordinary number of RVs and campers. I eventually pass a large flat area in the shadow of the Saw Tooth Mountain Range with a concert stage and mass of humanity followed by a multitude of vehicles. I learn later that I'm passing by the opening of the Mountain Home Country Music Festival this weekend. As I wind around the curvy, inclined highway covering the final twenty miles to Mountain Home, I'm thankful to be going in the opposite direction of the endless series of recreational vehicles. The day concludes with a delicious evening meal at a small Boise microbrew as the TV above the bar features an arm wrestling competition no one appears to be watching. I lack the motivation to request a different channel.

Saturday morning begins with a four-and-a-half-hour drive north to Spalding, Idaho, and **Nez Perce National Historical Park**. I visited a few of the historical park's thirty-eight sites spread across Idaho, Montana, Washington, and Oregon during our August trip last year. The park's locations protect the battle sites from the US Army's eleven-hundred-mile pursuit of Nez Perce tribal members in the summer and fall of 1877. The saga ended in October when the army forced the capitulation of the remaining members less than forty miles from the Canadian border at Bear Paw Battlefield near Chinook, Montana. I visited Bear Paw Battlefield last August, as well as Canyon Creek and Big Hole Battlefields, also in Montana.

The **Nez Perce National Historic Trail** commemorates the desperate five-month race for freedom. The historical park and trail's sad history characterizes Native American struggles against broken promises and a disappearing way of life. After an 1855 treaty grants the Nez Perce a reservation on their ancestral homeland around the Snake River's headwaters, the discovery of gold on reservation land triggered an invasion by miners and settlers. A new 1863 treaty confined the tribe to a reservation one-tenth the size of the 1855 treaty's land grant. Some tribal leaders accepted the new treaty, but many who stood to lose their land rejected it. The Nez Perce War of 1877 followed. Chief Joseph earned tremendous respect for his leadership and dignified, tireless advocacy on behalf of his tribe in the years after the war.

In route to Spalding on US Highway 95, a pullout overlooks the first battle at White Bird Battlefield, a Nez Perce victory in June 1877. After reviewing exhibits at the Spalding visitor center, I travel US Highway 12 through the Bitterroot Mountains. The route parallels two trails through the rugged peaks at Lolo Pass. Both the Nez Perce National Historic Trail and Lewis and Clark National Historic Trail penetrate the Bitterroots here. The National Forest Service visitor center in the pass makes an excellent break on the way to Missoula, Montana. A long day of mountain driving concludes in Missoula.

I considered and dismissed adding a day to the itinerary for a roundtrip to **Glacier National Park**. Kareen and I spent three days in Glacier last Labor Day weekend. We traversed the park on the Going-to-the-Sun Road twice for hikes on the Hidden Lake Overlook Trail at Logan Pass, the Trail of the Cedars and Avalanche Lake Trail, and stops at the Apgar Visitor Center, the park headquarters, and the West Glacier Amtrak station. Pat, an area resident and longtime NPTC member, met us in West Glacier with a piece of paper reading "300." I held the number for a park entrance sign photo, celebrating Glacier National Park as my three hundredth NPS unit visited. Since we stayed east of the park, we returned across Going-to-the-Sun Road at twilight in light rain. Sitting in the passenger seat as sheer drops of thousands of feet passed by her window, Kareen yelled at me every few minutes, "You're going too fast! We're going to die!" To which I would look down at the speedometer, reading 20 to 25 mph, and say, "Relax! We really can't go slower." Kareen declared, "I'm never going on this road again!" While her sworn avoidance of Glacier is a pity, we enjoyed the park's rugged mountain scenery. In another steady rain, a hike on the Many Glacier area's Grinnell Lake Trail highlighted our last day. The lake sits beneath the high peaks supporting the glaciers that feed it. We watched several bears snacking on huckleberry and dewberry on the adjacent ridges before our hike. Returning to the park during this trip would require driving over five hours roundtrip for a few hours in the park. I lack the strength.

Sunday morning begins at the National Bison Range. The Mission Mountains create a scenic backdrop for the refuge, which boasts the only confirmed genetically pure free-range American bison herd remaining. Limited testing on the Yellowstone herd have shown similar genetic purity, but the small sample size leaves the herd's purity in doubt to the folks at the range. Most bison in America today have some bovine genetics in their DNA due to cross-breeding over the past 125 years. As many as 60 million bison are estimated to have roamed North America at their peak, before the animal faced near extinction as herds fell from wonton hunting in the late 1800s.

After a two-hour drive southeast across western Montana, I reach **Grant-Kohrs Ranch National Historic Site**. Kareen and I toured the ranch and house last year. Today, I walk a couple of miles around the ranch, hearkening the days when cattle reigned in the wild west. Johnny Grant built the first ranch house in 1862, a wooden construction measuring four thousand square feet. Conrad Kohrs added a five-thousand-square-foot brick addition in 1890. Conrad and Augusta Kohrs met as children in their native Germany before immigrating to America. In 1868, they married in Iowa after a three-week courtship. Augusta transformed a dusty and dirty ranch house into an elegant western home, acquiring sophisticated furnishings and heirlooms. The ranch and its history remain preserved from efforts by occupants Conrad and Nell Warren, who recognized the site's historical importance. The Warrens promoted the property's conversion to a National Park Service unit in 1972.

From Grant-Kohrs, I return to the Nez Perce's story after another two-hour drive southwest to reach **Big Hole National Battlefield**. US Army troops under the command of Colonel John Gibbon attacked the Nez Perce encampment along the North Fork of the Big Hole River in the predawn hours of August 9, 1877. The fighting transitioned into a siege until the early-morning hours of August 10, when the last native warriors departed to join a retreat south. These warriors faced the military disadvantage of looking after women, children, and the elderly. The Battle at Big Hole results in more casualties than any other in the Nez Perce War. Many historians see Big Hole as the conflict's turning point. The fleeing tribal members now understood they would be pursued while they remained on US soil. Though Chief Joseph and the remaining combatants surrendered at Bear Paw on October 5, 1877, nearly three hundred tribe members safely escaped to Canada, including the other chief at Bear Paw, White Bird, who mistrusted the army's promises and led thirty to Canada the night after the surrender. Looking back through the lens of history, his judgment stands vindicated.

July ends having visited sixty-two parks. August begins Monday morning at **Little Bighorn Battlefield National Monument**, Lieutenant Colonel George Armstrong Custer's infamous military finale. Before last year's visit, I read two different battle histories, including Thom Hatch's brilliant and captivating narrative, *The Last Days of George Armstrong Custer*, published in February 2015. On June 25–26, 1876, a force of the 7th Calvary numbering about 600 men divided into three attacking forces after locating a large native village on the Little Bighorn River. A detailed battle history exceeds the scope of our story, but the separate forces consolidated into two groups separated by four miles. The five companies under Custer were annihilated. All 210 men, including Custer and his two brothers, Thomas and Boston, died strewn on or near Last Stand Hill's western face. Some were mutilated posthumously. Troopers discovered Custer's body the next day with his severed penis stuffed in his mouth. The remnants of the two three-company detachments led by Major Marcus Reno and Captain Frederick Benteen, along with the pack train, survived the battle under siege. The natives departed on the second day before the arrival of an army force led by General Alfred Terry. The Reno-Benteen group, including the pack train under Captain Thomas McDougall, suffered grievous losses with 53 killed and 52 wounded. Captain Grant Marsh, piloting the steamboat the *Far West*, set an unsurpassed speed record on the upper Missouri by steaming the wounded back to Fort Lincoln in the Dakotas, covering 710 miles in fifty-four hours.

The events surrounding the Battle at Little Bighorn have been the subject of dozens of volumes. Much of the earlier history published includes subjective accounts intended to avoid the army's embarrassment. Custer's widow, Elizabeth Bacon Custer, zealously guarded her late husband's reputation until her death in 1933. Fictionalized accounts of Custer and his men focused on their heroic defense against countless merciless savages. More recent works come much closer to a fair assessment.

Today, I walk up Last Stand Hill to gaze upon the markers for Custer, his brothers, and the forty men who died with them. Before leaving, I run into a ranger and the park superintendent in the parking lot. I share the exhibit plan. I purchased the park's pins last August, among the first I encountered. "Have a great finish to the centennial!" I say as I walk to the car.

Bighorn Canyon National Recreation Area surrounds 71-mile Bighorn Lake, created by Yellowtail Dam near Fort Smith, Montana. From the dam, it's a long, circuitous drive to the park's southern end. The route sends me on I-90 southbound to the Dayton, Wyoming, exit, where I take US Highway 14 west across the Bighorn National Forest, past Hunt and Bald Mountain, both topping out over ten thousand feet, on the way to Lovell, Wyoming, and the Bighorn Canyon Visitor Center. Listed as a scenic route, Highway 14 across the Bighorn National Forest reveals the Bighorn Range at altitude. The views across the high plateau of the peaks rising to either side make the three-hour trip to Lovell go quickly.

Last year, I took the park road to the Devil Canyon Overlook into the steep-walled confluence of Devil Canyon and Bighorn

Canyon. The view represents the park on its brochure. My 3:00 p.m. arrival leaves time to discuss favorite parks with the rangers on duty. I don't get a more appropriate experience into the wonders of Bighorn Canyon National Recreation Area until my third visit with Kareen during 2018.

It's impossible to truly see Bighorn Canyon without taking a boat trip to experience it at water level. Before the dam created the lake, a dangerous whitewater river once intimidated early travelers viewing the one- to two-thousand-foot walls dominated by Madison limestone stained red by iron oxide leaking out of more recent rock layers. The Laramide Orogeny, the mountain-building uplift that gave us the Rocky Mountains, raised the Pryor and Bighorn Mountains surrounding the canyon between sixty and 75 million years ago. We pass sediment layers near water level that appear so uniform they look like man-made rock tiles in the canyon wall. The layered rock walls, arches appearing near the rim, and the bighorn sheep walking on hopelessly precarious footholds high above us combine to keep us moving from one spot in the boat to another looking at this natural wonder.

We also explored the human history in our recent visit. The Two Eagles site near the canyon rim still features stone circles used to hold down teepees in the gales that pushed against us as we walked about these recycled tent rocks. The park also has four ranches preserved in various states. The former dude ranch at Hillsboro appears to have been taken over by rattlesnakes, which are seen everywhere here. The Lockhart Ranch is perhaps the most fascinating. Caroline Lockhart went from sensational journalist to fulfill her dream as a ranch owner. She owned the ranch, the most well-preserved in the park, from 1926 until 1955, growing it from 160 to 7,000 acres. Her life certainly seems to meet the definition of well-lived, if not always harmonious. Rangers at the site share some interesting stories of her series of ranch-hand lovers who didn't always get along. They point out a cliff adjacent to the property that Native Americans used for centuries as a buffalo jump. They hunted buffalo in mass by stampeding them over a cliff. They would slaughter the most grievously wounded first, allowing some with broken legs to wallow in agony for days. It served to preserve the meat while the harvest work continued.

Tuesday morning, August 2, begins entering **Yellowstone National Park** at the northeast entrance past Cooke City, Montana. Yellowstone hooked Kareen on the park system's wonders and special experiences over three full days last August. She's seen almost two hundred parks as of this writing. My first day in Yellowstone last August had been a drive around the park's famous loop road, entering at the east entrance and collecting passport stamps on the outer loop from Fishing Bridge, through West Thumb and Grant Village, Old Faithful and Madison, Norris and the Museum of the National Park Ranger, exiting through Mammoth Hot Springs and the north entrance at Gardiner. I picked Kareen up later that night in Billings. The next morning, we returned to the park via Beartooth Pass and the Northeast Entrance, the same entrance I'm using today. When we arrived among Lamar Valley's bison herd, Kareen got to see her first bison in the flesh. The park's wildlife and thermal features captured her imagination. We hiked at the Upper and Lower Falls of Yellowstone and through Mammoth Hot Springs and the Upper and Lower Geyser Basin. We finished our time in the park with a hike near West Thumb to an overlook of Yellowstone Lake and a West Thumb Geyser Basin tour. The natural wonders kept us in awe. Our park adventure started by observing a grizzly bear walking across a meadow outside of Cooke City and continued until we left the park through the south entrance near Snake River. When people ask about my favorite park, it's difficult to compare any place with Yellowstone. The park is simply in a class by itself.

This visit starts with a Lamar Valley wildlife show. I hit the day's first bison jam about ten miles into the park. Bison cross and travel the road as they wish. They don't care much whether they delay the tourists in their scenic home. At a second bison jam a few miles farther into the valley, a large bull walks right in front of my stopped car, almost brushing the bumper, then takes a step toward my open driver's side window before rocking back into the cow on his other side with a deep grunt. The bull's glare is piercing. "I'm not here for your lady friend," I say out the window, but move my hand to the window control in case he's not convinced. The bull, harem in tow, continues angling across the road. The possessive behavior isn't surprising, as we're in the middle of the annual bison rut. Less than a mile away, I stop at the Yellowstone Association Institute Buffalo Ranch and search for someone to open the gift shop so I can use the passport stamper kept next to the cash register. An older gentleman arrives to open the store. As I'm using the stamp, he talks me into joining the Yellowstone Association. I'm already a member of both Eastern and Western National Associations, affiliated with almost 250 NPS locations across the country. The membership gift lands Kareen another stuffed bison for her Chicago herd.

Before leaving the valley, I hit another traffic jam, this one caused by tourists watching a black bear sow in the trees at the wood line not more than 150 yards distant. Two little cubs scramble to keep up with mama, bopping up and down over fallen timber and rocks. I'm not one to fawn over cute, but the scene of the two cubs trailing mama bear through the woods brings a smile. From Lamar Valley, I stop at the Tower-Roosevelt Ranger Station to get a new passport stamp, added since last year. I share with the ranger how thrilling it is to be back in Yellowstone, even for a little while.

Continuing down the East Loop Road, I stop at Canyon Village for the usual routine and another park T-shirt in the gift shop inside the Visitor Education Center. The center's supervolcano exhibit fascinates me with its visual representations of the park's violent past. At Yellowstone National Park's center, a massive thirty- by forty-five-mile caldera stretches between Mount Washburn on the northern rim to the Red Mountains, forming the southern rim. The caldera covers the upper half of Yellowstone Lake and the Upper and Lower Geyser Basins. The hot spot responsible for Yellowstone's remarkable thermal features lurks three miles beneath the surface. One of forty such hot spots on earth, the magma chamber shook and shaped the land in three major eruptions. One of the most interesting visual exhibits I've seen anywhere in the parks is the trio of ash-containing cubes near the front of the exhibit area titled "The Big Blasts." The cubes demonstrate the relative size of the three eruptions. The Huckleberry Ridge Caldera Eruption, the largest, released 2,500 cubic kilometers of ash into the air 2.1 MYA. The amount of ash from the event is twenty-four hundred times the amount expelled during the 1980 Mount St. Helens eruption and covered the United States all the way to the eastern seaboard. Most of the Great Plains and the Midwest lay under eight to ten feet of ash after this cataclysmic event. The Henry's Fork Caldera eruption occurred 1.3 MYA and produced 280 cubic kilometers of ash. The Yellowstone Caldera eruption, the second-largest, occurred 640,000 years ago and released 1,000 cubic kilometers of ash.

Yellowstone contains three hundred geysers, two-thirds of all that exist on earth, and over ten thousand thermal features. Last year, Kareen and I watched the Grand Geyser, not far from Old Faithful in the Upper Geyser Basin, erupt in all its splendor. My favorite among the thermal features is the Midway Geyser Basin's Grand Prismatic Spring. Microorganisms that thrive in the spring's extraordinary environment ring the bright-blue pool of water with yellows, reds, and greens. I stood on the boardwalk passing the spring in a sort of trance, trying to internalize the hypnotic beauty.

Yellowstone, Grand Prismatic

Continuing south from Canyon Village, I stop at Fishing Bridge, West Thumb, and Grant Village before my final stop at the Snake River Ranger Station at the south entrance. I exit the park into the next unit, as the road leaving Yellowstone National Park to the south, US Highway 89/191/287, is also the **John D. Rockefeller, Jr. Memorial Parkway**. Created in 1972, the unit honors Rockefeller for his personal effort to purchase and donate thirty-two thousand acres to preserve the area's landscape.

Rockefeller's efforts also expanded the next park eight miles from Yellowstone's southern boundary, **Grand Teton National Park**. The parkway connects Yellowstone with Grand Teton. As previously mentioned in chapter 8, Rockefeller's generosity and interest in conservation played a major role in creating some of America's most beloved national parks, including Yellowstone, Yosemite, Grand Teton, Acadia, Shenandoah, and the Great Smoky Mountains.

My time in Grand Teton begins at the Colter Bay Visitor Center next to Colter Bay Village and Jackson Lake. I enjoy a two-mile hike on the Lakeshore Trail around the peninsula that forms Colter Bay. Extending the walk in the fresh air and scenery, I continue with the Heron Pond and Swan Lake Loops for another three miles. The trail time invigorates me.

At the top of 7,727-foot Signal Mountain, the overlook on the southern end of the summit parking area gives a bird's-eye view of the Grand Tetons. The tallest peak, Grand Teton, rises 13,770 feet above sea level and is flanked on the south by Middle Teton and South Teton, and on the north by Mount Owen. The Tetons present a spectacular alpine scene with twelve peaks above 12,000 feet. French-Canadian fur trappers named the rugged peaks "les Trois Tetons," which translated literally means the "Three Breasts." In homage to these early, presumably lonely explorers, I think of the mountains as the "Big Breasts."

These unique mountains are mere babies in geological terms, though the granite and gneiss rocks that comprise them are among the oldest on the continent. Between ten and eight million years ago, the mountains we see today began to rise along a north-south fault while the valley began to drop. These mountains are still rising at a rate of about three feet every thousand years. The valley drops at four times that rate, leaving the peaks towering seven thousand feet above the valley floor after rising thirty thousand feet since their ascent began. Like the Jeffersons, the Tetons are movin' on up *above* the east side. Hundreds of earthquakes each year testify to the fault's restlessness.

Grand Teton, Tetons in profile across String Lake

The infant mountains show their age in their rugged nature. But what makes this range special as a park also makes it a hiker's paradise. The fault's slippage created these peaks without foothills. A simple day hike leads visitors into the interior's alpine wonderland with peaks rising on all sides around meadows and lakes. During our most recent visit, Kareen and I hiked into Cascade Canyon to Cascade Forks, Paintbrush Canyon to Holly Lake and in the park's south end, around Phelps Lake into Death Canyon, a great name. I explained to Kareen, "The park service shortened its name from Bear Eats Chicago Doctor Canyon." The ability to penetrate the mountains in these canyons and return the same day makes Grand Teton truly extraordinary. Climbing into these valleys, evidence of mountain building and erosion lies all around. Collapsed walls leave massive rock fields spanning the valley. At Holly Lake, we listened to the thunderous report of rock falls on nearby faces. The rough nature of the peaks contributes to their changing appearance as the perspective changes. Grand Teton's lofty summit does kind of look like a breast as we hiked beside it in Cascade Canyon, one of the park's most popular treks for good reason. In the last phase of mountain shaping, glaciers thousands of feet thick carved out the canyons, transforming Cascade Canyon from a V-shape to a U-shaped valley. The terminal moraines they gouged out created the lakes at the foot of the mountains. The view of the Tetons from the valley is special, but you haven't really seen these mountains until you've hiked into them.

Grand Teton, Holly Lake

Back in 2016, my personal centennial exploration of the National Park Service's breasts continues farther down Teton Park

Road at the Jenny Lake Visitor Center and the Craig Thomas Discovery and Visitor Center. My final stop today is the Laurance S. Rockefeller Preserve Center. John D. Rockefeller originally planned to donate the 3,106 acres around the JY Ranch to the National Park Service as part of his land gifts to enlarge Grand Teton National Park. He loved the area's rugged beauty so much, he changed his mind and decided to keep the ranch and surrounding land as a family retreat. Laurance fulfilled his father's original intention when he donated the land and the ranch to the park service. The preserve center that occupies part of this land gift carries his name. I extend the day's hiking a few miles with a leisurely stroll on the trails. It's a relaxing way to finish the park portion of the day. Unfortunately, I have nearly three hours of driving to reach my hotel in Kemmerer, Wyoming. Sleep comes easy tonight.

After starting Wednesday with several hours of work in the hotel room, I drive thirteen miles west to the trip's last park, **Fossil Butte National Monument**. Neither Kareen nor I had great enthusiasm for this park last year, but that was before Ranger Stephan converted me into a born-again paleontologist. I forgot to ask him at Kings Mountain whether he's begun Revolutionary War transformations. On this visit, I have a full day to explore the park in detail. My flight back to Chicago doesn't leave Salt Lake City, two hours away, until tonight.

The butte at the park's center contains sedimentary layers compacted into sandstone in the millions of years after the 1,000-square-mile Fossil Lake covered the area. The present-day Fossil Butte sits near the ancient lake's center. The butte's large quantity of fossils date to the Eocene epoch of the Cenozoic era around fifty million years ago.

After visiting with the ranger on duty and watching the park film, I travel the five-and-a-half-mile park road, climbing up and beyond a high ridge at an elevation of nearly eight thousand feet after the paved road turns to unpaved on the monument's north side. The views of the butte and the landscape from the top of the ridge and the other side impress me with sweeping slopes and plateaus near and far. Returning to the park's south side, I leave the car for the two-and-a-half-mile Historic Quarry Trail. The trail climbs six hundred feet to the side of the butte, where visitors who trade some sweat for the view can see the fossil layers up close. The return hike from the butte face passes a small, A-frame shack on the dusty, sparsely vegetated hillside at the base of the bluff. It's hard to imagine anyone staying in this tiny structure, with a hole in the roof near the entrance for the stove's chimney. David Haddenham used the shack as a summer shelter during the fifty years he collected fossils here beginning in the early 1900s, scratching out a meager living from their sale.

From Fossil Butte, I drive south to I-80 westbound through the Wasatch Range. The main travel corridor through the mountains passes through Echo Canyon, following the path blazed by the 1840s western trails. As I sit in the Salt Lake City airport, I reflect on the seven-day trip. I regret not having more time to linger in these special places, but I'm also tired and happy to be coming home, if only for a little while.

26 *Delaware River Blues*

AFTER A WORK trip to Dayton, I drive north to Port Clinton on Lake Erie. Wednesday morning. August 10, I'm on the ferry to Put-in-Bay, Ohio, and **Perry's Victory and International Peace Memorial**. The 352-foot Doric column rising above Lake Erie on South Bass Island's western shore commemorates the September 10, 1813, naval engagement between Americans led by Master Commandant Oliver Hazard Perry and six British ships commanded by Captain Robert Barclay. The fleets clashed about ten miles northwest of South Bass Island. The American victory altered the Old Northwest theater in the War of 1812, as the critical British supply route to troops in the upper Midwest closed, forcing a withdraw to Canada. The naval engagement immortalizes Perry, following Captain James Lawrence, the American flagship's namesake. Lawrence perished earlier that year in a June engagement uttering his final words, "Don't give up the ship." The park and monument honors both the naval victory and over two hundred years of peace between the United States, Great Britain, and Canada.

The memorial's observation deck commands the whole island and others across the lake. Following a delightful conversation with a park volunteer in the visitor center, I walk about the town and island, adding an element from my first visit when I kept to the park. After the exercise, I catch the ferry returning to Port Clinton.

The third week of August, I'm on a Monday-morning flight to Philadelphia. Around business meetings Friday morning, the balance of the week will be spent touring New Jersey and Pennsylvania parks. Monday afternoon, I stop at Eastern National Association's headquarters in the Philadelphia suburb of Fort Washington to ask for contacts who might be able to help me find some of the missing pins for the exhibit. I leave with the name of the operations manager, Mark, who will provide some critical assistance later in the year.

Scranton is home to **Steamtown National Historic Site,** the only park dedicated to steam locomotive and railroad history. At Steamtown, the railroad of American history comes alive again. The park offers rail excursions into the northeastern Pennsylvania countryside in warmer months. Authorized in 1986, the park opened in July 1988.

The 10:00 a.m. locomotive shop tour highlighted my 2014 visit. A customized lathe cuts wheels, shedding large, coiled steel ribbons. A massive press fits heated tires around engine drive wheels, which are usually a smaller diameter for hauling freight and larger for speed in passenger service. This metalworking equipment is on a grand scale. Volunteers with their highly specialized knowledge and skills rebuild and restore the engines. Pictures of the facilities dating to the park's inception testify to the tremendous work required to realize its present condition.

Climbing into the engineer's cab exhibit near the turntable at the center of the roundhouse and visitor center, the array and complexity of the engineer's controls leaves me surprised that these steam engines remained operational and served as the backbone of American commerce for the better part of a century. The steam locomotive eventually faded into the pages of history after the introduction of diesel-electric engines in 1925.

A railway post office car on exhibit and the park film that demonstrates its use fascinate me. These cars retrieved and dropped mail bags from a moving train, requiring precise timing and coordination. Attendants grabbed bags with long straps hanging from an L-shaped rod that rotated to release the bag. They left bags via another rod in the reverse. My reaction to Steamtown surprised me. Examining the massive locomotives on display and exploring the exhibits, I felt like a little kid.

Scranton is also home to **Lackawanna Valley National Heritage Area** headquarters. The heritage area presents area history, focusing on the American industrial revolution. The coal, steel, and textile industries of northeastern Pennsylvania supported the growing country's demand for these materials. The surrounding Pocono Mountains offer plentiful natural attractions. After stopping at the heritage area office, I travel northeast for the next park.

Upper Delaware Scenic and Recreational River preserves 73.4 miles of the Delaware River separating Pennsylvania and New York. During my first visit, I examined the Roebling Bridge in the middle of the park. One of four suspension aqueducts built starting in 1847 for the Delaware and Hudson Canal, John A. Roebling's bridge is the oldest surviving wire suspension bridge in the United States.

Today I begin at the park headquarters in Narrowsburg, Pennsylvania, to collect passport stamps. I follow the Delaware on New York State Highway 97 and cross the single-lane Roebling Bridge to return to the Pennsylvania side and the Zane Grey Museum. The rural house Zane and his wife Dolly called home from 1914–1918 reflects on his success authoring popular western novels. The couple met in 1900, while Zane canoed on the river. Their ashes are interred in a cemetery next to the Delaware.

Paralleling the Delaware south, overlooks high on the river bluff reveal the valley's beauty as the river cuts through the wooded heights on either side. By early evening, I'm scanning the river bend as it turns out of sight from the Eagle's Nest near the unit's southern boundary. Upper Delaware has a lot to offer, even to those on land. The beauty and interesting aspects of Upper Delaware make it a favorite among the Lower 48 river parks.

Tuesday morning starts in the **Delaware Water Gap National Recreation Area**. The recreation area includes seventy thousand acres on both sides of the forty-mile **Middle Delaware National**

Scenic and Recreational River. At the park headquarters in Bushkill, Pennsylvania, I arrive a few minutes before 8:00 a.m. to find the parking lot empty. As I approach the door, I meet Ranger John posting a note about a water outage delaying the building's opening until 10:00 a.m. I planned to be in the southern end of the park by that time, continuing into New Jersey. I share a synopsis of my park journey and ask if I might use the passport stampers inside in case I can't return after ten o'clock. He lets me do my stamping and offers some stories of his own. I ask about his role after he mentions his thirty-six years in the park service. "I'm the park superintendent," he shares.

In John's office, he shows me a panther footprint cast in plaster from his time at Everglades National Park, one of many parks on his résumé. During our conversation, he shares a surprising and fascinating Delaware Water Gap fact. The largest black bears on US soil live here. Wildlife biologists tagged one of them in his backyard. The largest black bear confirmed in the United States over the past century, shot in November 2010 in Pike County, Pennsylvania, weighed 880 pounds. Typical adult black bears weigh from 150 to 550 pounds. Only the Kodiaks, their well-fed coastal brown cousins, and polar bears weigh more than the largest eastern black bears.

I can see the superintendent has plenty to do today, so I bid him farewell and a happy centennial. "Thanks for sharing your experiences." I see the Delaware Water Gap lapel pins for sale on the wall opposite the front desk, but I don't want to take any more of John's time this morning. I'll have to return later.

Next up is a stop at the Pocono Environmental Education Center for the passport stamp, then it's south to the Kittatinny Point Visitor Center. The building sits beside I-80 in the mountain gap for which the park is named. The river wore an S-shaped passage through the Appalachian Mountains as it flowed from the north to its Atlantic outlet in Delaware Bay. The park contains over one hundred miles of hiking trails, including twenty-seven miles of the Appalachian National Scenic Trail.

Before returning to headquarters, I climb the ridge south of the visitor center to a series of pullouts overlooking the river valley as it cuts through the mountains. I missed these spots in earlier visits. The beautiful views of the curving river and steep green heights around it underline the water gap as a park with many layers to explore.

Being from the Midwest, I didn't understand why New Jersey held the nickname the Garden State until I noticed the jet-black soil and learned of the state's extensive agricultural production on my first trip to the state in my twenties. Many Midwestern areas have this familiar color of rich agricultural land. Vegetables and fruits grow in abundance from central New Jersey's fertile soil.

Thomas Edison National Historical Park includes Edison's largest laboratory complex and Glenmont, Edison's home. Ten times the size of the Menlo Park facility, the West Orange lab rose after he became a household name and synonymous with scientific progress and invention. There's a major planning issue with today's visit. I forgot to check the park's operating hours and didn't remember it's closed today. Oops. I'll have to return later in the week.

Paterson Great Falls National Historical Park came into the system in 2011. Founded as the brainchild of Alexander Hamilton, his Society of Useful Manufactures did not realize the success he envisioned, though Paterson did develop into an important industrial city during the nineteenth century. Hamilton's vision of an industrial America proves correct but was ahead of its time when Patterson's first manufacturing facility arose in 1792. The driving force behind these early visions is water power from the Great Falls of the Passaic River. The falls drop seventy-seven feet at Paterson as the river descends from the continental shelf to the coastal plain.

Unlike my first visit, the visitor center and walkway to view the falls are open. I feel the mist hit my face as I stand above the roaring water crashing against the bedrock. I can see how early entrepreneurs would be impressed by the river's natural power.

Morristown National Historical Park commemorates the Continental Army's winter quarters site twice during the American Revolution. Washington and his army spent the winters of 1776–1777 and 1779–1780 encamped in Morristown. The winter of 1779–1780 proved especially brutal for its bitter cold and prodigious snowfall. The ill-equipped army, struggling for survival, faced starvation over the long winter. Washington's headquarters and the Jockey Hollow encampment are on my itinerary today. Morristown lies within the **Crossroads of the American Revolution National Heritage Area.** I'll stop at several more heritage area locations this week.

I cross the Delaware again for today's last two stops. The first is the **Schuylkill River Valley National Heritage Area** headquarters in Pottstown, Pennsylvania. The heritage area features the history of southeastern Pennsylvania's 125-mile river valley.

Hopewell Furnace National Historic Site is the day's last stop. As the colony's relationship with England deteriorated, operations such as the 1771 ironworks became critical to America's survival. My first visit here during the government shutdown in October 2013 had a clandestine feel. Sneaking past the closed visitor center, I studied the interpretive panels around the ironmaker's home and furnace operations, staying to my caution's limit. Fortunately, I escaped with a park memory and no one the wiser. I returned in 2014 for a thorough tour. Today's visit is the shortest of the three. After the visitor center tasks, I'm off to Middletown, Pennsylvania, tonight in route to the next park.

The Pennsylvania Turnpike westbound is uneventful except for a little rain after reaching the Allegheny Mountains. After working this morning with some lingering fatigue, I arrive at **Allegheny Railroad Portage National Historic Site.** The railroad portage, built from 1831 to 1834 as part of Pennsylvania's Main Line canal system between Philadelphia and Pittsburgh, solves the most trying obstacle on the route. Ropes and pulleys over a series of ten inclines transported cargo shipped over the mountains. Improved locomotive power rendered the portage obsolete after twenty-three years in operation.

The short walk through the woods to the No. 6 incline engine house, restored to enough of its original appearance to educate the visitor on its operation, also leads to the 1832 Lemon House, long removed from its former glory as a stop for refreshments and lodging. Walking into the 184-year-old home and tavern, one can imagine a group of dusty men playing cards and having drinks at tables placed across the wooden floor.

Thursday starts with a few hours of work followed by another trip through the Delaware Water Gap on my way to Thomas Edison National Historical Park. After getting the pins and stamps in West Orange, I head east to Gateway National Recreation Area's Staten Island subunit. Fort Wadsworth sits at the west end of the Verrazano Bridge, completed in 1964 as the first direct road between Staten Island and Long Island. I love the axial view down the bridge's length.

At the water's edge, Fort Wadsworth's Battery Tweed faces The Narrows to New York Harbor with its multilevel armament capacity. Named Fort Richmond through and after construction from 1847 to 1862, the brick fortification became Battery Tweed in 1902. The British made their first landfall near this location when they captured New York City in 1776. They held the key strategic position and the city for the duration of the American Revolution.

Gateway, Battery Tweed next to Verrazano Bridge

Fort Wadsworth, originally named Fort Tompkins until after the Civil War, was built between 1859 and 1876 as part of the Third System of American Coastal Defenses. The fort stands as one of the country's oldest surviving military installations and represents one of multiple eras covered within Gateway National Recreation Area.

Miller Field, a short drive south on Staten Island, is built on land once owned by the Vanderbilt family. A law enforcement ranger educates me on the site's history when I stop in the visitor contact station, tucked away among the post's surviving buildings adjacent to the air strip. Converted to an Air Coast Defense Station in 1920, Miller Field served as an active military installation until 1969.

Gateway's Sandy Hook Unit is named after the six-and-a-half-mile barrier peninsula extending north from the Jersey Shore. A natural breakwater for the southern side of Raritan Bay, the peninsula forms the south end of New York Harbor's entrance. The subunit includes the US Army's artillery proving ground and test range for nearly one hundred years, and the expanse of Fort Hancock, established at the end of the nineteenth century. Fort Hancock protected New York Harbor from 1898 until its closure in 1974. The fort hosted a Nike air defense missile location from 1954 until the system's deactivation nationwide the same year as the fort's closure.

This afternoon, a ranger leads me up the circular concrete stairwell of the nation's oldest, continuously operational lighthouse. Guiding mariners past Sandy Hook since June 1764, the light overlooks New York Harbor and Fort Hancock. He points out the harbor's two shipping lanes, a single-lane and a larger, two-way channel as I squirm past the large Fresnel lens in the oppressive heat. I enjoy this second visit as much as the first two years ago. The lighthouse views of the harbor entrance, backdropped by the Verrazano Bridge and New York City, are unmatched elsewhere on the peninsula.

Before leaving the area, I stop for an early dinner at a seafood restaurant suggested by a park volunteer. While waiting on the meal, I review tonight's lodging options. It's after 7:00 p.m. when I leave the restaurant, and night has fallen as I arrive at my Staten Island hotel.

Gateway, Sandy Hook Lighthouse

Friday morning, I drive the New Jersey Turnpike the length of the state to Wilmington, Delaware, skipping the only Mid-Atlantic NPS unit that I will not revisit this year, **Great Egg Harbor Scenic and Recreational River** in the **Pinelands National Reserve**. I walked several of the river's 129 protected miles last year. Great Egg Harbor is one of only ten contiguous US NPS units I will not visit this year.

After a business meeting in Wilmington, I drive to New Castle, Delaware, and **First State National Historical Park**. I toured the park's six separate locations last year. Established as a national monument in March 2013, Congress designated Delaware's first NPS unit a National Historical Park in December 2014, expanding it in the process.

Called Lower Pennsylvania among the British-American Colonies until the cusp of the American Revolution, New Castle Courthouse served as Delaware's original capitol in 1776–1777. After separating from Pennsylvania, the colonial legislature voted for independence at the courthouse in June 1776.

I find another NPTC member in the area for the club's Philadelphia convention on Saturday. We get carried away talking about recently visited parks and slink from the courthouse after a docent trying to give a tour stares a hole through us from the middle of the lower courtroom.

From New Castle, the next stop is Fort Mott State Park on the **New Jersey Coastal Heritage Trail Route**. Constructed in the last decade of the nineteenth century and completed in 1902, Fort Mott's purposed design against land attack is unique among East Coast military installations.

It's still early afternoon as I pull beside Philadelphia's Citizens Bank Park to buy tickets for the next two games here. The Cardinals play the Phillies this weekend, making the weekend trip multi-purpose between work, baseball and the NPTC annual convention, not necessarily in order of importance.

After checking in at our airport hotel, I take a cab to the ballpark. Despite the harsh reputation Philadelphia sports fans have earned, I've enjoyed my visits to this stadium in the city's south side sports complex. In addition to Citizens Bank, the complex contains Lincoln Financial Field, home of the Eagles, and the NHL's Flyers' home ice in the Wells Fargo Center. After a week of running between parks and historical sites in four states, I enjoy relaxing at the game, a 4-2 Cardinals win. Returning to the hotel, I visit with several club members enjoying cocktails in the lounge. I share the excitement of my pin project with fellow NPTC member Carl, a trim, dark-haired Florida radiologist, who peers through his wire-rimmed spectacles to share a picture of the Greenbelt centennial pin he earned volunteering at the park. "I'm not sure how you're going to get this one for your collection, but good luck!" Carl's enthusiasm for the national park system equals my own, and we banter over countless shared experiences. Carl typifies the unique and interesting individuals I've met through the club.

Convention Saturday disheartens me. Though the club prearranged free parking for eighty vehicles behind the Arch Meeting House, I miss the narrow entryway in the brick wall surrounding the parking lot. Two cars clinging to my rear bumper dissuade searching for the small gap. I pay twenty dollars to park a half-mile to the west. I don't mind walking.

I'm joining one of the club's group tours of Independence Hall. It's the fourth time I've toured this historic American landmark, and it never gets old to stand in the room where both the Declaration of Independence and the US Constitution were debated and adopted in 1776 and 1787, respectively. To stare across the tables and chairs to the large chair facing us, George Washington's chair during the Constitutional Convention, connects us to the nation's founding so many generations ago. The sun carved into the chair backing famously inspired Benjamin Franklin's musing about whether it represented a setting or rising sun.

Before our own convention's noon start, I walk a few blocks south of Carpenters Hall, the meeting location of the First Continental Congress in 1774, to join other club members at a small square brick ex-boardinghouse, the NPS's smallest unit in acreage, **Thaddeus Kosciuszko National Memorial.**

The memorial celebrates the Polish patriot who lent his considerable talents to the cause of the American Revolution. Kosciuszko helped choose the all-important Saratoga defensive position and established other military fortifications, including those at West Point. Regarded as a hero in the young nation, he stayed for a short time in the boarding house upon his return to America in 1797. The building's interior tells of his lifelong struggle for freedom in America and, less successfully, in his Polish homeland.

At the Benjamin Franklin Underground Museum bookstore, I stop to use a collection of passport stampers for Philadelphia area sites. The bookstore wasn't among my stops in the city back in

March. After waiting for about ten minutes to stamp my centennial passport book, I'm careful to leave some space to my left for someone else to use the stampers as I finish. A younger guy steps up to the space, banging into me, and starts grabbing stampers I've arranged on the desk. He reaches across me, hitting my arms and torso each time he snatches a stamper, tossing them in a pile after examination. I'm amazed that he doesn't seem to notice or acknowledge my presence. There's no "Excuse me" or even a nod. I think I'm seeing the obnoxious side of OCD. The experience portends events to come.

Upon arriving at the Arch Street Meeting House, the hall outside the convention meeting room looks like a triage area for a MASH unit. One table has extra centennial impressions from around the country that various members have left for anyone who might want them. Another table contains park brochures, junior ranger information, and other materials brought by members to share. The giveaways are scattered about each table, having been rifled through by the mass of humanity milling about the room. At my first convention last year in El Paso, I took advantage of the largess to collect a few missing brochures from unexplored parks. It's very kind of people to bring materials and items like this for the benefit of others and representative of the general spirit within the club. This year, I don't need any of the giveaways but instead shuffle through the crowd to the sign-in table. I walk past a table with special passport stampers the club has ordered for the convention and centennial. The people crowded around the table remind me of a hungry wolfpack eating a fresh kill. Elbows and asses obscure the round table. After checking in, I walk away without my prepaid convention T-shirt. Others have taken all the shirts in my size. I pass the frenzied hyaenas tearing the last meat from the carcass at the stamping table. The good, highly interesting people in our club seem washed away in chaos and madness.

I'm exhausted and dehydrated from walking in the heat toting my backpack, and the boorish behavior spoils my normal enthusiasm for park-related activities and this convention specifically. I retreat to the basement and slump on a wooden bench opposite the restrooms. It's cool down here, a sanctuary from the unaircon-ditioned main floor above. July temperatures and animal body heat make the main floor a claustrophobic sweat box. I'll wait until the convention starts, make copies of the stamps upstairs, and leave. After the throng oozes from the hall upstairs into the meeting room, I climb the stairs into the now quiet hall.

Deciding to stay for at least a part of the meeting, I enter the back of the hall and sit on a wooden pew as the Independence National Historical Park superintendent welcomes our group. I sit in my purgatory long enough to applaud the ten members who've achieved "platinum" status, meaning they have completed visits to all the current NPS units. The club had thirty-five platinum members going into this year, and ten is by far the most to achieve the accomplishment in a single year. No confirmation of park visits takes place, nor is there any standard applied to the definition of a visit. It's a self-reported, "on your honor" accomplishment. Some consider collecting the stamp to be sufficient for a park visit. Others have a long list of activities and experiences they check off before declaring a park visited.

It becomes obvious this year that some members are hyper-competitive when it comes to counting park visits and collecting passport cancellations. Many passport enthusiasts hope to acquire all the unique centennial cancellations. That aspiration spawned the competitive banter between Lee and me on the club internet forum. An array of tremendous claims and stupendous feats via the self-reporting system make my year look pedestrian. I don't know if these accomplishments are exaggerated, real, or spurious. None of it diminishes my respect and appreciation of the good people I've met through the club and in the parks.

Fortunately, I've got a built-in reason for an early exit, as I'm attending tonight's game at Citizens Bank. I quietly slip out the door during the 3:15 p.m. break and head to my car. Tomorrow I catch a flight home to Chicago, thrilled with the week's park adventures but trying to forget the way it ended.

27 *Carnivorous Redwoods*

KAREEN AND I take our annual vacation in the last two weeks of August as we have done the past four years. We've structured each trip around NPS locations. It was on the first of these trips that Kareen triggered my goal to see the parks in the Chancellorsville Battlefield bookstore. Thus, I blame her for the ensuing madness. It's clearly all her fault.

This year's vacation starts Monday morning. Our flight from Chicago to San Francisco lands about 8:45 a.m. We're driving into downtown San Francisco an hour later. Winding our way through traffic, our first stop is the Golden Gate Bridge Pavilion at the iconic bridge's south end. **Golden Gate National Recreation Area**, the most frequently visited NPS unit with over 15.6 million centennial visitors, has a distinct advantage in visitation with its large number and spread of locations in this major metropolitan tourist destination.

From the pavilion, we descend the hill to **Fort Point National Historic Site**. Part of the Third System of Coastal Defenses previously mentioned, Fort Point is the system's only Pacific Coast fortification, though the fort on nearby Alcatraz Island also dates to the Third System. Built between 1853 and 1861, Fort Point never saw combat. The strategic location, nestled under the Golden Gate Bridge's southern anchor, defended the bay entrance. Rifled artillery made masonry forts obsolete during the Civil War, leaving the impressive structure outdated soon after construction. Atop the fort, the Golden Gate Bridge runs axially to the Marin Peninsula, its main 4,200-foot span towering 220 feet above the one-mile wide strait for which it's named.

Nearby Crissy Field served as an army airfield in the decades before World War II. The site now includes a promenade and an urban recreation area. While Kareen and I are visiting the field, I stop at the Crissy Field Center and meet some park staff who celebrate my centennial journey by taking pictures of me with my centennial passport book held high for the park's social media page.

We continue to Fort Mason and the recreation area headquarters. I toured the grounds last year but use today's visit to find a cache of passport stampers kept here. It takes about fifteen minutes to find someone who can open the correct office. The regular occupant is out on sick leave. Fort Mason commands high ground above the near side of San Francisco Bay and the passage between Alcatraz Island and the mainland. The strategic position, improved by the early Spanish settlers in San Francisco's mission days, is called Point San Jose. Although the army owned the land, civilians occupied it until the army began Civil War-era development of Fort Mason.

We leave our car parked at Fort Mason and descend a curved lane to the waterline and the Aquatic Park Bathhouse. A short distance past the bathhouse, we stop in the **San Francisco Maritime National Historical Park** visitor center. The park features six vessels moored along the Hyde Street Pier. I explored the vessels in some detail last September. Kareen is more interested in eating a late lunch than boarding the ships. I'm hungry, too. We eat mediocre seafood at one of the tourist traps between Hyde Street Pier and San Francisco's famous waterfront landmark, Fisherman's Wharf. After our meal, it's time to check in at our downtown hotel for the night.

The next morning, we exit the city north over the Golden Gate Bridge to the Marin Headlands Visitor Center in Golden Gate National Recreation Area. The Marin Headlands overlooks

San Francisco, offering a great view of the hilly peninsular city by the bay.

Though administered by Golden Gate National Recreation Area, **Muir Woods National Monument** is considered a distinct NPS unit. Muir Woods protects 553 acres of old-growth coastal forest populated by the state's iconic symbol, the redwood. Some Douglas firs blend into Muir Woods' shaded hillsides. The park's proximity to San Francisco produces heavy crowds. Parking can be a challenge. At the park, we walk through Redwood Canyon under the big trees. I tell Kareen, who's been here before but not seen the redwoods farther north, "These trees are the appetizer before the main meal at Redwoods National Park." She nods without comment.

From the big trees, we travel north and toward the Pacific Coast, eating lunch at a small restaurant outside the next park, **Point Reyes National Seashore.** I often skip lunch when I'm in the parks alone. Kareen must be fed. A hungry Kareen is an unhappy Kareen. I've learned not to skip her regular feedings.

Our visit starts at Bear Valley Visitor Center and the half-mile Earthquake Trail. The trail runs along the San Andreas Fault and the spot where a farmer's fence over the fault separated, moving twenty feet during the 1906 San Francisco earthquake. The park service reconstructed the fence in its position after the disastrous quake. Kareen and I pose for pictures standing in the gap. Kareen looks irresistibly cute standing defiantly over the fault in her black fleece jacket and striped scarf, with her head tilted back. I caution, "Show some respect. The fault might open beneath you and swallow you whole." She retorts, "If it eats me, it's going to eat you, too!"

California's mainland rests on the North American plate, while the Point Reyes Peninsula sits on the edge of the Pacific plate. Testimony to the power of the fault and tectonic forces exists in plain view. The peninsula's geological fingerprint does not match the mainland here. The rocks matching those on the peninsula are found 280 miles south near Malibu. The Pacific plate moves an average of one to two inches per year, but the complexity of the many faults at the plate boundary builds enormous stored energy. The energy released in the 1906 quake moved the peninsula twenty feet in seconds. Point Reyes is a park in motion.

Point Reyes. Earthquake Trail

We continue farther into the peninsula to Point Reyes Lighthouse. An interpretive panel on the bluff above the lighthouse identifies Point Reyes as the windiest spot on the Pacific Coast. An anemometer maintained here for years by the US Coast Guard measured an average wind speed of about 20 mph and a record wind speed of 133 mph. Storm winds often exceed 70.

A three-hundred-step stairway descends to the lighthouse at Point Reyes. The scene of the vast Pacific against the lighthouse and northbound bluff is one of my favorites in the parks. The view north from the top of the sea cliff across Point Reyes Beach extends its entire eleven-mile length. My two visits here have both been under clear skies. That's not always the case. Heavy fog is common. Cooler water near the coast, especially July through September, frequently creates a blanket of fog as moisture formed above warmer water condenses. This fog can extend as far out as fifty miles into the ocean.

Our next activity is the 1.75-mile hike to Chimney Rock. Point Reyes is shaped like a whale's tail. The left oceanside fluke features the lighthouse. The right mainland-side fluke leads to detached rock formations. Among them, a roughly cylindrical column is named Chimney Rock. The views of Drake's Beach to the left and the battered sea cliffs over the Pacific are at once serene and fierce. We extend the hike further, careful not to get too close to the unstable cliff edge. Our walk passes the historic Chimney Rock Life Boat Station on the thin peninsula's northern shore. It's a thoroughly enjoyable experience that alternates between hot and chilly as the sun and wind hit our skin.

We leave Point Reyes for the four-hour commute to our hotel in Redding, California. Our route takes us past the north end of San Francisco Bay south of Napa Valley to I-5 north. I'm grateful for Kareen's patience, allowing me to schedule this road trip to the northern California, southern Oregon, and Bay Area parks. It's past 9:00 p.m. when we reach our hotel. Our dinner tonight consists of a rotisserie chicken and items from a local supermarket. Our limited cuisine is a small concession for the wonders ahead. We're staying in Redding two nights while we visit the next four parks. Including three Oregon sites, the next seven parks are new to us.

Wednesday begins in the **Whiskeytown-Shasta-Trinity National Recreation Area**. Among the park's three subunits, the National Park Service manages Whiskeytown while the US Forest Service manages the Shasta and Trinity sub-units. All three feature man-made lakes built to stabilize the California Valley's water supply. The Shasta Dam created the oldest of these when completed in 1944. From our hotel, I make a directionally challenged error and head north on I-5 for a quick, unplanned visit to Shasta Lake. Realizing the mistake, we turn around at the marina and head south and west to Whiskeytown.

Our visit starts eight miles west of Redding at the visitor center off California Highway 299. After collecting the Whiskeytown lapel pins for the exhibit and reviewing our options, we decide on the hike to Brandy Creek Falls.

The Whiskeytown unit's main road wraps around the south end of Whiskeytown Lake and is named J. F. Kennedy Memorial Drive. The September 28, 1963, dedication of the Whiskeytown Dam, the last of the three dams to be completed, proved to be one of President Kennedy's final public appearances. The lake flooded the original Whiskeytown site under 120 feet of water.

After the January 1848 gold strike at John Sutter's mill in the Sierra Nevada Mountains, the second major gold discovery in California comes from Pierson Reading in Clear Creek. The California gold rush of 1849 gives rise to multiple shanty towns, including Shasta City and Whiskeytown five miles to the west. Whiskeytown rises at the junction of Clear, Whiskey, and Brandy Creeks. Although the prospectors disappeared long ago, their history lives through several historic sites in and near the park.

We exit Kennedy Drive for two and a half miles of winding gravel road to the Brandy Creek Falls trailhead. Our hike, mirroring the creek's path through the heavily wooded, mountainous terrain, runs over four miles. A serene trek leads us to the sound of cool mountain water rushing over the rocks about halfway to the falls. About a third of the way down the trail, I hear rustling noises from the cliff above and to our left. The path hugs the side of the steep ravine cut by the water tearing downhill. I get a strong feeling that something's watching us. It makes me uncomfortable enough that I wait for Kareen, dawdling behind me. "Stay close," I urge her. I never see the source of the sounds, but the unsettling feeling and unnerving noises follow us for half a mile. At the falls, we walk past the lower falls to the uppermost waterfall, taking pictures against the backdrop. Dressed all in black and wearing sunglasses, Kareen smiles under a ray of sunlight piercing the forest canopy.

After an hour's drive east, we enter **Lassen Volcanic National Park** from Highway 44 near Manzanita Lake. We stop at Loomis

Museum for Kareen's bathroom break. I'm relieved too, as Kareen's been asking how far away we are for the past half hour. At Loomis, we're introduced to the park's explosive history.

Lassen Peak forms the south end of the volcanic Cascade Range. Lassen's last major eruptions occurred over three years beginning in May 1914 and continuing into 1917, though smaller eruptions continued until 1921. The largest eruption in the series, on May 22, 1915, created a swath of destruction a mile wide and over three miles long. Lassen Peak is the largest of the park's thirty volcanic peaks with eruptions in the last three hundred thousand years.

On our way through the park, we take pictures at Summit Lake but save our hiking time for Bumpass Hell. Little Hot Springs Valley stretches far below the trail. Our trek is rushed to make the Kohm Yah-mah-nee Visitor Center's closing time. The visitor center has an excellent exhibit on volcanism and the Cascade Range's volcanic history. Models lining the wall describe the four major volcano types: cinder cone, shield cone, composite cone, and plug dome. We'll see more examples of these different volcano classifications farther north in the Cascades.

After an early start Thursday, we travel north on I-5 before turning northeast on US Highway 97. At the turn, we get a clear view of the snow-capped, 14,162-foot Mt. Shasta to our right. Mt. Shasta, the tallest Cascade peak, rises sharply above the mostly flat foreground. It's classical volcano profile is unmistakable. Continuing near the Oregon-California border, we turn south on Highway 139 to the small isolated town of Tulelake, California.

The former Japanese internment facility at Camp Tule Lake and the Tule Lake Segregation Center National Historic Landmark comprises one of nine **World War II Valor in the Pacific National Monument** subunits and is the only one in the contiguous United States. Tule Lake, the most heavily fortified of the internment camps, held Japanese Americans deemed the highest risk to national security. The camp's core, now protected within a fenced area, maintained a segregated high security prison-within-a-prison.

We stop at a small visitor contact station wedged into the county fairground. The volunteer on duty offers us a cupcake to celebrate the National Park Service's centennial anniversary. I greet her with, "Happy Founder's Day!" The National Park Service, born on August 25, 1916, turns one hundred years old today.

Our next park is a short distance away. **Lava Beds National Monument** covers forty-seven thousand acres of lava flows and dormant volcanoes bordering the south side of Tule Lake National Wildlife Refuge. After the obligatory visitor center stop, we explore lava tubes along the Cave Loop Road. The tubes are dark away from the entrance. Descending into the first hole ahead of Kareen, I turn to watch her step down the ladder and stand in the column of light from above, looking like she's in a tractor beam. Our weak flashlight is overmatched by the inky blackness of the void. We repeat the process in more tubes, moving as much by touch as by vision. Kareen asks, "What are we seeing, exactly?"

"I don't know. You're the one with bat vision," I reply. When we started dating, the lack of light in her condo shocked me. She had no light whatsoever in her living room and bedroom beyond what came through the windows. One of my first gifts to her was a full set of lamps. She still takes a shower in a darkened bathroom with no artificial light. These caves should feel like home.

After seeing essentially nothing underground, we continue in the park with the short walk to Skull Cave and finish with a hike up the Schonchin Butte to the fire lookout atop the rock, elevation 5,302 feet. In the station, we meet Ranger Craig, who explains the tools used to spot wildfires and monitor fire risk. He also points out some landscape features, such as the massive shield volcano that produced much of the lava flow and tubes found in the park today. Ranger Craig bears a strong resemblance in appearance, supplemented by his deep, smooth baritone voice, to the famous actor Sam Elliot. Sam's, or rather Craig's wife, is on duty at the entrance station. I promise to say hello on our way out. Kareen hangs with us for a short time but loses interest when I share a few of this year's adventures. He wishes me safe travels and good luck with the final third of the year as I leave to catch up to Kareen on the trail down the butte.

After a night in Medford, Oregon, Friday morning we're off

to another new park and my final NPS cave unit, **Oregon Caves National Monument and Preserve.** The park's caves tunnel through the marble of the southwestern Oregon's Siskiyou Mountains. The unit sits directly between the Siskiyou and Rogue River National Forests. Visitors travel here by scenic US Highway 199, connecting Grants Pass, Oregon, and Crescent City, California. In the Illinois River Valley town of Cave Junction, Highway 46 goes east and dead ends at the monument. Part of the experience at Oregon Caves is navigating the park road. The paved two-lane road is in excellent condition, but one switchback after another leave us a little dizzy during the winding, slow climb. We arrive as the visitor center opens, ready to join the first cave tour.

The standard Oregon Caves tour covers a half mile under-ground, entering the cave at an elevation of 4,000 feet and exiting at 4,220. The caves feature limestone versions of the most common speleothems, including draperies, columns, flowstone, stalactites, and stalagmites. Not counting lava tubes or repeat visits, today marks the seventh NPS unit cave tour I've taken in the past two years. Our guide is professional and polite but somewhat cheer-less and likes to ask "gotcha" questions. I love to learn from park rangers and do so at practically every park. An interpretive panel, no matter how interesting or well designed and written, cannot convey the sense of enthusiasm for a subject that a human being can. But I don't enjoy exercises to demonstrate the guide's abstract knowledge at my own expense.

We're entertained by a lady in our group that asks a few stunning questions, like "Were there stairs in the cave when it was discov-ered?" and "How does air get in the cave?" As we move between the chambers, I whisper to Kareen, "Has the cave always been hollow? Are all caves hollow?" She whispers back, "Don't ask that!" She waits to hear my voice, but I leave her in suspense. Back in the car, I declare, "I've now toured all the NPS cave units, completing my descent through the bowels of the park service."

"Doesn't that make you a bowel movement, then?" asks Kareen, failing to conceal a devilish grin.

One hundred miles to the northeast, we enter our next, much

anticipated destination on Highway 62. The highway shadows the Rogue River for nearly forty miles, crossing it several times before turning to the east in the Rogue River National Forest and leading into **Crater Lake National Park**. About six miles after the western park boundary, the road crosses the **Pacific Crest National Scenic Trail** (often shortened to "the PCT"). I crossed the trail earlier this year near Cascade Locks when I drove over the Columbia River on the Bridge of the Gods in late June. The PCT crosses the bridge over the river but more importantly to PCT thru-hikers (the term used for long-distance trekkers as opposed to the modest day hikes defining my year), it marks the final 500 miles of the 2,650-mile Pacific Crest Trail. The bridge also happens to be the lowest point on the trail, at 180 feet above sea level. The highest point is Forrester Pass, north of Mt. Whitney, at 13,153 feet. I also crossed the PCT in the south this year, between Mojave National Preserve and Tehachapi, California, during our visits to Sequoia, Kings Canyon, and Cesar Chavez. I will intersect the trail over a dozen times before year's end.

Aspiring long-distance hikers start in the spring at the Mexican border with a goal to finish in September or October at the Canadian border. The south-to-north strategy is forced due to the heavy snowfall and late spring at higher elevations. The trail's most dangerous section is California's approximately five hundred-mile-long stretch in the high Sierras. Some high-altitude trail sections have nearly year-round snow and ice on narrow ledges with steep drop-offs and considerable elevation change. Conditions often render parts of this trail section impassable. Many thru-hikers bypass it, returning to the trail north of I-80 and Donner Pass. The PCT's immense challenge creates a culture all its own. Terms like "trail magic" and "trail angels" represent the best of human nature, when locals or others render assistance to thru-hikers. Although I can't pretend to understand the rigors of hiking over two thousand miles through the wilderness, I can sympathize with trail spirit and appreciate the better attributes of human character sought along the way.

We're tired and need a slow day at Crater Lake. We review

the day's objectives at the Rim Village Visitor Center and plan to circumnavigate the lake on the main park road, called Rim Drive, taking advantage of any hikes that supersede our malaise.

Crater Lake is the deepest lake in the United States, with a maximum depth of 1,943 feet below the surface, which is 6,173 feet above sea level. The roughly round lake varies between four and a half and six miles across. On East Rim Drive, we stop at the Sun Notch and take pictures of the deep-blue water. The isolated lake water, lacking any tributaries, tests among the purest of any large body of water in the country. The water purity explains the color. Pure water or ice absorbs reds and other shorter wavelengths and reflects longer blue wavelengths. Early visitors might have thought the lake's cavity created by a massive meteor, but it's the collapsed 12,000-foot volcano, Mount Mazama. The volcano fell in on itself after a major eruption seventy-seven hundred years ago.

We continue our drive around the east side with a stop at the Cloudcap Overlook to see the lake from a different perspective. The essence of the thing, a large, round deep-blue lake, dominates the panorama. A few brief stops on the north side offer subtle variations in profile. Kareen is out of steam and must be fed. Being careful not to expose my neck or any fleshy body parts, I slide behind the wheel and guide us out of the park on the north entrance road. We're staying in Chemult, Oregon, which offers nothing other than its proximity to the park. We check into an ill-used room at a motor lodge, inspiring us to check for bed bugs under the mattress. Finding no food options that meet Kareen's standards, she eventually orders some chicken from a quick stop (not our best option in my humble opinion) and retires to our room, leaving me to hunt my own meal. I walk to a place down the street and order a steak after I ask, "Is the meat good? I can't eat lots of fat." The older gentleman I presume to be the bar owner assures me, "I order the meat personally." The meal is edible, meaning I don't get sick from it. The steak loses about half its weight when I remove the fat. The best part of the meal is the cold draft beer. When I return to the room, I admit to Kareen, "I should have had the chicken."

On Saturday, I've planned a 360-mile roundtrip to **John Day Fossil Beds National Monument** in central Oregon. I give Kareen the option to join me or rest and relax while I run myself into the ground to see a new park. Predictably, she opts for the latter. As we gained experience with park trips, I learned that if our itinerary requires a lot of driving or hiking, or both, I need to insert rest days for her. Especially this year, I don't expect anyone to maintain my grinding pace. It would be more relaxing to slow down, but I enjoy the thrill of seeing something new. I figure we'll have time for slower, longer park trips in the coming years. An older and grayer version of me can chastise running children, shaking my cane as I shuffle down the path with suspenders holding my pants up past the navel. "Those damn kids!" I envision being a crotchety old man.

Managed by the US Forest Service, Newberry Volcanic National Monument lies in route to John Day. It's one of many irresistible, non-NPS sites I encounter this year. I wish I had a whole day reserved to see Newberry and its seven-hundred-acre obsidian flow, dating to thirteen hundred years ago. I walk through the immense lava flows, past chunks the size of cars and small buildings. My visit is brief, as the destination is still two and a half hours away.

John Day Fossil Beds National Monument contains three separated units. Spread across the John Day River and Highway 19, the Sheep Rock unit anchors the park. The Painted Hills unit is off US Highway 26 about thirty-five miles west of Sheep Rock. The Clarno unit is over twenty miles north of Painted Hills. My visit starts with the exceptional exhibits in the Sheep Rock unit's Thomas Condon Paleontology Center and Visitor Center. The displayed fossils are interesting, but the interpretation is brilliant. One exhibit explains the age and extent of John Day's various fossil-rich rock layers. Other exhibits expound on specific layers and their origin. Specific fossil finds, like the Clarno unit's Hancock Mammal Quarry, are reviewed in fascinating detail. The Painted Hills' Bridge Creek flora is covered likewise. The John Day Strata holds Oregon's richest fossil collection. An interpretive display explains that the strata's middle and upper portions include three different fossil-bearing sections, deposited between thirty and eighteen million years ago. Visitors view the fossil cleaning room through a window. The room appears like a hybrid of an operating room and a high-tech lab.

From the exhibits, I walk the Island in Time and the Blue Basin Overlook Trails. The scenery and its powerful color stun me. The Blue Basin merits the name. Rocks rising to the trail's left feature shades of green against beige. Returning to the trailhead, the nearer mesa, now on my right, contrasts with the crimson butte across the road.

At the Painted Hills unit, various shapes and sizes rise from the ground striped with crimson red and hints of yellow and green. I'm awed by the intense color at John Day Fossil Beds.

We have two days to explore the last park in our vacation's northern swing. I'm excited to return to **Redwood National Park** and the adjoining state parks. I came here for a day in the summer of 2008, during a break in the US track and field Olympic Trials at Eugene where I officiated. Big trees attract me like bees to honey. Southern California's sequoias are amazing. The Pacific Northwest's Douglas firs, especially on Vancouver Island, are incredible. The giant cedars and firs of the Olympic rain forest are surreal. But no park fires my passion for old-growth forests like Redwood National and State Parks. Passing beneath these three-hundred-foot monsters brings a serenity unique among park experiences. Time and space melt away. The feeling of being small among these giants, yet part of something larger and more important, consumes the senses. Walking among Northern California's coastal redwoods brings the kind of blissful peace John Muir must have felt in the wild. Redwood National and State Parks is a place of transcendence.

Before the year started, I told Kareen, "You haven't seen the 'big' trees!" We remedied the omission in part at Sequoia and Kings Canyon in March. Though we had way too little time during that trip, standing beside General Sherman and his brethren planted the seed. Though she had visited Muir Woods years earlier, I cautioned, "You haven't seen *the* redwoods until you've been to Redwood National Park." She replied, "We'll see."

We enter the park's northern boundary Sunday morning on US

Highway 199, stopping at the Hiouchi Information Center for a trail map. Before venturing into the woods, we drive across the highway to the Jedediah Smith Redwoods State Park for their passport stamp. In 1828, Jedediah Smith became the first nonnative to reach California's northern coast by land. When Smith arrived, over two million acres of old-growth redwoods covered the northern California coast. Today, Redwoods National and State Parks protect thirty-nine thousand acres of old-growth forest, approximately half of the remaining coastal redwoods.

After driving east on Highway 199, turning on South Fork and then Howland Hill Road, we reach the Stout Grove. I walked through the grove during my first visit and didn't want to miss another chance. We explore the grove and area trails, shaded by the high green treetops. I take pictures of Kareen standing in front of several massive specimens. Redwoods grow to more than 22 feet in diameter, and many exceed 300 feet, some 350 feet in height. The park boasts the 379-foot world champion redwood named Hyperion. Redwood bark thickens to more than twelve inches. The bark's chemical composition of tannins and other compounds resists fire, insects, and disease. A mature tree can weigh up to five hundred tons. The sequoias are heavier, having the distinction of the largest living thing by volume in General Sherman. However, redwoods are the tallest trees on earth. Douglas firs are one of the few species capable of contesting the redwoods lofty reign above 300 feet.

An interpretive panel explains the trees' limited four-hundred-mile range from Big Sur north to the Oregon border, and rarely more than forty miles inland. Redwoods receive about 35 percent of their water from the air! A large redwood can consume up to five hundred gallons of water a day. That's a thirsty tree! Winter storms supply sixty inches of annual rainfall near the park's coast from November to May. The slopes of the coastal highlands receive the most water from orographic rainfall, or rain that occurs when moisture-bearing clouds are forced to higher elevations. During the dry summer months, the trees collect most of their water from adsorption and condensation of moisture in prevailing fog and low ceilings. The big trees condense water vapor so efficiently, studies show the ground under a large redwood receives as much as fifty percent more water above annual rainfall. Furthermore, seedlings cannot tolerate extended freezing temperatures, another important factor limiting redwood range. The drier climate to the southern end of the tree's range narrows the tree's distribution to the coast and limits growth compared to Northern California.

During our two-hour hike in the Stout Grove area, we marvel at one giant after another. Finding a split trunk with three enormous redwoods growing from a shared root system, I snap a picture of Kareen perched in the notch between the massive trunks dwarfing her on three sides. I tell her, "This would be a bad time to learn that redwoods are carnivorous." Amused, I post two photographs of Kareen with her new redwood friends to social media with the explanation, "The last known photographs taken of Kareen alive. We didn't know these trees are carnivorous!"

Redwoods, Kareen's last photo

Refusing to dwell on Kareen's tragic outcome at Stout Grove, I head to the park headquarters and information center in Crescent City for a stamping stop and debriefing on hiking suggestions followed by a late lunch in Crescent City.

The redwood attack has not diminished Kareen's appetite. We find an elevated seafood restaurant at the town's public pier, climb the stairs and eat with a view of the Pacific. Checking into our Crescent City hotel, Kareen burrows into bed to digest her kill. I use the remainder of the day for a return to Jedidiah Smith State Park and more hiking nearby. I return to a darkened hotel room to find my alpha wolf fast asleep.

We devote our second day to the southern half of the park, beginning at Prairie Creek Redwoods State Park's visitor center off the Newton B. Drury Scenic Parkway, part of the old Redwood Highway and an eight-mile alternative to US Highway 101. Noting trail suggestions from the staff, we park a mile north at the Big Tree Wayside, a trailhead for several popular hikes. We start on the 1.4-mile Cathedral Trees Trail and the short Circle Trail, extending the hike to sections of the Foothill Trail and Cal-Barrel Road, a gravel lane up the shaded slope. National Geographic shot footage from the Foothill Trail for a recent film featuring the park. The adjacent gullies and fern-covered forest floor provide a classical temperate rainforest setting.

We return to the trailhead after our four-mile forest trek. Our walk proves fitful as I'm taking pictures of one tree after another. Time blurs in the cool, moist air. At the trailhead, Kareen poses for a picture in front of the "Big Tree," a redwood over three hundred feet tall, sixty-six feet in circumference, and estimated at fifteen hundred years old.

After the morning hike at Prairie Creek, we stop at Thomas H. Kuchel Visitor Center near the point where US 101 enters the thirty-seven miles of park coastline from the south. After a quick lunch in Orick, our afternoon activity starts down Davison Road, a rough gravel road accessing Gold Bluffs Beach and our destination.

Fern Canyon served as a film location for *The Lost World: Jurassic Park*. The steep, fern-covered walls support all six major fern varieties among one of the most biodiverse fern populations on earth. We scramble over fallen trees on our trek, climbing large and small rocks resting beside or in Fern Creek. The obstacles grow more numerous and intimidating deeper into the canyon. In a few places, the canyon walls narrow and give the impression of a large plant enveloping the trail. Near the end of the trail, we retreat from the last of the boulders and fallen trees blocking the path. The natural jungle gym, complete with flowing water, harmonizes with this place that time forgot.

Redwoods, Fern Gully

After retreating from the gully, we venture to the shoreline on another trail. Standing atop a tree trunk on the flat ground between the cliffs, the gully, and the ocean, I look north up the coast, a narrow strip of sand between the ocean and a modest cliff bathed in trees and foliage. I pose for a picture on the trunk, a perfect exhibition platform as well as viewing stand. At Kareen's insistence, I raise my hands and do a bodybuilding pose, flexing my left biceps with my right arm extended and right hand pointing to the sea. Kareen shouts, "Take off your shirt!" Spying a mischievous grin across her face, I refuse. Just as she's snapping another picture, a family pours through the bushes on the trail toward the water, stopping to take in the scene before laughing. Realizing the good doctor has spoofed me, I throw my hands in the air, still on the tree, and say, "And you wanted me to pose naked?" The family scurries by with nervous sideways glances, lest my question be a confirmation.

28 El Capitan

FROM REDWOOD, OUR vacation transitions south starting with a six-hour drive to Sacramento for a short night of sleep. Tomorrow, we complete the five hundred miles to our destination, **Yosemite National Park**. Both Kareen and I visited Yosemite Valley before we met. Over the next two days, we will enjoy the park together, with another light day scheduled for Kareen.

We reach the park at the Big Oak Flat entrance, taking Big Oak Flat Road as it winds its way down to Yosemite Valley. I start at the park headquarters and Yosemite Valley Visitor Center. The headquarters has a passport stamper cache representing the park's sixteen stamping locations. After the successful raid on the stamper collection, I join Kareen in the theater for a park film. She's watching her second film when I find her. I confess, "I purchased a couple of unique centennial shirts in the bookstore, to go with the forty-plus centennial T-shirts I've got at home."

Kareen shakes her head. "Well, that's nice." I, however, am pleased with my purchase.

Returning through the valley, we make several stops for pictures and short walks. It takes a few minutes to reorient ourselves among the park's famous landmarks. "Is that Half Dome?"

"No, that's the North Dome, next to the Royal Arches." I'm

relying on the park map—a lot. We stop at the Four Mile Trailhead and decide on a longer walk over the Swinging Bridge crossing the valley's Merced River and back to Sentinel Beach, which isn't really a beach. We circle past Yosemite Village again.

Kareen offers the comment, "We've already been here."

"Your genius overwhelms me," I reply.

Once again heading west, I stop beneath El Capitan at the Ribbon Creek parking area off Northside Drive. I ask Kareen if she wants to walk with me to get some pictures of the giant, granite rock from within its shadow. She opens the door, puts one foot out of the car, and snaps a couple of pictures with her phone. "That's good enough," she says.

It's feeding time again. "Ansel Adams would be proud. Well, I'm going to get a better view. Here's the car keys. Don't leave without me," I say. A few steps from the car, I turn around and repeat, "Don't leave without me!"

A clearing ahead offers an unencumbered view of the granite monolith standing three thousand feet above the valley floor. Climbers have coveted this giant rock since the first ones arrived. El Capitan's popularity, for its technical challenges, beautiful view, and simple exhilaration, continues unabated today. I'm not thinking about climbing, even as I spot some freestylers working the face in the afternoon sun. Staring up at El Capitan, I'm comparing it to the human version waiting in the car. Kareen is about as unmovable, resolute, and indomitable as this massive piece of granite. She combines this with one of the most powerful minds, when it's engaged, that I've ever witnessed in action. When her mind is turned off, it absorbs information at the same rate this granite absorbs moisture. She describes herself as an action-potential. "You ain't a kiddin'," I say in response. Both are beautiful creations in their own manner but share much more in common. They both change, albeit s-l-o-w-l-y. You might call both willful and stubborn. Most definitely, both are forces of nature. It's a challenging climb, but a hell of a view.

Returning to the car, I explain my epiphany to Kareen, that she's the human El Capitan. She's amused but preoccupied with finding our El Portal lodging and her next meal. My alpha must be fed or she might turn on me. In her defense, we've had two long days bridging Redwoods and Yosemite, and a sketchy night of rest between. I exit the park with all due haste, passing the Arch Rock entrance and the Arch Rock cancellation kept at the entrance station to check in for our two nights at the Yosemite View Lodge. I'll come back and get the stamp tomorrow. It's an act of self-preservation.

Day two in Yosemite is another rest day option for Kareen. I plan to traverse the park over Tioga Pass to the east side and another new park, **Devils Postpile National Monument**. In route, I'm looking forward to the scenery and views in an unexplored part of Yosemite National Park. Leaving early morning, I plan to return midafternoon. A rested Kareen can rejoin me for the drive to Glacier Point and its valley views.

The morning sun breaks free of the horizon as I enter the park at six o'clock. I'm fatigued, too, but excited to see the park's interior and parts beyond. After entering the valley, I turn left to climb Big Oak Flat Road. My ears pop with the altitude, and soon I'm turning off Highway 120 on to Tioga Road. Winding its way through the high country, Tioga Road is a short-season passage since the wind and snow come early and stay late. I pass the alpine scenery, intending to stop for pictures on the return. Only once on the outbound journey do I give in to the urge to capture the view. As I enter Tuolumne Meadows, where the PCT and the John Muir Trail meet, I'm compelled to stop and take a picture of the alpine prairie set against the high Sierra Nevada peaks in the distance. It's more accurate to say the two trails split at the meadows, since most hikers are northbound on the PCT. The trails join inside my destination, Devils Postpile.

The Tuolumne Meadows Visitor Center is not yet open, so I'll stop here on the return. Continuing east, I exit the park at the Tioga Pass entrance. I stop to use the entrance station's passport stamp. Thus begins a fight with wind gusts pouring through the pass at an elevation of 9,945 feet. I'm forced to hold down everything lest my passport page be stolen by Aeolus in his Sierra Nevada vacation home. I return the stamper and ink pad to the ranger slightly chilled.

The descent to the Mono Basin, past Tioga Lake and then Ellery Lake, offers a dramatic vista, as if driving off the face of the earth as the road winds around high precipices to fold back into the side of the mountain. The overlook above Ellery Lake reveals a steep-sided valley and the basin's flats beyond. If I had a lion cub to hold up, I could be in a Broadway musical.

Having descended all the way to US Highway 395, the same highway that passes by Death Valley National Park and Manzanar National Historic Site farther south, I turn right and continue the three-hour trip past June Lake to the town of Mammoth Lakes, California. The first park stop is at the Inyo National Forest—Mammoth Lakes Welcome Center. I want to make sure I understand the trip into the postpile. Public vehicles are not permitted all the way to Devils Postpile National Monument. Visitors park at the Mammoth Mountain Ski Area and buy tickets to a shuttle bus for park access. The monument area gets about four hundred inches of snow each winter, limiting its months of operation most years to June into October.

Running on schedule, I get my ticket for the shuttle and make it to the park's visitor contact station about 10:00 a.m. After visiting with the rangers and getting the cancellations, I hike to the postpile. The roundtrip trek covers two miles past the pile and over the top of it on the return.

Between eighty and one hundred thousand years ago, a massive eruption created a lava pool four hundred feet deep contained by a natural dam, likely a glacial moraine. As the lava cooled into rock, cracks formed creating mostly hexagonal columns. The columns vary, with a lessor number being three, four, five, or seven-sided. Some of the columns are exposed up to sixty feet above ground. Climbing to the top of the rock, the column patterns show from above, with added scrape marks from subsequent rock-bearing glacial movement through the valley. Similar mostly hexagonal columns are found elsewhere, such as throughout Washington State's Lower Grand Coulee, below the rim of the Grand Canyon of the Yellowstone, and of course, the massive columns in Wyoming's Devils Tower.

After exploring the postpile, it's another three-hour drive, longer with the planned stops, back to El Portal. Before picking up Highway 120 westbound back into Yosemite, I stop at the Mono Basin Scenic Area Visitor Center administered by the US National Forest Service near Mono Lake. Mono Basin is a high-altitude, endorheic basin, created by the deformation resulting from the interaction between the North American and Pacific plates. It's a closed hydrologic system that doesn't drain to the ocean.

The climb on Tioga Road isn't as dramatic as the descent. The return includes stops at Tuolumne Meadows Visitor Center and Olmsted Point to photograph a few of the high peaks amid the alpine landscape. In another hour, I'm working my way down to the valley and then on El Portal Road to stop at the Arch Rock entrance station for their passport stamp.

Back in our room, Kareen is awake, lounging in the bed watching TV and looking refreshed. Peering at me over her reading glasses, she greets me with, "I thought you might summit El Capitan before we go to Glacier Point."

Dropping my pack, I reply, "I'll free climb."

"Don't forget your three points of contact. You don't want to fall off," replies Kareen with a demure grin.

Standing 7,214 feet above sea-level, Glacier Point offers a great overlook of the valley and many of its most recognizable features, particularly the sawed-off, 8836-foot Half Dome, perhaps Yosemite's most famous landmark. John Muir loved this place at first sight in 1868 and enjoyed it with President Theodore Roosevelt in 1903. The pair chronicled their time together, camping near Glacier Point during a three-day trip. They awoke to five inches of fresh snow. The Glacier Point picture of John Muir and Theodore Roosevelt represents a pivotal moment in American history to conservationists and those invested in protecting our most treasured public lands. Muir convinced Teddy the valley needed additional protection, but Roosevelt, the foremost presidential advocate of public land conservation in American history, didn't need a lot of convincing. Over seven decades later, Jimmy Carter expanded on Theodore's legacy with his park system expansion, especially in Alaska.

Yosemite Valley

Our trip to the point today is filled with iconic views of the upper Yosemite Valley between Half Dome and the North Dome, and moving to the other side of the overlook, views down the valley of the Three Brothers and El Capitan glistening in the afternoon sun. In late August, the flow is near its minimum over the beautiful waterfalls that line the valley. The most famous of the waterfalls into the valley are Yosemite Falls on the north side and Bridalveil Fall on the south side. We're so taken with the beautiful valley and its famous granite monuments, we barely notice the omission. It's another excuse to return to this wonderful place. When we do return, earlier in the season and two years later, we'll climb two thousand feet from the valley floor on the Mist Trail, making a loop with the John Muir Trail, to see Vernal Fall and Nevada Fall up close and in all their roaring glory.

After enjoying a relaxing meal at the lodge and a good night's sleep, we're off early the next morning for the three-and-a-half-hour trip across Southern California to visit **Pinnacles National Park**. I visited the park last September, starting in midmorning at the western entrance. I learned firsthand that this landscape is a harsh and unforgiving place. Starting my first hike at the Chaparral Trailhead and intending to explore the Balconies Cliffs and Balconies Cave Trails, I got turned around and wound up hiking the Juniper Canyon Trail, climbing in elevation to the High Peaks Trail. I realized my error about a mile into the trail but decided to continue climbing. As the temperature moved into the mid-nineties baking me on the exposed trail, I considered a turnaround point with the water on hand. I hadn't planned for a five-to-six-mile hike in extreme heat. After trudging back to the parking lot, I ventured another half mile down the Balconies Trail but didn't have the strength or water to complete the loop.

Retreating again, I drove around the park's south end to the east entrance and Bear Gulch Day Use Area. From the trailhead, I climbed up the Bear Gulch Cave Trail, through the cool cave passage in the rock-choked gulch. From the top of the trail and the Bear Gulch Reservoir, I noted a second marked hiking trail returning to the parking area that descended around the caves to the left. I decided to try the alternate route, a scary mistake. About a third of the way down, the trail disappeared at a cliff. I couldn't find any markers, a rock cairn, or identifiable path. I felt a sudden urgency with temperatures now in triple digits. I had no choice but to climb to the top of the gulch and retrace my ascent. The cave's coolness offered less respite from the heat this time. My one-liter bottle of water for the intended 1.25-mile roundtrip hike now felt like a warm cup of coffee in my hand. I guarded the last gulp of hot water. I also noticed my motor control suffering. It's the closest I've come in the parks to a serious heat-related incident. Looking back, I failed to fully cool and hydrate from the morning excursion. Back at the Pinnacle Visitor Center, I bought a cold gallon of water and consumed it within fifteen minutes.

Kareen and I are only visiting the park's east side today, and I've made our goal modest, a return to the Bear Gulch Reservoir. We take plenty of water, and the temperature peaks about five to seven degrees cooler than my prior visit. We maneuver around the boulders and fallen rock obstacles on our short hike. We still have a one-and-a-half-hour drive north to San Jose for our hotel tonight and jumping off point for Friday's parks.

A trio of parks are lined up for the start of Labor Day weekend. We begin the day at the **John Muir National Historic Site** in

Martinez, California. John Muir married into the Strentzel family with his marriage to Louisa Strentzel in 1880 at the age of forty-two. Muir's father-in-law, Dr. John Strentzel, a successful fruit grower in the Alhambra Valley, built the large home on the hill and the park's centerpiece in 1882. Muir lived here until his death in 1914. His legacy as one of America's first prominent naturalists and an advocate for natural environments and America's public lands survives through untold multitudes and numerous entities, including our National Park System.

Kareen and I tour the grounds and the home. From my visit here a year ago, I try to fill in the big picture of John Muir's impact to Kareen as we read the home's interpretive displays. We return to the visitor center to view the film for our next park, a new one for both of us, **Port Chicago Naval Magazine National Memorial**. Reservation-only tours leave from the John Muir visitor center. Visitors must allow two weeks advanced notice for the required security clearance. The national memorial is located within an active army base, the same base that supplied naval ships during the memorialized World War II disaster. These restrictions leave Port Chicago the second least visited NPS unit in the contiguous United States with 1,942 centennial visitors.

On the night of July 17, 1944, two navy ships, the *E. A. Bryan* and the *Quinault Victory*, were being loaded with munitions. High explosives in sixteen railcars lined up on the pier awaited transfer on board. At 10:18 p.m., a tremendous explosion followed by a much larger one annihilated the ships, pier, railcars, and 320 mostly black servicemen loading the cargo. The navy pushed the mostly black munition-loading crews for faster times with little or no allowance for safety. Those in the remaining crews expected action by the navy that never came, and 258 among them refused to resume loading ships. The navy threatened the mutineers with death by firing squad. All but 50 returned to duty, resulting in the largest mass-mutiny trial in naval history. The 50 dissenters were convicted and given sentences of eight to fifteen years in prison. The navy granted clemency after the war, allowing the 50 to serve out their enlistments aboard ships. Racial discrimination's injustice, on full display throughout the Port Chicago tragedy and its aftermath, increased public pressure to desegregate the US military. President Harry Truman signed the order desegregating the US military in 1947, but the fight for equal treatment and racial justice in our armed forces would continue for decades.

We leave the visitor center on the 12:45 p.m. tour. After signing in at the base security post, we continue to the waterfront memorial. Decaying wooden pilings sticking above water, where the entry and exit rail lines converged to the pier, are all that remains of the wartime site. The memorial features a tiled plaza with concrete and bronze tablets listing the casualties. A flag pole flying the Stars and Stripes at half-mast stands to the right of the tablets. Two NPS interpretive panels at the plaza's waterfront explain the events and show the original structure. A mangled piece of metal lies beside the plaza, a piece of plating from one of the ships. A railcar bunker sits across a paved road behind the memorial. The unloading shelter consists of two reinforced earthen berms sandwiching the car. The ranger leading the tour explains the extent of damage resulting from the explosion and its aftermath.

On our ride to the memorial, a middle-aged man with short hair sat with an older gentleman in the bench seat behind us, discussing everyday life on the base. Curiosity getting the best of me, I turn to him as we leave the memorial. "Do you work on the base?"

He replies, "I'm the base commander. I transferred from a post at Scott Air Force Base a few months ago." He averts his eyes up to my Cardinals hat when he mentions the St. Louis–area post. "I've been waiting for my father to visit to take this tour. I wanted to hear the park service's presentation."

I ask him, "How is it that the army runs a naval supply depot?"

He replies, "The army operates the base, but its purpose is primarily naval supply and support."

I tell him, "My parents are navy veterans, and I have eleven veteran uncles who served in World War II and the Korean War. I guess that's one reason I'm a history buff. Port Chicago is the 380th NPS unit I've visited lifetime. I hope you guys enjoy your time together. Have a wonderful Labor Day weekend, and thank you for your service."

Friday ends with the less-than-glamorous experience of Bay Bridge rush-hour traffic. It takes almost ninety minutes to reach our Geary Street hotel. We're thankful to finish the miserable commute. The shopping district and square next to our hotel teems with a surging mass of humanity. Kareen parks the rental while I haul the bags to our room. A relaxing meal by the bay soothes a tinge of disappointment that our trip is nearly over.

Saturday morning, we head east over the Bay Bridge, turning north in Oakland to reach Richmond and **Rosie the Riveter / World War II Home Front National Historical Park**. The park honors and remembers the hundreds of thousands of men and women who came together under trying circumstances to assist the war effort.

US production capacity proved paramount to World War II's outcome. Lend-Lease Act shipments to Great Britain and the Soviet Union bolstered resistance after tremendous Axis gains early in the war. As Germany took control on the European continent, Japan overran a three-hundred-mile swath of the Chinese mainland, Indo-China, and a vast area of the Pacific Ocean, capturing critical natural resources. The attack on Pearl Harbor forced the United States out of isolationism. The Richmond park highlights the countless unsung contributors on the home front. Without their hard work and record-breaking production, the Allies lacked the resources necessary to prevail. Millions of people learned new trades, breaking barriers in the process.

The Kaiser shipyards on San Francisco Bay's north end produced 747 ships during the war. Liberty or Victory ships, designed to haul cargo and supplies to the front, dominated among the new vessels. An industrial avant-garde, Henry Kaiser innovated consistently while building his military-industrial colossus. The Kaiser yards are among the first to employ women in traditionally male-dominated trades. At peak production in 1944, females made up 41 percent of the welders. Almost none of these women had prior welding experience. Before war's end, an estimated six million women joined the American workforce. They provided America's winning edge against global totalitarianism.

Since the park's establishment in October 2000, area residents who worked at the shipyards during the war have spent time at the park to share their stories. Arriving at the visitor center as it opens, we preempt the scheduled agenda. As we explore the exhibits, we have the special privilege to meet Mary Torres. It's rare that you get an opportunity to hear the personal story of someone who lived the history being celebrated.

Mary Torres worked as a journeyman welder in Oakland from 1942 to 1945. Born May 26, 1923, Mary left her hometown of Donora, Pennsylvania, two days after her high school graduation in May 1942 to support the war effort. A newspaper advertisement soliciting shipyard workers spurred Mary into action. The ad provided an Oakland-area phone number and promised training for new workers. Knowing her parents would disapprove, she gathered her savings collected from a job at JCPenney, a year of babysitting, and a small cash graduation gift, and purchased a bus ticket. Thus, the eighteen-year-old embarked on a five-day trip to the West Coast with no job, place to stay, or guarantee of any type.

Rosie the Riveter, Mary Torres and Kareen

She arrived in Oakland with a suitcase of clothes, a few dollars, and the classified ad and phone number. The phone call landed her a temporary job as an inventory clerk at McClellan Air Force Base, but she grew restless for a more substantial position. Mary applied and was accepted as a welder at Moore's Shipyard in Oakland, where she would work for the duration of the war. She waited two weeks before contacting her parents to explain her decision. When Mary mentions her hometown, I recognize it for one of her classmates. A few years ahead of Mary in school, Stan "the Man" Musial retired as the most venerated player in St. Louis Cardinal history. Mary tells us she knew him well and played catch with him and others when they were children. It's a small world.

Mary's courage and humility shine through her story. She explains her actions as necessary. "There was really no choice in the matter," Mary says. "We were fighting a war on two fronts, and everybody had to pitch in. I just wanted to do something to help. I knew I couldn't sit at home and not try to help." Mary poses for a picture next to Kareen with both flexing their right biceps, portraying the famous war propaganda poster that proclaims, "We Can Do It," now a symbol for the park. Mary's a positive force, as determined today as her actions show her to be as a teenager. She honors us with her inspiring story.

Leaving the visitor center, we drive to the park's SS *Red Oak Victory*. The last of the ships built at the Richmond shipyards, *Victory* served the country in three wars. Richmond Museum Association volunteers restored and maintain her. During our tour, I snap a picture of Kareen in the captain's chair on the ship's bridge. It's not hard to imagine her in charge of something large, barking orders and thoroughly self-confident.

We make our way back into San Francisco with time to explore further today. Our next destination is the Presidio Visitor Center at the former military installation's main post. The Presidio's history extends more than two hundred years, from the first Spanish garrison established here in 1776 until the location became part of Golden Gate National Recreation Area in 1994. We walk the Presidio grounds enjoying the beautiful, sunny day.

Our behind-the-scenes tour of Alcatraz Island leaves at 4:00 p.m. from Pier 33 on San Francisco's waterfront. Our trip counts us among the 1.5 million tourists attracted to the island's history and mystique each year. The island's western history began with the Civil War–era post of Fort Alcatraz. Converted into a military prison in 1907 and a maximum-security federal prison in 1934, the federal penitentiary became the most notorious and remains the most famous prison in American history, popularized in pop culture with the release of the 1979 film, *Escape from Alcatraz*. Based on true events, Clint Eastwood starred as Frank Morris. Morris escaped from the island in June 1962 with two brothers, Clarence and John Anglin. What became of the trio remains a mystery. The prisoners used incredible ingenuity to plot and execute their escape. Morris's cell exhibit includes one of the papier-mache heads they made for their bunks to decoy the night watch.

The park service began offering this tour two weeks ago, a combination of normally inaccessible prison locations with the night tour. The guided tour takes us all through the prison. A ranger and a volunteer take turns sharing information. Among the areas normally off-limits to the public, we walk an underground passage dating to the military era. Prison authorities sealed the passage out of concern that it could be used for escape. We also visit the basement laundry area and, by a set of stairs in A-block, the original citadel underneath the prison. The old citadel became famous as a "dungeon," and its appearance matches the description. We descend into the dark and damp base of the building and past a row of twelve-by-twenty-three-inch "torture cages" used during the military prison era. The heart of the dungeon are walkways lined by casemates, originally built to shelter artillery and later converted to cells. Inscriptions made by former occupants and staff adorn the walls. Authorities discontinued the use of these lower-level cells in the 1930s due to public pressure brought about by reports of prisoner abuse and inhumane living conditions. As we walk past, it makes me shudder to think of being confined in one of these cells. We are only in the dungeon about ten minutes, but the atmosphere discomforts us enough to be relieved when we reemerge in cell block A.

Our stop in cell block D, home to the most dangerous prisoners, starts down the corridor at the last five cells, used for solitary confinement and better known as "the hole." Inmates experienced complete darkness in these cells, with only a small opening in the solid steel door for passing food trays and communication. The ranger asks for volunteers to step into the cell and have the door closed behind us. I raise my hand first. A few other brave souls join me, including Kareen who doesn't raise her hand but follows me into the hole anyway. The door slams shut and casts us into total darkness. A few whispers cease in a hush, and silence rules the pitch black, interrupted after a few seconds when I yell, "But I'm innocent!" The group laughs, as much to relieve the nervous tension as at my sense of humor. Kareen adds into my ear, "It was only a matter of time before the park service locked you up."

Our guided tour ends near the gift shop. We pick up a pair of headphones and small handset to go back through the public areas on the self-guided audio tour. Night has enveloped the island when we finish. Both Kareen and I visited the island years ago, but not this thoroughly. We complete our visit wrapped in our jackets against the chilling wind. I've heard it explained as heat loss due to humidity and frequent Pacific winds, but there is no place I've been in the country that is quite as chilly as San Francisco at night. Layering up in sweaters and jackets doesn't keep the body warm. We shiver in the night air as we admire the city skyline lit up against the darkness. The beautiful nighttime skyline adds a special scene to the Alcatraz night tour. It's a perfect way to end our West Coast adventure.

29 The Long Drive

IN THE WANING days of summer, September shifts the priority to parks that will soon be inaccessible. Complications arise when the southern trips include roads through higher elevations. Although some park services cease after Labor Day, most parks remain open through September.

The week following Labor Day gives me a chance to catch up on work, followed by the next-to-last St. Louis games in the baseball season. For the first time in six years, my October schedule is void of playoff games. In a twist, I'm grateful to be without the distraction. I can't imagine scheduling the remaining park trips around playoff baseball.

Two northern Minnesota parks Kareen and I visited last July are on my list. After a business meeting Monday morning, September 12, I return to several Mississippi National River and Recreation Area locations before crossing rural Minnesota to Duluth. In route, I stop on the North Country National Scenic Trail at Jay Cooke State Park in Carlton, Minnesota. Jay Cooke protects the Dalles of the St. Louis River, viewed from a pedestrian walkway called the Swinging Gate Bridge. The Dalles feature sharply tilted rocks lining the river on both sides. The river exposes slate and gray-wacke rocks in the Thomson Formation. After getting the park's passport cancellations, I enjoy a walk across the river and into the park in the remaining daylight. It's nice to get out of the car and move after covering 765 miles in eleven and a half hours of driving since leaving St. Louis twenty-four hours ago.

I sleep well Monday night, trying not to dwell on Tuesday. It's going to be a brutally tiring day. By 6:35 a.m., I'm in the car headed northwest, cup of coffee in hand, for the three-hour drive to **Grand Portage National Monument** in Grand Portage, Minnesota, six miles short of the Canadian border. Kareen and I visited the park last July around the boat trip to Isle Royale.

Grand Portage National Monument celebrates the overland bypass of the Pigeon River that eighteenth-century fur trappers and traders, known as "voyageurs," used on their passage across the Great Lakes to the fur-rich northwest frontier. The park maintains a living history exhibit, allowing visitors to glimpse the frontier camp and daily life of these early pioneers and outdoorsmen. I tour the living history area again today, reading interpretive panels. A stockade, Great Hall, and other buildings make up the reconstructed outpost.

Ojibwe lived near Grand Portage during the fur-trading era. They named the portage Kitchi Onigaming, which translates to "the Great Carrying Place," and the massive lake before us, Gitchi-Gami. We know it as Lake Superior. The Grand Portage climbs 639 feet over eight and a half miles, from the Lake Superior shore to the Pigeon River's Fort Charlotte site.

After the refreshing walk and a lively discussion with the rangers on duty and a fellow park traveler in the visitor center, I'm back in the car for a drive I swore never to repeat. It takes almost five hours to cover the 270 miles between Grand Portage and **Voyageurs National Park** headquarters at International Falls, Minnesota, but the drive over mostly two-lane roads feels much longer and tests my patience. I arrive at the headquarters at 3:30 p.m. to use a collection of stampers at the reception desk. I add the cancellations to my centennial year passport in silence, as there's no one in sight. It feels abandoned.

Water dominates Voyageurs National Park. The park includes more than five hundred islands and 655 miles of shoreline stretching across 55 miles of the US-Canadian border. Water makes up 40 percent of the park's 218,054 acres and provides the best means to see it. The first day Kareen and I spent at Voyageurs last July included a Rainy Lake boat tour to visit Little American Island, the site of a gold mine. The fur-trapping and trading Voyageurs navigated this collection of lakes, rivers, and streams through wilderness untouched by man during the North American fur trade. The park's name celebrates that frontier history. Last year, Kareen and I made it to all the park's visitor facilities, stopping at Kabetogama Lake, Ash River, and Crane Lake. Today, I truncate my visit at Rainy Lake Visitor Center 12 miles east of International Falls.

I choke down some bad chicken wings for an early dinner in International Falls before moving on. The next park is 1,250 miles away. Five hours of driving take me to the limit of my fatigue near Chippewa Falls, Wisconsin. I trudge into the motel room exhausted. I'm starting to realize that this trip marks a turning point in my centennial journey. The adventure has become a grinding test of endurance to see if my motivation can delay debilitation from chronic fatigue. The schedule from this point forward offers no respite, only a relentless test of willpower.

In a brief pause Wednesday, I stop at my home along I-39 for a night's rest on the way south. I'm out the door again at four thirty Thursday morning. A brief stop at the Trail of Tears State Park near Jackson, Missouri, provides my next break. The Mississippi River park north of Cape Girardeau, Missouri, lies where nine of thirteen Cherokee groups crossed the river in harsh winter conditions from late 1838 into 1839. Dozens of Native Americans lost their lives at this place, among thousands that perished on the trail.

The drive continues through the Missouri Bootheel's pancake-flat land and similar terrain in northeast Arkansas. I make my way across mostly rural farmland, past countless cotton and rice fields. It's 3:30 p.m. when I reach **Arkansas Post National Memorial** seven hundred miles from home. Arkansas Post sits on the Arkansas River upstream about fifteen river miles from its confluence with the Mississippi. The location serves as a military outpost and trading center from the first French permanent settlement in the lower Mississippi River Valley here in 1686. Six national flags fly above the flood-prone post over 150 years, including the Confederate flag over Fort Hindman, a resupply post guarding the water approach to Little Rock. An 1863 Union attack forced the fort's surrender. Today marks my second visit.

Inside the visitor center, I meet Ranger Kary. He's a little shocked when I tell him I've driven seven hundred miles today to reach the park. I might be the first visitor to arrive at Arkansas Post directly from Voyageurs. I called the park weeks ago, asking the staff to save a pair of the unit's lapel pins for the exhibit. Ranger Kary pulls the saved lapel pins from beneath the counter before I finish asking. When he sees the worn condition of my Eastern National membership card, he offers to laminate my nonprofit park association membership cards while I'm walking the grounds. I return to find the newly laminated cards lined up neatly on the counter. As I exit, I thank Kary for his kindness and wish him a great finish to the centennial.

I will experience chronic fatigue throughout the remainder of the year, but my exhaustion as I pull up to my Southaven, Mississippi, hotel has me in a mental fog. The week's numbers tell the story. Today's trip odometer reads 870 miles covered in thirteen hours of driving over the past sixteen. The Voyageurs to Southaven journey spans 1,400 miles over forty-eight hours, twenty-two of them driving. Since Tuesday morning when I awoke in Duluth, Minnesota, I've traveled 1,800 miles in sixty-two hours, twenty-nine behind the wheel. In the last three and a half days, I've covered 2,500 miles in over forty hours of driving. That's averaging almost twelve hours of driving per day. Although I manage to stumble over to a barbeque joint adjacent to the hotel, I'm not mentally there as I pick my way through a half rack of mediocre ribs. We're still not in Kansas City, Toto. At least the beer is cold.

The Voyageurs to Arkansas Post trip materialized as my goals became clear by midyear. I would have never sequenced the parks this way if I had foreseen and planned to revisit over three hundred parks while exploring seventy-six new ones in 2016. I need the pins at nearly all the parks on this trip. Moreover, this trip through fourteen NPS units spread across seven states completes centennial visits to every Midwest and Southeast region NPS unit.

Friday morning, I'm off to **Shiloh National Military Park**. Shiloh's sleepy, rural setting belies the scene of one of the Civil War's bloodiest conflicts. The Battle of Shiloh raged across two days, April 6 and 7, 1862. The tale of reversed fortunes began when southern forces swept the Union army, under the overall command of General Ulysses S. Grant, from their camps in a surprise, predawn attack on April 6, pushing them back to a position around Pittsburg Landing on the Tennessee River. During the night, a division of Grant's Army of the Tennessee and three divisions from Major General Don Carlos Buell's Army of the Ohio arrived on the river. A reinvigorated and reinforced Union army reversed their losses during the second day and forced the Confederates from the field.

I enjoy an abbreviated battlefield tour. I first visited Shiloh in April 1994, and the battlefield left an impression. It's the first Civil War battleground I toured as an adult. I could better understand the scale of carnage. After the battle, Grant wrote of the peach orchard, "So covered with dead that it would have been possible to walk across the clearing, in any direction, stepping on dead bodies, without a foot touching the ground." The hail of lead denuded the blooming trees. The South paid dearly at Shiloh with the loss of one of its best commanders in General Albert Sydney Johnston. He bled to death after being shot in the leg during the first day. The battlefield's peaceful silence today masks combined losses over the two days exceeding 23,700 in killed, wounded, captured, or missing. The pale of death stays with this place.

A Shiloh subunit, the Corinth Civil War Interpretive Center in Corinth, Mississippi, highlights the campaign through this southern rail center. I visit Corinth's Veranda House, a Greek Revival mansion dating to 1857 that served as temporary quarters for a succession of generals, including Confederates Braxton Bragg and Earl Van Dorn and Union General Henry Halleck.

My hotel tonight is in Huntsville, Alabama. After a string of bad meals, I breakthrough with an outstanding chicken dish at a little bar downtown. I walk the mile from the hotel to the establishment to get some circulation after the week's car time. It's a refreshing break to finally enjoy what I'm eating instead of choking it down to avoid hunger. I sink into the hotel's soft bed and fade away.

Saturday's itinerary keeps me on the run. It's less about distance and more about keeping my schedule. Driving east, I notice crowds waiting beside US Highway 72. About ten miles from Huntsville, police have the divided highway shut down for a bicycle race crossing the road. Fortunately, the start must be near, as stragglers only trail the leaders by fifteen minutes. I discover the crowds hadn't been for the bicyclists after passing larger groups along the road. I can't afford long, unexpected delays today, and this makes me a bit nervous. After another fifteen to twenty miles, the attraction appears. Motorcycles pass in the other direction adorned in red, white, and blue. They are not turning in my path, so I'm able to keep moving on my way to **Russell Cave National Monument**, the three hundredth NPS unit visited during this centennial journey.

Located in northeast Alabama's hills, Russell Cave contains an archeological record of human habitation dating back over ten thousand years. Due to the importance and vulnerability of the cave's artifacts, visitors view the entrance from a boardwalk and viewing platform. It's the only NPS unit named for a cave that isn't open to public tours. I pass a young ranger who's building a dugout canoe under a hut using only tools and methods available to the prehistoric Native Americans who occupied Russell Cave. I'm the only visitor present, but he discusses the living history project anyway as he stokes a fire to burn out part of the log's interior. I ask him, "Where are you going in that canoe when it's finished?"

He smiles. "Well, nowhere. No one's asked me that question until now." We share the smile and chuckle.

After an hour's drive to the southeast, I stop at **Little River Canyon National Preserve**, another beautiful place I didn't know existed until I started traveling to parks. During my first visit two years ago, I drove Canyon Rim Drive, a road shadowing the canyon's western edge and the most common and easiest way to see this southeastern canyon.

Today, I cross the Little River north of the canyon on Highway

35 and go south on Highway 273. To keep my schedule, I've got to keep moving in the direction of the next unit. After passing through Shinbone Valley east of the canyon, I turn west toward the canyon mouth. Coming from the valley, I climb what feels like the world's steepest road back to the canyon rim, but don't have enough time for sightseeing. The park road approaching the canyon from the southeast ascends at the steepest incline I can remember. San Francisco's Lombard Street runs one way downhill, so I can't make a reliable mental comparison. It takes a low gear to make the grade. I add the Little River Canyon mouth to my list of places I hope to explore further.

Due south of Little River Canyon, **Horseshoe Bend National Military Park** protects the scene of Andrew Jackson's first significant military triumph. On March 27, 1814, Jackson led thirty-three hundred US Army soldiers, Tennessee militia, and Cherokee and Creek allied warriors into battle against about one thousand Creek warriors encamped at a sharp 180-degree bend in the Tallapoosa River. The Creek warriors painted their war clubs red, gaining the moniker "Red Sticks." The battle ended the Creek War of 1813–14. The resulting treaties stripped the Creeks of their ancestral homeland. The victory launched Jackson's career in the public arena. He cemented his military legacy with the aforementioned victory against the British in January 1815.

I toured the battlefield last year. Today, I visit with Ranger Matt and his colleagues at the visitor center, buying the lapel pins they saved for me, and explain the project. They are excited to see what comes of the effort. I am, too.

The last two parks are another hour's drive south to Tuskegee, Alabama. I stop first at one of my favorite park units, **Tuskegee Airmen National Historic Site**. Moton Field served as an air field training location for the Army Air Corps' first African American fighter pilots. The segregated facilities at Moton Field and the nearby Tuskegee Army Air Field were the only two World War II–era pilot training facilities in the country for African American pilots. The first group of thirteen prospective pilots started training here in July 1941. Five graduated. One of them, Captain Benjamin O. Davis, earned promotion to Lieutenant Colonel and took command of the 99th Fighter Squadron. As World War II continued, more pilots completed training, and the 332nd Fighter Group and 477th Bombardment Group B-25 Medium were formed. The war ended before the 477th entered combat, but the 99th and 332nd fighter groups, combined in July 1944, achieved an unparalleled service record.

The air field's second hangar had been restored and opened as a new visitor and exhibit space months before my first visit. I sat alone in hangar 2's large new theater, watching an outstanding thirty minute park film reviewing the Tuskegee Airmen's story. The moving film elicited an emotional reaction unique among the park films I've watched. The courage and determination of these men in the face of gross unfairness and hostility honors the best attributes of humanity. The pilots not only overcame tremendous obstacles but achieved a stunning combat record. A hangar 2 exhibit displays some of the 332nd Fighter Group's extraordinary accomplishments and accommodations. Primarily assigned to bomber escort duty in Italy and North Africa, the 332nd exits World War II as the only fighter group never to lose a bomber to enemy attack. The painted red tail sections of the group's planes gave them the nickname Red Tails. With profound merit, the Tuskegee pilots, their mechanics, and the support staff disabused tired, deeply imbedded notions of racial prejudice. The "Tuskegee experiment" proved unequivocally that race is not a prohibitive factor to the highest level of achievement. The inarguable Tuskegee success and countless other examples of exemplary service by African Americans championed President Truman's 1948 Executive Order 9981 desegregating the US Armed Forces.

In hangar 2, I meet Ranger Shelton, who opens the small gift shop and sells me the pair of lapel pins the park staff has saved for the exhibit. It's a slow afternoon. We discuss the pin project and reflect on the park's newest exhibits. "That's so exciting and cool," Shelton says about the year's tour of the National Park System and the exhibit. "I've committed to fulfill my mother's request and write about all this. I hope I can do justice to the park system in the retelling," I reply.

"Can't wait to read about your journey in the book," he adds.

We share a mutual respect for the parks in general and the history at this park, specifically. Shelton tells me he's transferring to Charles Young Buffalo Soldiers National Monument in south central Ohio soon. "Well, good luck on your new assignment. But I think you're gonna miss the weather in the spring. And maybe the food," I say.

"Maybe so, but I'm excited about the new challenge," he says. His broad, infectious smile follows me through the exit door as I step out into the late-afternoon sun. I'm smiling, too.

The day's last park is four miles away, the **Tuskegee Institute National Historic Site**. Created in 1881, the formerly enslaved Lewis Adams, supported by former enslaver George Campbell, recruited twenty-five-year-old Booker T. Washington as the school's first president. Washington secured an abandoned, one hundred-acre plantation in eastern Alabama for the school grounds. Steadily improving the school's facilities and academic capabilities, Washington brought a major contributor to the campus in 1896 to lead the new agricultural department. Dr. George Washington Carver developed the Institute's academic, scientific, and research footprint until his death in 1943.

I park on the campus next to The Oaks, the Booker T. Washington home designed and built by Tuskegee faculty and students in 1899. From there, it's a short walk to the George Washington Carver Museum near the center of campus. The museum features many items personally used or developed by Carver during his forty-seven years at the school. I'm thrilled to learn the unit has a set of lapel pins for the exhibit, with several of each in stock. I didn't reach anybody when I called a few weeks ago. A kind lady, over ninety years young, helps me purchase the items and tells me where to find the Washington and Carver gravesites on the far side of the campus chapel, which happens to be my other planned destination. The volunteer encourages me to see the chapel's beautiful stained-glass windows.

I confirm her accurate assessment as I finish the visit and day touring Alabama's five NPS units with the chapel, pausing at the gravesites. The day closes with a relaxing dinner at the steakhouse next to my Columbus, Georgia, hotel. As I watch college football on TV at the bar, enjoying a delicious steak and cold beer, Kareen calls on her drive back to her condominium after working ten hours. It's another brutal Saturday on call for her. At least she can enjoy a description of the great meal I'm having and the day's experiences. When I explain how exhausted I feel, she offers no sympathy.

Sunday brings a chance to slow down. Today I'll visit the two Georgia NPS units I missed earlier this year. I start in Plains, Georgia, at the **Jimmy Carter National Historic Site**. The park features the Carter boyhood farm and house, the former Plains High School, and the Plains Depot that played an interesting role in Carter's 1976 presidential campaign.

This park has grown on me since my first visit in January 2015. I remember Jimmy Carter's presidency, amid the economic recession of the late '70s, the Iran Hostage Crisis, and general doubt over the future. Carter lost his reelection bid a month before I turned ten years old, yet I remember his administration's last year and thought I understood him. What comes out in specific relief after three visits to Plains is the man's goodness and decency. I always thought of Carter as an honest man trying to do the right thing. His leadership style projected a weakness, unfair at times, but reinforced by the helplessness the country felt as the Iranian mullahs openly taunted America while the Russians did likewise, invading Afghanistan. Most Americans felt the administration's economic policies failed to improve daily life in Middle America. My parents certainly felt that way. The trials and tribulations of 1979 have faded in time. What remains vivid at Jimmy Carter National Historic Site is the decency and humanity, the fight for good and for disadvantaged people at the core of the man and his postpresidential legacy.

Plains High School, operational from 1921 until 1979, serves as the visitor center, with a small gift shop inside. I buy the park's pin set from the kind lady staffing it today. She wishes me well with the exhibit after I tell her I've managed to acquire over four hundred of the pins. I share, "The Eastern National parks are the most difficult to complete, since I'm visiting all one hundred seventy–plus locations this year."

From the book store, I sit with another couple through the park film and revisit exhibits on Carter's life. After revisiting the depot, I stop at the Golden Peanut Company in a building once owned by the Carter family. The peanut ice cream and peanut brittle are irresistible. I get a large peanut ice cream milkshake and buy two pounds of peanut brittle, one as a gift for my parents, and the other that will disappear within days after I return home.

At the Carter farm to the west of town, I walk through the home and around the property. Rounding a fenced pasture, a curious pair of mules follows me around the perimeter. They must associate humans with feeding time, as they seem to be looking for a meal. "I can't help you, pal," I say to the nearest mule, looking around when I realize what it must look like if anybody's watching me converse with a mule. It's nice to walk a bit before getting back on the road.

Andersonville National Historic Site protects the Civil War's most notorious military prison. The prison held an estimated total of forty-five thousand Union soldiers in fourteen months of operation. The space, originally sixteen and a half acres and expanded to twenty-six and a half, held up to thirty-two thousand prisoners at its peak population in August 1864. Approximately thirteen thousand inmates died at Andersonville. The enclosure's horrific conditions defy the modern imagination. Only a single creek, called Stockade Branch, flowed through the prison from west to east, providing all the stockade's water and toilet facilities.

The site's National Prisoner of War Museum remembers and honors POWs from all our nation's wars. After purchasing the park's pins saved below the front desk, I watch the park film, perhaps the most harrowing presentation offered within the park system. Among this place's grim stories, the film reviews the fate of the prison commandant. In 1865, Captain Henry Wirtz became the only Confederate soldier executed as a war criminal after cessation of hostilities. Wirtz arguably earned his fate, but the reality of Civil War prison camps points to broad neglect and requires no embellishment. Of the 194,732 Union soldiers in Confederate prison camps, about 30,000 died during captivity. The statistics in the North aren't substantially better. Among 220,000 Confederate prisoners of war, 26,000 incarcerated soldiers perished.

I revisit the prison grounds behind the visitor center, including the living history area at the stockade's northeast corner, providing visitors some representation of the camp's living conditions. After stopping at the reconstructed areas and interpretive panels on the drive around the stockade outline, I finish my time at the site in Andersonville National Cemetery.

A welcome rest Sunday night near Montgomery, Alabama, has me awake and ready to see a new park location Monday morning. The **Selma to Montgomery National Historic Trail** covers fifty-four miles, beginning in downtown Selma, Alabama, and finishing at the Alabama State Capitol in Montgomery. The commemorated events of March 21–25, 1965, exposed Jim Crow laws disenfranchising blacks throughout the Deep South. Selma's Dallas County voting rolls included only 156 of 15,000 voting-age African Americans. The brutal county sheriff, Jim Clark, became a symbol of the region's deeply imbedded racism. Clark used violence and scare tactics to prevent minority registration efforts. The nation took notice. Authorities suppressed initial attempts to march for voting rights with the violent force of law. On Sunday, March 7, Alabama State Troopers and Clark's county force beat back six hundred marchers on Selma's Edmund Pettus Bridge over the Alabama River. The event earned the moniker "Bloody Sunday" and served to galvanize national support for the movement's civil rights goals.

I travel the entire route in reverse, starting at the Alabama State Capitol. Montgomery leaped to the front of the national civil rights debate in December 1955. Rosa Parks' brave refusal to comply with segregation law on a public bus, and the resulting Montgomery Bus Boycott, put racial segregation's basic unfairness on a national stage. During the boycott, a young local Baptist preacher, Dr. Martin Luther King Jr., emerged as the face and leader of the American civil rights movement.

Today's first NPS stop comes in the middle of the trail at the Lowndes Interpretive Center. Voter suppression in Lowndes County exceeded that of Dallas County. Violence worsened as voter registration efforts built momentum. The center tells of the march through the county, starting with a brilliant park film that brings the story together and continuing with an excellent exhibition. Lowndes Interpretive Center's overall historical presentation and exceptional interpretation covering a difficult topic is among the park system's most impressive.

The trail concludes at the Selma Interpretive Center. I meet Ranger Theresa at the center, sharing accolades for the trail's facilities. I continue the visit, walking past the Dallas County Courthouse and across the Edmund Pettus Bridge, turning around to pass the Brown Chapel AME Church, the march's starting point.

Late afternoon Monday, I'm pulling into Decatur, Alabama, to begin a long-awaited exploration of the **Muscle Shoals National Heritage Area**. Tuesday will be devoted to the heritage area. My first and only heritage area stop Monday afternoon is the Old State Bank in Decatur. Dating to 1833, the bank building is one of only four town structures to survive Civil War occupation. An enthusiastic docent explains how the bank served as a field hospital and the vault an operating room. The heritage area includes Hellen Keller's birthplace, W. C. Handy's home, and the Oakville Indian Mounds State Park. The Oakville Mounds Education Center shelters a magnificent collection of Native American stone artifacts. Another heritage area location is the state's oldest, continuously used post office, built in 1840 and still handling the mail in Mooresville, Alabama. I visit twelve heritage area locations before driving north to stay near Murfreesboro, Tennessee.

Wednesday morning at the **Obed Wild and Scenic River** visitor center in Wartburg, Tennessee, I stride to the desk and say, "I think you have something for me."

The ranger reaches beneath the counter, and lifting a brown envelope, says, "You must be the guy who wants the pins!"

"How did you know?" I ask, smiling.

"Well, the hat is a strong clue," he says, gesturing to my Cardinals hat.

"I guess it is," I reply. I explain the planned exhibit and that it will be turned over to the parks to display.

"That's cool. We hope to see it someday," says a second ranger who's joined us at the counter.

The second park today is an hour's drive north. **Big South Fork National River and Recreation Area** extends across the Kentucky-Tennessee state line and is a personal favorite. Big South Fork holds another distinction, as the site of my most embarrassing park experience. My first serious girlfriend and I visited the park in the fall of 1994. We hiked the trail to the Twin Arches, among others in the cool, damp early-November weather. The arches and scenery made the time go fast, despite the barren trees and light rain. We hiked for hours without seeing anyone. We seemed to have the whole place to ourselves. Walking another trail late afternoon, my girlfriend tugged my arm as we passed a wooden bench. "Let's rest a minute," she said. She waited for me to settle on the bench and jumped on my lap, her legs straddling my waist and protruding through the open space behind the small of my back. She kissed me, and I realized she didn't have rest in mind. I remember the hiker appearing around the corner, the only human being we saw in the park all day. It's debatable who was more embarrassed, me or the bewildered hiker who turned around faster than he'd appeared. I turned beet red while my lap-mate smiled, seeming pleased with herself. After we gathered ourselves, I hurried my amorous partner to our car. I moved like a deer fleeing a forest fire, blushing all the way home.

Nearly twenty-three years later, today's first stop is Bandy Creek Visitor Center in Tennessee. My message about the lapel pins didn't reach the right person, and the centennial Big South Fork pin appears to be out of stock at Bandy Creek. The seasonal ranger on duty, without other visitors, devotes almost forty-five minutes seeking one of the gold-colored pins. At the suggestion of the bookstore manager who he calls at home, he phones the ranger at the

Blue Heron Visitor Contact Station in Kentucky and confirms they still have a few in stock. He asks the ranger to set it aside for me and bids me good luck. I'm blown away by his kind effort.

I hoped to see some of the Kentucky side of the park this afternoon. The visit to the Blue Heron Mining Community is my first, despite four prior trips to the park. I marvel at the view of the Big South Fork of the Cumberland River at the Devil's Jump and Gorge Overlooks near Blue Heron. The sign at the top of the trail down to the Devil's Jump Overlook is a real motivator. It reads: BEWARE OF SNAKES, STAY ON TRAIL. Well, that's hard to resist. But the view is worth any added anxiety.

The Blue Heron visitor area features an outdoor exhibit of the site's coal mining history. Waiting on the wooden platform outside the contact station are Ranger Tommy and Ranger Niki, the park superintendent. I explain the exhibit project and my grand centennial adventure. They offer a few suggestions for placing the displays in the parks once they're completed. Niki proves to be a particularly helpful resource for suggestions on how to communicate with the parks. I greatly appreciate her feedback. We take some pictures for the Big South Fork National Recreation Area social media page to close the visit.

The visit's downside are the stories shared by the seasonal ranger at Bandy Creek and the park superintendent about rude stampers. When I asked about some old stampers formerly kept in the visitor center's back room, the seasonal ranger explained the supervisor removed them after an incident in May. Apparently, two gray-haired gentlemen asked for them. He had no knowledge the stampers existed or where they might be. The two guys got nasty, berating him for not knowing how to help and insisting, "We have a database that says they're here!" That last revelation indicates they are NPTC members. How disappointing. The seasonal ranger had started two weeks earlier. I could tell by the extraordinary effort he made to help me that he's a kind, helpful person. I'm ashamed to be a passport enthusiast with idiots like this running around. I mention to Ranger Niki why I enjoy stamping during park visits and apologize on behalf of all passport enthusiasts for the account shared earlier.

Unfamiliar with the seasonal ranger's story, she shared another incident about an ugly stamper. A middle-aged, tall, bulky guy requested an older stamper not kept out on the counter. The ranger on duty, a diminutive young lady barely breaking one hundred pounds, had no knowledge of it. The angry visitor leaned over the counter and started screaming at her from inches away, physically intimidating her. Another ranger called law enforcement and asked him to leave. They locked the door after he left so he couldn't reenter. "What's wrong with these people?" I ask, puzzled and disappointed. "It defeats the whole purpose of the hobby to behave in such a way." She nods in agreement, without answering the hypothetical question. The stories at Big South Fork aren't the only ones I hear across the country about hostile stampers. Most experienced rangers have at least one similarly bad experience. I intend to call out people who behave like animals by sharing these stories in the club's forum. At year's end, I'll do exactly that.

Wednesday night is spent with my parents in Lawrenceville, Illinois. I share a few stories from the year and assure my mother I will write it all down for her. "I'm going to write your book," I promise.

Smiling, she says, "Make sure they make a large print edition."

"I don't think we're quite at that stage yet, Mom."

30 Farewell to a Faithful Friend

THE HOME SOJOURN on Thursday night, September 22, is a short one. Less than eight hours after walking into my house, I'm in Chicago with Kareen for the weekend. It's the next-to-last weekend of the MLB regular season. The Cardinals are playing at Wrigley Field against the Cubs, who are running away with the division en route to a 102-win season. I'm going to enjoy this brief rest to attend the three-game series.

Meanwhile, my twelve-and-a-half-year-old chocolate Labrador retriever is in surgery Thursday afternoon at a Rockford veterinary clinic to remove a fatty tumor limiting his mobility. Our only option to keep him alive is to have it removed and take the significant risks inherent in a geriatric dog undergoing an abdominal operation. Buddy's recovering at the clinic through the weekend. I'll retrieve him Tuesday afternoon. He's got one major thing going for him. He's got a highly skilled and experienced veterinary surgeon looking after him. After the surgery, she informs me, "The large fatty tumor inhibiting his movement weighed four pounds. We removed seven fatty tumors from the area. Our concern now is infection."

In my constant wanderings and time away, Buddy weighs on

my mind. He's in the last days of his life and misses me. He has a good home in my absence with his dog sitter, my ex-colleague and friend Judy, who lives thirteen miles north in Beloit, Wisconsin. But she works long days in Madison, often gone twelve hours at a time. He's struggling with separation anxiety as he ages. I can sense the strain in his mannerisms.

The Labrador retriever became my idealized dog breed at the age of fifteen. Though I have no passion for hunting, I joined my father on a goose hunting trip to a Western Kentucky preserve. We started from the hotel at 4:00 a.m., sitting in concrete blinds built like baseball dugouts with metal benches, a camouflaged, hinged lid that could be thrown open, and steps at either end. Four blinds occupied a wooded field next to a pond. Each blind held four or five paying customers, a guide, and two or three Labrador retrievers.

My father and I occupied the blind guided by the owner and manager of the guide business. I thought I recognized him when we met in the early morning. Indeed, he hosted an outdoor-themed TV show for several years. My father's boss joined us and drank so much whiskey the night before, he threw up several times in the morning. He smelled like bourbon from a distance. I sat at the end with two of our dugout's three chocolate Labs. I marveled at their intelligence, self-control, affability, and indefatigable spirit. I started the weekend after geese and left it wanting the dogs.

The first Lab in my life came through a relationship. She moved in with her yellow Lab in tow, and when we broke up three years later, Wags stayed with me. It seemed like a bad country song. Wags typified the best of the breed: smart, full of energy, and well-mannered. Wags passed away in July 2011 during my expat assignment in Europe. I had come home to visit my fiancée, parents, and friends and could discern a subtle change in his behavior. When I left to catch the flight back to Amsterdam from Chicago, I turned around less than ten miles away, eyes filled with tears. I delayed the return for three days to spend them with Wags. I knew it would be the last time I saw him alive. He was thirteen and a half years old.

The second Lab, six years younger, came to me from an acquaintance. My friend wanted a Lab for a long time, but after he got his eight-week-old chocolate puppy from a local breeder, they discovered his wife had a serious allergy to dog dander. He finished house-training the dog, who he named Buddy, when the antihistamines prescribed for his wife proved insufficient. I ran into him looking despondent, on the verge of taking Buddy to the local animal shelter. He couldn't identify anyone who would take him. I told him, "We've already got a yellow Lab at home. If your puppy is well-behaved, what's the difference between taking care of one or two? We'll come over this evening and meet your dog." Of course, this meant we now had two dogs. It broke my heart to back out of the driveway and see my friend turn away so we couldn't see him cry. I would learn that feeling well.

When I pick Buddy up at the clinic, I'm surprised at his energy level despite his weakened state and bandaged midsection. Once we're home, I let him lay on the cool concrete of the garage floor, his favorite spot to rest, and watch him grow weaker over the next two days. He needs help to stand. It appears that we're getting close to the end. I take a picture of him in the driveway, as a sort of final photo. The vet adds another antibiotic to his meds on Thursday afternoon, and I drop him off at Judy's house with detailed care instructions. Judy will spend most of her weekend with him and watch him closely. At least, that's the plan. A six-hour drive for a morning customer visit in North Dakota awaits. I hope for the best as I depart.

After a fitful sleep Thursday night followed by Friday's meeting, it's time to head south for St. Louis and the end of baseball's regular season. On the way, I stop in southwestern Minnesota at **Pipestone National Monument**. The park manages the preferred quarry among Great Plains' tribes for the prized red stone. The soft yet durable nature of pipestone makes it excellent for ceremonial pipe carving. The exhibits highlight the master craftsmanship in the elaborate pipes and other tools worked from pipestone by Native American artisans. Pipestone artifacts dating back two thousand years have been found across the Midwest. The legislation that created the monument in 1937 incorporates provisions allowing Native American carvers to mine specific quarry claims, continuing the long artistic and cultural traditions connected to pipestone.

At the back of the visitor center, a couple of three-sided recesses form carving areas. Today, two carvers are chipping and sanding their latest pieces. I enjoy watching the carvers and examining their most recent creations. Pipestone lends a smooth beauty to the worked pieces. Perhaps it's the relative softness of the stone that is easy on the eye. The gift shop a few feet away sells completed items from the carvers who work at the park or sell their work here. Items carved in the park are sold at the gift shop, or so I ascertain when I ask one of the carvers for the price of a fist-sized bison he's just finishing. He whispers, "We're not supposed to sell anything directly, but it's thirty dollars." I quietly slip him the money, and he hands me the stone bison wrapped in paper. Now I'm dealing in the illicit bison trade. Kareen's right. The park service is going to lock me up.

The shop does have something else I want. Much to my surprise, the unit has the centennial and Find Your Park lapel pin set. Pipestone is not affiliated with either Eastern or Western National, therefore I hadn't even considered the possibility they might have them. The timing is fortuitous. They've got them deeply discounted on this last day of September.

It's perfect weather for a relaxing stroll on the Circle Trail past Winnewissa Falls near the quarry center. On the way out of the park, I take a picture of the Three Maidens, large granite erratics dropped here by glaciers. With the park's pins and Kareen's new pipestone bison in the trunk, it's time for the ten-hour drive to St. Louis.

Saturday morning, Judy calls me in distress. Buddy's abdominal wound is weeping. The surgeon has left a small opening for this purpose, but nothing happened while I had him. It sounds like the drainage is worse than anticipated. I advise Judy to take Buddy to the emergency clinic managed by the group that performed his operation. Buddy's running a fever. The surgeon's concern about infection proves prophetic. The clinic keeps him for nearly a week, administering a cocktail of potent antibiotics to bring the infection under control. The surgeon puts him under again to open and clean the area. Judy retrieves Buddy from the clinic when he's able to come home.

Buddy's medical condition perpetuates angst going into October. The month starts with developments on multiple fronts. An internal team meeting in Cedar Rapids, Iowa, runs for three days of the first week. The discussion triggers an unexpected action out of my boss. Having sat next to me throughout, he calls me after the meeting and asks if I might be willing to consider working in our marketing group. It's as if he'd forgotten that I have over twenty years of experience. My contributions during the meeting suggest I have more to offer than my current role demands. Of course I would be interested in an opportunity to work with marketing and product development again. I managed global marketing for my business segment during a two-year stretch a decade ago. He emphasizes that he's merely brainstorming, suggesting his query lacks genuine resolution. A brief call with him the following Monday to confirm my interest is the last I hear of the subject.

Before leaving Cedar Rapids, I drive a few miles into the southeastern part of downtown to the National Czech and Slovak Museum to refresh the site's passport stamp. The museum is part of **America's Agricultural Heritage Partnership**, more commonly known as the **Silos & Smokestacks National Heritage Area**. The heritage area covers most eastern Iowa counties and features the region's agricultural and industrial history.

On the drive home, I stop in West Branch, Iowa, at the **Herbert Hoover National Historic Site**. Taking advantage of the clear, sunny October day, I walk the grounds, snapping a picture of the thirty-first president's birth home. The nearby presidential library's exhibits show Hoover a much more accomplished and capable figure than popular history has acknowledged. After the market collapse of 1929, his minimalist approach to government intervention failed to address the dire situation for many Americans, ushering in the age of FDR and big government. Popular sentiment and some historians unfairly vilify Hoover, hanging the Great Depression on him. Such a view of Hoover and the Depression simplifies a complex set of events to satisfy the need to lay blame. The library exhibits help correct the record.

I'm leaving on another trip tomorrow morning to some of the last new parks for the year and to complete visits to the Arizona and California parks in 2016. I also got exposed to a virus at the business meeting. I'm starting to experience flu-like symptoms. It's disconcerting going on the trip, knowing Buddy is clinging to life, and for the first time this year, I'm getting sick too. I've got to keep moving and finish this journey. Knowing it might be the last time I see him alive, I stop at Judy's house to spend a few minutes with Buddy before heading into Chicago to catch a morning flight to Phoenix. I'm hoping he has a miraculous turnaround, and that I don't get deathly sick on the road. I need the parks to heal this tired traveler's heavy heart.

31 *So Cal, So Good*

OUR UNITED JET touches down in Phoenix a few minutes before noon. The sun's warmth on my skin welcomes me back to the desert. I hope to squeeze every minute from summer's waning days.

After a one-hour drive southeast, I arrive at **Casa Grande Ruins National Monument** in Coolidge, Arizona. The ruins of a large adobe structure the early Spanish explorers called a "great house," or casa grande, towers over smaller ruins in the ancient Hohokam village. A large, open-air roof supported by four metal poles protects Casa Grande from further degradation. The desert dwellers completed the structure around AD 1350 and later abandoned the village for unknown reasons.

From Casa Grande, I return north on I-10, passing through the boundary of the only NPS unit closed to the public. **Hohokam Pima National Monument** protects ruins on Gila River Indian Community land. The community considers the site sacred and prohibits outsiders. It is possible to get within the boundary on a few public roads, as I do this afternoon on the interstate south of Phoenix.

I hoped to make it to Santa Monica tonight to stay with a friend and work colleague, but it's too far. A dinner in Goodyear, Arizona, satiates my hunger before crossing the desert to a Palm Springs, California, hotel. Slipping past Los Angeles after the morning rush hour, today marks my first visit to **Santa Monica Mountains National Recreation Area**. The recreation area covers 156,700 acres, though the NPS owns only 23,410. The conglomeration of state and federal parks and preserves interspersed with privately owned land spans nearly fifty miles across the rugged, dusty terrain of the Santa Monica Mountains between LA and Oxnard, California.

My park experience starts midmorning at the Santa Monica Mountains Visitor Center on the King Gillette Ranch. I'm scouting a good hike both to see the park and hopefully burn up some of the virus that's giving me a sore throat and cough. A kind park volunteer reviews trails and helps me pick one. After collecting the information, I inquire with the bookstore manager about the set of pins she saved for me three months ago. Luckily, she's working today and finds the note she made from our conversation.

I travel west on Mulholland Drive, a winding, scenic road that crosses the park east to west. Mulholland Drive passes through Malibu State Park, which provided the outdoor scenery for the long-running television show MASH. After clearing the state park, I turn right on Cornell Road and then left into Paramount Ranch's gravel lot. The movie studio owned the ranch and maintains a mock western town set that's still in use. On the way to the set, I pass a catering spread for a film crew. Noticing the staff's inattentiveness, I think about making a sandwich. Instead, I follow the park volunteer's directions to a small convenience store for a delicious hot pastrami and swiss on rye, a perfect fill-up for the afternoon hike to the park's highest point, Sandstone Peak.

The Sandstone Peak trailhead starts from a former Ventura County Boy Scout Camp now called the Circle X Ranch. The one-and-a-half-mile trail starts at 2,030 feet above sea level and climbs 1,080 feet. It's a warm, sunny day with a light southwesterly ocean breeze, more pronounced near the peak. The first mile of the trail showcases the Conejo and San Fernando Valleys to the north and northeast. Despite the beautiful scenery, I'm struggling with the climb, coughing and hacking every thirty to fifty feet. The middle section follows the Backbone Trail, a sixty-seven-mile path crossing the park. After leaving the Backbone Trail, the gain outpaces the run, and soon I'm scrambling up the side of tilted rock. These mountains once rose above 10,000 feet before geological forces and erosion wore them down. The rocky outcrops and ridges challenge the visitor seeking the best overlook. The terrain at trail's end is more suited to mountain goats than men. Unbalanced footing over the steep angle forces a gorilla scramble up the last hundred feet. A concrete marker with a brass tablet inset identifies MT. ALLEN, EL. 3111 feet.

Good visibility allows me to look south over Malibu to the Pacific Ocean and west across the Santa Barbara Channel to the Channel Islands. As I take in the panorama, I get pictures in all directions, particularly thirty to forty miles west to the Channel Islands of Anacapa and Santa Cruz. More than sixty miles out, Santa Rosa appears in faint profile. The Sandstone Peak pictures represent my first photographs of tomorrow's destination, **Channel Islands National Park**. This ridge creates these islands on a section of the Continental Shelf extending into the Pacific. The four northern islands originate from a large, continuous island called Santarosae, dating to lower sea levels typical of the ice ages. An ocean channel has always divided the distant ridge from the mainland. Looking at relief maps with underwater terrain reveals the topographical connection.

From Circle X Ranch, I drive to the Pacific Coast Highway and arrive at the Robert J. Lagomarsino Visitor Center at Ventura's harbor to confirm tomorrow's boat trip. The boat leaves Ventura at 8:30 a.m. for the eastern end of Santa Cruz Island and doesn't return until 5:00 p.m.

The four largest islands in Channel Islands National Park extend in a line across ninety miles of ocean. The five northern-most of eight Channel Islands comprise the national park. Island weather can be unforgiving. Westernmost San Miguel Island receives the worst battering. North and northwesterly Santa Ana winds can average 20 to 25 mph and gust to over 100 mph.

We arrive at Santa Cruz Island's Scorpion Ranch about 10:00 a.m. Small launches shuttle passengers to the shore in groups of six. I get behind the kayakers, who go first, to maximize my hiking time. Santa Cruz, the second-closest island to the mainland after Anacapa, is the largest in the park at almost sixty-two thousand acres. The ranch's visitor contact station exhibits explain island history. Years of ranching activities prior to the national park denuded the island's east end of its natural flora. Scorpion Ranch only transitioned to the National Park Service in the 1990s.

Park service handouts caution visitors to be mindful of the island's organized crime syndicate. Nature's own interspecies La Cosa Nostra consists of two full-time island residents, the endangered island fox, which is among twelve species of plants and animals found nowhere else on earth, and the incorrigible ravens. Both the foxes and ravens are notoriously creative, persistent, and bold thieves. One of the rangers explains he's observed a raven flip open a wallet left on a picnic table and remove one of the bills inside, flying off with its loot before the unsuspecting victim could react. "What do the birds do with the money?" I can't resist asking.

"No one knows. We can only guess," the ranger answers.

These avian kleptomaniacs will steal almost anything they can carry away. The cash withdrawal is not an isolated incident. The ravens seem to enjoy looting tourists. It's a literal example of "feathering your own nest." The foxes comprise the ground attack. They prowl near picnic tables looking for anything interesting and neglected long enough to grab and pack away. Unattended bags don't have to be open to be at risk. Both the ravens and foxes have learned how to open zippers.

I clear out of Scorpion Ranch's high crime district to hit the 3.7-mile trail to Smuggler's Cove on the island's south side. The trail switchbacks up to sea cliffs beside the ranch. Temperatures soar into the nineties with no shade to be found. Removing my shirt a mile into the trek doesn't help until I feel a cool breeze across the island's spine. The undulating topography atop the island doesn't block the northerly wind. I stop to get pictures of the view, including the Santa Monica Mountains and Sandstone Peak across the water. Visibility is excellent again with clear skies. The opposing perspectives from above Santa Cruz Island's San Pedro Point to

Sandstone Peak and yesterday's picture across the channel comprise complimentary scenes.

The descent to Smuggler's Cove begins at a low grade but steepens the last quarter mile. Tucked away between the surrounding cliffs, the cove pleases the eye from above. I enjoy the cove's tranquility alone, well ahead of any other hikers. I covered the distance in ninety minutes despite stopping for pictures. Smuggler's Cove is a transitory personal paradise before black flies render the beach unbearable. Wind drives the irritating insects away at higher, less sheltered elevations. I shorten my rest at the shore and ascend the seashell-covered access road cut into the cliff. Not until I recover the immediate heights and most of the subtle incline to follow do I pass the first pair of hikers from the boat. Gorgeous wildflowers on the island's southern hillsides supplement views of the rocky coast and Anacapa Island five miles east. The three-hour round-trip to Smuggler's Cove, including the spur trail to the Scorpion Rock overlook, totals eight miles.

Returning to Scorpion Ranch, there's plenty of time to explore further. I photograph a massive eucalyptus tree shading the campground access trail. Returning to the exhibit area, numerous ravens are posted, watching visitors gather at the picnic tables. Foxes lurk behind the bushes, peaking around the side. I haven't seen a criminal threat this obvious and shameless since passing Tijuana's dark alleys on a Saturday night. On a weekend excursion with friends, we drove to the border and crossed on foot for a night of drinking and general debauchery. The crowded and brightly lit main streets had intersecting dark alleys every block or so, complete with shadowy figures lingering in the depths, visible only in profile. We shuddered to think of the fate of any inebriated tourist stumbling down an alley.

Our boat ride back to Ventura stars a surprise attraction. Five miles into the channel, we find ourselves among countless leaping dolphins. In any direction, five to ten dolphins are airborne at any one time, swimming northeast. One of the crew explains over the PA that we're passing through a megapod with perhaps thousands of dolphins hunting together. Megapods form when large amounts of prey fish, usually sardines or herring, render hunting in large groups strategically advantageous. Normal dolphin pods number fifteen to two hundred mammals. Superpods are considered multiple pods swimming and hunting together, and megapods are combined superpods. As many as ten thousand dolphins have been noted in one group off the California coast, earning the moniker of a super megapod. Super megapod sounds like a dolphin heavy metal band. I'm imagining a grinding speed metal tune for dolphins with a title like *Sardine Insurrection* when it occurs to me I've been in the sun too long. The dolphin show in the channel caps a great park day.

I find a Ventura microbrewery and sports bar to watch the baseball playoffs and enjoy a relaxing Saturday night. Sunday morning, I'm driving south past downtown Los Angeles. It's 8:00 a.m., and I'm zipping along at full freeway speed, the first time I've seen the 101 moving at full speed past the city. Apparently, many southern Californians sleep in on Sunday morning.

At the end of the peninsula opposite downtown San Diego, **Cabrillo National Monument** celebrates the first West Coast landfall on present-day US soil by a European explorer. Juan Rodriquez Cabrillo, representing the King of Spain, made landfall in San Diego Bay on September 28, 1542, with a flotilla of three vessels. Cabrillo did not survive the expedition, but his accomplishment and legacy endure at Cabrillo National Monument.

From the coast, I drive east through the desert landscape of extreme southern California on I-8, re-entering Arizona at Yuma. The **Yuma Crossing National Heritage Area** tells of the Colorado River crossing here during southwestern exploration and settlement. I stop at the heritage area headquarters inside the Yuma Visitor Center to read about this wild and remote frontier location.

Sunday night, I cross a busy Glendale, Arizona, street from my hotel to a Mexican restaurant and bar in a strip mall. I stay only long enough to eat my mediocre meal, grimacing from the loudest music I've ever experienced in a public establishment. Even indoor concerts I've attended had lower volume. It doesn't occur to me to leave until I've already ordered. I only survive the half hour it takes to get my food by wadding up pieces of napkin for makeshift ear plugs. It's a disquieting experience.

The week of October 10 exemplifies the year's remaining trips. It's a shortened version of a prior trip, with days inserted for new parks and new experiences at familiar parks. Monday's itinerary repeats a January 2014 trip. After a ninety-minute drive, I pull into the visitor center parking lot at **Montezuma Castle National Monument**. Montezuma Castle is a twenty-room structure built in a recess under a cliff between AD 1100 and 1300. A half hour to the northwest, **Tuzigoot National Monument** protects a Verde Valley stone-and-mortar hilltop village. Built by the Sinagua people between AD 1000 and 1400, the village consists of 110 rooms, 87 on the ground floor.

Continuing north on I-17 to I-40 east, **Walnut Canyon National Monument** is a few miles south of the interstate less than fifteen minutes east of Flagstaff. Twenty miles long and as much as 400 feet deep, Walnut Canyon's remarkable cliff dwellings date between 1125 and 1250. Visitors explore the dwellings via the one-mile Island Loop Trail after a 185-foot descent below the canyon rim. Passing through dwellings constructed at a sharp bend in the canyon, the trail provides 180-degree canyon views and a good look at the dwellings under the far canyon rim in multiple directions.

Twenty miles north, **Sunset Crater Volcano National Monument** boasts the most recent eruption, between 1040 and 1100, in northern Arizona's long volcanic history. During our 2014 visit here, Kareen and I found the lava flows and surreal landscape unlike anything we'd ever seen. The six hundred mountains and hills in the area immediately north of Flagstaff form the San Francisco volcanic field. Eruptions over this hot spot date from six million years ago to the most recent at Sunset Crater. Humphrey's Peak, the field's highest, doubles as Arizona's highest point at 12,633 feet.

Sunset Crater is contiguous with **Wupatki National Monument**, sharing a thirty-five-mile park road. Occupied at the start of the Sunset Crater eruptions, the Wupatki's ruins stood abandoned by 1250. Wupatki Pueblo next to the park's visitor center is the largest single ruin. Other structures and ruins are found throughout the monument.

With the remaining time this afternoon, I make the first two stops in **Grand Canyon National Park**. The Desert View Visitor Center is the easternmost visitor facility on the South Rim. After taking the obligatory photographs from Desert Watchtower, I discover the park's centennial pin in the set I'm collecting. I purchase the pin and a couple of centennial-themed shirts at the general store because, as Kareen will point out on the phone tonight, I needed more centennial shirts.

The Tusayan Museum and Ruin sits a few miles west of Desert View. I refresh my passport cancellation before revisiting the museum exhibits. I'll stay tonight at a hotel in the town of Grand Canyon outside the southern park boundary.

Tuesday morning, I start at the Horace Albright Training Center, named after the second director of the National Park Service, 1929–1933, and the invaluable assistant to the first director, Stephan Mather. The training center keeps a passport stamper for the site.

Next, I stop at the Backcountry Information Center, Verkamp's Visitor Center and General Store, and the Kolb Studio, adding each location's cancellation to my centennial passport. Kareen and I enjoyed a ranger-guided Kolb Studio tour two years ago. The Kolb brothers amassed an amazing photographic record and built an equally impressive home and studio, constructed over the canyon rim as if defying gravity. Today, I walk under clear skies, taking in the rim views across several miles of this grand irregular rock void.

The park headquarters also keeps a passport stamp. After I explain this year's journey to over 320 parks year to date and share the pin project, the rangers at the desk suggest I should meet Ranger Ted, librarian for the Grand Canyon National Park Research Library. They direct me across a courtyard to the building's far corner and Ted's office. Ted and I engage in a diverse conversation about the parks and park service. I explain, "I've enjoyed this year so much. The whole year has been a once-in-a-lifetime experience. But I'm starting to get tired, a deep kind of fatigue that doesn't go away after a single night's rest or even a few days off. And I've been fighting a chest cold the past week. I'm afraid I'm wearing thin."

Ted responds, "You're near the end. You must finish now if you're going to write about it. And you should finish. It'll be a great story. I would love to read it when you're done."

"Thanks for the kind offer," I reply before turning to leave. Almost as an afterthought, I pivot and say, "You know, everywhere I go in the park system, your colleagues validate the reasons behind the pin project. I'm deeply touched by the kindness and encouragement. As I've started to falter down the home stretch, some ranger or volunteer will give me a mental boost when I need it most. Even my wife, who thought I was crazy the first six months, is telling me I have to finish."

A warm smile spreads across Ted's face, and he replies, "You get what you give. Now go finish and be safe!"

My final stops are Yavapai Point Visitor Center and Geology Museum and the Grand Canyon Visitor Center near Mather Point. During our first visit here, I told the rangers I had visited a park recently that had its passport stamper stolen and pondered why anyone would want to steal such a thing. "What would you do with it?" I asked. The rangers told me they had a visitor *at the ranger desk* who turned around in full view and tried to shove a stamper into his pants. Shocked, the rangers managed to ask, "Sir, what are you doing?" before he got it past his belt. Since that time, I've learned that visitors steal stampers across the system. Many go missing during visits by groups of children. One park told me that they've lost three stampers to visiting Boy Scout Troops. Hearing these stories disappoints me.

After finishing my stops on the South Rim, I start toward Page, Arizona, where I'm staying three nights to see the last two unexplored parks in Utah's Colorado River Plateau. I will also enter the south end of Glen Canyon National Recreation Area after traveling through the north end in March. Today, I have three late-afternoon destinations. From the Glen Canyon headquarters, I drive to the park's Carl Hayden Visitor Center. From there, today's last stop is a personal favorite.

Five miles south of Page, the Colorado River makes three sharp turns at a place known as Horseshoe Bend, part of Glen Canyon National Recreation Area. The horseshoe is carved with a straight drop over one thousand feet from the rim to the river below. Kareen and I stopped here in 2014. A wind storm blew across the desert, with sustained winds over 35 mph and gusts over 70 that tore my hat off. Despite the wind, I was determined to see this place. Horseshoe Bend's grandeur in person surpassed the attraction's popular aerial photographs. I wanted to take a picture of the whole "shoe" from the rim. With no guardrails or man-made barriers, the only way to get the picture is by extending the camera over the edge. I pulled my hat from under my wind jacket where I had tucked it away, handed it to Kareen for safekeeping, laid flat on the ground, and crawled to the precipice. As gale force winds tore over us, blowing dust in my eyes and flapping the back of my jacket, I reached the great abyss, shuddering at the thousand feet of open space straight down to the winding river below. Carefully reaching out with my camera, the strap wrapped around my neck, I hear Kareen yelling something into the wind. Unable to understand her and stunned by her sense of timing, I yell back, "Good grief! Whaaat?"

She yells louder, *"Do you have life insurance!"* We hadn't reached our first anniversary at this point and already she's weighing her options.

Today under calm skies, I stand over the abyss enthralled by Horseshoe Bend. My peaceful solitude is free of hurricane-strength winds and a wife hoping to off me for cash. It's lovely.

Wednesday, I'm taking the park boat tour from Wahweap Marina near Page to **Rainbow Bridge National Monument**, a separate unit located within Glen Canyon National Recreation Area. The fifty-mile Lake Powell boat trip passes Glen Canyon's towering cliffs and carved rock. The two-hour passage climaxes at the world's largest natural bridge, spanning 275 feet across and rising 290 feet from base to top. The massive arch's center measures 33 feet wide and 42 feet thick. Melt and flood waters from 10,388-foot Navajo Mountain, six miles away, cut through a protruding fin of Navajo sandstone to produce the shape we see today.

Glen Canyon, Horseshoe Bend

Rainbow Bridge

Considered sacred by Native American tribes, the park service asks visitors to avoid walking under the bridge, a sign of disrespect.

Most visitors observe the bridge from a viewing area about two hundred feet away. A trail from the boat dock leads into Rainbow Canyon and the bridge. At higher water levels, boats could travel to within a few hundred feet. The current drought and low water level leave almost a mile hike. I walk ahead of the group and reach a ranger under a small shelter. She has a traveling case with interpretive aids, junior ranger booklets, and other supplies.

After most of the group is nearby, she points out a fossilized dinosaur footprint in the sandstone. Native Americans guided the first white people to see the bridge in 1909. Early outside explorers needed weeks to make the journey. Those early visitors included Theodore Roosevelt in 1913.

The next day I head north and west to the Bureau of Land Management (BLM) Grand-Staircase Escalante National Monument Visitor Centers in Big Water, Utah, and Kanab, Utah. Continuing north on US Highway 89 and then left on Utah Highway 14 brings me to **Cedar Breaks National Monument**, a massive rock amphitheater at 10,500 feet. The eroded west face of southwestern Utah's Markagunt Plateau features an amphitheater over 2,000 feet deep and over three miles in diameter. The monument's eroded red sandstone looks like a smaller, flipped version of Bryce Canyon, facing west instead of east. The visitor center is already closed for the season, so I travel the rim south to north stopping at overlooks.

From Cedar Breaks, I drive to lower elevations through the Dixie National Forest. Brilliant yellows decorate the clustered trees for miles. I pass Bryce Canyon on my way to the Grand-Staircase Escalante National Monument visitor center in Cannonville, Utah. Scenic Highway 12 works its way up ridges and around plateaus through the eroded landscape of the grand staircase stepping down through the Colorado River Plateau from the north to the Arizona border.

Friday morning begins with a drive across Navajo Nation. **Navajo National Monument** protects two Native American ruins. The Betatakin dwelling lies in a recess in the base of a cliff over

2 miles to the northeast of the visitor center. The Keet Seel ruins require a 17-mile roundtrip hike. That's an item for a future visit. Today, I take pictures of Betatakin from the overlook down the hill behind the visitor center, a 1.3-mile roundtrip hike. During the walk, I meet a couple in the NPTC and we share a few road stories before returning to our respective schedules.

It takes another ninety minutes to reach the next park. **Canyon de Chelly National Monument** is remarkable for its natural beauty as well as its archeological ruins. Visitors access Canyon de Chelly and Canyon del Muerto via the thirty-seven-mile (round-trip) South Rim Drive or the thirty-four-mile North Rim Drive. From the visitor center, I venture down South Rim Drive. I explored both park roads last year and plan to return for more hiking in this brilliant red sandstone canyon.

Next is **Hubbell Trading Post National Historic Site** in Ganado, Arizona. John Lorenzo Hubbell established a trading business here in 1876. Over subsequent decades, he became a trusted friend to the Navajo and area settlers. The restored trading post and supporting structures provide visitors a glimpse into southwestern history.

I drive west to reach **Petrified Forest National Park**. The Painted Desert landscape stretches across I-40. The interstate splits the park into a northern and southern section. Visitors view most of the petrified artifacts near the south end, in the Crystal Forest next to the Rainbow Forest Museum. Today's my fourth time in the park. Unlike prior visits, I don't drive the park road but collect cancellations and chat with the rangers. Sporting a broad smile, Ranger Jaquacia brightens my day with her energy and enthusiasm. Unsolicited, she runs upstairs to the park offices to retrieve the park's stamper archive so I can add the older stamps to my centennial passport.

Holbrook, Arizona, finishes the day. I tour the eighteenth century Holbrook Courthouse and the especially grim jail. Prefabricated in St. Louis and reassembled in Arizona, the solitary confinement cell imposes an image of living hell. Exiting, I shudder at the thought of experiencing Arizona's desert heat in a metal cage. I have another ninety-minute drive east on I-40 to my Gallup, New Mexico, hotel.

About an hour southeast of Gallup, **El Morro National Monument**'s centerpiece, Inscription Rock, stands above lower terrain as the park comes into view. I visited the park last year but left unfinished business. After walking the half-mile Inscription Rock Trail Loop and reading carvings on the rock from early settlers and US Army soldiers, I started the Headland Trail north of the rock to climb to the summit and pass over the top when nature intervened. First, a pair of badgers blocked the trail. Crossing perpendicular to the path from a fallen log about fifty feet off the trail, they got defensive when a brain-dead visitor, oblivious to the animals, walked right up to them and almost stepped on one. The high-tempered animal chased the idiot toward me, necessitating my own retreat until the badger returned to its business. Stalled for ten minutes waiting for the badgers, I noticed the western sky darkening. The storm seemed distant when I started the Inscription Rock Trail. After the badgers tactical withdraw, I ran into a group of rangers descending from the rock. They noted the coming storm clouds and suggested I turn around with them, advice I heeded, but too late to avoid getting totally drenched. Not having the time to wait out the weather, I missed traversing the top of the rock and viewing the Indian ruins found there.

Today, I correct the omission. I walk the Inscription Rock Trail Loop and the two-mile Mesa Top Trail in succession under sunny skies. Inscription Rock contains some two thousand entries. A reliable water source attracted travelers to the sandstone bluff. Early eighteenth century Spanish explorers' etchings remain legible. From the top, views of the Zuni Mountains to the north and east compete with the eroded, brush-covered cavity on the backside of the mesa. Mesa Top Trail passes two Anasazi pueblos, one on each wing of the *V*-shaped bluff. Looking eastward, I can see across the boundary into **El Malpais National Monument** less than fifteen miles away.

New Mexico Highway 53 connects El Morro and El Malpais,

straddling the El Malpais boundary before turning north. About a mile into El Malpais National Monument from the west, the thirty-two-hundred-mile **Continental Divide National Scenic Trail** bisects the park. The trail follows the Continental Divide, where the North American continent splits between the Pacific and Atlantic Ocean watersheds. After passing over it many times earlier this year in Colorado, Wyoming, and Montana, I'll cross the Continental Divide again farther south in New Mexico several more times.

An arid, volcanic landscape with a diverse list of natural features attracting hikers and backcountry explorers, El Malpais translates from Spanish as "the badlands." After the most recent eruption at McCartys Crater two to three thousand years ago, lava flows ran across the park's landscape. Last year, I traveled Highway 117 to the Sandstone Bluffs Overlook, a great place to observe the varied terrain and La Ventana Natural Arch, one of New Mexico's largest natural arches.

Off I-40 in Grants, New Mexico, the Northwest New Mexico Visitor Center is the only visitor facility open for El Malpais on this October Saturday. I show the ranger a copy of the National Park Service centennial systemwide map marked with an orange high-lighter over the parks I've seen this year. Yesterday evening, New Mexico became the forty-ninth state I've visited in 2016. Hawaii will be the fiftieth. Until recently, I had no intentions of traveling to Hawaii this year, but given the opportunity to visit all fifty states in a calendar year, how can I not?

Petroglyph National Monument protects several Albuquerque locations with Native American petroglyphs. The monument contains more than twenty thousand images, mostly drawn between four hundred and seven hundred years ago. Outside the visitor center off Unser Boulevard, I'm greeted by a three-and-a-half-foot snake crossing the sidewalk. Inside, I share, "You've got a nonvenomous snake in front of the building. I follow the ranger outside to identify the gopher snake. Even though I described it as nonvenomous (by the narrow, rounded head), he says, "We get plenty of rattlesnakes in visitor areas." Good to know.

A seventy-two-mile drive through the Cibola National Forest ends in Mountainair, New Mexico, at **Salinas Pueblo Missions National Monument**, which protects three seventeenth-century Spanish mission churches. I toured all three missions last year. The Salinas Valley communities organized around these churches are roughly centered about Mountainair. The Quarai Mission is eight miles northwest, Abo is nine miles southwest, and Gran Quivira is twenty-five miles south. Today, I'm after the unit lapel pins saved for me here. When I ask, the volunteer has no knowledge of the saved pins, and the manager's off and not answering her phone. The small bookstore appears to be sold out. We're about to give up when I notice a wall display with both pins in it. I pull the pins off the display and purchase them. They can replace them with the set saved for me in the locked office. Mission accomplished.

Before flying out of Phoenix late Sunday afternoon, I have one Arizona park on the itinerary. The route follows US Highway 60 for 356 miles before turning northwest for the final 27. It's a six-hour drive on US 60, which joins I-25 south for 25 miles before the highway goes west in Socorro, New Mexico. The drive on I-25 puts me on the **El Camino Real de Tierra Adentro National Historic Trail**, which covers the 404 miles north of the border among the 1,600 miles from Santa Fe, New Mexico, to Mexico City, Mexico. The trail translates to "Royal Road of the Interior Lands." Spanish explorer Juan de Onate led the first colonizing expedition up the route in 1598, creating the first Euro-American trade route into the present-day United States.

In Socorro, I pass a closed restaurant with the name Yo Mama's before the highway goes west through the Magdalena Mountains. The peaks give way to the high desert on the Plains of San Agustin at almost seven thousand feet above sea level. These high plains host the National Radio Astronomy Observatory VLA Telescope, most commonly known as the "Very Large Array." The VLA features twenty-seven radio telescopes in a Y-shaped configuration. The telescopes measure eighty-two feet in diameter and weigh 230,000 pounds, a little big for the roof. The telescopes sit on rails to allow adjustment of the array's configuration and total size.

After crossing the Continental Divide, I'm tired, hungry, and ready to stop for the night in Springerville, Arizona. When a sheriff's deputy pulls up next to me at a gas station, I ask him for restaurant suggestions. He motions to a small Mexican restaurant across the road and says, "The food is excellent, but the dishes are a little bit hot." I feel a sense of alarm when he says, "a little bit hot." After considering it a moment, he offers, "If you don't like hot food, stay away from the green chili." I already had my eye on the Mexican place before I asked, thus I enter the culinary gauntlet. The stuffed pepper special sounds delicious. I order it with the "mild" chili and learn "a little bit hot" is a dangerous description in the Arizona desert. The stuffed pepper is too good to turn away, but I'm consuming ice water and cold beer after each bite to mitigate the heat. I wonder if the people nearby, who can see me sweating while tears fall from my eyes, think I'm an overly emotional guy having dinner alone. The scene must look like something between sad and pathetic.

A three-hour drive on US 60 from the Arizona-New Mexico border to **Tonto National Monument** includes breathtaking scenery through the Salt River Canyon area. The Salt River forms the boundary between the White Mountain Apache Tribal land to the north and the Tonto National Forest to the south. The highway goes from vanilla, uninteresting high desert to a group of steep mountain canyons, as if entering a magic tunnel to a different land. The road hugs the canyon walls as it descends to a bridge over the river, then climbs again on the other side. I had never heard of this place.

I arrive at Tonto National Monument about 9:30 a.m. and climb the half-mile trail from the visitor center to the Lower Cliff Dwelling built into the dry, steep hillside. The monument's Upper Cliff Dwelling requires a strenuous, three-mile round-trip hike on a ranger-guided tour that isn't offered today. The ranger on duty at the twenty-eight-room Lower Cliff Dwelling takes my picture standing before the ruins. It's time to go home.

After arriving at my flight's Sky Harbor gate, United has an overbooked plane, and no one seems willing to stay. I don't have any commitments and volunteer to fly Monday morning for a $500 flight credit, a room, and a first-class seat tomorrow. When I ask for a good place to eat and watch LA and Chicago in the NLCS, the hotel recommends a local sports bar, and the shuttle driver drops me off. I walk into the crowded, rowdy sports bar to find everyone wearing Chicago Cubs gear. About half of them are drunk. Dozens of faces turn, staring at my Cardinals hat. I feel like a steak dropped into a school of piranhas. The desk clerk must have a sense of humor. The bar and restaurant proclaims to be the official Phoenix playoff location for Cubs fans, according to a banner hanging from the ceiling. The hostess pauses before seating me. I can tell she's thinking, "Where can I put this guy so he won't get killed?" And I'm imagining some Cubs fan in the bleachers at Wrigley next season bragging about the guy wearing the Cardinals hat that he shanked in a Phoenix bar during the playoffs. The trip's "last supper" ends well when I pay for the check and slip away undetected into the cool, crisp desert night.

32 Sunset on the Great Plains

ARRIVING HOME MONDAY afternoon, October 17, I'm thrilled to hear glowing reports about Buddy's recovery. The trio of antibiotics brought the infection under control, and he's regaining strength. He convalesces at home the next few days, weak but healing. We're both convalescing. I've traveled in seven of the past nine weeks, away from home fifty-three of the past sixty-two days, a stretch that included sixty-six parks in nineteen different states, nine Major League Baseball games, and one dangerously ill, geriatric Lab. And a prolonged rest must wait. Centennial madness gives no quarter. Can I reach the finish line with only adrenaline and enthusiasm? I'm going to find out.

Mercifully, it's a light week devoted to pressing work items and a business meeting Thursday morning in Blair, Nebraska. With great reticence, I leave Buddy with Judy Wednesday afternoon and begin the six-and-a-half-hour drive to Blair. A quarter of the way there, I find myself in a hospital emergency room.

When I retrieved Buddy, I put a sheet over my car's rear bench seat. His shedding coat left it covered in hair and dander. Hurried, I left the filthy sheet in place, flapping with the wind rushing through the open windows for the first twenty miles. I realize the terrible mistake as my breathing grows labored in the fog of hair inside the car. Removing the sheet does not resolve my breathing difficulties. As the drive continues, it feels like someone's suffocating me with a pillow. I'm in trouble.

I make it to Davenport, Iowa, and call Kareen to explain the predicament. She looks up the closest hospital and demands I go to the ER immediately. In hindsight, what happened became clear. Almost a decade spent with one or two large Labrador retrievers sensitized me to dog dander, and the self-inflicted car exposure triggered a reaction. I leave the ER breathing normally two hours later, but the car needs a thorough cleaning. I reach Omaha about 10:00 p.m., exhausted.

Despite an exciting Thursday morning meeting, it's a struggle to keep my eyes open, though I'm very interested. With a large coffee in hand, I go south to continue the planned travel, pledging to pull over if I feel my eyes grow heavy. This weekend, I'm swinging through seven midwestern parks visited last December, if I hold up.

Thursday afternoon brings me to the Heritage Center at **Homestead National Monument of America** in Beatrice, Nebraska. Homestead commemorates one of the most impactful congressional acts in our nation's history, The Homestead Act of 1862. The law opened millions of acres of public land to settlement. Any citizen or intended citizen claiming a 160-acre homestead of surveyed government land could own the land if the claimant met the law's conditions. The homesteader must improve the land with a dwelling and cultivation and reside there for five years. Over 270 million acres in thirty states transferred to private ownership under the act.

Union army scout Daniel Freeman made one of the first claims by persuading a Brownsville, Nebraska, land agent to accept his claim shortly after midnight on January 1, 1863, the date the law took effect. The monument includes a small portion of the Freeman homestead. Freeman's cabin site lies by a trail across restored prairie habitat between the park's Heritage and Education Centers.

A Heritage Center visual aid extolls homesteading's national impact. The visitor center walkway displays metal cutouts of the thirty homestead states with an area removed in each state relative to homesteaded land. Kenneth Deardorff claimed the last patented homestead on a southwestern Alaska parcel in 1974. Congress repealed the act in 1976 for the Lower 48 states and in 1986 for Alaska.

During my last visit to Homestead, I stumbled on an exhibition of thirteen quilts made by the local quilting association in honor of the centennial. I've never been passionate about quilting but found the exhibition a delight. Each quilt features a representative design for a park chosen by the quilter. The exhibition traveled to each of the thirteen featured parks during 2016, beginning with Homestead in December and ending with Homestead in 2017, after appearing at the National Quilter's Convention in Omaha, Nebraska. A fourteenth quilt from 1972 celebrates the hundredth anniversary of the first national park, some place called Yellowstone. The thirteen parks are Everglades, Homestead, Hawai'i Volcanoes, Saguaro, Shenandoah, Statue of Liberty, Joshua Tree, Jefferson National Expansion Memorial, Wolf Trap National Park for the Performing Arts, Wind Cave, Rocky Mountain, Glacier, and Mount Rushmore. I considered offering to chaperone the quilts, but I hoped for my own park journey in 2016. The never ending series of diverse and surprising experiences like the Homestead quilts motivates these travels. You never know what you'll find or who you'll meet.

Thursday night concludes in Topeka, Kansas. I get a message from a work colleague thanking me for recommending the newest member of our work team, my former customer. I never had any doubts. But a tinge of melancholy reminds me the end is near at work. Soon, these people I've known for two decades will be in the past. It's likely I will never see any of them again. I turn my attention to a meal in my hotel, Topeka's Capitol Inn. I'm feeling better and praying for some rest.

Brown v. Board of Education National Historic Site occupies one of the schools in the landmark 1954 Supreme Court decision. The *Brown v. Board* case was filed in 1951 after thirteen African American parents in the Topeka school district attempted to enroll their children in all-white schools. The most challenging exhibits, located down the hall from the front door, expose the hate-filled, racist reactions of segregationists to the struggle for equality. The Topeka parents lost their case in the district court, citing the 1896 *Plessy v. Ferguson* decision that declared "separate but equal," making segregation the law of the land. The umbrella of *Brown v. Board* consolidated five separate court cases challenging *Plessy*. The cases are deliberately selected, based on their locations and circumstances, in a strategy to overturn segregation's legal protection.

The highlight of today's visit materializes like a Topeka tornado. Stepping into the bookstore, I meet Robert, a retired university professor, and Ranger Randal. Referencing my park journey's civil rights stops initiates a storm of passionate historical discussion and personal reflection. Any nonhistorian or sane person would leave faster than they arrived upon the intellectual tempest. In this perfect historical storm, dates and names fly like trailers and trees. The Kansas plain's proffer no shelter until my next park.

In the Flint Hills of Kansas near Strong City, **Tallgrass Prairie National Preserve** protects 10,894 acres of the tallgrass prairie ecosystem that once covered 140 million acres across North America. Less than 4 percent of tallgrass prairie survives. In my two previous visits, I walked about Spring Hill Ranch reading interpretive materials, but lacked the time and appropriate weather to hike. Today, I intend to take a walk.

About a mile into the Scenic Overlook Trail, I run into the resident bison herd. Prospective hikers and visitors behind me stop, too. About 150 yards ahead, a bison bull stands on one side of the trail with two bison cows opposite him across the trail. Davis Trail, the normal workaround for such roadblocks, is closed today, leaving us to sidestep the bison in a wide arc through the tallgrass prairie or walk the bison gauntlet between three two-thousand-pound hunks of burning love. Even Elvis couldn't buffalo through this trio. The walkaround brings the prairie rattlers common to the area into the picture. They'll soon go into hibernation, but no one's sure. Where's a herpetologist when you need one? With warm weather and mostly sunny skies, I'm wearing shorts and athletic shoes, not ideal anti-snakebite gear. The bison show no inclination to move, even after I shout to the bull across fifty yards, "I know kung fu! You don't want any of this!" The other visitors shuffle several feet farther away. Thus, the slow-motion bison jam ends my prairie excursion and that of those behind me.

About ninety miles south of Arthur Bryant's Kansas City rib joint, **Fort Scott National Historic Site** anchors the line of frontier outposts extending from Fort Snelling in Minnesota, to Fort Jesup in Louisiana. Built in 1842, manifest destiny's westward push over the next two decades extended the frontier well west of Fort Scott. After abandonment in 1853, Fort Scott regained importance after the Kansas-Nebraska Act of 1854 brought popular sovereignty to Kansas, inciting a clash of arms between proslavery and antislavery forces that would become known as "Bleeding Kansas." Troops garrisoned the fort in 1857 and periodically thereafter to quell the violence. As peace settled in Kansas, the Civil War unsettled it. Fort Scott remained an essential military post throughout the war and briefly thereafter, from 1869–1873, to protect railroad workers expanding the nation's railways.

I relax on a walk around Fort Scott's surviving and restored buildings before driving to my Joplin, Missouri, hotel. Saturday morning, I return to the birthplace of a remarkable man of science and education, born enslaved at a small Diamond, Missouri farm in 1864. **George Washington Carver National Monument** celebrates the life of a great American and pioneer in the fields of science and agriculture. The visitor center exhibits explain Carver's life and legacy, including his impact as a teacher for nearly a half century at Alabama's Tuskegee Institute.

Next, I stop for my third visit to **Wilson's Creek National Battlefield** near Republic, Missouri. I toured the battleground two years ago but use today's visit to walk more battlefield trails, including those around the Ray House, cornfield and the Gibson Mill and home site. Passing Wilson's Creek near the Gibson Mill site, the quiet stream gives no indication that it once flowed through a bloodbath.

On August 10, 1861, five hundred men in the prime of their lives breathed their last in the Civil War's second major engagement and first west of the Mississippi. Though tactically a Confederate victory, the outnumbered Union force's stubborn resistance slowed the advance into Missouri long enough for pro-unionists to rally and save the state for the Union.

As I climb the low grade on Bloody Hill, I pass a massive black snake in the concrete drainage channel to the left of the park road. The snake's moving faster than I am. This hill witnessed the heaviest fighting and holds a stone tablet acknowledging the site of Union commander Brigadier General Nathaniel Lyon's death. Lyon, a well-respected officer, became the first Union general to die in Civil War combat.

Saturday's final stop, seventy-five miles to the southwest into Arkansas, is **Pea Ridge National Military Park**. The Union victory at Pea Ridge, March 7–8, 1862, secured Missouri's Civil War status as a border slave state under federal military control. The ground remains in much the same condition as during the battle.

My agenda for Pea Ridge conforms to that of Wilson's Creek. I complete the seven-mile driving loop through the battlefield, extending walks and photographing the field more thoroughly than I did during my first two visits. Pea Ridge's second day marks one of the few times an entire army from either side gathered in formation on one visible field. It's after 5:00 p.m. when I exit the battlefield to return north.

This trip completes my third time through the seven-park sequence of Homestead, Brown v. Board, Tallgrass Prairie, Fort Scott, George Washington Carver, Wilson's Creek, and Pea Ridge in that order. Last December, I added an eighth unit, traveling to **Buffalo National River** in the northern Arkansas Ozarks. Buffalo River stands out to me as one of the more isolated units in the Lower 48. There's no quick or easy way to stop by this unit. Buffalo is named the first "National River" per a 1972 congressional act. My day at Buffalo National River, December 23, 2015, marks the start of 360 days spent in 387 parks. Thankfully, at the time I didn't yet realize that I'd lose my sanity in the year to follow.

Saturday night, I stay in Springfield, Missouri, ready to begin the 515-mile trip home. Leaving early Sunday morning, I have time for an afternoon stop at the Lincoln Home in Springfield, Illinois. I take another tour of the home, though I'm unsure why, and enjoy a couple of hours in the sunshine around the restored historical neighborhood. I visit Lincoln's Tomb in Springfield's Oak Ridge Cemetery for the first time. I might have seen it as a boy but can't recall. After paying respects to one of American history's most beloved and respected presidents, it's time to go home.

33 Tarantulas and the Texas State Patrol

To REACH AS many NPS units as possible, I'm repeating two of last year's trips this November. The first returns me to Albuquerque on the morning of October 31. The second trip begins in San Antonio and covers the parks of Central and East Texas, when I hope to see my last two unexplored units in the southwest.

While planning the year's final trips in the Lower 48, I schedule a December week in Hawaii. The finish line beckons. Repeating the parks of Texas and New Mexico tests my endurance against two more grueling itineraries. Tuesday starts a sequence of four consecutive days driving between 500 and 650 miles a day. I'll cover over 3,000 miles this week. With notable exceptions, most revisits must be time efficient. I'm stretching myself and the schedule to the limit. The payoff will be one of the most memorable trips of the year.

After landing in Albuquerque at 8:00 a.m., I go north toward Los Alamos, New Mexico. **Bandelier National Monument** protects Puebloan ruins occupied from the late twelfth and thirteenth centuries through the sixteenth century. More than three thousand archeological sites lie within the park. Last March, I toured the park's most popular sites. The Main Loop Trail follows Frijoles Canyon to village sites like the town of Tyuonyi with its circular plaza ringed by four hundred rooms. The trail hugs the northeastern side of the canyon to access impressive structures like the eight-hundred-foot longhouse and cliff dwellings accessed through ladders. A trail following Frijoles Creek extends off the Main Loop Trail, leading deeper into the canyon to the Alcove House. Touring the Alcove House requires negotiating four successive ladders ascending 140 feet from the canyon floor.

Twenty minutes away, the Los Alamos unit of Manhattan Project National Historical Park features a downtown walking tour. At the visitor contact station, I find the staff moving exhibits across the street to the Los Alamos History Museum. Having visited the Oak Ridge, Tennessee, and Hanford, Washington, sites in December and June, respectively, Los Alamos is my third and final subunit in the park.

Created in December 2014, **Valles Caldera National Preserve** lies in the Jemez Mountains running across north central New Mexico. One of three supervolcanoes on US soil, the thirteen-mile-wide caldera dominates the preserve landscape. The present-day caldera derives from an eruption 1.25 million years ago. This afternoon, I'm looking for a good hike to close the long day of travel. The ranger at the visitor contact station suggests I hike the History Grove Loop around Cerro la Jara, a massive rock mound. I navigate the five-mile loop trail over subtly rolling terrain on the floor of Valle Grande in one hour and forty minutes. It's only a sample of the preserve's terrain, but it does get me out of the car.

After an early bedtime in Los Alamos, I'm up and out by 5:00 a.m. for the three-hour drive west to **Chaco Culture National Historical Park** in northwest New Mexico. Chaco Culture manages and protects the extensive Native American ruins discovered in Chaco Canyon. I spent hours walking through the canyon dwellings last year and felt I could have spent several days here. Any Chaco excursion includes the mandatory experience of one of the park system's worst access roads. Visitors reach the park from US Highway 550 via two county roads, 7900 and 7950. The former is paved and in good condition, but the latter transitions from paved to gravel, and then to dirt and gravel for the last five or six miles. After crossing a washout and poorly maintained private sections, the final two miles of grated road rides like continuous, bone jarring speed bumps. I bounce into the park shortly after 8:00 a.m.

The canyon shelters nine "great houses" and hundreds of smaller sites. The great houses are constructed between AD 860 and 1150 along the valley's Chaco Wash at an elevation of sixty-two hundred feet. The San Juan Basin's high altitude yields seasonal weather extremes. As opposed to my visit last July with temperatures in the high nineties, I'm forced to don a hoodie on this cold October morning.

From Chaco Canyon, I have a ninety-minute drive northwest to the Farmington BLM field office to collect a pair of Old Spanish Trail cancellations. From there, it's a thirty-minute drive northeast to **Aztec Ruins National Monument** in Aztec, New Mexico. The park contains a Puebloan village with four to five hundred rooms situated around a Great Kiva and several smaller kivas. Puebloans built and occupied this place between AD 1100 and 1300. Chaco Culture National Historical Park and Aztec Ruins National Monument are grouped together as the Chaco Culture World Heritage Site, one of twenty-three UNESCO World Heritage sites in the United States and US territories.

I follow US Highway 64 for a three-hundred-mile trek across northern New Mexico with two destinations in route. The first stop is the Rio Grande Gorge Bridge over the Rio Grande River. This northern New Mexico section of the Rio Grande is part of the BLM-managed Rio Grande del Norte National Monument. The bridge's pedestrian walkway spans the steep river canyon and its striped tan and dark-brown sedimentary layers. The second stop is Taos Pueblo, another UNESCO World Heritage Site. These locations are part of the **Northern Rio Grande National Heritage Area**. The heritage area extends south to Santa Fe and covers the region's extensive human history, from the earliest Native Americans to subsequent Spanish settlement beginning in 1598.

As I'm navigating through the Cimarron Mountains, I notice a dark object on the road. Slowing to 30 mph for a curve, I brake to a crawl as I see the strange object moving. A large black tarantula crawls across the westbound lane as I creep forward at about the same speed. In a dozen trips to the desert southwest, this tarantula is the first I've seen in the wild. The large, hairy spider engenders an unexpected sympathy. I stop and watch as it reaches the edge of the road and disappears into the sparse clumps of grass and dirt.

A few minutes later, I'm back to 75 mph, ten over the speed limit, when I see a black SUV emblazoned with "County Sheriff" on the side. I hit the brakes, but it's too late. With few safe pullover spots, I continue to a dirt driveway and watch in my rearview mirror as he turns around and races toward me with lights flashing. By the time he gets to my open driver's side window, I've got my driver's license ready and am sheepishly apologizing for speeding. He asks, "Where are you going in such a hurry?"

I explain, "I'm in the last hundred of five hundred miles today, visiting New Mexico parks. I started early, and I'm hungry and tired. I've traveled through forty-nine states visiting 350 parks this year."

"That's quite a bit of traveling," he says. "I'll be right back." After a few minutes, he returns, hands me the license, and says, "I'm gonna give you a verbal warning. Slow it down a little so you get there safely, wherever you're going."

I give the deputy a tired smile. "Thank you, officer. And be safe." The tarantulas and police aren't done with me yet. Both reappear in the desert.

Continuing east on US 64, I pass through the Cimarron Mountain Range and Cimarron, New Mexico to Raton, New Mexico. Wednesday morning, I'm back on the road by 6:00 a.m. for the three-hour drive to **Lake Meredith National Recreation Area** and **Alibates Flint Quarries National Monument** in the Texas Panhandle. The combined park headquarters and visitor information station in Fritch, Texas, is my first destination. South of town, my second stop is the Alibates Visitor Center at the Alibates Flint Quarries. The kind and cheerful rangers at the headquarters and quarry visitor center add some joy to my day.

I enjoyed the ranger-led quarry tour last July, though it moved at a deliberate pace. The tour highlighted fascinating details about the quarry and local ecology. Discussing snakes, the ranger explained how some indigenous rattlesnakes have adapted to domesticated surroundings by not rattling. "Cattle will stomp and kill rattling snakes," she shared.

"That's reassuring," I think as I contemplate future trail mileage through rattlesnake country. At the quarry, the various colors and shades of flint lend to a beautiful array of artifacts on display at the visitor center. Native Americans traded these items and unshaped flint across vast distances. I find myself comparing Alibates to Pipestone, both raw material sources for a broad range of Native American artisanship.

Created by the construction of Sanford Dam across the Canadian River, Lake Meredith serves the panhandle as a water source and host of recreational water activities. My experience with Lake Meredith is limited to pictures from the flint quarry and Sanford Dam.

I drove past **Capulin Volcano National Monument** early this morning on my way to Texas and stop now on the return. Capulin's cinder cone, rising 1,300 feet above the ground to an altitude of 8,182 feet above sea level, stands out from a distance. From the rim, the terrain reveals tremendous volcanic activity across the eight-thousand-square-mile Raton-Clayton volcanic field. I walked the Crater Rim and Crater Vent Trails last July. Today I tackle the Lava Flow Trail, interesting until the trail narrows to eighteen inches through tall grass. Maybe the nonrattling rattlesnakes have gotten into my head, but I move faster through the tall grass. It's time get back on the road.

Fort Union National Monument marks the location of three forts built to protect the Santa Fe Trail and western settlements, garrisoned from 1851 until 1891. Fort Union sheltered the critical junction of the Mountain and Cimarron branches of the Santa Fe Trail. The post remained active for over a decade after the railroad's 1879 arrival. I repeat last year's walking tour on the fort grounds. Building foundations on the quiet prairie hint at the bustle of activity that once filled this place. Trail ruts remain visible on the grounds. In softer, wetter ground, the ruts became ravines that identify the trail yet today.

Glancing at my watch, I realize my walking here and at Capulin pushed my schedule. It's almost 3:30 p.m., and I have an hour's drive to reach **Pecos National Historical Park**. I spent a day at Pecos last July, touring the fifteenth-century Puebloan cultural and trade center and the Spanish mission church completed in the early 1700s after the original church was destroyed in 1680. I reach the visitor center door one minute before closing time. This week's unforgiving itinerary won't permit a second stop here. Calling the park, I reach a ranger and ask, "I'm right outside your front door. Would it be too much trouble to let me in for just a couple of minutes to use your passport stamps?"

"Of course," the ranger replies. I can see him through the open window blinds.

Pecos National Historical Park also manages the Civil War battlefield at Glorieta Pass. Visitors access the battlefield after checking in at the visitor center to get the necessary gate code. Last year, I walked the 2.25-mile battlefield trail, noting the challenging terrain and importance of this narrow mountain pass. Union forces fought a Confederate invasion force here March 26–28, 1862, with the principle engagement on March 28. Federal troops defeated Brigadier General Henry Sibley's rebels, forcing their retreat south along the Rio Grande and back to Texas. It would be the last time a Confederate army threatened New Mexico.

My last ninety miles brings me to an Albuquerque hotel. Game 7 of the World Series plays on TV as I eat chicken wings for dinner. I'm too exhausted to watch the whole game, needing sleep before tomorrow's 5:30 a.m. wake-up call. I'm awakened later when my phone buzzes with the news that the Chicago Cubs won the World Series. I roll over and return to a deep, peaceful sleep.

In south central New Mexico, **White Sands National Monument** protects nearly 225 square miles of the southern Alkali Flats. The world's largest gypsum dunefield covers 275 square miles and reaches sixty feet high. Rock bearing gypsum, or calcium sulfate, dissolves in the mountains. Melt and rain water carries the salt into the Tularosa Basin and is evaporated in ephemeral (sometimes dry) lakes. Crystals ground into fine sand are then blown by the wind to the dunefield. This process over the millennia created the dunes we see today.

At White Sands last July, I walked the five-mile Alkali Flat Trail, marked by posts in the dunes. I carried three liters of water, but under a blazing July sun found myself short on water and time as dark clouds developed over the San Andreas Mountains to the west. The dunes are no place for a person in a thunderstorm. Having lost track of distance in the exotic, soft white sand hills, the safety of my car miles away, a kind visitor happened upon me and we walked to the trailhead together preoccupied in conversation. These dunes provide a harder, more stable walking surface than common sand due to gypsum's water retention.

My three-hour drive across southern New Mexico's rugged terrain passes through the Lincoln National Forest, a mountainous area thick with pines before giving way to arid plains. **Carlsbad Caverns National Park** impressed Kareen and I during our visit last year. We marveled at the amazing features during our self-guided tour of the cavern's Big Room. We joined the next two-hour King's Palace tour but underestimated the impact of spending over four continuous hours in the cool, underground air. Though we enjoyed the King's Palace tour, used the bathroom, and restricted our fluid intake beforehand, we ended the tour struggling not to wet ourselves. Our tour spent a long time in the Queen's Chamber and sitting in the cool, moist air became torture. As we exited, the ranger allowed us to walk ahead to the underground bathrooms. Our narrow escape didn't diminish the cave, though our precautions failed to prevent the unpleasant physical reaction.

At Pine Springs Visitor Center, I amuse the rangers with a few stories from the year. **Guadalupe Mountains National Park** remains a largely unexplored park for me. Kareen and I walked a few short trails and visited the remnants of a Butterfield Stage station, but we didn't have time to explore the park's interior. Over half the park's 86,367 acres are designated wilderness. It's another ninety minutes to my stopping point today near El Paso.

Kareen and I visited **Chamizal National Memorial** during the NPTC's annual convention here in July 2015. We enjoyed posing next to a giant, bronze bison sculpture placed in a rock island fronting the visitor center. I knew nothing of the park's story before our visit.

The Treaty of Guadalupe Hidalgo ended the Mexican-American War in 1848 and established the Rio Grande, called the Rio Bravo del Norte in Mexico, as the one-thousand-mile international border. A subsequent 1884 treaty clarified the boundary as the middle of the river's deepest channel, and further states that, should the river change its course, the original boundary will apply. The Rio Grande shifted its course to the south in the latter half of the nineteenth century, leaving Mexican land, including a farmer's section called the Chamizal tract, on the north side.

A 1963 treaty called the Chamizal Convention resolved these issues with the construction of a new, concrete-lined channel for the Rio Grande through El Paso. The new river channel opened in 1967. Provisions in the treaty allowed area residents to choose their country. The treaty also created a park from disputed land on each side. Congress authorized Chamizal National Memorial on June 30, 1966.

Across from my Clint, Texas, hotel, a small Mexican restaurant with excellent food and inexpensive draft beer supplies my evening calories. Friday morning, it's 6:15 a.m. when I enter eastbound I-10 for the first of 670 miles I'll travel today. The first stop is at **Fort Davis National Historic Site** in Fort Davis, Texas.

Established in 1854, Fort Davis protected early settlers, mail, and trade routes through the American southwest. African American troops serving in the Plains and Southwest, called "Buffalo Soldiers" by Native Americans, served at the fort from 1867 to 1885. After the last hostile Native American bands dissipated, the army abandoned the post in 1891. I walk around the fort, viewing exhibits and taking pictures of the remaining structures against the scenic mountainous background.

The next stop is the Persimmon Gap Visitor Center at the northern entrance to **Big Bend National Park**, covering 1,250 square miles of arid, mountainous terrain in the Chihauhuan Desert. Next up is the Panther Junction Visitor Center, followed by Rio Grande Village twenty miles to the southeast. Kareen and I noted the temperature at ninety-seven upon entering the park last year. The temperature gauge read one hundred at Panther Junction. As we descended to Rio Grande Village, the temperature climbed to 109 in ten miles. At the river, the triple digits didn't do full justice to the outdoor sauna. Humidity created stale air that made breathing outside uncomfortable. I asked Kareen, "Do you want to go for a hike?" This was brave or foolish, or a combination, considering her hot and hungry state. Her glare answered my question. We noted one could walk across the placid Rio Grande without getting your shirt wet. We guessed that the harsh desert acts as border control. The river at Rio Grande Village is part of a 196-mile section protected as the **Rio Grande Wild and Scenic River.**

I'm taking the thirty-mile Ross Maxwell Scenic Drive to Castolon, the only visitor center we missed last year. When we left Chisos Basin last July, taking the drive would have added three hours to our day. I chose between driving to Castolon and being killed by Kareen there, and perhaps eaten, or driving out the western entrance to our room in Lajitas.

Beyond Castolon, thirteen-mile Santa Elena Canyon empties downstream from its vertical fifteen-hundred-foot rock walls. Santa Elena is the westernmost of the three Rio Grande park canyons, the other two being Mariscal and Boquillas.

After passing Panther Junction, I see a dark object on the road ahead. It's moving, another tarantula! I slow, getting a good look at the little guy. A few miles later, another tarantula crosses the road. This one's dark brown rather than black. Another mile down the road, I spot another tarantula. Amid a half dozen tarantulas, I stop on Ross Maxwell Scenic Drive for pictures of the Chisos Mountains and 7,832-foot Emory Peak. I'm starting to wonder if a plane carrying Guatemalan coffee beans crashed in the park. For the unfamiliar, spiders hiding in coffee beans invaded a town in the 1977, made-for-television horror movie *Tarantula: The Deadly Cargo.*

The Ross Maxwell Scenic Drive to Castolon accesses some of

the more picturesque areas in the western half of the park. Named after Big Bend's first park superintendent, Maxwell laid out the drive during his tenure here. Off Maxwell Drive, the Sotol Vista offers a great western landscape featuring the Black Mesa, the Mesa de Anguila, and smaller foreground peaks. The other side overlooks the Chisos Mountains and the Homer Wilson Ranch in the valley below. Continuing the drive, I stop at the Mule Ears View Point to snap a picture of the Mule Ear Peaks two and a half miles southeast. From Castolon at the drive's twenty-two-mile mark, I continue the last eight miles to Santa Elena Canyon.

The Santa Elena Canyon Trail, a modest 1.7-mile roundtrip hike, stops today at the raging Terlingua Creek feeding the Rio Grande on the left. The often-dry creek reaches chest high at the trail crossing. I'm driving three hundred miles soaking wet if I wade the creek. I content myself with pictures of the canyon and flowing river from the bank. A beautiful butterfly lands on a leaf next to my head while I'm surveying the swollen creek and poses for a close-up. The river carved the canyon's high vertical walls through the mesa as a fault lifted the rock, deepening the passage as the earth rose. Ongoing erosion clouds the river emerging from the canyon.

Big Bend, Sant Elena Canyon

After a hike at Tuff Canyon, I reengage the tarantulas. I slow down for them but resist stopping for a picture, a mistake I'll regret. After spotting the seventh or eighth large spider on the road, I resolve to stop for the next one. The next arachnid appears as I'm heading west in the park. I'm doing the speed limit at 45 mph with some guy behind me in a massive black SUV riding my bumper. I can see him messing with his phone in the rearview mirror. He's not paying attention and won't pass, even when I slow to 30. When I spot the spider, he's still tailgating. A sudden stop will cause the clueless idiot to crash into me. The tarantula is crossing from the right into our wheel track. I slow down and move to the left to avoid it, hoping the idiot will stay glued to my bumper. He does not and runs right over it. I see a couple more outside the park, but I'm determined by then to keep pushing. It's a missed opportunity.

As to the desert spider rave, I'm clueless. I learn much later that male tarantulas migrate to mate, and wet and humid weather tends to coincide with high traffic days for the hairy critters. Most surprising, beyond the high number wandering the desert, is the beauty of these little creatures. Among the specimens I see, distinctive color and patterns decorate them. The majority are all black, but some have red markings on their body or legs. Others are brown or reddish with striped legs, or beige and black. It's a noteworthy and unexpected biology lesson.

As I leave the west entrance on the drive to El Paso, I skirt the edge of Terlingua, Texas, following Highway 118 north. Terlingua is so isolated, remote, and tiny, it's debatable whether you've been there or seen a mirage. Highway 118 crosses seventy-eight miles of nowhere to US Highway 90 in Alpine, Texas. Turning north, I notice a Texas State Patrol car at the gas station and think it odd. Kareen and I didn't see a single state trooper last year between the interstate and Big Bend. It's already after 6:30 p.m., with four hours remaining on the road to El Paso. I hope to make good time through the desert. I set the cruise at 80 mph in the 70-mph speed zone for Texas rural highways. About ten miles from Terlingua, another state trooper appears in a black SUV. I brake as he activates his lights. I'm thinking, "It's the middle of the desert!" I pull off the road and wait for the trooper.

As he approaches my open passenger window, I feel a sick sense of déjà vu when I hear him ask, "Where are you going in such a hurry?" I explain my day in Big Bend and a concise summary of the year's totals.

Trooper Tim suggests I step out of the car, and for a moment, I think, "Oh no! He's going to arrest me! My year's going to end in a Texas prison, doing hard time in a cell with an axe-murderer named Bubba!" Standing beside my vehicle, he asks questions about the parks, places I liked, and my favorite memories. Tim is courteous and professional. And nice people interested in the parks bring out the best in me. My enthusiasm overflows. After about the fourth park question, I admit to him that I thought he was hauling me to county.

He laughs and says, "No, I've got less than ten years until I can retire, and I'd like to do something like what you're doing." Our conversation lasts over thirty minutes. We walk back to his SUV, where he prints off a written warning, and shares, "My birthday is just a few days after yours." A little printer connected in his truck spits out the warning. I'm impressed by the setup. "That's cool," I say. "I've never seen a printed ticket like that, not that I'm experienced on the subject."

Tim smiles. I promise to slow down, and Tim waves and says, "Don't worry about it. Just be safe."

"You too," I reply.

As Tim turns his vehicle south, I resume the drive north, smiling at the delightful conversation and most interesting traffic stop I've experienced. Eyes on the road, I set the cruise at 77, thinking that's modest for the Chihuahuan Desert. Five miles later, another southbound black SUV appears. It's another Texas State Trooper! I pump the brakes, hoping slowing from seven over won't be worth his time. His lights activate as we pass. How could this be? The first thought I have is a blistering Texas day in a hot box circa *Cool Hand Luke*. Then I think of Texas's death row and its transient living accommodations. They're probably all Yankees who thought they could speed on rural Texas highways!

I pull over, again, and wait for the trooper to pull behind me, shutting my blue Ford Fusion rental down, and imagine it being towed away as I sit handcuffed in the back of his SUV. The trooper approaches the open passenger window, and before he can say anything, I hand him my license and say, "I thought I slowed down, officer. I really did. Sorry."

"No problem," he says, and takes my license back to his truck. Certainly, he will see the warning time-stamped not ten minutes ago. I'm contemplating my plight when he returns a few minutes later, hands me another written warning with my license, and says in an even, polite tone, "Just slow it down a little bit. There are curves and wildlife on this road, and you want to arrive safely."

As he turns to walk away, I blurt out, "Sir!"

"Yes?" he says, turning around.

"I've seen three troopers down here in the middle of nowhere. Do you guys have a big bust or something going on?"

"Oh no," he says. "It's the district state troopers chili cook-off tonight in Terlingua."

"Thanks," I reply, as his last sentence hangs in the air as if in a cartoon bubble. It's hard for my mind to process in the moment. From a Food Network show playing at Kareen's behest a year later, I learn that Terlingua hosts an annual chili cook-off competition the first Saturday of November. Terlingua? And this is the weekend I picked to visit Big Bend.

Friday night ends with another great meal and a couple of cold beers at the little Mexican place by the hotel as I contemplate my narrow escape. They're going to post an APB on the little blue Fusion. Good thing I'm leaving Texas tomorrow morning. The bad news is I'm coming back in two weeks!

Saturday starts early for a four-hour drive to the trip's final and only new park. After a pitstop for the Silver City, New Mexico, Continental Divide Trail stamp, Highway 15 to **Gila Cliff Dwellings National Monument,** a legendary road among park travelers, beckons. A sign outside Silver City warns motorists the forty-four miles will require two hours. I reach the monument in an hour and fifteen minutes, but it takes complete concentration to focus on the road and not be distracted by the wooded mountainous scenery of the Gila National Forest.

Gila Cliff Dwellings consists of six natural caves in the Cliff Dweller Canyon wall. Structures built in five caves create about forty rooms. The one-mile Cliff Dwellings Trail climbs 180 feet above the canyon floor. The canyon alcove structures date to the late 1200s. Scientists and scholars still speculate why these dwellings were abandoned in the early 1300s after one generation. Non-natives rediscovered them in the late nineteenth century.

Tomorrow's afternoon flight to Chicago leaves Albuquerque, and there's no reasonable way to get there from here. Warned to avoid the eastern route in favor of the roundabout southern route through Silver City and south to I-10, I cave to my GPS despite the predictions of doom. The eastern route follows Highway 152 through the Mimbres Mountains and earns my enmity as the longest, never-ending road I've driven. Built into mountains and cliffs, the two-lane highway snakes through endless blind curves, wrapping around so many corners direction ceases to have meaning. The shadows and changing elevation intensify the fun. Behind 8,228-foot Emory Pass, a wilderness terrain of steep mountain walls emerges. I've crossed the River Styx. Abandon all hope, ye who enter are condemned to drive this road for eternity, also the approximate duration of your commute. The southern route from Gila Cliff Dwellings becomes the best good advice I didn't take all year. It's appropriate that I spend my last night on the road in Truth or Consequences.

Waiting to board at my Albuquerque gate, I total the past six days. I drove 3,150 miles in fifty-three hours behind the wheel to visit eighteen parks. Charon's heavy toll includes nine hours of driving a day plus the hiking, heat, tarantula hoard, and Strother Martin's voice in my head, "He wants it. He gets it. Some men, you just can't reach."

34 Don't Mess with Texas

THE SUNDAY NIGHT return from Albuquerque concludes four weeks of travel across thirteen states. Amid the frantic pace, I've spent only two nights with Kareen, who's caught a bug for the third time this year. Each of the first two illnesses lingered for weeks. I roll my bag through the condo door to Kareen standing in the entryway. She offers, "I'm sick. You can't kiss me."

"I'm exhausted. It's bedtime," I reply. After setting my bags aside, I shed some clothes and enter the master bath to brush my teeth. Emerging from the bathroom, Kareen's lying on the bed naked, a beige towel over her head with the color and texture of a burlap sack. I think, "I'm about to break evil and violate a prisoner!" All I can manage is, "What's this? You look like a hostage!"

Pulling the towel down just far enough to reveal her eyes, she answers through the cloth, "Well, it's practical," and throws the towel back over her head.

I respond, "Okay, Dr. Love. Should I get some rope?"

The first full week in November is a welcomed week at home, focusing on work and enjoying Buddy's company. He's almost fully recovered, a miracle for an old dog. We walk about in the mild autumn weather, rejuvenated by our daily strolls through our community park. Tuesday evening brings an interesting experience. I'm eating dinner at a local sports bar and find myself in a conversation with a gentleman and lady sitting next to me. He asks about my NPS T-shirt and the pins on my hat, so I share a centennial summary. He replies, "You've spent all your money seeing parks, but you could have spent it on prostitutes." Both he and the lady laugh as he gives me a wink.

After a moment of stunned silence, I reply, "I never thought about it that way."

Saturday, I join an NPTC member meet-up at Trainfest 2016 in Milwaukee, Wisconsin. The annual convention boasts a subtitle of "America's Largest Operating Model Railroad Show." The club of train enthusiasts based in La Plata, Missouri, the May stamping stop, call themselves the "Rail Rangers" and have a booth in the convention hall at the Wisconsin State Fairgrounds. Exhibitors vary from suppliers of every conceivable model railroad part or component to the most elaborate model railroads one can imagine. Most of the operating model displays are complete with multiple tracks, towns, industries, and landscape. The Rail Rangers booth contains information on the National Park Service's Rails and Trails program. Among the booth's guests is Aida Frey, a teen junior ranger extraordinaire from the Chicago suburbs who's gained attention for her book about exploring over 250 NPS sites titled, *America, Can I Have Your Autograph: The Story of Junior Ranger Aida Frey*. In addition to meeting Aida, I reconnect with my park-traveling friends Lee and Deborah.

After milling about the exhibition, the NPTC members attending gather at the Rail Rangers booth. While counting heads at our prearranged meeting time of 10:00 a.m., we notice the first signature on the sign-up sheet is a gentleman in the club—we'll call him the Duke—who's apparently collected more stamps and visited more parks than either Lee or me this year. As with Lee (and me next month), the Duke visited all fifty states this calendar year. The Duke's stamp confirmations are consistently flawless, except for the one for which he forgot to center the date in the image of a cancellation Lee and I happened to obtain a few days before and after the date of his visit, respectively. Today, he's driven hundreds of miles to attend and remain invisible. Lee and I both mentioned our attendance in advance on the forum. If I had the chance to meet someone who's simultaneously engaged in a unique and rare challenge such as visiting close to four hundred parks and all fifty states in one year, I would jump at the chance. Neither Lee nor I had any idea the Duke would attend the meet-up but found it perplexing why he made a point to slip into the convention, get the cancellations, sign the sheet, and avoid everyone else attending the event. With members near the booth all morning, that's hard to do and defeats the purpose. The level of competitiveness in the club, and resulting shenanigans, distort the purpose of the club's park travel awards. Worst of all, I might have inadvertently encouraged this behavior with the "Centennial Madness" forum thread. We're getting more madness than expected.

Kareen and I spend Saturday night in Chicago. She's working long hours and still fighting the virus. She needs some fresh air. I invite her to join me for a Sunday afternoon at our two local parks.

A short, twenty-mile drive delivers us to the newest park, **Pullman National Monument** in the Pullman neighborhood of South Chicago. George Pullman founded the Pullman Palace Car Company in 1867. His name became synonymous with luxury in the late nineteenth century. Observing the poor living conditions common for Industrial Revolution workers, he built a town around his South Chicago factory hoping to attract "the best class of mechanic." A few flaws develop in Pullman's utopian vision. His paternalistic tendencies controvert the burgeoning labor movement. The issue comes to confrontation after he lowers wages 25 percent but not rent during the economic panic of 1893. Pullman's refusal to hear worker concerns results in the Pullman Strike of 1894. Congress created the Labor Day holiday in a conciliatory gesture as the strike spread, disrupting rail traffic nationwide. After federal intervention, the strike dissipated by August. Though Pullman's workers failed to achieve their economic gains, the strike illustrated the trap in company towns and businesses, leaving workers in debt with a cost of living higher than income. Though Pullman died in 1897, his company survived to supply most of the sleeping cars used during the rail era, peaking in the first half of the twentieth century.

The historic Pullman neighborhood is one of Chicago's most visited and notable neighborhoods for its red brick construction, attractive row houses, and landmark buildings that include the factory clock tower, the Hotel Florence, and the Greenstone Church. Pullman's model town became a major attraction during the 1893 Chicago World's Fair. President Obama brought Pullman into the park system with the declaration of Pullman National Monument in February 2015. Today marks my fifth visit to the new local unit.

Soon, we're back on the Bishop Ford Expressway headed to **Indiana Dunes National Lakeshore**. Starting with the customary visitor center stop in Porter, Indiana, I consult with the rangers for a hiking recommendation. I've enjoyed my experiences among a half-dozen visits to the dunes. On my first visit, in 2012, I climbed Mount Baldy, the park's largest sand dune. Mount Baldy has closed to the public for the past couple of years after a tragic incident involving a young boy falling into a sinkhole within the giant dune. In October 2015, I attended the annual Saturday Century of Progress homes tour. The five experimental homes moved across the lake on barges after Chicago's 1933 World's Fair and Exposition. The Wieboldt-Rostone House, the Florida Tropical House, the Cypress Log Cabin, the House of Tomorrow, and the Armco-Ferro House stand today along Lake Front Drive in Beverly Shores, Indiana. Beyond unconventional building materials and designs, the homes contain future lifestyle projections. The House of Tomorrow includes an airplane hangar, as every family would have this modern necessity by the 21st century. During my last visit, I relaxed to the sound of Lake Michigan's waves crashing ashore at the Portage Lakeshore and Riverfront. Today, we choose the Dune Succession Trail near the West Beach bathhouse.

Starting at the lake and following boardwalks and stairs up successively higher dunes, the one-mile Dune Succession Trail unveils natural dune progression. The shifting sand near the water collects into larger, more stable dunes as plants and trees stabilize them farther from shore. Most importantly, Kareen enjoys the lakeshore's air and natural beauty on this beautiful October day. The sandy autumnal background blends with the good doctor's brown skin, all black outfit, and the high bun perched atop her head. It's nice to see her smile, a picture I must take with me. Indiana Dunes National Lakeshore is our last park visit together during my 360-day journey.

Indiana Dunes, Succession Trail

Sunday night in Kareen's condo, a "super moon" illuminates Lake Michigan. I take a picture of Kareen's stuffed bison herd's collective business end, dubbing it a "bison super moon."

I return to the air Monday with a 9:00 p.m. flight to San Antonio. The trip builds on an itinerary from March 2015. I'm extending the route to a larger loop through Central and Eastern Texas, passing through Houston and Beaumont, then north and west to Waco to visit the last two unexplored parks in Texas and the southwest region. The trip starts roughly when I show up at National Rental Car to find the only vehicles available are massive nine-passenger vans. Not having an alternative, I drive the bus to my downtown hotel. I'm back by 6:30 a.m. to exchange for something suitable and leave with a white Ford Fusion. The color and license plate are different, so hopefully the Texas State Patrol won't know it's me.

The adventure starts at Mission San Jose in **San Antonio Missions National Historical Park**. San Antonio Missions includes four Spanish missions established in the early 1700s along the San Antonio River. All four remain active churches. From south to north, they are Mission Espada, Mission San Juan, Mission San Jose, and Mission Concepcion. The fifth mission in the series is managed by the state of Texas as one of the state's most sacred historical shrines, The Alamo. The Mission Trail, a popular recreational and exercise destination, connects all five missions and the famous San Antonio Riverwalk. I toured the three southernmost missions last March, but not Mission Concepcion due to a special church event.

In 2015, San Antonio Missions became the United States' newest World Heritage Site. A bronze plaque acknowledging the honor adorns the visitor center's front wall. We'll return at the trip's end. The second park lies two and a half hours due west, upriver of Del Rio, Texas.

Amistad National Recreation Area administers the US half of the international reservoir and its banks, created by the Amistad Dam's 1969 construction on the Rio Grande. After stopping at the recreation area's visitor information center, I cross the reservoir on US 90 West to reach Seminole Canyon State Park and the Pecos River, a Rio Grande tributary. A spur road leads down to the river bottom, mostly dry today, but includes views of rock-strewn Pecos Canyon. I assume that flash floods deliver most of the water passing through the canyon. Or perhaps the water's been diverted. There's no way the tiny stream and otherwise dry riverbed below me could carve this passage. Aside from the scenery, I love the local names. North of here, Dead Man's Canyon feeds into the Pecos. The Amistad Reservoir covers the confluence of the Rio Grande and Devils River. An S-curve in Devils River north of the reservoir is known as Slaughter Bend, where Satan Canyon feeds into Devils River. About six air miles northwest of the reservoir, Rattlesnake Canyon feeds into the Rio Grande from the US side. One shudders to think of the experience the poor fools who named that canyon had all those years ago. I'll accept that each place has been appropriately named without confirmation.

The remainder of the day is spent visiting sites along the "Old San Antonio Road," known now as **El Camino Real de los Tejas National Historic Trail**. The trail includes multiple routes across Texas and into Louisiana, representing roads established in the 1700s to connect Mexico with its northern missions. The combined routes through Central and East Texas add up to twenty-six hundred miles. My stopping point tonight is a few miles north of Laredo, Texas.

Wednesday morning, I'm off to Brownsville, Texas for the next park, **Palo Alto Battlefield National Historic Site**. The first battle of the Mexican-American War occurred on May 8, 1846, when Mexican forces clashed with the US Army north of the Rio Grande. A boundary dispute between Mexico and the Republic of Texas created the opportunity for Democratic President James Polk, an ardent expansionist, to force annexation with military conflict. Palo Alto developed as an artillery duel and American military success when Mexican troops retreated south. The Battle of Palo Alto proved the war's only significant engagement fought on present-day US soil.

Today's second park requires passing north through Corpus Christi to **Padre Island National Seashore**. After checking in at the visitor center, I enjoy a two-hour beach walk. A barren tree that's somehow washed up about thirty feet short of the beach now has birds on each extended branch and fascinates me enough to merit several pictures. It's almost 6:00 p.m. before I exit the park, continuing north.

Padre Island, bird tree

Wednesday night I pass through Houston, traveling from I-69 to I-10 east to Port Arthur. I stop near Beaumont at 11:30 p.m., with 324 miles behind me. The next park, and a new unit for me, is **Big Thicket National Preserve**. Big Thicket is spread out among twelve separate subunits over Eastern Texas north of Beaumont. Wetlands once dominated 3.5 million Texas acres near the Gulf of Mexico. The park preserves some isolated land representative of premodern East Texas.

I focus today's hiking in the Turkey Creek Unit near the visitor center. The ranger educates me on the most representative hike I can target to see the terrain. He suggests the Kirby Nature Trail, followed by the Sandhill Loop. Together, they total over six miles through traditional Texas wetlands. He adds he's had two Texas coral snakes slither over the trail behind him on treks in the past week. The coral snake is the only United States venomous snake with neurotoxin. The vipers that represent America's other venomous snakes have hemotoxin. Rattlesnakes, copperheads, and cottonmouths are all vipers. Neurotoxin tends to be far more lethal and is the type of venom deployed by the world's deadliest snakes, including African mambas and the cobra. Coral snakes are less dangerous since they are typically less aggressive around humans than vipers, though most snakes will avoid human contact if possible. I'm standing at the trailhead in shorts and hiking shoes, unsure what awaits. As I learn after my hike, Big Thicket provides natural habitat for thirty-seven different snake species, five venomous.

The Kirby Nature Trail leads me through mostly dry woodland, with some standing water in low spots off the broad, clear trail. As I cross a creek into the Sandhill Loop, the fallen leaves bury the trail. I proceed left about a quarter mile when I hear leaves rustling. I look down to a snake sliding over my shoes! I've never had a problem with snakes, admiring their critical ecological role controlling rodents. We had large black and king snakes around our house during my youth and left them alone to do their thing. However, unexpected snake appearances startle nearly everyone. And I'm no exception. Someone watching me would have learned white men can jump when motivated. With leaves obscuring my view, I turn around and satisfy myself with completing the nature trail loop. But the snakes have found me, and now they're everywhere. The next one I hear, since the rustling of the leaves is my only warning from the deep cover, is an eastern hognose moving to nab a frog that stays ahead of the frustrated snake. I'm sure my return to the trailhead beats my outbound time.

Wednesday concludes with several trail stops and a drive from Nacogdoches to Palestine to finish the day. Thursday morning, it's another new park at **Waco Mammoth National Monument**. The Waco Mammoth site, a state historic site before becoming part of the National Park System under a cooperative agreement on July 10, 2015, includes a ranger-led tour through the fossil bed. The site represents the only nursery herd of Columbian mammoths known to exist in the United States. Scientists have discovered twenty-three mammoths at the site. The Columbian mammoth is the largest mammoth, fourteen feet tall at the shoulder compared with ten feet for the woolly mammoth. The Columbian mammoth weighed up to twenty thousand pounds and consumed three to seven hundred pounds of grass and other plants daily. The site was discovered in 1978 when two guys noticed an unusual bone in the ancient creek bed and took it to Baylor University for identification. The most popular theory as to why an entire herd died here is that they were trapped in mud at a water hole during a flash flood.

Wednesday concludes with additional trail stops in the Austin area, before the night ends at an airport hotel. Thursday starts with another El Camino Real de los Tejas National Historic Trail site at Monument Hill and the Kreische Brewery in La Grange, Texas. The monument serves as the final resting place for thirty-six Texans who died fighting Mexican forces in September 1842 near San Antonio and another sixteen executed in April 1843 by order of Santa Ana in Salado, Mexico. The property, owned by German immigrant Heinrich Kreische, contains an 1850s–era house on a bluff overlooking the Colorado River and town of La Grange. The brewery was added below the bluff in 1862 and operated until Kreische's death in the 1880s.

Lyndon B. Johnson National Historical Park, sixty miles west of Austin, consists of the Boyhood Home and Johnson Settlement in Johnson City and the Texas White House at the LBJ Ranch east of Stonewall. After collecting the unit's lapel pins at the Johnson City visitor center, another Texas White House tour caps the visit. The LBJ Ranch entertains through all the aspects that speak to LBJ's personality. The house contains thirty-seven phones, including one under the dining room table. LBJ's family room and bedroom have a three-TV console for each major network. Perhaps my favorite item among the many interesting articles is a stack of mint condition currency enclosed in glass and sitting on the bookshelf behind his office desk at the western end of the home. The currency features LBJ's picture, a gift from his longtime political ally and friend, Secretary of the Treasury Henry Fowler. Fowler enclosed the money in a secure case to prevent Johnson from spending it.

Saturday concludes with another trail stop in San Antonio at the Navarro State Historic Site. Jose Antonio Navarro became a key player in two revolutions, the Mexican separation from Spain in 1821 and the Texas Revolution of 1832. The site protects homes he built in 1832 and 1855 in downtown San Antonio. Navarro served as one of two Tejanos (Texans of Spanish or Mexican descent) in the state's constitutional convention and played a critical role in securing rights for Tejanos and other nonwhite Texans.

Sunday morning begins at the Alamo. The mission earned a permanent place in Texas and American history when Mexican forces under Santa Ana defeated and executed the garrison on March 6, 1836. The remaining Texas State Historical Site structures dating to the battle are the church proper and the long barracks. From the Alamo, I visit Mission Concepcion, the next mission downriver. I navigate around parishioners enjoying a picnic at the 1731 stone church with two square towers at its front and stone archways leading away on the right side. The palm trees beside the structure and the domed chapel to the rear give its profile a Middle Eastern feel.

The grand loop through Central and East Texas makes a 1,900-mile tour. The United flight from San Antonio to Chicago, scheduled for 1:50 p.m., doesn't leave until 7:30 p.m. due to mechanical issues. It's the first significant delay I've had flying this year. Tired doesn't adequately describe my condition when I shuffle into our lakefront condo after 10:30 p.m.

35 *Miles to Go Before I Sleep*

SINCE I COMMITTED to this writing project, I don't want to omit parks I visited with my father last December. On Monday, November 28, I drive through Indiana and Ohio to West Virginia and my Beckley, West Virginia hotel, arriving after 11:00 p.m.

The **National Coal Heritage Area** tells southern West Virginia's extensive coal mining history. The heritage area covers a 5,300 square mile area once dominated by coal. The heritage area has a personal connection. My father left his electrical engineering job at General Electric to work for a southern Illinois coal company in 1976, launching a thirty-five-year career in the industry. After my sophomore year at Illinois, I worked two summers in a Galatia, Illinois, underground coal mine. Underground mining presents a unique and dangerous working environment. The four summer interns worked in two pairs, each assigned an experienced senior miner, making us a crew of three. My duo had a good man, a senior miner named David, looking out for us. He expected his two college boys wouldn't respect someone who started in the mines after high school. That couldn't have been further from the truth, as I explained to him before our summer ended. I'll never forget one shift. We entered a dangerous area behind a new longwall section about to be mined. We built cribs (stacked blocks of timbers, two feet long by four inches square) to support the roof and keep an air entry (mined passage) open behind the longwall mining face. Near the rear area, I leaned against the entry rib (wall of coal), before David pulled me away and directed me to shine my headlamp on the wall. There before us, a huge crack worked back into the seam. At the end of our shift, we passed that spot to find a ton of coal piled where I stood. It's a lesson about respecting knowledge and experience that stays with me.

Tuesday, November 29, starts at **New River Gorge National River** headquarters in Glen Jean, West Virginia. There are three NPS river units managed here. The other two, **Gauley River National Recreation Area** and **Bluestone National Scenic River,** round out today's itinerary. The New River's scenic gorge runs north through south central West Virginia. One of the world's oldest rivers predates the Appalachian Mountains around it. All three rivers attract boaters awed by the thousand-foot gorges in this river system. The New and Gauley offer renowned whitewater experiences.

The Canyon Rim Visitor Center off US Highway 19 overlooks the gorge and the famous New River Gorge Bridge. I can never resist the bridge overlook during my visits here. The second highest American bridge and second longest single-arch steel span closes the third Saturday of October in celebration of its 1977 completion.

I continue north on US19 to Highway 129 and the Gauley River. The Summersville Dam serves as the primary entry for rafters navigating the popular rapids over the recreation area's twenty-five river miles. The dam offers a water-level view for those staying dry. Next, Carnifex Ferry Battlefield State Park protects a Civil War battleground and overlooks a sharp bend in the Gauley, offering a glimpse of the scenery river goers enjoy as they ride the current down this green-walled, twisting passage.

From the Gauley, I take a more scenic option south for fifty miles on State Highway 41 to Sandstone Visitor Center. From there, I follow the New River on Highway 20 through the town of Hinton to reach Bluestone State Park. The state park includes a riverside gravel walking trail entering the NPS boundary. Trying to stretch my legs, I enjoy a four-mile round trip hike along the Bluestone National Scenic River. The unit includes a ten-and-a-half-mile section of the Bluestone River contiguous to the southern boundary of the state park.

Returning north, I explore the river's west side at Brooks Falls, and farther north, Sandstone Falls, two of many New River attractions. Following the New River's west bank, Highway 26 gives access to the falls at water level, whereas Highway 20 hugs the river's east side bluff and overlooks both falls.

Moving eastward near Charlottesville, I stop at Monticello, Thomas Jefferson's historic home and estate, to get a passport cancellation for the Journey Through Hallowed Ground National Heritage Area. Kareen and I toured the home in 2012. Monticello is one of four US World Heritage Sites outside the National Park System.

My next stop is the former home of our fifth president. James Monroe purchased the estate of Ash Lawn-Highland in 1793. Monroe kept the home for twenty-four years after he moved his family here in 1799. He sold the estate in 1825 to pay debts.

After staying near Richmond Tuesday night, I begin Wednesday at the **Petersburg National Battlefield** Eastern Front Visitor Center. The battlefield protects most surviving earthen fortifications in Confederate defensive lines and Union siege lines during the action around Petersburg from June 1864 to April 1865. I took my father on the entire thirty-three-mile auto tour last December. He particularly enjoyed seeing "The Crater," one of the war's most infamous actions. On July 30, 1864, federal forces detonated an 8,000-pound cache of explosives underneath Confederate trenches. A unit comprised of Pennsylvania coal miners, under Colonel Henry Pleasants, spent a month digging a 511-foot-long tunnel for the purpose. The idea might have broken the Southern lines and taken Petersburg six weeks into the siege if not for poor planning by Union leadership and the divisional commander's criminal negligence.

A black division in Major General Ambrose Burnside's corps

had been trained and prepared to lead the postexplosion charge through the Confederate line. Concerned about criticism should the project fail and lead to substantial loss of life among the black troops, Meade and Grant ordered Burnside to have one of his three white divisions lead the attack. Instead of selecting a unit, Burnside left it to chance by having the three commanders draw slips of paper. The assignment fell to General James Ledlie, a notorious drunk who was widely considered a coward. The bomb detonation caused disarray in the rebel line as hoped, but Ledlie's troops penetrated the defensive line by running into the crater rather than around it. Meanwhile, Ledlie drank rum in a bombproof shelter behind Union lines during the attack. Burnside ordered the black troops into the crater behind the initial attackers. These moves left the crater, at 30 feet deep, 60 feet wide, and 170 feet long, a mass of confused Union soldiers unable to climb out of the hole before Confederate troops rallied, shooting them and tossing grenades into the hole at will. The whole sad affair led to four thousand Union casualties and no strategic gain.

Today's second destination is Grant's headquarters at City Point. City Point sits at the confluence of the James and Appomattox Rivers, a natural choice for the transportation hub supplying men and materials to the Union army positioned around Petersburg. The Army of the Potomac exceeded 110,000 men during much of the siege, requiring an enormous supply chain. A quartermaster during the Mexican-American War, Grant stood well-qualified to judge supply matters.

Revisiting the James River location of Grant's cabin, I take a picture standing next to Grant's cabin door on display inside the visitor contact station in the Eppes family home on Appomattox Plantation, a 2,300-acre tract more than one hundred years old by the Civil War. Dr. Richard Eppes owned the plantation, enslaving 130 to maintain it before the war.

Kareen and I visited City Point in 2012. We marveled at views of the James slipping past the point and read interpretive panels throughout the area. One of the waterfront park panels at the end of Pecan Avenue reviews City Point's early history. The first

Englishman to see this place, Captain Christopher Newport, wrote of his intention to land English colonists near City Point before the shallow harbor and "many stout and able Savages" convinced him to return downriver to my next destination, **Jamestown National Historic Site**.

The Virginia Tidewater **Colonial National Historical Park** manages Jamestown as one of two subunits. Under Captain John Smith's leadership, English colonists landed at Jamestown on May 13, 1607. Though famine and sickness reduced their number, the colony survived as the first permanent English settlement in America. Historic Jamestown occupied the upriver end of Jamestown Island, judged a more defensible position than the lowland alternatives. After walking on the island, I return to the glasshouse to watch the park's glassmakers produce the 2017 "Pieces of the Year." The glass-maker heats the piece repeatedly in the stone-covered kiln, extracting it through an opening called "the glory hole."

After purchasing a piece of glass for Kareen, I'm off to the Yorktown Battlefield, the other Colonial National Historical Park subunit. Yorktown is the scene of George Washington's most important Revolutionary victory. The siege and capitulation of the British army under General Charles, Lord Cornwallis didn't end the war but decided the outcome in practical terms. Cornwallis's surrender, on October 19, 1781, paved the way for the 1783 Treaty of Paris.

Declared in November 2011, less than two months after the Department of Defense decommissioned the fort, **Fort Monroe National Monument** guards the approach to the famous water passage at the outlet of the James River to the Chesapeake Bay known as Hampton Roads. After visiting the fort's Casemate Museum, I walk around the fort for the next hour. From here, I'll head to Norfolk for the night.

My hotel Wednesday night in downtown Norfolk sits next to the Douglas MacArthur Memorial and Museum. MacArthur grew up in Norfolk. I'm having dinner tonight with another Norfolk resident, my park friend Deborah. She picks me up for dinner at a popular local seafood restaurant. We enjoy catching up on our travels. Deborah plans to do a grand tour of the park system in 2017. I'm down to one remaining trip after this one. It's been a long, rewarding effort, though I don't understand the full costs for another month. It warms my heart to see a friendly face so far from home.

I begin Thursday in Virginia Beach with a stop at First Landing State Park, inland from Cape Henry. The state park marks the April 26, 1607, first landing site in North America by Captain Christopher Newport, the same guy who was soon thereafter dissuaded by City Point's stout and formidable savages.

Modern visitors drive to Kill Devil Hills and **Wright Brothers National Memorial** in North Carolina's Outer Banks. When Orville and Wilbur Wright arrived in 1902, the brothers often endured rough boat rides to reach the location. The brothers chose the windy, remote spot deliberately. The park boundary includes the Wright Brothers Memorial on Kill Devil Hill, the launch site for their 1902 glider experiments. Orville and Wilbur returned in 1903 for their first attempt at man-powered flight. Markers behind the visitor center show the distance achieved in the first, second, third, and fourth flights. My father and I toured the site last December. I'm happy to be back, having seen all the Dayton park locations and finished David McCullough's excellent audio book on the Wright Brothers during the year's ample drive time.

A half hour from Wright Brothers National Memorial on Roanoke Island, **Fort Raleigh National Historic Site** marks England's first attempts at a permanent North American settlement. The first settlers landed in 1585 and returned to England a year later. The second settlement, in 1587, sent its leader John White back to England. White left 117 colonists behind. Upon his 1590 return, he discovered an abandoned colony with no obvious indication of the colony's fate. The word "Croatan" appeared on a wooden post at the abandoned settlement. The "Lost Colony" misfortune remains one of the most intriguing American historical mysteries.

The headquarters office at Fort Raleigh manages and administers the three local units, Wright Brothers National Memorial, Fort Raleigh National Historic Site, and the nation's first national seashore. **Cape Hatteras National Seashore** includes land on three islands. From north to south, Bodie Island, Hatteras Island, and Ocracoke Island each have visitor facilities. My father and I toured the three islands last December. We drove past Hatteras, North Carolina, to the end of the road system on Hatteras Island and took the free ferry to Ocracoke Island, staying the night there.

Cape Hatteras has intrigued me since youth. The seashore and Outer Banks parks became one of the last groups of parks I visited in the Lower 48. As with all barrier islands, natural forces sculpt Cape Hatteras. The Atlantic Ocean's pounding moves them west toward Pamlico Sound and the mainland. The seashore's most iconic feature, Cape Hatteras Lighthouse, testifies to the forces of change. A fascinating interpretive panel stands in front of the lighthouse's original 1870 location, showing the shoreline receding over fourteen hundred feet since the lighthouse's construction. By the 1980s the ocean encroached within sixty feet of the lighthouse. In March 1999, the park service moved the lighthouse twenty-nine hundred feet to the southwest over twenty-three days, adding fifteen hundred feet between the ocean and its present location. Cape Hatteras Light Station and its namesake island join their sister West Coast seashore at Point Reyes as parks on the move, though at the behest of different natural forces.

After a stop at the Bodie Island Visitor Center and Pea Island National Wildlife Refuge Visitor Center, I travel south on Highway 12 to Hatteras Island Visitor Center. There are stretches where the seashore isn't much wider than the road itself, giving the impression of driving in the ocean. Sand continually blows across the road, requiring regular maintenance. Hurricanes and storm surges that hit the Outer Banks must threaten to swallow the island whole. A serious storm surge transforms sections of Highway 12 into an underwater road. I think the question that had driven me to see this place and that I found most intriguing was: How can you maintain a road on a moving sand spit in the ocean?

The folks at the Hatteras Island Visitor Center seem amused by my centennial story. On the year, I've now visited every park in five of the country's nine regions. After a walk from the light station to the beach, I feel the weight of the travel as a warm ocean gust wraps around me. The Atlantic sends its waves crashing ashore, reminding me these waters aren't always so peaceful. Blackbeard once hunted his prizes from these islands three centuries ago. I'm too tired to channel my inner pirate and set sail tonight, staying near Manteo. I just want some rest.

Friday begins at a deliberate pace. I've got a four-hour drive inland in a wide, two-hundred-mile loop to make it to Beaufort, North Carolina, and **Cape Lookout National Seashore**. Cape Lookout forms the Outer Banks' southern end. The seashore comprises the Outer Banks' fifty-six southernmost miles over three main islands, North Core Banks, South Core Banks, and Shackleford Banks. Harkers Island Visitor Center serves as the departure site for island ferries. Harkers Island sits adjacent to Back Sound, sheltered from the Atlantic by the banks.

I'm too late for the park boat leaving for the islands. I occupy myself watching the park film and reviewing the new brochure, leaving unfinished business at Cape Lookout.

There are only two parks on today's itinerary. The day's modest aspiration misrepresents the effort. After this morning's commute, it's a three-hour drive to reach **Moores Creek National Battlefield**, about twenty miles northwest of Wilmington, North Carolina. We visited Moores Creek last December, touring the battleground.

The park protects the site of a small but important Revolutionary War engagement on February 27, 1776. A force of one thousand North Carolinian patriots defeated and turned back sixteen hundred loyalists under General Donald MacDonald at the bridge over Moores Creek. The loyalist force planned to join British naval forces in Wilmington to assert the Crown's authority over the colony. The British naval force, under Sir Peter Parker (no relation to Spiderman) moved south to attack Charleston, South Carolina, only to be defeated by the valiant defense of Sullivan's Island and its palmetto log fortifications. The victories at Moores Creek and Charleston secured the southern colonies' support for independence.

After staying Friday night east of Raleigh, North Carolina, I'm off early to return west on I-40 to Greensboro. **Guilford Court-house National Military Park** protects another Revolutionary War battleground. American forces under Nathanael Greene and British forces under Lord Cornwallis fought here on March 15, 1781. The British commanded the field after the battle but sustained significant casualties. It would be the last major engagement fought by Cornwallis before he ensconced his troops in Yorktown, awaiting resupply and transport from the British Royal Navy but receiving instead the French fleet and Washington and Rochambeau's combined force.

After a stop and hike at the W. Kerr Scott Reservoir on the Overmountain Victory National Historic Trail, I stop for the night in the Blue Ridge Mountain town of Boone, North Carolina. Sunday morning, I have a three-hour drive through the Appalachians to reach the trip's final park. **Cumberland Gap National Historical Park** brings back memories of my time in Knoxville in the mid-1990s, when I visited the park several times. On one visit, I arrived at the park's Pinnacle Overlook minutes after dawn on an early spring Sunday. I wanted to get out of my apartment and enjoy a hike in fresh air. Walking one of the paved trails not more than one thousand feet from the overlook parking lot, I heard a rustling sound and flash before me, a large animal leaped over the trail in one bound about thirty or forty feet away. A long, flowing tail trailed behind a tan- or light-brown-colored animal. Knowing there's only one animal in the US with a tail like that, I beat a hasty walk back to my car. That 1995 visit marks my first encounter with a mountain lion in the wild. I had no idea that it would not be my last.

The tunnel that takes US Highway 25E under the mountain did not exist during my earlier visits. Although it's an improvement for travel through the area, one unfortunate loss with the older wilderness highways is a historical marker for the Tri-State Tavern. The tavern sat directly on the Kentucky-Tennessee state line a few miles from the gap during an era when the legal sale of alcohol remained on a county basis. Local prohibition ordinances proved no match for the tavern owner's ingenuity. He constructed a bar

with wheels, simply rolling it over to the other state should authorities arrive. Like Daniel Boone through the historical gap more than
a century earlier, the rowdy mountain watering hole blazed a new
trail in interstate commerce.

Today's park activity is a four-and-a-half-mile hike on the Sugar
Run Trail and Ridge Trail. Nature supersedes the gap's substantial
human history and testifies to the inexorable march of time. This
path taken through the Appalachians by eighteenth-century frontiersmen and early settlers was first discovered by bison ranging
over most of North America in the centuries preceding European
settlement. Native Americans followed the bison, and frontiersmen followed the Native Americans. I follow them all in my visits
to the gap, enjoying a pleasant walk through the wooded ravine
on either side of the creek at its center. On my quiet stroll, I contemplate the last of the parks in the southeast region in 2016. After
the walk in the woods, it's six hundred miles to home. They will
be among the last of ninety thousand miles I've driven this year
to almost 380 parks in forty-nine states. For reasons yet unclear, I
reach the trailhead in tears. This feeling and the emotion of these
moments stays long after the journey concludes. The parks became
the essence of my life in these past twelve months. The exhilaration of the experience and its inevitable conclusion feels like saying
good-bye to a dear friend.

36 *Hawaii*

AFTER TWO AND a half days at home to collect myself, throw water on my face, and pack my roller bag, Wednesday night, December 7, I'm on a United flight leaving O'Hare at 4:00 p.m., arriving in San Francisco at 6:30 p.m. It's my last park trip of 2016. A couple of months ago, I scheduled a business trip to the company's R&D facility in Palo Alto, California. It's the only business flight I take in 2016. That sealed the deal on scheduling a trip to my fiftieth state of the year, Hawaii. I delayed the return flight for a week and paid for everything in between, a trip within a trip.

By the time I committed to the Hawaii trip, Kareen had come full circle on my crazy endeavor. She understood the sacrifices made to get this far. While initially circumspect, the idea of leaving the journey incomplete after so much time, effort, and personal and financial cost runs contrary to her nature. Her encouragement surprises me. When I complain about exhaustion, she reminds me, after asking for the number, that I have only four, then three, two, and finally, one trip left. Her most common statement is, "You did this to yourself. And now you've got to finish it." For someone who's running solely on adrenaline to a degree that isn't even fully apparent, her support means everything. She did extract a pound of flesh by way of a concession over this final trip. If I went to Hawaii in December, I had to return with her early in 2017. A second trip to Hawaii seemed no burden at the time. I had no way to know it would come at enormous cost.

After attending some work items Thursday morning, I'm headed north on US Highway 101, then east on the San Mateo Bridge. The sequence of I-880 to I-580, then I-680, leads north to Danville for a 10:00 a.m. tour of **Eugene O'Neil National Historic Site**. In 1936, O'Neil became the first and only American playwright to win the Nobel Prize for Literature. O'Neil won four Pulitzer Prizes, the last one awarded posthumously for his autobiographical work *Long Day's Journey into Night*. The material in that final work had been so personal and painful for O'Neil, he left it protected on the condition the play not be released during his lifetime. I toured his home in 2015 but found myself lost in a generational chasm. His works and popularity date to the first half of the twentieth century. I knew little to nothing about the man or his work.

While I can't claim a great familiarity with his work on this return, I can appreciate many nuances of the story that escaped me last year. The site features the O'Neil's Tao House, set against the backdrop of the San Ramon Valley at the base of the rugged Las Trampas Regional Wilderness. In a gated community, the home and grounds can only be seen on ranger-guided tours offered twice daily Wednesday through Sunday. The site is one of the ten least visited in the system with 4,287 centennial visitors.

Among Tao House's interesting aspects, O'Neil's work area in the second-floor study offers a window into the man. His small handwriting evolves to a barely discernible, tiny font as he ages. His passion for the sea is apparent from the model ships and nautical theme. O'Neil created an inner sanctum. His wife Carlotta guarded and respected his sacred creative space. It's one of many places in our National Park System where genius wrought accomplishment.

The tour brings down the curtain on California and the contiguous United States for the centennial journey. Friday brings another finale, though unclear at the time. The internal meeting I'm cohosting here turns out to be my last visit among dozens over the years at the company's Palo Alto location. Aware that this might be my last time at the facility, I try to talk to some of the many wonderful people I've worked with here, some for two decades, and share a redacted version of my grand tour of the park system. I make a point to tell those I see that I've never been happier. Late Friday night, I find myself walking the street, anxious to board the 9:30 a.m. Saturday flight to Kona and the big island of Hawaii.

Landing in Kona on time at 1:10 p.m., the first reminder that I'm on island time is the half-hour wait for my checked bag in the outdoor baggage claim. Nonetheless, I'm thrilled to be in Hawaii for the first time. My fiftieth state in 2016 is our fiftieth state. Today is also my birthday. Hawaii represents a forty-sixth birthday present.

After retrieving my rental car, I drive forty-five minutes up the coast to **Pu'ukohola Heiau National Historic Site**. The site's literal English translation is "Temple on the Hill of the Whale." Hawaiian King Kamehameha ordered the heiau, or temple, constructed in 1791 as a benefaction to the war god Ku. The temple's 22,400 square-feet and walls 16 to 20 feet high incorporates only water-polished lava rocks hand-carried from their source by a human chain twenty miles long. The painstaking construction required almost a year. For the heiau's dedication, Kamehameha invited his cousin and political rival and had him slain on arrival in sacrifice to Ku. Kamehameha's unique approach to ceremonial planning offers evidence that it's not just about the plan but the execution. Kamehameha unified the Hawaiian Islands under his rule by 1810, and they remained thus until his death in 1819.

Pu'ukohola Heiau National Historic Site and two other national park units on Hawaii's west coast feature native Hawaiian history and culture. **Ala Kahakai National Historic Trail** links all four of the island's parks. The 175-mile "trail by the sea" traces the important coastal transportation corridor from the northern tip of the island (Upolu Point) down the western coastline past Ka Lae (South Point) and the southeastern coast to Waha'ula Heiau. Established in 2000, Ala Kahakai National Historic Trail connects Hawaiian human and natural history. The coastal highway, called the Hawaii Belt Road, accesses all four parks and roughly parallels the trail.

Late Saturday afternoon, I arrive at my hotel in Kailua-Kona to find the street closed and a large crowd gathering. Following a detour marked for hotel guests, I snake my way around a building, down an alley, and into the parking lot to find an attendant. I ask, "What's going on?"

He responds, "It's the Christmas Parade."

"I thought the town was celebrating my birthday," I say with a straight face as a group of hula dancers make their way down the street next to us. He does a double-take before getting the joke and smiling. Turning down the normal entrance ramp, I find the last open spot.

Sunday morning, I travel a few miles to the next park's entrance one mile north of the airport road. **Kaloko-Honokohau National Historical Park** tells the story of how native Hawaiians managed and lived off the land. Ahupua'a, land allotments running from the mountain heights (mauka) to the sea (makai), demonstrate the philosophy of interconnectedness central to traditional Hawaiian culture. The ahupua'a encompassed diverse ecological areas with unique natural resources used to support the population.

I start walking Ala Mauka Makai, the 0.7-mile trail from the visitor information station to the Ala Kahakai National Historic Trail at the coastline. Traversing Honokohau Beach, I walk from the ruins of Pu'uoina Heiau alongside the ai'opio, or fishtrap, to the aimakapa, or fishpond. Between the fish pond and beach, a volcanic rock bed washed smooth by the ocean replaces the sand beach. Sea turtles frequent these rocks. Numerous turtles lounge in the morning sunshine. I pass two visitors who point out a pair of copulating sea turtles. Turtle love appears cumbersome. I wait until the mating Testudines take a smoke break before snapping their picture.

As the noon hour closes, I enter the third coastal park twenty-five miles farther south. **Pu'uhonua o Honaunau National Historical Park** protects a royal grounds and place of refuge. The grounds served as home to the ali'I of the Kona District. Reconstructed thatched buildings in a coconut grove represent the eighteenth-century royal residence. A stone wall dating to 1550 surrounds the pu'uhonua, or place of refuge. Noncombatants, defeated warriors, and those who violated the sacred religious rules and traditions of kapu could find safety within these walls. Otherwise, violators of kapu could face a death sentence. Kamehameha's successor ended the enforcement of kapu in 1819.

North of Pu'uhonua o Honaunau National Historical Park lies Kealiakekua Bay, Captain James Cook's landfall in 1779. The site represents the first known contact between islanders and Europeans. Subsequent interactions had a profound impact in the islands.

Ascending the Mauna Loa's steep grade from the park to the highway, I pass colorful tropical flowers blooming off the roadside. The floral color and beauty preludes nature's ferocity and power on display in **Hawaii Volcanoes National Park**. The best known and most popular among the island's parks, it's attracted a steady stream of tourists since Kilauea's current eruption began in 2008.

My exploration begins in the Kahuku unit on Mauna Loa's southwestern flank. Kahuku is the park's newest area, added in 2004. The unit only opens Friday through Sunday. My fortuitous Sunday afternoon offers a brief survey of the area before it closes at 4:00 p.m. I spend the first twenty minutes with the ranger in the entrance tent sharing my centennial story. At 383 parks into the year, Hawaii Volcanoes National Park proves one of the more memorable.

After a brief exploration of the Kahuku unit, I regain Highway 11 east to the main park area. At the Kilauea Visitor Center, two rangers review my plan of attack. The schedule serves me well, as I take advantage of this first day with a visit to Jaggar Museum to observe the venting lava lake in Halema'uma'u Crater. Until 2008, the park maintained trails and overlooks to the crater rim. Since the current eruption began, venting sulfur dioxide gas makes the area within a mile of the crater and its lava lake unsafe for visitors.

The Jaggar Museum tells the story of Kilauea's eruptions and the volcano's role in Hawaiian culture. According to island mythology, Pele, the goddess of fire, lives in the volcano. Pele is restless this evening. Activity in the lava lake is easiest to see at night. I'm ahead of the typical nighttime crowds and fortunate because the volcano is venting, causing the lava to shoot up thirty to fifty feet from the roiling cauldron. It's a thrilling and spectacular display. Shooting lava contrasts brilliantly in the gathering darkness as an intermittent light rain sputters from the sky. A little girl standing near me on the Jaggar viewing platform brings a smile to my face when she asks her mother, "Why doesn't the rain put the fire out?"

Monday, I set out for a day of hiking. I intend to go as far as my legs endure. First, I buy a pastrami and swiss sandwich at a little convenience store recommended by the lady who owns the Hilo bed and breakfast where I'm staying. Then it's off to the park.

Following the ranger recommendations, I start with the four-and-a-half-mile trail through Kilauea Iki and the Thurston Lava Tube. A thirty-five-day eruption late in 1959 shaped the crater and surrounding area at Kilauea Iki. The lava lake grew to a depth of four hundred feet. At the eruption's peak, the vent expelled lava and rocks more than eighteen hundred feet into the air.

The trailhead starts off the Chain of Craters Road, a few miles from the visitor center. It begins skirting the caldera's northern rim through a lush tropical rainforest. The trail crosses a large crack in the earth revealing a ruptured fault and some multiton rocks blasted from the vent. As the path turns with the northwest rim, it descends into the crater and across a jagged rock field before crossing the caldera floor past the main vent. The size and volume of the vent, caldera, rocks, and hardened lava expelled at Kilauea Iki extoll the power and fury below. The caldera's hardened lava rock floor buckles where it welled up from alternating cooling and venting. After crossing the crater floor from west to east, the trail climbs into the rainforest on the eastern rim. Bright orange and red tropical flowers contrast with the brown and black caldera.

After gaining the rim and passing a couple of excellent over-looks, the trail crosses the road to the five-hundred-year-old Thurston Lava Tube. After passing through the massive tube, the trail returns through a sparsely wooded area and continues a quarter mile up the road to the Kilauea Iki trailhead. The Kilauea Iki hike astounds me with its combination of foliage, scenery, and intimacy with nature's raw power. I consider the Kilauea Iki Trail one of my favorites in the National Park System.

Hawaii Volcanoes, Kilauea Iki

Continuing down the nineteen-mile Chain of Craters road, I pass among lava fields, cinder cones, and craters from past eruptions. Some vast lava fields extend to the horizon. The road descends thirty-seven hundred feet to the Pacific Ocean, abutted by a wall of hardened lava forming a one-hundred-foot sea cliff. Parking near the Roads End Ranger Station, I collect the location's passport cancellation before ditching the backpack for a small rucksack loaded with water, sunscreen, and my camera.

The spot where the lava flows into the ocean is clearly visible to the east by the steam plume rising into the air. It's a four-mile hike to the park service's rope barrier quarantining areas with dangerous sulfur dioxide. I pass the sixty-foot Holei Sea Arch near the ranger station and walk the gravel road to the barrier, about a mile from the active lava flow. The sun blazes, relieved somewhat by the ocean breeze. The cloud of steam rising from the water's edge grows larger on the walk. By the time I reach the ropes, I've removed my sweat-soaked T-shirt. The paths around the rope barrier to the left and to the ocean on the right leave the gravel road and pass over a recent lava flow. The jagged rock retains a shiny surface. Erosion gives older lava rock a flat black color after the brittle surface layer washes away. Newer lava is also slippery with sharper edges. Hiking over the new lava flow is tedious, unstable and treacherous. A fall could cause serious injury.

The path around the gaseous area to the left covers one and a half miles on the newer lava and would require a return after dark. Mindful of the afternoon heat, I scramble the half mile parallel to the ropes for pictures from the cliff. At the sea cliff, the massive steam cloud to the east bellows into the air, masking any daytime view of the lava pouring into the ocean at its center.

Hawaii Volcanoes, ocean vent

The return hike from the sea to the gravel road seems more difficult. A couple of times, I lose track of the ropes and wander off course, trying to use the flattest, most stable footholds. Balancing over the razor-sharp rock requires three or even four contact points. I recognize the symptoms of fatigue, by now a familiar aspect of park visits. Hiking over recent lava flows demands a higher level of concentration and exertion. I trudge back to the rental after nine miles of oceanside hiking.

Off the Chain of Craters Road, I stop to take pictures of the Mauna Ulu crater before walking the Devastation Trail south of Kilauea Iki. The trail explores landscape buried by cinders. Devastation also describes my own condition as I make a final stop at Jaggar to observe the lava lake. The lake is relatively quiet compared to yesterday. Steam rises from bright red surface cracks but no lava spews into the air. Satisfied I've given the park everything I had, I exit on Highway 11 to Hilo. I've hiked eighteen and a half miles today, a personal high for the year. The scenery and experiences make it all worthwhile.

By eight o'clock Tuesday morning, I'm on a Hawaiian Airlines island hopper headed to Kahului, Maui. The itinerary includes all four islands with NPS units. The mission revolves around the parks. Anything more is incidental. I've got a pleasant surprise awaiting on Maui.

Haleakala National Park covers 33,264 acres of eastern Maui. Like the National Park Service, Haleakala National Park and Hawaii Volcanoes National Park are celebrating their hundredth anniversary. They came into the park system together as separated units of Hawaii National Park on August 1, 1916. After securing the rental, I'm off on Haleakala Highway. The well-maintained road zigzags up the mountain. Multiple groups of bicyclists meet me, banking around the curves on the descent. Coasting down the highway attracts plenty of tourists.

From the park headquarters and visitor center at 7,000 feet, I continue to the Haleakala Visitor Center at 9,740 feet. The gusty wind and cool temperatures require a hoodie or jacket at 10,000 feet. Based on ranger recommendations, I hike two miles down the

Sliding Sands Trail, passing a split rock bracketing the path. The trek offers views of the summit crater's wilderness area across the valley to the Ko'olau Gap and the surrounding ridges and peaks against a Pacific Ocean backdrop. The wilderness area's rich red colors add a vibrancy to the panorama. The summit crater isn't a vent as it appears, but a product of erosion. Tropical rains carried by northeast trade winds washed away a massive chunk of the mountain.

Ascending on the Sliding Sands Trail, I'm feeling lingering fatigue from yesterday. My legs quiver up the 1500-foot climb. From the trail, I visit the Pu'u'ula'ula Summit at 10,023 feet, taking pictures of the island and ocean below and posing in front of the observation shelter's altitude sign. Viewing a sunrise or sunset from the summit is one of the park's most popular activities.

After exiting, I get a call from my mother, who tells me they are at the harbor near Kahului finishing a late lunch next to the aquarium. My parents decided to take a Hawaiian cruise, motivated in part by my adventure. I didn't know our schedules would coincide on Maui. I learn their summit bus tour arrived a half hour after I started hiking into the crater.

I catch up to them at the aquarium for a nice fifteen-minute visit. It's a pleasant surprise and makes my whirlwind trip less lonely. After seeing them off on their bus back to the ship, I eat an early dinner and head into Kahului to check into the Maui Seaside Hotel. Today's walking total of nine miles is easier than yesterday, but I'm beat. And I've got an early wake-up call for another island hopper to Honolulu tomorrow at 7:13 a.m.

Wednesday is a relaxed day. After an on-time landing in Honolulu, I drive to Waikiki and the Japanese Cultural Center. The center serves as a temporary visitor and information center for one of the newest park units, **Honouliuli National Monument**. Honouliuli is a Japanese internment camp established in March 1943 in southwestern Oahu, a short distance west of Waipahu, Hawaii. The site became a unit in February 2015 but is not yet open to the public. The closest visitors can get to the unit is a review of camp and Japanese-American history at the cultural center.

Additive to the history at Manzanar, Minidoka, and Tule Lake, the cultural center's interpretive materials are outstanding. I learn a great deal in two hours at the center, reading about early Japanese immigration to Hawaii, the impact of martial law after Pearl Harbor, the subsequent confinement, and the story of redress and recovery. Honouliuli remains distinct from the continental US internment camps as a prisoner-of-war facility. The camp held four thousand POWs versus four hundred internees.

Though I purchased the full Pearl Harbor tour for Friday, I head there now for my first visit to the Pearl Harbor unit of **World War II Valor in the Pacific National Monument**. Never spend one day in a park when you can spend two. The park completed events commemorating the seventy-fifth anniversary of the attack on Pearl Harbor a few days ago. I obtain a ticket to visit the USS *Arizona* Memorial today, marking the first of two visits to the memorial this week.

Having read a great deal of World War II history, I've wanted to visit Pearl Harbor and the USS *Arizona* Memorial since childhood. Standing on the memorial, I can see and smell the oil slicks floating on the water's surface below. The heavy oil smell hangs in the air. Reflecting on the lives lost, young men cut down so early in life, saddens me. The rusted ship below us, a metal tomb for many of the 1,177 officers and crewmen who lost their lives on December 7, 1941, magnifies the horror of these events and of war in general.

Thursday morning, I have an 8:30 a.m. flight to Molokai and **Kalaupapa National Historical Park**. Kalaupapa contrasts striking natural beauty with the park's profoundly sad story. The highest sea cliff in the world, varying from 1,600 feet at the point where a trail descends the cliff, to over 3,310 feet on the eastern side of the peninsula, isolates the Kalaupapa Peninsula on Molokai's north coast from the main part of the island, called topside. The cliffs derive from a massive landslide between 1 and 1.5 MYA, during which a third of the island fell away. Rock from this landslide can be found on the ocean floor as far as forty miles north of the island. An offshore volcanic eruption between 230,000 and 300,000 years ago created the peninsula, two miles from the cliffs to the northern tip and two-and-a-half miles wide at the base of the cliffs.

Beginning in 1866, officials arrested and involuntarily removed Hawaiians with Hansen's Disease (leprosy) to this secluded location. Patients remained segregated in the colony until 1969, over twenty years after an effective treatment was discovered. Islanders thought of Kalaupapa as a place where people came to die with no reprieve. Nearly eight thousand Hawaiians perished in isolation here over the colony's 103 years.

Kalaupapa history also includes great heroism and sacrifice, particularly by a Belgian priest, Father Damien de Veuster, and a nun, Sister Marianne Cope. Until he died from the disease in 1889, Father Damien devoted himself to the care and well-being of the colony's patients for sixteen years. Sister Marianne spent the last thirty-five years of her life in service to leprosy patients. She served Kalaupapa's residents for thirty of those years before her death of natural causes in 1918. The Catholic Church canonized Father Damien in 2009 and Sister Marianne in 2012. They remain an inspiration to those of all faiths for their selfless dedication to others.

Kalaupapa remains a closed community. Visitors must pay a fee and join a guided tour. The peninsula can be accessed by mule or foot on the cliff trail, or via plane from Honolulu or topside Molokai. Our plane stops at the topside airport before continuing to Kalaupapa. Our tour guide Steve arrives to pick me up in a minivan a half hour after the plane lands. We drive to the base of the cliffs on the west side of the peninsula to await a guest joining the tour after hiking the trail. A young man named Duy, who's touring Hawaii on the young adventurer plan, joins us as we watch several mules emerge from the end of the trail carrying other guests. The mule riders are with another tour, so we leave them and begin our exploration of the peninsula.

Only nine resident-patients remain in the Kalaupapa settlement on the peninsula's west side. Most residents elected to stay, considering the place their home after travel restrictions ended in 1969. Everyday life here moves slow and services are few, with around one hundred village residents at any one time. Common yet scarce sundries and supplies are purchased at the small local general store restricted to residents. Each November the settlement receives a barge. Receiving a large appliance or a major car part can be a yearlong process.

Steve drives us past the Kauhako Crater, the peninsula's highest point and a remnant of the offshore volcano that created this place. He continues to the original east side village, called the Kalawao Settlement. At the turn of the twentieth century, residents moved to the west side Kalaupapa Settlement for its milder weather. True to form, a heavy rain falls during most of our time on the eastern side, barely leaving time for pictures of the stunningly beautiful pali (cliffs) towering over the eastern peninsula and rocky shore. Cut with large ravines and adorned with lush green foliage above and anywhere on the rocky face that plants can gain a foothold, the east side cliffs soar into the sky high above the pounding surf.

Kalaupapa, sea cliffs

We finish our time in Kalawao listening to the pouring rain from inside one of the peninsula's oldest churches. I ask about the holes in the church's raised wooden floor at intervals among the pews. Those inflicted with Hansen's Disease produce excessive phlegm and regularly cough. Patients used a rolled leaf or plant stem to direct waste through the holes.

Returning to the Kalaupapa Settlement, our tour brings us to The Bishop Home for Girls, established by Mother Marianne Cope. Monuments to Sister Marianne and Father Damien adorn the grounds. The home's current manager, Sister Madeline Chin, talks to us in the chapel about life at the home among the Sisters of St. Francis and the legacy of Saint Marianne Cope, Beloved Mother of Outcasts. I find myself moved by this place. Kalaupapa is heartbreaking for its story, breathtaking for its scenery, inspirational for its heroism, and thoroughly unforgettable.

My last day in the islands, Friday, is devoted to a complete exploration of Pearl Harbor. A revisit to the USS *Arizona* Memorial elicits the same emotions as it had forty-eight hours earlier. Today's itinerary adds tours of the World War II submarine, USS *Bowfin*, the USS *Bowfin* Submarine Museum, the Pacific Aviation Museum, and the USS *Missouri*. The *Missouri* witnessed the end of World War II on its starboard deck. A circular bronze marker, in the shape of a porthole, designates the spot where the Japanese Instrument of Surrender is signed in Tokyo Bay on September 2, 1945. The *Missouri* harkens back to a time when battleships dominated naval warfare, a distinction held by aircraft carriers beginning in World War II. The *Missouri* is a floating museum and the last battleship on active duty not just in the US fleet, but worldwide. After being modernized in 1986, the navy retired the famous battleship from active service in 1992.

Saturday morning, I'm at the Honolulu airport early for a 7:00 a.m. United flight to San Francisco, connecting to a flight to Chicago. I'm happy to be finished with my last trip, but "tired" doesn't begin to describe my fatigue. I'm looking forward to home and rest. I'll get very little of either in the days ahead.

37 *Running on Empty*

AFTER RETURNING TO San Francisco on Saturday afternoon, December 17, the connecting flight to Chicago lands at 10:20 p.m. On my Uber ride from O'Hare to the lakefront, the driver asks where I've been. "Hawaii," I say.

He asks, "So, have you traveled much this year?"

"Oh, a little bit," I reply, staring at the passing storefronts on Irving Park Road like a dog looking out the window. I'm not all here.

Sunday, it's time to see my house again, but for less than twenty-four hours. I spend four painstaking hours organizing and numbering all the lapel pins for the exhibit displays. By Monday evening, I'm driving to Minneapolis for a Tuesday morning business meeting. After returning home Tuesday night, I've got another twenty-four hours at home before driving back into Chicago to spend Wednesday night through Friday morning with Kareen. Saturday, Christmas Eve, I complete the 350-mile drive to visit my parents in southern Illinois. I'm so exhausted on arrival, I sleep twelve hours Saturday and again on Sunday. Returning home Monday afternoon, I've got forty-eight hours to decompress before Kareen and I leave on a New Year's weekend trip to Mobile, Alabama. When I shoehorned the Hawaii week into December, I didn't consider all the calendar obligations to follow.

During the time at home on the twenty-seventh, I struggle with the simplest, most basic tasks. Opening a kitchen cabinet to retrieve a plastic cup for water, it falls from my hand. I can't concentrate on anything. Reading, a favorite pastime, is impossible. My neural wiring seems broken. My motor skills have vanished.

After buying sundries and other supplies Kareen needs Wednesday afternoon, I get in our black BMW sedan and set out for the interstate. As I approach an intersection to turn left, I see the entire bank of green lights and my mind processes it to include a nonexistent green left turn arrow. I make the turn and, too late, realize that both directions are green. Narrowly avoiding one car, the next one has insufficient time to brake in the 45-mph speed zone, hitting my car in the passenger-side rear quarter panel.

Fortunately, no one is injured. After shifting all the supplies into my company car, I elect to stay home tonight since it's after 9:00 p.m. and I'm too tired to drive. I feel like a prisoner being tortured on the rack. The typical, everyday events before Christmas would normally be enjoyable and anticipated. Instead, they have metamorphosized into an agonizing source of stress.

Chronic fatigue hit me hard about three months ago. In the interim, adrenaline and willpower fueled mind and body. The constant activity from mid-September through early November submerged me. I'm still waiting to surface. For the better part of a decade, I worked sixty-hour weeks and two to four jobs concurrently, but no fatigue, overwork, or exhaustion I've known compares to this suffocating debilitation. Thoughts of the year's accomplishments vanish in my mental haze. I can't think or function.

Our Thursday night flight to Mobile arrives after 10:00 p.m. We learn our rental car reservation cannot be honored. National is out of cars. The only two vehicles available at the airport are a minivan and a massive extended cab Dodge Ram pickup truck. We have a half-hour drive to our downtown hotel, and we're both exhausted. I choose the pickup, not realizing we must use a parking garage with two narrow 180-degree turns on each level. Hotel parking begins on the fifth level. I make it to the day of our departure before cutting the last turn too tightly in a momentary lapse of concentration and hitting the support column with the side of the pickup. There's no damage to me or the column, but the truck has $3,500 worth of damage. The fact that this happens in an unwanted and inappropriate vehicle forced upon us adds to the frustration. As a final insult, severe thunderstorms hammer southern Mississippi and Alabama much of the day and night of our departure, delaying us nine hours in the airport. We land in Chicago at midnight.

Our Mobile trip highlights include Fort Morgan, one of two nineteenth-century posts protecting Mobile Bay's inlet, and a day trip to Gulf Islands National Seashore in Florida. We pass a large beat-up boat beached beside the road to Fort Pickens. Two weeks ago, the park shared a picture of the boat on social media with the added comment, "We unfortunately do not have any information about the boat's story at this time. If we learn anything that we can share, we will." Yet, every other comment asks about the boat's origin. The park posts the same two sentences in reply to dozens of such inane questions.

Back at home, I focus on completing the lapel pin exhibit. After buying some supplies to make the displays, I enlist a local craft store to mount and frame the pins. Mounting the pins requires ten hours for each display. It takes over a month to complete the work. I pick them up at the beginning of February. The displayed collections are worth the wait, exceeding any vision I had at the project's onset. The shiny gold centennial pins are set against a flat black background. The green arrowheads in the "2016" on the pin catch the eye from about ten feet away, appearing as a field of green arrowheads against the black. The multicolored Find Your Park pins show nicely against a dark forest-green matting. A thick, dark-brown wooden frame holds the transparent acrylic protective sheet over the pieces. The acrylic is so clear that some who only see pictures think the pins are exposed and vulnerable to theft.

As January claws forward, so do I. When the adrenaline fueling the last few park trips subsided, I unwound mentally and physically. The battered body that hiked hundreds of miles, traveled almost one hundred fifty thousand, and spent over two hundred days on the road is all that remained.

With the exhibit moving forward, I turn to writing and planning visits to the remaining parks in 2017. Adding four to the total, three new national monuments are declared, and a previously authorized national historical park is established in mid-January. I visit two of the new monuments on February 1 during my return from the 2017 Cardinals Fantasy Camp in Florida.

Freedom Riders National Monument in Anniston, Alabama, tells of the fight to end segregation on public transportation through planned bus trips by civil rights activists across the deep south in 1961. On May 14, 1961, the freedom riders encountered a gang of armed white men, many of them Ku Klux Klan members. The gang attacked the bus at the Anniston station and again six miles out of town in route to Birmingham. One of the attackers threw a Molotov cocktail through a rear window, setting the bus ablaze. The mob assaulted some exiting riders. At the former Anniston Greyhound bus station where the initial attack took place, a painted mural in the adjacent alley details May 14 and the surrounding events. National broadcasts of the violent images shocked the country. On the Old Birmingham Highway, I stop at the spot where the bus burned to a charred shell. A historical marker identifies the bus location aside the old two-lane highway. More than four hundred men and women risked their lives on over fifty freedom rides in 1961.

An hour west, **Birmingham Civil Rights National Monument** includes Kelly Ingram Park, the Sixteenth Street Baptist Church, the A. G. Gaston Motel, and the Birmingham Civil Rights Institute, all in the Birmingham Civil Rights Historic District. Birmingham burst on to the national Civil Rights scene in the 1960s when local authorities under the leadership of the Commissioner of Public Safety, Eugene "Bull" Conner, used aggressive and intimidating tactics against nonviolent civil rights marchers centered about

Kelly Ingram Park. As with the freedom riders, news images of the marchers attacked by dogs and officers with clubs and sprayed with fire hoses shocked the public and galvanized support for the movement. The Birmingham Civil Rights Institute offers a detailed and compelling account of the city's civil rights history.

Violence and intimidation tactics against the movement lay bare on September 15, 1963. Four Ku Klux Klan members planted a bomb in a rear stairwell beside the Sixteenth Street Baptist Church, killing four girls ranging in age from eleven to fourteen. The fight for justice in the case continued for decades. Some participants had died by the time prosecutors won a conviction for the bombing.

Today, Kelly Ingram Park contains sculptures recognizing these events. I tour the institute, the park, and walk around the church. The exhibits at the Civil Rights Institute arouse my curiosity to learn more. Before leaving, I buy a copy of the Pulitzer Prize winning book, *Carry Me Home*, a remarkably detailed account of the Birmingham civil rights struggle.

After the exhibit pieces are completed upon my return home, I begin sharing the pieces with National Park Service personnel. I hoped to offer them as a traveling exhibit before finding a permanent park home. I learn that it takes a lot of effort and comes with plenty of rejection. The pictures don't do them justice. They need to be seen in person. I improve the explanation of the exhibit and its purpose over time. I wanted the pieces to communicate the gratitude that inspired them and encourage public support for our parks.

As February closes, Kareen and I leave for Hawaii, fulfilling my October promise. Kareen's worked incredibly long hours year to date. She expanded the trip from a week to twelve days in the planning process. The relaxed agenda allows a few new activities from the December trip.

Departing Tuesday, February 21, with a San Francisco layover, we land Wednesday afternoon in Kona. I again start with an afternoon visit to Pu'ukohola Heiau. The park is in the newly created exhibit. I share pictures of the displays with the rangers and park superintendent, who give me a tank top commemorating the heiau's 225th anniversary.

After a relaxing evening, we visit the two other west coast historical parks on Thursday and drive to Hilo. We have two full days in Hawaii Volcanoes National Park. I start by taking Kareen to Jaggar, where Kilauea is venting with force, throwing lava high in the air across the crater. We move to the Kahuku unit. After driving to the end of the six-mile park road, we enjoy a ninety-minute hike across an 1868 lava flow. The walk offers an education in ecological recovery from volcanic devastation. On our return to Hilo, we stop at Punalu'u (Black Sand) Beach to see its jet black shoreline of volcanic rock.

Hawaii Volcanoes, lava lake

This second time in the islands, I start absorbing more details about Hawaii. Originally dubbed the Sandwich Islands by Captain

Cook, the world's most remote major island chain is located 1,860 miles away from the nearest continent and over 2,400 miles away from the nearest point on the US mainland. Most people think of Hawaii as the eight main islands. However, the chain counts 137 islands extending 1,600 miles across the Pacific Ocean.

We start Saturday on the Kilauea Iki Trail. Kareen delights in the same blend of a lush, colorful tropical rainforest and ominous black and brown rock-strewn caldera that so captivated me in December. We have our picture taken in front of the main vent, a gaping hole in the caldera at the base of a mountain of rock and rubble. I enjoy the trail as much the second time as the first.

Our next destination is the Chain of Craters Road. At Roads End, Kareen and I hike a mile for a better view of the ocean vent to the east and the Holei Sea Arch.

Our next scenic excursion travels the Mauna Loa Road. Having seen Mauna Loa from multiple perspectives, I better appreciate the earth's largest mountain. The summit looms 13,677 feet above sea level. However, the sheer weight of the mountain's 19,000-cubic-mile volume depresses the sea floor. Measured from its base in the ocean depths, Mauna Loa rises 56,000 feet, 27,000 feet above Mt. Everest's 29,000 thousand feet.

We explore tree molds near Mauna Loa Road's junction with Highway 11. Tree molds form when fast-moving lava surrounds a water-soaked tree before it can burn, creating a rock cast of the trunk. On our way up the eleven-and-a-half-mile road, which narrows to one-way, we spot several nene, the endangered Hawaiian goose. As we make our way on the one-lane section, we pass several cars descending around blind corners at breakneck speed. After our third near head-on collision, I turn around halfway to the Mauna Loa Lookout. Kareen's only reaction to the near misses are vulgar utterances about the driver's intelligence. She doesn't suggest a retreat, but I've seen enough. No view is worth our lives.

Sunday morning, we fly to Kahului, Maui, for four nights at the Lahaina Hyatt Regency. Before driving to the island's south-west side, we visit Haleakala's summit. From there, we walk the half-mile Hosmer Grove nature trail near the park entrance. The

Hosmer Grove hosts the remnants of a failed 1910 forestry experiment. Before scientists understood the island's delicate and isolated ecological balance, twenty-three different tree species were planted here to determine those best suited to the unique climate and soil. The stand includes native O hi'a, pine, and eucalyptus varieties. The grove might be the most aromatic park location I've visited. The eucalyptus variants and pines produce a symphony of strong, pleasant scents. Some spots are so pungent I stop and fill my lungs with several deep breaths. Kareen looks at me and shakes her head. "You look like a dog sniffing a lamppost." I walk over to her side and raise my right leg before she scurries away. I tell her, "You can run, but you can't hide. Ruff!"

After a day relaxing at the hotel, we join a whale-watching boat tour through humpback feeding grounds off the island's southwest coast. We see several humpbacks, and a few leap above the waves, thrilling the home audience. The most impressive item on this excursion is land based. The amazing eucalyptus tree next to the 1859 Lahaina courthouse dates to 1873 and spreads across the whole block. Branches extend in every direction too far to be supported by the main trunk. These branches drop to the ground again for stability and further growth. Impossible to capture in one frame, it's one of the most extraordinary trees I've seen.

Wednesday serves as a rest day for Kareen. I will endure the five-hour roundtrip to Haleakala's Kipahulu unit. I tell Kareen, "Make sure the room service guy is fully clothed and gone before I get back!"

She retorts, "I can't promise that. If the in-room service is good, I might run up the bill."

Due to a mudslide on the road approaching from Hana in the east, the unit must be accessed from the west, increasing traffic on eight miles of unpaved coastal road approaching Kipahulu. After visiting with the rangers and getting the unit's one-page trail map, I'm off on the fantastic trek to the four-hundred-foot Waimoku Falls. The trail climbs eight hundred feet over two miles, passing the Falls at Makahiku before entering a thick, deeply shaded bamboo forest. The nonnative bamboo came here for agricultural reasons long before the park. Returning to the visitor center, I listen to the surf crash against the rocky shoreline on the half-mile Kuloa Point Loop Trail. I finish with the half-mile Kahakai Trail. The seven miles of hiking and two-and-a-half-hour commute back to Lahaina are trivial prices to pay for the experience.

Haleakala Kipahulu, Waimoku Falls

We finish our trip on Oahu, returning to Pearl Harbor and World War II Valor in the Pacific for another tour on our first day. I enjoy experiencing the history with Kareen, answering her questions and reviewing the exhibit for new details.

Our second day is an easy stroll down Waikiki Beach. Our nine-mile walk takes us from the Ala Moana Center to Diamond Head and back. On the return, we enjoy a second straight evening meal at the Crackin' Kitchen. The restaurant is a recommendation from my park friend Lee. I scouted it over two visits in December. Kareen loves it, and we repeat the successive meal plan to close our last evening in Hawaii.

We land in Chicago about five o'clock Sunday morning. At the condo, Kareen and I rest from our vacation. It's going to be the last peaceful rest for some time. I return to my house Sunday night and walk into a nightmare. Opening the door, I sense tremendous humidity. In the living room I feel water in the air. Striding to the hallway, water swooshes from the carpet beneath each step. I hear rushing water in the bathroom. Forcing open the swollen bathroom vanity cabinet, water sprays into my face. Trying again, but blocking the stream with my hand, I see the spray originates from the connection above the hot water valve, which I shut off to stop the leak. The nut fastening the tubing to the faucet is loose. Otherwise, the tubing, tiny plastic seal, and nut are undamaged. The same cannot be said for my house. All the carpeting in the finished basement is destroyed. The soaked drop ceiling panels lie in pieces on the carpet. Most of the basement drywall is water-laden. Every inch of carpeting is destroyed. I'm too stunned to process it all. I'm about to be homeless.

The road to recovery starts early in the morning. The leak destroyed the furnace and hot water heater underneath it. Within twenty-four hours, ServiceMaster begins removing soaked and ruined items, and everything I own that I can't pull out for immediate use or stack in the unaffected kitchen and dining room area is carted away for cleaning and storage. I'm fortunate not to lose any possessions of extraordinary personal importance. The exhibit displays are leaning against a wall downstairs, on edge against the floor. The frame and matting resist wicking the water, preventing significant damage. A month ago, I organized my park brochure collection in plastic bins. Prior, many sat exposed in a cardboard box. My father and I installed a large basement wall bookcase, and it kept many books and other items out of harm's way. Most of the items destroyed are of little importance. It could have been much worse.

Effective March 6, I'm homeless. And it's going downhill from here. It takes eight days for the remediation process to conclude. Over the rest of March, the insurance company and contractor they've chosen agree on an estimate, and I pick replacement flooring and other items for the home.

A week after returning from Hawaii, I resume writing. I set aside the essential reference materials among my possessions. I work for a week in a local hotel and then at the lakeshore condo. I'm still managing incoming work items and finding the daily interruptions incompatible with writing. By the week of March 20, it's clear a change is in order. I tell Kareen, "I've got to leave my job by the end of May, before I go to Alaska. I can't write and continue working."

She says only, "If you think it's time, do it."

Meanwhile, I'm working on the exhibits. I reach out to the Southeast and Midwest regional interpretation departments. During an aborted attempt to turn them over for display to the Southeast regional office, I show them to rangers for the first time at the Mississippi unit in Gulf Islands National Seashore. The rangers praise them. One says, "When the parks understand what you've got, they aren't going to give them up."

Stopping at Shiloh National Military Park on the drive home, I unwrap the displays from their protective cover of cardboard and blankets to take pictures inside the visitor center. Helpful park service personnel suggest photographs with people in a visitor center setting might present the exhibit more appropriately. I suspect the two Shiloh rangers on duty think I'm a little crazy for going through all the effort to unwrap the pieces for pictures. It's a struggle to get them rewrapped. The project didn't impress the Shiloh staff. I had emailed the superintendent a week prior asking if anyone at the park would like to see the pieces and never received a reply. The pictures taken by the ranger on duty were never shared or mentioned by the park. I realize I haven't yet learned how to explain the project well, but a few seem to perceive I have a hidden agenda. They are the exception.

As I'm working through the home disaster, starting the exhibit, writing, and handling normal work, a meeting pops up on my calendar for Wednesday, March 29. I don't notice at first that it's a face-to-face meeting with my boss with no other attendees. That realization dawns right before meeting time. As I'm heading from home, I call Kareen to tell her, "They've beat me to it. I'm driving up to Beloit to get fired. In the span of four weeks, I'm unemployed and homeless!"

She's emotionless, responding, "You're leaving anyway." My own feelings are complex, but the dominant sense is relief. A great burden is about to be lifted in a circumstance once unimaginable.

Shaking hands with my boss, I enter the conference room wearing a gray, NPS centennial hoodie and blue jeans. Sitting down, I start, "I have an idea why we're here. If this is something permanent, perhaps you can allow me the dignity to do it myself."

He responds, "Well, it is permanent, but that won't be necessary. Today is your last day of employment. You'll stay on the payroll like a full-time employee for two months through May." He proceeds to explain how I have no further responsibilities to the company effective immediately and agrees to allow me a few days to wipe all the personal files off my laptop and clean out my email. My work email will stay active for a couple of weeks to allow me time to clean it up. I'm not a malicious threat with such liberty and they know it.

I'm being downsized, not fired for cause. We talk for nearly an hour, saying little of importance, before he opens a manila envelope and hands me three bundles. The standard handout for downsized employees includes a hardcopy severance package summary, some information on available resources and programs, and a formal business letter from my boss, addressed to me, stating that in an evaluation of the people in my current job title, I'm judged the least competent and therefore am being let go. It's a standard format, but pride-swallowing, considering I hired, trained, mentored, or had done all three with the others listed. They are good people, but it's corporate legal bullshit. It would be more accurate to declare that I contributed the least among those in the role over the last two years.

The severance package plus the two months totals a year of continued pay for my twenty-one years of service. I'm elated. A few weeks from giving notice, I'm walking away with a year's salary gratis. I had thought long enough about all this beforehand to realize my boss and the company are doing me a great favor. This is the perspective I take away. From another perspective, my status and potential as an asset has sunk so low, the company is willing to pay me for a year to go away. In the end, I take responsibility. I made the decision to let go four years ago. It's another step. I've evolved into a new phase of life, and I wish it to include people who are honest and serve something beyond themselves. I walk away with a paid sabbatical to finish the park journey and write this book. All's well that ends well.

38 Return to the Midnight Sun

THE WEEK AFTER I'm professionally reengineered, I receive a welcomed response on the exhibit. Chris, in the NPS Midwest regional interpretation department, contacts the superintendents at Homestead National Monument of America in Beatrice, Nebraska, and the Lewis and Clark National Historic Trail based in Omaha. Both superintendents have interest in hosting the collections. I'm thrilled. I also receive interest from Indiana Dunes National Lakeshore to host the exhibit. It looks like they will stop in Chicago on their tour, punctuating the great news.

The exhibit opens at Homestead mid-April and will continue there through the park's host activities during the August total solar eclipse and the month of October. The park service will transfer the pieces from Beatrice to Omaha for its opening in the first-floor visitor center at the NPS Midwest Regional Headquarters, where it will remain through February 2018.

Back at what's left of my home, the repair project completion schedule calls for a three-week job. Work begins on April 10. During the first week, the drywall work proceeds with subcontractors who work hard and speak no English. I'm keeping an eye on things as I temporarily work from the end of my dining room table, surrounded by piles of possessions pulled aside for near term use. The drywall work stalls at week's end. Friday morning, I arrive from a local hotel to find the drywall guys with their van jacked up in my driveway, replacing the brakes. It's the first domino to fall on my journey into insurance contractor hell.

Over the next three weeks, a combined total of four working days are spent on my job. The contractor's personnel don't show up. At first, I get an explanation that there are emergency jobs in the Chicago area pulling away manpower. The contractor's project manager starts lying to me and doesn't stop until the job is completed. These aren't subtle lies but significant verifiable lies. Meanwhile, massive piles of trash and junk are collecting in and outside my garage. Empty fast food bags and drink cups, along with other litter, are scattered about the house, and beer goes missing from my refrigerator, the empties left in the basement. Consumables like trash bags disappear. I've little in the house of value, but what's there is pillaged.

After it's obvious I'm dealing with a company out of control, I demand a meeting with the project manager to explain that I would like to have the job finished by Memorial Day, a seven-week timeline. I hope to regain my possessions before I leave for a three-week trip to Alaska on May 31. We can't fix the past. I'm assured, face-to-face, that the job will be completed by May 24, giving me two days before the holiday weekend to accept delivery of my clothes and other property. Meanwhile, I'm staying with Kareen and traveling most of May. I return to the house on Memorial Day weekend to find little if anything done in the past two weeks.

The final week in May, I complain to the contractor, insurance company, and anybody who will listen. Giving them the benefit of the doubt for the days I've been away, work continued less than a third, and probably less than a quarter, of the working days since the job began. I get another round of guarantees, this time from the company's manager, that the work will "absolutely" be completed when I return from Alaska. You can guess what I find upon my return. Walls unpainted, trim uninstalled, bathroom installations incomplete, and other unfinished items indicate the rate of work remained unchanged during my absence. More disconcerting, the lack of attention to detail is stunning. Entire walls are painted so poorly, I can still see the old paint color across large sections. I inspect every detail and list the incomplete work. It's the first time in my life I've ever dealt with a professional service that repeatedly, directly, and verifiably lies. It will be nearly four months before I return home.

The first three weeks in June take me far away. I travel with a group of NPTC members, organized by Nancy, one of the club's founders and a former club president. Nancy's a travel agent and experienced park traveler. She's arranged and organized many trips to Alaska for NPTC members and others trying to see the Alaskan parks. Arranging trips within a group targeting the same locations creates substantial benefits, especially for places requiring charter flights. Small charter planes seat three passengers while the bigger ones can seat nine or more. My itinerary, over twenty-two days through June 21, contains thirty-six total flights. Of those, thirteen are commercial airline flights on Alaskan Airlines or Peninsula Air, eight are charter seaplanes, two are twin-engine charters, and thirteen are on single-engine planes. Nancy's careful planning means all the charters are shared, saving thousands of dollars.

The traveling circus begins with Alaska Airlines flights from Chicago O'Hare to Seattle, connecting to Sitka in southeastern Alaska. For the Seattle to Sitka flight, I'm joining two other NPTC members, Bill and Chris from New Jersey. They're both recently retired from long careers as a corporate attorney and a grade school math teacher, respectively. I meet them for the first time in SEATAC. During a six-hour layover, we'll visit **Sitka National Historical Park** together.

Sitka National Historical Park protects Alaska's first nonnative settlement, a Russian post dating to 1799. The Russians found enemies in the local Tlingit tribe, leading to conflicts in 1802 and 1804. After the Tlingit's drove them out, the Russians returned and regained their North American foothold under an uneasy peace. Although Russian American Company traders raised barriers for protection, the town's Russian Orthodox mission slowly created native connections. Americans replaced Russians after purchasing Alaska in 1867. Sitka became the US territorial capital. The park celebrates local tribal history and western civilization's introduction.

Bill, Chris, and I start our exploration at the visitor center, followed by the one-mile Totem Trail loop to the site of the 1804 battle between the Russians and Tlingit. Our next stop is the Russian Bishop's House, completed in 1843. The house and other original and reconstructed Russian-era structures are painted a bright yellow, making them easily recognizable. The Bishop's House interior features the Russian Orthodox Church's regional story. The most accomplished church leader, Bishop Innocent, arrived in Sitka as leader of the vast Kamchatka-Alaska diocese in 1841.

At the tiny, one-gate Sitka airport, we board a 7:00 p.m. flight to Alaska's state capital, Juneau. The next morning at Juneau's airport, I join a group of nine NPTC members on a 10:00 a.m. charter flight to Dry Bay, located in **Glacier Bay National Preserve**. Dry Bay has a ranger station and a gravel airstrip along the Alsek River, the only river that drains into the Gulf of Alaska through the coastal mountains. We read a park service information board at the preserve and get to snap a picture of the river before our pilot herds us back aboard for a flight up the coast to Yukatat, the site of another NPS office serving both Glacier Bay National Park & Preserve and Wrangell–St. Elias National Park & Preserve. At the airport, we struggle confirming the ranger station location. Finally, we're pointed to the correct building only to find it locked. Our repeated calls go to voicemail. Our pilot tells us he's the most experienced pilot at the charter service, yet he doesn't seem to comprehend why we're flying to these places. The morning highlights are the aerial views of the Alaskan Pacific Coast, particularly Fairweather Glacier and the Brady Icefield and Glacier in tomorrow's park destination, **Glacier Bay National Park**.

We arrive back in Juneau by 2:00 p.m. and continue our day with a visit to Mendenhall Glacier, a regular stop for travelers on Alaskan cruise ships on the Inside Passage. I enjoy the two most popular short treks, the Photo Point Trail, with its unobstructed view of the glacier across the water, and the Nugget Falls Trail with its voluminous rush of mountain melt water thundering into the bay. It's a great way to close the day before a dinner of Alaskan king crab legs at Tracy's Crabs in Juneau.

Friday, June 2, we have a 7:00 a.m. charter flight to Gustavus, Alaska, sixty-five miles west and slightly north of Juneau. At the Gustavus airport, we catch a shuttle to Glacier Bay Lodge at Bartlett Cove for the park service's daily Glacier Bay boat tour.

Glacier Bay serves as the penultimate destination for the Inside Passage cruises. The NPS now restricts the number of cruise ships allowed in the bay to two per day. Strict speed limits and other rules protect wildlife. Our park boat is at less than half capacity, making the all-day tour more comfortable. We travel sixty-five miles up the bay to view the highly active Marjerie Glacier at the terminus of Tarr Inlet. We spend an hour watching the Marjerie Glacier calve huge pieces of ice followed by a sharp thunder-like *crack* in quick succession, and a *whoosh* as the ice splashes into the water. The steep slope and dimensions of the bedrock under Marjerie results in a daily seven-foot advance. A massive section of ice the size of a house perilously leans away from the glacier face until the connecting ice at water level can no longer support it. With under ten minutes left in our time at the face, a crack and thunderous report announces the hour's climax as the section falls away. We next venture into Johns Hopkins Inlet as far as Jaw Point, so named because of the jaw-dropping view. The rugged beauty, with glacier-covered, jagged mountain peaks towering above the water on all sides, is considered the park's most spectacular scenic point.

From the Johns Hopkins Inlet, we get a close look at the Lamplugh Glacier's bright baby-blue ice. As we start our return through Glacier Bay, we pass Russell Island a second time. Russell Island, situated at the junction of the Johns Hopkins and Tarr Inlets, marks the location of the ice face at the time of John Muir's 1879 visit. The glacial ice that carved Glacier Bay advanced during the Little Ice Age, reaching a peak in 1750. The ice field extended beyond the current bay's inlet, burying Gustavus under a thick ice sheet. From its peak, the ice flow retreated about ten miles before Captain George Vancouver's 1794 exploration of the bay, then only five miles deep. The ice had retreated forty miles farther up the bay when John Muir arrived. The carved bay that the ice flow left behind thrills visitors with its scenery and wildlife. There is nothing else quite like it within the park system.

Glacier Bay, Margerie Glacier calving

On our way to the tidewater glaciers, we pass mountain goats perched hundreds of feet above us on Gloomy Knob, along with otters and porpoises at water level. Our boat crew excels at spotting wildlife. We spot multiple black bears on the shoreline, starting at the Grand Pacific Glacier's terminal moraine to the north and perpendicular to the Marjerie Glacier. The floating ice in Tarr Inlet hosts a healthy harbor seal population, and we see our first humpback whale in the Johns Hopkins Inlet. We stop for a time to observe a rare sighting of three wolves lounging on the rocky shore. The trio blend into their environment in a spectrum of colors: off-white, tan and black, and mostly black. We see and smell a thriving sea lion colony on Drake Island and tiny Francis Island. A variety of birds share the islands, including tufted puffins, bald eagles, common murres, pigeon guillemots, glaucus-winged gulls, black oystercatchers, and kittiwakes. Our ranger guide notes each wildlife sighting in blue ink on a park map.

After a late afternoon return to Juneau, we board an Alaska Air flight to Anchorage with Governor Randall T. Outlaw. He sits in the economy section exit row next to his plainclothes state trooper bodyguard and boards early. He acknowledges several Alaskans who notice and greet their state's chief executive as they pass. Our 10:00 p.m. arrival in Anchorage makes for a short turnaround, as we have a 7:30 a.m. flight Saturday to Barrow, the northernmost town in the United States. The Barrow airport might also be one of the world's smallest. The check-in counters border the baggage belt, all compressed into one large room in an aluminum, metal-framed commercial building on a concrete slab. We check into the Top of the World Hotel and depart thereafter on a tour of Barrow, bundled up against temperatures in the high twenties.

Our tour of Barrow highlights the fascinating history of this foreboding place. The town's official Inupiaq name, as of December 1, 2016, is Utqiagvik. Residents approved the change from Barrow in a narrowly decided October referendum.

Near the Arctic coastline, sixteen sod dwellings date to AD 800. Archeological evidence suggests settlement here as early as AD 500, making it one of the oldest permanent communities in the United States. Life underground, and the ability to make well-insulated clothing out of animal products, are essential to surviving frigid Arctic conditions. Barrow is Alaska's coldest town. The average low in February drops to negative forty-one degrees, the point where Fahrenheit and Celsius converge.

Situated 320 miles north of the Arctic Circle and 1,300 miles south of the North Pole, Barrow experiences no sunrise for sixty-five days from mid-November and no sunset for eighty days from mid-May through July. Winds of 40 to 60 mph, usually easterly, can occur year-round. Dense fog settles in the town sixty-five days a year on average. Polar bears roam into town during the colder months when the frozen ocean makes a continuous flat landscape from the Brooks Range two hundred miles south, across the North Slope's tundra plain to one hundred miles or more out to sea. The ice extends off the coast between thousands of feet up to several miles during our visit. The coast remains ice-locked until well into July each year. The directional signs at the Wally Post–Will Rogers Memorial indicate my home in Chicago is three thousand miles away. Post and Rogers died sixteen miles from Barrow in a 1935 plane crash. The town's airport bears their names.

Barrow is a semidry community. Residents may purchase up to six cases of beer per month and specified amounts of hard liquor, although alcoholic beverages must be shipped into town. Alcoholism threatens Alaskan native communities. Like other Native Americans, Inuit people have genetically lower levels of alcohol dehydrogenase than people of European origin. Centuries of alcohol consumption caused a natural adaption among people of European extraction. Native American populations lack this evolutionary adaptation. Signs in our hotel warn that alcohol consumption by guests is strictly prohibited and punishable by stiff fines and eviction.

Our tour highlight is a visit to the Inupiat Heritage Center. Three Inupiat dancers entertain us by performing traditional, storytelling dances. Inuits passed stories across generations by performing thousands of dances that incorporate motions of physical activities into a rhythmic routine.

The center is an affiliated site to New Bedford Whaling National Historical Park. New Bedford's whaling fleet made two thousand Arctic voyages to northern Alaskan coastal waters. The center's exhibits explain the Inupiaq culture among the town's 60 percent native population and across seven North Slope Inuit villages. On the coast, the culture centers upon traditional subsistence whaling. Most villagers participate as members of hunting "boat crews." Each village has an annual quota of bowhead whales, the most coveted whale species. Multiple celebrations, called Nalukataq, or the blanket toss, are held each year beginning in the third week of June. Each successful boat crew hosts a blanket toss festival to celebrate and share the bowhead whale harvest with the community. The bowhead whale remains an important part of the Inupiaq diet. I have deep admiration for the spirit of community and togetherness on display. Perhaps it's this remarkable aspect of human quality that has made Native American history so fascinating to me since the days of my youth.

Despite the harsh climate and challenging conditions, the residents who speak to us express contentment. The average family in town has three children, as opposed to the US average under two. The population here stabilized around 4,400 in the late 1990s. Amazon Prime is popular in Arctic communities, as nearly everyone relies on regular air deliveries. Perishables are a luxury. A gallon of milk costs $13.50 in the local supermarket. We travel to the northernmost point in the American road system during our tour, about three miles short of Point Barrow. Our group enjoys a good laugh when someone points out the dumpster sitting at road's end and says, "That's the northernmost dumpster in the United States!"

Sunday night, we're ready to leave Barrow to return to Anchorage. A few group members get together for a 10:00 p.m. beer in the hotel restaurant. We don't have much time. The next morning, we're on a 7:40 a.m. Peninsula Air flight to King Salmon, where we're staying two nights at the Antler Inn. We check in with our charter service and learn that the weather at our first destination is calm and clear. We waste no time getting in a six-passenger seaplane for the ninety-minute flight to **Aniakchak National Monument & Preserve**. Aniakchak is the least visited among the nearly 390 NPS locations tracked. An estimated one hundred visitors make it to the National Monument and Preserve during the year.

Halfway down the Alaskan Peninsula and 130 miles southwest of King Salmon, Aniakchak spans the peninsula where only thirty miles separate the Bering Sea and the Pacific Ocean. Weather fronts from both sides pound the area, leaving few clear sunny days and frequently preventing air travel by single-engine plane. The monument preserves a 6.5-mile diameter, 2,000-foot deep caldera, the site of a massive eruption 3,700 years ago that collapsed a 7,000-foot mountain in the Aleutian Range. The eruption is the largest in the Pacific's Ring of Fire over the last ten thousand years.

About two thousand years ago, the water in the caldera breeched the wall at a point now known as the Gates of Aniakchak, releasing a torrent down the path that the **Aniakchak Wild River** follows today. The most recent eruption came in 1931 at Vent Mountain, a 3,350-foot peak within the caldera. Despite the conditions and volcanic activity, sockeye salmon navigate the sixty-three river miles from the Pacific to spawn in Surprise Lake, the caldera lake remnant that remains today.

Aniakchak, Surprise Lake and Gates of Aniakchak

Sitting in the jump seat next to our pilot, Lenny, I'm fixated as the caldera and surrounding area come into view. The skies are clear across the peninsula, giving us a view from the Bering Sea across the Aleutian Mountains to the Pacific. The caldera dominates the stark, barren landscape. The eruption's devastation is evident for twenty miles or more around the caldera. There are

no visitor facilities in or near the park. The remote setting challenges survival skills of the few brave souls that attempt to hike
into the caldera from some remote drop-off point. Planning and
self-sufficiency sustain life here.

Lenny skims the surface of the preserve's Meshik Lake. The
small lake's low water level won't permit a landing, so he regains
altitude and turns to follow the river's path through the Gates. After
circling once inside the caldera, Lenny touches down on Surprise
Lake and taxis to a rock and cinder beach near an adjacent hill.
After we exit the plane, I scramble up the hill to view the caldera
surrounding us.

Vent Mountain rises to the east. We turn in circles on the
small promontory, taking in the landscape. Surprise Lake stretches
out below and the Gates rise to our north. The others followed
me up the hill, so I ask someone to take a picture of me with
Vent Mountain and the Gates in the background. It's a celebratory
moment. Aniakchak's two units are my 400th and 401st NPS units
visited. It's hard to think of a more surreal setting.

From Aniakchak, we fly north to **Alagnak Wild River**. Alagnak
winds and twists for sixty-nine miles from its origin at Kukaklek
Lake to Kvichak River, which flows into Bristol Bay and the Bering
Sea. Sockeye, pink, chum, king, and silver salmon all swim the
Alagnak to their breeding grounds in the freshwater lakes where
they spawn and die. Newly hatched salmon stay in freshwater
about two years before they begin their two- to three-year Pacific
sojourn. The Alagnak merits the description "wild." On the river,
Lenny sloshes in his waders through knee-deep water to help us get
out of the plane and on to the river bank. We take a few pictures
at ground level before we fly over the coiled, ever-bending river to
its confluence with the Nonvianuk. We continue east and slightly
south over the Nonvianuk to its origin, Nonvianuk Lake in **Katmai
National Preserve**. There is little for us to do after landing on the
lake without going in it. We look at the scenery, particularly the
eastern peaks, and we're off again. Back in King Salmon, we thank
Lenny and leave to check in at the Antler Inn.

Our last piece of park business today is a visit to the interagency visitor center a few hundred feet away. I pose with a piece of cardboard Nancy colored with "400." It's a thoughtful gesture. Today marks the last time I'll see four new units in a single day.

We rejoin Lenny Tuesday for the short trip to Lake Brooks in **Katmai National Park**. The park's western boundary begins six miles east of King Salmon, and Brooks Camp lies another twenty-seven miles farther east. The camp and park have light visitor traffic today. In a month, the place will be teeming with thousands pressed together to watch brown bears fish the Brooks River. The Brooks salmon run occurs in July and September. The salmon swim upstream from Naknek Lake, the largest within park service boundaries, to spawn in Brooks Lake. To do so, they must navigate the two-mile Brooks River and its famous obstacle, Brooks Falls. Crowds pack the fall's viewing platform, hoping to see bears catch salmon jumping the falls in midair. Our itinerary avoids the crowds, sacrificing the salmon run for access and flexibility with the float plane in case inclement weather forces a change.

Our day begins with the one-mile hike from Brooks Lake to Brooks Camp. We pause at the suspended wooden bridge over the Brooks River mouth. The rangers have closed it while a female bear and her three cubs search for scraps in the delta mud. As it turns out, these four bears are the only ones we'll see up close, though we spot several bears roaming the tundra below our return flight to King Salmon. There are an estimated thirty-eight to forty-two thousand bears living on the Alaskan Peninsula.

All Brooks Camp visitors attend a bear orientation. It's vital that visitors understand how to behave around these dangerous animals. After the orientation and park film, several of us take a side trail to a shelter protecting a reconstructed dwelling frame dating to AD 1200. People have inhabited this area of the Alaskan Peninsula for thousands of years though the archeological record suggests periods of abandonment, not surprising in a volcanically active area. There are fifteen active volcanoes along the Shelikof Strait to the east.

Most visitors only see a fraction of the park and preserve's 4.1 million acres, all isolated from the Alaskan road system. Visitors fly into the park as we did or land at one of the coastal stations.

I split from the group to hike part of the one-and-a-half-mile Dumpling Mountain Trail but retreat before finishing it. I'm reminded of solo hiking's dangers when I see Ranger Matthew at the Brooks River pedestrian bridge, remembering him from Great Basin last March. He worked the visitor center desk during my visit and heard of my mountain lion encounter firsthand and less than an hour afterward. We recognize each other immediately. He smiles, shakes my hand and asks about my centennial journey, and I congratulate him on his new assignment. We enjoy a mutual laugh when I tell him, "I'm not giving you the chance to finish this Yankee off by asking for trail advice!"

Catching up to the group by Brooks Lake awaiting our plane, we fight a persistent onslaught of mosquitoes. As we hear the loud rumble of Lenny's seaplane engine coming in from the west, I'm thinking about a future trip to Katmai to see more bears and the park's volcanic setting in the Valley of Ten Thousand Smokes.

After returning to Anchorage on an early Wednesday flight, the group splits up. Fellow NPTC member Joan and I elect the eight-hour roundtrip drive to Homer and the Alaska Islands and Oceans Visitor Center managed by the US Fish & Wildlife Service. The Alaska Maritime National Wildlife Refuge protects the habitat for seabirds and other wildlife over 25,000 islands and coastal areas in south and western Alaska. When compared to the contiguous United States, the refuge covers an area that would extend from California to Georgia. A popular birding destination, Homer hosts the refuge headquarters and the Kachemak Bay Shorebird Festival each May.

The town sits at the Kenai Peninsula's southwestern corner aside the bay. Joan and I walk the trail through the marshland behind the visitor center, observing cranes, gulls, and ducks. We end at the bay, enjoying the Aleutian Range towering across the water. The bay's tidal variations are twenty-eight feet near Homer. Farther up the Cook Inlet near Anchorage, tidal variance can measure thirty-seven feet.

After a delicious salmon dinner on the Homer Spit, Joan and I enjoy a pleasant conversation on our return to Anchorage. We spot moose grazing in the evening daylight. About an hour into the drive, we stop across the road from a bull moose eating grass in the ditch west of Highway 1. We're staring in astonishment at two guys in the road. They're taking pictures, alternately posing in front of the moose. As I ease the car to a stop, I roll down my driver's side window. They nod, moving to their car. One says, "You all gonna get yerself a picture next to the moose?" I nod and smile, too shocked to speak. I turn to Joan, whose baffled expression mirrors my own. She shakes her head. "Darwin's theory in motion," I suggest. "Indeed," she replies.

The next morning, I hitch a ride with Bill and Chris to Talkeetna. Our group reserved a charter flight to Denali National Preserve's Dall Glacier. In route, we stop at Iditarod Race headquarters in Wasilla. Next to the walkway, early-morning dew condenses on a cast of a husky in his racing accoutrements. Droplets dripping from the sled dog's extended tongue give the statue an astonishing life-like quality.

We arrive in Talkeetna to discover an overcast preserve prohibits a morning flight. I ask Bill and Chris to drop me at a lodge outside of town used by the cruise ship companies. Walking the resort's trails will give me something to do while we wait on a weather update and a final go/no-go decision. It's a pleasant walk but leaves more time to kill. Tour groups wander the village browsing souvenir shops. The day trippers wear identifying badges. One large group is kitted with matching jackets. After lunch, we hear our preserve flight won't happen. Fortunately, it's the only flight we lose to weather on the trip.

Friday, Bill, Chris, and I separate from our group for two days in Kotzebue, the gateway to the western Arctic national parklands. We land in Kotzebue at 7:35 a.m. We're a bit early to check in at our charter service, Golden Eagle Outfitters Air Taxi, with the slogan, "Trust us with your life, not your daughter or wife." I smile and think, "You think a grizzly is dangerous. Try my alpha. Summiting El Capitan sans invitation and permit means your ass."

We find the office open. Around 8:00 a.m., a well-built young man with short blond hair shows up in a pickup truck. He smiles and says, "Hi, I'm Jared. I'll be your pilot the next two days." Before our excursion, Jared has some cargo to deliver this morning. We take advantage of the time at the town's NPS's Northwest Arctic Heritage Center, the visitor center for three western Arctic parks. Among the exhibits, I'm particularly interested in a life-size beluga whale. The small Arctic whale almost seems to have a contented smile. I snap a picture of the beluga for Kareen.

She's always using the phrase "stuffed like a beluga" after consuming her evening meal. I didn't really know what it was until now. I watched Kareen eat a chicken for the first time long ago; my she-wolf reduced the carcass to a few splinters. And she does resemble the beluga sleeping off her meal, resting for the next hunt.

There's more truth in all this than one might think. All the pictures I've taken of her smiling broadly followed a large, particularly delicious meal. Partially eaten bones, shells, and other debris scatter about the table in a scene that leaves one scanning the area for a hyena. Servers return to our table with shocked looks that say, "Do you ever feed her?"

By 11:00 a.m., Jared's ready for us. We jump into the three passenger Cessna. Bill and Chris share the back seats, and I'm in the jump seat next to Jared. Our first heading lies across Kotzebue Sound to **Bering Land Bridge National Preserve**. Bering Land Bridge occupies 2.7 million acres in the north-central section of the Seward Peninsula. As with most Alaskan parks, no roads enter the preserve boundary. Jared approaches Cape Espenberg, the tip of the Seward Peninsula and preserve. The Arctic Circle bisects the cape. He touches down several times on the beach, rolling across a few hundred feet of sand each time before lifting off. Free from ice less than a week, wood debris bunched ashore won't permit a safe landing. Our roll across the beach and our aerial views will have to suffice.

From Cape Espenberg, we fly north over the sound to **Cape Krusenstern National Monument**. Jared picks a dry rise amid the flat tundra near the cape and makes a soft, easy landing. On our descent, several groups of dark shaggy musk oxen bunch in circles, their standard defensive posture. Each group sprints across the tundra in unison as we pass overhead. To the north beyond the Krusenstern Lagoon, the Igichuk Hills are the only close terrain rising substantially above sea level. A few shoreline fishing shacks are visible from the air, but no one's in sight. Other than the musk oxen, our only indications of life are some ivory-colored caribou leg bones on the tundra, and small, brightly colored, purple, blue, yellow, and white wildflowers dotting the ground.

After another short flight, we land on a sand bar in the Agashashok River, a tributary to the **Noatak Wild River**. Our rocky runway shares the higher ground with a couple of large tents occupied by academic researchers studying climate change. They either aren't in their tents or choose to remain hidden, as we see nobody. We are inside 6.59 million-acre **Noatak National Preserve**. The preserve includes the western half of the Brooks Mountain Range and runs to the Baird Range in the south. It is a stark, scraggy landscape. Pines grow in patches on the rises to either side of the valley. After about fifteen minutes, we're back in the air, climbing to clear the western end of the Baird Mountains. It's a short, forty-minute ride back to Kotzebue.

At the Nullagvik Hotel, Bill, Chris, and I enjoy a hearty dinner. Bill and I both order the day's special, reindeer sausage in pasta with red sauce. It's delicious and filling. I'm able to take a portion back to the room for later. The dish tastes just as good heated the next morning. We're sampling some excellent food thus far on the trip. I especially enjoy the fresh Alaskan king crab special at the Glacier Brewhouse in Anchorage. To supplement digestion of the caribou pasta, we venture out to the waterfront walkway to watch the ice flow moving past town. Every year when the coastal ice breaks up, the current carries it past this shoreline and into open water as it melts. A constant parade of ice flows past the rocky bank during our first twenty-four hours in Kotzebue. The thinning, brittle ice, broken into countless pieces, makes a continuous clinking sound as it passes as if thousands of thin champagne glasses are tapping. It's a unique and memorable experience.

We're doing a longer trip Saturday morning. Jared informs us heavy rain is falling in the Brooks Range, but we leave anyway. Another pair of visitors has chartered a second plane to join us today. Nancy made our reservation months ago, but these two guys showed up this morning looking for the same ride. We start with a 115-mile flight east to the Great Kobuk Sand Dunes in **Kobuk Valley National Park**. We take pictures on the massive dune field, covering twenty-five square miles and rising as high as two hundred feet. The NPS staff gave us little blue rally towels with "Kobuk Valley National Park" in bold, white print. The park service started giving these to visitors for pictures, in lieu of any entrance or boundary signs. We loan one of our towels to the guys in the other plane and discover they are from the St. Louis area. It's a father and son who are trying to visit all the fifty-nine national parks together before the son begins medical school and "faces the end of happiness."

Our second park today is another sixty miles northeast on a gravel bank in the Ambler River running through the Schwatka Mountains in Gates of the Arctic National Park. We fly above the valleys through isolated mountain wilderness. After landing, it's a life and death battle with the mosquitoes. With the warnings of heavy rain, I neglected to bring the repellent, a mistake heartily endorsed by the Ambler River's swarming mosquitoes. I take pictures of the views, holding out until it's obvious the insects are regrouping for an all-out attempt to carry me away down the valley. I execute a tactical retreat into the plane, closing the door behind me. The small birds, or rather mosquitoes, slam into the windows trying to drain the last few pints of my blood. I'm grateful when we take off and turn south for the 105-minute flight to Kotzebue.

Our return takes us back over Kobuk Valley National Park

and the Kobuk River. We land in Kotzebue before 2:00 p.m. Since our flight to Anchorage doesn't leave until 7:00 p.m., we're able to return to the Northwest Arctic Heritage Center, where we meet Ranger Julia, who enlivens our day. It turns out, she's a good friend to a young lady who sat next to me on the flight from Anchorage. They both studied media science in college and ended up in Kotzebue.

We share our park stories and the intention to write this book. Julia insists, "You can't leave out over a dozen Alaskan parks. That would be a crime!" I've heard something similar. A ranger at Glacier Bay said much the same thing, but with a *Godfather* twist. "We have lots of bears and know where you live." I agree that I'll find a way to include all of Alaska's parks. I imagine hearing a scratch on the door back in Illinois and opening it up to a thousand-pound coastal brown bear with the NPS arrowhead shaved in its fur and a collar inscribed with "Return to National Park Service–Glacier Bay after meal."

We spend our last two and a half hours watching the park service collection of films, including one starring Julia herself and another ranger dressed in an especially sad caribou costume. Julia is sufficiently impressed with our dedication to the parks and our film study that she gives us gold lapel pins with "Arctic Circle Film Series" on them. They are awarded to visitors who attend a minimum number of weekly film nights hosted at the heritage center during the long winters. Mine goes on my hat, to join the other gifted pins from special places throughout the park system. Julia warns me that she'll find me if I leave the four Western Arctic Parklands, totaling 11.8 million acres, out of the centennial story. I take her seriously. She's an energetic young woman and might be more formidable than Glacier Bay's bear.

Due to a flight delay, we don't land in Anchorage until 11:30 p.m. Mercifully, Sunday's an easy day. I've only got to exchange a ticket with Alaska Airlines and pick up a rental car for the next few days. The folks at Alaska Airlines are wonderful throughout the trip. Excepting the Caribbean island hoppers and charter flights, all my commercial air travel since the start of 2016 has been on United Airlines, Hawaiian Airlines, or Alaska Airlines. I've had enjoyable interactions with employees of all three, but the thirteen flights on Alaska Air during this trip reinforce their consistently high customer satisfaction rating.

From the airport, a four-hour drive awaits to our accommodations tonight at the Gakona Lodge. We have an early start the next morning to catch our 9:00 a.m. charter flight out of Chitina, Alaska, to McCarthy for a two-night stay at the Kennecott Lodge. Our current itinerary balances out my time across two visits between the northern and southern areas of Wrangell–St. Elias.

The Kennecott Lodge and Historical Mine complex sits above the convergence of the twenty-seven-mile long Kennicott Glacier and the Root Glacier. The combined ice flow's terminus lies west of the lodge. The Kennecott Mine, a National Historical Landmark, produced $200–$300 million of copper and silver from rich ore deposits between 1900 and 1938. Among my activities here, I join a ranger-led tour of the surviving ore processing facilities, the multilevel concentration mill, the machine shop, power plant, and leaching plant.

After a self-guided mine tour on the second day, I use the balance of the day to attempt the four-and-a-half-mile one-way Bonanza Mine Trail, which gains 3,800 feet in elevation over that distance. If that seems like a healthy climb, it's because it is.

Perhaps it's the physical challenge amid grand scenery or I can't leave well enough alone or I'm just plain stupid. All these thoughts occur to me over the next three and a half hours hiking the Bonanza Mine Trail. It's the most elevation gain and most physically demanding trail I've attempted in the park system. To climb almost four thousand feet in four-and-a-half miles, the trail ascends for three-and-a-half miles. The constant steep ascent lacks flat sections until near the end. It keeps going up, then farther up. The climb makes a workout, but the thin mountain air, with less oxygen and humidity, raises the difficulty. The sweating and thin air dehydrate me at an astonishing rate. My two-and-a-half-liter water supply needed to be twice as much. I'm also unaccustomed to adjusting my hiking pace for this combination of exertion and altitude. Those who've hiked with me can attest—I move.

I cover nine miles exploring the shorter trails and the mine on the first day and ten miles the second day, including the Bonanza Mine Trail. I make it within a mile of the trail's end, covering most of the elevation gain before the water shortage stops me. If I continue, I'll have to make the four-and-a-half-mile descent without water. There's no safety margin. To paraphrase famous American climber Ed Viesturs, the ascent is optional, the return mandatory. I can see the Jumbo Mine across the distance on the adjacent mountain side. The Jumbo Mine and Bonanza Mine Trails split about a mile up, with the Jumbo Trail going left and the Bonanza Trail going right. The Jumbo Mine Trail climbs 3,400 feet. I'm about even in altitude with the Jumbo Mine on the opposite mountainside when I stop. Though it's disappointing not to finish after climbing so far, the views across the peaks and down to the glaciers below captivate me. I contemplate the small glimpse I've enjoyed of this enormous park as I bounce down the trail, returning to the lodge a spent, dehydrated, and sweaty mess.

Wednesday, we take a 2:00 p.m. flight to Chitina and a leisurely drive to Anchorage. Thursday is a scheduled off day, but I use it to pick up a few stamps I missed last year and mail a box of dirty clothes and park materials back home via Priority Mail. I tell Kareen, "I'm mailing you a package!"

"What is it?" she asks with excited anticipation.

"It's a surprise," I reply.

Two days later, she protests, "It's your dirty laundry and park brochures."

"Yes," I acknowledge, "but arranged with love."

Thursday morning, I catch an 8:00 a.m. flight on Lake Clark Air from Anchorage's Merrill Field to Port Alsworth. Lake Clark Air uses the northern of two gravel airstrips at Port Alsworth to land their twin-engine turbo prop. I'm staying at the Farm Lodge. The family-owned business on the shore of Lake Clark's Hardenberg Bay maintains several lakeside cabins for guests. The cabin is comfortable, the home-cooked meals are delicious, and the people who run the Farm Lodge and Lake Clark Air are delightful. After leaving my luggage with the lodge, I walk to the **Lake Clark National Park and Preserve** Visitor Center next to Port Alsworth's southern airstrip. Reviewing the itinerary with the ranger, she provides local trail information and the same for tomorrow's destination, Twin Lakes.

The national park and preserve together cover over 4 million acres on the west side of the Cook Inlet. Over 60 percent of the land, or 2.6 million acres, belong in the National Wilderness Preservation System. The park covers the south end of the Alaska Range and the north end of the Aleutian Range, connected by the Chigmit Mountains. For such a massive area, there are only 6.9 miles of developed and maintained trails in the two units, all located near the Port Alsworth park headquarters.

I'm exploring the Tanalian Trail network that begins a short distance south of the two airstrips. I'm hoping to make it at least as far as Tanalian Falls, about 2.3 miles away from the trailhead. The ranger cautions me that bear activity increases nearer to the lake, an important piece of information. The trails consist of two, 1.7-mile trails running parallel to each other. The Falls and Lake Trail, my choice for the outbound trip, takes a line across elevated wooded terrain, offering views of the lake and Tanalian Mountain. A short distance up the trail, I pass the NPS boundary marker, signaling the transition from private property to Lake Clark National Preserve. The Beaver Pond Loop follows a lower course through marsh and wooded wetland, narrowing at times to a bare strip of earth. The 2.6-mile Tanalian Mountain Trail veers left at the junction of the three trails. Tanalian Falls is to the right. I follow the falls trail, which continues to the Tanalian River's source at Kontrashibuna Lake.

After leaving the Falls and Lake Trail, the falls trail exits the trees and passes through an open area before returning to a densely wooded, heavily shaded area near the river. The rumble increases in volume until the roar of the rushing water drowns out all other sound in the dense woods. As I enter these woods, I have the strong sense of being watched. This seems odd since I haven't seen anyone on the trails. Penetrating the woods another one hundred feet, I spot the first spur trail below the falls. At the spur, a pine tree aside the trail has four deep grooves gouged through the bark into the wood five feet up. It's a bear's territorial mark. A quick scan of my surroundings reveals nothing of concern but doesn't abate the uneasiness I've felt since entering the denser forest.

Proceeding down the spur, I take a few minutes to feel the rushing water's power on the misty bank aside the multilevel, multichannel waterfall. Returning on the spur, I turn right on the main trail toward a second spur above the falls. I stop dead in my tracks after a few strides, staring at a large pile of scat. I could see this spot clearly when I turned to go beneath the falls. It had been clear past this point. Berries are visible in this fresh pile, the size and shape of bear scat. Whether it's from a black or brown bear, I don't know, nor do I care to find out. Another nervous scan reveals nothing. After removing the bear spray from my small knapsack and clipping it to my belt, I continue to the second spur, intent on seeing the falls from above. I walked too far not to see the falls, despite the feeling it's time to leave. This might be unwise. But I figure, I'm already here, and this bear is either going to leave me alone—or not. I'm hoping for the former. I shorten my time at the top of the falls to a couple of minutes, retreating in good order. I leave the dense woods and pop back into the sunlight of the clearing without ever seeing a bear, but I'm not looking that hard either. I'm interested in what's between me and the trailhead. What can I do other than keep walking? Though I lose the sense of being watched by the trail junction, my return down the lower Beaver Pond Loop easily breaks the pace of the outbound leg, absent sightseeing or malingering.

Returning to the visitor center, I watch the park's collection of Richard Proenneke films. The NPS has four films featuring Richard Proenneke, whose friends called him Dick. See chapter 19. Three of these films are new to me. Proenneke's story, covering thirty years of wilderness life at his Twin Lakes cabin, captured the public imagination. After the film study, I return to the lodge to check out the accommodations. Before the family-style dinner in the main lodge, I enjoy a quiet stroll along Hardenberg Bay. I'm thrilled to have two full days in this place. Three others from my group are arriving tomorrow for a Twin Lakes day trip. The extra day allowed me to explore Port Alsworth and meet the good people at the lodge.

Saturday brings a trip highlight. My guide Jeff and I fly a float plane to Twin Lakes, about thirty-five miles north of Port Alsworth. We aren't waiting on the other three members of my group coming on the morning plane from Anchorage, as no one's sure exactly when they'll arrive. We fly over the mountains and swing above the western Lower Twin Lake. The water shines in a beautifully rich, striking blue hue. The plane clears the small stream of water connecting the lakes, and our destination comes into view. Situated on the southern bank of the eastern Upper Twin Lake, the Richard L. Proenneke Historic Site has become the most popular visitor destination in Lake Clark National Park after Port Alsworth itself. The park service maintains Dick's cabin as he left it in 1997, a permanent tribute to his legacy.

Ranger Danny, who's living in one of three nearby cabins just east of here, greets us on the rocky lakeshore. The sturdy log structure brims with Proenneke's personal items and character. He brought only the metal parts of the carpentry tools he needed to construct the residence. Proenneke fashioned the wooden handles himself. His tools are available for inspection today. Each tool handle matches the contours of my right hand perfectly, the kind of wear only possible after countless hours of use. A 1984 calendar showing June hangs above a small desk he constructed near the window. Handwritten notes, including weather conditions and his itinerary, fill the space for each day. Using only his canoe and legs, Proenneke covered impressive distances throughout the valley and sometimes over the mountains. Dick kept a map of the Twin Lakes area and used a pin stuck in the middle of a slice of tree trunk to put a hole in the map at the day's destination. Holding the map up to the light of the window presents a fascinating visual aid on

Dick's coverage in the surrounding area. He had a practical purpose for keeping the map. Should any visitors find him gone, they could look at his map and know his whereabouts.

Danny gives us a guided tour and walks us past Hope's Cabin and Spike's Cabin, two hundred and three hundred yards east, respectively. The park service uses them for staff housing. Dick first stayed at Twin Lakes in 1962 with retired navy captain Gale "Spike" Carrithers and his wife, Hope. Weisser's Cabin, built in 1967 by a mutual friend, sits one hundred yards east of Spike's Cabin. Due to complications with their Small Track Leases, Carrithers, Weisser, and Proenneke never owned the land around their cabins, which predate the permanent protection of the Twin Lakes area as part of Lake Clark National Monument in 1978 and Lake Clark National Park in 1980.

Danny takes a picture of me standing in the half-closed Dutch door. Among many interesting features, Danny points out deep scratch marks in the door frame. The grooves resemble yesterday's pine tree scar. Dick escaped a bear one morning, and the bear left a calling card after arriving at the door seconds after Dick shut it behind him.

Maintaining the cabins requires substantial effort from several master carpenters. One of the carpenters volunteering his time and expertise takes a short break to discuss his task. Tony has boards and tools laid out about fifty feet south of the cabin. He's building a new frame to support Proenneke's sod roof. The sod and wooden frame require replacement at intervals to withstand brutal winter weather. Dick lived here year-round, through the frigid winter cold, biting winds, and deep snows.

After our extensive tour and walkabout, Jeff and I hike the Teetering Rock Trail. The trail follows Dick's path through the pine trees and up the ridge behind the property to a plateau between two mountains where a massive boulder sits precariously on the slope. This multi-ton erratic rests where a glacier dropped it years ago. It's possible to rock the boulder side to side by pushing with both hands. The elevation overlooks Upper Twin Lake and the valley. The calm lake reflects the mountains opposite, casting a detailed reflection on the blue water's surface. It's one of my favorite park scenes. The beauty so enchants us, Jeff and I linger, sharing stories and exploring farther up the steep, narrow valley accessed from the plateau. Jeff tells me that Dick hiked up to the rock every morning upon waking. He called it his "morning constitutional."

It's past noon as we stand on the slope overlooking Upper Twin Lake and still no sign of the three day-trippers. Jeff entertains me with stories from his twenty years as an Alaskan guide. He's from northern Wisconsin but lives in Port Alsworth and guides for Farm Lodge guests. He shares some memorable experiences, including bringing a San Francisco woman here who thought she could live in Dick's cabin. He's also guided for some arrogant clients who made it clear Alaskans ranked below them in the social order. During one junket, a group of well-heeled political attorneys, including the chief of staff of a former presidential candidate, used Jeff's services for several days of tiresome babysitting and walked away without tipping or so much as a thank you. "That's obnoxious," I say. "They're probably making a few million a year. They might spend more on high-end escorts than we make in a year. Well, we can't all be gods among men. I'm going to stiff you, too...gotta pay for the lap dances in Anchorage."

Lake Clark, Twin Lakes

Jeff laughs, "I figured as much."

After wandering above the valley entertaining one another, we finally see the float plane appear over Lower Twin Lake, presumably with my companions. It's almost 2:00 p.m. Descending the trail, we learn inclement weather delayed their flight to Port Alsworth for four hours.

By day's end, we're enjoying the aerial view on our flight to Anchorage through the gap between the Aleutian and Chigmit mountains. I'm ecstatic, assessing Lake Clark as one of the park system's jewels and joining Glacier Bay as my personal Alaskan favorites.

Sunday's another off day. I'm using it for a piece of unfinished park business from last June. I leave Anchorage early morning for the drive to Seward and Kenai Fjords National Park. After stopping at the Seward visitor center, I arrive at the Exit Glacier Visitor Center for today's challenge, the Harding Icefield Trail.

I attempted to climb the 4.1-mile (one-way) Harding Icefield Trail twice last June, only to be turned back each time when the trail closed due to a black bear sow and her two cubs taking residence near it. Last year, I left under the impression the bear response team drove the bear off, reopening the trail. I learn of the aftermath today. The black bear proved to be more persistent than that, returning throughout the summer to raise havoc on this popular trail. Today, the trail is open and clear to the Top of the Cliffs, a point high enough to look out across the Harding Icefield.

I reach the Top of the Cliffs and a short distance beyond. From Marmot Meadows at 1.4 miles to Top of the Cliffs at 2.4 miles up, the trail views the Exit Glacier from above the midpoint of the steep ravine or chute the glacier has carved into the rock. Deep snow slows my ascent over the last mile, but I slog through it to 3.3 miles up the trail before it stops me. From about the three-mile mark, the snowpack, melting snow, and wet ice create treacherously slick conditions. The ascent's manageable but descending absent traction is a struggle. A pair of hiking poles would have been invaluable up here. A set of crampons would be nice, too, to reach the emergency shelter near the trail's end, in plain view ahead.

From the Top of the Cliffs, the view south of the Harding Ice Field astounds me. The field covers between three hundred and eleven hundred square miles, depending on how much of the forty glaciers originating from it are included. Wikipedia references the ice field as three hundred square miles in size, as opposed to the park service referencing seven hundred. A staggering sixty-foot average annual snowfall sustains this field. The adjacent 5,500- to 6,500-foot peaks surrounding the ice field look like small rocky pyramids. The ice must be more than a half-mile thick in places. This unique landscape crowns the trail's three-thousand-foot climb. After yesterday's Twin Lakes panorama and the Harding Ice Field today, I'm on sensory overload as I descend for the drive to Anchorage.

Kenai Fjords, Harding Ice Field

The trip's final adventure brings five from our group together again to the Aleutian Islands. We catch a 9:45 a.m. Peninsula Air flight Monday morning from Anchorage to Dutch Harbor and Unalaska. The Dutch Harbor World War II sites are part of the **Aleutian World War II National Historic Area** and one of the nine sites included in the World War II Valor in the Pacific National Monument.

The NPS covers two important historical threads at Dutch Harbor. First, on June 3–4, 1942, the Japanese attacked this lonely isolated North Pacific outpost. Second, the native Alaskans, the Aleuts and other native Aleutian Islanders, survived for centuries in this harsh, unforgiving environment and yet bore unfair treatment by the US government during the war. Aleutian Archipelago weather influences both stories. Notoriously awful conditions alternate between cold, foggy, rainy, windy, and often some combination of all four.

The port of Dutch Harbor, contiguous with the town of Unalaska, lies on Amaknak Island, connected by a bridge over a small channel to the main island, Unalaska. The port and town gained fame from the Discovery Channel's reality TV series, *The Deadliest Catch*, currently in its thirteenth season and airing in over two hundred countries. Dutch Harbor hosts the Alaskan king crab and snow crab fishing fleets. The show highlights the treacherous conditions these fishermen face in the Bering Sea during the October king crab season and January snow crab season. The stormy Bering Sea creates life-threatening conditions on a continual basis. Most deaths among the fishermen occur from hypothermia and drowning. Evidence of the fishing fleet pervades the town. Metal cages, or "pots," are stacked everywhere. The crab fisheries cover an area bordered by Dutch Harbor in the south and St. Paul Island to the north.

Humans aren't the only predators here. Unalaska has more bald eagle residents than humans. Every building has intermittent bald eagle sentinels. It's quite normal to see as many as a half-dozen bald eagles posted atop larger buildings. The huge birds blend into the landscape like pigeons in other US cities.

We tour Dutch Harbor and Fort Schwatka, the abandoned World War II–era military installation atop Mount Ballyhoo at Ulatka Head. The fort is the most extensive and best preserved of the four coastal defense posts built to protect the harbor. At 897 feet above sea level, Fort Schwatka holds the distinction of being the highest coastal defense post constructed on US soil. The Japanese invaded and assumed control of the western Aleutian Islands of Attu and Kiska within days of the Dutch Harbor attack. Though it galvanized the threat to the Aleutians, the two-day air raid on Dutch Harbor offered little strategic value to the Japanese. The Aleutian campaign served as a diversionary effort from the main thrust across the Pacific targeting Midway Island. The events of June 1942 proved a crucial turning point in the Pacific. American forces hit Japanese forces on Attu and Kiska hard from bases on Adak and Dutch Harbor. My own uncle Dean Kroese spent his World War II service stationed as a navy mechanic here, describing it as a lonely and inhospitable place lost to the world. By August 1943, American forces brought the Aleutian Islands under US control for the war's duration.

The Japanese threat triggered the US government to evacuate nearly nine hundred Aleuts from nine different villages across the islands, interning them under deplorable conditions in a primitive southeast Alaska camp. The southeast Alaskan Coast's rainforest environment was strange and difficult for the Aleuts, who were treated no better than prisoners, with little effort made by government authorities to provide necessities. While the story of Japanese American internment is well known and represented at four NPS units, the injustice and callousness of Aleut internment has largely been forgotten. The simplest way to relate the story is to say the military had the natives moved as a war expediency, then forgot about them, leaving them for dead in practical terms. The summary most sympathetic to the government claims the Aleuts are evacuated for their own safety and are lost in the bureaucracy of an overwhelmed government trying to manage a two-front war. In more realistic terms, it's part of the federal government's long legacy of treating Native Americans as something less than humans and citizens with equal rights.

On our second and final day in the Aleutians, we visit the Aleutian World War II National Historic Area Visitor Center in the airport's aerology building. The current Dutch Harbor airport sits on the World War II–era airstrip. Exhibits cover everyday soldier life at this remote outpost, explain typical duties, and review the war's progression through the Aleutians and its impact on the residents.

On the way to our next destination, our group walks past a supermarket, stopping to get some drinks. Parked in front of the market is a running pickup truck with a mixed-breed dog sitting on top of the cab. I snap a picture of the scene, posting it later with the explanation, "Aleutian vehicle theft prevention system." With refreshments in hand, we pass our hotel and continue to the Museum of the Aleutians, covering Aleut history and traditional life.

Our day closes with a 6:35 p.m. return flight to Anchorage. From there, I catch the 11:45 p.m. Alaska Air flight to Chicago O'Hare. After all this Alaskan beauty, I return home a richer man.

39 The Last Lap

WITH THE TRIP to Alaska, I've made it to 410 of the 417 NPS units. The first post-Alaska park adventure doesn't include any of the last seven units. I drive through Nebraska to the Black Hills of South Dakota and the annual NPTC convention hosted at Mount Rushmore National Memorial.

Kareen joins me Wednesday night in Rapid City. It's Kareen's first trip to the Black Hills parks. We start at Minuteman Missile National Historic Site. I repeated the Launch Control Facility tour with Ranger Jim on Wednesday afternoon, and Kareen joins a Thursday morning tour with Jim while I greet multiple NPTC members arriving for subsequent tours. Jim adds a lot with his uniquely suited background, having retired from active duty with the missile defense system and Strategic Air Command. From Delta-01, we drive eleven miles west to the missile silo, Delta-09, where the park has the silo open for a film crew and is using the opportunity to allow park staffers to venture underground. A ranger wearing a harness emerges from the silo as we watch. He smiles and asks, "How are you doing?"

"Fine," we answer in unison. He's familiar. I have met him but won't remember until the convention that it's the park superintendent, Eric.

Our next stop is Badlands National Park. We repeat the Door,

Window, and Notch trails explored last March, followed by the park driving tour. Kareen enjoys the trails despite the July heat. We complete all three, but I don't wander as far on the Door Trail as I had last March. "It's too hot for that," Kareen states. In addition to the endlessly complex, eroded, and colorful Badlands landscape, a large group of bighorn sheep traveling by the road greet us midway through the park. It's my first bighorn sheep jam.

Friday, we travel into eastern Wyoming to visit Devils Tower. After circumnavigating the monument on the main trail, we return east, stopping at Jewel Cave to find the tours filled. We finish the day at Mount Rushmore.

Saturday morning, we leave the hotel early for the drive south to Wind Cave National Park. Kareen's delighted to see part of the park's bison herd congregated over the road entering from Custer State Park. We join a 9:30 a.m. cave tour, returning to the Rapid City Best Western for the convention. The most interesting part of the convention is the guest presentations given by Ranger Ed covering Mount Rushmore, and Eric. Both do a tremendous job highlighting their respective parks. Ed discusses some of the lesser-known aspects of the giant sculpture, such as the secret vault behind the heads, featuring an inscribed tablet. Eric shares a preview of the park's upcoming film, which will be outstanding, and plans to accommodate increased visitation. The word's getting out about Minuteman Missile!

I drop Kareen off early on Sunday morning for her flight to Chicago and proceed to the South Dakota Air & Space Museum next to Ellsworth Air Force Base. The museum has an impressive collection of planes on the grounds, including the B-1B Lancer, B-52 Stratofortress, B-29 Superfortress, the C-54 Skymaster, and EC-135, known as Looking Glass. Looking Glass is the Strategic Air Command's mobile back-up to the underground command post that controls the US nuclear arsenal. The Skymaster did much of the heavy lifting during the Berlin Airlift from June 1948 to May 1949. The museum also has a Nike-Ajax antibomber missile and a Minuteman-II ICBM on display.

The indoor exhibits include a model and explanation of the Minuteman-II defense system. The US Air Force 44th Missile

Wing, commanding the 66th, 67th and 68th Missile Security Squadrons are based out of neighboring Ellsworth AFB. Each squadron includes five groups with ten missiles each. Minuteman Missile National Historic Site's Delta-01 and Delta-09 belong to the 66th Squadron's Delta Group.

From the museum, I drive southeast to address some unfinished park business. I've visited Badlands National Park six times now, but only the North Unit. I've never seen the southern Stronghold Unit. I stop at White River Visitor Center about noon to ask for hiking suggestions. I inquire about Cedar Butte, a bluff about three miles west. Ranger Matt overhears my question and asks if I would like him to take me to see the bluff. Matt is a seasonal ranger and familiar with the area. He calls the Pine Ridge Indian Reservation, encompassing the park's Stronghold and Palmer Creek subunits, home. I readily agree, not quite comprehending what Matt has in mind. He says he'll join me for the hike. That's a thrill. I'm elated to have the company, and Matt is an excellent guide for our five-and-a-half-mile roundtrip hike to Cedar Butte.

Matt is Lakota Oglala and regales me with stories about the butte's features and the Sioux legends behind them. Our trailhead lies through a locked, gated fence over a primitive ranching path. As Matt points to the butte's sculpted rock features, we walk along its length for a half mile over mostly open, dry ground. Our return takes a different route across tall prairie grass. I ask Matt how he avoids rattlesnakes on cross-country treks. "My grandmother told me not to walk in high grass where you can't see where you're stepping," he replies, as we start into an area of knee-deep, thick prairie grass.

"So, tribal wisdom suggests not doing what we're doing right now?" I ask.

"Yes," Matt replies with a straight face. It sounds like something I would say.

Matt seems too nice to be sarcastic like me. I stay behind my Sioux scout until we return to the shorter, less dense scrub grass. I find out later from other NPTC members that several stopped here and thoroughly enjoyed meeting Matt. One describes his enthusiasm as infectious. I'm so impressed that he would take me on a five-and-a-half-mile hike, I hardly know how to thank him properly after we finish. I make a point to get his email address and wish him well with the NPS or wherever his promising future may take him.

The next stopping point is a return to the Wounded Knee Massacre site. During my first visit in 1998, I found the site neglected, with two barely legible dilapidated signs the only markers. Today, the descriptive sign has been restored and a small shelter stands between a parking area and the former encampment.

On December 29, 1890, 356 men, women, and children of the Minneconjou and Hunkpapa under the leadership of Chief Big Foot camped here in a flat recessed area next to Wounded Knee Creek. A day earlier, the group had surrendered to the US 7th Calvary five miles to the north. Pine Ridge Agency troops arrived early on the twenty-ninth, totaling 450 soldiers surrounding the encampment. Troops placed four Hotchkiss guns on a western ridge overlooking the camp. A fight broke out while soldiers moved among the teepees confiscating weapons. In the ensuing melee, soldiers opened fire with the Hotchkiss guns, aiming indiscriminately into the encampment and hitting Sioux and soldiers alike. Many Sioux attempted to escape through an east-west ravine behind the camp, or down the Wounded Knee creek bed. The cavalry chased down and shot untold numbers whose immediate transgression consisted of fleeing for their lives. When the smoke cleared, 146 Native American men, women, and children lay dead. The seventh suffered thirty-six killed. Contemporary eastern newspapers hailed the event as a glorious battle, but history accurately labels the event the Massacre at Wounded Knee. It marks the final armed conflict between the Sioux and the US Army. I've always thought that Wounded Knee should be an NPS unit honoring the Native Americans who died here and during westward expansion. Many tribal members do not wish the US government to tell their story, and it's hard to criticize that opinion. It's important history for future generations to remember.

On Monday, I stop at Homestead National Monument to discuss the exhibit's duration. We left it open-ended. I'm thrilled and honored to have them at Homestead. I meet Mark, the park superintendent, as I walk into the Heritage Center. After a warm greeting, we agree the exhibit will continue through the total eclipse on August 21, moving to Omaha sometime after Labor Day. Homestead lies right in the middle of the path for the eclipse and is the official NPS host for NASA during the event.

The next park adventure begins the last two weeks of August. We start our travels with a trip to southern Illinois to watch the August 21 total eclipse with my friend Greg and his girlfriend, Michelle, at the Crab Orchard National Wildlife Refuge. We park at a wayside eleven miles northeast of the point of maximum duration at two minutes and forty-one seconds. The spectacular show stimulates multiple senses. The transition from near total to total eclipse alters the level of light dramatically. Cicadas begin buzzing as the sky darkens, adding a symphony to the dimmer switch. The onset of totality comes in a rush. We take full advantage of our southern Illinois back-road knowledge, returning to Greg and Michelle's house in my hometown, Sesser, Illinois, in less than thirty minutes. We learn the next day that some of the thousands from Chicago who came south needed twelve to twenty-one hours to complete the normal five-and-a-half-hour drive from Marion, Illinois.

Our next adventure is an eight-day trip to Maine and Acadia National Park. I'm driving from Chicago to visit parks en route. Kareen will meet me in Maine, flying from Chicago to Bangor on Thursday night.

On the drive east, I stop in Auburn, New York, to see one of the four newest units added in January. **Harriett Tubman National Historical Park** includes Tubman's Auburn home from 1883 until her death in 1913, and the Tubman Home for the Aged, a home for disadvantaged elderly founded in 1908. Tubman moved to Auburn in 1859. A fire destroyed her original home in 1880. The brick home being renovated dates to 1882–1883. In 1896, Tubman purchased twenty-five adjacent acres and later used it for the aged sanctuary.

Harriet Tubman withstands every historical test as a genuine American hero in the term's truest sense. Harriet Tubman Home, Inc., partners with the NPS at the site. The enthusiastic docents retell Harriet's story with an energy and passion fitting to her memory.

After joining Kareen Friday night, we leave Bangor about 8:30 a.m. Saturday, headed for Millinocket, Maine, and **Katahdin Woods and Waters National Monument**. The main street storefront visitor contact station displays a banner with the new park's name and the NPS arrowhead. It's the only NPS sign we'll see at this unit. The helpful station volunteer reviews the park and potential activities with us. Despite her laudable enthusiasm, the numerous signs posted by locals protesting the new park send the message "park visitors get out."

The parkland's previous owners, the Quimby family, long wanted it to become a park. Logging companies previously managed the land under a ninety-nine-year lease. After removing the valuable timber, they lost interest. The Quimbys purchased the acreage adjacent to Baxter State Park and Mt. Katahdin in this remote, hilly area of central Maine. In the ensuing years, many locals used the land as they wished. Some even built houses on it. This triggered an inevitable conflict with the legal owners, who donated the property to the federal government for the national monument declared by President Obama on August 24, 2016.

Before our park adventure, we eat lunch in the Appalachian Trail Café a few doors down the street from the visitor station. It's a tradition for those completing the Appalachian Trail to catch a ride from its terminus on Mt. Katahdin to the café and consume a hearty meal hearkening their return to civilization. Hikers originally wrote their name in ink on the wooden café door. Soon, the drop-down ceiling panels replaced the door. The café leaves the current panel down for the thru-hikers who wish to sign it.

We access the park via US Highway 11 north to Swift Brook Road west. The road passes through a detached section before reentering the park farther west and coming to the sixteen-mile Katahdin Loop Road. The loop offers access to Katahdin Woods and Waters National Monument's southern section. The road's condition forces reduced speed to avoid damage from sharp rocks and occasional potholes. We scan the green rises of Baxter State Park and

Mt. Katahdin to the west from The Lookout in mile six. Between miles seven and eight, a large bobcat darts in front of our car about twenty-five feet away, leading us down the gravel road for about one hundred feet before exiting stage left into the bush. Kareen and I agree to supplement our tour by hiking the Bernard Mountain Trail.

Before mile marker 12, a dirt logging road spurs from the loop. The first mile and a half on this road are the beginning of the Bernard Mountain Trail. As we exit the car, we greet a New Hampshire couple finishing the trail. They share their passion for Maine's beautiful backcountry. We wish them a safe journey and press on. About a quarter mile into our walk on the wooded lane, we freeze as a large black bear appears on the incline ahead, ambling out of the bush and down the road toward us. The bear's at least two hundred yards off, but it seems to notice us, wheeling about on its back paws and reversing course into the trees to our left. Kareen's ready to keep going, but this is the first time a bear has appeared before me on a trail, and I'm uneasy leaving it between us and the trailhead. It doesn't help that I watched the movie *Backcountry* a few months ago. After a minute or so of deliberation, I decide that discretion is the better part of valor, and we return to the trailhead. We are probably safe to continue, but after the experiences of the past eighteen months, I've grown more cautious. Moreover, the good doctor and her muscular legs can outrun me.

After staying in Millinocket, we drive to the park's northern section but abort before entering. Neither Kareen nor I have much enthusiasm. Maybe it's the lack of NPS presence or the unwelcoming signs displayed by residents who want to use the land however they please, or maybe we're just tired. It's an attractive place with room for improvement.

We drive east across Maine's countryside to Calais and Saint Croix Island International Historic Site. I introduce myself to Rangers Carole and Bill, who seem to appreciate the interruption for my park story. Kareen snaps a picture of the three of us and we bid them a farewell. Our next park visit will be longer by five days.

Last year, I had one and a half days to explore Acadia National

Park. The time allowed a basic tour of Mount Desert Island. I missed the other park areas, including the islands. This trip corrects that omission, addressing more unfinished park business. We start our adventure on Monday, August 28, in the Schoodic Peninsula. We walk across Schoodic Point's sea-worn volcanic rock to the ocean rolling up at its edge. The unique, rugged shore commands its own style of beauty.

Tuesday is devoted to Mount Desert Island. Kareen and I hike the Ocean Path, passing Thunder Hole and the Otter Cliffs. I let Kareen rest and trek farther south, well beyond the distance I covered last year, delighting in the subtle nuances of the tree-covered, irregular coastline south of the Otter Cliffs. Our next exploration is Cadillac Mountain and the Bubble Trails to the north and south Bubble and Bubble Rock. Kareen cracks me up on the North Bubble. As we're crossing the broad summit area, she asks, "Aren't we close to the Bubble Stick yet?"

"The Bubble Stick?" I ask. It hits me, she means the summit markers. I take pictures of Kareen smiling at both bubble sticks, El Capitan in Acadia.

Acadia, Kareen and her bubble stick

Our third day in the park, we take the ferry to Little Cranberry Island and the Islesford Historical Museum. Our afternoon includes a drive around Somes Sound to the Seawall area, where we walk the Wonderland Trail. We also stop at the park's Village Green information center, and we're greeted by Ranger Maureen. Kareen shakes her head and walks out as I share a summary of my centennial adventure and its projects. Maureen relishes the tale. I've found another kindred spirit.

On the fourth day, Kareen rests while I make the fifty-six-mile drive to Stonington for a day trip to Isle au Haut. Due to its remoteness, Isle au Haut is the least visited among the park's major areas and islands. The trails scramble along the coast over rocks and countless tree roots, challenging the visitor to watch their step. I meet Rangers Allyson and Charlie, who get copies of the island's passport stamp for me. It's kept farther north at the ranger station next to the Town Landing. I spend my time on the island wandering across the southern half, centered around Duck Harbor Landing. Allyson and Charlie tell me I must claim that Isle au Haut is the best part of Acadia, and I honor that promise now, confirming their subjective admission. I trek over eleven miles on the island and enhance the fatigue with four more near Bar Harbor. Kareen and I are lodging one-and-a-half miles from downtown Bar Harbor and walk into town each night. After eating another lobster dinner, I'm pleased with a day well spent.

Kareen and I close our time in Acadia with a five-and-a-half-mile walk around Eagle Lake. The hike is lovely, especially the areas around the lake's southwestern side. The trail navigates all manner of boulders requiring a rock scramble. As we pass the midway point, I learn that I'm the only one between the two of us who brought any water. About three miles into the hike, I raise the water bottle to my lips and say, "It's too bad you didn't bring any water. I'm really thirsty." Her look mixes puppy dog and wolf, half begging, half considering attacking me, consuming her kill and drinking *all* the water. I'm the one who's thirsty when we return to the car. I have reason to be. I've walked sixty-five miles in seven days.

After dropping Kareen off for her 6:00 a.m. flight Sunday morning, I begin the long drive home. Passing through northeastern Massachusetts, I stop at Salem Maritime National Historical Park and the Essex National Heritage Area on my way to stay in Hartford. Labor Day Monday, I take time to explore the city area near the Samuel Colt gun factory, soon to be part of Coltsville National Historical Park. The park's opening remains pending as of this writing. My next stop is a return to Weir Farm National Historic Site, where I enjoy another walk around Weir Pond before continuing into the southern part of the Hudson River Valley to visit a dozen or so locations in the Hudson River Valley National Heritage Area over the next two days, including the Military Academy at West Point.

While in the Hudson River Valley, I'm able to address another piece of unfinished park business with a visit to FDR's Top Cottage, part of the Home of Franklin Delano Roosevelt National Historic Site in Hyde Park, New York. Top Cottage is constructed on land three miles east of the main house on the banks of the Hudson. FDR purchased the land for a personal retreat in 1936–1937, and completed the home in 1939, months before the famous British Royal Family visit. Eleanor hosted a picnic for the king and queen at Top Cottage that charms history-lovers for its simplicity and the notable influence of Eleanor's personality on the event's planning and execution.

The final park stop of the trip is a real treat. At the James Garfield National Historic Site in Mentor, Ohio, I tour the Garfield home. It's fascinating, layered history, and worth the wait. The visit marks my third time at the site, but the first time I've been able to see the house. In part due to Garfield's premature death from an assassin's bullet in the first months of his administration, the house tour is more a history of the intelligent and gifted First Lady, Lucretia Garfield.

The Monday after returning from New England, I'm traveling to Washington state and two of the final five parks. Our Chicago-Seattle flight passes over the wildfire currently threatening northeastern Mount Rainier National Park. Our view of the mountain from the plane's window includes the shapely mountain and entire park proper, glorious except for the smoke billowing up in the foreground. The week's planned on a tight schedule. Tuesday morning, I'm up at four o'clock for the three-hour drive to Chelan, Washington and the Lady of the Lake Express boat to Stehekin, Washington in **Lake Chelan National Recreation Area.**

The boat ride north crosses the lake's deep blue water for fifty miles, culminating with our arrival at Stehekin Landing. Lined with high, sharp and snowy peaks, the V-shaped Stehekin River Valley corridor extends north from the landing into the heart of North Cascades National Park. Lake Chelan fills two glacier-carved basins. The deepest one, Lucerne Basin, is 1,486 feet deep, making Lake Chelan the third deepest lake in the United States. Steep rock walls towering over 1000 feet above the water bracket the basin. Not to be out done by Scotland, local myth tells of the "Monster of Lake Chelan." According to legend, the monster lives in the Lucerne Basin and consumes unsuspecting yuppies on holiday. Author's note: The latter part is my embellishment.

Lake Chelan, Stehekin River Valley

The park's scenery supersedes any notion I had before the visit. Unfortunately, the tight schedule this week gives me enough time to visit Stehekin's Golden West Visitor Center and the immediate surroundings before returning on the boat back to Chelan. I regret not having several days in this beautiful place to explore the hard-to-reach park. I'll have to return with Kareen. She needs to see this hidden gem.

One of the day's highlights is meeting John from Yorktown, Virginia. A retired army colonel who's hiking the Pacific Crest Trail, he's only ninety miles away from completing the 2,638-mile trail at the Canadian border. Exuding enthusiasm and positive energy, John's trail name among other thru-hikers is Colonel Buck. It's a thrill to spend part of the boat ride up the lake talking with him.

Late Tuesday afternoon, I enter the trip's second park at Grand Coulee Dam in **Lake Roosevelt National Recreation Area**. Lake Roosevelt is a 155-mile long manmade lake created in the Columbia River gorge by the ten-year Grand Coulee Dam project. After completion in 1942, the dam stands as the largest masonry construction ever built, surpassing Egypt's Great Pyramid, which held that distinction for forty-seven centuries. Presently, the dam is the largest producer of hydroelectric energy in the United States, and the world's third largest hydroelectric facility.

Wednesday, I travel over one hundred miles of the lake's length, stopping at the park's visitor facilities from north to south. After staying sixty miles away from the dam in Okanogan, Washington, my day begins crossing the Colville National Forest to Kettle Falls. I'm looking for the passport stamp. A volunteer at the ranger station suggests I ask at the NPS office. Having no luck calling, and seeing the ground floor deserted, I climb an outside stairwell to a second floor and get an employee's attention through the window. I feel like a cat burglar. He comes downstairs and lets me in, after which I share my park story in a few sentences. He looks around for the stamper with no luck. I thank him and leave, finding my prey at the town's chamber of commerce visitor information center.

From Kettle Falls, Highway 25 south passes Bradbury Beach, where I stop at the lakeshore. Highway 25 parallels the lake's eastern shore over the fifty-nine miles to Fort Spokane Visitor Center. Built in 1880 as one of the last frontier military outposts, Fort Spokane loses its garrison for the Spanish-American War in 1898. From 1900 to 1910, the buildings served as a Native American boarding school, then a healthcare facility for Native American tuberculosis patients until its closure in 1929.

After walking the fort grounds and reviewing the interpretive displays, I continue to parallel the lake for fifty-three miles to the park headquarters in Coulee Dam, Washington. A few miles outside of town, I stop at the Spring Canyon Visitor Contact Station, hoping to use the location's passport stamper. Some rangers returning from lunch see me bouncing down the trail and ask if I need help. Ranger Clint opens the closed building to let me use the passport stamp. He's recently transferred from Cane River Creole National Historical Park in his home state of Louisiana. I mention visiting all six of Jean Lafitte National Historical Park's visitor centers before realizing he said Cane River Creole. "At least you had the correct state," Clint says.

"The parks are merging into one in my brain," I concede.

At the Lake Roosevelt National Recreation Area headquarters, I enter a lobby with a receptionist and a smiling law enforcement ranger who greets me with, "You're the guy who's gone to all the parks and is writing the book! The Kettle Falls office called us and warned us you might show up."

"Yeah, that's me," I confess, glancing down at his taser, handgun, and handcuffs. "I hope you're not here on my account. Whatever it is, I didn't do it!"

I show the two NPS employees pictures of the exhibit while explaining its intent. They smile and nod, probably unsure what to make of their unusually exuberant visitor.

From Lake Roosevelt, I drive southwest generally progressing to Seattle and my 4:00 p.m. flight tomorrow. My last stop is Sun Lakes–Dry Falls State Park. Dry Falls, a few miles southwest of Coulee City, Washington, once formed the earth's largest waterfall. The waterfall ran over three-and-a-half miles and stood 350 feet tall. Incredible flood waters cut steep-walled canyons called coulees. The largest of these, the Grand Coulee, is up to eight hundred feet high and more than a mile wide in some places. Dry Falls forms the northern end of Lower Grand Coulee, whereas the Grand Coulee Dam seals the southern end of Upper Grand Coulee and Lake Roosevelt. The flood waters that gouged these canyons originated from two-thousand-square-mile Glacial Lake Missoula.

I photograph the dry falls and read the outdoor interpretive panels Wednesday afternoon, but the visitor center is closed when I arrive, so I decide to stay nearby tonight and visit again the next morning. Thursday morning, I'm greeted by Ranger David, a park interpretive specialist. David appears to manage and staff the visitor center solo and works at a frenetic pace to engage each visitor. He helps me visualize the Ice Age floods that carved east central Washington state. David's good spirits make the perfect bookend for this trip to complete the Pacific Northwest NPS units.

Saturday, October 28, begins my journey to the system's most remote parks. I fly thirteen and a half hours from Chicago to Tokyo, wait through a four-hour layover, then fly three hours to Guam. I land on the Northern Mariana island at 2:30 a.m. Guam is the southernmost of fifteen islands in the Mariana Archipelago. These islands, first contacted by Europeans when Portuguese explorer Ferdinand Magellan landed on Guam's southwest coast in 1521, are inhabited by the native Chamorros at the time Magellan claims the island chain for Spain. In 1668, a Spanish missionary names the islands the Marianas after the Spanish regent of Austria. Guam became a United States territory after the Spanish-American War. The Mariana Islands north of Guam, most notably Saipan and Tinian, are ceded to Japan after World War I, setting the stage for World War II and the events in the Pacific Theater told at **War in the Pacific National Historical Park**.

The Japanese attack on the island follows the attack on Pearl Harbor by several hours. With a force of a few hundred on the island, the navy commander surrendered on December 10, 1941. The United States moved to retake Guam in 1944, launching July attacks on two west coast beaches. Asan and Agat Beach lie north and south, respectively, of the strategic Orote Peninsula. The peninsula commands

Apra Harbor's deep-water port to the north and is home to the current US Naval Base Guam. The T. Stell Newman Visitor Center sits a few hundred yards away from the base's main gate.

Bill and Chris, the New Jersey couple I traveled with in Alaska, are visiting Guam this week. They pick me up at my hotel Tuesday morning. At the visitor center, we're greeted by the friendly park staff. Ranger Rufus offers suggestions on touring the park's seven units, spread over nine miles of the southwest coast and highlands overlooking the Philippine Sea. We're visiting the developed areas open to visitors.

At the Agat Unit, the two-mile beachhead extends from Apaca Point in the north to Bangi Point in the south. We walk to the water at Apaca Point, past concrete bunkers built into the rocky shoreline. Marines and army infantry took direct fire as they waded ashore from the reef five hundred yards out. Japanese fire knocked out as many as twenty-four landing craft approaching this beach. At Ga'an Point, the beachhead's center, a defensive stronghold opens to the island's tunnel system, built by the Japanese to support defensive operations. The Agat beachhead took three days of heavy fighting to secure. Today, the American, Japanese, and Guamanian flags fly together at Ga'an Point to honor the brave men who fought over these shores.

A short distance from the northern beachhead, the Piti Guns Unit contains three five-and-a-half-inch coastal guns placed on the heights of a mahogany forest overlooking the beaches below. Not yet operational during the American landings, some believe the Chamorro labor gangs slowed or sabotaged their installation. The short trail climbing the thickly forested hillside demonstrates the difficulties moving on this terrain. The oppressive heat and humidity creates treacherous footing. Stone-reinforced steps cut into the trail help visitors avoid sliding on the muddy jungle floor.

At the Asan Bay Overlook, a Memorial Wall lists over sixteen thousand Chamorro and American casualties from the hostilities. The overlook commands a view of the Asan Beach Unit, Apra Harbor to the south, and the Guam International Airport to the north. After stopping briefly at the Fonte Plateau Unit to peer through the locked gates to a tunnel system, part of a former Japanese naval communication center, we continue to Asan Beach.

War in the Pacific (Guam), Asan Beach

The northern beachhead stretches over one and a half miles from Asan Point to Adelup Point. Today, a quiet, narrow swath of sand and a thin row of palm trees mark the shoreline. Walking trails follow the beach and access the bluff at Asan Point, where entrenched Japanese defenders engaged the northern landing force. Almost three weeks of fighting on Guam left 7,000 American casualties, nearly 1,000 Guamanian deaths, and 17,500 dead out of the 18,500 Japanese defenders. American commanders declared the island secure on August 10.

After walking in tropical heat and humidity all day, my legs and feet are shot. I decide it would be a good idea to try out the massage place next to my hotel. It appears legit, as opposed to many of the island's massage parlors that are thin fronts for prostitution. It turns out the place adjoining my hotel is a little too serious. My social media post on the night of October 31, 2017, summarizes it best:

I've probably done some dumb things during park travels, but I might have accomplished the dumbest move yet here in Guam, park 415/417. After twelve miles of hiking in a tropical island battlefield, I relax with a shower and decide my battered feet can use a traditional Chinese foot massage. I could tell I was in trouble right away when it was obvious the lady had the forearm strength of your average, seasoned lumberjack. I was able to block the pain for a while by imagining how good it might feel if someone was amputating my lower leg with a bone saw after a pull of whiskey. After she discarded the pulp of bone, skin, and ligaments that used to be my left foot and ankle, she proceeded to my right foot, which has hurt in recent months from hundreds of cumulative hiking miles such that I've speculated I might have a stress fracture. I tried to be brave... It wasn't until she looked up at me, quivering with tears rolling down my cheeks, and said with a devilish grin, "Too hard?" that I managed a weak nod, fighting the urge to retract into the fetal position. I'm not posting for sympathy, rather as an object lesson for others.

Wednesday morning, we depart Guam at seven o'clock for a day-trip to the island of Saipan. We land after passing over the island of Tinian off Saipan's southern tip. The *Enola Gay* departed Tinian's North Field airstrip in the early morning hours of August 6, 1945, to drop the first atomic bomb used in warfare on Hiroshima. We're visiting **American Memorial Park**, an NPS affiliated site covering the World War II history on Saipan.

On the island's central west coast, the park includes the northern end of Micro Beach and the adjacent north-facing cove. Saipan's coastal waters have an intense blue color over the coral reefs and in the deeper coastal waters as well. Collectively, the shades of blue off Saipan's coast are among the most vibrant series of blues I've seen anywhere. The coral areas appear as lighter and brighter blues and remind me of St. Croix's Buck Island. Other coastal waters show a deep, dark blue reminiscent of Crater Lake. The beautiful ocean water stands in stark contrast to the island's historical horrors.

At the park's visitor center, Ranger Renee greets us and suggests island points of interest before starting the park's film. After the film, we tour the exhibits, memorial, and beach. A few Japanese bunkers remain. The memorial lists the US servicemen who died taking the island after attacks launched on the southwestern beaches. US forces, led by the 2nd and 4th Marine Divisions, and the army's 27th Infantry Division, took Aslito Airfield on the south end before sweeping north through rugged central highlands. Japanese forces anchored their resistance in the north, pushed back in bloody combat that's sometimes hand-to-hand. The fighting ended on July 9. Over 3,250 Americans died and 13,000 were wounded during the battle. Nearly the entire Japanese garrison of 30,000 perished. Only 921 Japanese defenders were taken prisoner.

American Memorial (Saipan), Banzai Cliff and Marpi Point

Saipan is best known for its civilian tragedy. The first Pacific Island with a substantial Japanese civilian population taken by US forces, over twenty thousand Japanese civilians died during the fighting. Japanese military authorities warned civilians that the Americans would inflict horrible cruelties. As a final sign of loyalty to the emperor, the military declared death preferable and more honorable than capture. As many as eight thousand civilians jumped to their deaths from Suicide Cliff, a couple of miles inland from Marpi Point, the island's northern tip. Hundreds of civilians and soldiers jumped to their deaths from Banzai Cliff, running east above the ocean-battered coast from Marpi Point. A navy lieutenant leading a patrol boat around Marpi Point after the tragic events reported the water near shore impassable due to the quantity of floating dead.

Modern-day revisionist historians who claim Truman's use of the atomic bombs unjustified ignore the inevitable and obvious conclusions of reoccurring Pacific Island events where Japanese soldiers fought until death and civilians died rather than be captured. Nothing can distort the horror witnessed on Saipan or refute the message it sends. The alternative to the bombing of Hiroshima and Nagasaki was the invasion of Japan's main islands. After the extreme loss of life on Iwo Jima and Okinawa in 1945, it became clear such an invasion would have cost hundreds of thousands of American lives and unknown multitudes of Japanese lives.

Our time in the Marianas ends with a relaxed Thursday. We travel to Ritidan Point at Guam's northwestern tip to the Guam National Wildlife Refuge. The gravel road leading to the refuge is in such terrible shape, cars must navigate a maze of potholes, sometimes leaving the road entirely due to clustered pits. The refuge includes a rainforest bracketed by a sand beach and high bluffs a mile or more inland. We come and go without ever seeing anyone working at the refuge.

Our last stop together in the islands is at the popular tourist destination, Two Lovers Point. The views are nice from the high bluff overlooking Agana from the north. Otherwise, it's a tourist trap on a grand scale. Bill and Chris bid me farewell as they drop me off at my hotel.

Friday night I'm on the 4:45 p.m. Hawaiian Airlines flight out of Honolulu to Pago, Pago, the capital of American Samoa. The **National Park of American Samoa** is my fifty-ninth and final national park and next-to-last NPS unit. (Author's note: Sixtieth national park declared in February 2018 from change in designation.) Hawaiian Airlines only schedules the five-and-a-half-hour flight on Mondays and Fridays. Each roundtrip makes a long day for the Hawaiian Airlines crew, who work both flights in succession, returning to their Honolulu hub at 5:50 a.m. I'll have three days to explore the main island of Tutuila.

American Samoa is easily the most isolated of the sixty national parks. The Samoan Archipelago consists of thirteen islands (nine inhabited) in the South Pacific Ocean approximately twenty-six hundred miles southwest of Hawaii. The only US territory south of the equator, American Samoa includes seven islands, five rugged volcanic islands, and two coral atolls. The Samoan Islands span three hundred miles. The country of Samoa occupies the six western islands, separated by the International Date Line. The country of Samoa stays an hour earlier tomorrow than American Samoa.

The word Samoa means "sacred earth," descriptive of the beautiful rain forest, tropical reefs, and coastlines protected by the park. Considerable interpretation shares *fa'asamoa*, Samoan customs, beliefs, and traditions. Island villages retain identities within one of the oldest Pacific civilizations, dating back three thousand years. One park film explains the extraordinary process of making woven mats that are prized as possessions and gifts, often handed down generationally. While the mats are woven from local natural materials, the entire Samoan culture is woven from the islands' natural world, built around fishing and living in harmony in the world's largest body of water.

My time in the park begins at 10:00 a.m. Saturday. Ranger Tai meets me on her day off to help me organize the weekend. I spoke to Tai a week ago. She got permission to open the visitor center, closed on weekends, for a couple of hours today. She also dropped off a packet of information at my hotel so I could review the materials after arriving Friday night. Both kind gestures contribute substantially to the quality of my visit. After initial greetings and my sincere thanks for her tremendous effort, we agree on a series of trails for today and tomorrow. The first trail is the seven-mile roundtrip Mount 'Alava Trail, starting at Fagasa Pass and finishing at the 1,610-foot Mount 'Alava summit. Tai cautions me to truncate the hike in the event it starts raining. The trail's dark, volcanic rock is often indistinguishable from mud, making walking treacherous. Otherwise, the rocks are covered with green algae creating a slippery surface. I will personally substantiate her words: "It's harder to go down than come up."

I've hiked a lot of trails in the National Park System over the past two years. While I rank the Bonanza Mine Trail in Wrangell–St. Elias as the most physically demanding trail I've tackled, the Mount 'Alava Trail takes the most out of me. The intense tropical sun, directly overhead this time of year, and the pervasive humidity enhance unusually high temperatures this weekend. Even the Samoans are wiping their brows and commenting about the heat. The midday sun causes a burning sensation more intense than the other equatorial climates I've experienced in Colombia and Brazil. Though I've layered on SPF 100 sunblock, I scramble to avoid direct sunlight and find shade whenever possible. The Mount 'Alava Trail's heavy shade makes it passable for less acclimated visitors such as me. If the whole seven miles exposed the hiker to direct sunlight, anyone not covered or otherwise protected would burn up. Despite the physical effort required to climb this trail, it's manageable with the shade and sufficient water. The summit's views of Pago, Pago directly below and Tutuila's east end are unforgettable. The rainforest-covered island spine shows on the green ridges running away from the summit in two directions. As I near the summit, I notice the first fruit bats flying among the trees. These large bats, with two- to three-foot wing spans, are ever-present "flying foxes." They don't eat insects but feed on the nectar of ripened tropical fruits. In the early evenings, they can be seen in large numbers everywhere. What surprises me is how majestic and beautiful they are. I never considered bats to be either, but it's true for these giant Samoan fruit bats. The bats are to Pago, Pago what seagulls are to most every other harbor or port. Their numbers dominate multiple shorebird species, at least to my eye in Pago, Pago. On the descent, I'm pointing the camera skyward at a bat gliding overhead when my foot loses purchase on an algae-covered rock, sending me crashing to the ground with a thud before sliding about ten feet downhill on my derriere.

Sunday, I explore the other areas Tai and I outlined. The

1.7-mile roundtrip World War II Heritage Trail navigates Matautu Ridge, the backbone to Blunts Point, commanding the western side of the Pago Pago Harbor entrance. Two large, six-inch coastal defense guns mounted in circular concrete emplacements sit one above the other near the point. Walking the trail, remnants of pillboxes, concrete foundations for barracks, offices, and a mess hall are visible on the heights along the trail. The farther one goes on the trail, the more the jungle reclaims the fortifications. Some concrete pads are hard to see. During World War II, Tutuila hosted a US Naval Base and the Tafuna Air Base. Although home defense forces prepared for an amphibious assault, the only Japanese attack on the island occurred on January 11, 1942, when a Japanese submarine about ten thousand yards off shore fired fifteen projectiles from a five-and-a-half-inch deck gun. The shelling proved inconsequential. The island's facilities were used in support and training for America's Pacific operations until more advanced, convenient bases became available after military victories to the north.

American Samoa, Pago, Pago from Mt. 'Alava

Next up is a drive around the harbor to cross Afono Pass to the north side of the island. The Lower Sauma Ridge Trail leads onto a small peninsula extending off the north coast through historical settlements indicated by the terraced land and offers a view of Pola Island and the Vai'ava Strait National Historic Landmark. Pola Island, a 420-foot, tower-like island, creates the north side of the strait. Passing east through the town of Vatia, the road ends at the Pola Island Trail. A short path leads to a large cobblestone beach. The smooth ocean-washed stones run up to the high bluff straight ahead that leads north to form the south side of the straight. Two sea arches are visible at the base of the cliffs extending into the ocean. The crash of the swell and rising tide on to the stone beach lulls me into a mixed feeling of peace and respect for the ocean's incredible power.

Monday, I decide to spend the day visiting the park staff in the visitor center and doing some writing. Ranger Pai greets me on arrival. She's staffing the desk and helps me find a place to sit and write for a while in the film room. Ranger Jason, the park's chief of interpretation, and I talk about the park experience and my motivation to write about the journey. We take pictures with a woven matt donated by a couple who finished the fifty-nine national parks here last February. Reflecting on my American Samoa experience, I believe the staff here manages the kindest national park. That's tall praise, and well earned.

During my layover on Oahu, I revisit the Pearl Harbor Visitor Center and drive to the site of Hawaii's newest NPS unit, Honouli-uli National Monument. Honouliuli is located about five air miles west of Pearl City in a gulch surrounded by Monsanto Corporation land. Since access to the site is blocked by corporate property, it's hard to see how this unit will be regularly accessible to the public. Given the other three NPS internment sites' interpretation and Honouliuli's primary function as a POW camp, the distinct contribution of this unit appears to be the excellent interpretation of Japanese-American history offered at the Japanese Cultural Center.

Sitting down for lunch in the Honolulu airport while waiting to board the flight to Chicago, I remove my worn, soiled, sweat-stained pin-adorned Cardinals hat and take a picture of it on the bar. Posting it to social media, I identify it as the only specific hat, particularly baseball cap, ever worn in all 59 US national parks, and soon to be the only one worn in all 417 NPS units. I intended to wash it and continue wearing it in the parks, but multiple rangers implored me to leave it as is. It has tiny particles of dust and dirt from Alaska to the Caribbean and Maine to American Samoa. Kareen insisted I retire the filthy hat, and so I've done as of this writing, moving the pins to a new Cardinals hat for park adventures to come.

After the Pacific trip, the next park task is a drive to the Lewis and Clark National Historic Trail Visitor Center on the ground floor of the NPS Midwest Regional headquarters in Omaha, Nebraska. The trail opens the lapel pin exhibit the second week of November. It will remain in Omaha through February 2018, when it will move to the Chicago area to be cohosted by Pullman National Monument and Indiana Dunes National Lakeshore. Ranger Julie greets me and takes some excellent pictures for the trail's social media page. I share an update on the ongoing writing project with Julie, Ranger Neal, and the trail superintendent, Mark. I thank them for hosting the displays and tell them I hope to return after the book is completed.

Meanwhile, I've planned an NPTC meet-up at my last NPS unit, **Reconstruction Era National Monument** in Beaufort, South Carolina, one of the four new units created in January 2017. I contact Fort Moultrie to inform them we'll have a group visiting their location in Charleston to close the meet-up. Since we will not interact with any NPS personnel in Beaufort, it seemed appropriate to finish our day in Charleston, where we might take a symbolic picture with a ranger or some similar thing.

I drive from Chicago to South Carolina the first week of December, routing through the Mississippi Gulf Coast National Heritage Area for a closer look at over a dozen participating locations. At the heritage area headquarters office, I meet Jeff and arrange a tour of the Charmley-Norwood House designed by Frank

Lloyd Wright and Louis Sullivan. The house, built on the coast in the 1890s, incorporates some signature Wright design features, such as the use of natural lighting to create an indoor "open air" environment and patterns in three, such as windows, wall panels, ceiling, and so forth. By coincidence, I'm joined on the tour by fellow NPTC member Gary. We know each other, having met a year earlier in the New Castle, Delaware, subunit of First State National Historical Park. The heritage area includes many interesting sites and nearly forty stamping locations across the Gulf Coast.

The Beaufort-Charleston meet up and visit to my 417th NPS unit coincides with my forty-seventh birthday weekend, a nice coincidence. Kareen flies to Charleston Thursday night. We start the hour-long drive south to Beaufort on Friday morning, December 8, arriving midmorning. Though the official meet-up is Saturday, we are previewing the sites today on our own. The first participating site is the Beaufort Visitor Center and History Museum, where we share our story with Lynda and the kind museum staff.

Beaufort and South Carolina's sea islands lay at the heart of newly freed people's struggle to integrate into a post–Civil War society as citizens. Union forces took control of the local sea islands early in the war. White residents fled ahead of the November 1861 military occupation. Thousands of newly liberated plantation workers created both problems and opportunities. How to support their transition from slavery to freedom? Our next stop helped answer that question.

All parties understood education to be essential for progress. Two Pennsylvania women, Laura Towne and Ellen Murray, arrived in 1862 to teach, using the Brick Church on St. Helena Island until moving across the street in 1864 to the Penn School, now known as the Penn Center. Kareen and I meet Michael, the director of the museum, after arriving. Michael shares how his great-great-grandmother knew and lived near one of the museum's featured subjects, Robert Smalls.

Robert Smalls gained permanent fame in May 1862. A steamboat pilot, Smalls ran the steamer CSS *Planter* out of Charleston past the harbor's defensive guns to turn it over to the Union navy blockading the coast. Smalls brought sixteen others with him. All would find refuge in Beaufort. Smalls became the first black Union steamboat pilot and played a key role in the Lincoln administration's decision to arm black troops for combat. Smalls later served five terms as a US congressman representing this South Carolina district. Robert Smalls' intelligence, determination, and courage combined to make a genuine American hero for all times.

We attend a meet-up dinner Friday night, and my fellow park travelers have busied themselves in anticipation. Twelve club members, Kareen, Mike—a former fantasy camp teammate and Beaufort resident—and I attend our dinner. As we near the end of our meal, Deborah brings out a round, white birthday cake decorated with green frosting trim. The top features the NPS arrowhead under beige letters and numbers spelling HAPPY 4 * 1 * 7 BIRTHDAY. Fellow traveler Chris pulls out a tube that contains a banner reading "Cardinal Dave's Platinum Celebration, 417 NPS units!" The NPS arrowhead and NPTC logo bracket the description. Deborah's cake is so amazing I hesitate to cut into it. I pose with another NPTC member, Carl, the radiologist from Florida, holding the banner aloft in anticipation of tomorrow's activities. Having no forewarning of these special preparations my fellow club members made, I'm thrilled and overwhelmed at the sentiment. Celebrating this special achievement with these people makes all the difference. Along with Kareen and a few well-traveled park rangers, they are the group that best understand the sacrifices necessary to see all these places. Their attendance crowns a joyful weekend.

Saturday morning, we start our meet-up with a tour Carl arranged at the Brick Baptist Church. We meet Ethel, an elder, who shares the building's history. The island's enslaved population built the church for the landowners in the 1850s. When the white population fled ahead of the Union army, the island's Gullah community took over the church's use and management. It has remained so ever since. After our church tour, the group crosses the road to the Penn Center for a museum tour and group picture.

St. Helena Island is home to one of the most protected, intact Gullah communities remaining in the United States. Many island residents trace their generations back to antebellum days when those traveling to the mainland had to go by water.

Reconstrcution Era, final park

I'm surprised by the complex layers of history that comprise Reconstruction Era National Monument. The park's hosts and cooperating entities are welcoming, enthusiastic, and full of fascinating knowledge about this important era and place in American history. The park experience educates me in unexpected ways. I'm grateful to have such a special place mark the end of my journey.

We conclude our day with a drive to Sullivan Island and Fort Moultrie. We arrive to discover no one aware or interested in my special day. After greeting the two rangers working the visitor center, I say, "We're celebrating my four hundred seventeenth and final park visited at Reconstruction Era earlier today."

The female ranger says, "Congratulations!" to which the male ranger replies, "I've met other people who've done it." Thus ends my idea that we might include the park service in our celebration.

Kareen adds, "You picked the wrong park if you wanted a handshake."

"I guess so," I reply.

The muted experience at Fort Moultrie in no way detracts from the wonderful experience I have this weekend with Kareen and my fellow club members. Nor does it reflect the countless times park service personnel have made exceptional efforts to assist me, showing kindness and enthusiasm that lifted my spirits and encouraged me to stay the course. Somewhere in my mind, there's a part of every National Park Service unit and trail that I can see, almost touch. These are the lasting memories I treasure and take with me forever.

40 *A Walk in the Park*

WHEN I FIRST made a goal of seeing all the National Park Service units in August 2012, I imagined it would take years to finish. The idea to visit every unit evolved. So many parks surprised me, regardless of prior knowledge.

At the journey's end, I saw the experience in new ways. Many characters, villains, and heroes live on in my psyche. I wanted to stand where Washington, Lincoln, Grant, and Hamilton stood. I wanted to see the same battlefields as Joshua Chamberlain and Red Cloud. I wanted to see the airstrip and walk in the same church where men proved and preached that human achievement and quality has nothing to do with the color of one's skin. I wanted to walk through the homes of presidents and the laboratories and recesses where genius carried the day. I wanted to celebrate the accomplishments of the working class and the underprovided men and women of American history.

This book serves as my testament to all these people. For those who never came home, for those who suffered unimaginable horrors and privations, to those who suffered discrimination and prejudice, for those who fought in their own way to guarantee I had a free land to call home, this book is my way of saying you have *not* been forgotten by the generations to follow. We are your living monuments. We are the vestige of your sacrifice. And we are forever grateful.

The yearlong centennial journey developed into a priceless life experience. I'm thankful I had the circumstances and opportunity to complete it. Having said all that, I have no plans to travel to all fifty states or visit four hundred parks in a calendar year ever again. The centennial will remain a unique life experience. When it began, I had no idea where it might end. Likewise, I didn't comprehend why I was doing it. Something moved me, drove me to the road and all these special places.

The travels are about much more than the mountains, valleys, lakes, deserts, rivers, forests, and hundreds of historical places. My story is a human story. The regular acts of kindness and words of encouragement shared with me along the way helped restore my faith in the basic goodness and decency in humans.

I knew I had lost something over the course of my adult life. And I wanted it back. I became lost in a never-ending series of meetings, budgets, and selfish personalities. When my career faltered, I received respect out of common courtesy as someone who used to be important but no longer mattered. Over a year removed, I wonder if the mountain lion blocking my path at Great Basin had been delivering a message. "You're on the wrong path. Find a new one." The parks formed the roadmap from a life of mediocrity to a life of joy and fulfillment.

I missed the burning curiosity and fascination with all new things I had so naturally as a child. Learning something new, thinking of new places, and discovering their stories always made me happy. I wanted to find that seven-year-old made a slave to the adult world and free him. I traveled 144,000 miles in 360 days, and tens of thousands of miles more to complete the journey. The anticipation of the parks pulled me through thousands of hours driving and flying. I completed the journey a better, more mature man because the parks reawakened the person within, the person I've always been. I learned the truest beauty known to humankind exists within us and shines outward.

Appendix 9

The Centennial by the Numbers

- 387 NPS units in 360 days, beginning December 23, 2015
- Visited 76 NPS units for the first time in 2016
- Traveled 146,000 miles in 2016, 90,000 driving and 56,000+ flying
- Visited parks in 50 states and the US Caribbean territories in 2016
- Drove over 1,800 hours in 2016
- Park-related travel cost in 2016: ~$30,000
- Conceived goal to visit all the units in August 2012. Initial visits by year: 125 in 2014, 97 in 2015, 76 in 2016, and 23 in 2017
- By the end of 2015, had visited 318 NPS units
- By the end of 2016, had visited 394 NPS units
- Four units added to NPS in January 2017.
- Completed visits to all 417 NPS units in December 2017
- Became the 15th person known to have visited the current number of units. Fewer than 100 are known to have visited all the NPS units since there have been more than 350.

The National Park Service by the numbers:

- There are 418 NPS units located in all fifty states and five island territories.

- Sixty NPS units are national parks as designated by Congress.

- Other unit designations include memorials, monuments, historical parks, historic sites, battlefields, military parks, preserves, recreation areas, rivers, seashores, lakeshores, and other less common designations.

- Six Caribbean units are spread among the islands of Puerto Rico, St. Croix, and St. John. Two are in the Pacific island territories of American Samoa and Guam, with an affiliated site on Saipan.

- Four Hawaiian Islands host eight NPS units.

- There are 382 units (solely or in part) in the Continental United States.

- There are forty units located outside of the Continental United States: twenty-four in Alaska, eight in Hawaii, and eight in the island territories.

- Several parks have subunits in multiple locations, states, or regions.

- US presidents can create units at their discretion under the 1906 Antiquities Act. Theodore Roosevelt's administration saw the introduction of twenty of the current NPS units.

- Pinnacles National Park, in California, became the fifty-ninth national park in 2013. Theodore Roosevelt originally protected the park in 1908, creating Pinnacles National Monument.

- In February 2018, during the writing of this book, Jefferson National Expansion Memorial in St. Louis had its name changed to Gateway Arch National Park by congressional act, making it the sixtieth national park as designated by Congress.

- In October 2018, Camp Nelson National Monument in Kentucky became the 418th NPS unit.

- There are forty-eight NPS-affiliated national heritage areas and twenty-five various affiliated sites, including national historical sites and national memorials that are not NPS units.

- There are thirty-one national trails, thirty created by the National Trails Act of 1968.

Appendix 99

The Centennial Journey

January 2016 Summary

Total NPS units visited: 32

January 2: Fort Sumter (Fort Moultrie), Charles Pinkney, Fort Pulaski; January 10: Effigy Mounds; January 14: Saguaro-East; January 15: Fort Bowie, Chiricahua, Coronado; January 16: Tumacacori, Organ Pipe Cactus; January 17: Saguaro-West; January 18: Lincoln Home NHS; January 19: Natchez Trace Parkway, Natchez Trace NST, Brices Crossroads NB, Tupelo NB; January 21: Vicksburg NMP, Poverty Point NM; January 22: Cane River Creole NHP, Natchez NHP; January 23: Jean Lafitte NHP, New Orleans Jazz NHP, Gulf Islands (Mississippi); January 24: Gulf Islands (Florida); January 25: De Soto, Everglades, Big Cypress; January 26: Dry Tortugas; January 27: Biscayne, Everglades; January 31: Canaveral, Fort Matanzas, Castillo de San Marcos, Fort Caroline, Timucuan

February 2016 Summary
Total NPS units visited: 25

February 1: Ocmulgee, Martin Luther King, Jr. NHS, Kennesaw,, Cumberland Island, Fort Frederica; February 2: Chattahoochee, Chickamauga and Chattanooga, Stones River; February 3: Fort Donelson, Mammoth Cave, Abraham Lincoln Birthplace, Lincoln Boyhood; February 4: George Rogers Clark; February 9: Mississippi NRRA; February 12, Dayton Aviation Heritage NHP, Charles Young Buffalo Soldiers NM, Hopewell Culture, William Howard Taft; February 13: River Raisin; February 18–19: San Juan NHS; February 20: Christiansted, Salt River Bay; February 21: Buck Island Reef; February 22: Virgin Islands Coral Reef, Virgin Islands NP

March 2016 Summary
Total NPS units visited: 53

March 3: Mississippi NRRA; March 5: Friendship Hill, Fort Necessity, Flight 93, Johnstown Flood; March 6: Independence (Philadelphia Flower Show), Edgar Allan Poe, Valley Forge, Gettysburg, Eisenhower; March 7: Catoctin Mountain, Monocacy, Harpers Ferry, Potomac Heritage, Appalachian NST, Antietam, Chesapeake and Ohio Canal; March 10: Knife River Indian Villages, Fort Union Trading Post, Theodore Roosevelt NP; March 11: Mt. Rushmore, Jewel Cave, Wind Cave, Minuteman Missile, Badlands; March 12: Agate Fossil Beds, Fort Laramie, Scotts Bluff, Chimney Rock; March 13: Nicodemus, Fort Larned, Washita Battlefield, Oklahoma City NM; March 14: Oklahoma City NM, Chickasaw; March 15: President William Jefferson Clinton Birthplace Home, Hot Springs, Little Rock High School, Fort Smith; March 22: Lake Mead, Pipe Springs; March 23: Zion; March 24: Bryce Canyon; March 25: Capital Reef, Arches, Canyonlands; March 26: Natural Bridges, Capital Reef, Glen Canyon NRA, Hovenweep; March 27: Great Basin; March 28: Death Valley; March 29: Manzanar; March 30: Sequoia, Kings Canyon; March 31: Cesar Chavez, Mojave, Castle Mountains

April 2016 Summary
Total NPS units visited: 35

April 2: Joshua Tree; April 3: Tule Springs Fossil Beds; April 13: First Ladies. Cuyahoga Valley, David Berger; April 14: James Garfield; April 17: Ulysses Grant, Jefferson National Expansion Memorial; April 18: Theodore Roosevelt Inaugural, Women's Rights, Fort Stanwix, Saratoga; April 19: Martin Van Buren, Vanderbilt, Home of Franklin Roosevelt, Eleanor Roosevelt, Weir Farm; April 20: Springfield Armory, Blackstone River Valley, New Bedford Whaling, Roger Williams; April 21: Cape Cod, Adams; April 22: Minute Man, Frederick Law Olmsted, John Kennedy, Saugus Ironworks, Longfellow House and Washington's HQ, Boston, Boston African American; April 23: Salem Maritime, Lowell; April 24: Acadia; April 25: Saint Croix Island, Roosevelt Campobello; April 26: Saint Gaudens, Marsh-Billings-Rockefeller

May 2016 Summary
Total NPS units visited: 33

May 4: Saint Croix, Apostle Islands; May 5: Keweenaw, Isle Royale, Pictured Rocks, Father Marquette; May 6: Sleeping Bear Dunes; May 12: Missouri, Niobrara; May 16: Rocky Mountain, Florissant Fossil Beds, Great Sand Dunes; May 17: Curecanti, Black Canyon of the Gunnison, Mesa Verde, Yucca House; May 18: Colorado, Dinosaur; May 19: Bent's Old Fort, Sand Creek Massacre; May 20: Harry Truman; May 26: African Burial Ground, Stonewall; May 27: Castle Clinton, Statue of Liberty, Federal Hall, General Grant, Hamilton Grange; May 28: Governors Island, Saint Paul's Church, 9/11 Memorial; May 29: Sagamore Hill, Fire Island, Gateway (Jamaica Bay)

June 2016 Summary
Total NPS units visited: 18

June 3: Ozark; June 7–8: Denali; June 9–10: Gates of the Arctic; June 11: Yukon-Charley Rivers; June 12–13: Wrangell–St. Elias; June 14–16: Kenai Fjords; June 24: Klondike Gold Rush; June 25: North Cascades, Ross Lake; June 26: Olympic; June 27: Mount Rainier; June 28: Lewis and Clark, Fort Vancouver; June 29: Fort Vancouver- McLoughlin House; June 30: Manhattan Project, Whitman Mission

July 2016 Summary
Total NPS units visited: 62

July 12: Arlington House, Lyndon Baines Johnson Memorial Grove, Theodore Roosevelt Island, George Washington Parkway, Clara Barton, Great Falls, Wolf Trap NP for the Performing Arts, Manassas; July 13: Cedar Creek and Belle Grove, Shenandoah, Fredericksburg and Spotsylvania, Prince William Forest; July 14: George Washington Birthplace, Thomas Stone, Piscataway, Fort Washington; July 15: National Capitol Parks–East (Anacostia Park), National Mall, Washington Monument, World War II, Korean War, Vietnam Veterans, Lincoln, Constitution Gardens, Ford's Theatre, Franklin Delano Roosevelt, Martin Luther King, Jr., Thomas Jefferson, Pennsylvania Avenue, World War I, White House, Frederick Douglass; July 16: Oxon Hill Park, Kenilworth Gardens, US Botanical Gardens, Rock Creek, Mary McLeod Bethune, Belmont-Paul Women's Equality, National Mall, Carter Woodson; July 17: Greenbelt, Fort McHenry, Hampton, Assateague; July 18: Harriet Tubman Underground Railroad; July 19: Richmond, Maggie Walker, Appomattox, Booker T Washington, Blue Ridge Parkway; July 20: Andrew Johnson, Carl Sandburg, Great Smoky Mountains; July 21: Cowpens, Kings Mountain, Ninety-Six, Congaree; July 22: National Capitol Parks–East (HQ), Frederick Douglass, Washington Navy Yard; July 28: Timpanogos Cave; July 29: Golden Spike,

City of Rocks, Hagerman, Minidoka, Craters of the Moon; July 30: Nez Perce; July 31: Grant-Kohrs, Big Hole

August 2016 Summary
Total NPS units visited: 33

August 1: Little Bighorn, Bighorn Canyon; August 2: Yellowstone, John D. Rockefeller Parkway, Grand Teton; August 3: Fossil Butte; August 9: Dayton Aviation; August 10: Perry's Victory; August 15: Eastern National HQ, Steamtown, Upper Delaware; August 16: Delaware Water Gap, Middle Delaware, Paterson Great Falls, Thomas Edison, Morristown, Hopewell Furnace; August 17: Allegheny Railroad Portage; August 18: Delaware Water Gap, Thomas Edison, Gateway (Staten Island-Sandy Hook); August 19: First State; August 20: Independence, Thaddeus Kosciuszko; August 22: Golden Gate, Fort Point, San Francisco Maritime; August 23: Muir Woods, Point Reyes; August 24: Whiskeytown-Shasta-Trinity, Lassen Volcanic; August 25: Valor in World War II (Tule Lake), Lava Beds; August 26: Oregon Caves, Crater Lake; August 27: John Day Fossil Beds; August 28–29: Redwoods; August 30: Yosemite; August 31: Devils Postpile

September 2016 Summary
Total NPS units visited: 18

September 1: Pinnacles; September 2: John Muir, Port Chicago; September 3: Rosie the Riveter, Golden Gate (Alcatraz); September 12: Mississippi; September 13: Grand Portage, Voyageurs; September 15: Arkansas Post; September 16: Shiloh, Natchez Trace Parkway; September 17: Russell Cave, Little River Canyon, Horseshoe Bend, Tuskegee Airmen, Tuskegee Institute; September 18: Jimmy Carter, Andersonville; September 19: Selma to Montgomery; September 21: Obed, Big South Fork; September 22: George Rogers Clark; September 30: Pipestone

October 2016 Summary
Total NPS units visited: 32

October 5: Herbert Hoover; October 6: Casa Grande Ruins, Hohokam Pima; October 7: Santa Monica Mountains; October 8: Channel Islands; October 9: Cabrillo, Yuma Crossing; October 10: Montezuma Castle, Tuzigoot, Walnut Canyon, Sunset Crater, Wuptaki, Grand Canyon; October 11: Grand Canyon, Glen Canyon; October 12: Rainbow Bridge; October 13: Cedar Breaks, Grand-Staircase Escalante; October 14: Navajo, Canyon de Chelly, Hubbell Trading Post, Petrified Forest; October 15: El Morro, El Malpais, Petroglyph, Salinas Pueblo Missions; October 16: Tonto; October 20: Homestead, October 21: Brown v Board of Education, Tallgrass Prairie, Fort Scott; October 22: George Washington Carver, Wilson's Creek, Pea Ridge; October 23: Lincoln Home; October 31: Bandelier, Manhattan Project, Valles Caldera

November 2016 Summary
Total NPS units visited: 30

November 1: Chaco Culture, Aztec Ruins, Rio Grande del Norte, Taos Pueblo; November 2: Lake Meredith, Alibates Flint Quarries, Capulin Volcano, Fort Union, Pecos; November 3: White Sands, Carlsbad, Guadalupe, Chamizal; November 4: Fort Davis, Big Bend, Rio Grande; November 5: Gila Cliff Dwellings; November 13: Pullman, Indiana Dunes; November 15: San Antonio Missions, Amistad; November 16: Palo Alto Battlefield, Padre Island; November 17: Big Thicket; November 18: Waco Mammoth; November 19: Lyndon B. Johnson; November 29: New River Gorge, Gauley, Bluestone; November 30: Petersburg, Colonial, Fort Monroe

December 2016 Summary
Total NPS units visited: 15

December 1: Wright Brothers, Fort Raleigh, Cape Hatteras; December 2: Cape Lookout, Moores Creek; December 3: Guilford Courthouse; December 4: Cumberland Gap; December 8: Eugene O'Neill; December 10: Pu'ukohola Heiau; December 11: Kaloko-Honokohau, Pu'uhonua o Honaunau, Hawaii Volcanoes; December 12: Hawaii Volcanoes; December 13: Haleakala; December 14 World War II Valor in the Pacific, Honouliuli

Index

Page numbers with park pictures are indicated in bold

I

J

K